Governments and Leaders

Governments and Leaders

An Approach to Comparative Politics

Edward Feit, Contributing Editor
University of Massachusetts, Amherst

Gerard Braunthal
University of Massachusetts, Amherst

Lowell Dittmer
State University of New York, Buffalo

Jerome King
University of Massachusetts, Amherst

Harvey F. Kline
University of Massachusetts, Amherst

Karl W. Ryavec
University of Massachusetts, Amherst

HOUGHTON MIFFLIN COMPANY BOSTON

*Dallas   Geneva, Illinois   Hopewell, New Jersey
Palo Alto   London*

Contents

Contents

Contents

Contents

Contents

Contents

Contents

xi

Contents

Contents

Preface

There are so many sound books on comparative politics at the introductory level that a new one must be more than ordinarily justified. One immediate defense might be that this book combines the traditional and the novel—the study of political institutions with political biography. Yet to make this claim is not to answer the charges: Why this book? Why biography? And how is this book to be used? This preface addresses these questions.

Why This Book?
For several years now, increasing numbers within each successive student generation have voted against the study of foreign languages and foreign cultures. They have voted in the only way they can—by avoiding courses in these areas. In our discipline, political science, this trend is reflected in declining interest in comparative politics. Why should this be? It is surely odd that at a time when the interdependence of the world is evident to even the most parochial, students are turning their backs on the study of other nations. Can it be that after a quarter-century of "pax Americana" there is a growing isolationism among students against which academic disciplines are powerless?

This question permits no simple answer. As teachers of comparative politics, we are convinced of the importance of renewing student interest in the ways in which foreign countries are governed. After all, we have a vested interest in this effort. But there is more to it than that. Comparative studies are the realm in which political science must justify its claims to universality. If this

cannot be done, it risks becoming, as Bernard Crick has put it, merely the "American science."

Believing in the importance of winning back the thinking young people, we have directed this book to that end. Biography is emphasized, and lives are related to institutions. There is little of what might be termed a "self-consciously political science approach." The language has deliberately been kept simple, the approach is descriptive, and jargon has been avoided. Our teaching experiences convince us that if interest is to be recaptured, students must be approached differently than in the past.

Humans are characteristically interested in other humans. If a painted landscape has figures on it, it is the figures that capture attention. Many people who would not read formal history read biography or historical novels, the biography of fantasy. Gossip is ever popular, as are those serialized tales of gossip, the soap operas. The aim in using biography in teaching is not to trivialize political science, but to attempt to harness this obvious fact to the study of foreign governments, to give the subject meaning for beginning students.

Most texts have followed the development of American political science since the 1950s. The trend they indicate, until very recently, has been the restatement of formal concepts, taken as reflecting universal human behavior. The importance of these laws was accepted as self-evident and their discovery presented as the means by which whole societies and individual institutions could be reconstructed on bases more rational than human history or chance human events. It was an advantage to be "outside" the culture studied, as it was presumed to insure the instructors' and the students' value-free objectivity.

Yet students felt that something was wrong with this approach even before the most recent philosophers of science realized it. The most recent political thought argues that to treat political life as operations analysis is to misunderstand the fundamental nature of culture. Told on the one hand to regard freedom as a fundamental value, and on the other to embrace an allegedly scientific approach "beyond freedom and dignity," students retreated from us. The dominant forms of political analysis, in which political "systems" were presented much as electronic circuit diagrams, seemed to confirm many of their fears: they were governed by abstract processes that they could not fully understand, and they had no control over their own lives. It is not surprising that students should avoid studies that confirm their worst fears and turn inward either to psychology or to the solace of a variety of religious and spiritual cults.

Added to the spiritual retreat was the subject matter itself. Many textbooks were overly detailed and boring. Instructors, faced with the problem of teaching three or four governments in detail, could not develop interesting themes in the framework of the texts. Much of what was taught— strange legislatures, parties, groups, names —seemed to students like the parts of a machine that would not come together and match the chart. Students gained little of the flavor of politics in the countries they studied or of the differences in political culture that made these nations what they are.

Political analysis, formal and informal, is an invaluable means to understanding. As political scientists, this is our meat and drink. Yet we cannot expect students, new

to the subject and uncertain whether they will like it or not, immediately to share our enthusiasm. If they are to be won, students must be eased in, by being presented with material that can hold their interest. In no way is this an argument against academic rigor, yet if ours is to remain a vigorous field, it must attract new minds. We cannot expect students to come to us already motivated to study comparative governments; we have to create motivation by showing that what we have is interesting and important.

Why Biography?
Political biography as a teaching tool responds to the newer philosophical and psychological developments. It suggests both the ways in which individuals can be free and the fashion in which their lives are guided by institutions and by chance. The use of biography allows inwardness to be turned to advantage: it encourages students to "put themselves in the other fellow's shoes," an act that most recent philosophers of social science tell us is of great importance in understanding both the world and morality. The effort to see through the eyes of others takes hard work and imagination, and imagination cannot work on abstract forms. It takes the stuff of life to spur the imagination. Thus we believe that political biography is a better means of fostering knowledge and imagination than any other form.

Political biography, taken together with the description of institutions, has the following advantages: It gives students an identifiable figure whose metaphorical shoes they can use. The interplay of institutions and the politician's career puts the individual, groups, parties, legislatures, and electorates into clearer focus. Students learn not only the forms but also the flavor of politics in the different countries. Providing both biography and institutional information, this text cannot be as comprehensive as the more conventional works. But what students miss in mental cataloguing they may gain in understanding.

Although breaking new ground with the emphasis on biography, the text retains much that is traditional. The countries featured are those usually found in beginning courses in comparative politics: Britain, France, Germany, and the Soviet Union. China and Cuba are added because of the interest in both regimes and the potential importance of the former. Each country is described in a brief historical chapter and in a longer chapter on its political institutions. These are followed by a treatment of an individual politician: Harold Macmillan for Britain, Valéry Giscard d'Estaing for France, Willy Brandt for Germany, Nikita Khrushchev for the Soviet Union, Chou En-Lai for China, and Fidel Castro for Cuba.

A caveat ought to be entered here: this is *not* intended to be a book about great figures in world politics. Our choice of the less-than-great was deliberate. Those selected are important politicians who certainly are skilled, capable, and more important, representative. In Montesquieu's words: "When societies first come to birth, it is the leaders who produce the Republic. Later it is the institutions that produce the leaders."

In addition, these politicians were chosen because biographical material was available on them and because their lives could be satisfactorily presented in a brief format.

In sum, then, the text tries to introduce a new approach without sacrificing all tradition. It is novel in its use of biography and traditional in its use of countries and institutions.

How to Use This Book
Because this book considers countries, institutions, and individuals, it is extremely

flexible in use, more so, perhaps, than the more standard texts. Some suggestions for use are therefore included below. First, however, a summary of the general layout might be helpful.

This book follows no formal political science model, but biography in and of itself provides a structure and a basis for comparisons. Assuming the importance of both institutions and political culture to be evident, we attempt to show how they interact by examining the life of an individual politician for each country. Therefore, each part is organized broadly on the following plan:

1. The political and social culture of a country is briefly described.
2. Its political institutions are briefly explained.
3. The early life of the political leader, his socialization into politics, and his first steps on the political road are presented.
4. The politician's career is carried to its high point, accompanied by a discussion of what is presently happening and why.
5. The failure of the politician's career (if it has failed) and reasons ascribed to it are described. If the politician continues in power or if he died while in power, reasons for success are adduced.

Institutions are treated formally and informally—formally in the overview of each government and informally in the course of biography. The politician, his role, and the influence of institutions on decisions is emphasized in each part, but the political figures are subordinated to the institutions, rather than the reverse. Given proper guidance, students should emerge from a course in which this book is used with a deeper understanding of the politics of the six countries described and a broader grasp of politics in general.

To this end the book permits several approaches, none of which is mutually exclusive. Some of the approaches might be:

1. *Country-by-country direct.* Each country is treated as a whole and presented in any order that the instructor finds most comfortable. Instructors who already have lecture notes based on this approach can no doubt continue using them, making adjustments only to include the biographies.

2. *Country-by-country topical.* Topics are selected from each part and presented in turn. Thus the section on political socialization and recruitment of the leaders might be compared and attention drawn to the political culture and existing institutions in their respective countries. That is, the third chapter in the British, French, and German parts might be compared with their counterparts in the sections on the Soviet Union, China, and Cuba.

3. *Comparison by political organization.* Here the democratic polities, Britain, France, and Germany, are first compared among each other and then contrasted with Communist regimes. The similarities and differences in recruitment, role, and opportunities could be discussed.

4. *Contrasts between the "First" and "Third" Worlds.* A beginning is already inherent in the text, as both Cuba and China can be considered Third World. However, the contrasts might be expanded by comparing countries that started out with something like the Westminster system (Ghana or Nigeria, perhaps) with others that started out with the French system. Kwame Nkrumah might be compared with Felix Hophuoet-Boigny or with other figures at the head of African, Asian, or Latin American countries.

These suggestions are by no means exhaustive and are offered to show how flexible the book can be in use.

Acknowledgments

As always, the authors owe many debts to others, which can only be inadequately discharged in a preface such as this. We owe a particular debt to Professor Robert W. Clawson of Kent State University, who from the outset acted as constructive critic, adviser, and guide. We also benefitted from the advice, criticism and guidance of Professors Henry Albinski, Pennsylvania State University; Dale Krane, Mississippi State University; Keith Legg, University of Florida; Sanford Lieberman, University of Massachusetts, Boston; Alan P. L. Liu, University of California, Santa Barbara; Bradley Richardson, Ohio State University; George Romoser, University of New Hampshire; Lawrence Scheinman, Cornell University; Philip Taylor, University of Houston; Walter Weiker, Rutgers University; and M. F. Whitemore, University of Kent; and we thank them all for their help. We are, in addition, grateful to our editors for seeing the project through its many stages. Although all these friends enabled us to avoid at least some errors, we alone take responsibility for everything set out in these pages.

E. F.
G. B.
L. D.
J. K.
H. F. K.
K. W. R.

Governments and Leaders

Introduction

Why Individuals?

This is an introductory text on national political systems that assumes that leaders—the ordinary as well as the great—do count and that those who lead nations have a particularly important place in the study of comparative government. A second principal assumption is that political institutions matter. The book is designed to illustrate how national political systems work by looking at their operation through the lives and careers of political leaders chosen to highlight most effectively the interplay of people and institutions.

Some of the political actors picked for this study have essentially been inheritors and perpetuators of institutions and practices initiated by others. Harold Macmillan, Valéry Giscard d'Estaing, and Willy Brandt fit that description. Others—Chou En-lai and Fidel Castro—have played crucial roles in the creation and growth of their national systems. Finally, the career of a leader who changed the nature of an inherited political system by his own ambition and skill is illustrated by Nikita Khrushchev.

The impact of these individual leaders on the histories of their nations and the world varies, but there can be no doubt that history would be much different without their participation. In other words, political events are neither predetermined nor inevitable. They depend not only on circumstances but also on those who bear personal responsibility for the politics of their nations.

The principal method of this text is to use the career of a distinguished political figure as the central theme around which each of the political systems is presented. This approach has a number of advantages for the beginning student of comparative politics. First, tracing the career of a national leader will involve readers in the life of a real figure with whom they can identify, introducing an experiential element into the learning

1

process. Second, the influences contributing
to the advancement or retarding the progress
of an individual who is climbing up the political ladder can be viewed in relation to
the institutions and practices of the political
environment; parties, interest groups, national political institutions—all take on
added meaning through this "ground level"
view. Finally, the flavor of politics emerges
as the reader discovers what kinds of people
succeed, as well as why they succeed and
why they opt for some strategies over others.
After completing this text, the beginning
student of comparative politics should have
a comprehensive grasp of the essential nature of each national political system, as
well as an understanding of many basic
generalizations about politics in *any* system.

Why Comparative?

A key step toward the understanding of a
particular phenomenon is gathering as many
examples of that phenomenon as are available and comparing them. If all possible
examples are exactly alike, then the phenomenon will be one about which explanatory
generalizations are easily made. The more
variation displayed by examples, the more
likely it is that many cases will have to be
studied before reliable generalizations will
be possible. Thus it is with the social phenomenon known as politics. We know that
it is an interpersonal activity. We know that
it is an activity related to gaining influence
over the making of rules. But aside from
such basic statements, it is not possible to
make very many accurate general observations about politics around the globe. Can
scholarly specialists in American politics assume that their generalizations about political participation in the United States are true
in, say, France? And although some general

statements about American interest groups
may also be applicable to France, will they
have any relevance to politics in China?

As the number of national political systems studied scientifically increases, and as
the resulting information is compared, the
likelihood of obtaining accurate and comprehensive knowledge about the phenomenon
of politics in general increases directly. But
the total number of nations on earth is too
large and their complexity too great to allow
such a comprehensive, scientific approach.
One alternative, which can accommodate a
significant increase in cases and can reduce
the problem of complexity, involves looking
at *segments* of political activity. The segment characterized by individual political
leaders' interaction with the institutions and
practices of their national systems is obviously our choice for this introductory text.
Analyzing only that segment, using examples from a number of countries and from a
number of different historical periods, permits a broader perspective than the comprehensive approach does. More important, it
introduces the kind of diversity that will
enable the beginning student of comparative
government to acquire a knowledge not only
of the politics of nations but of their *people*.

This book contains sections on the political careers of leaders from Great Britain,
France, the Federal Republic of Germany,
the Soviet Union, Cuba, and China; each section is presented in six chapters. The introductory commentary that follows is designed
to preview for the reader the basic focus of
each of those six chapters.

Basic Data: Environment and Political Culture

The environment and the political culture of
each country are outlined in the first chapter

2

of each part. The term *environment* refers to the geography, society, and demography of the nation under consideration. But what is political culture? The word *culture,* in this instance, is an anthropological idiom referring to the social attitudes, the customs, the arts and the conveniences of a particular civilization at a certain time. Definition of a distinctly political culture requires that nonpolitical actions be distinguished from political. Such distinctions, though often difficult to make, are not impossible. If people smoke in a public place, one might ask them to stop; this would not be a political act. If, however, one agitates for the enactment of laws to prohibit smoking in public places, this action would be political.

Just as the broad social culture predisposes people to act in certain ways toward objects, so political culture predisposes people to act in certain ways toward political objects. Political predispositions are influenced by such cultural elements as traditions, history, legend, motives, emotions, norms, and symbols. The predispositions themselves can be broken down into three parts: knowledge and awareness of the political system, emotional dispositions to the system, and evaluations of the system—judgments of the system and its performance. *Political objects* are the parts of the political system: legislatures, executives, judiciaries, parties, and pressure groups. All the elements of the political culture are closely interwoven; separating them, as this book does, can be done only for purposes of analysis.[1]

Political culture allows us to give meaning to political acts. It helps us to understand why similar institutions work differently in different countries and how nations have borrowed institutions from elsewhere and adapted them to their own political culture.

The relative homogeneity of British political culture has meant that the widespread acceptance of the authority of government has been tempered by the belief that government should be responsive to the voters.[2] In France, the fragmentation of the political culture has resulted in the contradictory beliefs that government should be autonomous and that it should be under popular control. Each group of voters, whether of the left or the right, will trust the government only if its own party is in power. This schizophrenic political culture has been ascribed to the alternation throughout France's history of "regimes of order" with "regimes of movement."[3] Political culture also provides some explanation of why the Germans, though relatively well informed about their institutions, lacked commitment to them in the early postwar years.

The Soviet experience shows the difficulty of attempting to homogenize diverse cultures. Although the regime strives continually to transform political behavior and political values and claims to have produced a new Soviet citizen, large parts of the country remain loyal to traditional attitudes, a situation that significantly affects the functioning of government. This is particularly the case in the rural and minority areas. The Communist party is still trying to eliminate nepotism in the Islamic areas without success. The Chinese Communist approach to the transformation of political culture has been more intensive than that of the Soviet Union—and sometimes more spectacular. Small-group remolding programs such as

[1] Dennis Kavanagh, *Political Culture* (London: Macmillan & Co., 1972).

[2] Eric Nordlinger, *The Working Class Tories* (Berkeley: University of California Press, 1967). See also John H. Goldthorpe et al., *The Affluent Worker: Political Attitudes and Behavior* (Cambridge: Cambridge University Press, 1971).
[3] Eric Nordlinger, "Democratic Stability and Instability: The French Case," *World Politics* 18, no. 1 (1965):127–157.

"thought reform" and self-criticism are directed to this end, and the people are encouraged to transform their view of the world by participation in great mass movements.

Basic Data: Institutions

Political culture has been said to permeate all political systems. One component of the political culture is its political institutions. Partaking of both social structure and cultural pattern, these institutions give form and focus to politics. Thus, political institutions are discussed throughout this book, but they are expressly described for each country in the second chapter of each section.

The relationship of political institutions to political culture can perhaps be made clear by analogy. Karl Marx tried to prove that goods gained value because of the labor added at each stage of their production. Only the addition of this labor turned raw materials into finished goods; therefore, each article contained a certain quantity of "crystallized labor." In turn, the products and structures of a society can be described as containing "crystallized culture," for the products were made to forms and by techniques that were culturally determined, and the institutions were formed by the development of enduring and organized patterns of behavior. It is through political institutions that social control in the largest sense is exerted and fundamental political desires are met.

Institutions, clearly, are made up of individuals following certain practices and rules within the framework of organizations that embody these formal and informal rules. Again, an analogy may be helpful in explaining this conception. Imagine a tropical island, a palm-fringed coral reef. This reef is built of the skeletons of coral that lived in the past; it provides a home for the living coral, which, when they die, will add their skeletons to the building of the reef.

Institutions, like individuals, have their own institutional subcultures, each of which adds to the political culture of the whole. Heinz Eulau has pointed out that in a very real sense a political culture can be considered an aggregate of political subcultures.[4] These subcultures rest on such things as location, religion, social class, language, occupation, and generation. They combine, in turn, with role cultures, role being the function or expected behavior of an individual in an organization or a group, whether this be a political party, legislature, bureaucracy, or interest group. The biographical parts of the text illustrate something of the opportunities and constraints arising from the institutional and cultural framework in which politicians operate.

Institutions and Leadership
Institutions can be studied at various levels of development. One might almost say that the degree to which institutions have developed determines the constraints or opportunities of leadership. In the British legislative subculture, for instance, high office comes only to those who have served a fairly long apprenticeship as ordinary Members of Parliament. This custom puts limits on the degree to which candidates for high office can develop independent styles and ensures a general conformity among those with high aspirations. In France, on the other hand, legislative impasses often encourage legislators to turn to the "heroic leader" who acts to liquidate crises.

Institutional political culture has its effect on leadership in the Soviet Union and Cuba as well. Robert C. Tucker describes this

[4] Heinz Eulau, *The Behavioral Persuasion in Politics* (New York: Random House, 1963).

when he speaks of the "deradicalization" of Marxist elites, which takes the form of an adjustment to the international political culture, a willingness to accept other countries as they are, and a weakened desire to alter the status quo abroad.[5] At home it means adjusting goals more realistically and conceding at least some of the things needed to increase the contentment of Soviet citizens. On the other hand, Tucker points out, this deradicalization may lead to an increase in the flow of ideological rhetoric rather than a decrease. The reason for this may be that the political culture sustaining and legitimizing the Soviet regime is radical, and to deny the rhetoric of revolution would destroy the base by which the regime makes itself lawful. As a result, maintenance of a version of the Marxist ideology is necessary for the Soviet leadership, and their actual behavior therefore continues to an extent to be affected by this ideology.

Deradicalization was the major issue in Chinese politics in the 1960s and early 1970s. One segment of the leadership, the radicals, was determined to fight this process tooth and nail, while another, the moderates, showed greater willingness to accept deradicalization as an inevitable by-product of modernization. Chou En-lai, while making stylistic concessions to the radicals, seems to have been among the most consistently effective advocates of moderation. At the end of his life he was able to ensure continuation of this moderate philosophy, although it remains to be seen if China's revolutionary legacy can be transformed without further unrest.

Recently deradicalization seems also to have begun in Cuba, though the regime is still so young that it is difficult to be certain.

[5] Robert C. Tucker, "The Deradicalization of Marxist Movements," *American Political Science Review*, 60, no. 2 (1967): 343–358.

Since 1970, Fidel Castro has adopted a less idealistic and more decentralized rule at home and, with the possible exception of Angola, is showing less desire to change things in other countries. Castro's rhetoric, at the same time, has remained just as radical as ever, as his calling for changes in the relationship between the United States and Puerto Rico indicates.

In general, the more established and settled a system of government is, the greater the emphasis is on "the rules of the game," both internationally and at home. These rules are to be interpreted, of course, in the broader, rather than the narrower, sense.

These issues and the political activities of the leaders to be studied should indicate that elites are by no means homogeneous. There are serious divisions within elites, in terms of both personality and policy. The long conflict that Churchill, and also Macmillan, waged with successive Conservative party leaderships is a case in point, as is Macmillan's later rivalry with R. A. Butler. Specific events, such as the invasion of Egypt at the time of the Suez crisis, again highlight differences within elites. In France the bitter personal relationship between Georges Pompidou and Valéry Giscard d'Estaing from 1966 to 1969 and, more recently, the tension between Giscard and the new challenger on the right, his former Prime Minister Jacques Chirac, show that even within a long-established governing group there can arise fierce interpersonal competition. The last years in office of West German Chancellor Konrad Adenauer brought out serious differences between him and his successor, Ludwig Erhard. The Social Democratic elite, as Brandt's career so clearly shows, has not been spared its share of feuding, either.

The leadership groups in dictatorships are no more cohesive than those in democracies. In the Soviet Union, Khrushchev was involved in intense factional struggles with those in the leadership favoring the continuation of Stalinism. This tension continued as he attempted to decentralize the economy, make agriculture more profitable, and reduce the costs of the military. Each attempt was opposed by the groups affected, and a coalition of those threatened by his policies were able eventually to remove him. In China, also, leadership was long assumed to be centralized and monolithic. But this conception disintegrated when it suddenly became apparent in 1966 that a "two-line struggle" was taking place over a number of basic political issues. Since that time, dissension in the leadership has been evident on occasion, resulting in two major purges.

In addition to differences in personality and in policy, generational differences add another dimension. This is, in a sense, most evident in political cultures based on reward for length of service, thereby forcing the young to "wait their turn." The older generation, on their side, try to hold back impetuous and impatient youth by a variety of compensations for loyalty and demonstrated ability. The method used in Britain is the provision of junior ministerial positions, parliamentary secretaryships, and other ranks that offer the opportunity to train for higher office and to further demonstrate both loyalty and skill. When Fidel Castro came to power, he came as representative of a new generation in Cuban politics. But since the old regime had been discredited, intergenerational conflict was less important. Most of the infighting was between individuals of roughly the same age. Fidel Castro appreciated that the emergence of other leaders would detract from his own power and took many steps—some of them quite ruthless—to rid himself of any competition. So it is clear that the absence of an older generation does not remove the source of conflicts within elites. Indeed, much political conflict is less of the old versus the young and rather more of alliances of some old and young politicians versus other alliances of old and young.[6]

The Chinese revolutionary leadership also seized power in 1949 as representatives of a younger political generation and in the first decade of their rule took steps to organize the youth and the women. Such organization was aimed at giving these groups more power within the Chinese family, thereby undermining the power of the older generation. The Chinese leadership has itself aged since that time, due to lack of turnover in the highest ranks. Thus the Cultural Revolution and the steps to revive it in the 1970s display some of the elements of generational conflict, with the young and more venturesome bureaucrats siding with the radical forces.

Political Culture, Conflict, and Bureaucracies

Bureaucracies have subcultures of their own, just as have all other institutions. Ideally, this subculture rests on three broad bases, irrespective of country: rationality—decisions are governed by reason embodied in rules and not based on emotion or whim; organization—all positions are structured through rank, with clear jurisdictions and lines of authority; and agency—the administrative machine responds to instructions from outside itself and acts on behalf of principals who decide policies. Bureaucracies, in practice, never quite conform to this ideal. They are seldom as disinterested as they seek to appear, a fact that emerges in this book.

British administrators, for instance, seek to "capture" their political heads, the Minis-

[6] Edward Feit, "Generational Conflict and African Nationalism in South Africa," *International Journal of African Historical Studies* 5, no. 2 (1972):181–202.

ters in charge, and to persuade them in various subtle ways to represent the views of their departments within the Cabinet. Departments also discourage Ministers' taking too active a role in their affairs. An independent Minister is quickly and firmly brought back into line, and it takes a very strong man or woman to resist the kinds of pressures a determined Permanent Secretary can apply.

China has, perhaps, the oldest bureaucratic tradition in the world and was the first to establish examinations as a criterion for recruitment and promotion in the bureaucracy. Since the revolution, the Communists have returned to the earlier bureaucratic pattern, although wary of the tendencies of the bureaucratic tradition to insulate the rulers from the people and to foster a sense of its elitism. The attempt to regulate the bureaucracy and to prevent distortion of the party's will was first made through the institution of parallel control bureaucracies. Later, it was attempted by cultivating a more activist, and critical, perspective among the citizenry.

France's bureaucracy, at least at its highest reaches, long had a reputation for autonomy. Governments came and fell, but the bureaucracy carried on. This autonomy has become somewhat less visible in recent years because of the domination of the French executive by Gaullists. Their long term in office has enabled them to appoint men and women sympathetic to their point of view to the highest permanent positions in the civil service. Nevertheless, the underlying sources of bureaucratic power remain largely intact and are bound to reappear strongly as the parties' struggle for control of the executive surfaces once more.

The ability to appoint the higher civil servants does not in itself ensure control of the bureaucracy. During his first years in office, Castro tried to minimize the importance of the bureaucracy. He was free to determine its structure and appointed many of the bureaucrats himself. Yet, he soon discovered, bureaucracies seldom merely apply the laws. Rather, through interpretations of the law, they develop power bases of their own. Castro found that this detracted from his own power, a condition that he could not tolerate.

The political culture of a bureaucracy has an important effect on its behavior and on the extent to which bureaucracies will obstruct policies they oppose. In the Soviet Union, for instance, the bureaucracy quietly impedes the implementation of policies it does not like, such as it did to Khrushchev's economic reforms. This happens despite the fact that the bureaucracy is represented in top party bodies such as the Central Committee and the Politburo. In West Germany, on the other hand, although senior civil servants are politically conservative and therefore dissatisfied at times with ministerial decisions, they will normally carry them out efficiently and impartially. The German tradition of respect for authority may be a contributing factor, as it is in East Germany, a country often said to be the only one in which communism works efficiently.

Political Parties and Pressure Groups

Political parties differ greatly in their patterns of subcultures. Much depends on how the dominant culture and its exponents received them when the interests they represented first surfaced as important political forces. For example, after some resistance by propertied classes, the emerging British working class was handled in a conciliatory way. The political wing of the labor movement, the Labour party, was incorporated smoothly into the course of political competition. This generated a trust in parliamentary institutions as a means to desired social change. The attitude that came to dominate in Britain was that bargaining was the best way of getting reforms. In France, on the other hand, different groups—landowners, merchants, capitalists, and laborers—were not smoothly accommodated, and as a result each had an incentive to gain control of the state as a means of advancing its specific interest.[7] Those with something to defend sought to retain control of the state and so to defend their interest against the interests of others. No group trusted the state, and no group felt its rights secure unless it controlled the state. Each subculture, then, was structured into exclusive institutions, each tending to parallel all the others and so to reinforce the subculture. Thus a French Communist will have friendships largely within the party and will seek to satisfy even nonpolitical interests, such as hobbies and recreation, in clubs organized by the party. Unlike Britain, with its independent national newspapers, newspapers in France generally are subscribed to on party lines. Antagonism between groups of different subcultures is increased by strong religious, political and social loyalties.

West Germany, in contrast, has seen a decline in the ideologically based parties so characteristic of the period prior to the Hitler era. Before 1933 the German parties, like the French, had their own subcultures and their own press. But since 1945, as the West German parties have become less ideological and more pragmatic, the importance of these subcultures has declined. To maximize their electoral appeal the parties seek a broad base of support, and, unlike some of their predecessors, they are strongly committed to a democratic order. The "new look" does not mean that policy differences do not arise in

foreign and domestic affairs, but these differences are more muted than they were prior to 1933.

Parties in the communist world emphasize their role in training their peoples. Through initiation of their members into the political culture, they aim to bring the values of the regime to the broader public. The parties have a strong ideological bent, and ideological training is an important part of socializing people into the political culture. One could argue, indeed, that this is the major function of the parties in communist countries. The parties also provide the leaders with a way of finding those who manifest ability in leadership and display the greatest ambition. These members can be recruited to be the leadership cadre of the future. To this end, the Communist party of the Soviet Union has established special party schools, some with terms of post-university study lasting four years. Although today the Cuban Communist party (CCP) is becoming more important as a source of future leaders, it was the smallest Communist party of any Communist nation in the 1960s. Its position reflected, in part, Castro's desire to ensure that power, unconstrained by party or bureaucracy, remained in his hands. With the deradicalization that began about 1970, this is changing and the role of the party is becoming more important.

The Chinese Communist party includes at most 3 percent of the Chinese people, but it has made a strong comeback since it was temporarily eclipsed by the youth movement and then by the army in 1966–1968. The party is organized along the same formal lines as that of the Soviet Union, but has tried to introduce informal mechanisms to keep in closer touch with the people. These have taken the form of the "mass line" and the occasional call for "mass criticism" of the party leadership. Party leaders are also sent

[7] Michel Crozier, *The Bureaucratic Phenomenon* (Chicago: University of Chicago Press, 1964).

down to the masses from time to time. Formally, the Communist party is part of a coalition that includes a number of small "bourgeois democratic parties" in a "united front," but the real power of these parties has dwindled down to almost nothing.

Executives and Legislatures
In the nineteenth century political activists pressed for constitutional government with the executive responsible to the legislature. Representative democracy would curb the arbitrary power of governments and, it was hoped, turn popular aspirations into law. The twentieth century has disappointed these hopes. Legislatures have largely lost ground to executives; in their struggle each legislature has, at one time or another, had the upper hand, but executive power has usually been reasserted.

There are a number of reasons to account for this change. First is the impact of World War I and its demonstration of massive organization of men and materials for a common purpose. The harnessing of entire nations not only showed what could be effected through modern management, but also led to immense expansion of administrative bureaucracies. The second reason, perhaps, was the Great Depression of the 1930s, which discredited private enterprise and encouraged people all over the world to look to their governments to meet their needs. Again administrative control was enhanced. The expansion of administrative power was accompanied by the spread of a socialism that envisaged large-scale government planning as a permanent feature of the modern state. Finally, the bureaucratic expansion was further reinforced in World War II, which once again called large government bureaucracies into being to manage the ever increasing involvement of government in every sphere of life.

Mass participation in government has, thus, led to demands for state intervention in fields from which the government was precluded in the past and has created a vast web of social legislation culminating in the so-called welfare state. In turn, the welfare state has required incursions into the private life of citizens that even the most radical democrat of the nineteenth century would have rejected. The rise of executives reflects the extension of political culture into general culture, or the politicization of social culture. This process has been carried furthest in the Soviet Union and other Communist states, which simply declare that since everything is political, everything is within the command of the state.

The decline of legislatures does not mean that legislatures no longer pass laws. These bodies have interested themselves in more fields than in the past and have put more time into considering and drafting legislation. But in the political subculture of legislatures, with their cumbersome rules and procedures, it is impossible for them to act swiftly and effectively. In addition, the matters calling for laws are increasingly complex and technical, forcing legislatures to rely on the knowledge of the executive and its experts for guidance. Balancing the bureaucracy in this task are pressure groups, much of whose function is to supply this information to both the legislature and the executive. And last, though not least important, the very complexity of modern government bureaucracies, operating by their own rules and sometimes in a jargon bearing little resemblance to ordinary speech, has made investigation and evaluation a difficult task.

The importance of executives, and consequently of those in the positions of chief executives, has determined the focus of this book. Although it explores many aspects of politics in each country, the emphasis is on

Introduction

the political leaders—where they come from, why they succeed, and why they fail.

Socialization and Recruitment: The Early Years

The way individuals acquire their political culture—that is, the way they acquire predispositions to political objects—is termed political socialization. Political recruitment is the process by which individuals are drawn into the political process.

The agents of political socialization, broadly speaking, are such bodies as the family, the school, youth movements, teams and associations, and (in some countries) the church. The sources of socialization may be formal or informal, conscious or unconscious, latent or manifest. In addition to these, other factors, such as social class and ascribed status, can be important in socialization. The influences of these various agencies are not always complementary; often they reinforce each other, but at times they may contradict each other. Children from politically conservative families will usually be conservative, but they may, in some cases and under some conditions, become radicals. The early Russian revolutionaries, for instance, were not drawn from the peasantry or the industrial working class, but from affluent and often socially prominent families. For some complex of reasons, they were socialized into a new political culture—one might almost say a political counterculture—breaking with that into which they had originally been socialized. Fidel Castro is another example of this kind of political development. Born into a wealthy family, he attended the university, as did most wealthy youths of that time. Like many of his fellow students, Castro became a radical, but unlike them, he

retained his beliefs. His contemporaries generally became deradicalized on getting their first job after graduation. Several of his professional associates, who also had been young radicals, tried to draw Castro into the "democratic circle" so that he could share in the benefits and rewards of the political system. But they failed to convince Castro, who remained firmly on his own path and emerged eventually as leader of a revolutionary group.

Another leader who also rejected many of the beliefs current in his time is Willy Brandt of West Germany. Yet Brandt did not rebel against his own socialization; rather, he followed the path it dictated. The socialist atmosphere of his surroundings and the social class into which he was born were decisive. He rejected the conservative values of his schoolteachers and was uninterested in church activities, which he saw as supportive of that same conservatism. Instead, he avidly espoused socialism as propounded by his socialist grandfather and by his journalist mentor, Julius Leber, who was also a leading Social Democratic party official. Brandt soon became a political activist, his activities reinforcing his viewpoint.

Rebels, it would seem, develop in two ways: either they reject their socialized political culture or, having been brought up in a subculture opposed to the ruling order, they accept the role of rebel.

Nikita Khrushchev began his career as a soldier in the Red Army in the civil war that followed the Russian Revolution of 1917. His service in the Red Army brought him into contact with the socializing forces of communism, and his socialization was continued by studying in party schools and by serving as a party official. Khrushchev's rise followed what were ordinary lines for a man aiming for the top in the Soviet system.

Military service, indeed, has played a powerful role in the careers of many political figures. Castro, of course, led his own forces in the bid for power in Cuba; and Macmillan's contact with the working classes of Britain in the trenches of World War I awoke him to their worth. War certainly can be said to be a significant instrument of socialization, especially in those countries in which having served is a passport to politics. In Britain few, if any, Conservative leaders who had not served the King or the Queen in the army could hope for the highest office.

In a broad sense, socialization can be said to take place in two stages. The first stage begins with the family and establishes the general perspective of political culture. The second stage is that in which the individual links his or her own personal advancement directly to political activities. These two stages hold true for rebels and conformists, and this process, at once formal and informal, continues throughout life. The array of socializing agencies is vast and becomes more complex as the individual passes from birth to death.

Macmillan's political perceptions were molded by the family tradition of ambition and hard work, to which was added his mother's drive toward the social and political advancement of her children. Macmillan's socialization into an elite role was continued in school and at the university and by his wartime service in an elite regiment of the British army. Marriage after the war into the family of the Duke of Devonshire, one of the leaders of the Conservative party, served to further socialize Macmillan into politics. The process was continued when he entered the party and became a candidate competing for the votes of the working class.

Destined by his father for the role of a leader of France, Giscard went to all the right schools and was prepared for the prestigious Polytechnique and the National School of Administration. In the course of his socialization, Giscard, like Harold Macmillan, must have learned what would advance his career, and his educational background gave him the right sort of contacts. He also learned how to deal effectively with those who could either advance his career or retard it. But for Giscard and Macmillan the same kind of education had to take place in the broader framework of parliamentary experience. Here formal training in the ways of a parliamentary government was to be gained in the Assembly or in the House of Commons; and informal training, in "the corridors of power." This training was essential for both men before they could hope for the highest office.

Pathways to Power: The Middle Years

The chapter following that on the socialization and recruitment of the political leader deals with his rise to power. The first consideration is, obviously, how a person comes to be recognized as a leader, and this, in turn, demands a definition of leadership. As Lucian Pye showed for Burma, it is one thing for a politician to come to power and another to understand how power is to be used.[8]

The meaning of the term *leadership* has been debated among political philosophers for centuries. Nonetheless, the term can be defined in a common-sense way. Leadership is the exercise of influence over a long time in a variety of situations in a consistent way. In addition, all the members of the group, party, or legislature *expect* the leader to exercise this influence consistently.[9] In essence, the public's belief that certain individuals

[8] Lucian W. Pye, *Politics, Personality and Nation Building: Burma's Search for Identity* (New Haven, Conn.: Yale University Press, 1962).
[9] Peter Kelvin, *The Bases of Social Behavior: An Approach in Terms of Order and Value* (London: Holt, Rinehart and Winston, 1970).

who exercise influence consistently should do so to fulfill their roles is what qualifies them as leaders. In political terms, these expectations will be molded by the dominant political culture. If the position of the leader is formally recognized in the political culture of the group, the position is not only one that confers power and influence but also one that is valued. Formal leadership separates person and office. The Prime Minister of Britain, for example, has institutional power, but may personally not be highly regarded. Neville Chamberlain is an example: although his policy of appeasement of Hitler brought him into personal disrepute, the powers of the office of Prime Minister remained unimpaired.

There is, of course, a difference based on how leaders came to power, whether they are appointed by popular choice, or actively seize power, or are selected by an inner grouping. The argument is that leaders selected through popular choice are more likely to impose their own ideas, as are individuals who create the basis of their own power. Leaders appointed by small groups in the absence of popular choice are more likely to see themselves as coordinators.[10]

British Prime Ministers, for instance, as the focuses of public interest, have become increasingly independent of their party colleagues and more likely to impose their policies on Cabinets. A comparison can be made of two German leaders: Konrad Adenauer, as the architect of post–World War II Germany, could be far more independent, indeed autocratic, than Ludwig Erhard, who was his successor as Chancellor. Erhard tried to avoid playing the role of leader and thus contributed to his own prompt downfall. In

France, even since General de Gaulle's departure, the same conditions are true: it is the leader who is the focus and who can dictate policies. The parties of the left—the Socialists and the Communists—would no doubt like to be popular for their ideology rather than their leaders' images.

Castro, by contrast, as the creator of his revolution and the incumbent of postrevolutionary power, has a more decisive voice in determining what happens in Cuba than did Khrushchev in the Soviet Union, who was appointed by a cabal in the Politburo. Khrushchev's power grew as he passed from government by committee to personal rule, but it was never as firm as that of the Cuban leader. Khrushchev was, for example, unable to expel his opponents from the party, though pushing hard for their expulsion on several occasions.

Political Leaders at the Top: How Do They Get There?

One of the most debated questions about political leadership is whether personal qualities or historic circumstances determine who is to be the leader and how effective that leadership is. Anatol Rapoport speaks of the "rational" and the "cataclysmic" views of history.[11] The rational view sees the leader as a person reasoning out the steps toward a goal; the cataclysmic view sees the leader as one who is caught up by historical forces and swept along by them, with no more control over them than human beings have over the forces of nature. Perhaps it is best to say that personality and situation interact with each other: they are not alternatives, but each

[10] This is the theoretical argument of William Whyte in *Street Corner Society: The Social Structure of an Italian Slum* (Chicago: University of Chicago Press, 1943).

[11] Anatol Rapoport, Editor's Introduction to Karl von Clausewitz, *On War* (Baltimore: Penguin Books, 1968).

contributes to leadership. This is true even in political systems with highly traditional pathways to power, such as Britain and France. It is also true of Germany and of the Soviet Union, where the pathways to power have been routinized more recently.

The interplay of personal ability and historic circumstance is very evident in British politics. In the British Parliament seniority counts more than age, and so entering the House of Commons early in one's career increases one's chances of reaching the top. Hence, anything that facilitates entering Parliament at a young age—being born rich or titled, or receiving the right education—gives the politician possessing them a head start. Macmillan, backed by the wealth of a family publishing business, and encouraged by marriage within a political and aristocratic family, had just such a head start. In his case, it helped put him in Parliament; his failure to progress for a long time was due to his pressing his convictions, which often were unpopular with his party. Nonetheless, any British politician must count on the period from bottom to top taking some fifteen years.[12]

Loyalty is another factor that must be taken into account with long service, and it was on this score that Macmillan was considered deficient by leaders like Stanley Baldwin and Neville Chamberlain. Macmillan was loyal to Churchill, however, and so was rewarded with office when Churchill came to power. Loyalty may be to faction, rather than to party leader, and if a faction becomes powerful enough, its leaders will have to be drawn into the government. No matter how Macmillan and R. A. Butler felt toward each other, the Prime Minister had to place Butler in every Cabinet he formed. A parallel with France is suggested here: despite their mu-

tual dislike, President Pompidou and Prime Minister Giscard each found it necessary, in advancing his own career, to cooperate with the other.

The career of Willy Brandt again shows the interesting way in which circumstance and skill combine. Brandt's rise was certainly aided by personal qualities—his skills as a speaker, his attractive personality, and his intelligence. He was known to be loyal to the party and to accept its ideals. Further, Brandt had gained the support of party leaders, a support he had skillfully cultivated. Matters of chance were equally evident. Brandt was in the right place (Berlin) at the right time (during the postwar chaos). He achieved public prominence first as a party leader, then as a member of the city legislature, and then as its President. Finally Brandt became Mayor of Berlin when this city represented an outpost of the West, at the height of the Cold War. The climb up the political ladder was paralleled by a climb up the party ladder. By the time he became Party Chairman, he was already the designated Chancellor candidate. The next steps were from Vice-Chancellor and Foreign Minister to the top, as Chancellor.

The closely structured character of the Western democracies seems to determine that becoming a leader is more a matter of situation than of personality. The juxtaposition of historical circumstances with the appropriate service and commitment, as shown above, determines who will rise to the top.

In Communist systems, the trend is in the same direction as regimes become deradicalized and routinized. It is interesting to contrast the Soviet Union, China, and Cuba in this regard. The Soviet Union may be termed a mature Communist state, whereas both China and Cuba are less mature in terms of development and systematization. Cuba is still in its first generation of leaders,

12 W. L. Guttsman, *The British Political Elite* (London: McGibbon & Kee, 1963).

with Castro in full possession of power; the Chinese system is in its second, following the deaths of Mao Tse-tung and Chou En-lai. The Soviet Union has now experienced at least four changes in leadership. In Cuba personality, particularly the personality of Castro, dominates the regime. In China a trend toward depersonalization of the leadership seems to be underway, while in the Soviet Union the means by which a leader is selected has begun to assume rudimentary shape and to influence the scope of individual leaders. The changes were not clear at the time of Stalin's death, just as they are not so soon after the death of Mao. Khrushchev, however, showed that the operational leader of the party apparatus could edge out all opponents in other parts of the political system for the topmost position. This remains true and seems to have become a permanent factor in Soviet politics.

Political leaders depend on administrative bureaucracies for their information and for the execution of their policies. Information is perhaps the more important, for policies are based on what is known of a situation. Who controls information, therefore, to a great extent controls policy. Although policy making is increasingly falling to bureaucracies, the political leaders still have to give the impression that everything originates with them and with their political associates. The need to convey this impression to the public has led to a heightened emphasis on leadership style, an emphasis so great that some political thinkers have come to wonder whether leadership is anything other than style.[13]

What is style? It has been defined as any distinctive (and therefore recognizable) way that political acts are performed or ought to be performed. Thus, Murray Edelman argues, the important question is less one of *how* leaders lead and more one of *why* followers follow.[14] Followers follow, he asserts, because they are *reassured* by the belief, deliberately fostered by leaders, that the latter are competent, know what to do, and will take responsibility for what happens. Leaders provide hope for a public that finds the world too difficult to influence and too complex to understand. All that leaders must do is to reassure the people, for the goals they profess to pursue cannot be assessed, and there is no way of knowing whether the leaders will or will not bring about desired change. It is even more difficult for members of the public to judge the success or failure of political acts. Leadership, as a result, resembles acting. The political leader plays the actor-hero, reassuring the public, while the real decisions are made elsewhere.

In emphasizing style to the extent he does, Edelman may have pressed the point too far. Significant historical facts cannot be explained in terms of style alone, and the same can be said for acts that are of less profound significance. The fate of nations or even of civilizations has often depended on one individual, on that individual's ability to endure the stress of decision at a time of crisis without breaking. Would the present century have been the same had Lenin died before the Russian Revolution? Had de Gaulle been killed in 1940? Had Churchill died in 1938? Or had Mao died on the Long March? Yet, to claim this is not to denigrate Edelman's point. Style was important to the great who acted to move and shake their world. It is even of greater importance in our time, due to the immediate impact of television. Television has become an important element in political culture,

[13] Murray Edelman, *The Symbolic Uses of Politics* (Champaign-Urbana: University of Illinois Press, 1964).

[14] Ibid.

projecting the image of the leader into virtually every household. This image, moreover, depends heavily on the leader's style. There seem to be common elements in this style in all political cultures. The leader must, by both appearance and actions, convey a sense of competence, intelligence, calm under stress, eloquence, and likeability, among other qualities. What specifically conveys these qualities to publics is, however, a matter of political culture.

Britain, with its deferential political culture, turns largely to leaders who either are upper class or appear to be. Other voters look to leaders who are aggressively lower class, though this image is primarily confined to Labour. Generally, as one goes up the political ladder in Britain—from constituency, to party activists, to local government, to Parliament, to the Cabinet—the emphasis is increasingly on the upper and upper-middle classes, *regardless of party*.[15] A recent survey has shown that voters in Britain attach greater importance to the personal qualities of the leaders than to the goals to which the leaders are seen to be committed.[16] The sense of the leader's being from the upper classes seems one of these qualities, as long as it is not combined with snobbery. Edward Heath, for instance, was disliked not only because he was unmarried ("he wouldn't understand family problems"), but also because he was seen as a snob.[17] Macmillan was much appreciated because he was seen as hard-working and "unflappable"; he would not, people thought, panic in times of crisis. However, Macmillan's age was held against him. Age and other personal qualities unrelated to politics play their part, as do

appearance and the ability of a leader to make himself liked.

There is, of course, a considerable gap between the image, as seen by the public, and the reality, as seen by other politicians. Many insiders in the Labour party held a far less flattering view of Harold Wilson than did the public. Wilson could project an image of honesty and bluff forthrightness to the public, while most of his colleagues considered him devious and unreliable.[18]

The French, with their traditional admiration of logic and figures, were influenced by Giscard's mastery of economic facts and theories. This was, indeed, how he first made his mark in the French parliament. France also prides itself on its literary tradition, so Giscard's occasionally expressed desire to be an author, rather than a politician, and his admiration for Flaubert have both amused and flattered French sensibilities, for Flaubert was certainly one of the masters of modern literature. Giscard subtly combines two qualities much admired in French politics today—technical skill in a technical field and a strong sense of the importance of language, of political rhetoric. While perhaps lacking some of the verbal flair of General de Gaulle, Giscard expresses himself publicly in a fashion that makes his nearest rivals, as well as leaders in other nations, appear stodgy and unimaginative by comparison.

Although each of the German politicians who rose to prominence after World War II had a different career and different style of leadership, there is something of a common pattern. Brandt was appreciated by the supporters of the Social Democratic party and the coalition government for his personal style of leadership and for his successes in foreign policy. In postwar years, with national memories of Nazism and with a desire

[15] Guttsman, *British Political Elite*.
[16] David Butler and Donald Stokes, *Political Change in Britain: The Evolution of Electoral Choice*, 2d ed. (London: Macmillan & Co., 1974).
[17] Ibid.

[18] Ibid.

to regain respectability, Brandt represented much of the "new Germany": he was democratic and not authoritarian, he used power sparingly, and he was able to relate to an ordinary German citizen as easily as to a foreign dignitary. Brandt was, however, also a very moody man, easily depressed, and not the sort to maintain party unity. Yet, despite these weaknesses, historians of the future may well class him as one of the more noteworthy German leaders of our times.

Interestingly enough, Khrushchev's image corresponds somewhat to the reverse upper-class image adopted by some Labour party figures in Britain. He was the rough peasant come up in the world and, it was often suspected, played the part with gusto. Like many other leaders, he appeared different to those with something to lose. To the new Soviet middle class Khrushchev appeared "nekulturny"—crude and uncultured—and, in addition, provided the image of one who is erratic and prone to institutional changes that threaten the established elites, such as the state planning bureaucracy and the officer corps. This made him dangerous to colleagues in the Politburo, who combined against him in 1964. Khrushchev was the nearest thing to a popular leader in the Soviet Union, and when he came to Moscow to vote after his fall, he was given a warm reception by the crowd. His public appearances were understandably kept rare.

Lady Violet Bonham-Carter has said that there is no occupation, profession, or vocation in which personality is more important than in politics. But one senses that she is concerned with both image and reality, for she adds that politics involves the obligation not only of appearing and speaking, but also "thinking and feeling—or at least appearing to think and feel—in public." [19]

[19] Violet Bonham-Carter, *The Impact of Personality in Politics* (Oxford: Clarendon Press, 1963).

The Decline of Leaders

Two of the leaders considered in this book, Giscard and Castro, remain in power as it goes to press. Chou En-lai died in office. Three fell from power: Macmillan because of illness and the gradual erosion of his influence; Brandt because of the scandals that began mounting around him; and Khrushchev because of a loss of support by the politically powerful in government and party. Macmillan and Brandt, at this writing, remain influential, but Khrushchev ceased all political activity with his fall.

To understand why leaders fail we must look to what they are expected to provide. They are expected to exercise continuous influence and to reassure the mass public that their needs are being or will be met. They are at the same time guardians of order within their own parties, founts of reward and patronage; and they are expected to demonstrate success—whether apparent or real—at suitable intervals. Failure to provide these things erodes the leader's image and causes followers to look elsewhere for influence and reassurance.

In the British case, Prime Ministers are expected to provide leadership by offering new ideas to the party that will, in turn, appeal to the voters in the constituencies. They are expected to hold the party together, to prevent the factions from moving apart and thus breaking the party, a condition that would occasion either its falling from power or its appearing in disarray to the voters. They are expected to control the kind of legislation that is passed, to ensure that it is consistent with the government's declared policy and not too different from what was promised the voters. And finally they are expected to maintain Cabinet loyalty—not by acting like vigilantes, not by sacking Ministers at the smallest sign of weakness—but rather by reassigning them or giving them a graceful period of time to prepare their resignations. Macmillan, by sacking several Ministers at one time, damaged his reputation for loyalty and calm, both important ingredients in his leadership image. Voters also expect Members of Parliament, and Ministers in particular, to be more moral than they themselves are. The Keeler-Profumo scandal, in which a Minister (but not a Cabinet Minister) was involved in a sordid scandal with a call girl, further tarnished the reputation of Macmillan's government though the Prime Minister was personally exonerated. Together with Macmillan's age, ill-health, and seemingly waning powers of command, this incident led many Conservatives to doubt his ability to lead the party to victory in the next election. Macmillan was, therefore, persuaded to resign by circumstances. He resigned with reluctance, and had he not overestimated the seriousness of his illness, he might have tried to continue leading the Conservative party.

Brandt resigned from the chancellorship for a number of reasons, but remained on as head of the German Social Democratic party. Plagued by dissension within the party and sniping by two other top party leaders, he was also influenced by adverse economic developments and a spy scandal within the chancellery. The capacity of Brandt's administration had been brought into question by the scandal, as it was felt that the spy's employment indicated a breakdown in communications within the intelligence services, and there was some fear that Brandt's private life would be drawn into the case. Though Brandt was not entirely blamed for the spy scandal, the stigma and remaining ill-will made continuance in office impossible.

It is more difficult to determine the reasons for the fall of a leader in the Soviet Union. According to news reports, Khrushchev asked to be removed "for health reasons" but the absence of praise made it clear that he was in disgrace. References were later made to "hare-brained scheming" and "hasty decisions." Khrushchev may have been able to hold his enemies in check, but seems not to have been able to prevent his friends from ousting him when they grew discontented with his leadership. His successors began, as the former Politburo had done on changing leaders, by emphasizing the collective character of the leadership group.

Summary

The purpose of this chapter has been to explain the structure of this book and to introduce some of the topics it covers. The book uses the lives of important, but not necessarily great, politicians to help explain the political systems in which they work.

The importance of comparison in learning is emphasized, as are the conceptions of political culture, political socialization, and recruitment, within the framework of political institutions. In the course of the discussion, supplemented by examples, democratic and communist systems are contrasted, revealing some of the similarities and some of the differences between them. The role of bureaucracies, which increasingly are gaining control of legislation and making their executive heads their hostages, are aired, as are the roles of the pressure groups.

Much of the rest of the chapter concentrates on leadership, for much can be learned of political systems by looking at the kind of leadership that succeeds in politics. The discussion follows the chapter order of the book, beginning with the way in which the leaders enter politics, how they rise to the top, what they do once there, and why they fail—if they do. In the course of explanation, such things as the political image, the role of personality, and the role of circumstances are considered.

I

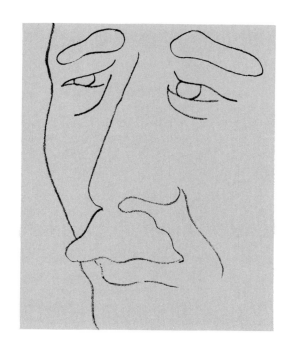

Harold Macmillan and British Politics

Edward Feit

Harold Macmillan
Short Biographical Sketch

Born in London on February 1, 1894, Harold Macmillan was educated at Eton and at Balliol College of Oxford University. He served in World War I as an officer in the Grenadier Guards and was wounded three times; he then served as aide-de-camp to the Governor-General of Canada, 1919-1920.

He sat as Conservative Member of Parliament for Stockton-on-Tees, 1924–1929 and 1931–1945, and then for Bromley, Kent, 1945–1964. Governmental positions have included Parliamentary Secretary, Ministry of Supply, 1940–1942; Parliamentary Under-Secretary of State for Colonies, 1942; Minister Resident at Allied Headquarters, 1942–1945; Secretary for Air, 1945; Minister of Housing and Local Government, 1951–1954; Minister of Defense, 1954–1955; Secretary of State for Foreign Affairs, 1955; Chancellor of the Exchequer, 1955–1957; and Prime Minister January 1957–October 1963.

He has been chairman of Macmillan & Co., a British publishing company, since 1963, and its president since 1974. He has also served as Chancellor of the University of Oxford since 1960. Macmillan married Lady Dorothy Evelyn Cavendish, daughter of the Duke of Devonshire, in 1920.

1

Introduction:
Britain–Land and People

Britain and the British

Britain is a group of islands located off the coast of Europe and divided into four countries: England, Scotland, Wales, and Northern Ireland. Once independent kingdoms, they are now united under the British Crown and, thus, are often referred to as the United Kingdom. The Scots, Welsh, and Irish become annoyed if their counties are spoken of as "England" or they themselves as "English," yet England is by far the largest county, with over 80 percent of the whole British population concentrated there in a strip measuring roughly 100 by 300 miles.

Britain is highly urbanized, more so than any European country, with most people living in cities, large and small towns, and villages. Seven cities contain 40 percent of the total population, with London alone housing about half that figure. Much of this heavy concentration has taken place in the past one hundred years, though Britain was highly urbanized even before then. There

was one country man for every townsman in 1851, and the proportion has changed to one in twenty today.

Until the early 1960s Britain could boast of a vast colonial empire on which "the sun never sets." London was the hub of Empire, and British cities manufactured the goods bought in the colonies. Now, though the sun has set on Britain's once proud empire, London remains the center of British life— geographically, commercially, and politically. Industry, commerce, banking, and government are concentrated in London. Most Britishers can visit London for the day and be home that night. The centrality of London has given all Britishers a national, rather than a local, outlook (as evidenced by the national focus in television and in the press). Because of its accessibility and its history, Britishers have a bond with London that is lacking in countries where the capital is distant and rarely visited.

Great Britain

*Ailing Economy and New
Commonwealth*

Despite the fall of the pound sterling and
talk of economic collapse, Britain remains a
rich country. It ranks seventh among the
world's nations in gross national product,
and Britishers are among the wealthiest 10
percent of the world's peoples. Yet, to say
this is not to deny its severe economic problems, which successive British governments
have been unable to resolve.

As the first country to industrialize,
Britain grew rich and powerful in the nineteenth century. It became known as "the
workshop of the world," and marveling
foreigners said that "God must be an Eng-
lishman." But the advantage of being first
eroded as other nations developed industries
of their own. British industries became obsolete, especially those that had been the
foundation of its wealth: coal, engineering,
iron, shipbuilding, and textiles.

Britain also pioneered the labor movement
and succeeded to such an extent that today
the power of the trade unions inhibits the
remodernization of the economy. The unions
have become virtually "a state within the
state"—an autonomous power beyond the
control of either Conservative or Labour governments. The power of the trade unions is
so great that they comprise, in essence, a
second government. The power of unions
and the antiquated work rules they seek to
perpetuate have led many British industries
to set up plants outside the British Isles.
Britain has not only exported industry; it has
exported some of its most talented citizens in
a "brain drain" that causes serious concern.
In addition, it supplied many present competitors with the machinery they have used to
drive Britain out of the world's markets.
Britain now has a high rate of unemployment: it must find new industries to absorb

its workers and new ways to hold on to its
shrinking share of the world trade.

In addition to fragments too small and too
scattered to become independent, many of
Britain's former colonies remain linked to it
through the Commonwealth—a loose association of independent states with the British
Monarch as nominal head. The "old Commonwealth" consisted of countries bound to
Britain by sentiment, similar institutions, and
a common culture: Canada, Australia, New
Zealand, and the former Union of South
Africa. The ties within this old Commonwealth were close. Since the sixties a "new
Commonwealth" has emerged with the grant
of independence to most of the British colonies that opted for Commonwealth membership, countries such as Ghana, Malaysia,
Nigeria, and Sri Lanka. This new Commonwealth comprises nations vastly different in
populations, cultures, and forms of government. Many are republics and one, Malaysia, has a monarch of its own. Ties now are
looser, and the Queen's role is purely titular.
Economics and sentiment bind this Commonwealth, which allows Britain to retain some
of the tattered trappings of an empire whose
time is past.

The "Class-Ridden" Society

Few terms are as misused as *social class*.
Measures such as income, education, and
occupation are often applied, possibly in an
attempt to quantify this variable. These are
important measures, but social class is far
more subjective, especially in Britain, where
class rests on intangibles such as birth, rank,
lifestyle, accent, and, to some extent, achievement and identification.

The best way to understand the role of
class in British society, is, perhaps, to look at
it from the top down, beginning with the
Monarch at the apex of the class pyramid.

Britain is a monarchy and the Monarch is obviously the highest personage in the land, followed by members of the royal family. Below them is the titled aristocracy, beginning with the title of highest rank, that of duke, and ending with the lowest, that of knight. Sharing titles and common interests, the aristocrats form an integrated body, which enhances their importance. The aristocracy is not a useless ornament but rather serves to set many standards for the society as a whole, notably those of disinterested public service and a tradition of "fair play." Their services in peace and war, often distinguished, have earned the aristocrats the respect in which most of British society holds them.

The Monarch, as "fount of honor," confers titles, and new ones are created each year in a Birthday Honors List. All titles other than knight used to be hereditary, but since 1958 most titles are granted for the life of the recipient only and cannot be inherited. These new titles form a layer below the old aristocracy and absorb the most successful and creative people in Britain. A Birthday Honors List may include not only the most successful of academics, authors, industrialists, and professionals, but rock stars and football players as well. Thus considerable prestige is conferred on men and women who may have begun life in quite humble circumstances.

Merging with the new aristocracy is the upper-middle class, which is closest to the aristocracy, new and old, in strivings. It resembles the American upper class and tries to emulate the aristocratic lifestyle. Members either attended or send their children to the "right school" (the large and more prestigious private schools) and the "right college" (one of the "blue bricks"—Oxford or Cambridge), take up the "right profession" (banking, law, literature, or medicine), and achieve the "right level" of success (substantial, but not flashy). Cultivation of an aristocratic accent and lifestyle is also customary, as are efforts to join either the "literary set" or the "country house set." The influence of the aristocracy has been debilitating to many members of the upper-middle class, who tend to look down on industrial management as a career even though their fortunes, earned or inherited, were made in industry. While workers, unions, patterns of investment, and other causes are commonly cited in explaining Britain's decline, the attempt to carry aristocratic attitudes into industry must take its share of the blame.

The class structure in the lower reaches comes closer to the pattern in America and other countries. The influence of the aristocracy and their imitators is increasingly diluted as one descends the class ladder. Yet the class structure, despite increasing intellectual criticism, is broadly accepted and voluntarily upheld. It could not be maintained in any other way than by general implicit assent; it could not be imposed.

Nationalism and Change
One other observation might be mentioned: in a quiet way the British are extremely nationalistic and suspicious of foreigners and foreign ideas. They have a firm belief that Britishers are superior (this is considered to be so obvious that there is no need to boast) and that, in spite of everything, "British is best." Their confidence has been shaken by the country's rapid decline; but if this fact is mentioned, achievements in the arts, humanities, and sciences are offered in rebuttal. The sense of national superiority and the resulting solidarity have helped ensure the stability of British society. They have also contributed to a sense of smugness and self-

righteousness that has prevented Britishers from benefiting fully from the experiences of others. After all, if things are already being done the right way—"the British way" —why change?

Despite such shortcomings, the sense of being British and the love of things British have enabled its democracy to survive without a formal constitution. The broad acceptance of the British way, playing fairly by the rules, is deeply entrenched. This attitude, perhaps stronger than it would be if it were embodied in formal documents, is what makes the British system workable.

2

British Government:
An Overview

British political institutions are deeply rooted in the past and, like many things ancient, seem complicated when described for the first time. The present chapter will attempt to present their working in simple terms, to be elaborated on later when Harold Macmillan's career is discussed.

The Unwritten Constitution:
Some History

The British Parliament has evolved over hundreds of years, and its history could not be presented in detail in so brief a section as this. Certain historic events are set forth as particularly important here, but this does not mean parliamentary evolution was an uninterrupted forward movement. Rather these events can be considered convenient markers of change.

The most significant of such markers are the revolutions of 1642 and 1688. The Revolution of 1642 marked the decisive phase in the struggle of Monarch and Parliament. Charles I claimed to rule by divine right—as God's anointed, he was not subject to any earthly authority—and was beheaded for his pains. Britain then had a brief experience of republican government and returned with relief to the "Merrie Monarch," Charles II, who could no longer claim his father's powers. Parliamentary supremacy was again confirmed in the Revolution of 1688, which toppled James II and installed William of Orange and his wife, Mary, as joint Monarchs. Parliament passed a Bill of Rights that stated among other provisions, that the King was forbidden to pass or amend laws or to raise taxes or imposts, without the consent of Parliament. Elections to Parliament had to be free, and Parliament was to meet frequently. The system established informal checks and balances between Monarch and Parliament, but the monarchy grew weaker as Parliament grew stronger. Politicians soon learned how to manipulate Monarchs and how to manage all affairs among themselves. The power of the Crown was further curtailed when the office of Prime Minister was established by Sir Robert Walpole in 1721 and the Prime Minister was made broker between Parliament and Monarch.

Two historic facts must, however, be borne in mind: first, despite the revolutions of 1642 and 1688 Britain did not need to reconsider its constitution in the face of rapidly changing events, as did continental revolutionary regimes. Continuity was maintained through Parliament, and this continuity has made it unnecessary for the British to spell out the terms of government. Second, the Crown has remained at the center of British government (except for Cromwell's short republican experiment in 1649–1660) even when its powers have been greatly reduced. British Monarchs, in any event, have always had to face challenge. In the past they ruled with the cooperation of the nobility, who still retain a role in the House of Lords. They had also to consider the power of the church, although this was largely settled by Henry VIII (of the many wives), who broke with Rome, established the Church of England, and made the Monarch its head. The mass conversion of Britishers to Protestantism helped enhance unity and the tie of Monarch and people. Today the Monarch is largely a figurehead, though royal influence varies with the personality of the incumbent of the Throne.

Everything in Britain's largely unwritten constitution is connected to the (often distant) past. The constitution is not a single document as is the American, but is instead a mixture of laws, customs, and generally accepted rules.

Although the foundation for democracy was laid in the seventeenth century, universal democracy came to Britain only recently. It was at the turn of the nineteenth century that a highly literate bourgeoisie and working class began to press for a say in the country's affairs. Parliamentary reforms enabled Britain to accommodate these new classes without a revolution. The Reform Act of 1832, the first of the great reform acts, enfranchised only 7 percent of the people, yet its passage made it clear to the working class that even though their wishes had not been fully met, they soon would be. The franchise was extended by another 9 percent with the Reform Act of 1867 and a further 20 percent with the Reform Act of 1884. The Representation of the People Act of 1918 extended the vote to most men and to women over thirty; and in 1928 women were given the vote on the same conditions as men. The secret ballot was introduced in 1872 and corruption successfully defeated in 1883 with the Corrupt and Illegal Practices Act, which limited how much each party and each candidate could spend in an election and imposed heavy penalties for corrupt practices. Nearly one hundred years had to pass before all Britishers were fully enfranchised.

Slow as the process may seem to have been, it did give the British political system time to absorb each new group of voters and spared Britain the travail of the European countries. Tranquillity has been bought at the price of flexibility. Britain's institutions, slowly and peacefully evolving, have tended to solidify, making innovation very difficult, if not impossible. Thus, despite the intense pressure on the economy and the growing need for new legislation, Parliament still works by the timetable of a more leisured age.

The British constitution, thus, is incorporated in no one formal document and consists partly of laws, partly of court decisions, partly of rules and practices, and partly of common law. For example, the Parliament

Act of 1911 limits the life of a Parliament to
five years. In practice, however, a government that has lost the confidence of the
House of Commons is expected to resign.
Although there is no law to this effect and
although Prime Ministers have, from time to
time, continued in office after being defeated
in the House, the practice is generally observed. It is very difficult (but not impossible) for a Government lacking a majority
in the House to govern.

The Structure of Parliament

Monarch, Lords, and Commons

British government is made up of three
parts: The Crown, the Cabinet, and Parliament. Parliament consists of two houses, the
House of Lords and the House of Commons,
much as the House of Representatives and
the Senate make up the Congress of the
United States. The important differences are
that the House of Lords is not elected and
that the powers of Lords and Commons, unlike House and Senate, are not equal. The
House of Commons is very powerful, the
House of Lords very restricted in influence.

Perhaps the best beginning is with the
Monarch, who still has a role in British government. The Monarch has the right to be
informed on all affairs of state, at home and
abroad. All Cabinet and department papers,
all foreign communiques, and all Cabinet
decisions are sent to the Monarch. All formal appointments are made by the Crown,
though only on the advice of the Cabinet.
The Monarch can accumulate considerable
experience in the course of a reign, perhaps
more than many Ministers, gaining informal
influence in this way. Otherwise, the Monarch can advise, encourage, warn, and even
privately criticize governmental decisions,
but it is Parliament or, more specifically, the
Cabinet that decides in the end.

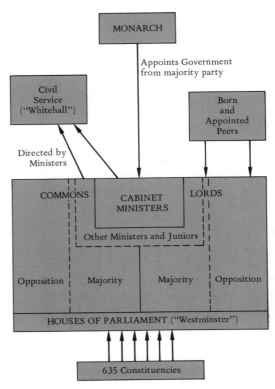

Schematic representation of British government

The House of Lords, like the Monarch,
remains with only a shadow of its once great
powers. Even the veto that the House of
Lords once possessed has been sharply reduced by acts of Parliament of 1911 and
1949. Delay is now for no more than one
year, and none is brooked on money bills.
The House of Lords has a minor legislative
role, in that bills of minor importance are
introduced there, the government sponsoring
some nineteen such bills each year. Membership in the House of Lords was hereditary in
the past. Today, though hereditary peers
remain members, the new rank of Life Peer,
created in 1958, has made members who
cannot transmit their titles or their seats in
Lords. Perhaps the strangest thing about the
House of Lords is that, according to the

30

polls, it more closely reflects public opinion than does the popularly elected House of Commons.

The major legislative body is the House of Commons, chosen in one general election by universal franchise every five years or less. There are 635 constituencies (electoral districts), averaging sixty-five thousand voters, though they vary in size. Each constituency sends one representative to the House of Commons as its Member of Parliament (often abbreviated to MP), election being by a plurality of votes cast.

Government and Opposition
Members of Parliament enjoy certain privileges and immunities to protect their independence of thought and decision. They are members for the duration of the Parliament to which they are elected. They cannot even be removed by their constituencies, but only by expulsion from the House. They are free of danger of arrest or lawsuit for anything said or done in Parliament. But there are equal responsibilities, due to the party system by which Parliament works. Though bound to no party by law, members are generally expected to sustain the Government if they belong to the ruling party and to oppose the Government if their party is in opposition. Knowing, as they do, that they owe their election to their party affiliation, they accept party discipline more readily than their American counterparts. Clearly, breakdowns in party discipline do take place, but the skill of the leadership usually ensures that a majority party can avoid a defeat on a major issue by holding its members together.

The building in which the House of Commons meets, steeped in an atmosphere of age and tradition, assures genuine debate. The small size of the debating chamber discourages oratory, while the division into two sets of benches—along the left and right sides of the Speaker's throne, with the Government

on the one side and the opposition on the other—makes clear the physical, as well as the political, separation of the two sides. This arrangement can be contrasted with the fan-like shape of American and Continental chambers, in which parties blend into each other. The voting method also serves to enhance the party distinction in Britain: members walk into their own party's lobby on their side of the House to be counted. To vote with the opposite party means, literally and metaphorically, to cross the floor—an action highly visible and not taken lightly.

Each of the two sides is divided within itself into front and back benches. The front benches are occupied by the party leaders. If the party is in power, the seats are those of Ministers and Junior Ministers; if in opposition, by the shadow Cabinet and other leaders. The party rank and file are appropriately known as backbenchers, as they sit behind the party leaders.

The time allowed for debate is distributed among Government and opposition, with the greater share going to the Government. As the source of all new legislation, the Government needs time to introduce, explain, and defend it, while the opposition, who can only argue in contradiction, requires relatively less. Such time as is accorded to a particular bill is largely given over to the leaders of both sides, backbenchers having little opportunity to state their views. And since Governments tend to make most bills matters of confidence, members are almost compelled to vote along party lines.

The opposition has important and recognized functions, the most important of which are to criticize Government policies and to propose alternatives. Its role is also to provide an alternative government, should the ruling party lose its majority to a sufficient extent to be brought down. The last is unusual, and so the role of critic is what remains. Indeed, as long as the Government retains control of the House, the opposition has no prospect of getting its way. It is sometimes granted concessions, such as amendments to a bill, but this is by the good grace of the government in power. On rare occasions, the opposition is able to provoke disunity in Government ranks, weakening discipline to the point of breakdown. Members on the Government side know that should they be too rebellious, they have to face an election at a time when their party is at its weakest and most divided, so usually they can be induced by their leaders to pull back from the brink. The opposition, thus, seeks to score moral points against the Government until such time as it can again appeal to the people.

The electorate is the true target of debate. Government and opposition speak over the heads of their opponents in the House to the people outside. The parties may have to wait until the next election to know the extent to which their suasion has worked, unless they accept the verdict of the public opinion polls. Ultimately, it is the electorate that decides. Then the Government knows how well it has justified its policies, and the opposition how well it exposed their weaknesses.

The Cabinet
As the Cabinet is the focus of much that follows in the biographical chapters, less will be said of it here than its importance warrants. Nevertheless, a few remarks are essential.

Effective government calls for Cabinet control of the House. The government must, therefore, be drawn from the party most strongly represented in the House of Commons. Cabinet members, called Ministers of the Crown, are usually selected from among the most important leaders of the strongest party. Unlike American Cabinet members, who cannot sit in Congress, British Ministers *must* be Members of Parliament. However,

not all Ministers of the Crown are Cabinet members; some head departments of less than Cabinet rank.

Originally a private council of the Monarch, the Cabinet in recent times has united in itself both legislative and executive leadership. Leadership is the key, as confining membership to the most important ministries signifies. Attainment of ministerial office is a high promotion for a Member of Parliament, but attainment of Cabinet rank is among the highest to which he or she could aspire.

Ministers, inside or outside the Cabinet, have one or more Junior Ministers and one or more Parliamentary Secretaries to assist them. A Junior Minister is not a Minister of the Crown; but invitation to a Junior Ministry is often a step toward higher rank, just as promotion to Parliamentary Secretary often precedes appointment to a Junior Ministry. Ministers, Junior Ministers, and Parliamentary Secretaries make up a sizable proportion of the House membership, perhaps as much as 40 percent of that of the ruling party. The system of promotions thus acts as a check on members and contributes to party discipline: a backbencher who is too unruly may be denied the fruits of office. As Labour leader Harold Wilson put it, a dog who bites all the time may find himself denied a license.

The importance of the Cabinet in general and the Prime Minister in particular has grown over the years. It is this body, with the civil service, that has increasingly been responsible for legislation.

Making the Laws
Any member on either side of the House of Lords or the House of Commons can introduce a bill, but only a small proportion of these are actually passed. Most bills originate with a government department, based either on the wishes of its permanent civil

servants or on some promise made to the electorate. In addition, interest groups sometimes succeed in getting legislation introduced or amended through their friends in Parliament. An emergency may also prompt the passage of bills.

A bill generally begins as a Cabinet memorandum circulated by the Cabinet Secretariat to all interested Ministers. Once approval has been obtained, it goes to the Committee on Future Legislation in the Cabinet, which examines it and puts it on a provisional priorities list. As more bills are

usually proposed than Parliament can handle in a session, proposals have to be ordered in importance. With the opening of Parliament, the Cabinet's Committee on Present Legislation takes over, and the Minister awaits the instructions of this committee before laying his bill before the House.

Once introduced, the bill goes through a number of readings and committee stages. The *first reading* is no more than a formality: the name of the bill is read out and printed copies are distributed.

The *second reading* is the more important

Simplified illustration of the passage of a public law in Britain

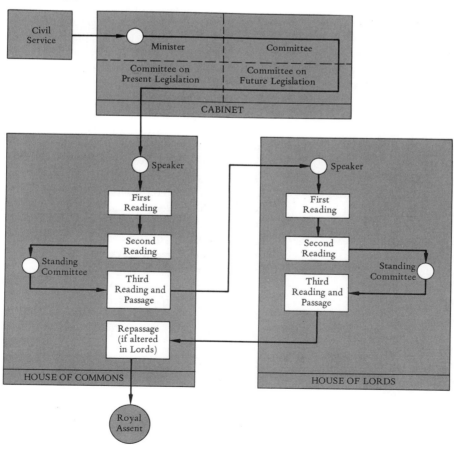

by far, for at this stage the principles of the bill are debated. The opposition now has the best chance to challenge the Government, as Ministers and opposition leaders exchange blow for blow. The Government wins, of course, but the opposition has had a chance to express its objections to the principles on which the bill is based.

After the second reading, the bill goes into committee stage, where it is closely examined and new clauses and amendments are considered. Government and opposition go over the bill paragraph by paragraph and word by word. Groups whose interests may be affected by the bill now have an opportunity to suggest amendments through friendly MPs. These legislative committees consist of Members of Parliament only and, unlike American committees, cannot call witnesses or withhold bills from the floor of the House. They also differ from American committees in being unspecialized; that is, they handle any legislation on any subject put before them and are labeled merely A, B, C, and so on. The reason is that the principles of the bill have been decided in the second reading, and all that remains for the committee to do is to perfect the wording.

The Government may decide not to send a bill to a legislative committee, but instead to have it considered by a Committee of the Whole House. This, simply put, is a debate by all members under relaxed rules, the Speaker leaving his throne. Once again, the principles of the bill having been decided earlier, it is only perfection of the bill that is at issue.

Committees cannot alter the substance of a bill, but changes in wording may introduce subtle changes in the principles on which it was written. If such changes are introduced, they are debated in what is, in effect, a repeat of the committee stage. The bill may then be recommitted to a committee or may pass to the *third reading*. The procedure of the third reading is similar to that of the second, except that debate is more limited. The bill usually passes this reading and is referred to the House of Lords, where a similar process occurs. Once through both Houses successfully, it needs no more than formal Royal Assent to become an act of Parliament— a law.

Political Parties

The Conservative Party

For all its ceremony and custom, the British Parliament is a political arena in which parties struggle for power. The Conservative and Labour parties are the major contenders, with the Liberals and other smaller parties on the sidelines. As our protagonist, Harold Macmillan, is a Conservative, that party will be considered first.

Although the name suggests inflexibility, the Conservative party has proved to be very adaptable. In the nineteenth century, the Tories (as the Conservatives still are nicknamed) freed the British economy of ancient laws and tariffs. To preserve what they believed best in British values, they curbed the unrestrained drive of British industry. They were responsible for some nationalization of industry, Conservative governments taking over broadcasting and electricity supply. To this day, the Conservative party expresses what average Britishers seem to feel are British values and remains more representative than Labour, which appeals in the main to intellectuals and to the industrial working class. The Conservative party gathers support from the aristocracy, landowners, smallholders, industrialists, professionals, businessmen, and a significant proportion of the working class as well. Indeed, were the entire British working class to vote Labour, the troubles of that party would be permanently ended.

British political parties are complicated, but fortunately there is some common pattern to the organization of the principal parties. Each is best seen as a combination of three distinct organizations: the parliamentary party, the constituency party, and the professional party—the party's bureaucracy.

For the Conservatives, the parliamentary party is comprised of all Conservative members of Parliament, actual or prospective. The constituency party, named the National Union of Conservative and Unionist Parties, is a federation of individual Conservative organizations in the constituencies. The professional party, known as the Central Office, has a permanent staff that keeps the party running.

British political parties, unlike American, are permanent and professional, so the Central Office has an important role. It is the secretariat of the party leader and includes several sections, all staffed by skilled men and women handling constituency organization, finance, and publicity. In addition, it contains a highly influential research department. It is the business of the Central Office to formulate and supervise the execution of party policies. Maintaining the party at a high level of preparedness for upcoming elections or by-elections is another responsibility. Lists of suitable candidates are made available to constituency organizations, and professional organizers are provided.

The National Union is made up of the Conservative associations in each constituency and in theory is governed by an unwieldy Central Council with 3,600 members. The Central Council is clearly too large to govern, and so actual management rests with a General Purposes Committee of 56 members and with a number of more specialized committees, such as those on policy, finance, and trade unions. Very important as an advisory body is the Committee on Candidates, which maintains a list of approved candidates for use by the constituency associations. The latter, however, are not obliged to accept any proffered candidate.

The constituency associations are literally the party in the country, spreading the party's propaganda and getting out the vote. They also are responsible for selecting the parliamentary candidate for the constituency.

The National Conference embraces all elements. Some 4,500 delegates put in an appearance at these affairs—about two-thirds of those invited. The conference is little more than a sounding board and can pass only nonbinding resolutions that are conveyed to the party leader, who cannot, of course, entirely ignore the wishes of the rank and file. The importance of the conference varies with the personality of the leader, who uses it to gauge the sentiment of those on whom he will depend in the next election.

The parliamentary party is the most important body in the Conservative party, as it is through this body that policies will ultimately become laws; and the leader has a crucial role in the party, as it is to the leader that the party looks for results. This individual must win victories or go, and almost unendurable pressures to resign are put on a leader who has failed to meet the party's criteria. On the other hand, with party support, the leader can employ many methods to ensure that its members behave. There is considerable patronage to dispense, as the leader appoints not only the Cabinet, but also the party Whips, who act as the leader's right hand in Parliament. The leader is the link between the various party bodies, creating and maintaining party policies.

Great as the power of the leader may be, it is not limitless. Restraint is exercised by a variety of party (not Parliamentary) committees, especially the 1922 Committee, whose members are all the party's backbenchers when the party is in power and all party MPs, including the leaders, when the party is out of power. The backbenchers on the various committees receive information from the research department and, of course, have some independent sources. In short, the party leader and those on the front bench cannot count on the uncritical loyalty of the backbenchers and must, to some extent, bow to their wishes. So the party remains essentially democratic, though greater stress is laid on the leader than is true in the Labour or Liberal parties.

The Labour Party
Labour, unlike the Conservatives, is entirely of this century, though its roots are in the industrial revolution. Beginning as the Labour Representation Committee in 1900, it was formally named the Labour party in 1906 and took its present shape at a conference in 1918 that permitted direct affiliation of trade unions and other organizations and decided on the establishment of constituency parties. Unlike the Conservatives, who pay vague tribute to the philosophy of Edmund Burke (1729–1797), Labour is avowedly ideological. Though not Marxist, their ideology is a British kind known as Fabianism, which emphasizes evolution rather than revolution as the way to socialism.

Despite considerable differences from the Conservatives' structure, Labour maintains a tripartite organization: an independent parliamentary party, constituency parties, and a Central Office.

The supreme authority in the Labour party is the Annual Conference, which directly elects a National Executive. The National Executive, in turn, stands in close relationship to the parliamentary Labour party (PLP). The party leader is elected by the parliamentary party and acts as an ex officio member of the conference and the National Executive. There are more restrictions on the leader's powers, and Labour on the whole is more open and democratic than the Conservatives.

Unlike the Conservative counterpart, the leader of the Labour party is elected each year. This person must, when the party is not in power, accept an elected Parliamentary Committee, whose members may be uncongenial. Once elected, however, the Labour leader enjoys much the same power as the leader of the Conservatives. The party has a Liaison Committee between leader and PLP members and a number of topical committees, much as have the Conservative members. So despite their differences, the parties do mirror each other in some respects.

Members of the PLP, though without a vote, can attend the Annual Conference. On its side, the PLP does not consider the conference resolutions binding. The independence of the PLP became an issue in 1960 when an important part of the PLP platform was rejected by the conference. The party leader, then Hugh Gaitskell, stated that the rejection did not bind the PLP and was able to silence the opposition. The rule was confirmed once again in 1962 and has remained in force ever since. Now the conference can do no more than advise the party, though Labour MPs cannot ignore those who provide funds and support any more than the Conservatives can.

The Labour party has two kinds of members, individuals and organizations. Individuals are organized into constituency Labour parties, while trade unions and cooperative societies can become affiliated members. Both are represented at the Annual Conference, the arena where power struggles among the different factions are played out. Generally, the constituency parties are to the left of the trade unions and press for socialist ideals. The unions vary in their ideology and on the whole are more interested in bread-and-butter issues. Block voting enhances union power, for each union gets one vote for every 5,000 members and its total number of votes must be cast as a block. Powerful union leaders can therefore play the different party factions off against each other by offering to cast their union's block of votes in their favor. The different factions in the Labour party are thus induced to make the union leaderships promises that might not otherwise be consonant with either party policy or the best interests of Britain's economy.

Of the two major parties, Labour is the harder to discipline. Leadership demands the highest skills, which often fail. Rules for the punishment of rebels exist, but they are applied as selectively as in the Conservative party: the more powerful and vocal rebels are seldom punished. Despite dissension that often seems close to chaos, the Labour party is strong and presently dominates British politics. The large and growing working population, though not unanimously for Labour, gives the party a solid base, reinforced by the unions.

Union leaders have a great voice in the Labour party even though less than half their members actually vote Labour. The "big five" unions—transport, engineering, municipal workers, store clerks, and electrical workers—have an absolute majority at the Annual Conference. In addition, unions control some eighteen of the twenty-eight seats on the National Executive. Unions also play a subtler part, as they will pay a large part of the election expenses of the constituency organization that nominates one of their candidates, a very tempting offer to constituency organizations lacking funds.

Labour, like the Liberals, has problems in maintaining voter appeal. It has largely accomplished its original objectives and has found little new and exciting to attract voters. British workers are becoming ever more interested in personal advancement and material possessions and ever less concerned with the class struggle and nationalization. Labour, like the Conservatives, has increasingly been forced to rely on the personality of the leader, his or her ability to attract votes and to reconcile the warring factions in the party.

Other Parties
Although perhaps deserving of more space, less will be said of the Liberal party and the various nationalist parties in Britain.

The Liberals, the third of the established parties, are the reduced heirs of a proud tradition. Until 1919 the major parties were the Conservatives and the Liberals, with the latter representing the party of reform. The Liberal party won for Britishers many of the freedoms taken for granted today, such as the universal franchise and the free press. But having achieved its professed goals and offering no new direction, it could not compete for worker loyalty with Labour, which supplanted it as the second party. The party continues to win some 20 percent of the popular vote, but the plurality single-member system limits it to between eight and fifteen seats. In view of the decreasing parliamentary majorities of the major parties, Liberals may have a future role as a "swing" party in the House, their support being necessary to maintain a Government.

Growing in importance, though still small, is the Scottish National party, which speaks with a stronger voice since the discovery of oil off the coasts of Scotland. Once polling only 2.4 percent of the popular vote, the party was not taken very seriously; but in October 1974, things changed. The party gained 30.4 percent of the Scottish vote and sent eleven of its members to the House of Commons. This upward trend has not yet peaked, and it could well be that the Nationalists will capture thirty of Scotland's seventy-one places in Parliament in the next election. For all its growing popularity, the party seems unclear in its goals. The watchword is Scottish independence, but no one is sure what this means: independence from England, or simply greater Scottish autonomy and a Scottish Parliament divorced from Westminster.

Nationalism in Scotland and Wales is more crucial for Labour than for the Conservatives. Labour has had a majority in England on only two occasions, 1945 and 1966, so it relies on support in the solidly Labour counties, Scotland and Wales, to win elections. If these countries go largely Nationalist, Labour's hopes of governing will fade.

Elections

The General Election of 1974 resulted in deadlock. Neither Conservatives nor Labour won a majority in the 635–seat House of Commons, Labour holding 301 seats against the Conservatives' 296. The Liberals won 14 seats; all other parties, 24. The Labour Government is, therefore, a minority Government, and the votes of the minor parties are critical. James Callaghan, the present Labour leader, might under other circumstances have called an election in the hope of increasing his mandate; but with the present state of the British economy, rising unemployment, growing regional nationalism, and other factors, an election would probably result in Labour's defeat. Labour must soldier on, remaining in power by buying the votes of the smaller parties through concessions to them. Indeed, the pattern of recent British elections has marked the failure of the major parties to draw voters, though both will doubtless continue to dominate the political landscape.

Callaghan's plight highlights the flexibil-ity of his position. Unlike an American President, a British Prime Minister is not bound to elections at fixed dates: the timing of an election is a political choice. Though the Parliament Act of 1911 limits the life of a Parliament to five years, it can be dissolved at any time on request of the Prime Minister to the Monarch. Once the decision is taken, the Prime Minister and the Cabinet offer the Monarch their resignations and within about ten days the King or Queen will dissolve Parliament. According to law, elections must be held within three weeks of dissolution, making election campaigns brief and low-keyed by American standards. Constituencies are asked to present candidates, and all a candidate needs is nomination by two voters and support by another eight. In addition every candidate must deposit about £50 ($90), which is lost if the candidate does not get one-eighth of the total constituency vote. The deposit is refunded if the candidate loses but gets above the minimum. The deposit is intended to discourage frivolous candidacies, but not to deter serious contenders, and so is relatively low.

The election itself is usually held on a weekday from 7:00 A.M. to 9:00 P.M., and the counting begins as soon as the ballot boxes are sent in, usually the evening of the election day. Unless the election is very close, the results are known by midnight.

The British electorate has one General Election in which each individual votes for only one candidate. This partly explains the higher voter turnout in Britain than in the United States. In 1974, for instance, 80 percent of the British electorate went to the polling booths, as compared to the usual American figure of 40 to 60 percent. The simplicity of British elections, and their relative infrequency, may encourage voter interest. Identification of the candidates is easier, in the sense that the voter casts a ballot for a leader and a party, and there are no primaries. On the other hand, as the election law does not recognize parties, the ballot papers do not state the party affiliation of candidates. Each party, therefore, must take great trouble to impress their candidate's name on the voters. Nevertheless, the ballot papers are simple when compared to the "bed sheet" ballots in America.

In the House there are some 400 safe seats held by the major parties. Any person nominated in a safe constituency is virtually assured of election. The difficulty is that the constituency associations, whether Conservative or Labour, that control such seats are often unrepresentative and select candidates more suited to their tastes than to the voters'. The electors, nevertheless, vote for the candidate because of party ties. This leaves the contested seats, roughly one-third of the House, on whom the swing from one party to the other depends. The change in government is often determined by a swing of a few percentage points in the marginal constituencies. Hence, much of the electoral contest is an attempt by both parties to capture the uncommitted vote in the contested constituencies.

Pressure Groups

Pressure Groups and Parties

The traditional distinction between parties and pressure groups does not hold in Britain. Custom dictates that parties seek political office and pressure groups try to exert influence on the elected legislators and administrators behind the scenes. But British trade unions were involved in the formation of the Labour party and with that party form part of the labor movement. Providing nearly 90 percent of the Labour party's members, the unions sponsored 112 of the 287 elected Labour candidates in 1970. The unions domi-

nate the National Executive of the Labour party and, unlike the AFL/CIO in this country, are directly involved in a political party. Hence labor unions, traditionally seen as a pressure group, operate directly on a British party. What is true nationally holds even on the local level, where the Labour party branch and the local trade union are often one and the same.

The Conservative party, unlike Labour, is independent of any one pressure group. Organized business and commerce do support it, though there is no formal connection between them, by providing both funds and candidates through sponsorship of individuals. Although Conservative members are expected not to allow their group affiliation to affect their actions, it is difficult to understand how this can be avoided, especially as interest groups look for people already supporting their position out of conviction. Candidates, in turn, link themselves to groups whose views they find congenial. Many members, in addition, are doctors or lawyers, who are certainly inclined to be influenced by their peers and the demands of their professional organizations.

Interest and Ideology

Pressure group action often has an unconscious ideological content, which also blurs the distinction between party and pressure group. Pressure groups often do more than support an interest—they defend a way of life. Uneconomic coal mines continue in operation because of the pressure of mining communities in England and Wales. The government is pressured into buying British aircraft for the government-operated British Airways, even if they are uneconomical, to avoid the loss of prestige and jobs that closing the industry would involve. The picture is further complicated by many groups who lobby hard for no tangible reward, such as some pacifist groups and the anti-apartheid lobby. Their satisfaction is gained from work for an ideal rather than from hopes of personal gain.

The spectrum of British pressure groups is vast, ranging from those opposed to "blood sports"—mainly fox hunting—to professional, labor, and employers' groups. The importance of the different groups varies according to which party is in power. Trade unions obviously receive a more sympathetic hearing from a Labour government, and employers from a Conservative one. Yet such is the power of the unions that they can virtually dictate to any government, Labour or Conservative. The unions were sufficiently powerful, for instance, to bring down the Conservative government of Edward Heath in 1974.

Size is an important determinant of pressure group power. The Trades Union Congress has a combined membership of 11 million, and the Confederation of British Industry, an employer's group, has some 12,000 companies affiliated with it. These pressure groups are attractive in differing degrees to the different parties, though the employers are very much less powerful than the unions.

In addition to working on their own, pressure groups form alliances when they believe that this best serves their interests. Employers and workers, despite their adversary relationship within an industry, may unite in the face of a common threat to the industry as a whole. Thus, in April 1974, fleet owners and fishermen united in blockading British harbors as a protest against the importation of cheap fish.

Pressure Groups and the Government

Because British government is central and not federal, British pressure groups are more limited in scope than their American counterparts. In the United States a pressure group can seek on the state or local level what it cannot obtain on the national. This is impossible in Britain: not only is government centralized in Westminster, but the Cabinet is all-powerful. Nevertheless, there is work for the pressure groups to do, for much that happens in politics—not being a matter of major policy—never comes before the Cabinet. Even minor policy matters do affect interests, sometimes to a considerable extent. For instance, certain questions relating to the shipbuilding industry might not warrant discussion in the Cabinet but would be negotiated among one or more Ministers, departmental officials, and the affected interests—shipbuilders, unions, consumers' associations, and so on. Decisions taken might never be discussed in the full Cabinet or in the House, if they were not contrary to general Cabinet policy.

The negotiations among the Ministers and the others go smoothly if the interests involved are not too difficult to reconcile. Generally, the groups seek to work for reconciliation, for each values their quiet cooperation. Indeed, the effectiveness of a pressure group is often judged by how little public attention it receives. Pressure groups also are important because of the information they provide for policy formulation. Legislation calls for specialized knowledge beyond the scope of any administrative department. Among the few sources of such information are pressure groups, so they are frequently consulted before laws are put before Parliament. Thus, when Harold Macmillan was Minister for Housing, he consulted with both employers' groups and trade unions in building before deciding the policy of his department. As the information offered is bound to be biased in favor of the interest concerned, Ministers will consult several sources, as Macmillan did.

Although Cabinet dominance has reduced the importance of ordinary Members of Parliament to pressure groups, representation in Parliament is actively sought. By a judicious question or two, a member can advance the group's interests; and as Ministers do not like to leave questions unanswered for fear of public criticism, the ensuing discussion can publicize the group's view and ensure that it is not overlooked. Members are also involved in the drafting of legislation in the committees, and small changes in wording can make great differences to the way a law is applied. Nevertheless, a pressure group whose only access to legislation is through ordinary Members of Parliament is in a very unfavorable position.

British pressure groups act under many constraints. No matter what any department has agreed to do, the approval of the Treasury has to be obtained if money is involved. The Treasury has the reputation of being tightfisted to special interests. Too, what benefits one group may harm another; and if more than one department is concerned, leading to a conflict of jurisdictions, this may result in stalemate on the issue. Much, therefore, involves the nature of the group, its support, and the direction of government policy. The result is that pressure groups try to get on as well as they can with the party in power, despite any ideological differences. They will eagerly offer information and advice to any government that will listen.

The Administrative System

Ministers and Administrators
The great powers of the higher British civil servant arise, in large part, from the combination of executive and legislative powers in the Cabinet.

Men and women who achieve ministerial rank are usually skilled politicians. They know the cut and thrust of party infighting;

they know on what to negotiate and where to hold firm; they know how to build and hold public support. But they do not have the specialized knowledge on how to run their departments, which is common coin to the higher administrator. Like all who lack expertise, the Ministers are in the hands of their experts. Many come to office fired with new ideas, set on initiating new policies, and —not having intimate knowledge of the subject—lacking clear objectives. Their ideas soon run aground on the department view. They find it is the administrator who knows the ins and outs of the department, has the connections to make administration run smoothly, and can reduce complicated technical questions into simple position papers. Ministers may not wish to take the advice of their senior civil servants, but they have little choice: there is no other well-informed and disinterested source to which they can turn. Attempts to introduce outsiders may antagonize the whole department and ensure the Minister's failure.

Choice is not what all Ministers want. Many want good relations with their senior civil servants and are prepared to be the spokespersons of their department in the House. Then many find it gratifying to head a department and to lead a group of subordinates, more gratifying than having to meet the criticisms and arguments of equals in the Cabinet. Administrators know how to seduce their Ministers with marks of respect and other blandishments. The lack of expertise is in this way compounded by a genuine willingness to do what the department considers necessary.

The majority of programs, as a result, originate not in Westminster but in Whitehall (headquarters of the civil service, which has come to characterize the British civil service much as the Pentagon characterizes the American military). Programs come less from Cabinet discussion than from bargains struck among the different administrative departments.

The Cabinet is where political and administrative strands are joined, yet it has time only for the most important matters. To keep overall control the Cabinet has a number of specialized committees that consider questions of insufficient importance to merit the whole body's consideration. The senior civil servants in departments that would be involved in administering the legislation establish a parallel committee of their own. If, for example, a Cabinet committee were to involve five Ministers, the senior civil servants from the same five departments would also establish a committee to consider the same questions. There they would work out an official solution to present to their Ministers, rather than risk their Ministers' coming to conclusions through political infighting. The Whitehall committee works quickly, as they want to brief their Ministers along the same policy lines before a Cabinet decision is reached.

If a Minister is troublesome, the administration has its methods of retaliating. One tactic is waging a "paper war," flooding the Minister with information, reports, recommendations, and regulations—six or seven boxes fully loaded with matters that must be decided, it is claimed, before the next morning. In addition, each paper has to be authorized in the correct form, a verbal authorization being unacceptable. Even a Minister who wishes to be a political dynamo and comply with the request is crushed under the sheer weight of paper. Most Ministers understand quickly and gladly fall back on the administration and its established ways.

If possible, the department tries to have one of its own as a link between the Minister, the Junior Minister, and any advisers the Minister brings along. A promising young Assistant Secretary is usually given this task. By advising the Minister of the department's attitude, and the department of the Minister's, this individual attempts to keep the Minister happy and to maintain a smooth working relationship.

Ministers cannot afford to antagonize their departments and thus lose their cooperation. Administrators, in turn, accept the two-party system as long as they can remain uninvolved. Realizing that changes in government are for the good of the system and that they need someone at their head to take responsibility for decisions, they like Ministers who enjoy prestige and can win the department what it wants. A former Labour Minister, R. H. S. Crossman, sums it up this way:

The effective Minister is the man who wins the support of his Department without becoming its cherished mascot. To do so he has to strike a balance. He needs the acquiescence, at least, of the Department in what he is up to, and for this he needs to be a success in the Department's eye. So he's got to appease them by winning a number of their battles for them in the Whitehall war.[1]

The Minister goes along with the department in matters that do not have a direct effect on the government's policies, but fights hard for what is considered essential. He or she can afford to be neither the department's captive nor its enemy.

Entry and Organization
Entry into the civil service is by competitive examination. The quality of entrants is usually high: many are graduates of Britain's best schools and universities, with excellent records of political honesty and personal probity.

[1] R. H. S. Crossman, *The Myths of Cabinet Government* (Cambridge, Mass.: Harvard University Press, 1972), p. 65.

Civil servants, once appointed, are supposedly apolitical. They are not to make their personal political views public nor to allow them to influence their decisions. According to theory, they faithfully execute the policies of any Government in power, through the Minister at their head. But there is more to it than that. Being a civil servant rather than a political appointee, the Permanent Secretary can establish a reputation for reliability and professional trustworthiness that the American counterpart cannot match. The Permanent Secretary, Deputy Permanent Secretary, Under-Secretaries, and Assistant-Secretaries, though keeping discreetly in the background, enjoy great popular respect. This and their reputation for honesty—cases of corruption are rare—buttress their claims with their Minister. The reputation of the service is cherished for reasons of both pride and power.

Conclusion

The British government is one of implied checks and balances. Many of the old checks and balances—the power of the Monarch and that of the Lords—have been reduced to nullity or delay. Yet, in its working, the system constrains even the most powerful of Prime Ministers. Although reference to some kind of providential influence is justly unpopular today, there is something almost uncanny about the restraints of the unwritten constitution. The restraints arise out of the opposed forces within the Cabinet, Parliament, Administration, interest groups, media, and public opinion, which together act as a concealed brake on the Prime Minister and other government leaders.

The Cabinet is at the center of power, binding people, party, Parliament, and Administration together. Despite the Prime Minister's growing authority, it remains the focus of government. The enlargement of Cabinet power has led to the view that Britain elects its governing committee.

The Prime Minister and fellow Cabinet members are judged not only by their policies but also by their success in keeping their party together. Only if party unity is maintained can the Government consistently defeat the opposition. The opposition is respected, in turn, both because of its essential role in British democracy and because of the knowledge, which haunts all Prime Ministers, that their day in the opposition will come. If they do not consider the opposition now, they may not be considered when they occupy the opposition benches.

It clearly is impossible to do more than touch on the parts of the British system in so short a chapter. The way in which these parts combine in the political process will become clearer as we discuss Harold Macmillan's career.

3

Macmillan's Early Years:
From School to Parliament

Introduction

The British system of government has been briefly described. The unwritten constitution, Parliament, Cabinet, monarchy, and administration, together with the parties and pressure groups, comprise the frame of British politics. Within that frame, effective British politicians build their policies and their careers. Knowing the political game, which rules to bend and which to hold rigid, is the mark of the professional in politics— Harold Macmillan was a professional to his fingertips.[1]

[1] Much use has been made in Chapters 3 to 6 of information drawn from the biographies of Harold Macmillan by Emrys Hughes, *Macmillan: Portrait of a Politician* (London: George Allan & Unwin, 1962), and Anthony Sampson, *Macmillan: A Study in Ambiguity* (London: Allen Lane, Penguin Press, 1967), as well as Macmillan's six-volume autobiography (New York: Harper & Row, 1966–1974). Specific footnotes are not provided.

Macmillan's appearance tells little of his capacities. Superficially he could well be mistaken for a polished and somewhat decadent aristocrat, but few who knew him made this mistake. Active, ambitious, and energetic, Macmillan served in the House of Commons for about forty years and was the Prime Minister for seven of these years, the longest consecutive period of tenure in this century. He steered Britain from the status of great power to one more within its capacities and in harmony with the times in such a way as to make the more modest role palatable. Because his career spanned so much change, it may be a suitable vehicle for understanding British political processes.

British government has been described as "Cabinet government," and leadership of the Cabinet falls to the Prime Minister. Increasingly what emerge as Cabinet policies are those of the Prime Minister. So, although no one life can encompass all of British politics and the use of Macmillan's life must leave gaps, the rise of a politician from his earliest training to the pinnacle of power and into decline must reveal much about politics in Britain.

The Education of a Future Prime Minister

Family Background
Harold Macmillan was born on February 10, 1894, at 52 Cadogan Place, in a fashionable part of London. His grandfather, Daniel Macmillan, had been one of twelve children of a small farmer. Through hard work and native shrewdness Daniel Macmillan made the family fortune: beginning as apprentice to a bookseller, he progressed to his own bookshop, then founded what became a publishing empire. He died when his son, Maurice Macmillan, was only four years old, so Maurice was brought up by one of Daniel Macmillan's brothers, a partner in the firm.

Maurice Macmillan was a reserved and taciturn Scotsman, a partner in the prospering publishing concern, and the author of religious books now long forgotten. Although deeply interested in religion, able in business, well-educated, his influence on his son, Harold Macmillan, seems to have been slight. It was Harold Macmillan's mother who was the dominating influence in both childhood and later life.

Macmillan's mother was an American, born in a small town in Indiana in 1856. A woman of extraordinary character and charm and of unusually strong character, she had made up her mind that Harold Macmillan would be a Prime Minister of Britain. Highly gifted, but restrained by the limited opportunities for a woman of her class at the time, she centered her ambitions on her sons and did all she could to lay the proper foundation for their careers. So successful

was she that Harold Macmillan was later to say that he owed everything he had achieved to her devotion, support, and advice. His very survival in World War I was due to her. Brought back seriously wounded from France, he persuaded the ambulance driver to take him home instead of to a military hospital in Essex. Because his wounds had been allowed to heal superficially without first being drained, he was dangerously ill and certainly would have died but for his mother's actions. She rushed him to a hospital run by American friends, where he received proper attention, including a long series of operations. Not content with this, she went to the War Office and berated several generals for their neglect of the wounded.

There was a negative side to the love and care Macmillan's mother lavished on her sons. She was very domineering and tried to enter into every aspect of their lives—their daily affairs, amusements, and friends. Macmillan and his brothers resented this and evaded her probings. On the other hand, she gave her children some of her own strength and confidence and the knowledge that under any circumstances, whether right or wrong, they could count on her support.

In short, Macmillan's mother was a determined woman, who could not be swayed from anything about which she had made up her mind. Having decided that Harold Macmillan was to be Prime Minister, she supervised every step of the way to 10 Downing Street (the official residence of British Prime Ministers) until her death in 1937.

Education for Leadership
The first qualification for a future Prime Minister is the right education in a system that is frankly and openly elitist. About 2 percent of British schoolboys are educated at what are called *public* schools but are really private, exclusive, and very expensive institu-

tions. These public schools are the fount of the British leadership, training young men for high office, imbuing them with a sense of public purpose and a corporate spirit. The corporate spirit remains long after the years of schooling are over and is expressed in the so-called old boy network—a loose association of public school alumni who assist graduates of their schools in finding suitable posts, advance each other's interests, and mix informally.

The public schools are residential high schools, which are run very much by and for the establishment. The schools are generally sexually segregated, there being separate public schools for women. An upper-class youth, then, leaves home at the age of thirteen, coming home only for vacations. Macmillan, a product of this process, approved of it. By being forced to leave home early, he has argued, a youngster learns to manage without his or her parents, whose selfish love or indifference could damage character. Nor did Macmillan find anything wrong with the schools' perpetuation of class distinctions. He did not feel that removing upper-class youth from all contact with those less fortunate increased their ignorance of their countrymen. This is a serious drawback, perhaps, because of the positions of leadership that fall so readily to alumni. Yet on the whole, public schools have produced a social class whose moral commitment to public service is unequalled elsewhere.

The political importance of the right school emerges from the statistics. Thirty percent of Conservative Ministers have graduated from one school—Eton—and many of the others are products of five other highly prestigious schools: Charterhouse, Harrow (attended by Winston Churchill), Marlborough, Rugby, and Winchester. The Labour party, in its turn, has a fair share of public school alumni. "Old boys" comprise about one-third of all Labour Ministers, although

they are graduates mostly of the less prestigious institutions.

Eton being "the mother of Prime Ministers," it seems natural that Macmillan was sent there. His stay was short, as he caught pneumonia after only a few months and had to be withdrawn. Few of his contemporaries would have singled him out then as a future leader. He was a very good-looking boy, but he made few friends, being shy and bookish. After leaving Eton, he was tutored privately at home for entry into Oxford, the next step appropriate for one aiming at high office.

Oxford and Cambridge are the two premier universities of Great Britain. Oxford has slightly more social status than Cambridge, but this varies from one college to the next, as these universities are made up of large numbers of semi-independent residential colleges. "Oxbridge," as they are often called, are the blue brick universities, corresponding roughly to the American Ivy League. The "red bricks"—the lesser (though often academically excellent) British universities such as London, Manchester, Liverpool, Leeds or Southampton—are less socially prestigious, resembling to some extent the better state universities in the United States both in character and student body. Not unexpectedly, Oxford and Cambridge have produced more of the Conservative leadership, and the red bricks much of the Labour leadership, though the Labour party on the whole has more Ministers with university degrees.

Tutored for Oxford by one of Britain's most brilliant young scholars, Macmillan entered Oxford and went into one of its most prestigious and intellectually demanding colleges, Balliol. Balliol men were known for their tranquil consciousness of effortless superiority, and Macmillan flowered in their company. His years at Oxford were the high point of his life, he was later to say, and his happiest moments came when he revisited

Balliol. Macmillan's nostalgia for his days at Oxford was accentuated by the deaths in World War I of all but one other member of his graduating class. Late in his career, weighed down with years and honors, Harold Macmillan seemed more delighted with his appointment as Chancellor of Oxford than with any other distinction.

The Dashing Soldier

Oxford brought out the best of Harold Macmillan's intellect, but for him, as for so many of his generation who survived it, World War I was the "great divide." The war had a shattering impact on the compact British upper class, an impact reinforced by the smallness of the class itself. Largely known to each other, they took it for granted that in war, as in peace, it was their duty to lead and to sacrifice. They supplied the bulk of the junior- and middle-rank officers who, in the nature of military action, bear the brunt of casualties.

At the outbreak of war, Macmillan accepted it as his duty to enlist at once. He was first posted to an ordinary regiment of the line, but his mother soon changed that. Exercising influence and using her considerable determination to the full, she obtained his transfer to the elite Grenadier Guards. Macmillan proved a model officer, courageous, disciplined, and energetic. Lightly wounded twice, each time returning to the front, he was taken out of combat by a serious back wound received in the Battle of the Somme in 1917. Lying wounded in a shell-hole, as fighting continued around him, Macmillan claims he read Aeschylus's *Prometheus* in the original Greek. Memory may have romanticized the incident for Macmillan, as it did for others who endured the conflict, but the story shows Macmillan as he liked to see himself—the dashing, imperturbable guards officer. To the end of his career, his speech was salted with military

terms and analogies. His cavalryman's moustache, which he wore long after leaving the service, became something of a trademark; and his wound, which troubled him throughout his career, gave him a peculiar shuffling walk, which like his moustache served to distinguish him.

The war had an unintended effect. Like others of his class, Macmillan had been removed from contact with other social classes. The war brought him into close contact with the common man, and Macmillan found that he was not so common after all. Sympathy and understanding for the less fortunate grew in Macmillan, marking the rest of his political life. In a sense, the war brought him back to his ideological roots: his grandfather and his father had professed a peculiarly British socialism, which was expressed in the Christian Social Movement. These ideas gained new focus in the comradeship of the trenches.

Service as a guards officer, together with his education, had equipped Macmillan for entry into the upper classes. He may not have been an aristocrat, but he looked like one, was educated like one, and had served in an elite unit. Yet, for all that, Macmillan remained proud of his origins, carrying a picture of his great-grandfather's humble cottage from office to office. He had the social compassion of his forebears and much of their toughness of mind and self-confidence. Knowing what his family had overcome served him well in later struggles.

At the end of the war Macmillan wished to remain a soldier a while longer, and again his mother exerted influence, gaining him a much sought-after post as an aide to the Duke of Devonshire, who was then leaving England to become Governor-General of Canada. Although Canada was a self-governing dominion, like other members of the Commonwealth it had a Governor-General sent from Britain to represent the

Monarch. Such rank was often bestowed on members of the higher aristocracy who, installed in office, received all deference that would have been accorded the Monarch. Macmillan greatly enjoyed the ceremonials and status that came with his post of aide. Indistinguishable in manner or appearance from the young noblemen who usually served as aides, he married one of the Duke of Devonshire's daughters, thereby becoming a member of one of Britain's most powerful political families. The marriage ceremony

was one of the events of the 1920 season, attended by the royal family and many famous authors affiliated with the Macmillan publishing firm. Macmillan's marriage was happy; and Lady Dorothy, though regretting his choice of politics over publishing, was a continuing source of strength and advice.

The political importance of the Devonshire family could have provided Macmillan with a platform from which to launch forth into politics, but there is no evidence that he exploited his marriage to further his political

Harold and Lady Dorothy Macmillan at the polling booths in the General Election of 1959

(Sport and General Press Agency)

ambitions. Exploitation was not really necessary because, as a relation of the Duke, he was in constant contact with people of importance in Conservative politics. And in the role of Colonial Secretary, the Duke had further access to the government and the party.

The importance of the Duke of Devonshire may seem strange in view of his title. Although the House of Commons is the major source of legislation, the House of Lords also has important functions. Each party must have among its leaders some Peers (as the Members of the House of Lords are called) who can act for the party in Lords. Members of Lords, therefore, are often included in the government, a circumstance that accounts for the Duke being Colonial Secretary.

Harold Macmillan, having married and worked briefly for the family firm, was now ready to enter politics.

Candidate and Constituency
By 1923, the year he entered Parliament, Macmillan had met all the requirements of a Conservative political candidate. Yet, many of his qualifications would have suited Labour equally well. Good-looking and well-connected, he had attended the right schools and university and had a good military background. The Labour party, for all its emphasis on the working class, is not immune to snobbery. Nevertheless, it was the Conservatives whom he chose and on whose behalf he became a candidate.

British parliamentary hopefuls cannot choose the seats they will contest. Safe seats go to seasoned candidates or to those the party considers essential to parliamentary or electoral success. The newcomer has to cut his teeth in a district that is extremely difficult to win or cannot be won at all. Macmillan was nominated by the constituency association of Stockton-on-Tees, a working-class

area he had never before visited. Unlike the United States, where candidates must reside in the district in which they stand for election, Britain has no such requirement, for it has very different ideas on representation. In the United States the candidate is of greatest importance, party being a secondary consideration. In Britain the reverse is true: it is the party rather than the candidate that is important. Voters know that few of the candidate's promises will be fulfilled unless they are party policy. So party label and party leaders' image matter the most. A good candidate can win a few more seats, and a less effective candidate can lose some, a significant factor in marginal constituencies. But the candidate runs for the party; and thus whether the candidate is or is not from the area matters little. This enabled Harold Macmillan, young and wealthy, to stand for a constituency unknown to him, to appeal for votes from the largely working-class electorate.

Stockton, which was to be intertwined with Macmillan's fortunes for much of his career, typified what had happened to many industrial towns when British industrial supremacy eroded. A boom town early in the nineteenth century, an early terminus of the first railroad line, it was hard hit by the post-war slump: misery and unemployment were widespread. Macmillan, made sensitive by his experience during the war, was deeply moved. After his election, a campaign that initially eluded him, he became the champion of the unemployed.

There are no primaries in Britain, and candidates are nominated either by the party associations in the constituencies or, in Labour's case, by unions and other member institutions. This is logical, for—as in Macmillan's case—candidate and constituency may know little of each other. In theory, in the Conservative party the Central Office has final say, but this does not always hold in practice. Safe constituencies jealously guard their independence, resenting intervention by the Central Office. Seats with little prospect of victory often have to go begging for candidates.

Stockton was considered to be virtually safe for the Liberals. When Macmillan asked the constituency association why it had come to him as its candidate, he was frankly told that none of the others it had approached felt inclined to waste their time or money campaigning for the Conservative party there. The chairman of the constituency association told Macmillan that he hoped for little more than a good fight.

On his side, Macmillan knew nothing of the constituency and equally little of what he was expected to do. Without any background in political work, he had no idea of the rough-and-tumble nature of politics. All he remembered was some political philosophy from college and the stories his father-in-law had told him. He knew nothing of industry other than a bit about printing; and he had never even seen the great steelworks nor the shipyards nor the people who toiled in them. To make matters worse, the party organization in Stockton was in confusion. When asked a question, the chairman of the association retreated into the fur collar of his coat and said little. Macmillan asked, Was there a headquarters? Were committee rooms taken? When would nominations be? He received few answers. Eventually, with the help of his agent, a barely literate Cockney of great political astuteness, order emerged. This man was to remain Macmillan's agent for five elections, after which he retired from politics.

Practical work in the constituency taught Macmillan much. His polished speeches, more suitable for Oxford, were scrapped, as he learned to let his own ideas emerge more directly. He learned about party organiza-

tion and the needs of the residents of Stockton. The seat was lost—honorably lost—the first time around. The Liberals held the constituency with 11,734 votes, but Macmillan had gained 11,661—far more than expected. Labour, the opponents of the future, won 10,619.

Macmillan had expected his defeat to keep him out of Parliament for five years, its usual life, but that Parliament lasted only from 1923 to 1924. None of the parties could form a government with a clear majority, so a new election was called for 1924. His chief opponent was a Labour candidate, not a Liberal, and yet Macmillan succeeded. He was embarked on his political career with everything apparently in his favor. He had turned defeat into victory, gaining for the party a seat it had not expected to win. He had all the credentials of a leader, yet he remained outside the party leadership until 1939 and came into office only later. Why did he fail to fulfill his early promise for so long? The reasons teach much of the nature of British politics.

The Years of Frustration

The New Member

Harold Macmillan came to Parliament with ideas at variance with those of his party's leaders. His efforts to propagate his own views, and the frequency with which he expressed them, made the party leadership distrust him. For a Conservative, his ideas were radical, challenging the more orthodox views of the leadership, who responded with mistrust. He was considered to be far too impractical to be invited into the Cabinet.

Macmillan had other drawbacks, one of which was his limited skill as a speaker. He was nervous, aware that his recitals of statistics of distress among the unemployed bored his colleagues. The unemployed became Macmillan's obsession, haunting his thoughts and actions throughout the 1930s. He was their determined advocate, and his passionate espousal of their cause ensured his remaining on the back benches from 1924 to 1940. Macmillan later admits that this long spell in the political wilderness was partly his own fault, for he pursued his own plans whether or not they coincided with what the party wanted. None of this was apparent when his parliamentary career opened, seemingly so full of promise, in 1924.

A newly elected member has certain privileges, among them the right to a "maiden speech"—the first speech he or she makes as a member. Macmillan describes the thrill of first taking a seat in the historic House: the sense of gratitude to supporters, the determination to earn everyone's confidence, and the emotions of having achieved a long ambition, coupled with a sense of responsibility to the community. He was enthralled at being a member of this ancient assembly and determined to watch, wait, and learn.

As other newly elected Members, Macmillan had much to learn of procedures so complicated that even at the end of his long career he had to admit he could not have passed a first examination in them. The Clerks of the House, skilled in the rules, assist the members with such things as traditional regulations, printed standing orders, case law, and the rulings of previous Speakers of the House. Ministers or members are sometimes impatient with these procedures, though the impatience often arises out of interest and enthusiasm. The traditional methods are intended to protect the rights of the opposition, rights vital to the functioning of the system if it is to remain democratic. The opposition needs protection; the Government can usually look after itself. Min-

isters impatient with the rules when in power are usually eager to invoke them when in opposition.

Few Members of Parliament can give their entire attention to the House. Parliamentary salaries are too low even today to allow membership to be a full-time career. Therefore, sessions are held in the afternoon and evening to give members time for their jobs, and many members come to the House quite late. Macmillan admits that he seldom got to the House from his publishing business until 4:00 P.M., which meant that he missed Question Time—the best way of getting to know the names and faces of fellow members. Macmillan tried to make up for this by attending the debates, a method that served his purpose, but would be less helpful today. Nowadays, members give more time to party committees, though these have sometimes been described as devices to keep backbenchers agreeably and harmlessly occupied.

Macmillan successively attacked the Governments of his own party, for he believed that they were unable or unwilling to keep the promises they had made to the unemployed. He spoke out about the grimness of unemployment, of men without work or hope, their families barely subsisting in shabby back streets. He became the conscience of the Conservative party; and if lack of personal advancement is a measure of sincerity, Macmillan's sincerity is undisputed. His career seemed firmly stuck.

In addition to attending the House, Members of Parliament must do much work in their constituencies. They are expected to attend local festivities—from football matches to mayoral dinners—and to ensure the efficient working of the party machinery. Macmillan, in addition, had to bear the burdens of his depression-starved constituency. Letters, each containing the story of an individual tragedy, poured in, filling file after file, and there was little Macmillan could do. As an ordinary member he could hope only to prod the government by continually bringing the plight of the unemployed to its attention.

The Rebel

The Conservative party at that time was determined to hold back on government intervention in the economy. Macmillan, on the other hand, favored government planning and some control of industry. He wanted money to be spent on bridges, roads, and houses; he favored government boards that would invest in agriculture; he was for anything that would provide work for the unemployed. He wanted the government to plan, so that it knew what it wanted and how to get it. On this topic Macmillan often spoke more like a Labourite than a Conservative.

The Labour party courted Macmillan from time to time, but he rejected their advances. He aimed at improving capitalism, not at encouraging socialism, and at forestalling what he saw as unpleasant revolutionary change. People deprived of hope would not act constitutionally, and so he saw the Conservative leadership as the unconscious begetters of revolution. He described the party as dominated by "second-class brewers and company promoters" who represented only themselves. But he was equally contemptuous of the wealthy who turn to socialism while enjoying lives of luxury and derided economists and planners who opposed full employment from the comfort of their easy chairs.

Critics are seldom popular, and Macmillan suffered from the usual prejudices against critics who voice their views too openly. He was suspected of being one who opposed for the sake of opposition, who thirsted for office and wanted to show the leaders that they were wrong in leaving him out. His conduct

was seen simply as disloyal, and disloyalty was not to be rewarded: Macmillan remained firmly on the back benches.

Party leaders prize unity most highly and have considerable—though not unlimited—powers to pull reluctants of their own party back into line. The most drastic remedies, of course, are the dissolution of Parliament and the holding of new elections. Alternatively, the party leader can expel recalcitrant members from the party, leaving them to run in the next election as independents—almost certainly guaranteeing their defeat. Yet steps such as these may do more harm than good to a party leader. A leader who consistently offends a fair proportion of his followers is likely to be pressed to resign, rather than to dissolve Parliament and risk damaging the party: leadership is maintained not by brute threats but by persuasion.

Constant persuasion is frustrating and fatiguing, so a Prime Minister seeks people who are both able and loyal for office. Loyalty is sometimes overvalued. But as each Cabinet must include the leaders of the principal factions within the party—some of whom disagree with the Prime Minister, others being actual or potential rivals—a Prime Minister without a base of loyal supporters in the Cabinet is indeed in trouble. Leaders, quite naturally, watch for faithful support and reward it accordingly.

On their side, members offer loyalty because they owe their places in Parliament largely to the party label. Candidates for office, no matter how rebellious, try to avoid expulsion—the denial of the party endorsement. This assists the party leadership in exacting discipline. Voting on the bases of the party label and the leader's image, many electors have neither the time nor the inclination to even learn their member's name. Often the party has difficulty, before an election, in impressing the member's name on the voters. A party member who steps too far out of line and loses party support is likely to find that the voters will simply switch to the party's replacement. Unlike United States Senators or Representatives, who run on their own records with the assistance of their own organizations, the British politician owes all to the party. As a result, the pressures to conform are considerable.

Nonconformists can prod the leadership by forming or joining a group of others of like mind. The group can then try to build support in the party until it becomes strong enough to command the leader's attention. Macmillan joined such a group, which called itself the YMCA and had within it some of the brightest of the young Conservatives. They aimed at reform, planning, and a constructive alternative to socialism. Many of its members were to become prominent later, but at that time they were struggling with the party leadership (for reasons now of interest mainly to historians). The existence of this group and others like it shows that backbenchers, though limited by their dependence on party, need not become "rubber stamps."

Macmillan was still a relatively obscure backbencher, though his visibility was increasing, when the Conservative party was rejected by the electorate. Unable to solve the problems of economic depression and unemployment, it tottered to defeat in 1929. Macmillan took this defeat hard. With tears streaming down his face, surrounded by cheering Labour supporters, he vainly called for "three cheers for [Conservative leader] Baldwin."

The Pendulum
Labour did not long endure in office. Under pressure of events, the Labour leader, Ramsay MacDonald, formed a national govern-

ment of all parties, Conservative, Labour, and Liberal. The Labour leadership could not, however, convince all in their party of its necessity, and the Labour party split. New elections were called, and Macmillan returned to the fray.

Macmillan was in Germany, ironically, for treatment of his war wounds when the elections were announced. Although able to walk only with the aid of two canes, he fought an active campaign and was returned to Parliament with a large majority. Once more, the voters had put their trust in him.

Yet Macmillan remained dissatisfied with the new Parliament. The Great Depression of the thirties was then at its zenith. Unemployment rose again and again, and the government seemed to have neither plans nor solutions. Macmillan himself was growing older; younger men had gained office, while he remained on the back benches. Still, he seemed concerned more with the government's laggard behavior in economic questions than with the stalemate in his career.

Macmillan's discontent found new focus in foreign affairs. A Conservative government, which had been elected in 1936, abandoned sanctions against Italy. These sanctions had been imposed by the League of Nations in the hope of halting Italy's aggression against Ethiopia, an independent African state. In the face of the government's decision, the opposition moved a vote of "no confidence."

A vote of no confidence is nothing new in Parliament. The opposition continually moves such votes, for the ensuing debate provides an opportunity to criticize the Government and to put alternative policies to the electorate. Were the opposition to win the motion, the Government would fall. But as the Government usually commands a majority in the House, the opposition sets its sights simply on discrediting the Government's policies. Members are expected to vote with their party on such a motion, and it is a serious blow to a Government when members of its own party vote with the opposition. This is what Macmillan did, crossing the floor to vote with Labour.

Macmillan voted according to his conscience, believing that he had been elected because of the party's promise to stand up to Mussolini's aggression and that he would fail his constituents if he voted with the party when they failed to do this. At the same time, Macmillan resigned the party whip, a gesture that meant he ceased to be a member of his party. This was Macmillan's own decision: the Chief Whip had intimated that Macmillan need not leave the party, but Macmillan felt he could no longer conscientiously remain in it. Resignation of the whip need not be permanent. When Neville Chamberlain replaced Baldwin as party leader, Macmillan asked to resume the whip, and his request was gladly granted.

The term *whip* has two meanings. Whips are party functionaries in Parliament, whereas whips are party documents. The Whips are there to ensure party discipline and to make certain that members are in attendance when an important vote is to be taken. Whips are powerful party figures, but like the party leader, they try more often to persuade than to intimidate. They also act as conduits from the backbenchers to the party leadership, informing the latter of sentiment in the party. Most important of the Whips is the Chief Whip, who is in overall control of party discipline and is aided by one or more Whips under his instructions. Consulted on all important party matters, the Chief Whip must know on which issues the party is divided and on which united.

The whip is a notice sent to Members of Parliament telling them when votes are to be taken and so ensuring their presence in the House. Its importance is indicated by the number of underlinings on it: an item of little importance to the party need not be underlined at all, while a "three-line whip" —underlined three times—indicates a crucial vote. Members ignore it at their peril. Voting against the party on a three-line whip is tantamount to treason, and even absence or abstention must be for a very good reason. The gradation of the whips allows members to arrange their lives with some degree of order and ensures support for party policies on those issues that matter most.

Macmillan, then, first refused the whip, resigning membership, and then resumed the whip, rejoining the party. Of course, the decision whether to return or to withhold the whip remained with the party, though the question did not arise in Macmillan's case. Why, however, did Macmillan rejoin? The main reason seems to have been the replacement of Baldwin with Neville Chamberlain as party leader. Macmillan believed Chamberlain to be the "robust" leader that he sought and was impressed with Chamberlain's logical mind and record of social reform. But Chamberlain disappointed him in his policies both at home and abroad, and Macmillan soon was as critical of Chamberlain as he had been of Baldwin.

International Crises and War
Following his disillusionment with Chamberlain, a new and decisive influence entered Macmillan's life: Winston Churchill. Impressed by Churchill's personality and vision, Macmillan became increasingly aware of the dangers represented by the European dictators. As one of a circle of younger Members of Parliament around Churchill, he became more and more absorbed with foreign affairs. Churchill's group gained strength when Chamberlain's Foreign Secre-

tary, Anthony Eden, resigned from the Cabinet in 1938 in opposition to Chamberlain's policy of appeasement of the European dictators.

Eden's resignation illustrates both the relationship between a Prime Minister and his Foreign Secretary and the principle of collective Cabinet responsibility. Because a Prime Minister has overall responsibility for the policy of his government, he must be in touch with all departments. Two departments are, however, crucial: the Foreign Office and the Treasury. The Treasury has greater independence, for it is obliged to consult the Prime Minister only on matters of major policy. The Foreign Office, on the other hand, has daily contact with the Prime Minister. As the Prime Minister usually takes a special interest in foreign policy, there must be harmony if they are to work well together. But if there are differences, complete frankness is essential, neither making a move without consulting the other. It is generally disastrous for a Prime Minister to deal directly with the heads of other states and to keep the Foreign Secretary in ignorance. Chamberlain, determined to pursue his independent contacts with Mussolini, again and again left Eden uninformed of his dealings. This behavior provoked Eden's resignation in February 1938.

Why did Eden resign? A Cabinet is collectively responsible for all decisions taken, and a Minister who remains a member—even if in personal disagreement with its policies—is bound to identify publicly with Cabinet decisions. The only public way of signifying disagreement is by resignation. On resigning office, a Minister is permitted to state his or her reasons in the House, yet even then, a former Cabinet Member may be under constraint. Although resigning under dramatic circumstances, Eden could not tell the full story. He could not reveal all the facts

without damage to British policy elsewhere, nor could he make too much of the discreditable and unorthodox methods Chamberlain had used in his blind search for appeasement. To do so might have broken the party and brought the Government down, a step Eden was not then ready to venture.

Many Conservatives rallied around Eden and, after consulting Churchill, abstained when the opposition moved a vote of no confidence. Abstention, though not the most courageous form of protest, can be effective if it is made clear to the public, and especially to the press, that it is motivated by disapproval of government policies.

Desperately pursuing the policy of appeasement, which Chamberlain sincerely believed would bring "peace in our time" by giving Hitler and Mussolini what they wanted, he drifted from one crisis to another. The dictators' appetite for aggrandizement seemed to grow with the eating. When Germany attacked Poland in September 1939, the policy of appeasement was finally and manifestly discredited.

The War Years

Despite an active parliamentary career Macmillan entered the war largely unknown to the wider public. Considered a malcontent by the party leadership, thought to be intelligent—albeit somewhat smug and boring—by those in the party, he was respected by many of ability, such as Churchill. But his admirers were in no position to reward him. The war wrought a dramatic change in Macmillan's fortunes, for he at last came into his own. He knew this well; as he later reminded Churchill, had it not been for Hitler, Churchill would not have been a Prime Minister, nor Macmillan a Minister.

Macmillan remained frustrated in the months immediately following the outbreak of war. Chamberlain remained Prime Minister till the end of the months of "phony war" early in 1940. Propaganda had predicted massive air raids on London on declaration of hostilities, but they did not come. French, British, and Germans sat behind fortified lines without firing a shot. Although Britain had gone to war to protect the independence of Poland—now overrun by German armies, her freedom extinguished —Chamberlain could think of no motto more inspiring than "business as usual."

Criticism of Chamberlain mounted, and what was left of his waning prestige vanished with the fiasco following the German invasion of Norway. Discredited, his government fell on May 10, 1940, defeated on a Vote on the Adjournment. This vote is usually taken in the last half-hour of the parliamentary day and provides the opposition with yet another opportunity for criticism. On this occasion there was a widespread defection among the Conservatives, many of whom, including Macmillan, crossed the floor to vote against the Government. Chamberlain resigned, to be replaced by Winston Churchill, soon to live his and his country's greatest hours.

Churchill was at last in power and could use his position to reward those who had stood by him in the political wilderness. A British Prime Minister, like other politicians, uses patronage to assure loyalty and reward the faithful, but Churchill was more restricted than usual in what he could offer his followers. To conduct the war with utmost vigor, he had drawn all parties into a national government and had to reserve important offices for their leaders. Thus, fewer offices were available for Conservatives. Macmillan was included among those to be given office, but could not be offered as high a position as he might have received under ordinary conditions. He was made Parliamentary Secretary to the Minister of Supply.

Although this was Macmillan's first promotion, a Parliamentary Secretary is not a Minister, not being appointed by the Crown and having no constitutional powers. The Parliamentary Secretary assists the Minister and makes decisions—consonant with the Minister's policies—on minor matters in the Minister's absence. The Secretary also assists the Minister by providing information to be used in question time. Macmillan was, however, in a position to profit from the experience of his Minister and, like other Junior Ministers, was considered a man to watch. Parties use these positions to discover men and women of talent, to train the more able for office, and to weed out the less able.

Macmillan learned much from both Ministers he served. He greatly admired Labour's Herbert Morrison, and, as Morrison rather wryly commented, such was Macmillan's ambition for them both that Morrison had to caution him that winning the war came first.[2] Macmillan almost idolized the second Minister, Lord Beaverbrook, whose influence was thought to be almost too pronounced by some of Macmillan's friends. They felt that Beaverbrook, whom Macmillan sedulously imitated, had coarsened him and made him less pleasant a person. Perhaps Macmillan lacked a firm identity: he imitated those he admired, first Beaverbrook and then Churchill. Macmillan's mysticism, not far below the surface, found a complement in Churchill's encompassing visions that swept over vast expanses of history and human destiny. So, despite differences in age, appearance, and personality, Macmillan seems to have felt impelled to imitate Churchill's mannerisms and speech.

The effects of office manifested themselves in Macmillan's character. As a Junior Minister he gained political insight that he had

2 Herbert Morrison, *An Autobiography* (London: Odhams Press, 1960), p. 300.

lacked on the back benches. He also showed two traits that were to be evident throughout his career: impatience with the public aspects of politicking and mastery of working in committees. On the floor of the House, where as Parliamentary Secretary he had to answer questions on minor issues, he showed impatience and irritation, frequently becoming short and sarcastic. Within the Department of Supply Macmillan was a different person. He could now put into effect the policies he had so long contemplated, and in so doing his success was great and obvious. He helped reorganize the ministry and to set up boards of employers and workers, all of which contributed to efficient production of the means of warfare. He also established contacts among industrialists and unionists, contacts that were later to stand him in good stead.

After two years in Supply, Macmillan became Under-Secretary of State for Colonies, a position providing another opportunity to display his administrative skills. But his greatest chance came in November 1942, when Britain needed a Resident-Minister at Allied Headquarters in Algiers.

Removed from the centers of power, the office had been spurned by two other politicians. Macmillan accepted it with reluctance. Yet the very isolation of the post allowed Macmillan to wield great power. He was on his own in North Africa and could display his mastery of administration and politics with no one to overshadow him. He had to steer a careful course, taking into account the all too delicate susceptibilities of the French, whose two generals—de Gaulle and Giraud —each claimed to speak for France. The Americans were easier to handle; but whether military or civilians, they were only too conscious of America's power and their own importance. In this complex knot of personalities and relationships, Macmillan was able to win the trust of the Americans and the French, while at the same time expanding British influence. He established a close and lasting friendship with Dwight Eisenhower, and even the ever prickly Charles de Gaulle later said that Macmillan had "all his esteem"—an achievement in itself.

Macmillan's sphere of power expanded again, embracing Europe itself, when he became Resident Minister for the Central Mediterranean in 1943. Europe was devastated by war, and Macmillan was closely involved in the initial steps to reconstruction. With the Americans opting out of Italian politics in 1944, Macmillan could reshape the Italian state virtually on his own. He also dealt effectively with Marshal Tito of Yugoslavia and helped settle the civil war in Greece. Once again Macmillan could put his ideas to the test and once more he showed that they could be translated into practice.

Macmillan was now no longer the theoretician boring the House with figures. Having shown that he could handle situations of great delicacy and difficulty, that he could solve problems, Macmillan returned to Britain a new man, more confident and less shy. He was still not a major public figure, for his work had been largely outside the focus of public attention. But to Churchill and to the Conservative leadership, Macmillan had established his right to office.

Brief Office and Long Opposition
Macmillan was appointed Secretary for Air, but his spell in office was to be short. The government could do little more than wait for the new elections, which had been called for July 26, 1945, precipitated by Labour's resignation from the national government.

Labour's leaders decided, once the war in Europe had ended, that they no longer wished to serve in Churchill's Cabinet. They believed that the tide of voter sentiment was

running in their favor and that their representation in Parliament did not accord with
their strength across the country and in the
armed forces. They also wanted to put their
socialist principles into practice at once and
could do this only if they controlled the
government. In addition, they knew that
their organization was largely intact while
that of the Conservatives had run down.
Labour's strength derived from the trade
unions, which had continued functioning
throughout the war, while the Conservatives'
power, based on local associations, had been
weakened as members were drawn into the
armed forces or into war work. Besides, the
existing Parliament had sat for ten years,
and it was time to go back to the people.

Labour's landslide surprised even its own
supporters, as the party emerged with 388 of
the (then) 640 seats in the House. Churchill and his government were overwhelmingly
rejected. The rejection was not of Churchill
personally; he was appreciated and popular.
But the public wanted a change and believed
that socialism could effortlessly bring instant
utopia. The Conservatives seemed dated and
stale, with little new to offer the people after
so many years of sacrifice and war.

Macmillan was soundly beaten. Indeed,
he had sensed what was to come during his
drab campaign. Things passed too quietly;
meetings were well attended but uneventful.
The special courtesy and consideration opponents showed him were signs that they felt
confident of victory. In defeat Macmillan
wondered if he should not quit politics but
shrewdly decided to carry on. He reasoned
that the very magnitude of the Labour victory would work against the party; such high
hopes had been built that Labour could never
realize them. In one or, at the most, two
Parliaments the tide would turn.

Having lost Stockton, Macmillan needed
to win an election to return to Parliament.

As a leader important to his party, there was
little difficulty in finding him a safe seat:
Bromley in Kent. Successfully contesting the
by-election, he resumed his seat on the
Conservative front bench on November
20, 1945.

The Frontbencher
Macmillan was now establishment—no
longer the rebel he had been before the war.
He seemed more of an actor, more mannered,
less sincere. Nevertheless, he was a redoubt-
able debater, who could easily raise the
Labour government's temperature as he
taunted them in ways they could not ignore.
Labourites resented his sallies, and his own
party was delighted. Below the surface,
however, Macmillan was depressed. He did
not relish being in opposition and found
criticism—without the opportunity for action
—to be tedious and uninspiring. Government bills were fought in debate and in
committee, but the Government always got
its way in the end. Having tasted office,
Macmillan found his membership in the
Conservative shadow Cabinet little to his
liking.

To criticize effectively and to be ready
with an alternative government if called to
office, the opposition in Parliament maintains a shadow Cabinet. Each leader "shadows" a government Minister, challenging the
policy either of that department or of the
government as a whole. The shadow Minister also chairs a party committee that provides advice and information and considers
the policies of the department. Macmillan
became shadow Minister for Fuel and Power,
concentrating his attacks on the government's
plans to nationalize the coal mining industry.
Macmillan's position was embarrassing to
him, for he was attacking policies similar to
those he had advocated before the war.
Macmillan did not seem fully engaged in the

debate and, in the end, paid tribute to Labour for the way they had fought to gain their goal.

Planning had become part of Conservative policy, though some die-hards found the word hard to tolerate; to soothe their fears it was called "national housekeeping." Leaders knew that if the party was to recapture power, it would have to drop the catchwords of the 1930s and to restate its positions. Economic issues were most important in meeting the Labour challenge, and the Conservative party would have to have realistic plans of its own. Churchill set up an Economic Policy Committee, which was chaired by Macmillan's long-time rival R. A. Butler, but which adopted most of Macmillan's ideas. Some of Labour's nationalization of industry was accepted as inevitable and irreversible. Never-

theless, private enterprise was emphasized in the framework of a centralized economy under government guidance.

Meanwhile, as Macmillan had predicted, the mood of the country was changing. Labour was on the retreat. The public was tired and disillusioned, for the Labour party's plans seemed to lead not to utopia but to an ever harsher austerity. Not surprisingly, the Conservatives won the General Election of 1951 with a majority of twenty-six seats. Macmillan now expected high office. Close to Churchill, respected by his party, he hoped for the Treasury or Foreign Affairs. He was given the Ministry of Housing, an important, but not a prestigious, position. Yet, like his office in North Africa, this unpromising post was to be a great opportunity.

4

Macmillan's Middle Years: The Minister

The Housing Crusade

The Problems of a New Minister
Housing was a crucial problem in postwar Britain. Two million people needed housing, and both Conservative and Labour leaders doubted that it could be built. Nevertheless, the Conservative party had pledged itself to build 300,000 houses in a year, a task that now fell to the newly appointed Minister of Housing, Harold Macmillan.

A Minister taking over a department is expected to be an amateur. Macmillan knew nothing of the housing industry and was committed to a task the experts declared impossible. Macmillan was fortunate enough to inherit competent civil servants, but his handling of his department demonstrates what a skillful Minister can accomplish in administering programs and devising unusual methods.

The power of civil servants in the success of a Minister was mentioned in the previous chapter. This was one of Macmillan's first problems. The Permanent Secretary knew little of industry or production, while the first Deputy Secretary was on the point of retirement. It was the next Deputy Secretary in rank who was to be the linchpin of the program. Evelyn Sharp was able and endowed with a strong personality, dominating the department of which she later became Permanent Secretary. Known for her ability to dissect a problem for ministerial decision, she was a useful ally and, in good measure, the person responsible for the success of Macmillan's housing program.

Macmillan's program was drawn from his war experience and his prewar ideas on planning. He aimed at setting up production boards of industry and labor, which were intended to secure materials, bring them to the right places at the right times, and supervise their use in housing construction. Needing an able administrator for effective coordination of the various boards, Macmillan turned to a man with whom he had worked in the war, Sir Percy Mills.

The introduction of an outsider is often resented by the administrative staff, so the way Mills was brought in illustrates another facet of the relationship of Minister and administration.

First, the problem was to obtain Mill's release from a job in private industry. This was done by getting Churchill, whom Mill's employer revered, to write a personal letter asking for the release. Although reluctant, Churchill was prevailed on to write the letter. Then there were the problems with Whitehall. What was to be Mill's rank? How was he to relate to the various Permanent Secretaries? What were his functions to be? Although Macmillan said he would ignore it unless problems arose, a long paper was prepared, setting everything out. As Macmillan expected, Mills soon won the confidence of officials, and there was little friction.

A new Minister, to succeed, must make the principal pressure groups aware of his future plans. Macmillan approached the building unions, telling them frankly that he knew little about housing and asking for their advice and sympathy. The union leaders were both amused and impressed, finding this a welcome change from Ministers who, they said, believed they already knew everything and were unwilling to listen. The wholehearted cooperation of employers was also obtained through visits to Macmillan's office. With the two principal pressure groups inclined to cooperate, Macmillan proceeded to organize his office.

Effectiveness in office depends not only on the Minister but also on the choice of Junior Ministers, who can greatly contribute to the success of their senior's policies. Macmillan chose a recently elected, ambitious business tycoon, Ernest Marples, as his Junior Minister, knowing that he would turn the same skills that had led to business success to the success of the building program. Macmillan's Parliamentary Private Secretary, Reginald Bevins, has provided interesting insight into the way Macmillan worked. Macmillan was patient, encouraging the others to talk, seldom saying anything himself; he just puffed on his pipe. At the end he would thank them and carry out the decision he had made before the meeting began. Although encouraging able civil servants, such as Evelyn Sharp, Macmillan never let them initiate policies. "Ministers are the kings," he would say, "against the civil servants who are the modern barons. Your job is not to accept what they say but to criticize them and go on criticizing them."[1]

The dimensions of the housing problem are apparent from even a brief recital of the facts. In 1951 the housing shortage was due partly to neglect and partly to laws passed at different times. A spate of construction in the nineteenth century had not been enough to keep up with growing population nor to avoid overcrowding and slums. Rent controls during both world wars led many owners to neglect their properties, which fell into disrepair. Building virtually ceased during World War II, while bombing destroyed many dwellings, with the rubble impeding rebuilding. The result was that families exceeded dwellings by about 1 million; and of the 13 million dwellings, 2 million were shared by two or more families. Materials and labor were in short supply,

[1] Reginald Bevins, *The Greasy Pole: A Personal Account of the Realities of British Politics* (London: Hodder & Stoughton, 1965), chap. 3.

and building was hampered by a maze of codes and regulations.

Building the Houses
Macmillan announced a three-point plan to the Cabinet on November 19, 1951. It called first for a great increase in the ratio of privately built houses to those built publicly; second, it allowed the sale of municipally owned houses, under proper safeguards; and finally it allowed the construction of smaller houses.

Macmillan's proposals were approved by the Cabinet and were announced on November 27. The similarity of some of Macmillan's proposals to those Labour had advanced when in power rendered Labour's criticism ineffective. The press was friendly, the public patient. The stage was set to build the houses.

And Macmillan did. The Conservative party had set the goal of 300,000 houses a year more as a pious hope than as a realistic goal. Macmillan triumphantly realized the hope: 327,000 houses were built in 1953, and another 354,000 in 1954. Macmillan's housing crusade having exceeded the wildest expectations, it is little wonder that he was given a hero's welcome at the Conservative conferences from 1952 onward.

New materials and new ideas had aided success. Marples's "boneless wonder"—a house with a cement frame—and Macmillan's "peoples' house" were examples. Macmillan himself was photographed sitting uneasily in a peoples' house at a Good Housekeeping Exhibition in London.

Macmillan now had the reputation of a man who got things done, a reputation a British Minister who aspires to bigger and better offices must achieve. There were critics, it is true, on both sides of the House. Some argued that the houses had been built at the expense of industrial development, others that this was just a Conservative trick to lure working-class votes. Macmillan countered with the argument that badly housed workers could not be productive. One fact remained: the houses had been built—a very persuasive argument to voters.

Man and Minister
Now sixty years old, Macmillan remained an enigmatic figure. To the general public he seemed aloof and unglamorous. The *Daily Mirror* had run a poll to pick Churchill's likely successor, and Macmillan had captured less than 2 percent of the vote. The charisma that receives so much attention today seemed totally lacking.

Macmillan presented striking contrasts in private and in public. A master of give-and-take in small groups, he took an interest in the families of his staff and showed great personal warmth. He was witty in conversation, and though possessed of a monumental temper, he never displayed it without cause. His Parliamentary Secretary, Bevins, described working with Macmillan as an adventure because he exuded such enthusiasm and infectious zeal. By those outside his circle Macmillan was either much admired or much disliked. He was a very private man whose ambition drove him to assume a public role.

More significant, perhaps, is the change from the radical of the thirties to the establishment man of the fifties. Changes of this sort are difficult to explain, due partly to age and experience and partly to the change in perspective, from back bench to front bench.

Macmillan exhibited the narrowing of attention that occurs as a politician moves into power. The whole range of policy, in the most general terms is open to a backbencher—foreign affairs, the economy, all aspects of national life. Once in office, the business of the department circumscribes the Minister's outlook. Cabinet papers, Foreign Office telegrams, memoranda covering the whole range of government business are circulated to each Cabinet Minister. They are overwhelming in volume and uninviting in style. As a result, Ministers will concentrate on the business of their own departments and leave the papers of other departments unread.

Ministers are also encouraged to concentrate on their own department by the different degrees of power and authority inherent in different offices. The de facto governing body of the Cabinet consists of the Prime Minister, the Foreign Secretary, and the Chancellor of the Exchequer, together with one or two other specially experienced or influential Ministers. Their colleagues are expected to listen in silence and do their own work. Of course, on matters of supreme importance, all Ministers are duty-bound to express their views and even to threaten resignation in their support.

Many situations do not erupt into crisis or demand drastic action. Problems tend, instead, to drag on from day to day, or even from one Cabinet to the next. Cabinet Ministers engrossed in their own work find it difficult to do more than keep up with the larger affairs of government. The rest of the time is taken up with the needs of the department, the necessity for placating some of the party powerful, and routine business.

In the many volumes of his autobiography, Macmillan speaks of the difficulties that face a Minister who wishes to maintain a broad perspective of the government. In Housing, for instance, Macmillan could take an interest in general economic and financial problems. Other questions, such as defense, foreign affairs, or European unity, to which he had devoted so much work while on the back benches or in opposition, could only occasionally receive attention. "The fierce and almost frantic pursuit of the housing target filled my mind," he writes, "to the exclusion of everything not directly related to the achievement of our purpose." Day by

day they worked to reach the target, and debates in Parliament "were an irritating, sometimes galling distraction." [2]

Defense, Foreign Office, and Treasury

The Upward Path

Possibly because office narrows vision, Cabinet posts are not intended to be permanent. Ministers are moved from department to department in reshuffles of the Cabinet. After his great success in Housing, Macmillan could now expect a promotion, which was not slow in coming.

Every Prime Minister reshuffles his Cabinet, sometimes more than once or twice in a session. Reshuffling enables Prime Ministers to weed out the weak—Ministers and Junior Ministers who have not fulfilled their potential—and to improve the Cabinet position of those with demonstrated abilities. Prime Ministers themselves are not appointed permanently, as the statistics tell. From 1951 to 1961 the Conservative party had three Prime Ministers. Of the seventy-five people invited to office under Churchill in 1951 only sixteen remained in office ten years later. Of about fifty Junior Ministers, only ten had entered the Cabinet, and six more had survived as Juniors. Of course, not all were fired. Some Junior Ministers, feeling they could get no further, had retired from politics in frustration; others had returned voluntarily to the back benches. Nonetheless, only the strong survived. Macmillan, certainly one of the strong, steadily improved his position, reaching in the end the pinnacle of power—the prime ministership.

Macmillan advanced even though his

[2] Harold Macmillan, *The Tides of Fortune 1945–1955* (New York: Harper & Row, 1969), p. 377.

performance in later offices was somewhat disappointing: he held three different Ministries without conspicuous success. How did he survive? The reasons are complex, but one factor was his colleagues' recognition that Macmillan's position in each of these offices was impossible, through no fault of his own.

In the Ministry of Defense, much of Macmillan's time was taken up with Churchill's increasing incapacity due to age and illness, coupled with the Prime Minister's reluctance to admit these realities. Macmillan had been one of Churchill's most faithful followers and owed much to his encouragement and support. Yet, by January 1955, even Macmillan was convinced that Churchill would have to go. On his side, once Churchill realized that he no longer had Macmillan's support, he felt that the time to resign had come. He did so on April 5, 1955, and, declining a seat in the House of Lords, became again an ordinary Member of Commons.

Anthony Eden, for so many years Churchill's heir apparent, was the obvious choice as successor. He had the right social credentials coupled with a record of achievement: graduate of Eton and Oxford, officer in World War I, courageous opponent of appeasement. Few would have believed when he took office that he would be gone and forgotten in a mere two years.

Eden, unlike Macmillan, was a man with a strong public image. Public faith was not, however, shared by Eden's colleagues, who felt misgivings at his vanity, indecisiveness, and jealousy of power. Many also believed that having played a secondary role to Churchill made him unfit for the role of leader. Nonetheless, all felt he should be given a chance. In turn Macmillan was accorded another promotion. Though not Eden's first choice (he would have preferred

Macmillan and Churchill, 1958

(The Press Associated Limited)

Lord Salisbury), he became Foreign Secretary.

Macmillan was chosen because he was not a member of Lords. At that time Peers could not renounce their titles, nor could they speak in Commons. Thus Salisbury could not appear to defend Government policies, a task that would fall to his Junior Minister. Great burdens would be thrown on the Junior Minister and on the whole Government. To avoid these difficulties, Macmillan was selected. Strangely, when Macmillan became Prime Minister, he appointed Lord Home to be *his* Foreign Secretary. The problem was not insurmountable, but Eden judged the situation differently, and Macmillan accepted with alacrity, as he had long coveted the foreign secretaryship.

Macmillan's misfortune was compounded in that after Housing, he went into ministries without defined tasks. He had difficulty, therefore, in creating a sphere in which the department could operate. Though many characterized Macmillan as one of Britain's worst Foreign Secretaries, it is difficult to discern how many of the policies he administered were his and how many were Eden's. In addition, the Foreign Office seemed to bring out the visionary in Macmillan, for like so many practical men he had an intuitive and romantic side. His belief in the effectiveness of summit talks—meetings of heads of state—is a case in point. He traveled all over Europe trying to convince the American Secretary of State, John Foster Dulles, and the Soviet leaders to attend such a meeting. The summit, held from July 18 to July 23, 1955, led to little, and Macmillan was overshadowed by Eden. Nevertheless, Macmillan continued his efforts for more summits then and later.

Macmillan's shrewdness showed through even when he was an apparently unsuccessful Foreign Secretary. He recognized before others the changes taking place in the Soviet Union and realized that the new forces there could be harnessed to peace. He was one of the few foreign politicians able to maintain good relations with Dulles. Macmillan also came to the Foreign Office at a time when problems that were to vex Britain for many years were beginning to emerge: the Middle East, Cyprus, the economy, the Common Market.

Meanwhile, Macmillan's standing in the party seemed unaffected by his showing as Foreign Secretary. He was now seen as a prospective Prime Minister by many backbenchers. When Eden reshuffled his Cabinet at the end of 1955, it seemed inevitable that Macmillan be promoted to the Treasury, one of the key ministries. The Chancellor of the Exchequer—in effect the Minister of Finance—ranks just below the Prime Minister in importance. The Chancellor is in charge of all finance; his department coordinates all other departments and is in charge of economic planning. For all its importance, it is a relatively small department, a condition that helps to concentrate its considerable powers. All other departments must make overtures to the Treasury if any funds will be expended. So the Treasury has an overview of all pending legislation and can coordinate all departments. Its control of the budget, deciding what is to be spent where, gives it control of economic development. In addition, the Treasury collects taxes, duties, and imposts. The Chancellor is, therefore, a very powerful figure.

The appointment as Chancellor did not completely please Macmillan because of the tradition that Chancellors seldom rose to be Prime Ministers. On taking office, he amused his colleagues by insisting it be clearly understood that this was a step toward being Prime Minister and not away from it. Otherwise, man and office seemed well matched. Macmillan had always been interested in planning and public finance, and his interests and expertise harmonized with the Treasury.

Macmillan introduced his first and, as it happened, only budget to the British people in 1956, one in which he had to demand that Britishers tighten their belts. Britain's economic plight was growing and the prestige of Eden's government on the wane when Macmillan took office. Gallup polls showed that in one year voter support had fallen from 70 percent to 40 percent. Macmillan would be obliged to introduce new measures bound to be unpopular, as they included cutting the subsidies on bread and milk. The question now arose as to the timing of the public announcement. Most of the Cabinet wished to delay announcement until the budget speech, while Macmillan wanted the policies made public earlier. His reasons were national necessity and political expedience: the opposition was bound to ask for a debate as soon as the House met, and the Government had to be ready. Macmillan felt that he could not carry on unless the whole Cabinet supported his policies and prepared a letter of resignation. Lady Dorothy, his wife, delayed moving into the official residence of the Chancellor, next to that of the Prime Minister, at 11 Downing Street. Happily for Macmillan's career, an acceptable solution was found.

Although Chancellor for only a short time, Macmillan left his mark on the Treasury. First of all, he improved the collection of statistics so that the government was not, as he put it, trying to look up "tomorrow's trains with last year's timetables." He also devised the premium bond scheme, an imaginative way of raising moneys for the government.

The British government faced the problem of stimulating savings in its bonds. Macmillan believed that private savings might be encouraged with an element of lottery. Prizes would be small, and unlike ordinary gambling, the capital invested would not be risked. Winnings would be financed out of interest. The limit to which investments could be made was to be £500 (about $800), and prizes were to range from 1 of £1,000 to some 200 of £25 each. Before putting the scheme into final form, Macmillan had to consult with all lobbies concerned with savings. Support by the National Savings Movement—a lobby that encouraged individual saving—had to be won. Then there were the churches and the savings banks, who feared that their customers would transfer their funds to the new issues.

This highly innovative scheme met the re-

ception Macmillan expected. Some churches opposed gambling as morally wrong, but others gave it qualified approval. Harold Wilson, leader of the opposition, made a witty attack, saying that it was a shame that the future of Britain should depend on the proceeds of a "squalid raffle." The public loved the scheme from the start, and the premium bonds sold. They paid no interest but did offer the chance of a tax-free prize. The very jokes made about them in the media served to publicize them. The success of the bond issue did nothing to hurt Macmillan's career.

Macmillan was an able Chancellor. Britain's balance of payments improved from a deficit of £92 million in 1955 to a surplus of £192 million in 1956. Yet Macmillan found the role of Chancellor trying, as he had to spend days telling old friends why they could not have the funds for their pet departmental schemes.

In his memoirs Macmillan points to the difference he found between the Foreign Office and the Treasury. The Foreign Office could be likened to a daily newspaper: announcements of events and crises come without foreknowledge or warning, and decisions have to be made from hour to hour or minute to minute. The Treasury he likened to a weekly magazine, whose editor has more time to consider events as they occur. Both departments, and especially the Minister, must work out long-range policies under the pressure of immediate events; it is the time frame for decision that is different.

The Suez Crisis and the Fall of Eden

The Political Setting
The Suez Canal had been a vital link when Britain had a vast empire. One of Egypt's major national assets, it was leased by a cor-

poration in which the British and French governments were the major shareholders. Egyptian President Gamal Nasser nationalized the canal on July 26, 1956, putting the British and French governments on the horns of a dilemma. How were they to respond? The distrust of Nasser added a cutting edge, for in terms of a 1954 agreement between Britain and Egypt the British had abandoned their bases on the Suez Canal in return for Nasser's promise to protect their interests. Eden had sold this plan to a reluctant Cabinet by assuring them that Nasser could be trusted. Nationalization was a humiliating blow to Eden personally and to his Government. Everyone in the Cabinet felt that some response was required. The question was what form this response was to take.

Macmillan emerged as one of the Cabinet "hawks," urging military action even more strongly than Eden himself. This position was enigmatic: Macmillan was under no pressure, and his duty as Chancellor was to urge caution and thrift. Indeed, he had just cut social services. Except for costs, the invasion of other countries was not the business of the Chancellor. Yet Macmillan, more than many of his colleagues, advocated invading Egypt.

Eden's situation was different and easier to understand. After only a few months as Prime Minister, he faced rising discontent in both party and Cabinet, and to this was now added the appearance of appeasing both Egypt and the Soviets. The party right wing and some newspapers urged a strong stand. These pressures were reinforced by attitudes shared by a broad sector of the public: a nostalgia for the war, for Britain's lost greatness, and a frustration with Britain as it now was. Eden had every reason to take action, even rash action.

Since Macmillan had no such motives, why did he, clear-headed man that he was, take the line that he did? Several factors may

have influenced him. One, perhaps, was the fear of repeating Chamberlain's mistaken attempt at appeasing a dictator. Another was a misapprehension of the American view. In his memoirs Macmillan points to American vacillation, with Eisenhower and Dulles alternatively encouraging strong action and then retracting their advice. Macmillan believed that the Americans would publicly protest invasion of Egypt to recover the canal while privately hoping for Nasser's fall. He felt that they suspected Nasser of bringing the Soviets into the Middle East (not without reason) and feared the Egyptian President would work to undermine friendly Arab governments.

Yet, after the British invaded Egypt along with the French, Eisenhower and Dulles seemed to take the invasion as a personal affront. They seemed particularly to resent the fact that they had not been consulted in advance. Dulles's hostility, indeed, amounted almost to frenzy, and American pressure forced the British and French into a humiliating retreat. Britain and France had to face not only the threats of the Soviet Union but also those of the United States, both acting in an unnatural coalition. The reasons why the Americans acted as they did, and the steps taken by the different parties, are beyond our scope. There is little d
however, that Britain and France
enjoyed a strong position
States not intervened.
had suffered a hu
hands of the Is
their Russian
then, have
the area.
sisted o
1955
soil

over the handling of the Suez crisis. This discontent raised the question of Cabinet responsibility once again. According to theory and practice, the Cabinet is collectively responsible for all government decisions. Nevertheless, the level of Cabinet consultation has varied. Churchill made most of his decisions himself or, at best, consulted only a small group of Ministers. Attlee, the Labour Prime Minister, did much the same during his term in office, and Eden, in turn followed the pattern. This was acceptable as long as things went well, but when failure was due to the Prime Minister's having willfully embarked the nation on a disastrous foreign venture, the challenge of consultation was raised once more. Eden was blamed for having made decisions without consulting the whole Cabinet or even keeping them informed. A strong claim was made for the more traditional procedures to be reinstated, though when Macmillan replaced Eden, he also kept much of the decision-making power in his hands, as, indeed, have his successors.

It would be a mistake to blame Suez entirely for Eden's downfall. In some senses Suez strengthened his position for a time. Both front and back benchers in the party felt it their duty to rally around their leader, and Macmillan displayed greater loyalty to before. It was the dissatisfaction Eden's ways of dealing failing health that Eden's resignation with him, Suez

the of

had mainly to discuss costs. His support of the Suez venture was sufficiently strong to earn him the backing of the majority of the party but sufficiently vague so as not to tie him too closely to its failure. Harnessing all the arts of the politician, he was able to make the Suez venture and even its outcome sound good. Macmillan was an obvious candidate for the role of Prime Minister when Eden, after a reasonable wait intended to refute the claim that Nasser had driven him from office, finally threw off the mantle on January 9, 1957.

Selection of a New Prime Minister
Macmillan's major rival was R. A. Butler, who had at first opposed the Suez venture and then given it lukewarm support. Butler was the candidate of the party left, Macmillan of its right. Butler had correctly assessed the Suez situation; Macmillan had assessed it wrongly. Why then was Macmillan chosen? The answer tells us much of how political parties actually work.

Eden's decision to resign, revealed to the Cabinet on January 8, made urgent the question of succession. After Butler and Macmillan left the meeting, the other Ministers were consulted. It was clear that the senior Ministers were for Macmillan. Determined that the selection of Eden's successor should not fall to the Party Meeting, they adopted the unorthodox procedure of individual polling. Each Cabinet member was called to the office of Lord Salisbury and asked whether it was to be Butler or Macmillan.

By tradition—the Royal Prerogative—the Monarch may make anyone he or she wishes Prime Minister. It is customary for the Monarch to choose the leader of the majority party in the House as Prime Minister or, if the matter is unclear, the person most acceptable to the majority. If a Prime Minister resigns without naming a successor, as did Eden, the Prerogative acquires some semblance of reality. The question of what the Queen ought to have done remains debated. She should, one argument runs, have sent for the Leader of the House of Commons, then R. A. Butler, who also was leader of the majority party. He would have said he could form a government. He expected to be summoned, but the summons never came. Instead, the Queen sent for Lord Salisbury, Leader of the House of Lords, and for Sir Winston Churchill, to consult with them. Strangely enough, Eden was not consulted; and Churchill, though high in honors, was only an ordinary member without official position in the party. Perhaps the Queen was badly advised on the rules, for when she exercised the Royal Prerogative, its exercise seemed manifestly unfair.

Macmillan was not the most obvious choice, for Butler had much to his credit. Indeed, on the face of it, he had the stronger claim. He was Leader of the House, that is, the Minister who arranges the order of legislation together with the Whips, and thus functions as a one-man Rules Committee, in the American sense. Butler had presided over the Cabinet with distinction in Eden's absences and during his illness. Yet steps were obviously contrived to keep him from office. Why?

Butler had the reputation for being unreliable. He had opposed the Suez venture but had not resigned from the Cabinet, fearing his resignation would be described as wrecking the party. Instead he urged caution and restraint. Rumors spread that he had undermined Eden and weakened Government resolve. In fact, Butler had been loyal, but this did not help him with the strongest element in the party. The Conservative right had favored intervention and determined that Butler would not be Prime Minister. With the party already divided and discontented, Macmillan was seen as able to hold the party together, and so the choice fell to him.

After a week in office, Macmillan later said, he still seemed to be living in a kind of daze. He could not yet believe that he really was Prime Minister. It had the unreal nature of a dream or nightmare. Yet it was true: he had attained the highest office and was to hold it without interruption from January 18, 1957, to October 13, 1963.

5

Macmillan at the Top:
The Prime Minister

Introduction

After some thirty-three years in Parliament, Macmillan now was Prime Minister. He was confirmed by the Party Meeting (not to be confused with the Annual Conference), a body consisting of all members of the House accepting the Conservative Whip and the party executive. This body in theory elects the leader, but in fact merely ratifies a choice already made. Later the method of selecting a Prime Minister was to change and to become more democratic. But at that time, on January 22, 1957, the expected confirmation came automatically. He now was Prime Minister, facing the aftermath of the Suez crisis and having no guarantee that his government would last more than a few weeks.

Macmillan was, however, superbly suited to pulling together the party. The fatigue that had seemed to set in at the end of the Suez debates disappeared, and a revitalized Macmillan appeared. He had been regarded as aloof, but now he seemed careful, friendly, and sensible. Conducting himself with dignity and composure, he consolidated his position in the House. He established lines of communication with backbenchers and invited Ministers to informal conferences at Checkers, the official country residence of British Prime Ministers. Perhaps he was just acting the genial host, as his enemies have asserted, but the act was good enough to be accepted. In addition, he had to learn how to appeal to a wider public on television and radio. For a man as reserved as Macmillan, it was an ordeal, and he never was to feel himself expert, however much his performances were praised.

First, Macmillan had to appear in the House, on the same afternoon as the Party Meeting had confirmed him. His own party received him without great enthusiasm, and the opposition with a reasonable amount of derisive shouting and laughter. (Shouting interjections in Parliament is common to both sides; there is not that formal decorum the public expects. The British people themselves were surprised, when Parliament was broadcast live in 1975, at how much of this goes on.) The reception Macmillan received was not unexpected. Also in accordance with tradition, the leader of the Labour party, Hugh Gaitskell, rose to make a few kind comments, promising a tough fight but also expressing personal goodwill. With this customary courtesy, the customary battle between Government and opposition was joined.

"The middle way" (*title of the book written by Mr. Macmillan in 1938*)
Macmillan balances the factions in his Cabinet

(By permission of Beaverbrook Newspapers, Ltd.)

The Cabinet and Its Crises

Forming the Cabinet

Forming a government was obviously the first task facing Macmillan. This is a matter on which Prime Ministers can expect little advice. They can consult with the Chief Whip and their own staffs, but the choice is theirs alone in the end. Clearly Prime Ministers cannot discuss with one colleague the merits or faults of another who may also be a contender for the same post. Then, when it comes to the less vital junior ranks, other things must be borne in mind. Senior Ministers press the claims of younger members who have served them, yet those who have ability but lack sponsorship cannot be ignored. This makes the formation of a government a matter of fitting together a jigsaw puzzle of more than eighty pieces.

The formation of a Cabinet is more than the construction of a government; it is also a way of holding the party together. The factions of the left and the right must be accommodated. First there was Butler, still a major party figure with a following among the party left. Much depended on Macmillan and Butler working smoothly together. Butler had hoped to be Foreign Secretary, but instead accepted the post of Home Secretary, much to Macmillan's relief. The Home Secretaryship was important but unglamorous, and it offered no opportunities of diverting the spotlight from the Prime Minister. The remaining portfolios were carefully balanced between individuals who had urged action at Suez and those who had opposed it. In addition, new and promising members were brought into the Cabinet.

Balancing a government brings other advantages. Although Prime Ministers do not often consult with their Cabinet colleagues, all members are expected publicly to support the Prime Minister. Including opponents in the Cabinet assures that they are bound by the Prime Minister's policies. And including some of their strongest supporters ensures that they will receive more than passive compliance.

Resignation and Rebellion

Ministers are not completely helpless, for they can resign if a Cabinet adopts policies to which they are opposed. As we saw when Eden resigned from Chamberlain's government, the resignation of a Minister can be very embarrassing. Resignations have even brought governments down, when the Minister was sufficiently well known and held in high esteem. Faced with a threatened resignation, a Cabinet may well compromise, if that is possible within the framework of policy. On resignation, a minister is given the opportunity to state the reasons to the House, and these can weaken a Prime Minister's reputation. Prime Ministers often have to face some resignations during a term of office, and much depends on the way the resignations are handled. Macmillan emerged from these crises with an increased, rather than a diminished, reputation.

The first resignation was that of Lord Salisbury, the man most instrumental in securing Macmillan's nomination as Prime Minister. Salisbury was reputed to be a powerful figure. A scion of the Cecil family, which had long roots in British politics, he was related to many of the leading Conservatives. An outspoken champion of empire, he fell out with Macmillan over the latter's handling of the Cyprus problem.

Macmillan had drawn the lesson from Suez that Britain and France could no longer impose their wills on smaller powers. Britain would have to reach an accommodation with the Greeks struggling for the independence of the British colony of Cyprus, of whom Archbishop Makarios was the principal leader. Makarios had been exiled, and Macmillan ended his exile and allowed him to return to Cyprus. Salisbury, rightly interpreting this as the first move towards decolonizing Cyprus, resigned. He had hoped to shake or even bring down Macmillan's government, but was outplayed. Macmillan treated Salisbury's resignation as insignificant, for he realized that Salisbury was isolated in his archaic imperial stance. Despite his name and connections, Salisbury did not have much support within the party. Resignation, therefore, ended his career, not Macmillan's. Salisbury, like many others, was to discover that the country could be governed without him.

A more important, and potentially embarrassing resignation was that of the Chancellor of the Exchequer, Peter Thorneycroft; and his two Junior Ministers, Enoch Powell and Nigel Birch, followed his lead. (These resignations involved more complex matters and will be discussed later in this chapter.) Thorneycroft, Powell, and Birch resigned just as Macmillan was about to begin his Commonwealth tour, the first by a Prime Minister. Macmillan, in his calm way that was to become famous, said that he was "not going to let little local troubles stand in his way" and proceeded with the tour. It proved an unqualified success, Macmillan making an excellent impression wherever he went and showing remarkable stamina for his sixty-four years. The publicity he gained distracted attention from the resignations and made the public aware of the new and greater stature Macmillan had achieved in his transition from a man of the old order to one of the new. From champion of empire, Macmillan had become champion of a multiracial Commonwealth and broker between its black and white members. He showed once more that he was the only man on the Conservative side who could lead the country after Suez.

Resignation from the Cabinet ended Salisbury's career, but this is not always the case.

Thorneycroft and Powell found places in later Cabinets.

Macmillan's Foreign Policy

The Visit to Moscow

Macmillan returned from the Commonwealth tour with greater self-confidence and a renewed passion for foreign affairs. His ultimate aim was to find a new and important role for Britain as "honest broker" between the superpowers, the United States and the Soviet Union. The role was to be achieved by Macmillan acting as go-between at summit meetings.

Macmillan's continual drive for summit meetings was not without critics at home and abroad. The British Foreign Office believed such meetings muddied the waters of diplomacy and provided the Prime Minister with opportunities for unwise concessions. Leaders like to return from meetings with something to show and will often give up much to show their own people a little. The Foreign Office also feared that summits encouraged exhibitionism and invited break-

Macmillan, in his tall fur cap which was to be the butt of endless jokes, with Nikita Khrushchev

(By permission of Beaverbrook Newspapers, Ltd.)

down of established policies. Significantly, Macmillan's first summit was a fiasco. It may serve, however, to illustrate his style.

The most sensational event of 1957 was unquestionably the Soviet launching of the first space satellite, Sputnik. The Soviet Union's claim that it would launch a space satellite had not been taken seriously, although the world knew that the United States was about to make the attempt. The shock of American failure and Soviet success created the unfounded impression that the Soviet Union was ahead of the United States in science. A fresh approach to the Soviets seemed necessary, and Macmillan, in his role as broker, saw himself as the most suitable man to open the negotiations. To this end Macmillan dropped a minor international bombshell: he would accept a long-standing invitation to visit the Soviet Union.

The proposed trip met with skepticism and scorn. The Conservatives were lukewarm, while Labour accused Macmillan of an electioneering stunt. Americans and Western Europeans were suspicious and doubted that anything of value could come from the encounter.

Macmillan went ahead with the trip. His welcome was warm but unspectacular. Looking rather ridiculous in a foot-tall, Russian fur hat—a hat that soon became the favorite butt of cartoonists—the Prime Minister was met in Moscow with the usual honor guard. The British party was well received at the conferences and events they attended. Such thaw as there was at the outset soon froze over. Khrushchev began to play a cat-and-mouse game with Macmillan, apparently designed to pry Britain loose from America and Western Europe. It culminated in an election speech by Khrushchev in which he attacked the British government over Berlin and Suez and asserted his determination to conclude a peace treaty with East Germany. It contained many friendly references to

Macmillan and offered a nonaggression pact to Britain, but this speech robbed Macmillan's visit of much of its point. Again displaying his famous control, Macmillan tried to salvage what he could by making it clear to Khrushchev that Britain was not about to abandon her Western friends. Khrushchev then became very angry or pretended anger—Macmillan was never sure which—and developed a diplomatic toothache. Macmillan was told that because of this toothache Khrushchev could not join the British party on its tour of the Soviet Union as planned; they would have to go on accompanied by lesser officials.

Khrushchev's withdrawal was an obvious slight, which became more insulting when Khrushchev, obviously in excellent spirits, appeared at a reception for an Iraqi delegation. Macmillan was now faced with the choice of ordering his plane and leaving in a mood of affronted dignity or of going on with the tour. To go home, though it might arouse sympathy, would end the hopes for a summit, so Macmillan decided to carry on with the tour and await any favorable turn of events. This came when Macmillan was visiting Leningrad—Khrushchev announced that he was cured and would meet the British again. Meetings were held, and some, on arms limitation, proved fruitful later. But no immediate gains resulted.

Macmillan returned to qualified approval at home and to irritation and suspicion abroad. His visit to Moscow had to be followed by visits to allied capitals to justify the trip and to explain that Britain had not surrendered her interests or those of her allies. Macmillan, to some extent, was able to allay his allies' fears.

Britain and America
The Conservatives won the General Election of 1959 handily. Macmillan had presented himself as the universal peacemaker to a

74

British public hungry for peace. The Conservatives won 365 seats and Labour took 258, with 6 seats going to minor parties. Macmillan's leadership was confirmed, and barring any untoward events, he had another five years to govern.

Changes in America were perhaps more significant. President Eisenhower, Macmillan's old friend, had served his two terms. John Fitzgerald Kennedy was elected President in 1960. Macmillan's relationship with Kennedy was, perhaps, to be even stronger than that with Eisenhower, although he was never to have the same influence over Kennedy. Young, energetic, supported by an able team, Kennedy needed no broker to arrange affairs between Khrushchev and himself. Although Macmillan's services were less necessary, he was able to establish an almost avuncular relationship with the President, their closeness being reinforced by the fact that the British Ambassador, David Ormsby-Gore, was related to them both. This background permitted Macmillan to play a significant role in the achievement of the Test-Ban Treaty, a lasting contribution to world peace and a step on the road to limiting nuclear arms.

Macmillan and President Dwight D. Eisenhower breakfasting together at the President's suite in New York, September 27, 1960

(Wide World Photos)

First Steps to the Treaty

Disarmament had been talked about for centuries but became a major issue only after the slaughter of World War I. It was discussed by the major powers with little result and died a natural death in the 1930s, with the rise of the European dictatorships, all of which were committed to increasing their armed forces. Development of nuclear weapons during and after World War II confronted the human race with the real prospect of annihilation, and the issue of disarmament or arms control was resurrected.

Control of the construction of nuclear weapons or the reduction of nuclear arsenals had been discussed by the United States and the Soviet Union, but no agreement could be reached. The Americans demanded that on-site inspection be part of the treaty, and the Soviets, ever suspicious and secretive, refused. Details of a possible settlement had been worked out by a committee of experts in 1958 and 1959, but their talks were stalled. Matters seemed more pressing with recurring crises over the status of Berlin in 1961 and the Soviet attempt to force the West to accept a separate peace between the Soviet Union and East Germany. Europeans had been further roused by the sealing off of West Berlin by the infamous Berlin Wall. Both sides, then, were amassing nuclear weapons, and the atmosphere was increasingly polluted by fallout from tests of nuclear devices.

Yet hope remained. Despite the breakdown of the 1960 summit, the idea of a test-ban treaty, an agreement to ban tests in the atmosphere, remained alive. Because such a

Macmillan meets President John F. Kennedy on his visit to Britain, June 29, 1963

(Keystone Press Agency)

ban would not involve general disarmament, agreement seemed within reach. President Kennedy, in his inaugural address, had stressed the need to discontinue tests and was pressed by Macmillan to put his precepts into practice. Kennedy stopped further tests, and the Soviets tacitly followed his lead. Yet the treaty evaded signature. With no treaty in sight, American experts pressed for renewed testing. Their pressure grew when the Soviets resumed testing, exploding a massive nuclear device of fifty megatons with particularly "dirty" fallout, which much disturbed the United States. Kennedy now wanted further tests, but they would have to be run on Easter Island, a British possession, and Macmillan's agreement was required.

Further Negotiations
Macmillan was emotionally committed to the idea of disarmament, an issue to which he could wholeheartedly devote his energy and intelligence. The first step was to get the Cabinet to agree that the Americans could use Easter Island, but its use would be tied to some treaty that would limit testing. Then Macmillan met Kennedy in Bermuda in December 1961 and tried to persuade Kennedy not to resume testing, predictably suggesting yet another summit. Kennedy was moved, but believed that testing had to be resumed. New tests were announced for March 1962.

The Cuban Missile Crisis, which Macmillan termed "one of the great turning points of history," brought about change by demonstrating how easily the world could come to the brink of a nuclear holocaust. It showed the Soviets the limits of their power, and the United States the dangers of an unchecked arms race. After the crisis had passed, Macmillan urged reconciliation. His insistence led to the first moves to detente between the two superpowers. Macmillan drew Kennedy's attention to the common cultural bonds between East and West. Although the

Soviets seemed strange and different, they were not all that alien, as their art, literature, music, and history showed. It was not right, therefore, to treat the Soviets as barbarians.

Macmillan's ideas may seem commonplace now, but they were daring at the time. He believed that the Soviet leadership's outlook had changed since the death of Stalin in 1953 and that Soviet politicians were of the traditional Russian mold. Nor had he, in the welter of events during the Cuban Missile Crisis, lost sight of the goal—the Test-Ban Treaty. Kennedy now was receptive, the Soviets interested, and the stage set for serious negotiations.

Ratification of the Treaty
Bargaining between the United States and the Soviet Union soon showed that a treaty was possible only if underground testing were allowed, and this point was agreed upon. The final treaty was initialed in Moscow on July 25 and ratified on October 8, 1963.

Macmillan rightly regarded this as a great achievement and was always to value the part he had played. He did not doubt that once rivalry in testing was ended, progress would be made in other limitations on nuclear arms. The signing of the treaty also gave Macmillan a much needed boost on the domestic scene in the wake of the Profumo scandal, which had shaken his government. The Test-Ban Treaty was well received in Parliament with many members on both sides rising to cheer and wave their order papers.

Macmillan's role was generously acknowledged by President Kennedy, who attributed the success of the negotiations largely to Macmillan's commitment, steadiness of purpose, and determined perseverance. Certainly, other factors contributed to the successful conclusion of the treaty. Both superpowers were interested in ending the tests. But, as Kennedy pointed out, Macmillan's continuous interest and urging kept lines of communication open.

Entering the Common Market
Macmillan's difficult and unenviable task was to lead Britain through the transition from the glory of great power status to a lesser role. Britain had been acknowledged as one of the Big Four—together with the United States, the Soviet Union, and China—more out of courtesy than fact. Churchill's stature at the war's end had concealed from the British their diminished stature in the world. Macmillan had tried to maintain some sort of a role as broker between the superpowers, but as Britain's international role shrank, the possibilities of acting as broker diminished. Britain, willing or not, had to face the prospect of being a part of Europe.

The Foreign Office, originally opposed to entry into the European Common Market, now favored entry. Lord Home, the Foreign Secretary, and his Junior Minister, Edward Heath (both of whom later became Prime Ministers), were enthusiastic. The British public, however, was apathetic, and Macmillan's support was wavering at best. It was only with the collapse of the 1960 summit that Macmillan changed his mind. Britain needed a new goal for her foreign policy, and the Common Market well might provide the basis for a new crusade.

Once he had decided to promote Britain's entrance into the Common Market, Macmillan timed his announcement shrewdly. He knew that among the Conservatives there was discontent over joining and that the Cabinet was itself divided. To prevent opponents from mounting a serious counterattack, he announced the decision to Parliament just before adjournment and on a day before a public holiday. The matter had then to wait until the fall session of the House.

Controversial and divisive issues present a particular problem to a ruling party. The Cabinet must be kept together, for the resignation of key Ministers could provoke a crisis. To ensure that the Cabinet did not collapse, Macmillan shunted those against entry into the Market into positions either where they had to work *for* entry or where they could not do any harm. Skeptic Kenneth Maudling went to the Colonial Office; R. A. Butler, another critic, was put at the head of the negotiating committee for entrance into the Market.

Butler accepted the position because he was in a double bind. Had he refused, he would have lost all influence over the shaping of British policy toward the Common Market. By accepting, he was committed to Britain's entry, but could shape the conditions under which this was done. Butler doubtless felt that, were he to resign, he might have embarrassed Macmillan, but could not have changed the course of events.

Enthusiasts for the Common Market, in turn, were placed where they could do the most good. Britain faced the problem of Commonwealth preferences: Commonwealth members received favorable trade terms from Britain. Many Commonwealth countries, such as New Zealand, depended on Britain as their main customer for agricultural products. Duncan Sandys, Minister for Commonwealth Affairs and "half a New Zealander," was designated to set their doubts at rest. British farmers also feared European competition, so Christopher Soames, an enthusiast both of the Common Market and of British agriculture, became Minister of Agriculture.

Macmillan enjoyed power and knew how to use it. He surmounted the remaining hurdles: the Commonwealth Prime Ministers' Conference and the Conservative Party Conference. The first meeting was stormy, but Macmillan was able to reach agreement with the Commonwealth Prime Ministers that British negotiations would not be hindered by Commonwealth demands. In any case, the Commonwealth Prime Ministers could not have prevented Macmillan's doing as he pleased, though relations might have grown strained, and this could be reflected in the Conservative party. Macmillan's major triumph was, however, the Conservative Party Conference. The supporters of the Common Market were well organized and logical; even Butler was now enthusiastic for entry; the antimarketeers were confused and ineffective. Everything seemed to be going Macmillan's way.

French President Charles de Gaulle upset Macmillan's plans. Although de Gaulle had, for a time, seemed willing to accept Britain's entry into the Market, his overriding priority was to make Europe a "third force," independent of the United States. His vision was as strong as Macmillan's, and as negotiations wore on, de Gaulle began to doubt that Britain would relinquish her special relationship with the United States. The British, thus, had first to convince de Gaulle if he was not to block Britain's entry.

Macmillan visited de Gaulle in December 1962 in the hope of clearing the air. Priding himself on his command of French, Macmillan conducted all negotiations without an interpreter; it is doubtful, as a result, that de Gaulle and Macmillan fully understood each other. De Gaulle made it clear that he could not encourage Britain to continue negotiations for entry into the market, but Macmillin seems to have missed this point. The result was painful and embarrassing: in a press conference in January 1963, de Gaulle vetoed Britain's entrance into the Common Market. This refusal was a bitter blow, for despite the care and patience of the chief British negotiator, Edward Heath, the talks had failed. Macmillan could hardly contain himself at what he saw as French duplicity. His foreign policy seemingly a shambles, he sank into pessimism. Except for the Test-Ban Treaty, his initiatives seemed to have led nowhere.

Yet politics is a continuous process and not a series of separate incidents. Many things attempted by Macmillan failed at the time, but they also pointed the way to the future. One was the Common Market, for ten years later Macmillan was to have the pleasure of attending at the signing of Britain's entry—by invitation of Edward Heath, then Prime Minister. Also the Test-Ban Treaty was to be a permanent monument to the wisdom of some of Macmillan's policies, as was his reappraisal of the Soviet leadership.

Domestic Policy

Building the Image

Prime Ministers are much occupied with foreign policy, partly by tradition. Another important reason is that Prime Ministers, heading no specific department, find that laurels are to be gained most quickly in successes abroad. Issues of foreign policy are more glamorous than are the dull and workaday problems at home. Issues can be more readily simplified for public consumption, heroes and villains more easily identified. However, although foreign policy tends to capture the public's imagination, it is domestic policy, particularly what happens to the economy, that determines whether elections are won and lost.

The Conservative party's popularity grew after their 1959 victory, largely because Macmillan was better than Labour's Hugh Gaitskell in choosing issues and gaining public affection. Gaitskell, despite his merits, could neither unite his party nor convince voters that he would make a better Prime Minister than Macmillan. The Labour party under Gaitskell was in disarray, saddled in the public mind with memories of postwar austerity and rationing. Yet, even if the weakness of Labour is allowed for, much credit for the Conservative successes must go to Macmillan.

Macmillan had his roots in the past and his mind on the future. He realized the importance of the media and the need to turn it to the benefit of his party. Television allowed politicians to take their personalities into every home, and under the single, critical eye of the camera every expression and nuance was evident. Drama could be injected into issues, but the style of presentation had to be more relaxed and intimate than had been the rule at the large public rallies of the past.

British political television is much more limited than that in the United States. Yet, like an American President, a British Prime Minister can always command public attention. As the leader of the majority party, what the Prime Minister says is likely to become law. His appearances are thus more interesting than those of the Leader of the Opposition, who can only criticize. Macmillan made a hesitant start but soon became comfortable with the new medium. He proved adept at capturing news time, familiarizing the electorate with his appearance and presenting himself as relaxed, genial, and clear. The opposition, helpless in what seemed a flood of Macmillan propaganda, tried to ridicule him with nicknames such as "Supermac" and "Macwonder" and pictures of him in Superman tights and cloak. This backfired, and the nicknames became part of the Macmillan image, which did much to boost the Conservative party's fortunes.

"They Never Had It So Good"
Important as Macmillan's image was for Conservative success, the rising tide of prosperity contributed more. The years of sacrifice during the war, the "blood, sweat, and tears," had been followed by years of ration-

ing and shortages. Britishers had watched in frustration as even defeated countries like Germany and Italy rebuilt their economies and overtook Britain in trade and development.

The economic boom of 1959—though proved to be deceptive by subsequent events —was heady stuff for a hard-pressed public. Macmillan's association with this sudden prosperity was at least partly a matter of luck. Had Gaitskell been Prime Minister he might have reaped the political benefit. But Macmillan was Prime Minister, and he knew how to capitalize on the improvement in living standards. His reputation for economic expansionism and opposition to deflation made him appear the author of the good fortune.

The economic boom, no matter how precarious, was very real to voters. Britishers could now buy things that were beyond the dreams of their parents—cars, refrigerators, television sets, and even washing machines. In keeping with the materialism of the time Macmillan coined a slogan that would haunt him when times turned bad: "They never had it so good."

Resignation of the Chancellor
The boom was not Macmillan's first, and like later booms it could not last. Earlier, Macmillan's handling of the depression of 1957 had earned him a reputation that was to magnify his role in the later boom.

In 1957, it seemed as if Macmillan's government were hurtling headlong to disaster. There was a sudden rush on British gold reserves, and the Chancellor of the Exchequer, Peter Thorneycroft, opted for deflation. This action saved the pound, which recovered in the following months. No sooner was recovery evident than Macmillan reinstituted his expansionist plans. Thorneycroft continued to urge deflation, and when this policy was not adopted, he resigned, taking his two Junior Ministers with him.

Macmillan feared the disintegration of his Cabinet, with all senior men resigning. In that case, there would be no alternative to a dissolution of Parliament and an election in which the Conservative party would be in a hopeless position. This had to be avoided at all costs. Macmillan tried to pass off Thorneycroft's resignation as best as he could and immediately appointed a new Chancellor, Heathecoate Amory. Partly by luck and partly by skill, Amory was able to maintain expansion without undue inflation. Then, by removing most controls, Macmillan and Amory sparked a spectacular boom in 1959.

What of those who resigned? A Minister who resigns is seldom popular with his party or his constituency. He usually tries to minimize the harm to both by avoiding excessive criticism. He must discreetly convey that his jump overboard is not a criticism of captain or crew, but just that he happens to prefer the water. Thorneycroft, after a courageous resignation speech, took a long voyage to Australia and New Zealand. For such discretion he and one of the Junior Ministers, Enoch Powell, were later rewarded. The other, Nigel Birch, who had been overly critical to press and public, remained outside.

The Great Election—1959

British elections, though they must be held at least every five years, can come largely at the discretion of the Prime Minister. The Prime Minister decides when Parliament is to be dissolved and can so time things that elections take place either at the time most advantageous for the fortunes of his party or at the time least disadvantageous.

Given the economic boom, the choice of 1959 as an election year was not unexpected. Parliament was four years old, and the

Conservatives were well prepared. Macmillan, therefore, resigned on behalf of his Government on September 5 and announced an election for October 8.

Macmillan did not like elections, for it was very difficult to conduct the business of government and campaign for reelection at the same time. Elections were times of mounting tension: not only was the fate of the party at issue, but so were the careers of many people. Too, this was Macmillan's tenth election. As Prime Minister, Macmillan's campaign differed from those of backbenchers. In his earlier campaigns he worked in his own constituency, but as Prime Minister he had to assist other candidates, covering virtually the whole of Britain, making speeches in the great cities at night and in smaller towns by day. A backbencher, what is more, could make the same speech in different parts of his constituency. Since the speeches were not widely reported, the same points and even the same jokes could be repeated. But the Prime Minister had to spend his daytime train journeys preparing a rejoinder to some point raised by the Labour leader the night before.

The 1959 election was astonishingly active by the more subdued British standards, which means fairly tame by those of the United States. There is a legal limit in Britain on what can be spent in campaigns, as there is in America, but British limits are set far lower. A candidate is limited to about $750, plus about four cents for each registered voter in urban centers and five cents in rural areas. (The amounts in sterling are £450, one and one-half pence, and two pence, respectively.) The average sum that can be spent is no more than $3,500 in total. Loopholes do provide candidates some leeway; for example, there is no limit to what can be spent before an election, which enabled large employer associations to rally to the Conservative cause. As a result, the party was able to spend some $1.2 million on press and poster advertising alone. The heavy investment in the campaign, together with more imagination and better management, helped hammer the Conservative message home. The Conservative majority in the House increased from fifty-nine to one hundred.

Before an election each party issues a manifesto to the voters, and that of the Conservatives hopefully pointed to greater prosperity to come. The Labour party's, "England Belongs to You," was uninspiring. It did not make clear how ordinary voters would benefit from "ownership," and the promises proffered could not be compared with the Conservatives'. Despite the backing of organized labor, the Labour party's campaign was dull and lackluster.

The Conservatives also tried to escape their upper-class image by displaying posters of middle-class and working people with the slogan "You are looking at a Conservative." They also showed a typical British family enjoying their new possessions with the slogan "Life's better under the Conservatives. Don't let Labour spoil it." Prosperity was the Conservative theme. The facts seemed to support them. For instance, automobile ownership had increased from 3.5 million to 5 million, while in the previous generation a motorcycle was the height of a working man's aspirations.

Macmillan personally campaigned hard, covering some 2,500 miles—a great distance in the small British Isles—and speaking personally at seventy-four meetings. He gave an impression of vigor and confidence and seemed to enjoy the struggle.

The election was influenced by two new factors, television and the polls, both of which were used to the full. The British Broadcasting Corporation, a government-owned monopoly, regulates the amount of

air time accorded each candidate. Each of the two major parties usually gets equal time, with less for the other parties.

Macmillan's television campaign was carefully planned by experts. He was to stay on his feet during the performance, his only props consisting of a globe, a map of Britain, and some letters to be picked up and read at random. Macmillan found the early rehearsals discouraging. So much was at stake, and he wondered if he could convey the desired image. On the whole, Macmillan's appearance made a good impression, certainly better than that made by Hugh Gaitskell, who was seated in an ornate chair at a desk, making his performance static and dull. Macmillan's appearance did lend itself to merciless parody, with Macmillan shown as petting the globe rather like a pet dog. However, even teasing wins attention, and it is attention that a politician craves. It is better to be funny than boring.

The other new element, the polls, did not make the election seem a foregone conclusion. The polls indicated that the Conservatives could at best hope for a narrow margin of victory; and Gaitskell even thought victory could be within grasp, as the Conservatives had not done particularly well in by-elections from 1955 onward. In fact, British polls were in the future to be wrong as often as right, despite the great attention they receive.

On polling day Macmillan and his wife toured their constituency and spent the evening quietly at 10 Downing Street. They watched television anxiously at first, but their fears were soon allayed. The Conservative victory was established by 1:00 A.M., and Gaitskell conceded victory—an American habit till then foreign to British politics.

The results of the election were dramatic. This was the first time that a British party had won three elections successively with increased majorities in each election. The

Conservatives were jubilant. Labour, on the other side, was in disarray, fearing that their party had outlived its purpose. If working men and women identified with the Conservatives, if they no longer sought social revolution, how was Labour to compete? Britain, which had seemed firmly set on the road to the left a few years before, now seemed to be marching equally steadfastly to the right. Could the Government ever be defeated? The Conservatives had defied the fourteen-year cycle, and with Macmillan at their head were again the Government of the country.

Supermac was now at peak form. He did his "humble duty" by informing the Queen of the election results, informing her that she need not interrupt her vacation. Macmillan had led his party to an almost impossible victory and was again Prime Minister. He knew difficulties lay ahead, but he felt sure of his ability to withstand them.

Fading Fortunes

The Economic Storm

Macmillan's confidence seemed justified. With its large majority the Conservatives seemed securely in power, while the opposition was despondent and divided. Yet the apple had worms. The electorate soon grew bored with the Conservatives after so long a period in power, and even the Conservatives seemed to be growing bored with one another. Too many Ministers had to be ousted for incompetence. Most of those who were asked to resign did so and accepted peerages without too much embarrassment to the government. The younger members remained disappointed, as it seemed to them that there were still too many of the "old guard" in the Cabinet. In addition, the Government was burdened by the presence of a number of ex-Ministers who maintained a barrage of criticism.

What was more, by 1960 the economic storm so long brewing had broken. The time when the good life was ever getting better had ended by 1961. The British economy was overheated—more jobs than workers to fill them. Britain owed foreign countries more than she could pay, and the gap was growing. Prices rose and the pound fell.

The sick economy resisted all the recommended cures. Wages rose and unemployment grew. "Stagflation"—a combination of inflation and stagnation—was something new. It seemed, as Macmillan put it, that the country was in an Einsteinian world where cause and effect no longer followed expected rules. The public, unaware of the complexity of the problem, resented being the victims of government policies when life could be so agreeable.

A new approach was needed, but it was hard to discover what this new approach should be while the economy spiraled downward. Sterling, more than ever in danger, threw the Treasury into something of a panic. The Chancellor, Selwyn Lloyd, came out with a "little Budget" that increased interest rates, raised consumer taxes, and cut back government spending and bank loans. A "pay pause"—resented by workers who found their wages frozen—was particularly unpopular. The policy, which had originated with Macmillan and was administered by Lloyd, was sound. It had the seeds of an income policy that became a standard measure of later governments, and it gained the government part of its objectives. The British public, though, remained as unconvinced as unemployment rose, discontent increased, and the image of Supermac was tarnished.

Public dissatisfaction found expression in Conservative defeats in by-elections for safe seats. The Conservative candidate in Blackpool narrowly held off a Liberal challenge.

Orpington, however, was the major portent of what was to come: a Conservative majority in this safe constituency was turned into a loss to the Liberals by more than 8,000 votes. The interesting fact is that the Conservatives were not losing to Labour, which also suffered apparently from a loss of voter confidence. Both parties were losing to the Liberals in what seemed much like a protest vote. Voters went Liberal, not because they necessarily found its program convincing, but because they wished to express their dissatisfaction with the two major parties. This was evident in Pontefract, where, in the absence of a Liberal candidate, the swing from the Conservatives was small.

The Party Purge

Macmillan concluded that the party needed a younger image if it was to face the voters with any prospect of success. Another election seemed imminent in 1961, and the party needed leaders who could win or, if worst came to worst, fight effectively in opposition. The Central Office had already begun to warn of disasters in store, and pressure mounted on Macmillan to do something to restore the party's fortunes.

Macmillan was on the horns of a dilemma. Having built his base of power on loyalty, he faithfully supported colleagues if they got into difficulties and expected support in return. As a result, the party was burdened with an aging and sometimes incompetent leadership. Many older leaders had indicated their willingness to retire, and over time they could have been removed without damage to party unity. But Macmillan did not allow the necessary time. Pressed by prominent party leaders and the Chief Whip to make a drastic reshuffle of his Cabinet, Macmillan apparently panicked. Usually imperturbable in crisis, he had been shaken by a story leaked to the mass-circulation *Daily*

Mail; it detailed what seemed to be a plot by R. A. Butler. Driven to act precipitately by external pressure and his own suspicions, Macmillan abandoned his usual political skill and purged his Cabinet with an abruptness felt by many Conservatives to have been unwarranted.

Without making his plans clear, Macmillan called to his office each of the Ministers to be purged and demanded their resignations. The majority agreed, but were angered and hurt that their hurried resignations would appear as dismissals, disgracing them when they were not at fault.

The major problem had been the Chancellor of the Exchequer, Selwyn Lloyd. Lloyd was criticized for his handling of the Treasury, and his pessimism did not inspire confidence among the backbenchers. On the other hand, Lloyd stood very close to Macmillan. The pressure for a reshuffle had, however, come about largely because party leaders wanted Macmillan to get rid of Lloyd.

Dismissal of a Minister is always painful in Britain because of the intimacy of the party leadership. Macmillan tried to mask Lloyd's dismissal by massively reconstructing his Cabinet, but Lloyd was not to be so placated and an emotional scene ensued. Lloyd dismissed Macmillan's suggestion that he return to business and stated that he would remain in Parliament, continuing to press his financial policy from the back benches. Lloyd's action was most embarrassing. First, Lloyd published his letter of resignation in the *Times,* Britain's most prominent newspaper, pointing to the unfairness of his dismissal as he had merely carried out Macmillan's policies. Lloyd garnered much sympathy, and Macmillan much criticism. In addition, by remaining in the House, the leadership had to face another knowledgeable critic. Lloyd exploited his advantage over Macmillan largely because of the clumsy way Macmillan had handled the reshuffle.

Nonetheless, Macmillan rode out the storm, the blow to his prestige having been serious, but not fatal. None of the dismissed Ministers had much of a following among the backbenchers, so there was no support for a revolt. Above all, the dissidents could not agree on who was to replace Macmillan were he to fall. So the party settled down and Macmillan recovered the skill he had momentarily lost. He rallied the party with a great display of legislative energy and a whole new series of policies on incomes, consumer affairs, and other issues. Complacency was at an end, and on the adjournment, twenty-one days later, Macmillan was once more in control.

The End of the Road

The New Cabinet

The individuals brought into the government by the reshuffle were considerably younger than their chief. Macmillan was nine years older than the next oldest Minister and seventeen years above the average age. He could not be as much in tune with the new Ministers as he had been with their predecessors, who had shared so many experiences with him. Even though his flexibility and intelligence stood him in good stead, the gap in age remained. Perhaps the heavy preponderance of Etonians in the Cabinet helped Macmillan understand his new colleagues better, for there were more now than in previous Cabinets.

Macmillan had not survived the purge unscathed. He had owed much of his reputation to his calm in crisis and his loyalty. Now these were in doubt. Trust was the cement of government and party, and Mac-millan's ruthlessness—whether real or apparent—had undermined trust. It affected the loyalty seen owing to him. Macmillan was now largely isolated and had to face coming crises alone.

The Profumo Affair

When the newly reconstituted Cabinet met in the fall of 1962, the mood in Britain had changed. Gone were the heady days of 1959, for the economy had deteriorated and the level of unemployment was rising. Britain's "stop-go" economy was stopping more often than going. The Common Market, which Britain had been debarred from entering, was succeeding. The government was the butt of endless satire, a measure of popular disillusion. Macmillan's flurry of legislation, while uniting the party, had not raised hopes or bolstered public optimism. Despite these setbacks, Macmillan held his grip on the party, and there were few signs that his political career was soon to end.

Blow after blow descended on the government. The United States cancelled the Skybolt missile, which was to be the basis of the British nuclear deterrent. The winter of 1962–1963, one of the coldest in history, caused the antiquated heating and water systems to break down. Though the government could hardly be blamed for the weather, discontent grew. Public opinion polls showed Labour with its greatest lead in seventeen years. Numbers of security cases in which government officials had betrayed secrets to the Soviets further discredited the government. The press generated a climate of sensation and suspicion. It is against this background that the Profumo case must be seen. The case, which broke in June 1963, was discussed as both an issue of security and one of scandal in high places. It also affected the role a member of the government and a Prime Minister were expected to play.

Because of these considerations, it merits a brief discussion.

John Profumo was Minister of War (not to be confused with the Minister of Defence), a position not a Cabinet rank. After a distinguished military career and marriage to a well-known British film star, Profumo had become involved in a sexual relationship with Christine Keeler, a prostitute who was twenty-seven years younger than himself. The affair apparently began at Cliveden, the country home of Lord Astor, and was continued by visits arranged through a procurer, Steven Ward. Ward was an open admirer of the Soviet system and had made many of his clients suspicious by the way he had praised that regime.

In the cause of promoting the Soviets, Ward became very friendly with Captain Eugene Ivanov of the Soviet navy. Known to be an intelligence officer, Ivanov acted, it seems, less to gather information than to compromise prominent people so that Ward could blackmail them. Profumo was an obvious target. His friendship with Ward and Ward's relationship with Ivanov—though not Profumo's relationship with Keeler—were known to British intelligence. Intelligence asked the Secretary to the Cabinet to warn Profumo, who seemed grateful and broke with Keeler. Though he saw her once or twice more, the relationship seems definitely to have ended by December 1961.

Christine Keeler continued her rather sordid life and became involved in a court case between two of her lovers who had tried to kill each other. In the course of these proceedings, Keeler's connection with Profumo came to the attention of a Labour leader, Colonel Wigg, who saw himself, as Macmillan put it, "as the unofficial keeper of morals and protector of security." The press also had the story, and pictures of a scantily clad Christine Keeler began appearing in the daily press. Rumors about Profumo began circulating, and the opposition demanded that the Government confirm or deny them. The question of particular concern was whether security had been breached. The Chief Whip and the Attorney-General visited Profumo, who declared that he had not seen Keeler since December 1961 and that *no* impropriety had taken place with her. He would sue if such allegations were made outside the House.

Profumo's denial and Macmillan's actions are important. As Prime Minister, Macmillan was specially responsible for the Security Services. He should not have left the investigation to the Chief Whip and Attorney-General, but should have intervened personally. Coming with all the authority of his office, he most likely would have shamed Profumo into an admission. But Macmillan was known for his prudishness and probably shied from having to ask a colleague about his sex life. As a result, he opened himself to a charge of negligence. His avoidance was apparently justified by Profumo's successful libel suit against the Paris magazine *Match* and the Italian *Il Tiempo*. He could hardly be expected to believe that Profumo would lie to his fellow members and to the courts. With this explanation, Macmillan hoped that he could put the Profumo case behind him, but this was not to be. New rumors began circulating, which claimed that Keeler had been asked to obtain secrets about nuclear weapons from Profumo during their relationship.

The blow fell while Macmillan was vacationing in Scotland: Profumo made a full confession. Macmillan now faced a very unpleasant case, worse in many ways than Suez. Why was it so serious? A man approaching middle age, still attractive, had taken up with a young woman. Surely this kind of thing happened all the time. What mattered was that Profumo had lied to the House. Ministers and politicians, as Macmillan well knew, did not always tell the whole truth; Winston Churchill himself had spoken of "terminological inexactitudes." But this term referred to political issues subject to interpretation in different ways. Formal statements, which members of the House made on their honor, were regarded as absolutely binding. The whole of British public life was based on confidence in Parliament, party, and government. To lie to the House was unforgivable.

The Profumo case gave rise to wild rumors about other members of the Cabinet who now were accused in the popular press of all kinds of perversions. Macmillan appointed a Commission of Enquiry under Lord Denning to investigate whether there had been any breach of security. Profumo paid the penalty, being forced to resign from Parliament. But Macmillan—though able to convince Parliament that he had acted honorably and justly—could not convince it that he had acted with sufficient prudence.

The Profumo case weakened Macmillan's position in the party, for he seemed slack and unable to maintain control. His state of mind was disturbing—almost that of a sleepwalker. He did not seem to grasp what was going on around him. When he attended a garden party in his constituency, Bromley, he posed for a photograph with a young child. A heckler whispered in his ear, asking whether he did not wish it was Christine Keeler. Macmillan seemed not to hear, as his face betrayed no expression. Even at a reunion at his beloved Oxford, he shuffled around like a man of ninety, as impassive as a waxwork.

This state of mind gave Labour some advantages. Shrewdly, Harold Wilson decided that Macmillan would make a more suitable opponent than the new, younger leaders coming up in the Conservative party. He therefore threw support to Macmillan, upbraiding the Conservatives for not supporting their leader. Angry at hearing their leader patronized by the Leader of the Opposition, the Conservatives rallied around him, just as Wilson wished. In addition, Labour did not make morality an issue, but seized upon security, a weaker issue soon shown not to have been imperiled. Macmillan, as a result, was able to carry the House in a vote of confidence by a narrow majority. The Whips rallied support by promising that Macmillan would soon resign, when the time was appropriate. There matters rested for the time being.

Resignation and Succession

Macmillan, to the dismay of the party, made it clear that he did not intend to resign. The Gallup polls of 1963 showed that though the Labour party retained its lead, it had been cut to 14.5 percent. Macmillan was heartened, and though he did seem willing to resign on occasion, his small band of followers always persuaded him to remain. This he would doubtless have done had illness not intervened.

Macmillan awoke just before the conference of 1963 in great pain. The complaint was diagnosed as a blocked prostate gland. After routine treatment he felt well enough to conduct a Cabinet, but his colleagues noticed that he hardly seemed fit enough to travel to the conference at Blackpool. Macmillan's condition deteriorated, and hospitalization became necessary. Believing that his condition was serious, Macmillan sent a letter of resignation to the Conservative Party Conference, which was read by Lord Home. Later Macmillan learned that he was not as ill as he had supposed, but it was too late. His resignation had been accepted. It was now time for the processes by which Conservatives selected their leaders to work.

Using the privilege that permits an outgoing Prime Minister to select his successor, Macmillan chose Lord Hailsham. Such a choice is not binding on the party. Whether the choice holds depends on the record of the Prime Minister, his willingness to promote his successor's cause, and the state of the party at the time. The party had, then, no obvious successor in view. The need to select a leader in the glare of publicity was embarrassing to the Conservatives, for these matters were usually settled behind closed doors in respectable privacy. The intrigues and muddles that resulted from the un-

wonted openness were more than the old rules could survive, and new procedures were adopted soon after the conference. Meanwhile, events had to run their course.

Hailsham was a surprising choice, for Macmillan had never shown him particular favor or even seemed to agree with his ideas. The reasons for the choice remain unclear. Macmillan says little more than that he found Hailsham to be "in the Disraeli tradition." A political deal is alleged by some while others argue that Hailsham—popular, tempestuous, and colorful—could have held the party together. It is more likely that the old rivalry between Macmillan and Butler may have been involved. Macmillan may

Macmillan's successors try to fit his clothes

(By permission of Beaverbrook Newspapers, Ltd.)

have seen the matter of leadership as between Butler and Hailsham and wanted to block Butler's bid.

Involuntarily, Hailsham reduced his prospects for nomination. He began to push in an almost American manner, contrary to tradition in Britain. He appeared with his family on television and played the demagogue at public meetings. The inevitable "Stop Hailsham" movement gathered strength. Hailsham was stopped, but this did not really benefit the other candidates. They were expected not to promote their causes, but instead to emerge as contenders out of party discussions. Yet, in the heated atmosphere of the conference, it was difficult for them to remain silent. Butler threw his hat in the ring, as did Iain McLeod and Reginald Maudling.

Macmillan continued to pull strings behind the scenes from his hospital bed. He asked for "soundings" in the Cabinet, by the Chief Whips in Commons and Lords, and by the chairmen in the constituencies. Given Macmillan's interference, and the generally heated atmosphere at the conference, it was likely that the choice would be the candidate with the fewest political foes. Macmillan,

his soundings complete, produced such a candidate from the wings—Lord Home. A "Stop Home" movement by Butler and Hailsham failed. Macmillan, determined that Butler should not be Prime Minister, promoted Home's cause. Only when Home's candidacy was secured, did Macmillan formally send his letter of resignation to the Queen.

When the Queen visited Macmillan in hospital shortly after his formal resignation, he read her the result of his soundings and suggested that she invite Lord Home to form a government. The invitation followed a few days later, and Lord Home became the first British Prime Minister in this century to sit in Lords. But Home soon resigned his title, becoming Sir Alec Douglas-Home, and was then permitted to take his place in Commons. His term as Prime Minister was not a success. He knew little of economics, as he admitted, and had little interest in domestic affairs. He attracted little support in the party and was hardly an effective foil to Harold Wilson. The Conservative party had, in fact, chosen Home because Macmillan had so engineered things as to give them no choice.

6

Assessment
and Conclusions

Summation

Macmillan retired from office and from politics, saying in the last pages of his autobiography that his political life ended in 1963. He did not wish to extend it artificially, for "enough was enough." He had sat in Commons for more than forty years, been a Minister for seventeen, and served as Prime Minister for seven. An enigmatic, complex character, Macmillan will always be a controversial figure. He enjoyed power and understood its use, and yet his achievements, seen with the perspective of time, do not appear to amount to a great deal. The Test-Ban Treaty, indeed a great achievement, will mark his place in history, but other than this no clear accomplishments emerge. Macmillan will not be spoken of as another Disraeli, Gladstone, Lloyd George, or Churchill. His time in power had little effect on the course of British history, and few of his goals for Britain were realized.

The summits failed, Britain's entry into the Common Market was blocked, the economy threatened living standards at home and undermined Britain's position abroad. Had Macmillan resigned in 1960, he might well have gone down as a great Prime Minister, for it was not until 1961 that the realities of Britain's situation became painfully clear. Circumstances may have been against him, for as he showed in North Africa, at another time greatness might well have been his.

The crucial question remains, then: Could anyone else have done better? On the whole one must answer no. Neither Butler, Heath, Gaitskell nor Wilson could have arrested Britain's decline. The present Prime Minister, James Callaghan, is trying to save the sinking ship, but will probably fail. Nor is Margaret Thatcher, leader of the Conservatives, likely to do better, although she reveres Macmillan, who has been her model. Britain is just quietly running down. Macmillan's sense of style, his ability to dramatize issues and to exploit situations, could partly hide the slowing of the mechanism; he could still impress Britishers with the notion that Britain played an important role in world politics.

Power and Personality

Lord Acton, in a well-worn aphorism, said that all power corrupts. The powers of a British Prime Minister are great, especially those of a man who has three times led his party to victory. Did power corrupt Macmillan? Does it corrupt others and contribute to their decline? Character of politicians alone cannot account for change in politics; situation is also important. Yet as politics consists of an interplay between these two factors, personality must be considered.

At the height of his powers, Macmillan seemed to have moved far from the young reformer of the 1930s. He was less sincere and more dramatic. His affectations were becoming more pronounced: the shake of the head, the drooping of the mouth, the baring of the teeth, the wobbling of the hand—all the tricks of the stage. He would tell stories, often with tears in his eyes, of the different stages of his life: the veteran of World War I, the champion of the unemployed, the trustee of his nation's future. He seemed not only to act but also to change roles at bewildering speed. He could be one minute the sophisticated clubman, at another the shrewd Scottish businessman, and then, seconds later, the intellectual visionary or poet. Colleagues were often baffled and unimpressed.

Macmillan was aware of the divisions in his personality. Perhaps he was covering up an unresolved inner anxiety with a veneer of imperturbability. His public face—the calm leader firmly in control—concealed deep-seated insecurity, which only his upbringing enabled him to overcome. "I was always anxious lest I do something wrong," Macmillan wrote of his childhood. "I was oppressed by a kind of mysterious power which

was sure to get me in the end." [1] The future was more likely to be unpleasant than pleasant; the world was alarming, and people likely to be difficult. These feelings carried over into public life. He never went into Commons to make an important speech without feeling violently sick beforehand, even after seven years as Prime Minister. Question Time made him as apprehensive as he had been before battle. On those days Macmillan made it a rule to eat alone in order to conceal his nervousness from others. He accepted his discomfort, he writes, as something that was inevitable and had to be endured.

Macmillan's posturing may, therefore, have been the defense of a very private man having to act in a public role, rather than a cunning scheme to deceive friends and opponents. Among friends and with small groups Macmillan was a different man, pleasant and able to summarize arguments precisely and to win agreement. In public, however, the actor returned, eager to find flaws in an opponent's argument and to demolish him with sarcasm or incisive wit.

Yet other less desirable characteristics also became evident as Macmillan aged in office. He seemed to be closing himself off from others and becoming more and more of a snob. The close contacts Macmillan had developed with backbenchers fell into disuse, as he came to rely for advice on an increasingly small circle, particularly the Secretary of the Cabinet, Sir Norman Brooke. He no longer seemed to enjoy the company of intellectuals, which he had once prized, and seemed happiest when surrounded by the titled. This predilection might not have mattered, for Britishers often are snobbish, but it seemed to affect Macmillan's Cabinet appointments: the number of aristocrats ap-

[1] Harold Macmillan, *Winds of Change 1914–1939* (London: Macmillan & Co., 1966), pp. 40–41.

pointed to the Cabinet was unprecedented even for the Conservative party. Macmillan claimed that appointment rested on merit, but it seemed more than a coincidence that so many people of merit happened also to have titles. He might sometimes mock the titled, but his eagerness for their company was marked.

Strangely, Macmillan refused a title when it might have been his. A retiring Prime Minister is customarily offered a Peerage, yet Macmillan did not claim one. Macmillan's autobiography provides no explanation. Was it because he held that only the old titles were legitimate, or because to the end he wished to emulate Churchill? Did he perhaps believe his place in history secure without it? Or perhaps this was an inverse snobbery? Like Churchill, Macmillan accepted a knighthood, and now is Sir Harold Macmillan, still actively writing at the age of eighty-three years. He did publish and has not perished.

Lessons of British Leadership

The German theorist of war, Carl von Clausewitz, described war as a rational activity. War, he claimed, was directed toward defined goals by means thought out in advance. What differentiated the theory of war from the actual battle was chance events that could not be foreseen. These chance events, which Clausewitz called "frictions," distinguished theory from practice. A political career can, in this sense, be compared to theoretical and real wars. A political career has set goals, and the means by which they can be achieved are generally established. Yet, once again, chance events distinguished what happens in theory to what happens in practice.

Looking at British politics as a rational activity, one can say that the attributes of the successful politician are known and can be achieved with reasonable diligence: education, military service (though this is not always essential), apprenticeship in politics, and advancement in party and Parliament. Birth into the right family cannot, of course, be planned, but choice of party can offset accident of birth. Chance enters not only into historic period, some offering better opportunities than others, but also into such randomly distributed factors as intellect and emotional stability, which combine to form talent. Trained talent allows an individual to make the right decisions on how chance and career are to be harnessed. No objective attribute of success helps in the absence of talent, yet the objective attributes, being most easily understood, might warrant first examination.

Being born into a political family is an advantage. Political need not mean being devoted to a party and actively working for its cause, though these conditions often help; it means having a family with a more than ordinary interest in politics. Macmillan's father and grandfather had such an interest, manifested in their espousal of Christian Socialism. Macmillan's mother saw a more orthodox political career for her son and planned the logical steps to that end. Yet, but for the chance event of meeting the daughter of the Duke of Devonshire and convincing her to marry him, he might have gone into publishing and remained there. Nor need one look only to the Conservative party. Labour Prime Minister Harold Wilson came from a family where parents and grandparents were deeply concerned with politics, though none entered Parliament.

Education is a second factor. British education is avowedly elitist, and the better educated are almost expected to play a part in politics. Children are sorted out in primary school into those who can benefit from higher education and those who must be satisfied with a less rarefied role. Because of educational advantages originating at home, class and status as well as intelligence influence who gets what kind of education. Level of education and kind of education determine how far a person can go in politics and in much else. Only 2 percent of Britain's population have university degrees, but half the Members of Parliament are graduates. And this holds for Conservatives *and* Labour. In this century eleven of the sixteen Prime Ministers of *all* parties have been university graduates, and two of the five nongraduates came from political families. Trade unions provide an alternative route, though this applies mainly to the Labour party.

Social class pervades British life. Conservatives generally, and Labourites often, come from the upper-middle class. Their university training leads them to follow upper-middle-class careers, and there is little marked difference between the parties in this respect: 50 percent of Conservatives and 55 percent of Labourites have such backgrounds. Because of the importance of the trade unions to the Labour party, 41 percent of its Ministers have had working-class backgrounds. Nevertheless, had Macmillan turned to Labour as his vehicle to power, his background would not have differed very much from that of many Labour leaders. In short, on the career ladder—whether in politics, the civil service, finance, or industry—the better the education, the higher the status, the better the start, the greater the chances of major success. There is no single path to prominence, and all obstacles can be overcome in Britain as almost everywhere else. But the right attributes smooth the way.

Other things being equal, coming to politics early helps ensure success. Experience counts in the British system, and those who want to reach the top must start early. Mac-

millan's career is an illustration, for he sat in the House seventeen years before winning recognition. (However, his wait was extended because of his unorthodoxy.)

It should be evident that the British and American systems differ in important respects. Americans run for office, whereas in Britain office is the reward given by the party in power. A young American male or female can run for any office they choose, from President to dogcatcher, but in Britain this is impossible. As promotion comes from the party in Britain, what gains promotion is behavior that the party values. For example, support is given an individual leader; if his faction wins out, this loyalty is rewarded. Macmillan's following Churchill serves as an example. Loyalty, then, is one of the keys to office.

Gaining office, however, is no more than a first step. Loyalty must still be displayed. Butler failed to advance to the highest office because his loyalty was suspect after Suez. On the other hand, Ministers of only moderate competence but great loyalty may be retained by a Prime Minister until pressure for them to be dropped becomes too strong.

Even a Prime Minister is not immune. He is expected to display loyalty to colleagues and party and to hold the party together so that it works effectively in Parliament and wins elections. A Prime Minister who fails to hold the party together and who cannot provide victory, no matter how much he may be liked or valued on other grounds, will be driven to resign.

Experience is the other attribute highly valued in British politics. Ministers are usually drawn from those who have served an apprenticeship in either House. This practice has been criticized, yet all efforts to alter it have failed. Harold Wilson tried appointing five people without previous parliamentary experience to the Cabinet with, at

Two former Prime Ministers attend the funeral of a third. Harold Macmillan and Harold Wilson at the funeral of Lord Avon, formerly Sir Anthony Eden, on February 15, 1977

(United Press International)

best, dubious success. The most noted case, that of Frank Cousins, showed that a powerful trade unionist could be an ineffective Minister: Cousins resigned after only two years in office. An experienced person, after all, knows how to transact business and get results in the parliamentary environment.

Macmillan's career, unique in some respects, similar to his contemporaries' in others, shows how common characteristics and talent play their part in a political world that continually changes. Britain faces serious problems, some old and some new, but at least for the immediate future those entrusted with their solution will be men and women produced by processes similar to those that made Macmillan.

Selected Bibliography

The number of good books on British government is almost embarrassingly large. The books that follow are selected as suggestions only.

For a good general survey of British government and politics, see Richard Rose, *Politics in England* (Boston: Little, Brown, 1974).

For insiders' views, see R. H. S. Crossman, *The Diaries of a Cabinet Minister,* vol. 1 (London: Hamilton, 1975); and Herbert Morrison, *Government and Parliament: A Survey from the Inside* (New York: Oxford University Press, 1954).

Roland Young, *The British Parliament* (Evanston, Ill.: Northwestern University Press, 1962), is a good survey of the institution. A useful analysis of the Cabinet is in Bruce Heady, *British Cabinet Ministers* (London: George Allen & Unwin, 1974). Backbenchers have their turn in Peter G. Richards, *Honorable Members: A Study of the British Backbencher* (London: Faber & Faber, 1959).

British elections and their effects on candidates are in Fred Willey, *The Honorable Member* (London: Sheldon Press, 1974).

Two interesting books on parties and their workings are Michael Rush, *The Selection of Parliamentary Candidates* (London: Thomas Nelson, 1969); and David J. Wilson, *Power and Party Bureaucracy in Britain: Regional Organization in the Conservative and Labour Parties* (Lexington, Mass.: D. C. Heath, 1975).

Then, of course, for Macmillan himself, there are the biographies of Emrys Hughes, *Macmillan: Portrait of a Politician* (London: George Allen & Unwin, 1962); and Anthony Sampson, *Macmillan: A Study in Ambiguity* (London: Allen Lane, Penguin Press, 1967). There are also the six volumes of autobiography, *Winds of Change 1914–1939, The Blast of War 1939–1945, The Tides of Fortune 1945–1955, Riding the Storm 1956–1959, Pointing the Way 1959–1961,* and *At the End of the Day 1961–1963* (New York: Harper & Row, 1966–1974). The author has drawn heavily on these biographies and autobiography.

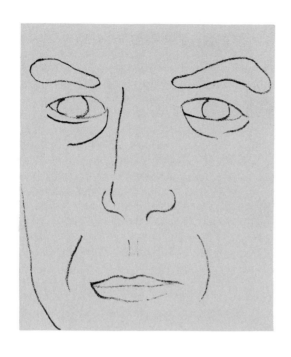

II

Valéry Giscard d'Estaing and the French Government

Jerome King

Valéry Giscard d'Estaing
Short Biographical Sketch

Valéry Giscard d'Estaing was born on February 2, 1926, in Coblenz during the French occupation of Germany. He studied at the Janson-de-Sailly and Louis-le-Grand lycées in Paris and at the Blaise Pascal lycée in Clermont-Ferrand. At the age of seventeen he joined the Resistance and took part in the liberation of Paris. Enlisting in the First Army at eighteen he fought in the French and German campaigns and was awarded the croix de guerre.

Giscard was admitted to the Ecole Polytechnique in 1946 and later to the Ecole Nationale d'Administration. He was named an *inspecteur des finances* in 1952 and was officially made deputy director of the staff of Premier Edgar Faure in 1955.

On January 2, 1956, he was elected Deputy from the Puy-de-Dôme Department and in April 1958 was elected general councilor of the canton of Rochefort-Montagne. In November 1958 he was reelected Deputy from the Puy-de-Dôme Department (from the second district of Clermont-Ferrand).

Giscard was appointed Secretary of State for the Budget in January 1959, the youngest minister of the Fifth Republic. He was named Minister of Finance and Economic Affairs in January 1962 and held that post until December 1965. In September 1967 he was elected Mayor of Chamalières, a town near Clermont-Ferrand. He was reelected Deputy from Puy-de-Dôme on the first ballot in March 1967 and in July 1968 and held the office of chairman of the National Assembly Finance Committee.

President Pompidou, after his election in June 1969, appointed Giscard Minister of the Economy and Finance, a post he held throughout three Cabinet changes (July 1972, August 1973, and March 1974). Valéry Giscard d'Estaing was elected President of the French Republic on May 19, 1974.

He was married in December 1952 and he and his wife Anne-Aymone have four children, two daughters and two sons.[1]

[1] Services de presse. Ambassade de France.

97

1

Introduction:
France – Land and People

Social Diversity

Like all other advanced industrial nations of the world, France lies in a temperate zone. Its geography has as much variety as its climate, and its items of trade are even more diverse: artichokes from Brittany and Provence, steel from Alsace-Lorraine and the Rhône Valley, apricots from the Midi, supersonic airplanes from Toulouse, wheat from Beauce, ships from the Côte d'Azur and Normandy, skis and hiking boots from the Alps, and wine, of both international and local reputation, from virtually every river valley. Along with this variety of physical production, there is also a great variety of social production. "How can France have a two-party system," the late President de Gaulle once asked, half plaintively, half proudly, "when she insists on producing 438 varieties of cheeses?"

The contrasts and variety of the country are not just metaphysical. There are obvious differences in lifestyle, in economies, and in culture from one region to another, even as each has its own regional cuisine. The mystical Bretons, whose religious feelings have their roots deep in their Celtic past, are terribly irrational by the standards of Latin rationality held by the people of the southern littoral. Yet these same Latins are generally seen as all talk and no work by the peoples of Alsace and Lorraine, who thereby probably reflect their more nearly Germanic culture. Then there are the differences between country and city and the special ambivalences arising within a formerly peasant population that has become largely industrial and urban within the past one hundred years—differences first of all between rural people and the various provincial bourgeoisie and then again between the country in general and Paris.

Paris and Centralization

Like Britain and the Soviet Union, France has a capital city, a thing alien to the Amer-

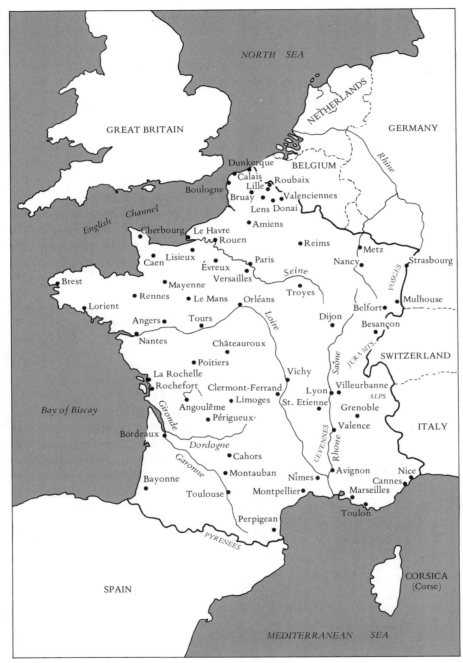

France

ican experience. Paris considers itself, and in most respects is, the leader of the country in all ways—intellectually, culturally, commercially, financially, administratively, and politically.

Measured against the standards of a London, a New York, a Mexico City or a Tokyo, Paris is only a small megalopolis of about 3.5 million. Yet its metropolitan region is where more than a sixth of the population lives (8.6 million out of 51 million), where a third of the country's cars are registered, where nearly half the telephones are connected. By virtually every measurement of economic well being, Parisians are ahead of those of their fellow citizens who live elsewhere, without even taking into account the great cultural amenities, such as museums, the opera, and the public buildings, with which the capital abounds.

Life goes on elsewhere in France, of course. But those who live outside of Paris tend to look to the center either with envy or for the purpose of identifying themselves as being against Paris. The *idea* of Paris is thus everywhere. It is perhaps the one factor, apart from language, that French people everywhere share in one way or another. For centuries, anyone who wanted to make a mark on the world dreamed of going, or went, to Paris. Paris is where people either became rich, famous, and powerful or learned to live off those who did. So Paris is both the seat of government and the center of cultural life. Its history is not just a microcosm of French history; it is almost that history itself. French kings lived in Paris long before Louis XIV built the palace at Versailles, just outside of Paris, in the early eighteenth century. The French Revolution of 1789 was largely made in Paris. So were the Revolution of 1848, the Commune of 1870, the events of May 1968. The coming and going of governments and regimes, of kings, emperors, presidents, premiers, for-

eign dignitaries, and tyrants, as well as of theologians, authors, poets, musicians, professors, and philosophers, have so long been associated with Paris that many French people regard it as the center of the world, beyond which lies an outer darkness.

The centralization of France in Paris is both symbol and fact, reflecting the relatively rapid industrialization and urbanization that have taken place during the last century, particularly since the end of World War II. These processes occurred at a later date in France than in either England or Germany. No doubt the relatively low density of the French population, combined with the general wealth of the soil in so many regions of the country, made the attraction of the land and the way of life of the small landholder endure longer than in much of the rest of Western Europe. In some respects France still has, sentimentally speaking, a peasant culture, even though what may properly be called a peasantry has long since disappeared, replaced by agribusiness on the one hand and small freeholder and tenant farmers on the other.

The great demographic fact remains the rapid movement of rural populations to industrial centers. This movement, which began with the first of the postwar economic plans, has been deliberately stimulated by government policy and has continued to be a centerpiece of official economic planning ever since. By current official census figures, more than 80 percent of the population is now urban, while 20 percent remains rural. At the same time, even rural life has been unimaginably transformed by the development of broader regional and even international markets and by the coming of television and the automobile to the poorest of isolated pockets in the countryside.

Until very recently, however, this process of industrial development especially favored the greater metropolitan region of Paris over all other areas. Marseilles, the second largest city of France, still basks in a relatively provincial torpor, traffic jams aside. Marseilles is the economic and political center for the lower Rhône valley, just as Lyons is for the upper Rhône and Bordeaux is for the Garonne valley. But these cities, and others like them, will forever remain just regional centers. The center of the *nation* is Paris.

Industrial Life
With the rapid growth of French cities in general, and of Paris in particular, the quality of urban life has not attained those heights hoped for by those aware of the common root linking *civilization* with *civitas*. The escape from what Marx once called "rural idiocy" has for a vast majority of urban French meant a falling into a daily round of *"métro, boulot, dodo"* (subway, job, sleep), occasionally lightened by an afternoon in a park, an evening at the movies, and the annual escape from the city for the four weeks' paid vacation that French employers are obliged by law to provide all regular employees.

It is true that ever since Rousseau, the French have flirted with the idea of a return to nature. But this idea has little to do with the average American's hope of having a single-family dwelling unit on a patch of grass. To the French, nature is more a cultural idea than a woods or a windowbox with petunias and geraniums. The rediscovery of nature is for them not a biologist's task. It involves, rather a search for the moral roots of human life and association beneath all the layers of acquired social conventions accumulated over a long history of national self-consciousness. The pursuit of nature, therefore, has far less to do with earning one's subsistence by one's own hands than with trying to rethink the age-old conundrums of the meaning of personality and individuality

in the face of a contemporary culture that, as Rousseau wrote in his *First Discourse,* evaluates each person in terms of his capacity to consume.

So the travel bureaus' pretty pictures of the Alps and the Côte d'Azur, and the pleasant American belief that the French really "know how to live," must give way, on closer inspection, to a harsher reality. An officially sponsored public opinion poll taken in 1973 seemed to suggest that the happiest place in France is Morbihan, a district in Brittany, which is among the poorest in the nation, with the lowest per capita income, and which, like many other rural districts, has been losing young people to industrial centers for several generations. Further, the poll suggested that unhappiness increased as one lived closer to large cities, despite their higher standards of living. Of course one must be careful in interpreting any poll about something as difficult to define as happiness. Whatever the relative degree of unhappiness in Paris or Lille or Marseilles or Toulouse, there has been a continuing net gain in their populations, while great regions of once cultivated countryside have become largely depopulated, their villages abandoned to the old and dying. It is not happiness that makes a modern industrial economy go.

At the same time, the desire to escape from the disamenities of contemporary urban life has not yet produced a wholesale move to the suburbs in France as it has in the United States. On the one hand, French cities are generally surrounded by villages as old as themselves, which are in turn surrounded by lands already cut into small private parcels. Hence the great tracts of field and forest ready for leveling by the bulldozer at the command of the real estate developer have not generally been available in France. More important yet, French understanding of what civilization is has not yet embraced the suburban lifestyle. It must in some respects even repudiate it because the city is the model of the French idea of civilization. This model gained ascendancy for many complex political and historical reasons, but perhaps chief among them is an idea of equality. Far from proving that all men are created equal, French historical experience, with its succession of feudal barons, kings, and, today, capitalists, has tended to show just the opposite—that men are very unequal indeed. Equality is, therefore, not something that in the French view can be taken for granted. It is, rather, the product of great and continuing political effort, of human contrivance, against a world of natural selection that, if left to itself, would create ever greater inequalities. Now the city itself is a human invention: one can go for weeks in a city and never touch, see, or hear anything that is not the work of human hands. The city is thus a symbol of the fundamental political task. This task, as the French see it, is to *create* a justice wholly out of human ingenuity, for human purposes, a justice whose key is the goal of equality.

Class Politics

How different, therefore, is the class situation in France from that in Britain. There are enormous disparities of wealth and power in France today, probably even greater than those in England.[1] There is a system

[1] The Organization of Economic Cooperation and Development made a survey of income distribution among its twenty-six nation members in 1976 and concluded that France had, after Italy, the most unequal distribution of any. The richest 10 percent of the population in France gained twenty-two times the amount of annual income as the poorest 10 percent. The comparable relationship for the United States was fifteen times; for the

of elite education, of which President Giscard d'Estaing is one of the typical, if more notable, products. And yet none of these differences of wealth and power has any standing in the idea of justice so far as the vast majority of Frenchmen is concerned. Of course, these differences have been more or less accepted for long periods of time. But at no time since the French Revolution of 1789 have they had legitimacy. Thus there is always something uneasy rumbling somewhere in the depths of French society, despite apparent political routine.

Political Values

This shadow of unease points to a critical factor in the spirit of modern French nationalism. What no French person can forget, no matter where his or her sympathies lie along the political spectrum, is that France is a revolutionary nation. Far more than 1776 for Americans, 1789—the year the French Revolution began—represents for the French the beginning of an understanding that the nation had thenceforth to be totally self-conscious and self-created, lifting itself out of the routine and the injustice of history by its own political efforts. There is little agreement among French people even today at what particular purposes those efforts should be aimed, as the continuing vitality of ideological disputes between the left and the right shows. But there is nevertheless a common understanding that politics must transcend the bargaining processes of economic and other private interests in order always to look to a public and national interest as an ideal. And this understanding has in turn given rise to a common attitude about

Netherlands, eleven times. The distribution of wealth, as opposed to income, is widely believed to be far more unequal, although no survey of wealth has been done.

103

politics. It is an attitude of cynicism, born of the realization of an unbridgeable chasm separating practice from ideal.

French political experience and political culture are, therefore, exclusive, as Americans and other foreigners have sometimes learned to their chagrin. French patriotism is not expressed as British national sentiment has traditionally been. Rather than an understated, often smug, and unquestioned point of view that everything British is naturally best, without anyone's having to say it, the French take the stance that there is no virtue in pretending to hide France's light under a bushel. What matters is that the *idea* of France is constantly being refined and clarified, lest what all French people feel to be their identity become lost in the shuffle of events.

In other words, the French are open to a pessimistic view of the passage of time. If it may be said of Americans, for example, that they think of their nation as a field in which many different kinds of growth are inherently desirable because growth is life, then one should say of the French that they tend to think of their nation as a work of art—a picture that must be protected from all unskilled artists who add a dab too much paint here, the wrong color there, and so on, finally ruining the original design and balance. Of course, events do add all kinds of things to their picture. And so from time to time the French feel the urge to start over again with a clean canvas, to get rid of all the messy things history has added to their personal images of an ideal France.

This urge has found the most obvious historical expression in the long succession of new constitutions and political regimes that have followed one another since 1789. What other modern industrial nation has had so many? A consulate, a directory, two empires, a restoration, and five republics have been established, to speak nothing of several interim periods that have only particular names, such as the July Monarchy and Vichy. Thus, in any discussion of the political institutions of the Fifth Republic, it is important to remember that this pattern of repeated formal changes enters into every French political system; it is, indeed, part of the system itself.

2

French Government: An Overview

History of the French Presidential System

The current written constitution of France dates from 1958 and is an expression of the political views of the founder of the Fifth Republic, General Charles de Gaulle, who served as President from 1958 until his voluntary retirement from office in 1969. Like all the earlier democratic constitutions of France, the Constitution of 1958 formally proclaims the principle of popular sovereignty. But in practice, the Fifth Republic, like its predecessors, has reflected continuing disagreements and uncertainties about the kinds of representative institutions and procedures through which the will of the people should find expression. As long ago as 1688, sovereignty was practiced in Great Britain in terms of "the king in parliament," a convention that later evolved into a form of popular rule through the supremacy of the House of Commons and its executive

committee, the Cabinet. But popular sovereignty came to France as a revolutionary idea, confronting monarchical and authoritarian traditions in both public and private life, in both state and church. As a consequence, this idea has had to fight to make its way into contemporary political usage. And although it may be said to have won many important battles since 1789 against the positivist and authoritarian mentality, the war between them is by no means over even today.

Legislative-Executive Relations
From the beginning of the Fifth Republic—even in its very genesis—the clearest evidence of this struggle has lain in the evolution of the powers of the presidency. When the Fourth Republic collapsed in 1958, it was widely believed that the cause of failure stemmed from its parliamentary system's inability to make decisions on such critical matters of policy as whether or not to continue

the war in Indochina, and later in Algeria, against the native forces seeking self-determination. The consequence of this lack of decisiveness was that these wars dragged on futilely for years, embittering French political life and draining men and resources away from needs at home. Critical of the way the parliamentary system operated in the Fourth Republic, many argued the necessity of enhancing the powers, and above all the stability, of an executive who could act decisively in a way that a legislature, representing many different and conflicting interests, could never hope to. So long as the chief holder of power was elected, the argument went, the practice of democracy would in no way be compromised. For is not regular accountability to an electorate the essential element in popular sovereignty? If so, should not a president, chosen by a majority in a free and fair electoral campaign, represent the people even better than a legislature, whose members, after all, are elected by local areas according to local interests?

Citizens of the United States should have no difficulty in identifying with the issue so raised. Ever since the Constitutional Convention of 1789, Americans of nearly every generation have had to wrestle with it. One way it has been handled is through making a sharp distinction between domestic and foreign matters. In domestic affairs the predominant power was given formally to Congress, where debate and discussion may take a long, even indefinite, time. In foreign affairs, on the other hand, the power to act quickly and decisively is often vital. So here the President was given the power to act before, and sometimes even despite, Congress. Over the years, and particularly since the Cold War with the Soviet Union and a hot one in Indochina, Americans have discovered that it is not as easy to separate domestic and foreign affairs as traditional constitutional practices had implied. When concern for national

security and related problems becomes large enough, politics no longer stops at the water's edge. The problem is only heightened by the fact that the nuclear balance of terror, under which we have been condemned to live since 1950, has given the President alone power to "push the button," despite Congress's constitutional authority to declare war.

The kinds of constitutional problems between decisiveness and debate, between secrecy and an informed public, between liberty and security, that the United States is now beginning to confront have in fact faced France for centuries. A relatively small part of the Eurasian continent, France is ringed about with potential enemies whom, since the Treaty of Westphalia of 1648, it has had to face as one sovereign nation against others of the same kind. The wars of Indochina (1946–1954) and Algeria (1956–1962) are but recent examples of its perennial difficulties. Unlike Germany, which once dealt with similar problems in a militaristic manner, France has since 1789 been guided by democratic aspirations. But these aspirations have never been fully embraced in a practical way. As a consequence, French political practices have been torn between the opposing values of liberty and security, of spontaneity in growth and positive protection of existing interests.

However, physical security against an outside enemy is no longer the only factor in national welfare. Economic competition has long been recognized as yet another reason to govern decisively. The problems of economic recession and economic growth demand a response: the first produces unemployment; the second, increasingly scarce and expensive resources. And together they now mean inflation. For both economic and military reasons, then, the political systems of all democratic nations have been evolving toward greater power in executive hands, leaving less in the hands of the legislatures. The French political system has been no exception to this general rule.

Traditional Parliamentarianism
Under the parliamentary systems of the Third (1875–1940) and Fourth Republics (1946–1958), the parliament, or National Assembly, was the dominant branch of government. Formally, this supremacy was comparable to that of Parliament in Great Britain; but practically, there was a profound difference between the two systems. In Britain the House of Commons has long lain under party discipline and the leadership of the Prime Minister, so policy and legislative programs have generally been the effective responsibility of the party that controlled the prime ministership by means of winning a popular majority, or at least a plurality, in national elections. In France, however, the existence of seven or eight parties dividing the electorate among them, combined with an electoral system that tended to encourage the predominance of local men and issues over national ones, meant that there was little effective long-term policy making, even in domestic affairs. Under the French parliamentary system, cabinets could have great powers for brief periods of time. But they could never be sure of staying in office long enough to carry out broad legislative programs.

The Third and Fourth Republics were perhaps not really less competent than the governments of Britain or the United States during the same period of time. But their image was consistently bad, nowhere more so than among the French themselves. Most thought of the French parliamentary system in terms of either revolving-door or do-nothing cabinets. An activist Premier would often be turned out of office within a period of six or seven months, while one who confined his efforts to fence mending among his parliamentary supporters might be allowed to stay for more than a year, but have absolutely nothing to show for it.

Between the end of World War I and the beginning of the Fifth Republic, no French Premier ever developed much control over parliament. The splintering of parties in the nation as a whole meant that none was large enough to elect a majority in parliament. Thus every Cabinet existed at the mercy of one or another coalition of parliamentary groups. The art of becoming Premier seldom had anything to do with being the leader of a party capable of mobilizing the public around national issues or programs in general elections, but a great deal to do with being a broker of interests in the corridors of the National Assembly. And in this insiders' game of coalition making, leaders of the smallest parliamentary groups were often the most effective, since they were less of a threat to the influence of the larger groups when they attained the position of Premier.

The intricacy of these parliamentary processes of the Third and Fourth Republics finally succeeded in alienating much of the French electorate. So when the crunch came, as it did twice—once in 1940 with the Nazi invasion and once again in 1958 with a threatened military coup d'état by the French Army fighting against national independence for Algeria—there was simply not enough support to keep the old parliamentary machinery going. Indeed, this lack of support for the system was shown even by the constitutional referendum of 1945 that brought the Fourth Republic into existence after France's liberation from Nazi occupation. In that referendum, scarcely more than a third of the electorate voted in favor of the new constitution, while another third—rather uncharacteristically of the French voting public—simply stayed away from the polls. So the Fourth Republic was born with opposition and indifference as its principal midwives.

And yet it must be obvious that this creaky parliamentary system was not an arbitrary imposition on an unwilling nation. Although the idea of legislative supremacy was in keeping with the revolutionary ideas of 1789, the parliamentary systems of the Third and Fourth Republics developed historically because they softened real differences among the wide variety of interests in the country at large. The Constitution of 1946, for which the public showed such little enthusiasm, had been intended in the minds of many of its makers, in fact, to provide an antidote to the weaknesses of the Third. And yet these weaknesses reappeared almost immediately and continued to drain away popular support until the collapse of 1958.

One moral of the story is clear: in France, attitudes toward political power are usually circumstantial. In other words, when you and your friends are in office, the greater the state's power, the better. When your opponents are in office, the weaker the government, the better. The best thing to do is to capture the power and machinery of government for yourself and use it to the hilt. The next best alternative is to weaken the government so as to minimize harm to your interests.

What such attitudes mean in practice, of course, is that apparent agreements about the processes in government also tend to be circumstantial. French political history has produced many practical checks and balances from which French citizens have drawn and still do draw considerable security. But the practice of checks and balances has never been accepted in French political thinking. Rather than regard government as an inherently dangerous thing, the French have tended to think of it as a tool, one of potential for unlimited good when correctly used, but subject to misuse when in the hands of fools or knaves. Knaves and fools are, of course, people whom you fear, or distrust.

And so modern French political systems, whatever their form at any moment, have been locked in ambiguous conflict between an abstract desire to have a strong government that will do good and a very practical fear of the power of government for the actual harm it is likely to inflict. The parliamentary systems of both Third and Fourth Republics came to reflect the reluctant triumph of fear—a triumph assured by the fact that no single party was able to get a majority of the popular vote in any election, any more than a leader in parliament could put together anything but a coalition cabinet. Under these circumstances, a cabinet was as likely to include opponents as friends; it was better, therefore, to have cabinets short-lived, while keeping your fingers crossed that no emergency requiring effective government action would arise.

Fall of the Fourth Republic
But history has seldom taken finger crossing very seriously, especially in times of crisis. France found itself in just such a crisis in Algeria in 1958. An independence movement led by Arab nationalists was in direct and violent confrontation throughout the region with ethnic Europeans, who had held power in the region ever since the French conquest of Algeria during the nineteenth century. A large French army was sent to Algeria to bring the Arabs' revolt under control. But the desire and even confident expectation of winning a military victory against the Arabs made it only too easy to forget the political dimensions of the matter (an error repeated by the Americans in Vietnam a decade later). So with the success of each succeeding military operation, the French army and leadership found themselves ever more embroiled in a bitter struggle between European residents and Arabs, with all the cruelest overtones of a race war.

French public opinion, consistently misinformed by official military sources, was at first slow to react, but gradually became more and more appalled. Succeeding revolving-door cabinets in Paris increasingly asked themselves what France was trying to do, especially whether the cost of keeping Algeria French was worth the prize. These doubts quickly got back to the highest officers of the French army in Algeria, who, fresh from the 1954 defeat in Indochina, became extremely sensitive to the charge that they might be either not very competent in their conduct of military operations or not very objective in their view of the political situation. They easily fashioned a stab-in-the-back theory to account for their lack of political success in Algeria. According to them, the hand that held the knife was the Fourth Republic, willing to push the army into war, but unwilling to provide sufficient means for winning it. It thus occurred to some of the military leadership, in conjunction with leaders of Algeria's Europeans, that the only way they could keep Algeria French was to win a political battle in Paris against supporters of the parliamentary system.

Now enter General Charles de Gaulle. The year 1958 did not mark his first appearance in French politics, but rather a remarkable comeback from what most public opinion had deemed a state of permanent retirement. This apparent retirement had seemed to take place in two stages. The first came in 1946, when—as hero of the Liberation, standardbearer of Free France, and President of the Provisional Government ruling in the interim between the flight of the Germans and the drawing up of a new constitution—he had warned his fellow citizens against accepting the 1945–1946 draft constitution of the Fourth Republic. In General de Gaulle's view, this draft constitution was bound to reestablish the old, detested political system of the Third Republic. His warn-

ing, buttressed by his unexpected resignation as President, had its effect, and the final vote showed it. But this effect was insufficient to keep the Fourth Republic from coming into being.

Indeed, instability marked the Fourth Republic for the fourteen years of its existence. Party squabbles quickly brought back the old familiar pattern of revolving-door and do-nothing cabinets. The public complained about constant inflation, and lack of decisiveness led rapidly to the development of that war in Indochina which the United States was to inherit in the 1960s. These troubles confirmed General de Gaulle in his already long-standing opposition to the parliamentary system. They also confirmed his determination to act. Thus was launched in 1947 what he called the *Rassemblement du peuple français* (RPF), not a party, but a movement designed to refashion French political institutions through an upsurge of popular enthusiasm and led by himself. Ironically, the RPF proved to be a great party, but a poor movement. In the general elections of 1951 it won nearly a third of the seats in the lower house of parliament. But its impressive strength was far less than adequate to the goal of remaking the political system in keeping with General de Gaulle's vision. He himself lost interest, returning once more—many people thought definitively—to his country home in Colombey-les-deux-Eglises to work on his war memoirs, while the Fourth Republic was left to its own failing devices. Without his light, the RPF began to wither on the vine.

It is worth noting, however, that the Fourth Republic was not altogether hopeless in terms of results. It may have been inadequate in fighting wars and inflation. But it nevertheless produced one of the highest economic growth rates in the world (second only to the Japanese in the long term), full employment, and a range of public and so-

109

cial services that Americans are unlikely to enjoy for a generation or more to come.

Civil Bureaucracy and the Fourth Republic

In trying to explain how such an unstable system of government was able to attain such remarkable results, most observers have decided that the French civil service was really the key. Undoubtedly there is much validity in this assertion. It is true that the French civil service has a much longer experience of professionalism—from Napoleon's reign, if not from that of Louis XIV—than either the American, which dates only from the late nineteenth century, or the British. But an effective civil service needs more than technical expertise; it needs a great deal of both political savvy and support. If the French civil service was an effective instrument for social and economic policy during the Fourth Republic, as most agree it was, then it must have had fruitful relationships with the parliamentary system. The latter, therefore, cannot have been all bad, however discouraging its appearance. Indeed, the great variety of political interests and partisan conflicts characteristic of both public and parliamentary life from 1946 to 1958 meant that the flexibility of the civil service and its own potential for relating effectively to diversity were essential factors in the economic effectiveness of the Fourth Republic.

But if publics are more likely to take happiness for granted than to thank governments for it, blame for their troubles is easily passed into politics. And if one thinks, as the French political culture inclines French people to do and as General de Gaulle most definitely did, that the essential art of politics is to keep up appearances, then the Fourth Republic has to be accounted a failure, not so much because it actually did fail in 1958, but because it looked like a loser from the very beginning. It did not seem to stand for anything in particular and was incapable of identifying its purposes. It had a bad press, and the citizens found nothing in its ways or means to protect them from a military coup, much less to catch their imagination or hopes.

Structure of the Presidential System

Commanding the army and catching the public's imagination and hopes, however, was what General de Gaulle had already shown himself to be a master at, long before 1958. From the vantage point of the present, one may say that he was a great leader—very likely the greatest among all those of the North Atlantic democracies so far in the twentieth century. And the Fifth Republic, which he brought into being in 1958 by playing dissident army officers, European leaders in Algeria, and French public opinion off against one another, created a presidential regime designed to enhance his style of leadership.

The argument for such a new system was based on the following logic: no one party could ever hope to obtain a majority of popular votes in France; therefore, the National Assembly would always be fractured into a number of conflicting groups whose respective leaders would always be competing among themselves for ministerial posts; therefore, no effective executive could ever arise from a base in the traditional parliament. The only answer to this state of affairs, according to General de Gaulle, was to create an executive whose election and term did not depend upon parliamentary coalitions.

Although there were some formal features

—the fixed term in office, for example—that made France's new presidency resemble the American, there were and still are great differences. In fact, one early similarity—election of the President by an electoral college—gave way in France to direct popular election of the President in 1962. The change was of great symbolic significance, because direct popular election of a President had last been tried in 1850, with Napoleon III, and the results for the Second Republic (1845–1850) had been disastrous: Napoleon III declared himself Emperor in 1852 on the basis of a popular plebiscite, thus beginning the so-called Second Empire, with all

its restrictions of civil liberties and personal freedom. To reintroduce direct popular election of the chief executive seemed to many French people, with their long historical memories, to risk a new plebiscitary dictatorship. By using a succession of plebiscites, President de Gaulle did little to dispel such fears. Increasingly, it came to be recognized that the presidency was more his personal vehicle for power than an office adapted to future circumstances.

The Dual Executive

Although this point needed no emphasis, the written constitution itself contained a poten-

Executive and legislature of the Fifth Republic

* The number of additional ministers depends on the political needs of the President.

METHOD OF HOLDING OFFICE

Direct popular election by whole nation → PRESIDENT

PREMIER

| Finance | Foreign Affairs | Justice | Education | Commerce Industry |

| Health | Interior | * | * | * |

Appointed by President, dismissed by President →

COUNCIL OF MINISTERS
(Weekly meetings, presided over by President)

Indirect election by electorate composed of members of local governing councils (mayors and municipal councillors)

Direct popular election by district (single-member districts) →

Legislative Program — Censure

NATIONAL ASSEMBLY — Bills — SENATE

Legislative Program

PARLIAMENT

111

tial ambiguity. It arose from its creation of a dual executive—the office of President, on the one hand, and the office of Premier, on the other. So long as General de Gaulle was President, few could have any doubts about where power lay; a Premier would have to do his bidding or he would not stay Premier for long. Yet this office is a traditional aspect of parliamentary, not presidential, regimes. A Premier is normally elected by the parliament and holds executive power at the pleasure of a majority of the parliament. But when de Gaulle was President, the Premier was appointed and held power first and foremost at his pleasure. As if to make the point quite clear about who was responsible to whom, de Gaulle's constitution made it mandatory for members of the legislature whom he chose for Cabinet posts to resign their seats in the parliament immediately. It was not that de Gaulle felt any compunction about appointing people to ministerial posts who were *not* elected representatives. The major thrust of his rule was to make the National Assembly into a rubber stamp for his own decisions.

Separation of Powers

And yet, while the 1958 constitution transferred to the executive some of the formerly exclusive power of the legislature to legislate —most dramatically by Article 16, which gave emergency powers to the President— that power was by no means taken away altogether. Articles 49 and 50 allowed the National Assembly to pass a motion of censure of the Premier and his Cabinet or to reject their legislative program in order to oblige their resignation. Moreover, the power of the Senate or upper house, as opposed to that of the National Assembly, was somewhat enhanced; under the 1946 constitution, the Senate had had barely a delaying capacity. But of course the real catch in the relationship between Cabinet and National Assembly came in the provision of Article 21

that authorized the President to order the lower house's dissolution and to hold new general elections within forty days. So long as General de Gaulle remained President, the practical effect of this article was plebiscitary, since the general policy and program of the Cabinet were obviously his. In 1968, for example, after the crisis of the "May events" (as the student riots and ensuing wildcat strikes in 1968 are usually called in France) the lower house was dissolved on the President's command. In the ensuing general elections, the Gaullist party won an absolute majority of seats—358 out of 497—marking the first time in French republican history that a single-party majority has ever existed. And this majority was continued in the general elections of 1973, thus providing President Giscard with his support in parliament until the general elections of 1978.

The provisions of the 1958 constitution thus make possible relations between executive and legislature that have not yet come about. The condition for such relations would be deadlock between National Assembly and President. Dissolution of the National Assembly and a call for new general elections would probably be a first step in any President's attempt to break such a deadlock. But if these new elections produced a legislative majority as hostile as the previous majority had been, the President would then be in a singularly difficult position. Resignation would entail a new presidential election, constituting an invitation to the electorate to elect an individual compatible with the new legislative majority. Refusal to resign would presumably require the President to adjust both program and choice of members for the Council of Ministers in such a way as to satisfy the legislature. In either case, a transfer of power from President to National Assembly would be the result, and the Fifth Republic, as it came from General de Gaulle's hand, would be radically transformed.

The Party System

Another formal similarity with the American Constitution has led in reality to another profound difference. Neither constitution makes any mention of political parties. General de Gaulle, like General George Washington, was often thought of, and certainly wanted to be thought of, as a person above all partisanship. But parties are integral to democratic regimes, for they help voters identify with broad political viewpoints and thus serve to mobilize public opinion in such a way as to make it the basis for legitimate power. Parties can also make possible some measure of political responsibility and thus organize both legislative and executive branches in predictable patterns and processes, without which political life would degenerate into a wholly private matter of negotiation without apparent public rhyme or reason. The importance of parties to democratic government made itself felt in Britain and the United States as early as the turn of the eighteenth century and soon became recognized as such. Yet General de Gaulle wrote his 1958 constitution without any reference to parties whatever, constantly claiming that he was not the leader of any party, but the leader of the nation as a whole.

Party and Parliament

Although de Gaulle's favorite political epithet for the Fourth Republic was "party regime"—by which everyone knew him to mean a regime destined to chaos by the activities of partial interests—his friends and supporters knew well that party support in the National Assembly for his legislative programs was going to be indispensable. So they promptly organized a new national political party, called the Union for the New Republic (UNR), which won 17.6 percent of the votes in the legislative elections of November 1958 on their very first try, sec-

ond only to the Communists, who won 18.9 percent. And since President de Gaulle then rewarded the UNR by naming one of their leaders, Michel Debré, as Premier, the idea rapidly spread, and has validity even today, that the principal function of the Premier is to act as chief organizer of the President's support in the National Assembly. Debré was, in fact, so good at organizing party affairs that in the general elections of 1962 the Gaullists won 40.5 percent of the popular vote, making the UNR the largest single party in the Assembly at that time and, with the support of some Independent Republicans, the basis of a relatively stable parliamentary working majority. Ironically, however, the UNR's triumph was Debré's undoing. President de Gaulle came to think he had real reason to fear his Premier's ideas, since they could be associated with the Gaullists' parliamentary strength. Debré was therefore dismissed, to be replaced as Premier by Georges Pompidou, who had never previously run for public office or engaged in politics at all. Thus was asserted a basic principle of the Fifth Republic's first ten years: personal loyalty to the General was more important than any other political consideration.

Once this fact of General de Gaulle's presidential power had become clear, the structures of the party system inherited from the previous parliamentary system began to change. It was not simply a matter of new parties, such as the UNR, appearing or of new names being given to old political persuasions, for these things had long been common prior to the Fifth Republic. What was different now was that all parties increasingly began to define themselves and their positions with respect to the President. General de Gaulle had effectively nationalized power, and the parliamentary parties had to follow suit or go out of existence. Thus, by the time of the parliamentary election of 1967, the old alphabet soup of French political parties had been reduced to five distinct groupings, in which the permanent opposition to de Gaulle was made up of the Communists, the Socialists, and some small splinter groups on the left and the extreme right, while his more or less steadfast support came from the Gaullists (UNR), the Independent Republicans (center right), and the Center Democrats. In terms of electoral percentages, this meant that in 1967 some 51 to 53 percent voted for representatives generally favorable to the General, while 44 percent voted for representatives generally opposed to him, leaving about 3 to 5 percent voting for representatives who might go one way or the other. The parliamentary result was somewhat akin to American parties in Congress, where being for or against the President often gives the appearance of a two-party system, although there are in fact intermediate groups (the southern Democrats prior to 1970, for example) whose political game involves issues; nominal opposition to or support of the President's party is secondary.

No doubt a political scientist would have told General de Gaulle in 1958 that the most likely way of effecting a permanent reform of France's political system would have been to use his leadership abilities to establish a party capable of bringing about a two-party system—not just a party that would carry on his name, but a political organization that he, as President, had been willing to create and maintain as a function of the office itself. General de Gaulle chose not to act in that way, preferring to develop the presidency on a basis of personal popularity. But his successors do not have, and are not likely to be able to gain, his kind of personal authority and thus must now come to terms with a party system whose evolution is anything but predictable.

The party situation in France today, as in the past, remains fluid. Of the five major party groups now represented in parliament, the Socialists are the oldest, having organized in 1905; and the Communists are the next oldest, dating from 1920. The Gaullist party came into existence only in 1958 and has already changed its name—from Union for the New Republic (UNR) to Union of Democrats for the Fifth Republic (UDR), and now to Movement for the Republic (RR). As for Giscard d'Estaing's party, the Independent Republicans, its formal birth occurred only in 1966. Its support came largely from an earlier party known as the Independents and Peasants, established in 1949. In the so-called moderate center, Jean-Jacques Servan-Schreiber, former publisher and editor of the weekly magazine *l'Express*, has recently led the Democratic Center party. This group was founded in 1966 by Jean Lecanuet, who had been an unsuccessful presidential candidate in the 1965 election, in which the voting was dominated by General de Gaulle and François Mitterrand, now leader of the Socialists and the alliance of the left. The Democratic Center has always hoped to make its rather small weight felt by doing a balancing act between the Gaullists and the combined left, trying to make themselves necessary either to the majority in the National Assembly or to the opposition on specific questions. But the tactic has not yet worked for them, especially since the legislative elections of 1968 and 1973, which gave the Gaullists an absolute majority in the National Assembly.

Except perhaps for the Communists and the Socialists, then, the national existence of French parties depends very much on current events and current leadership. While it is true that the presidential regime has transformed the current behavior of French political parties, emphasizing conflicts between left and right and reducing the center to a nullity, the permanence of this change cannot yet be taken for granted.

Not only is the present alliance of the left dependent on a very tense working relationship between the Socialists and the Communists, but the Gaullists themselves reflect centrifugal tendencies, which are likely to become more pronounced as they lose some of the political patronage that has been the principal source of their unity since de Gaulle's departure in 1969. This loss is not just a speculative possibility, since the presidency is no longer in the hands of even a de facto Gaullist; and they are very unlikely to be able to repeat in 1978 their legislative electoral successes of 1968 and 1973.

As long as de Gaulle was President, his popular authority was such that party developments drew little public attention. But as the 1960s wore on, the charge of personal power was ever more frequently leveled against the General. These charges foreshadowed a time when the whole issue of legitimate organization of political power would again be raised. The attack on his methods drew particular force from his only slightly disguised plebiscites, designed to face the electorate with all-or-nothing questions. As the Algerian crisis, which had brought the Fifth Republic into being, receded into the past, President de Gaulle's often explicit threats to resign began to lose their effect. The stability and prosperity of the regime began to appear sharply at odds with the advancing age of the President. And although the great riots and strikes of May 1968 at first seemed to give renewed life to the idea of a catastrophe to follow, their consequence was just the reverse. On the one hand, they helped produce an absolute majority of Gaullists in the National Assembly in the general elections the President had called in July 1968 after dissolving the previous Assembly;

this result made it easier for the public to believe in the stability of parliament itself. And on the other, apparent stability and prosperity were reestablished with good speed, suggesting that the benefits of the Fifth Republic were based on more in political life than merely the General's power. So when in the spring of 1969 de Gaulle once more decided to play his familiar trump, in a constitutional referendum aiming at reforms of the Senate and local administration, the public was no longer with him. The defeat of the referendum gave the aging General no choice except to pack his bags and leave the Palais Elysée. And this he promptly did, without even designating an heir apparent.

After de Gaulle

This discussion of the institutions of the Fifth Republic has so far focused on the presidency not merely as an office, but also as the creation of one man. And this emphasis is quite warranted for the period of General de Gaulle's ascendancy. But with his departure, the Fifth Republic entered into a new stage, just as George Washington's replacement by John Adams meant a change in American politics. It is never easy to succeed the founder of a new state, as the next President, Georges Pompidou, no doubt like Adams before him, was to discover. The machinery of the system inevitably became less flexible. Pompidou found that he had neither de Gaulle's freedom nor the same kind of popular support. The institutions themselves had not yet developed to their fullest, either, because as long as the General was still in control, they had to be prepared to bend to his will, being, after all, his creatures. But they were *not* Pompidou's creatures. Under him it was necessary that they develop a life of their own, on their own, in order to continue at all.

*General de Gaulle taking his leave after the
1969 referendum*

(*Ah! quelle année!* by Auclert et Calvi © by Editions
Denoël)

The incumbency of President Pompidou,
elected in 1969 against a divided field of
opponents that included centrists like Alain
Poher and Socialist François Mitterrand, was
marked especially by the fact that he had
never been a leader of the Gaullist party, or
even a member of it. Nor was his public
reputation similar to de Gaulle's. He was
widely considered to have been a loyal personal friend of the former President and, as
Premier, a more or less competent executor
of de Gaulle's wishes. But he was certainly
not a man of broad political vision. Political
cartoonists of the day sometimes drew him as
a Sancho Panza to de Gaulle's Don Quixote,
and the comparison was altogether believ-
able. But Pompidou was more than just
short and fat; he also had the character of a

Sancho Panza. He was intensely practical,
and in his relatively brief political career he
had learned well and quickly how to manipulate the political forces immediately around
him. He cared little for the public limelight,
preferring inconspicuous corners to arrange
the deals and compromises that would carry
things on from one day to the next. As for
ultimate destinations, he had little concern.
Politics was for him a matter of daily problems and routines.

Among the daily problems inherited from
his famous predecessor, however, none was
more continually pressing than the choice of
his Premier: not only was a Gaullist party
then holding a majority of seats in the National Assembly, but its leadership was being
actively contested by individuals whose only
common bond was that each imagined himself or herself to be the true spiritual inher-
itor of General de Gaulle's charismatic gifts.
Pompidou had to choose one of them as his
Premier, in order to maintain control of the
parliamentary majority. But in choosing one,
he had to reject the others. And since each
had a group of followers, both in parliament
and throughout the country, he risked losing
more support than he gained.

De Gaulle's party legacy, in short, was a
peculiar one. No doubt all party machines
are of use only to their creators: Mayor
Daley's successor in Chicago, for example,
will have to create a machine of his own, for
in future elections he cannot expect simply
to rely on the late incumbent's. But the
Gaullists after de Gaulle's last retirement
from politics were not just a party machine.
The General had consistently maintained the
pretense that he would never stoop to merely
partisan politics; and the office of the Presidency that he had designed for himself owed
much of its apparent legitimacy to widespread public agreement with de Gaulle's
criticisms of party politics. As President,
able. But Pompidou was more than just

Pompidou had therefore to deal with parliamentary figures who considered themselves true apostles of Gaullism though he knew them to be ambitious leaders of factions in a partisan grouping. Simultaneously, he had to pretend, as his successor had always done, that the office of the presidency was above all partisanship. Yet one method his predecessor had used for doing this—the plebiscite—was closed to Pompidou. Even with his enormous popular authority, de Gaulle had exhausted that tactic. The very idea was inconceivable for Sancho Panza.

Pompidou's choice as his first Premier was Jacques Chaban-Delmas, Mayor of Bordeaux and a notable left Gaullist. Despite their representation of great vested interests, the Gaullists were, in fact, broadly spread out along an ideological spectrum from moderate left to far right; and Pompidou, whose own inclinations were rightist, wanted to secure his left flank. But the Gaullists were also divided between those who had found membership in the party useful for electoral and patronage reasons and those who joined through conviction that the General's message for the world had to be carried through history by apostles. Chaban-Delmas claimed to be an apostle. His appointment as Premier was thus intended to assure spiritual Gaullists that the faith was in good hands (and perhaps also to discredit the whole idea of a spiritual successor to the General). Having thereby placated those attracted by faith, Pompidou then set out to satisfy those Gaullists interested in the power and money of politics—interested, in short, in things that make action on a day-to-day basis possible.

In French political life, this group of doers (as distinguished from the thinkers, of whom Chaban-Delmas was ostensibly more the type) may be further divided into two classes. On the one hand, there are private business and commercial interests, especially the largest enterprises—steel, chemicals, pharmaceuticals, aircraft, oil, textiles, banks, insurance, and so on. On the other, there are public agencies, both local (municipalities and cities) and national (health and education). Pompidou knew there was a coincidence of interests between these two groups. Both wanted and needed affluence, economic growth, and the expansion of credit. Private interests want this because increased profits are what their world is all about. And the public agencies need it because increased private profits mean increased tax revenues, and hence, expansion of their respective realms. Pompidou's basic policy was thus to expand private and public financial credits and thereby to earn political support from among those Gaullists for whom the appointment of Chaban-Delmas, with his talk about social justice and creation of a new society, was anathema. In short, unlike General de Gaulle, Pompidou had no substantial capital in public opinion that he could spend at will to undertake great things. On the contrary, his prepolitical experience as a financial adviser in the Banque Rothschild had long since given him to understand that the world turns on money. His position as President made it possible for him to decide who was to get how much, and when, from the work of public policy.

What instrumentalities does a French President have for gaining political support? To answer this question requires a brief review of the possibilities of interaction between the centralized state agencies, the business world, and the patronage available for each.

The Administrative System

Finance

In all democracies the question of public money—where it is to come from, where it is to be spent—is basic to politics. To get a sense of how the French political system operates, therefore, one must look at control of the Ministry of Finance and Economic Affairs. The most obvious feature is the high degree of concentration of financial and economic power in this particular administrative service. The power formally comes from the legislative grant of authority to collect taxes and to prepare the government's budget. Practically, it is based on a vast amount of information available only to the Ministry of Finance and through it, at the Minister's discretion, to the Premier and the President. The Premier can know many useful things about political moods in parliament and about the political situation in the big cities. But knowing in detail where the money is coming from, whom it is going to, at what rate, and with what probable effects on business activity, employment, inflation, and the strength of the franc among world currencies gives the Minister of Finance and his department an ability to influence the President that even the Premier does not have, as we shall see in the rise to power of Giscard d'Estaing.

Like the entire public administration of France, the Ministry of Finance is organized along hierarchical lines. This general form was imposed on the French civil service as long ago as Louis XIV and perfected by Napoleon Bonaparte, dictator in the period from 1800 to 1814. Specialization of function, combined with specialization of knowledge, is the rule for all positions below the very top. No one need know or understand any more or any less than is required by the precisely defined functions of his particular position. Communication is always up and down, never across, from equal to equal. Napoleon's thinking was, of course, dominated by his military experience. His need, like that of Louis XIV before him, was to be able to mobilize all civilian resources for war.

Yet some general picture and information about the work of an entire department is an obvious necessity for the head of an organization structured this way, and it is provided in France by various so-called inspectorates—special groups within each department who report to the Minister himself and who are authorized to roam through all ranks and levels of a department, checking, confirming, correcting rules and procedures, and above all informing themselves across all divisions, subdivisions, and normal lines of authority about what is really going on.

Each major department of the French civil service has such an inspectorate. However, the Finance Ministry's inspectorate operates not only internally; its members are authorized to explore all the other departments of the civil administration. The logic of this authority is clear: since every public service spends money, and since that money comes out of the state's total budget, which is prepared in the Finance Ministry, it is necessary for the Finance Ministry to be able to account for the whole public bureaucracy. In all politics, information is power, just as lack of knowledge is weakness. Since the Finance Ministry both directs the preparation of the budget and knows, through its own Inspectors, about the real internal operations of every public agency—often more than the nominal heads of those agencies, in fact—it is necessarily the most powerful ministry of all.

This power extends, moreover, even to the operations of local governments—from the mayors of the largest cities to the municipal councils of the smallest communes. The reason for this lies in the tax structure of the country, whereby general taxes—income, sales, and value-added taxes—provide the overwhelming majority of revenue for all levels of government, while local real estate taxes, the only kind local governments are authorized to collect on their own account,

118

remain minimal. The result is inevitably to strengthen further the power of central government, since even the largest cities, like Paris itself, are thereby reduced to begging on a competitive, annual basis for the funds to carry on their essential municipal services. Consequently, local elected officials are inclined to decide on priorities and policies that will please the Finance Minister in order to increase, or at least maintain, their access to the Treasury for the benefit of their own local electorates. To put the matter the other way around, the Finance Minister, by the control of subsidies to local government, has a vast power of political patronage.

. As the French administration is organized basically along military lines, it must, like any army, distinguish institutionally between field (or line) and staff functions. The Ministry of Finance's major tasks—collection of taxes and distribution of subsidies—constitute field work. Staff agencies, rather like the general staff of an army, help the central government plan how battles are to be fought in theory, while leaving the actual fighting to field officers. There are today two principal staff groups in France—the Council of State, which is very old, and the Commissariat for the Plan, which is rather new.

Council of State

The Council of State's roots go back to the eighteenth century, and its original purpose was to provide advice to the king. Its basic function today is still to provide advice to the executive, although the complexity of its operations has naturally grown along with the modern extension of governmental functions. It is one of the three *grands corps de l'état,* the other two being the Court of Accounts (*cours des comptes,* equivalent in function to the American General Accounting Office) and the Court of Cassation (roughly comparable to the Supreme Court of the United States, without the power of judicial review). Like the Finance inspectorate, the Council of State draws most of its 175 members from among the highest graduates of the National School of Administration. And also like the Finance Inspectorate, its members are considered elites in the French civil service.

The Council of State today is the principal internal regulator of the whole civil bureaucracy, except for the judiciary, which is excluded from its supervision by the principle of the separation of powers. But it is even more than internal regulator, because its members, like those of the Finance Inspectorate, can work throughout the whole bureaucracy as high-level advisers to other departments and agencies. So it has a very broad influence in the actual drafting of all legislation presented by the executive to the parliament for adoption. The importance of this drafting is indicated by the fact that French legislators, like their counterparts in Britain, but unlike American Congressmen, have practically no facilities or staff for drawing up bills on their own. Consequently, neither the French nor the British parliament has a real investigative role—the power to subpoena witnesses or to gather expert testimony for the purposes of legislating—as can committees of Congress. The relative impotence of the French parliament is reflected in a corresponding strength and structure of the executive branch, within which the Council of State plays a key role. With powers over the form and much of the substance of legislative drafting, its members have in addition an almost exclusive authority to interpret those bills passed into law, because they draw up the mass of detailed regulations that all civil servants and operating departments must follow in application of the laws. And finally, in a system that really has no counterpart in either Great Britain or America, the Council of State can sit as judges in disputes arising between private citizens and the state on the application of laws and administrative rules and regulations, even awarding damages to individuals whose legitimate interests they judge to have been wronged by state activities.

Planning Commission

The newer of the staff agencies, dating from 1946, is the General Commissariat for the Plan. It has no counterpart in Britain or the United States, either, although all contemporary governments do engage in economic planning simply by drawing up massive budgets and controlling the money supply. In France, however, the Commissariat for the Plan has been authorized by legislation to draw up successive Five-Year plans that indicate what the planners believe to be suitable goals for all the principal sectors of the economy, both public and private. The key to this planning has been its basically informational character; it has no authority to compel producers to live up to the targets set for them. Each plan represents a model of an economy of balanced growth and a statement of the government's intentions on which private enterprises may, if they choose, base their own decisions. These intentions are often not realized in practice, however, for even within the government itself the plan is only advisory. And it is still the Finance Ministry that determines the national public budget, as it is the parliament that votes the budget into law.

Immediately after World War II the effectiveness of the first plan was relatively strengthened both by the importance of the national budget in a war-wrecked economy and by the widespread desire to get life back to normal as quickly as possible. But as one Five-Year plan after another has come along —the sixth covering the period from 1970 to 1975—general prosperity and abundance have replaced scarcity, and public and even parliamentary interest in the planning processes has declined. In spite of its obvious weakness, the Commissariat for the Plan has become a respected institution within government itself, since its processes prompt most agencies to think out loud, so to speak, about what they are doing and why. It is certainly true that the French public as a whole broadly accepts free-enterprise capitalism and could be persuaded to think in other terms only with the greatest difficulty. But the very existence of the Commissariat for the Plan shows that this acceptance of free enterprise must be understood in relationship to the statist (*étatiste*) tradition, according to which it is a legitimate function of the state to encourage and promote, both directly and indirectly, the development of commerce, industry, and technology, as well as certain broad social goals. To use again the metaphor of politics as art, one may say that a basic political attitude of the French is that a society arranged according to some formal pattern, which every member of the society understands, is the proper goal of politics. Although this outlook may on certain occasions have revolutionary implications—as 1789, 1848, 1870, and 1968 suggest—it can also be quite conservative and even pessimistic in its consequences; it can express a deep fear of just letting things happen without public forethought, public foreknowledge, or public permission. As we have seen, modern French history is caught between welcoming spontaneity and regarding it as a threat to all security.

Interior

This fear of spontaneity, which is understandable on the level of personal security (drunken driving is both spontaneous and dangerous), has yet another manifest reflection in a central institution of French government—the Ministry of the Interior (whose functions should in no way be confused with those of the Department of the Interior in the United States). The Interior Ministry is another Bonapartist refinement of a set of traditions, having to do primarily with military conscription, drawn from the monarchical system that preceded the French Revolution of 1789. Napoleon's reputation as a military genius depended, in the first place, on the fact that he was able to organize a mass army, something no other European nation had previously done. But to raise a mass army, one must know at the very least where the young men are and what their names are. In setting up the Interior Ministry, Napoleon I created a vast system of internal spying and policing, reporting directly to the Emperor himself. Since his time its functions have been somewhat changed—the military services now get most of their information directly—but the basic structure, if not the practice, of a police state is still there. The formal duties of the Ministry continue to include maintenance of a national police (*Gendarmerie Nationale*) and a special riot police, available for rapid service in any part of France, from the tiniest village to the middle of Paris. Added to this system of police are the local police forces of every municipality, which, through their offices (*commissariats*), also perform certain national functions, such as issuing passports, identity cards, and work visas, as well as keeping track of foreigners and tourists. More important to politics is the administrative division of the country into prefectures, each with its own Prefect, a career civil servant, appointed by and reporting to the Interior Ministry in Paris. Prefects serve as representatives of the central state to every local government unit in the nation and are, consequently, the central state's source of information on all local political activities. In national electoral campaigns the Prefects provide vital political information to those in power, thus tending to strengthen candidates favored by the President or the President's party.

This brief description of four characteristic administrative agencies of the French state allows some broad conclusions about the French political system in general. Perhaps the most important is that it encourages everyone's very practical dependence on the central bureaucracy. Whether it be for an identity card, which all French people are required to carry on them at all times, or a driver's license, or a school diploma, or a university degree, or permission to install a septic tank or to receive medical services, or a ticket for a train or air trip—or for a thousand other things that are either vital or desirable—the private citizens must usually turn to some state agency to present their claims (in the proper form, of course), wait their turn, and often be told that they have come to the wrong place, or have made a mistake, or must fill out yet another form to get the right rubber stamp for whatever it is they want or need. Red tape (*paperasserie,* they call it) became a French disease long ago and is still epidemic there in peculiarly aggravating forms. So this very practical dependence on the state is accompanied in virtually every citizen's feelings by a sharp sense of annoyance, injustice, and even rebelliousness. There is a dividing line between people who are in government and politics and people who are not; on a personal level this sense of division goes beyond all the differences attributable to party loyalties and convictions that otherwise divide people both in and out of government. This primary dividing line is between "us" and "them"—"they" being all those in authority, whether elective or appointive. And from the point of view of those who do have positions of authority, there is often a more or less abstract nervousness about what "those people out there" really want. So continues an unending microcosmic struggle everywhere in France between the private person and the official, coloring the political system from its lowest to its highest reaches.

Pressure Groups

This antagonism is not, however, the only factor entering into relations between the citizen and the state. Having called the peculiar administrative spirit of the country statist, we must now discuss the way this spirit is reflected in the organization and modes of action of pressure groups. The statist tradition assumes that centralized government may rightfully oversee any and all private activities within France, with the view to promoting the public interest. That is, the state is not only thought of as a negotiator among conflicting interests, however important in actual practice this task may be. Rather, the state is considered to be the ultimate repository of the public interest, an interest that in the French view is not to be confused with the many necessary compromises among private interests, which state agencies may help to facilitate. Inevitably, a corresponding outlook develops within nearly all pressure groups. Although they are trying to get the best treatment possible for their members, pressure groups feel their own legitimacy inheres in the completeness of the claims they make. Consequently, French pressure groups tend to develop broad political points of view designed to justify bread-and-butter claims, since they know that in French eyes no merely self-interested argument can be seen as formally legitimate. In other words, the persuasiveness of French pressure groups depends not on the narrowness of their material interests, but rather on the way these material interests are fit into a broad political ideology corre-

sponding to the total range of the state's responsibilities.

Labor
The organization, or perhaps one might say the disorganization, of the French labor movement illustrates this point. Labor unions have long been considered by American political science as pressure or interest groups—groups that by definition pursue some particular interest of their own, with a view to maintaining or increasing their share of power and privilege at the expense of some other. Labor unions, for example, try to increase their share of profits specifically at the expense of owners, stockholders, and, more broadly, consumers in general. Like the AFL/CIO, with its customary preference for the Democratic party in the United States, the major French unions tend to have party affiliations. In France, however, these party affiliations are both closer and more tense than is the case in the United States. In the first place, there is no overarching union organization, like the Trades Union Congress in Great Britain, to mediate relations between unions and parties. Thus, the *Confédération générale du travail* (CGT) is linked more or less directly with the Communist party, and the *Confédération française et démocratique du Travail* (CFDT) with the Socialists. The *Confédération française des travailleurs chrétiens* (CFTC), representing Catholic workers' interests, was once linked loosely to the *Mouvement Républicain Populaire* (MRP), a Christian Democratic party, until the latter's virtual demise with the advent of the Gaullists. Naturally, the political parties would like to make effective electoral use of their respective union associations; naturally, the unions themselves have other interests than electoral ones. Even where their broad interests correspond, workers' unions and workers' parties inevitably differ in their respective approaches to

these broader goals. So there is a good deal of internecine squabbling in their relationships, reducing both party and union effectiveness.

This weakness is compounded by two factors; only a small proportion (perhaps 20 percent) of the total work force is unionized at all, and this 20 percent is split among many different trade and craft unions, each of which is strongly inclined to act on its own without taking into consideration the activities of others. Indeed, small autonomous unions are so numerous that the open shop exists in nearly all industries, and questions of representation and bargaining are so terribly complex that management almost always has the dominant position in negotiations. Combined with the general tendency of all organizations to pattern their goals in the broadest possible social terms, rather than simply in terms of bread-and-butter issues, these facts have meant that the French workers, who as a class are relatively prosperous, owe their share in the national pie far more to general legislation guaranteeing them a pension, health insurance, paid vacation, and the like, than to the ability of their unions to extract concessions directly from employers. Many of these legislatively guaranteed fringe benefits come from the Fourth Republic, when the civil bureaucracy was itself dominated by Socialists and when the Socialist parliamentary party was necessary to successive governing coalitions: legislation guaranteeing the rights of state workers opened the door to the protection of all workers.

Working-class access to the levers of power was considerably reduced, however, with the coming of the Fifth Republic. General de Gaulle thought of unions and other pressure groups as he did of parties: inherently illegitimate intermediaries between the state and the citizen. And with the reduction of parliamentary power and the tightening of party discipline among the Gaullists, who

have dominated parliament, interest groups have found influence with individual legislators to be of relatively little account. By strengthening the executive, President de Gaulle strengthened the departments and agencies of the bureaucracy, thus making it the preferred target for interest group pressure.

Yet the civil bureaucracy has been very selective in listening to the claims of private interests. Learning the bureaucratic language comes much easier to some groups than to others. For example, we do not find the business organization, the *Conseil national du patronat français* (CNPF), having to demonstrate in the streets or even engaging in general public relations programs in order to be heard where it counts. Many other kinds of interests, however, find that the state often turns a deaf ear to their claims and that their only recourse is to make a fuss, in hopes of attracting someone's attention. Two examples will illustrate this phenomenon.

Agriculture

The first comes from agriculture and suggests that the state sometimes acts on claims even when it is not listening to those who put them forth. Farm products are a vital part of the economy, as France not only is very nearly self-sufficient in staples but also earns much foreign exchange from the export of agricultural goods. This fact is not altogether pleasing to some national elites, who like to think of their nation as being at the forefront of industrial and technological progress. But it is a fact well recognized by economists in the Finance Ministry and reflected in the consistently hard bargains France has driven with the other members of the Common Market in negotiations at Brussels on farm prices. So in terms of effective government support, French agriculture does rather well. Yet thousands upon thousands of French farmers feel themselves to be neglected by Paris, and their principal organizations, unable to get routine access to government, encourage them to feel this way. Over the years the result has been periodic demonstrations in which roads are blocked with tractors and farm produce, crops and even animals are destroyed, fruit is given away to passing tourists, all in attempts to make the farmer's sense of injustice known to the public.

State Employees: Broadcasting

Another example may be drawn from the government monopoly of radio and television broadcasting, which is financed largely by funds raised from sales and use taxes on television receivers. Since, in this context, program content is not left to commercial interests, as in the United States, the questions of who programs and what should be the content of programming have long been matters of political dispute, not least among the state employees of the monopoly, *Radio-Télévision Française* (RTF), itself. The executive branch constantly intervenes both broadly and specifically in news programming and in the presentation of material that may affect the public's interpretation of the news, censoring outright certain figures whose views are considered inimical to the government in power.

During the Fourth Republic this intervention was rather diffuse and discreet, since the open manipulation of programming by one political group risked alienating other groups necessary to maintenance of the governing coalition. But during the Fifth Republic, in which the executive has enjoyed relative stability and the support of a relatively permanent majority of Gaullists and their allies among other right-of-center parties, this intervention has become more obvious and correspondingly more resented by employees of the service, who feel that

they should be treated as professionals, not as agents of the President's or the Premier's views just because they are civil servants.

The result has been an unending conflict, usually remaining subterranean, but occasionally breaking out into the open. During the events of May 1968, for example, many of the best-known television figures were transferred or dismissed outright because General de Gaulle considered their reporting of the events disloyal to himself and the Fifth Republic. Since the General's retirement, this continuing clash between the civil servants' professionalism and the executive's political needs has been reflected in twenty-four-hour strikes by RTF personnel, leaving the public nothing to watch. And these have been sufficiently troubling, at least to the image of the executive, so that Giscard d'Estaing felt it desirable to make an electoral campaign promise during his race for the presidency in 1974 to reform the broadcasting service in order to assure it of greater professional autonomy, like that of the British Broadcasting Corporation—a promise that has yet to be fully realized.

In sum, it appears that pressure groups in France, like society itself, are highly fragmented and compartmentalized, especially at the lower end of the scale of power and money. This fragmentation is the work of cultural history. It results from the felt need to justify the smallest economic claim by reference to some broad social vision and the consequent belief on the part of each organization that it is engaged in a zero-sum game with all the rest, even those smaller than itself. This situation is made to order for the centralization of power in Paris, since every group turns to Paris in hopes of satisfaction of its claims and frustration of the claims of its competitors. The agents of the central power are thereby convinced, not unreasonably, that they may pick and choose at will among those who importune them, since the likelihood of a concerted campaign for common goals is virtually nil.

Big Business

Thus, as a general rule under the Fifth Republic, it is big business interests that have had the most routine access to the levels of power. A sinister interpretation may of course be placed on this fact, and many ordinary French do so. But it should be remembered that for at least two hundred years, most elites in France have wanted to create a powerful industrial and technological society, organized on scientific principles, with efficiency and productivity as the highest goals. To such leadership, France's reputation as a producer of fine wines, perfumes, clothing styles, and leather goods is no satisfaction at all. Insofar as these things earn foreign exchange they are not objected to. But they have the wrong symbolism; the dominant leadership would far prefer to have France known overseas by the Concorde SST, computers, medical technology, and social systems in which all workers go about their daily tasks in the most efficient, productive, and uncomplaining manner imaginable. But the diversity of France still remains, perhaps paradoxically encouraged by the fact that every organized group tends to think of itself as representing the whole of a social vision about what France should be.

Conclusion

French political attitudes are torn, as we have seen, between high expectations of justice in the abstract and great cynicism about politics in practice, between the desire to get the whole power of the state in one's own hands and the fear of what would happen if one's opponents managed to get the whole power of the state in their hands. As a model of rationality and efficiency, the French theory of government proposes a system whereby those who have majority popular support should govern without checks and balances until they cease to have majority popular support. This model assumes an informed and intelligent electorate, freedom of speech and press, and free elections. But it makes no allowance for checks and balances in the internal workings of government itself. It sees no point, as America's founders did, in setting up political institutions so related to one another that internal friction and inefficiency were assured.

The historical practice of French government may be related, almost sequentially, to these attitudes in conflict. The Fourth Republic, with its endlessly shifting coalitions among parliamentary groups, was a period in which fear of one's political opponents appeared uppermost. Looking merely at the outward forms of its governmental institutions, one might conclude that there was no reason why the French parliamentary system could not have worked very much like the British. But the multiplicity of parties meant that the way in which the legislature and executive related to each other, to the administration, and to the public was in practice very different. The image of the parliamentary system of the Fourth Republic confirmed public memories of the Third: a parliamentary system in the context of French society produces revolving-door cabinets, on the one hand, and governmental inability to act effectively, on the other.

The widespread fear of a military coup d'état in 1958 undid the parliamentary system that, in the classic words of one of its founders, "divided Frenchmen the least" and brought General de Gaulle to power with a constitutional blank check. Thus the Fifth Republic, with its presidential system, came into being. The written constitution of this republic, like that of its predecessor, is a long and carefully wrought document. But so long as General de Gaulle was still President, the importance of its written provisions appeared secondary to the leadership of the man himself. With his retirement in 1969 (and death in 1971) the Fifth Republic entered upon a new stage in its political history—a period of the founder's successors. The first, President Georges Pompidou, had none of the General's popular support for legendary charisma. He made every attempt to reassure France that his presidency was continuing along the line established by the General, but his relative success in this task was largely guaranteed by his having inherited a Gaullist parliamentary majority from 1968, when the May events had again revealed how much easier it is to unite a French majority around fears than hopes. While fear may create a majority, it cannot

carry on the day-to-day business of politics. And so Pompidou's successor, Giscard d'Estaing, long ago had to orient his own political career around his own ideas, personality, and political performance, recognizing not only that General de Gaulle had at some time to leave the political scene but also that the period of "after de Gaulle" must sooner or later be invigorated with more than memories of a great man.

So we now turn to a political biography of President Giscard d'Estaing, whose career began in the Fourth Republic and led rapidly to the highest office in the Fifth. Its study should help to illustrate how the political scene in France is constantly changing on the surface, like the foliage of a tree, while the roots that nourish the tree develop at a slower pace.

3

Giscard's Early Years: From Childhood to Government

Family Background

Born on February 2, 1926, in Coblenz, Germany, where his father was financial director of the French High Commission in the Rhineland after World War I, Valéry Giscard d'Estaing seems to have been destined for a career as man of state long before his birth. On his mother's side his ancestry has been traced back to an illegitimate daughter of Louis XV, who reigned from 1715 to 1774. Among more recent maternal ancestors were Count Montalivet, Napoleon Bonaparte's Minister of the Interior in 1809, and his son, Camille, who later held several ministerial posts under King Louis Philippe. Giscard's maternal grandfather was Jacques Bardoux, who for most of his life was Deputy or Senator from Puy-de-Dôme, having almost inherited the parliamentary seat from his father, Angénor Bardoux, Minister of Education from 1877 to 1879. Though Jacques Bardoux never succeeded in getting

a ministerial portfolio himself because his conservative views never fit the needs of a governing coalition in the Third or Fourth Republics, his rural constituency nevertheless returned him to parliament again and again, much as if he had been a feudal lord representing his manor at court.

As for Valéry's father, Edmond Giscard, business was more his concern than was statecraft. The paternal genealogy is also less distinctive than the maternal. Despite appearances, the addition of d'Estaing to the family name does not mean that the Giscard family had an aristocratic lineage. The person from whom the name comes, Admiral d'Estaing, was a hero of eighteenth-century battles in India and North America against England. He was guillotined during the revolution, leaving no children, but being survived by a female cousin who was a distant ancestor to Edmond Giscard. Thus, when the latter applied in 1922 to the Council of State to have d'Estaing tacked on to his

127

own family name of Giscard, there was no legal difficulty about the matter, as there were no other persons with the name to object. The fact that Giscard's father should care to apply for and receive an aristocratic name for which he could claim no corresponding title gives perhaps a good indication to his social, not to mention his political, ideas. This curious circumstance did give rise in 1962 to a possibly apocryphal joke at Giscard's expense, made by President de Gaulle, whose noble lineage was not in doubt. As Minister of Finance, Giscard asked the President whether he might use his own name for an issue of treasury bonds he was then considering floating. The General replied, "H'mm, Giscard d'Estaing. . . . Yes, you're right. That should be an excellent name for borrowing." Giscard's younger brother, Olivier, who is a banker, financier, director of IBM Europe, and graduate of Harvard Business School, has some legitimate claim to the name because he, at least, has been elected representative from the town of Estaing in the Auvergne, where the family owns several properties.

Inherited Wealth

The Giscard-Bardoux clan has country properties, chateaux, town houses, and apartments in many different places. But since its various members have long had ambitions to serve—as well as direct—the state, they could hardly afford to nurture their ties to the provinces alone. When Valéry's parents returned to France from Germany two years after his birth, they went to live in the Auvergne in a small chateau that Edmond had just bought. This so-called Chateau de la Varvasse was a fifteenth-century priory, to which its previous owner had added two imitation fairy-tale towers, located in five acres of apple orchard. Full of fears in his early years, especially afraid of animals and the dark, Valéry was overprotected by his

Chateau de la Varvasse, where Valéry spent his early childhood

(Documentation *Le Crapouillot*)

mother and never played outside the extended family circle until he was ready for school. That date reached, however, the country would no longer do. His parents took him to their apartment in the most exclusive section of Paris.

Schooling

In this part of the capital, the parents had no hesitation about sending the boy to public school, since both his teachers and his fellow students were bound to be of appropriate social standing. Valéry received most of his secondary schooling at the Lycée Janson-de-Sailly in the wealthiest section of Paris. The German occupation little delayed his studies, for during that period his parents moved to another property they owned near Clermont-Ferrand, where Valéry attended tenth and eleventh grades at the Lycée Blaise Pascal. He then returned to Paris for his final year in high school to prepare for the *baccalauréat* examinations. Administered by the state, these exams are the door through which all must pass if they hope to obtain salaried positions in either government or private industry, or if they wish to go on to higher education.

Valéry's preparation for the baccalauréat exam was more than adequate. In spite of his exceptionally young age—sixteen—he was ready to take both the classical part, oriented to Latin, Greek, and philosophy, and the mathematical part. At a time when not more than a third of *lycée* students, which then represented hardly more than 25 percent of the school-age population, passed what they call the *bac*—even on a second try—Valéry sailed through both parts with flying colors. His parents had expected and, in fact, demanded no less. His father had already foreclosed another possible career for which Valéry was naturally gifted. At age twelve, he had been inspired by a passion for music by a young, blind piano teacher. Edmond Giscard's reaction to this interest was first violent, then subtle. After banging the keyboard cover on Valéry's fingers while the child was playing for his mother, he replaced the inspiring musician with a teacher who believed that music both began and ended with scale practice. The results were predictable, and the child's passion soon cooled. His talent for music was, however, only one gift among many, and it was perhaps not entirely wasted. It later enabled the political candidate Giscard to play the accordion at rallies and cafés during his electoral campaign and thus to appear more nearly a "man of the people," one to whom the life of ordinary citizens is not totally foreign.

In fact, of course, the luck of birth—not only natural endowment, but also social and financial situation—opened doors to a rapid advance in a public career. Politics and the desire for power were in his family's blood long before Giscard's appearance; so were money and business connections. Even events, over which neither he nor his family had any control, appear to have conspired to advance his career. How it provided vehicles for his rise will be described in later sections. Here, we shall see how, under his family's careful guidance, he was prepared to make use of political opportunities as they arose.

Considering his success in both classical and mathematical baccalauréat exams, all of French higher education lay open to him. He himself had chosen the mathematical part of the exams because he had long thought of a career in the French colonies, building roads and bridges. Such a career would have fit well with the idea of duty that his social class had instilled in him. And with a diploma in mathematics, he would have been able to enter what was then perhaps the most prestigious of all France's *grandes écoles,* Polytechnique, graduation from which would have assured him a good position in any private business or branch of public administration, either in France or in the overseas dependencies. But before any of these possibilities could develop, he found himself caught up in the Resistance movement.

Wartime Experiences
By the summer of 1943, Hitler's plans for the complete subjugation of Europe and Russia were in disarray. Several German divisions had already sunk into the abyss of Stalingrad, and British and American troops were occupying North Africa preparatory to the invasion of Italy. Within France, these changes in Nazi fortune had considerably strengthened the various Resistance groups, while the population as a whole had begun to despair less of Germany's eventual defeat.

Even the usual fence-sitters began to think it might be sensible to place a small bet with those who had been on the side of the liberation of France from the beginning as a matter of principle.

Thus it was that Giscard, in his eighteenth year, became a courier for the clandestine press, bringing to an end what he later told a journalist was the "anguish of trying to decide whether to participate or not in the events of the time." His parents were anything but happy about this particular form of participation, since the dangers involved were perhaps more evident to them than to Giscard. But it also is certain they weighed the advantages less and the dangers more heavily than did their son. Like many in the highest bourgeoisie of France, their broadest political concern was for the maintenance of a strong state; and it was part of the general opinion among this class at the time that Marshal Pétain, seconded by the German army, did in fact represent law and order—sufficiently to make private and tacit acceptance of the Vichy regime a morally and politically acceptable position. Wealth, of course, made prudent abstention from choosing between collaboration and resistance easier for them than for many others. But their abstention reflected the attitude of many Frenchmen at the time.

By becoming a courier, Giscard soon came into contact with men whose class and political opinions were very different from his own. As a consequence—and perhaps because of his youth, too—he went through a period of repudiating everything his parents stood for: the political right, wealth, the bourgeois way of life, and business. In spite of all the shaping of his political destiny by generations of ancestors, he had at this time only the vaguest of political ideas, made up of generalities and abstractions capable of being neatly labeled "good" and "bad."

Over the strenuous objections of his family, he planned to leave France for England in order to join the Free French under General de Gaulle. But his contact man was caught and executed by the Germans before the flight could take place. By then the liberation of Paris was at hand. The parents begged their son to return immediately to his studies so that he could prepare for the entrance exam to Polytechnique. But Giscard refused. Further, he refused their offer to find him a safe spot in the Liberation forces under General de Lattre. Instead, he hitchhiked to the French army, which had just debarked in Provence, and joined a tank corps, most of whose units were composed of Arabs from North Africa. With that group he was engaged in several battles against the Germans, including one in which his tank was hit by a shell and caught fire, killing one of the men aboard and burning Giscard's face. He returned from Germany with a croix de guerre and a Bronze Star from the American command under which his tank corps had been operating.

Grandes Écoles

Training at ENA

The winter of 1945 found him back at school, cramming for the entrance exam to Polytechnique, which he passed in the fall of 1946. He entered Polytechnique immediately and graduated two years later, sixth in his class. This ranking gave him the right to choose his next step in public administration. He selected the National School of Administration (ENA), a new grande école that had been opened by the Provisional Government in 1945 to train higher civil servants in a manner more congenial to parliamentary institutions than had the old *École libre des sciences politiques.* Nationalized in 1945 and renamed the Institute of Political Studies, this formerly private school had dominated the formal training of higher civil servants in the 1920s and 1930s. It had tended to indoctrinate them with a conception of public duty that accorded closely with the interests of the great industrial firms, financiers, and bankers—in short, with the bourgeois interests of that period.

By the time he entered ENA in 1948, Giscard's intention had changed from bridge building in the colonies to entering the Finance Inspectorate, to which admission is restricted to only the best graduates. His youthful flirtation with socialist ideas now behind him, Giscard could devote his full energy and skills to the theoretical and apprenticeship training in public service provided by ENA, in the highly competitive company of young people almost as clever as he. Graduating again near the top of his class in 1951, he entered the Ministry of Finance as staff assistant in 1952 and was appointed an Inspector of Finance in 1954.

Thus some of the most basic steps in his extraordinarily rapid rise to power had already been completed by the time he reached the age of twenty-six. These steps were perhaps not determinative in themselves, but they did make available opportunities that he would not otherwise have had. And these opportunities were determinative. The relationship between education, opportunities, and power helps to explain why, despite nearly two hundred years of *"liberté, egalité, fraternité,"* France today still seethes with social resentments and political tensions.

Ever since Napoleon I, the French state has ostensibly opened careers to talent. This sounds like equality of opportunity. But of course, in practice, talent is not a pure gift from heaven; it requires education to become socially useful. And when Giscard was going through school, French education was rigorously elitist, as it still is today. First, it was geographically elitist: public schools in Paris were generally superior to schools in provincial cities, and schools in large provincial cities were generally superior to schools in small provincial cities. As for the countryside, there was no local secondary education available at all. Assuming that they had the drive and their parents' support, rural and small town children had to leave their homes when then entered the secondary system, to become boarders at some possibly distant city lycée. The break with family thus had to come early for such children, and it had to be made completely, so that the culture "down on the farm" would not taint the bookish culture the system taught.

Nor were workers' children much better able to advance than those of farmers, even though they were more likely to be located near a city lycée. For France has always treated education as learning how to deal wholly in abstractions. The long adherence to classical—and dead—languages was an indication of this tendency. Good thinking was taught without reference to personal experience, so when the capacity to learn Latin and Greek finally was given up as a touchstone for talent just a few years ago, its place was promptly taken by an even more abstract subject—mathematics. Secondary school students in France today are offered, in practice, more than five different routes of preparation for the baccalauréat, including those represented by classical languages, modern languages, social sciences and history, philosophy, and mathematics. But ambitious middle-class parents know well that only the last offers any real chance of their children's success in passing the entrance exams of the grandes écoles and that only a diploma from one of these schools offers the opportunity to rise in the ranks of either civil service or business bureaucracies.

Elitism

So in both geographical and cultural senses, education has long been elitist in France. It is available to money and social class; that is, if it is perhaps more available to old money than to new, it is in any case available mostly to families of wealth. The reason is fairly clear: to be successful in a highly competitive school that emphasizes abstract thinking and ideas virtually to the exclusion of daily reality, students must be insulated from the ordinary world on a day-to-day basis. Few children can arrange such insulation for themselves. For most families it demands the constant vigilance of the parents, who understand its importance and are willing and able to make the sacrifices necessary to maintain it. Indeed, children must be convinced that academic work *is* the real world and that all of life outside school is merely illogical, sentimental, and in some measure unreal. This constitutes, of course, a form of moral education in itself. For middle-class children determined to succeed in competitive exams, regular work and no (fundamental) questions asked must be the basic rules. They are required to forget themselves in one sense in order to re-create themselves successfully in the terms that the system requires, in order to act on the promises of power and status that it makes for later life. For successful students, like Giscard, these rewards can come very early.

A brief description of the grandes écoles will clarify their function as an integral and, in some ways, symbolic part of the fast track for advancement in both private and public bureaucracies, especially the state's. The grandes écoles are not universities, nor do they provide the kind of education offered by universities. Nor are they schools of liberal arts. They are rather preprofessional schools,

specializing in a certain range of subjects. Polytechnique, for example, has a physics and engineering orientation. At present the most prestigious of the grandes écoles, it was created by Napoleon I to provide engineers for his armies. Even today students are formally incorporated in the military, receive pay, wear uniforms on special occasions, and owe either military service or payment to the state for their training upon graduation, since that training is provided at taxpayers' expense. Today, Polytechnique's reputation is based, not on service to the military, but on its graduates' contribution to rapid economic growth or productivity—growth "Japanese style," as the French call it—which has been basic public policy throughout the postwar period and especially since 1968.

Economic growth, it is assumed, is better supported by schools of a technical orientation, so the notion of grandes écoles now includes the study of electricity at Grenoble, mines and mining at Lille, business in Paris and Lyon, forestry and agriculture in schools around the country. And, of course, there are the Institute of Political Studies and ENA in Paris.

Despite the diversity of subject matter, all these schools have certain things in common. They admit students only by highly competitive examination, for which one or two years of intensive study, often at expensive private schools, is customary. They rank their students competitively. And they give their top graduates—as was Giscard at both Polytechnique and ENA—first choice of the best or most promising civil service jobs available. They are, in short, schools where one learns first and foremost that "nothing succeeds like success," that nothing is to be gained by questioning "the system," but that everything, rather, is to be gained by adopting its methods and style.

Under the circumstances of Giscard's rapid rise in and through this system, it is not difficult to see why he early gained a reputation for being rather cold and ruthless—a "computer on stilts" or, in the words of one of his later close and loyal political associates, Prince Michel Poniatowski, "a nice guy who was straightened out by Polytechnique."

A Foot in the Door

A member of his social class would not find many doors in politics closed under any circumstances, but his success at Polytechnique and ENA opened new doors to Giscard. The question is: Who was behind these doors? Where did they lead? That is to say, what people already in political life became useful in furthering Giscard's career? Certainly two men did more than any others to provide the groundwork for the Giscard career: Edgar Faure and Charles de Gaulle.

The first meeting with Faure took place in 1949 while Giscard was still at ENA; common acquaintances introduced them at a dinner party at the Palais Royal. At the time, Edgar Faure was a young (forty-one), up-and-coming Deputy, who had begun his career through the electoral, rather than the administrative, route. Soon after this first meeting, Faure was named by one of the more forgettable Premiers of the Fourth Republic to be Secretary of State for the Budget. This was during the period when the revolving-door cabinets made familiar during the Third Republic had again become the mark of postwar parliamentary practice. And Faure was beginning to show himself very clever at moving into the door as it turned. He became *ministrable,* which means that he was a bright and useful young man who thought that all political problems could be solved by clever economists like himself. Nominally left of center on the political spectrum, Faure was in practice a Keynesian of technocratic tendencies who preferred the maintenance of economic expansion even at the price of that persistent inflation which Giscard, as Minister of Finance, was later to call the "leukemia" of the French economy. Faure was also a member of the Radical Socialist party, which was then a party in name only. It had long since ceased to represent any particular views, much less radical or socialist ones, being little more than a disjointed and localized electoral machine committed—like all other French parties, including the Communist—to the defense of small private property.

Faure and Giscard much impressed each other, their conviction that all political problems were basically economic providing a common bond. Although there was no official relation between them in the next five years, they maintained frequent private contacts, which were, Giscard is reported to have said, as important in his political education as his later contacts with de Gaulle. This probably means that he found himself sympathetic to Faure's general Keynesian outlook. On the other hand, the two men represented different views on which economic solutions were applicable to political problems. Even then, Giscard was committed to the maintenance of the value of the franc as indispensable to sound policy and thought of a balanced state budget as the major support of its value.

Whatever their differences, when Faure was named Minister of Finance in July 1954 by Premier Mendès-France, he asked Giscard, who had by then been admitted into the Finance Inspectorate, to be his principal administrative aide. Both men regarded it as a highly fruitful collaboration. For Faure, however, it marked almost the apogee of his political career, while for Giscard it was just the beginning. This disparity of political fortunes was increasingly to separate the two men until, for a brief moment in the spring of 1974, they appeared as rival candidates for the presidency. Although both men were technocratic and pragmatic in their approach to political problem-solving, some political differences did distinguish them. It is worth noting Faure's appreciation of Giscard's orientation:

Valéry does have a profound sense of social justice. But he believes social justice can be realized only if there is a harmonious sharing of the wealth. In order to share wealth, however, you must first produce it. And in order to produce it you must have free enterprise.[1]

In Giscard's view, the strength of a nation lies in private wealth, which permits the state to tax for the benefit of those who do not have it, thus advancing productivity, social peace, and civil order.

A Bourgeois Marriage
Early in his career, Giscard had assumed this political position:

France wants to be governed from the center right. I shall place myself at right-of-center, and I shall one day govern France.[2]

It is entirely possible that this political orientation was a deliberate choice, for it can hardly be called irrational. Yet it is also the view of the social class to which Giscard was born. Moreover, this perspective was undoubtedly reinforced by his marriage in late 1952 to the former Anne-Aymone de Brantes, scion of another family at once aristocratic, rich, and powerful. One of the bride's grandfathers, a member of the Schneider family, had been owner and man-

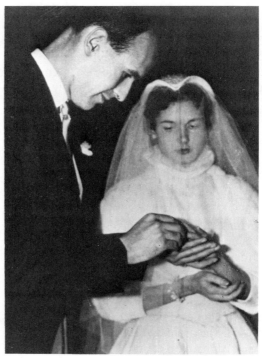

The marriage of Valéry Giscard d'Estaing and Anne-Aymone de Brantes in 1952

(Documentation *Le Crapouillot*)

aging director of le Creusot steel mills, once the largest in France, and an important member of the steel industry's former *Comité des Forges* (which during the 1930s had bought up controlling interests in two of France's leading newspapers, *le Temps* and *le Journal des débats,* in order to help purvey the merits of private property and the hatefulness of all forms of public regulation of economic enterprise).

In keeping with the manner of girls of her social class at the time, Anne-Aymone was not sent to a lycée nor prepared for competitive examinations, as her husband had been. On the contrary, she was educated at

[1] Quoted in François Lancel, *Valéry Giscard d'Estaing,* (Paris: Belfond, 1974), p. 44.
[2] Lancel, *Giscard,* p. 42.

134

a religious school and then in secretarial classes, as if her upbringing should reflect Napoleon's dictum that the "function of women is not to think but to believe." Their four children, two girls and two boys, have been raised in a less conservative way. Since her father's election to the presidency, the oldest daughter has held a post in the public information section of the Ministry of Foreign Affairs. During the electoral campaign of 1974 the face of the second daughter figured prominently in one of her father's campaign posters to indicate the candidate's understanding of youth. Using one's family publicly as campaign material is a political technique that was virtually unknown in France until Giscard did so in the spring of 1974. He claimed to have taken the idea from American politics, particularly from the Kennedy family. Perhaps he suspected that in comparison with those of the other candidates, his family looked especially appealing. His opponents, at any rate, even Socialist François Mitterrand, preferred to follow French tradition in the matter, keeping their families as much out of the public eye as Giscard's new style allowed. Even with the new style, the Giscard family members ended up by retaining as much of their private lives as they had when the race began, their campaign personalities being the product of public relations rather than of nature.

First Election
Service on Edgar Faure's Ministry of Finance staff gave Giscard a taste for electoral, as well as administrative, politics. Hardly had his ascent in the civil service ranks of the Finance Inspectorate begun when he decided to seek election as a Deputy from Puy-de-Dôme, the constituency of his maternal grandfather, Jacques Bardoux, who had more or less inherited the seat from his father, Angénor Bardoux. The occasion came in December 1955, when Faure, then Premier,

tried the dramatic and, until then, unused device of dissolving the National Assembly in hope of the electorate's being able to produce a more coherent legislature through general elections. At that stage of the Fourth Republic's brief history, parliamentary politics were more unstable than usual. Faure's Cabinet had followed after that of Mendès-France, who had succeeded in extricating France from Indochina, but whose coalition had fallen apart after only seven and one-half months. Mendès-France had been probably the most memorable parliamentary leader in the Fourth Republic, but his obvious popular appeal had particularly nettled the Assembly, ever jealous of its own supposed governing powers. So Faure's attempts to govern in Mendès-France's wake produced virtually no policy at all.

Election day was to be January 2, 1956, so Giscard traveled to Puy-de-Dôme to campaign, thinking that his family's reputation in the region and his grandfather's unvarying success in being reelected, would assure his own success. This assessment of his future constituency ultimately proved correct, but his immediate difficulty derived from an unexpected source. Jacques Bardoux, though eighty-four years old, saw no particular reason why he should withdraw his own, assuredly successful candidacy just to make way for a young whippersnapper like Giscard. Ultimately, blood proved thicker than water, at least from the young man's point of view. Giscard's parents spared no effort to convince the old parliamentarian to retire from active politics immediately, and he finally acceded to their pleading. In withdrawing from the race, however, Bardoux refused to endorse his grandchild's candidacy.

Casting about for the help of another prestigious figure, Giscard's thoughts turned to Faure. But Faure also refused endorsement. Giscard had been useful as an economic adviser, so long as he remained in the position as expert from the Finance Inspectorate. But Faure knew Giscard's conservatism well, and endorsement of a man holding such opinions would have taken a great deal of explaining to Faure's own left-of-center public. So Giscard had to undertake the campaign in Puy-de-Dôme with little but his good looks, fortune, sharp intelligence, superb education, pretty wife, and accordion to help him. He neither had nor needed a party affiliation.

Party affiliation indeed meant little in Puy-de-Dôme, which—apart from Clermont-Ferrand, home of Michelin tires—is an agricultural district. Elections there are more likely to turn on the price of milk or the possibility of getting a village snowplough than on ideology. There is really only one philosophy among the small farmers: the preservation of their small holdings. And this point of view came without struggle to Giscard, who had long since declared his conviction that the center right was the perspective from which most Frenchmen wanted to be governed. So without party platform, but with some suggestions about how the

The tyro campaigner in his first constituency, Puy-de-Dôme, in 1956

(Documentation *Le Crapouillot*)

local farmers might increase the value of their produce by making cheese instead of selling raw milk, Giscard won his first election handily, just one month before his thirtieth birthday. He thus began a mandate in the old parliamentary system the very year that the first flickerings of the war for Arab independence in Algeria came to public attention. But in becoming a Deputy in the National Assembly of a republic that was to be put to death in 1958, Giscard had not bet on a dying horse. On the contrary, he had, as usual, carefully hedged his future.

First, he always had his status as a Finance Inspector to fall back on. Thus, even if his political luck should not carry him to the top, he would still retain an excellent chance of being appointed a financial and economic manager in some public agency. The second hedge came with his seating in the 1956 Assembly. Without party affiliation, he was free to move in the Assembly where he chose. That place was going to be somewhat right of center. But he was in the position of being able to offer his support instead of having it merely taken for granted. And as several parliamentary groups were then trying to form, each needing the required minimum of thirty members, he was solicited by several. One of these, satisfyingly enough, was led by Edgar Faure, who was trying to create a group to be called the *Rassemblement* of Left Radicals and was short just one member. His appeal to Giscard was summarily refused. Giscard chose to join instead a parliamentary group called Independents and Peasants for Social Action (IPAS).

Parliamentary Life

The political views of this group were, in the French context, clearly to the right. The peasant side of the group, of course, represented private agricultural interests. And in the French world, where big agribusiness and small farmer could more or less join

forces politically, the IPAS could claim, without too many contradictions, to be representing the interests of both. On the independent side lay industrial, banking, and financial interests, with which Giscard clearly felt comfortable. As for the social action part of the name, that meant working to get state aid for these interests. The parliamentary leader of the IPAS at the time was Antoine Pinay, who had once been Minister of Finance and whose public reputation rested on his having taken some vigorous and temporarily effective anti-inflationary measures in the early 1950s. So Giscard was personally introduced to Pinay by none other than Jacques Bardoux, the grandfather whom Giscard had peremptorily retired, but who was apparently not one to bear a grudge against his own flesh and blood.

Word soon went around the Assembly that Giscard was likely to be among the comers. He even succeeded in satisfying Assembly traditions by limiting his activities and speeches to technical matters he had studied so that he appeared rather as an expert than as an ideologue, more as a man of facts than of philosophical commitments. He showed little inclination to attend floor debates or take part in rhetorical contests. But he prepared his appearances before the Finance Committee (equivalent in the United States to the combined Ways and Means and Appropriations Committees) with great care. At the same time he strengthened his local support by getting himself elected as representative of the canton Rochefort-Montagne to the General Council of Puy-de-Dôme and as Municipal Councilor of the village of Chanonat. In November 1956, he was chosen to serve on a parliamentary delegation at the eleventh session of the General Assembly of the United Nations in New York, to taste international negotiations.

But there is no doubt that it was in the

committees of the National Assembly that he made his greatest impact. His effectiveness came from his technical commentaries before the Assembly's Finance Commission, at which he appeared, in the words of one journalist, as

imperious, absolutely unflappable, speaking as if from a stage, sometimes for three hours at once, without notes, sovereignly dominating the most difficult subjects, lining up budgets, analyzing economic forces, pointing out various perspectives, juggling figures, fiddling with his glasses, never faltering on a single word, a single sentence, or the slightest detail, and silencing even his most recalcitrant opponents with a deluge of facts.[3]

Outside of committees, his parliamentary activities led to the formation of an informal study group of new Deputies, of a variety of political shades, whose common bond was that they were all under the age of forty and personally ambitious. This last trait being the most obvious of their characteristics, it was not long before the older members of the Assembly began to think of them as the "young wolves" and of Giscard as the one with the longest teeth. The experience of organizing the "under forties" was in fact a dry run for the later and more important group organized under the name of Independent Republicans, which was to become the party vehicle for his ascension to the presidency.

Yet Giscard's first two years in the Assembly were not marked by the kind of success that journalists and newspapers of the time would note. Although his grand-

[3] Albert-Paul Lentin, *Les héritiers du Général* (Paris: Denoël, 1972); cited in Lancel, *Giscard,* p. 57.

father Bardoux had introduced him to the leaders of the center right, the 1956 elections had not produced an Assembly favorable to conservatives. Pinay was himself unable to form a governing coalition, and Giscard's chance to become a Minister during the Fourth Republic thus evaporated.

In the meantime, the Algerian struggle for independence came increasingly to dominate, and to poison, French political life. The European colony in Algeria had always played an important part in economic policies of the Third and Fourth Republics. Now history was about to assign it a direct political role as well.

The events arose from a number of different sources, among which were both the practical inability of the French to suppress the Algerian Liberation Front and the unwillingness to grant it the kind of recognition that could eventually have led the way to accommodation. It was the European colony's fear of vacillation on the part of the French government, strengthened by repeated ministerial crises that were ever more difficult to resolve, that finally led the colony's leaders, on the night of May 13, 1958, to declare the formation in Algiers of an independent Government of National Safety. This body was committed in the first instance to mastering the Arab revolt and, as a necessary corollary to this ambition, to mastering the government in Paris to assure a sufficient supply of fresh troops and arms for the purpose. The Fourth Republic and its constitution were about to be replaced by the Fifth and its grand master, Charles de Gaulle. This story is so closely related to that of Giscard's ultimate rise in French political life and to the possibilities of action that the presidency offers that it must now be sketched.

4

Giscard's Middle Years: Political Manners and Morals of the Fifth Republic

De Gaulle as President

With the revolt of the European colony in Algiers, backed by some of the highest military officers in the French army then engaged in pacification in North Africa, the last parliament of the Fourth Republic panicked. In the throes of its final ministerial crisis, it immediately elected as Premier a nonentity whose function was to hold the fort until such time as Charles de Gaulle could be persuaded to accept leadership once more, to become the savior of France again, as he himself had claimed to be during the period of the Vichy regime and the liberation from the German occupation.

Seizure of Power
The developments of 1958 were already proving themselves to be much to the General's expectations. Having always been one of the Fourth Republic's liveliest critics, he

was sure that France was essentially ungovernable under a parliamentary system. As noted earlier, he had in 1947 formed a broad movement, called the *Rassemblement du peuple français,* with which to undermine the uncertain stability of the Fourth Republic in its earlier years. So it was not surprising that he had carefully prepared for the later crises he was sure would arise. In May 1958, the key to his coming to power was his ability to reassure both the French military in Algeria and the French public at home that he had their respective, and opposite, interests at heart.

In Algiers his men had already been active as catalysts in the revolt of May 13. When General Salan stood on the balcony of Government House in Algiers to announce to the assembled European multitudes the formation of the Government of National Safety and found himself wondering whom to propose to the crowd's enthusiasm, one of de Gaulle's agents was at his side, whispering, "Vive de Gaulle!" At a loss for other names, General Salan promptly took the suggestion, and de Gaulle's political support in Algeria was assured at a critical moment.

As for France, support there was quickly mobilized, too. General de Gaulle could pose, with some justification, as a bulwark of legitimacy against the military putsch in Algeria—the only man with sufficient moral authority to keep the dissident officer corps under control and to prevent a right-wing takeover of the enfeebled French democracy. So the French National Assembly obligingly voted to make way for de Gaulle on the only terms he would accept—permission to write the kind of constitution for France that he wanted.

Thus entered onto the scene in the rebellious spring of 1958 a leader in French history whose curious mixture of personal ambition and devotion to the national welfare shaped French politics for the better part of a generation and created the Fifth Republic's office of the presidency, which Giscard was so ardently to seek almost from the moment of its inception.

This presidential office is both more and less than a symbol. It is a symbol of the victory of one traditional conception of French political needs as against another. At the same time, its powers are very real, even though their use depends greatly on the person who occupies the office and the nature of the political circumstances.

We have already seen something of the symbolic value of the office. It reflects a broad political conviction among the French that they are ungovernable by traditional parliamentary means: they need a strong hand at the top to keep order and to protect the national interest from the partial, vested, and private interests that are thought to find characteristic reflection in Parliament and would otherwise tend to dominate political life. At the heart of this conviction is the feeling that no compromise of private interests can represent the national interest, which must go beyond a mere accord among existing political forces to express the aspirations of France as a nation. When de Gaulle spoke about his "certain idea of France," it was to this sentiment he referred, and the French public understood.

A "Certain Idea of France"

But, of course, there is paradox about a national commitment to a certain idea of France being expressed through one man. If the nation needs common aspirations, can this need be fulfilled simply by appointing a strong man whose own personal idea of France becomes the object of passive acceptance by the rest of the citizens? Is not some form of active democratic and participatory input required if the need is to be met in a genuinely common way? The answer to this question has made detestation of one-man rule as much an element of the French political tradition as the desire for a strong regime. For in practice, the strong man's order is a passive order, in which private interests are perhaps protected to some extent from assault by other private interests. But at the same time, the common idea of France receives so little opportunity for expression that it is soon forgotten. Thus has arisen a countervailing thrust for a parliamentary system that through public debate may become a seedbed for the growth of common aspirations. In comparison to this system, one-man rule, though less confused, is at best negative in character.

General de Gaulle's occasional attempts to listen to the public, particularly by way of his referenda, were meant to overcome the tensions between those opposing political sentiments. But the desire to have security, accompanied by de Gaulle's frequent threats to resign immediately if any of his referendum proposals were defeated at the polls, always foreclosed the possibility of a genuine exchange of views. Under de Gaulle, political dialogue was far more a tacit understanding than a give-and-take between the public and the executive.

This tacit understanding involved three elements. The first and most obvious concerned the maintenance of order. Here General de Gaulle was given, and exercised, almost a free hand. His power and authority were based first on historical memories; for he had been the liberator of France, the leader above party and partisanship, the prophet who foresaw the evolution of political forces and thereby mastered them without being mastered by them. His control was also facilitated, however, by his attackers, particularly that group of European colonists and dissident army officers who unsuccessfully attempted yet another coup d'état in 1962 and his assassination in a futile struggle to keep Algeria French. For although by many standards slow to do so, General de Gaulle did finally back the idea of self-determination for Algeria in 1960; combined Algerian and French referenda to that effect took place in 1962. The official announcement of this policy in 1960 set in motion an increasingly violent opposition by European diehards in Algeria, led by the Secret Army Organization (OAS) under General Salan, who thus entered into rebellion against the very man he had helped bring to power only two years before.

The OAS's principal means of action included terrorism in Algeria and attempted assassinations in France, including several dramatic tries on the life of de Gaulle, who in one instance escaped narrowly when his car was machine-gunned at a Paris intersection. Even those who disliked de Gaulle's rule nevertheless tended to think him preferable to the OAS terrorists and hard-liners from Algeria, whose conception of politics was far more concerned with the maintenance of a dying colonial order in Algeria than with the national interest, as the vast majority of people living in France understood it. So in the context of French public opinion, de Gaulle had the advantage of posing as a leader in the middle—between the extremes of military and colonial reaction on the right and communism on the left.

The second element of the tacit understanding between the French and the General came out of his foreign policy. The basic theme of this policy was creation and maintenance of a realm of diplomatic independence, wherein France was free to define and to be responsible for her own national interests, without consulting Washington, or the Pentagon, at every turn. In practice this meant weakening France's ties with NATO, delaying England's entrance into the Common Market, and undertaking detente with Eastern Europe, the Soviet Union, and China, while asserting France's interests with her former colonies in Africa by means of economic and military aid.

It is probably true that the majority of French people were less enthusiastic about the practice of this policy of "grandeur" than was de Gaulle. But the broad spirit of it appealed to them strongly, especially as the previous decade of economic growth had made them aware of both the increasing Americanization of their lifestyles and their growing dependence on the American dollar as their medium of international exchange. Added to their perceptions of a milder form of Cold War and the possibility of maneuver involved in the growing split between China and the Soviet Union, they generally found reason for supporting de Gaulle's foreign policy of independence.

Questions of Social Justice

The third element in France's tacit understanding with de Gaulle and his Fifth Republic is the most difficult to describe because it concerns peculiarly French conceptions of, and aspirations for, social justice. It is also the element most influenced by the class and political temperament represented by Giscard. We have already noted that France has a tradition of conflict over this issue: by some, the theory of social justice is perceived to be separated from its practice only by realities that time is bound to overcome, whereas by others they are seen as inherent opposites. Jean-Jacques Rosseau once characterized the opposing views in terms of those whom he called, respectively, *subject* and *citizen*:

The subject boasts of public law and order, the citizen of the freedom enjoyed by the individual. The first prefers the security of property, the second that of the person. The first will maintain that the harshest government is the best, the second the gentlest. The first wants to see crime punished, the second to make crime impossible. The first thinks it is fine thing that a country should be feared by its neighbours, the second prefers that they should ignore it. The first is happy when money circulates, the second demands bread for the people.[1]

Ancient politicians incessantly talked about morals and virtue, those of our time talk only of business and money.[2]

The difference between these two perspec

tives indicates a difference of attitudes toward public purposes. If one has great hopes for the moral development of humanity, if one thinks individuals capable of learning how to put the welfare of the community ahead of private interests, then the development of this willingness must be the goal of political life. Every citizen must be committed to a form of justice by which every other is equally a beneficiary of this moral education. If, on the other hand, one thinks that the members of the human race are more reliably selfish than generous and that stability depends on human qualities most commonly displayed, then it has often seemed reasonable (at least until the rise of environmental concerns) to try to turn the problem of social justice into a pursuit of economic growth, on the theory that active concern by all citizens for their own interests would contribute to the aggregate well-being of society, whether they individually cared about it or not.

It is clear why there is a conflict between these two approaches to justice. The latter, "trickle-down" approach depends for its efficacy on stimulating the very sentiments of self-interest that the other theory of justice would repress in order to cultivate compassion toward others. While in the French political tradition these opposing viewpoints have often been exploited in conflicts between right and left, they may indeed identify poles toward which all political sentiments are oriented, even within the minds and hearts of individual French people. For is not the French citizen characterized, as the old joke says, as someone "who wears his heart on the left and pocketbook on the right"?

De Gaulle's Balancing Act
With respect to these poles of left and right, General de Gaulle held a marvelously ambivalent position. There was much in his

[1] *Social Contract,* book III, ch. 9, E. Barker, ed. (New York: Oxford University Press, 1960), p. 249.
[2] "Discourse on the Sciences and Arts," in Roger D. Masters, ed., *The First and Second Discourses* (New York: St. Martin's Press, 1964), p. 51.

political stance to recall the radical, the revolutionary, the man of the left whose basic aspiration for political life is an ideal of social solidarity, above parties and private interests. This ideal often found reflection in de Gaulle's rhetorical disgust at the pettiness of the people whom history had called him to govern. But the other side was also there, in terms of a dependence on the alliance with the managers of France's economic and financial affairs. Thus it was that de Gaulle performed a balancing act, or at least tried to perform one. And in the measure that this appearance was convincing to the greater part of his fellow countrymen, his regime enjoyed the essence of legitimacy.

But General de Gaulle was called on to perform a balancing act in another sense, too. On the one hand, he needed to convince the public that his Fifth Republic represented a degree of constitutional stability that it had never before known, and could never hope to know, under a parliamentary system. On the other, he had to show them that his own person was the key to the regime's stability; he feared that if they came to believe too much in the success of his institutions, they would find him superfluous.

In this enterprise he had to prove that he was above his own creation, that since he had made the institutions of the Fifth Republic, he could just as well remake them whenever it seemed desirable to him to do so. He was thus always engaged in an implicit struggle with his own past work. This is one reason why the device of the referendum figured so importantly in his presidency. It demonstrated publicly that he could revise his constitution whenever he cared to appeal to the people.

He was not dependent upon referenda alone to prove his superiority to the constitution he had drawn up, however. The very existence of the Communist party helped to serve the same purpose. However suitable

the institutions of the Fifth Republic might appear in the light of de Gaulle's presidency, the danger of a Communist's winning the presidency by popular vote was clear to virtually all noncommunist electors: an office that was reasonably safe in the hands of a person of liberal disposition could become a terrible thing in the hands of a possible tyrant. For this reason de Gaulle made the Communist party stand as a symbol for all opposition to him. It was not his intention to give legitimacy to his adversaries; they were by definition disloyal not merely to himself, but, more fundamentally, to his idea of France. And yet, precisely because of the use to which de Gaulle put it, the Communist party became an institutional part of the Fifth Republic, as useful to political stability in the person of its first President as any other state institution.

The Opposition and Its Conflicts
De Gaulle's attitude in this respect became determinative, as it was for so many other things, including both the form the political opposition has since tried to take and the strategy Giscard was to develop in his own pursuit of the presidency. A brief history of the French left, and especially that of the relations of the Socialist (SFIO) and Communist parties, will help to show why.

The French socialist movement goes far back into the nineteenth century, with antecedents at once revolutionary, utopian, and Marxist. By the last decade of that century, the movement's future looked dim: their formal espousal of revolutionary doctrine precluded participation in the governments of the Third Republic, but the possibility of a workers' revolution seemed fairly remote to increasing numbers of French socialists. The same problem was being faced by all the Marxist parties of Europe at the same time. As the number of their adherents grew, so grew the potential advantage of participation in whatever political institutions were available in their respective countries. This perception of potential advantage ultimately led to a fundamental revision of revolutionary schema, along with the adoption of the generic name *social democrats* to indicate that although perhaps still Marxist in their broad sympathy with the working classes and their analysis of the contradictions of capitalist society, these parties would in fact work for change through existing parliamentary institutions instead of concentrating their efforts on an unlikely social revolution. In short, socialism tended more and more toward reform and less and less toward violent overthrow of capitalist institutions.

World War I was to prove a watershed for this revisionism, however. Along with the familiar idea of the workers' revolution there came another item of Marxist faith: the working classes of all nations were fundamentally allied against the capitalist classes. It was thus taken almost for granted among socialists that the existence of substantial social democratic parties in the parliaments of all Western European nations was going to make war impossible because workers from one country would never be persuaded to fight workers from another. Yet when mobilization in 1914 came, the working classes of the respective European nations went—if not always with enthusiasm, at least willingly enough—to kill and be killed by their working-class brethren on the orders of those very capitalist and bourgeois classes whose authority they had long challenged in theory.

The shock of this state of affairs was far from being digested by social democrats in France when the Russian Revolution occurred, accompanied by the refusal of the Soviets to continue in a war that had already bled Russian workers and peasants white. This double trauma produced a great split in the French left that continues to this day.

It was formally recognized at the congress of the French left at Tours in 1920, in which the French Communist party (CP[F]) came into existence, with support from a majority of the delegates present. This new party repudiated revisionism and social democracy following a hard line on the absolute necessity of a violent overthrow of capitalism in every nation.

Although the Communists were never wholly outlawed by the Third Republic as an avowedly revolutionary party, their leading members were subject to constant legal harassment, which served only to strengthen their conviction that the revolutionary path was the right one. As a consequence, social democrats were inevitably displaced from the left and increasingly abandoned their ostensibly radical talk for parliamentary action. Indeed, ironically for a supposedly Marxist party, the French Socialist party during the 1920s and 1930s became in substantial part one of petty bureaucrats and teachers in the state schools, whose theoretical commitment was to international peace and whose practical commitment was to improved salaries and working conditions. In their new place they came increasingly close to putting on the mantle of power legally as the years of the Third Republic passed.

The chance came in the early 1930s with the collapse of a center-right coalition ministry, after a series of financial scandals culminating with the mysterious death of one Stavisky, a chief figure in them. It was widely believed at the time that he had been murdered by the French police, on orders from the conservatives in power, in order to forestall any embarrassing revelations he might make in court about their financial shenanigans. Since this event came to a head in France just as the full weight of the Great Depression was felt, a mood of profound concern gave the major Socialist leader of the time, Léon Blum, a chance to form a Cabinet.

Based on a left-of-center parliamentary alliance of Left Radicals (a party of moderates, despite the name), Communists, and his own Socialist party, this coalition was known as the Popular Front.

In the whole dreary period of revolving-door cabinets during the 1930s, Blum's was the only one to leave its mark on legislative history. In spite of its very short life, his government produced a series of broad social reforms including bringing the banking system under public control; recognizing collective bargaining; enacting old-age pensions, the forty-hour workweek, and guaranteed annual vacations for workers; and introducing systematic government intervention to reduce unemployment. But Blum's coalition collapsed in 1936 when the Communists withdrew their support, thus throwing doubt among Socialists and other leftist groups as to the Reds' real intentions. So the Popular Front left very ambiguous results and memories.

Some thought it showed that the Communists were willing to relegate violent revolution to the background and to cooperate with existing parliamentary institutions to define and protect specific working-class interests. Others considered the Communists' abrupt defection from the Popular Front to be proof of their willingness to put doctrine ahead of bread on the working person's table. Meanwhile, events in the Soviet Union suggested still a third possibility: that French Communists were merely a tool of the Kremlin. For immediately after the fall of the Blum Cabinet, the notorious Moscow trials began, by which Stalin brought about the systematic purging of the old Bolsheviks, leaving him sole master of Russia. The French Communist party was put in an embarrassing situation by the revelations of torture and brainwashing made throughout these trials. To the extent that its members looked to the Kremlin as their

Vatican and to Stalin as their pope of international communism, they generally refused to see what the dictator's purposes were, pretending that he was merely weeding out the corrupted and the revisionists from Soviet political life, as Stalin claimed. It was still too early for most French Communist party members to face up to the possibility that communism as an ideal was being corrupted in Moscow or that at the very least there was a difference between Stalinism and communism.

The second and even greater shock to the French Communists came with the signing of the 1939 non-aggression pact between Hitler and Stalin. This accord gave Hitler permission for his attacks upon Poland and, later, Western Europe, by ensuring that the Soviet Union would not enter the war to create the kind of second front that had been the undoing of the German armies in World War I. Even after the invasion of France in the spring of 1940 and the collapse of the French army, French Communists officially pretended they were bound by Stalin's agreement with Hitler. It was not until Hitler invaded Russia in July 1941 that they came to oppose the Nazi occupation of northern France.

Hence, in French noncommunist opinion in general, there arose the feeling that the French Communist party was far more responsive to the Kremlin's interests than to France's. And in the postwar period this sentiment was in no way weakened by the Soviet-backed "revolution" in Czechoslovakia in February 1948, which installed a one-party Communist dictatorship there. Thus, when the winter of 1948 brought a series of Communist-led coal miners' strikes in the pits of northern France—though based on what certainly were justifiable local conditions—a Socialist Minister of the Interior, Jules Moch (later France's representative to United Nations disarmament conferences) got public support for using the force of police and army against the strikers, defeating both the strikers and their grievances summarily. Thus was reconfirmed the deep split between the two officially Marxist parties of France, the Socialists and the Communists. At the same time, the virtual exclusion of Communists from all political participation in any coalition was also confirmed, in spite of the facts that more than a quarter of the French electorate continued to vote Communist and that the second largest group in the National Assembly—although far from a majority—was then made up of Communist Deputies.

Since the formation of the French Communist party in 1920, its formal participation in a Cabinet has been limited to the period 1945–1947, when de Gaulle's Provisional Government recognized the Communists' important role in the Resistance by granting a few portfolios to Communists. But these Ministers of the Fourth Republic were forced out of the government in May 1947 as a result of their voting against a new wage policy recommended by their erstwhile associates in the Ramadier Cabinet. Not to have voted against that wage policy would have alienated them from their power base among industrial workers. Since then no Communist has held national office in either the Fourth or Fifth Republics, a fact that reflects the deep alienation from the state that has characterized the French industrial worker since the beginning of the industrial revolution.

Later opportunities for the French Communist party to mark its independence formally from Moscow—the revelations contained in Khrushchev's secret speech in 1957 and the outright Soviet suppression of the revolts in East Berlin in 1953 and in Hungary in 1956—were passed up by the official leadership of the party, although notable supporters, like Jean-Paul Sartre, vigorously criticized the Kremlin for its role in Hungary. So right up to the fall of the Fourth Republic, the Communist party remained an outcast in the French political system, a fact of enormous political and social significance in light of its consistently large electoral support. Finally, under the first legislative elections of the Fifth Republic, by some gerrymandering and a new single-member district system of representation, de Gaulle even succeeded for a time in reducing the number of Communist Deputies in the Assembly to ten.

The exclusion of the Communist party from the governing power of the Fourth Republic set the stage for General de Gaulle's use of the symbols of anticommunism. His constitutional style, even more than his constitution, was presidential, meaning not only that he always pictured himself as the leader of the nation, above all parties and partisanship, but also that he particularly identified himself as the only effective dike against a revolution in France itself. In September 1958, shortly after he came to power, he referred to himself as "above the political struggles, a national arbiter." In 1962 he said of himself that he was entrusted with the "destiny of France and of the Republic," while in 1964 he referred to himself as the "source" of all power. Under the circumstances, it is not surprising that in 1966 about 60 percent of the French people regarded him as having set up a regime of personal power.

Personal Power and Ideology

Two Sources of Power

In some democratic nations such a judgment would have to be taken as unqualified criticism. This is not always so in France, however. Two factors have always given some legitimacy to personal power there, especially under such circumstances as those which made de Gaulle Chief of State. The first of these are familiar enough to Americans: a combination of political apathy and complete privatism. It is an attitude characterizing a very substantial proportion of the French electorate, especially in that part of the political spectrum vaguely associated with the center. In turning this part of the electorate into his own political capital, de Gaulle found that the French Communist party came in very handy.

First, its revolutionary doctrine and its refusal to dissociate itself not only from Moscow but even from Stalinism made it a perfect symbol of evil for those who thought of politics primarily in terms of law and order. Second, the Communist party has long been associated both in the minds of its own members and in public opinion generally with parliamentary, rather than presidential, institutions. Even today, when they have recently supported the Socialist candidate, François Mitterrand, for President, Communists are still seen as more hearty defenders of the parliamentary system than of the Fifth Republic. Third, there is the feeling that somehow the Communists are simply old-fashioned in almost all respects, organizationally and doctrinally. Their assumed preference for the institutions of the Fourth Republic in part supports this feeling. But their own internal structure also contributes to it, for that structure is typical of heavy-handed and over-centralized bureaucracies in general and, ironically, of the French state bureaucracy in particular. And this characteristic of their organization is underlined by their tendency to conserve very shopworn Marxist phrases in their official pronouncements, often applied without much discrimination to very disparate political, social, and economic phenomena. There is a good deal of lively Marxist and leftist thought in France today, but it is very little nourished by the French Communists—any more, indeed, than it is by the Soviet Communist party. This state of affairs is made only too clear to the average noncommunist Frenchman by the proliferation of little political groups—the famous *groupuscules* first brought to public attention by the events of May 1968—that repudiate the French Communist party in the names of a truer Marxism, Maoism, Trotskyism, or leftism in general. Even the Unified Socialist Party (PSU), a splinter of the SFIO brought to life by Mendès-France in 1968 and for a time led by Giscard's one-time associate in the Finance Ministry, Michel Rocard, has done more for the quality of recent political debate on the left in France than has the CP(F). So in all these ways, the Communist party offered itself as a large target for de Gaulle's criticisms of all that was wrong, rigid, unimaginative, inefficient, and not in keeping with his idea of modern France.

The second factor in apparent French approval of de Gaulle's exercise of personal power is perhaps related not to too little knowledge of politics, but to too much. More exactly, it is related to too long a historical memory. The French are necessarily aware that many regimes and many political dreams have come and gone and that none has ever been able to win the permanent or universal assent of humanity. Under these circumstances, it is easy to suppose that even laws have little that is inevitable or natural about them. They are at their best expressions of passing human conventions that one challenges, or even examines, only at the peril of all social order. From this point of view society is a social contract that specifically forbids the illusion that politics involves the pursuit of truth and justice. Pretense of belief is thus the highest civic virtue, and proof of this pretense is asking no questions, taking no general interest.

In politics, this attitude puts a tremendous burden on leadership, which must be able to call forth obedience by force of personality rather than by reference to rules and conventions that everyone knows to be artificial and fragile, even in the very act of pretending to believe in them.

Leadership

The real leader, therefore, does not merely apply old political values within the web of history, but is charismatic—having the gift of prophecy and being able to invent values appropriate to new times.

The often noted ideological character of French politics is thus of a limited nature. The function of political doctrine is to prepare the way for new social contracts, the adoption of which future events may make necessary, not because such contracts will in some ways be more progressively true than old ones, but only because history is always reducing the latter to absurdity. Consequently, the one thing that all the so-called families of France have long had in common, despite their differences, is the feeling that political order and political meaning are not natural or discovered things, but are invented and imposed by force of will.

With some, this force of will may express itself in terms of adherence to the orthodoxies of a doctrine, regardless of the consequences. With others, it may express itself in loyalty to a leader like de Gaulle, who was, of all contemporary political figures, the one who appeared to come closest to having a genuine gift of prophecy. Third, it may express itself by adherence to written or positive formal rules, combined with broad rejection of personal responsibility for their application, exemplified best by the passion for red tape for which the French civil service bureaucracy has long been notorious. And last, it may express itself through cynicism toward all politics, combined with a tight adherence to the customs of the family and social class within which one happens to have been born, in order to protect private property and the interests serving to maintain it.

In France, the consequences of these diverse attitudes have been double. On the one hand, they have resulted in the practical exclusion from political power of large segments of the population, especially the working-class population. On the other, they have produced a feeling that runs surprisingly far up the socioeconomic scale, a sense that the country is divided between us and them. They are those who rule, and we are ordinary people who are trying to protect ourselves the best we can by the means available to little guys. If the material situation of millions upon millions of little guys in France is not worse than it is, the fact is certainly due more to the hope of "killing socialism with kindness" on the part of the leading capitalists than to affection for the principles of liberty, equality, fraternity.

Consequently, even the French themselves are uncertain about whether they are a fundamentally conservative or a fundamentally revolutionary people. History and circumstances seem to suggest that they may be both. About the only thing one can be more or less sure of is that the idea of progressive reform elicits little faith in any part of public opinion.

It is against this background that we can now come back to consider some of the more specific features and events of de Gaulle's presidentialism and thus to set the stage for Giscard's arrival in the office.

De Gaulle and the Legislature

Unique Relationship

General de Gaulle's presidency was formally characterized by unique relationships of the

148

office itself to the National Assembly and to the Premier. De Gaulle's solution to the problem of executive-legislative relations was unique because it involved two elements found in no other constitution, either parliamentary or presidential. First, while both the President and the members of the national legislature are elected by direct universal suffrage, their respective terms of office are of different length, the President's being seven years, the legislature's being five. Yet the President has authority to dissolve the National Assembly whenever it challenges his policies without having to put his own mandate on the line.

The second oddity of de Gaulle's constitution of the Fifth Republic is, as we have seen, the office of Premier. What possible function could a Premier have, what powers were available, if in fact the Premier was merely the President's creature? If de Gaulle needed to explain himself to the legislators, why shouldn't he go himself or send his Cabinet members, or heads of administrative departments, in a manner similar to that of an American President? It is hard to say whether de Gaulle's inclusion of an office of the Premier in his new constitution was more a concession to the forms of the parliamentary past or a device peculiarly suited to his own uses, to be taken as an expression of his contempt for traditional parliamentary forms and institutions. Perhaps it was some of both. At any rate, under the Fifth Republic's constitution the choice of the person to serve as Premier is entirely the President's, and twice General de Gaulle chose Georges Pompidou, who was a personal adviser with no prior political experience, belonged to no political party, and, once in office, showed great facility at angering leading Gaullists, as well as Giscard d'Estaing.

The Gaullists

The term *Gaullist* reflects another curiosity of the Fifth Republic. Who in fact, were and are the Gaullists? Were they members of a political party founded by the General? Or were they simply self-appointed and devoted admirers of the man? The answer has to remain ambiguous or, as the French say, nuanced, because none of the parliamentary and electoral organizations that formally supported de Gaulle, his Premiers, and his policies, ever formally received the General's blessing. It is true that his first Premier in the new Fifth Republic, Michel Debré, considered himself a leader of sorts of a party that the public thought of as Gaullist. But Georges Pompidou did not so consider himself and was, in addition, cordially disliked by the officials of the party that identified itself with de Gaulle. (He, of course, never identified himself with it.) This refusal to identify himself with a party or a parliamentary majority stemmed from the General's oft-repeated condemnation of all parties, as if their very existence was really the most offensive part of democracy.

The leading members of the specifically Gaullist party made the best of their ambiguous situation. The UDR has on the one hand been a national electoral machine, well financed and well organized, in the manner of any modern political party, for the purpose of electing representatives to both the National Assembly and local governing bodies. And its repeated electoral successes, dependent on de Gaulle's long coattails, enabled it to reward the loyalty of its members with various forms of patronage. On the other hand, so long as de Gaulle was alive its members had to pay a certain price. This price was not so much to vote a strict party line, for on many issues there was no particular party line. It was, rather, to express on every public occasion unwavering loyalty to the General and, if they were Deputies in the National Assembly, to vote for his Premier's policies unfailingly. The net effect of these two sides of the Gaullist party constitution was a state of affairs that in many ways suited French political life perfectly. Gaullist Deputies were able to associate themselves with the charisma of the great man while at the same time working for the benefit of their local constituencies without the least concern for broad national interests.

The political strength of the Fifth Republic under de Gaulle thus came from its embrace of both poles of the tension between local and national, private and public, economic and political, in which the idea of France was represented by the General, while his Gaullist minions stood for local and vested interests. And this was a division of labor at once practical and symbolically comfortable.

The fact that the UDR has failed to produce new leadership of de Gaulle's type is significant. Indeed, many of their leading figures came early in the Fifth Republic to be called barons, and the name has stuck. The feudal inheritance of the term expresses well its contemporary political aptness. For the nobility of prerevolutionary France were representatives of local, vested interests—interests kept in their proper and limited place only when they were mastered by a strong monarch who stood above them as an arbiter of national interests. That de Gaulle was frequently represented by the political cartoonists and commentators in the early years of the Fifth Republic as both Louis XIV and Joan of Arc is no accident.

Giscard's Rise into Orbit

To see what opportunities the Fifth Republic presented to Giscard, we must now turn back to his earlier career. He had been elected a Deputy to the last Assembly of the Fourth Republic, vainly hoping for a ministerial portfolio the very year that the Republic was to collapse. With its fall, in the face of the revolt by the Europeans in Algeria, the context changed rapidly in Giscard's favor.

His first step in the ladder of power came when de Gaulle, in order to reassure the French of the good financial intentions of his regime, appointed Antoine Pinay as Minister of Finance in 1958. Pinay, long-time parliamentarian and fiscal conservative, had made his name in the early 1950s as the only Premier of the Fourth Republic who had put control of inflation as his highest priority. Giscard had been introduced to him by his grandfather, Jacques Bardoux. And, of course, Giscard had made his own early parliamentary reputation on the basis of his apparent technical economic skills, keeping his opinions on the political crises of the moment fairly much to himself. So when Pinay became first Minister of Finance of the foundling Fifth Republic, he not surprisingly called upon Giscard to be his Secretary of State for the Budget. Giscard thus began to share in *le pouvoir,* as the French often call executive government, at the age of thirty-three.

Finance Minister

Under the 1958 constitution, appointment as a member of the Cabinet obliged resignation of the seat in the National Assembly. But since this body no longer held the keys to power, Giscard was happy to make this little sacrifice in order to move onto General de Gaulle's staff. Nor did it take him long to understand that those who deliberately crossed the will of the General were fated to long exiles. Indeed, he learned this rather more effectively than his mentor, Pinay, who, because of a disposition to argue with de Gaulle on policy matters, lasted but one year as Minister of Finance. Pinay was replaced by Wilfred Baumgartner, director of the

Banque de France. When after another year, Baumgartner had had his fill of kowtowing to the general, Giscard was ready to step up to Finance himself.

Having moved into the Minister's office on Rue de Rivoli, elaborately furnished in nineteenth-century style, he proceeded to collect taxes. His manner was so efficient that journalists told the public of a large Gobelin tapestry hanging on his office wall. It was entitled, they claimed, *Gathering Pears,* French slang for "fleecing the suckers." Two years later, as a mark of de Gaulle's more complete confidence in him, Giscard acceded to the title of Minister of Economics and Finance, to direct both receipts and expenses and thus to enter into more critical policy-making decisions. The tapestry was then removed. In terms of the hierarchy of state offices, Giscard had arrived at the third most powerful office in France, Premier Pompidou holding the second. Perhaps Giscard even had the General's ear on more important issues than did the Premier.

Although never a Gaullist nor a member of the UDR, Giscard had won de Gaulle's favor early in the history of the Fifth Republic. On the one hand, if his own political sympathies were on the side of those who wanted to keep Algeria French, he never adopted a hard-line stance. On more than one occasion he urged the "hawks" to be realistic and to accept the facts: by January 1960 de Gaulle had decided once and for all in favor of Algerian independence, and this was the only policy the vast majority of French citizens were going to accept. Otherwise, he kept his political opinions largely to himself, doing what his patron told him in an apparently loyal, conscientious, and obviously competent fashion. In the case of Giscard's first period as Minister of Finance (1962–1965), this meant applying de Gaulle's stabilization plan.

In terms of the General's foreign policy,

the scheme was rather a success. By the end of 1964 he was able to announce a great surplus of dollars and the largest reserves of gold among any of the advanced industrial nations except the United States itself. But within France the consequences of the operation were much less favorable, for it involved broad restrictions on credit, price and wage controls, and hence a drag on economic growth, with political dissatisfactions following along a broad front. Giscard's reputation, in the meantime, had hardly become one to excite popular admiration. Journalists referred to him as Fiscard, *le fisc* in French meaning the taxing power.

Giscard's Fall from Grace

The year 1962 had also marked the start of Pompidou's Cabinet career. As Premier he early showed concern about the presidential elections scheduled for December 5, 1965. In light of the general slowdown in the economy brought about by the stabilization plan, he began to urge a shift toward an expansionist policy, the effects of which would be felt in advance of the elections. But with the support of Giscard, whose economic forecasting services in the Finance Ministry were predicting that the economy was soon to pick up again anyway, the General refused to modify his restrictive policy. As for the presidential election, de Gaulle played coyly with public opinion, refusing for a while to say whether he would even be a candidate. It was only in November 1965, in fact, that he appeared on radio and television to warn against a "disastrous confusion" were he not reelected President, asking the electorate for "frank and massive" support.

He had every reason to suppose that his appeal would be answered. The only opposing candidate with anything like a national constituency was François Mitterrand, the Socialist, who was far from having been able

Finance Minister Giscard being dumped from de Gaulle's government in 1965

(Illustration by Jacques Faizant from "La nature des choses" [Denoël])

to organize the very diverse kinds of opposition to the General. Great was everyone's surprise, then, when the results of the first ballot were made known.[3] Far from having won a "frank and massive" mandate for a second seven-year term as President, de Gaulle had not even won an absolute majority of votes cast. Forced into what he personally considered a disgraceful run-off

[3] Under the Fifth Republic, elections take place in two successive ballots on successive Sundays. The first ballot (*le premier tour*) is in effect a nominating ballot unless a candidate wins an absolute majority thereon, in which case that individual is elected, not just nominated. At the second ballot a week later only a simple plurality is needed for election.

election with Mitterrand, he was to find that even the second ballot was far from being as supportive as he had obviously expected. Indeed, Mitterrand's percentage of the popular vote rose from 34.7 to 44.8 percent, while de Gaulle's went only from 44.6 to 55.2 percent.

The General's fury with his closest collaborators knew no bounds. After an opportune reminder of preelection warnings about the stagnant state of the economy by the Premier himself, his fury fell on Giscard, whose mistaken confidence in a spontaneous economic recovery had coincided with de Gaulle's own preference for maintaining the stabilization plan without modification. Thus was Giscard summarily fired from the Finance Ministry on January 19, 1966; "thrown out like a domestic servant" were the words the victim himself used to describe his dismissal. Before leaving office, he took the occasion at his final press conference to point out to reporters a piece of eighteenth-century furniture that had been started before the revolution with decorations of royal motif and finished after 1791 with those of a revolutionary motif. "The artisan's discretion," Giscard was careful to point out, "did not prevent his being guillotined. It was a case of human ingratitude." [4]

Thus began Giscard's three and one-half years "in the desert." Unbeknownst to him or anyone else at the time, being out of office in the spring of 1968 was to be a formidable piece of good luck for his presidential ambitions.

[4] "Le petit Giscard illustré," *Crapouillot,* May–June 1974, p. 54.

5

Giscard at the Top:
Rising to the Presidency

In the Desert

Thus to a political career already marked by intelligence, fortune, and social status was to be added the further gift of chance—a gift that consisted of being out of power during the period in May–June 1968 when an unexpected popular uprising showed de Gaulle's authority to be faltering. Having made a marriage of mutual convenience with the General early in the Fifth Republic, Giscard found himself released from that marriage by the General's displeasure just when further association with and responsibility for public policy could have marked his political future with confusion and failure.

"Thinking Gaullists"

Although no one foresaw the coming of the May 1968 "undiscoverable revolution," as one commentator was to call it, Giscard was able to put his exclusion from power to good use. As early as the spring of 1966 he undertook the creation of a new party under his leadership. This organization at first consisted of nothing but so-called study groups under the name of Perspectives and Realities. But by May 1966 enough of these study groups had been formed in various cities of France to make their conversion into a political party feasible. And so Giscard announced the establishment of the National Federation of Independent Republicans. The perspectives of the Perspectives and Realities groups became the perspectives of presidential power for Giscard, while the realities were those of an economist with close ties to the financial and business world.

The Independent Republicans' first electoral challenge came with the legislative elections of March 1967. Their special task was to make their differences with the UNR-UDR clear without making them so sharp that they would alienate General de Gaulle's large, if not always fervent, popular following. Giscard undertook this task in July 1966 when he called the Independent Republicans "thoughtful Gaullists." The implications were clear enough; he intended to support de Gaulle and the Fifth Republic at critical moments, but reserved the right for himself and his followers to criticize when they thought criticism was warranted.

Following up on his claim that the Independent Republicans were thinking Gaullists with a speech on January 10, 1967, Giscard declared that his party would take a "yes, but . . ." position on the government in power. The "yes" was intended to indicate general support of President de Gaulle himself, of the institutions of the Fifth Republic, and of political stability, which Giscard called the basic "condition for all active policy with respect to the future." The "but," on the other hand, expressed the Independent Republicans' reservations about what Giscard called the three failings of the regime in power.

The first was a failure to develop more liberal institutions—by which was meant the tendency to center all power in the great man and the refusal of the Gaullist majority in the National Assembly to undertake genuine debate with its closest critics, that is, the Independent Republicans. The second weakness of the regime Giscard identified as a failure to develop a true economic and social policy. This criticism was aimed at de Gaulle's preoccupation with foreign affairs and, in particular, with the accumulation of gold in the treasury, a policy that in Giscard's direct experience had relegated rapid economic growth to too low a priority. Finally, Giscard saw a failure of the regime represented by de Gaulle's refusal to be a more ardent European, specifically his blocking British entry into the Common Market on terms different from the original ones, which the British felt they could not accept.

Legislative Elections of 1967

The results of the 1967 legislative elections suggest that Giscard's cautiously critical stance was shared by a growing part of the French public at the time. In those elections, the ruling Gaullist majority in the Assembly lost thirty seats, the Independent Republicans gained nine, and Giscard personally won a first-ballot victory in Puy-de-Dôme with five thousand votes more than he had received in 1962. The strength of the Gaullist coalition in the Assembly was thereby sufficiently reduced so that the left opposition was tempted to call for a vote of censure in hopes of persuading de Gaulle to replace Premier Pompidou. The move forced Giscard to take a stand. The parliamentary group of Independent Republicans voted against the motion of censure, thus allowing Pompidou to stay in office without new legislative elections. But the margin was so slim that Pompidou was sent the message: either make concessions to the Independent Republicans or face the prospect that some future motion of censure might win their support.

However, Pompidou refused to accord a special status within the Gaullist majority to the Independent Republicans. In the first place, he was not in the habit of discussing policy even with that majority; there was no need to do so as long as he had the General's support. In the second place, he no doubt remembered what it was like to have Giscard as Minister of Finance: Giscard had had de Gaulle's ear as much if not more than Pompidou, because Giscard had the machinery of the Finance Inspectorate and the intelligence services of the Finance Ministry at his disposal, while Pompidou had nothing—not even a popular or party constituency in the country. In practice, Pompidou was willing to make some concessions to the Independent Republicans on matters of their special economic interests. But he did so not out of respect for their leader, but rather out of a desire to show his followers that they did not need Giscard to win favors from *le pouvoir*.

There was thus increasing hostility between the two men. Pompidou no doubt hoped that Giscard's growing criticisms of the government would eventually result in sapping the latter's support among both Independent Republicans and the public generally. Having thrown the Independent Republicans some economic tidbits, the Premier thus continued to act as if a renewal of threats by de Gaulle to resign would always be the trump card in domestic politics.

May 1968
The means Pompidou chose to weaken Giscard, however, were soon to prove disastrous for de Gaulle. Taking France's bulging gold reserves as proof of the success of his economic policies, the General continued to launch himself on foreign policy initiatives with little regard to what was going on in France. At this very time, vested economic interests were strengthening their advantages and power, and the resentments of the less favored were growing.

There is little indication that Giscard was aware of this development. But others were, including even some among the Gaullists. In particular, René Capitant, a loyal follower of the General from the earliest days, was appalled at the new concessions Pompidou had made to economic powers. In 1967 he warned the majority of a possible workers' revolt against the regime. The warning was to prove prophetic, but it was to no avail.

The attention of most political commentators, including Giscard, was focused largely on the President's foreign trips and pronouncements, all of which emphasized the uniquely personal character of his regime. Within France, discussion centered on bills that would permit the executive to act in some areas by decree, without even a pretense of legislative consultation. In foreign policy, attention was dominated by de Gaulle's visit to Canada, during which he made a call for *"le Québec libre!"* thus appearing to favor the dissolution of Canada, and by his position of studied neutrality in the Seven Day War in the Middle East, a position that appeared to many as more favorable to the Arabs than Israel.

These policies provided occasions for the strongest criticism of the General ever launched by Giscard, culminating with a speech in which the outcast declared:

We simultaneously feel an aversion and anguish. The aversion is inspired in us by the wretched political regime France used to have [under the Fourth Republic]. . . . The anguish is inspired in us by fear that if the solitary exercise of power should become the rule, France would be ill-prepared to assume direction of her affairs in the future in an atmosphere of calm, broadmindedness, and national consent.[1]

This attack brought forth an immediate and unusual response from Premier Pompidou in an interview given to *l'Express* on September 4, 1967:

Mr. Giscard d'Estaing's statement is unfortunate because in one blow it reawakens those old French demons—the taste for political crisis and the mania for new political coalitions, and because it attacks the authority of the Chief of State and thus leads us, whether we wish it or not, according to our own tendency, toward our natural inclinations, toward a return to weakness.[2]

As for the General's personal reaction, expressed in private, it was that Giscard was

[1] Cited in Lancel, *Giscard,* p. 107.
[2] Ibid., p. 126.

"Bad luck, [one] who brings bad luck to everything he touches."

In any case, Giscard now missed no chance to declare and vote his opposition to Pompidou. Insiders began to speak of hatred between the two men, and the spring of 1968 seemed likely to make the political atmosphere even warmer. As a matter of fact it did do so, but not in a way the insiders had expected.

On April 18, while Pompidou and Giscard were still arguing over the relative merits of supporting public radio and television by private advertising, the May events were rapidly gestating in what at first appeared to be a minor quarrel at the University of Nanterre. Yet barely three weeks later, bourgeois university students were battling riot police throughout the Latin Quarter, where streets had been laced overnight with barricades raised in a quixotic and short-lived demonstration against the injustices of industrial life and perhaps even against industrialism itself.

Aside from trying to wrest control of the Sorbonne and the surrounding streets back from the students, the government remained strangely unresponsive. And this unresponsiveness was matched by nearly all the other institutions of French society, including the major unions and parties. Only when wildcat strikes throughout the country followed the student demonstrations did the government take positive steps to mediate the conflicts.

On the side of the Independent Republicans, Michel Poniatowski, close friend and collaborator of Giscard and Minister of the Interior after the latter's election to the presidency, argued in the Assembly that

methods of brutal repression cannot in any way be an effective response to the problems brought to the fore by French youth; the police are now

acting under orders whose effects will only lead to excesses of repression.[3]

As for Giscard, he waited prudently for the worst to pass before continuing his quarrel with Pompidou:

A government that, in spite of a breathing spell, shows itself neither capable of re-establishing the authority of the state, nor of getting France back to work, ought to resign of its own accord by the rules of democracy. Its prolonged maintenance, which no longer answers any national interest, is going to make the social crisis become a crisis of the regime.[4]

He proposed that France should keep de Gaulle as President, but that Pompidou be replaced by someone capable of uniting a popular majority sufficient to reestablish authority; then the nation could proceed to new legislative elections. As for the person capable of organizing this new majority, should not the leader of the Independent Republicans be the man who could succeed?

The General's reaction was very different. He wanted to know whether the French people still felt need of him. At first he thought the way to find out was to hold a referendum on his continuation in office. This he proposed in a speech on national radio and television on May 24:

For very nearly thirty years, events have imposed on me on several serious occasions the necessity of leading the country to assume its own destiny, in order to prevent certain others from taking it in charge in spite of itself. I am ready to do this again now. But this time—above all this time, I need—yes, I need!—the French people to say what they wish.[5]

[3] Ibid., p. 125.
[4] Ibid., p. 126.
[5] Ibid., p. 127.

The appeal totally failed to produce its desired effect on the public. In the words of one commentator, de Gaulle

did not turn the situation around. His charisma no longer came down from on high. The magic effect had evaporated. What had become of those accents which moved, those words charged with glory and heroism which touched the heart, those formulas of hope which brought forth great patriotic sighs? [6]

Legislative Elections of 1968
In an about-face, the General canceled the referendum and ordered dissolution of the National Assembly instead, setting new elections for early July. Giscard and his independent Republicans now had to follow the principles set forth in the "yes, but . . ." speech in earnest. They had to stay close enough to the majority in order to profit from the moral caution of the General and the wide fears engendered by the May events, while at the same time distinguishing themselves enough from the Gaullist majority, and Georges Pompidou, to appear to the public as having the strength necessary to move the Assembly toward their views.

But the legislative elections of July 1968 undercut this strategy, at least temporarily. Fears caused by the May events so dominated the electorate's mood that the Gaullists won an absolute majority in the Assembly. Although the Independent Republicans gained some seats, they were no longer needed to form a parliamentary coalition. Giscard seemed to be more lost in the desert than ever.

But the great Gaullist victory in the 1968 elections did not cause Pompidou's star to rise immediately, either. Having what he

took to be new proof of his own popularity, de Gaulle promptly dismissed Pompidou as Premier, probably largely because of the latter's failure to foresee the events of May, followed by his failure to take them sufficiently seriously when they occurred. In any case, the General now brought forth one of his old, but previously rather neglected, political themes to respond to what he had called the *chienlit* of May. This was the theme of participation, by which he meant that all the nongovernmental institutions of society, even business and academic ones, should establish regular means of allowing the participation of all their members in deliberating policies for their respective organizations. Banker that he was, with secretive instincts, Georges Pompidou was hardly a man to put such a theme across. De Gaulle now offered the premiership to a diplomat, Couve de Murville, hoping that skills in mediation would calm the recently ruffled waters.

De Gaulle's Departure
The General's personal regime had, however, been mortally wounded by the events of May. And as 1968 wore on, Giscard returned to the attack on Gaullist policy on such fundamental matters as the budget and the possible devaluation of the franc. The final break came in the spring of 1969 when the General decided to call for a new referendum on two issues that had been little discussed outside the government itself and were apparently of little interest to the public at large. These issues were reduction of the powers of the Senate, already with scant power anyway, and a proposal for a new system of regionalization, aimed at overcoming the defects inherent in the traditional division of France into small administrative *départements* (districts).

Although the Independent Republicans were by no means opposed to the creation of

[6] Raymond Tournoux, *Le tourment et la fatalité* (Paris: Plon, 1972), p. 83.

Marianne, the symbol of France, catches Giscard tip-toeing out the door just before the 1969 referendum, the defeat of which brought about General de Gaulle's immediate resignation as President. She is saying, "You're going out this late?" suggesting the last-minute nature of his refusal to support the referendum.

(Illustration by Jacques Faizant from "Figaro")

new regional entities, which they saw as being a potential aid in the long run to a united Europe, they were totally opposed to reducing the powers of the Senate, in which they enjoyed considerable influence. Furthermore, Giscard said that he saw no reason to distract the voters with such peripheral matters while the nation was still reeling from the blows inflicted on its morale and its economy by the events of the preceding summer.

The Gaullists led the campaign for a favorable referendum vote badly. They were little aided by the General himself, who appeared to think that his usual threat of resignation would be quite sufficient to insure a favorable vote. Giscard's first instinct was to abstain from public comment. But as the date for the referendum came closer, he stated his personal opposition to the reforms while speaking as the Mayor of the little village of Chamalières, a post to which he had been elected in 1967. The Gaullist press replied with virulent personal attacks against him. Thus the break between him and the old general became both public and final just before the referendum vote. Indeed, even some Independent Republicans saw no reason why he should have made anything of his personal opposition. Three Independent Republican Ministers denounced Giscard's position publicly, specifically accusing him of a willingness "to engage the country in an adventure and to throw his votes in with those of the Communist Party."

Such threats were to prove fruitless. On April 27, the proposed reforms were rejected by 53 percent of the popular vote. At 11 A.M. the following day General de Gaulle resigned. Some Gaullists accused Giscard of stabbing the old man in the back. As for the General himself, he had already been reported as saying some time previously that he knew Giscard would betray him, adding, "I just hope he does it thoroughly." [7]

Presidential Elections of 1969
If de Gaulle's resignation hardly caught Giscard by surprise, it nevertheless did seem to upset the timing for his own try at presidential office. Ideally, the General's term would have run to its appointed end in 1972, at which time it would be clearer whether Giscard ought to seek his political blessing or whether it would be best to run as an independent in fact as well as in name. As it was, de Gaulle had already correctly predicted what would happen after his disappearance

[7] Cited in Lancel, *Giscard,* p. 136.

from the political scene: "You won't have to fear a vacuum. There will rather be an overflow of candidates." [8] The question suddenly confronting Giscard was whether he should be one of them. Should he stand on the sidelines for the time being, in order to improve his chances at some later date? If he did abstain, which of the several other candidates should he back?

Since Giscard had never made any secret of his presidential ambitions, it was therefore with some surprise that the public learned of his decision not to run. On the other hand, the presidential lists did contain Georges Pompidou. In the scramble following de Gaulle's resignation, what had transpired between them?

It appears that although Giscard had certainly been thinking of declaring his candidacy, Pompidou outmaneuvered him in getting the backing of the UDR, the majority party of which neither was a member. For directly after de Gaulle's resignation, instead of seeking the immediate endorsement of the majority party, as Pompidou had done, Giscard sent one of his closest political lieutenants on a mission to the aging Antoine Pinay in hopes of persuading him to seek the presidency for the remainder of de Gaulle's term, with a quid pro quo in the form of the Finance Ministry for Giscard during the interim, so that the latter could more effectively prepare the way for his own candidacy in 1972. While waiting for Pinay's response, Giscard held a press conference in which he argued that

France now needs a calming candidate. . . . To take over after an exceptional man, we need a man of experience who has not been engaged in the political conflicts between majority and opposition in these past few years, a man who is open to Europe, who can re-unite rather than divide, and who will restore to all of us our lost confidence.[9]

But Pinay was not to be rushed. His characteristically cautious reply came in an interview on Radio Monte-Carlo, in which he said he would re-enter the political scene only to forestall a collapse of the regime.

Giscard's ploy had failed; his own Independent Republicans were already calling for a meeting with Pompidou to see if the latter would provide sufficient return on an investment to warrant their endorsement. The meeting ended to everyone's satisfaction, except Giscard's. Pompidou proved himself to be both conciliatory and diplomatic, and he was disposed to settle the quarrel he had previously been carrying on with the Independent Republicans' leader. As for the rank and file of the party, they won satisfaction from Pompidou on what most of them considered five essential points: European unity, negotiations for England's entry into the Common Market, systematic development of a policy of industrializing France, liberalization of control of radio and television, and respect for the constitutional rights of parliament. Giscard still held back, reluctant to back a man who had been his personal enemy, yet equally reluctant to back another candidate who had neither the time nor the authority to unite the Gaullist opposition. But most of Giscard's parliamentary followers saw an opportunity to increase their influence in government with the election of Pompidou. So when Pompidou was declared the winner, among the first telegrams of congratulations was one from Giscard, reading, "Bravo, Mr. President, for your magnificent victory."

8 Ibid., p. 137.

9 Ibid., p. 142.

The Pompidoulean Presidency

When the new President announced the formation of his Cabinet, the Premier was Chaban-Delmas, committed Gaullist and long-time member of the UDR. And Finance Minister was none other than Valéry Giscard d'Estaing.

In light of France's economic difficulties of the time, it is not certain that Pompidou intended to offer the Finance Ministry purely as a gift for the purpose of ensuring Giscard's future success. Having lost the better part of two months' production due to the wildcat strikes in 1968, France had suffered a real economic setback. And this setback had necessitated abandonment of the last remnants of de Gaulle's stabilization plan, both to stimulate the economy to the maximum and to have the money to pay the increased labor bill resulting from the so-called Grenelle Agreements of July 1968, which had provided the major unions, including the Communist-affiliated CGT, with a means of leading workers back to their jobs. By April 1969, however, when de Gaulle resigned, this shift in economic policy had produced a badly overheated economy, generating international monetary speculation on what was coming to be regarded in financial circles as an inevitable devaluation of the franc.

Finances Again

Thus when Giscard again took over the Finance Ministry in 1969, he was faced with hard choices. There were a seriously unbalanced budget, a balance of payments so out of line that France was routinely dipping into her gold reserves to pay her foreign debts, an inflation rate already running at more than 5 percent a year, and active speculation on international money markets aimed at forcing devaluation. Talk about the pos-sibility of revaluation had already been heard a year earlier, when de Gaulle was still in office. But the General had vigorously denied the possibility of such a move, virtually linking the question to a matter of national grandeur.

So almost the first steps taken by Giscard after his appointment were to devalue the franc and to try to balance the budget. Devaluation was easily accomplished, in the middle of August 1969. The second feat was not so easy. However, due to the economy's generally overheated condition, good profits were being made. Thus tax receipts were also larger than had originally been expected, enabling the new Finance Minister to reduce the budget deficit to its smallest amount since 1965.

Yet his three years of involuntary exile from power had brought relaxation of Giscard's previous strict insistence upon balanced budgets. Emphasis was no longer placed on what the state could take from the private sector, but rather on what it could give. When spectacular growth of the French economy in 1969 allowed him to forecast a budget surplus for 1970, he proceeded to use it not to increase social services but to cut taxes. These cuts were made in part for those with the lowest incomes. But in keeping with Giscard's general economic beliefs, taxes on corporate dividends were also reduced. This step was based on his conviction that personal savings in France were increasingly falling behind real investment needs and that it was therefore a critical matter to persuade those with substantial amounts of discretionary income—the rich, in short—to put their money to work for future economic growth. This attempt to encourage capitalists to invest their capital productively has been always at the heart of Giscard's view of the state's intervention in the economy. At an international meeting of economists he was to organize in Paris in June 1972, he made this point clear once again:

I believe that in an evolving world the enrichment of some does not occur ineluctably at the expense of impoverishing the rest. We ought therefore to put our purposes on a scale in order to attack poverty first of all . . . [while at the same time] keeping the basically just system whereby a person can enrich himself by his own merits and his own effective work.[10]

Economic Policies

Pompidou's election to the presidency thus not only brought Giscard again into formal control of the state's relationship to the economy, it did so at a time that appeared peculiarly congenial to his own political and economic outlook. It was a time of widespread uncertainty shaped by the unexpected events of 1968 and de Gaulle's sudden resignation, with their hints of fundamental change to come. For although de Gaulle had given the Fifth Republic a new constitution, everyone knew that his going must mark the end of an era.

Giscard's dropping his quarrel with Pompidou when the latter became President, if startling to those who had been aware of their previous feelings, was yet a very expeditious step. For at his best, Pompidou had shone largely by reflecting de Gaulle's light. A man of considerable shrewdness, he had developed a skill at political infighting since his first appointment as Premier in 1962. But he had never had a broad political base and for a long time was so little interested in acquiring one that de Gaulle had ordered

him, prior to the 1967 legislative elections, to "get out and make himself known"—curious advice to a man who had already been appointed Premier for a second time. Hence his winning the presidency in 1969 indicated not so much the strength of popular support as the disarray in which de Gaulle's sudden resignation had thrown parties and electorate alike and the strong desire of most people to return to normalcy as a way of escaping the fears generated by 1968.

Whatever their personal differences, in any case, Pompidou and Giscard shared rather similar policy outlooks. They had traveled in much the same financial circles, even though Pompidou had not been born into them, as Giscard had been. Both believed that state intervention in the economy should be largely reserved to stimulating it when it began to slow down, and they believed that this stimulation should take place not through increasing government spending for public welfare, but by measures that favored private investment. They both subscribed to the view that what the poor most lacked was money and not public services, whether in the form of housing, education, transportation, or access to culture in general. And so when Giscard became Minister of Finance for the second time in 1969, he found willing support from President Pompidou for a policy of stimulating economic growth without deficit financing. And this policy enabled Giscard to strengthen still further his hold on the constituency of "responsible people," especially useful in his coming struggle with the left over the presidency.

In a curious way, the association with Georges Pompidou perhaps helped Giscard's own public image. Whatever Pompidou's merits, he was hardly a popular figure or a "man of the people," even less a warmhearted sympathizer with popular causes. In

---

[10] The various papers presented at this conference were published in *Economie et société humaine* (Paris: Denoël, 1972). Cited by Lancel, *Giscard,* pp. 157–158.

contrast to him, a person even of Giscard's reputation as a cold technocrat from a mon-eyed background could, with a little public relations effort, appear relatively open and friendly. Furthermore, the time of Pompidou's presidency was not especially propitious to good feelings in politics. This was perhaps another and surely not the least of de Gaulle's several legacies, even if unintended. The public's attitude was summed up in a comment on de Gaulle by a French journalist who had known the vicissitudes of both the Fourth and Fifth Republics:

De Gaulle, that man of grandeur, had he not broken the springs of grandeur? . . . [He] was the artisan, in spite of himself, even without

knowing it, of a consumer society which stood at the very opposite of his own outlook. . . . [By 1969] the only thing left to him was a "nice" death, because the French, in their middling way, only wanted to live comfortably, without trouble, without history, without blood, without legends, satisfied with quibbles about political successions, with the tax collector, and how to spend their leisure time.[11]

President Pompidou liked to claim that he was carrying on the Gaullist tradition; but his term was in fact increasingly marked by a widespread and increasingly frenetic rush

[11] Lucien Bodard, *Les plaisirs de l'hexagone* (Paris: Gallimard, 1971), p. 338.

Finance Minister Giscard and President Pompidou in 1969

(Documentation *Le Crapouillot*)

to maximize private gains. Just as Louis Philippe (1830–1848) had made *"Enrichis-sez-vous!"* ("Get rich!") the motto of his reign, so the same motto came to seem equally applicable to President Pompidou's presidency, with able technical support from his Finance Minister. It was also a regime marked by increasingly flagrant financial scandals, especially in urban real estate speculation, where the largest returns in the shortest time were to be made.

As for social policy, Pompidou's term of office was characterized largely by three elements. One was the encouragement of the private automobile industry, especially by providing hidden export subsidies[12] and by personally insisting that speed limits be lifted after the first effects of the 1973 oil crisis had passed (Pompidou himself drove a Citroën-Maserati) against the express wishes of his own Premier, Pierre Messmer, who thought the reduction in accidents and deaths was a good trade-off for the lower speed. The second element was to encourage speculative real estate interests by permitting the continuing desecration of Paris through the construction of high-rise office buildings and inner-city four-lane highways on the grounds that nobody, not even Parisians, should want to continue to live in a "museum." [13] The third policy was to encourage

the production of meat by a variety of subsidies directed to specific types of farming, on the theory that since the French were on the way toward enjoying one of the highest standards of living in the world, they should also learn to have sirloin steaks on their tables. While much of traditional French cuisine was based on solutions to the problem of taking the less expensive cuts of meat and turning them into something delicious, Macdonald's has since 1972 been showing Parisians how to turn them into quick profits. This shift in culinary goal suited the temper of the Pompidou regime perfectly.

On its negative side, these social policies tended toward the relative starvation of what the French call *biens collectifs*—schools, hospitals, libraries, public transportation, telephones—and the aggravation of certain social problems. Of these, perhaps the most troubling has been the use of laborers from Spain, Portugal, and particularly North Africa for the performance of menial jobs —trash collection, highway construction, semiskilled and unskilled factory labor, field work—for which French workers can no longer be recruited in sufficient numbers, because the pay is low, the benefits minimal, and the career future virtually nonexistent. As in many other Western European countries, including West Germany, much of the economic miracle, although owing its original stimulus to postwar American aid, has developed its continued strength on the basis of a secondary labor market consisting of immigrant laborers. Now estimated at some 15 million in Europe as a whole, and at 1.5 million in France, these workers fill the unpopular jobs and are employed and laid off with fewer of the social protections accorded by

[12] Export subsidies are formally illegal among members of the Common Market. The device used is to rescind the value-added tax on goods sold outside the country of manufacture.
[13] More than any other city in France, Paris is subject to policies imposed upon it by the national government, whatever the city council may think. For example, Pompidou intended to impose a Left Bank superhighway on Paris, and he won a vote in the city council by a certain amount of arm twisting of Gaullist representatives. The first dramatic move of Giscard's presidency was to announce cancellation of these plans, much to the relief of lovers of "old Paris." The issue of self-rule for Paris has now engendered a reform

whereby the city is entitled, like other French cities, to have an elected Mayor, presumably more responsive to his Parisian constituents than to pressures from President or National Assembly.

law to citizens. Some of Western Europe's high growth rates during the past twenty years, then, is due to making practical use of an economic view once held by Joseph Stalin: labor is capital.

The Electoral Campaign of 1974

Since the Finance Ministry is really the nerve center of French government, Giscard was particularly aware of these problems. But his position also made him aware of another fact about which the public was deliberately kept in the dark and which only other members of the inner circles of government knew. This fact was Pompidou's failing health, leading to his progressive abandonment of daily and then even weekly supervision of the affairs of his government through 1972 and 1973. Of course, no one could know whether Pompidou would die before the expiration of his term in 1975. But what Giscard and the others of the Cabinet did know was that under no circumstances would Pompidou be a candidate again, nor could he stand in the way of another right-of-center figure's rise to power. So far as Giscard in particular was concerned, Pompidou was a lame duck President as early as 1971. Thus Giscard had an advantage over other future candidates for the presidency in being able to create contingency plans, according to whether Pompidou would live through his mandate or die in office.

Pompidou's Death
As it turned out, he died in office on April 3, 1974, two years before the expiration of his seven year term. In the light of this circumstance, Pompidou's last real political efforts—an attempt, wholly unsuccessful, to

put through a constitutional amendment reducing the presidential term from seven to five years—raise interesting questions, which have not yet been answered, about his later personal relationship with Giscard, who he knew would have an inside track to the presidency if the next election were to come by surprise.

Pompidou's death came as a shock to the French public. Though it had heard vague rumors about his illness, it had not been in the least prepared for the sudden news of its fatal nature. Giscard alone among the serious candidates had been able to prepare a plan of attack with right timing. His strategy aimed at beating candidates who were nearest to him in the political spectrum on the first ballot, while enhancing his strength against whichever candidate the combined left could agree on for the second. Timing was critical for the first, or nominating, ballot.

This was so because Gaullists still had a majority in the National Assembly and tended to think of themselves as a national majority as well, though they had in fact been without effective leadership ever since de Gaulle's resignation. The various currents within the Gaullist parliamentary group, which de Gaulle had been able to hold together by his own authority, had long since weakened the unity of the UNR-UDR. It had become a party held together more by the smell of power than by either a leader or an idea.

In the politically hectic days immediately after Pompidou's death, Giscard's strategy toward the UNR-UDR had thus to be the one he had already developed when he had been out of power: building and maintaining a nonpartisan majority, united on the basis of a broad spirit of pragmatism. This stance of Giscard's fit well with the outlook of most of the rank-and-file UNR-UDR members, who had been elected largely on the promise of patronage in the form of state subsidies for their constituents and who, in any case, had never thought of de Gaulle, their hero, or themselves as ideological. Although Giscard himself was not a Gaullist and had gained a reputation for being a prickly fellow among political figures like Pompidou and Debré, he had never attempted to make the Independent Republicans an exclusive group. On the contrary, all he had ever asked, when out of power, was that those in power share their intentions more broadly with his group in parliament. Consequently, when he was in a position to aim at the presidency himself, he did not appear a threatening figure to most parliamentary members of the UDR, who expected to be asked to support an eventual Giscard government and to continue to share in power and patronage in the measure that their numbers warranted. Although the Independent Republicans represented but a small proportion of the Assembly in numerical terms, Giscard already potentially enjoyed, long before Pompidou's death, the support of a substantial part of the majority group. And since, as Minister of Finance, he was fully informed on patronage matters, well knowing which constituencies needed which kinds of state subsidies to meet their local problems, common political sense for a large number of Deputies, City Councilors, and Mayors implied a very open response to a Giscard candidacy.

In any case, Paris was hardly in doubt about the likelihood of his ambition. Aware that his aim was known, Giscard was able to play a useful public relations game and to withhold the announcement of his intentions until a week of formal national mourning for the late incumbent had run its course. The situation facing Giscard's principal rival for the political favors of the Gaullist majority in the presidential race, Chaban-Delmas, allowed no such pretty maneuvers.

Scramble for the Candidacy

Pompidou had left no political testament; even his private secretary had been unable to get a statement of preference from the dying man about possible successors. This meant that the Gaullist majority was uncommitted and available, not only to its nominal leaders like Chaban, but also to interlopers like Giscard, whose stance in favor of continuation of the Gaullist constitution without de Gaulle had enormous attraction for those whose fear of disorder was their primary concern. This being the case, the fact that Chaban had held no national office at the time of Pompidou's death became a crucial factor. Not being close to what was going on in Paris in the weeks before Pompidou's death, Chaban was off to a late start. And the reason why Chaban held no national office at this critical time weighed heavily against delaying announcement of his candidacy. He had been dismissed from the premiership in 1972 by Pompidou after the satirical Paris weekly, *le Canard Enchaîné,* had published facsimile copies of his recent income tax returns—returns that showed that even though Chaban received salaries as both Mayor of Bordeaux and Premier of France, he had paid no income tax at all, due to certain tax-law loopholes.

Avoiding taxes in one way or another is a national pastime in France. But proof of Chaban's engagement in this pastime hardly endeared him to the electorate, for the French regard avoidance of taxes as a private, not a public, duty. To have avoided taxes as a public official confused the basic rules of the game of us and them in the mind of the average French person. In any case, among Gaullist barons Chaban had always appeared to pose as a defender of the cause of social justice. His political speeches making appeals for a "New Society," distinct from Pompidou's implicit invitation to self-interest, contrasted all too clearly with his

165

astuteness in avoiding taxes. Tax returns are presumably protected from prying eyes in France, as they are supposed to be in the United States. Some have suggested that if *le Canard Enchaîné* was able to make facsimile copies of Chaban's returns, it could have been because its reporters were able to photograph them at the Ministry of Finance, of which Giscard was then head. As Minister, he could not, of course, have overseen the activities of all members of his services. But if the leak was not intentional on Giscard's part, it certainly suited his plans very well. Chaban, in short, had a difficult comeback to make. Speed in announcing his race for the presidency as a true Gaullist was, he believed, the only way he could hope to reduce the danger of the majority party's falling apart in the face of appeals for a new unity around Giscard.

The Gaullists' Failure

Chaban's efforts were to prove but another example of bad timing. He had intended to make his announcement immediately after the termination of the funeral eulogy being pronounced in the National Assembly by its presiding officer, Edgar Faure. But the ceremonies had been delayed at the start, and Faure had barely made it to his most moving references to the late President when news of Chaban's announcement arrived at the Palais Bourbon, circulating in whispers among the nation's elected representatives, quite diverting their attention from the mourning ceremonies. One Gaullist, Jacques Chirac, found Chaban's haste especially unseemly. Shortly after a vigorous public expression of disgust, he led a group of forty-three Gaullists out of Chaban's camp, thus sounding the death knell of the latter's presidential hopes.

Chaban's untimely announcement also precipitated announcements from other presidential hopefuls more or less close to what

they hoped would continue to be a Gaullist majority—so many in such rapid succession that the UDR seemed to be dissolving before the public's very eyes. Journalists likened the circumstances to a wake in which the relatives of the deceased were busy dividing up the property even before the body of its former owner had cooled. All the more impressive, then, was Giscard's dignified insistence that he would announce his own intentions with respect to the presidential race only after the week allotted to official mourning had fully elapsed. The media pretended to find the suspense exciting, a stance that further directed favorable public attention to him.

Giscard made his announcement in the town hall of Chamalières, where he was still Mayor. If his decision was hardly a surprise, its terms nevertheless extracted the maximum of advantage from the circumstances:

Less than a week ago President Georges Pompidou disappeared. I thought then, and I think now, that those who were inspired by his memory ought to associate themselves with the mourning of the French people before worrying about who is going to succeed him.

I am speaking to you today, here, in this town hall in the province of Auvergne, to tell you that I am a candidate for the Presidency of this Republic. [Loud cheers from assembled crowd]

Why am I running? First of all, it seems to me right that someone who has served in Georges Pompidou's government, and in whom he had confidence to the very end, should run.

For many years now I have been stating publicly that France needs an enlarged majority. In the difficult situation we are now going through, and will continue to go through, we must create that enlarged majority. This is why I am now addressing myself to you, supporters of the UDR, Independent Republicans, Centrists and Reformers. And also to all those who share in common, in spite of their differences, certain fundamental political principles, and who refuse to accept a bureaucratized society. I am addressing myself to you all in order to create this new enlarged presidential majority.

How will I conduct my campaign? I shall look France deeply in the eyes, tell her my message and listen to hers. I will try to lead an exemplary campaign, making a larger place for ideas than for money. I will attack no one, whether candidates from yesterday's presidential majority, or opposition candidates.

For the 18 years that I have participated in public life, that has always been my rule. I have no intention of changing.

And now let each candidate propose his policies so that, in the end, France will be the winner.[14]

Shortly after this speech, Chaban's rapid eclipse was traced by the pollsters in excruciating detail. So far as winning over the Gaullists was concerned, Giscard had played his hand beautifully. In the brief time remaining he had to turn his attention to the left. Would he succeed in continuing its exclusion from national power, as his predecessors had done?

The Left

That, after all, was the ultimate crux of French politics. The Communists had been political pariahs ever since 1946, and the Socialists had involuntarily joined them in isolation with the collapse of the Fourth Republic in 1958. The exercise of political power on the national scene had thus fallen into hands further to the right from the mean of the political spectrum than the normal spread of the electorate itself. In shared misery, the Socialists and Communists had begun to explore the possibility of alliance early in the 1960s. Could a coalition of the

left be formed in country and parliament, either to confront the office of the presidency, to which the left had always been viscerally opposed, or perhaps even to win it?

The process of cooperation between the two major parties of the left proved extremely difficult because, as we have seen, the historical divisions between them were in many ways more immediate than the traditional divisions between the left and right. But the surprising showing of Mitterrand against de Gaulle in the 1965 elections encouraged leaders of both parties to try to come to some agreement. Their earlier efforts aimed at legislative elections of 1967, for which it was agreed that if, in the first ballot, either a Communist or Socialist stood relatively well, then the candidate with the lower number of votes would desist on the second ballot, asking his supporters to vote for the better-placed candidate of the left. Although this accord was not followed everywhere to the letter in the general elections of 1968, there was enough adherence to it to encourage continuing efforts at combination.

These efforts came to a head in 1972 with the writing of a Common Program to serve as a platform for the candidate of a federated left in the presidential campaign, then thought likely to come in 1975. So if Pompidou's death caught the UDR off balance, it was much less of a shock for the Socialists and Communists who, with their already prepared confederation, were in some ways almost as ready to campaign as Giscard.

This apparent entente between Socialists and Communists worried not merely the right, but also large parts of the center. What remained to be found out was whether Giscard would be able to add enough support from this center to win the ultimate contest with a unified left on May 19.

Unlike the left, Giscard himself refused to draw up a general policy platform. To

[14] Cited in Lancel, *Giscard,* pp. 18–19.

have done so would have been inconsistent with his pragmatism, he argued. This is another way of saying, of course, that he was broadly satisfied with the framework of modern French society and was convinced that management techniques, of which he often vaunted the efficacy, were what were most needed in government, rather than vague statements of more of less visionary goals.

Nevertheless, the tenor of much of his campaign indicated a feeling on his part that his approach was threatened by some parts of the Common Program. Some articles of that program—such as the call for nationalization of all banking and many key industries, a guarded and even unenthusiastic acceptance of the European Common Market (a point of view the left had shared with de Gaulle), and a promise to reform the electoral system and presidential powers so that the balance of power between legislature and executive should again tip toward the legislature—Giscard could attack with all the conviction and wit at his command. But much of the rest of the left's platform was not so easily disposed of before the general electorate, which was both increasingly dissatisfied with things as they were and increasingly nervous that the most probable changes were likely to be for the worse rather than for the better.

The leitmotif of Giscard's campaign thus became "change without risk." It combined promises about changing certain obvious wrongs with the image of a man who not only understood it was money that made the world go around, but knew how to use that understanding to minimize threats to private property and private enterprise.

The forces of the combined left thus faced the problem of convincing the center that the reforms and changes they proposed were not economically and financially irresponsible. In one of the rare interviews Mrs. Mitterrand accorded to the press during the campaign,

she assured the public that "socialism [did] not mean poverty." The conception of French society that the left did its best to propagate was the one of us and them. Of course, we were the vast majority of little guys, whose modest hopes for a modest amount of property and a modest degree of security and personal comfort were constantly being threatened by them, the forces of big business and big finance, which had long since seized the republic in the interests of private wealth. While this argument fell comfortably on Communist and Socialist ears, the extraordinary growth of the economy and personal real income during the preceding ten years or so made it less welcome to the amorphous center, which was vaguely aware that economic conditions had never been better. Yet the left's appeal had more than the strength of traditional sentiments of social justice behind it: for all the economic growth that had taken place during the Fifth Republic, the distribution of benefits was more unequal than before. The poor and the lower-middle classes might statistically be better off than they had been back in 1958. But it was apparent to virtually everyone that the upper-middle classes and the rich were much better off and seemingly more entrenched in positions of power than they had been back in the Fourth Republic.

Questions of Principle
The combined left took as its basic perspective what middle and upper classes have always been reluctant to admit—that class, not individual merit, is the major factor, in personal success in modern industrial societies. The common program, therefore, called for the nationalization not only of all major institutions of finance and investment, but also of all industries engaged in armaments, aeronautics and space, nuclear energy, chemicals, pharmaceuticals, and natural resources in general, plus some selective nationalization

of electronics and computer firms. In addition, it would reorganize domestic agricultural markets in order to protect small farmers and, where necessary, would block international control of agricultural prices through Common Market accords.

As to constitutional reform, the left promised to abrogate Article 16 of the 1958 constitution, in order to deprive the President of the authority to rule by decree during a national emergency. And they would otherwise limit the President's authority to act without parliamentary approval to things like nominating the Premier, sending messages to parliament, dissolving it, and to contacts with a special supreme court that they proposed to set up. In addition, the common program called for the reestablishment of elections to parliament on the basis of proportional representation according to lists of candidates established by the various party executives themselves.[15] Finally, the left called for a new partnership between legislature and executive, the principal instrument of this change being a modification of the constitution's Article 11, so that referenda could never again be used as a way of obtaining a plebiscite for presidential policy against the National Assembly.

That his major opponent on the left, François Mitterrand, should run his electoral campaign on this program posed both an opportunity and a dilemma for Giscard. The dilemma was evident: if it meant what it appeared to mean, and if it were to be applied with any degree of consistency, the Common Program would likely result in great changes in French social structure—changes that would certainly not be to the

advantage of the kinds of wealth and power that Giscard himself had virtually always represented, whereby both political and economic initiatives lay in the hands of a small elite. What if the vast majority had had enough of this elite? What if the Communist and (somewhat more reluctant) Socialist appeals for profound change were to catch the imagination and hopes of a popular majority? The problem thus facing Giscard in his campaign was to make what the left offered appear a threat. While picturing himself as an agent of responsible change, he had to paint Mitterrand as someone likely to unleash processes over which none could hope to maintain control and the end of which none could foresee.

The opportunity provided Giscard by the Common Program sprang from the fact that the center, including much of the "silent majority" in France, was little inclined to faith in politics. Fear of losing control of reforming trends would thus weigh more heavily in their final choice, Giscard believed, than would their hopes for some possible, but highly uncertain, good. Though Giscard was willing to commit himself to specific improvements, he made it clear that these reforms would depend on strengthening, not weakening, existing economic and political institutions.

This approach posed, in turn, a dilemma for Mitterrand. As leader of a more or less united left, was Mitterrand to insist on the necessity for tremendous change, and ensuing upheaval, that would accompany a rigorous application of the common program? Or should he appear, rather, as a man willing to work within the broad spirit of the Common Program, but with no timetable for its execution? If he put himself forward as the agent of great change, he would perhaps please some Communists, but likely frighten away some Socialists and certainly fail to attract those votes of the center vital

---

[15] This electoral system was used by the Fourth Republic and is still used in municipal elections. General de Gaulle introduced the single-member district under the Fifth Republic because he wanted to undermine any arrangement that might be favorable to party unity and discipline.

to his election. If, on the other hand, he posed as a man of leftist convictions, but in no sense a doctrinaire and therefore an advocate of merely the spirit of the Common Program and not its real substance, then he was likely to rupture the far from solid accord with the Communists.

Matters of ideology aside, Giscard could run as a man who, if elected, would be able to work with the existing presidential majority, since he already had been working with it for five years under Pompidou's presidency. Mitterrand, on the other hand, might find himself stymied as President in the face of a National Assembly whose working majority would be unalterably opposed to legislation designed to carry out any part of the Common Program. In that case, Giscard asked his opponent, would Mitterrand efface himself and choose a premier able to deal with this working majority? If he did so, he would in effect be abandoning the strong presidency bequeathed by de Gaulle and reinstating the unstable reign of parliament that had characterized the Third and Fourth Republics. If, on the other hand, he dissolved the National Assembly immediately after his own election in an attempt to get a new majority favorable to the left's program, he would be forcing a second national campaign hard on the heels of the presidential one. In that case, political uncertainties would distract France from the very real economic problems it faced, especially in light of the cruel rise in oil prices brought about by the OPEC cartel.[16]

This potential threat of months of furious politicking, with no certainty of eventual ac-

cord between executive and legislature, combined with discreet threats of a possible flight of capital to more salubrious climes, no doubt had an effect on the final outcome. Indeed, memories of the recent history of Chile were present enough in French minds to make troubling comparisons between Allende and Mitterrand a matter of reflection right across the political spectrum. Mitterrand's caution not to upset the center, and the image he projected of a well-heeled lawyer (which is just what he is by both training and disposition) even before the first vote, caused one of his opponents on the far left, Arlette Laguiller, who had been thrust into national prominence by her leadership of a strike of bank clerks earlier in the spring of 1974, to coin the only memorable phrase of the whole campaign. She told television viewers that they had the choice between "two real men of the Right [Giscard and Chaban] and one false man of the Left [Mitterrand]." [17]

---

[16] France is currently importing about 90 percent of her energy resources. One proposal would attempt to reduce dependence on foreign sources of supply to about 65 percent by 1990, but such a development would require heavy use of nuclear power, whose future now seems far more clouded than it did even two or three years ago.

[17] French law requires the state-run radio-television services to give equal time to all certified presidential candidates. This is arranged in practice by devoting an hour on two different occasions to the candidates' presentations. Lots are drawn to determine the order of appearance. In 1974 there were eight candidates; each was allowed seven minutes on each occasion, for a total of fourteen minutes before a national audience. After the first ballot, the two winners, Giscard and Mitterrand, met in television debate for two hours, the exchanges being timed in much the same manner as were the televised debates of Carter and Ford in the 1976 American presidential campaign. Prior to the first ballot, there were three candidates on the left besides Mitterrand: Alain Krivine, ex-graduate student turned Trotskyite radical in the events of 1968; René Dumont, agronomist-ecologist who conducted a consciousness-raising campaign against the dangers of modern industrialism, with which he associated both the destruction of nature and the oppression of the poor and working classes; and Arlette Laguiller, whose appeal incorporated feminism and the striving of the masses. The

Skillfully nurtured doubts about the left's own intentions and capacities could not efface, however, the fact that Giscard had by 1974 been Finance Minister for ten of the Fifth Republic's fifteen years of existence. So if he meant to take credit for the almost quantum leap in economic growth that France had made during that period, he would also have to take the blame for the very concrete inequalities and injustices that had thrown a disproportionate share of the benefits of this growth to the well-off and of its burdens onto those least able to defend themselves.[18] Mitterrand pointed out that for all the years Giscard had been Minister of Finance, he had refused to recommend as policy the very promises for better social welfare he was now making as a candidate.

Giscard's appeal to the electorate could not, therefore, be based exclusively on his economic expertise. His managers knew that the "selling of a President" would require all the devices and skills of public relations; if the consumer was to be persuaded to buy their product, the packaging would have to be at least as compelling as the contents. Even before the first ballot, polls had shown that the French public thought of Giscard not only as a knowledgeable economist and a person of integrity without political partisanship but also as a good family man and a

good Catholic. Of his two major rivals, Chaban had been divorced twice, while Mitterrand had to appear to his supporters as someone who had substituted socialism for Catholicism, so in the realm of bourgeois pieties Giscard had no peer.

Continuity was thus promised with Giscard for both political and social reasons. On the one hand, as he claimed before the television cameras, he was uniquely a political leader of the Fifth Republic. On the other, he was the only candidate really in tune with the public's contemporary expectations of pragmatic effectiveness in government. And to the charge that he was cold—nothing but a calculator of figures and dealer in abstractions—the candidate replied:

I don't think that's true. I believe that I am reserved, no doubt as many of you are; I am reserved because that's my temperament, and then also because I don't like just looking for effects, because I don't want to say more than I mean, and because, finally, what one feels most strongly is difficult to say. When I announced my candidacy, I said that I wanted to look France deeply in the eyes, but I would like to touch her heart.[19]

As to the center, despite their many past differences with de Gaulle and then Pompidou, they finally had much by way of political attitude in common with Giscard and his Independent Republicans—in particular, the belief that the terms *left* and *right* no longer served a very useful purpose, that political problems could be solved only when ideological postures were put aside and when economic technique replaced partisanship as the method of politics.

French system of the two successive ballots allows voters to express their preferences in the first, to compromise according to electoral realities in the second.

[18] In a striking book, *Les Exclus* (Paris: Seuil, 1973), René Lenoir, then Pompidou's Minister of Social Affairs, argued that at least 10 percent of the French population stood outside of the "normal" culture and that without appropriate public policy, this proportion would increase in ten years to 20 percent. The title, "the excluded," meant such groups as young drop-outs who were not assimilable through the ordinary educational system, the old, the chronically ill, certain categories of unskilled labor, and so forth.

[19] Cited in Lancel, *Giscard,* p. 175.

171

*Campaign photograph of Giscard with his wife
and children in 1974*

(Courtesy of French Consulate, Boston)

The vital importance of every gain in the second ballot was now made clearer in every succeeding opinion survey. Two days after the first ballot the difference in percentage points between Giscard and Mitterrand appeared to be barely 2 percent in the former's favor. Finally in the actual ballot itself, the difference came down to just over 1 percent. The election was the closest in French history for major office. It was also among those with the highest degree of participation —88 percent.

172

6

Assessment
and Conclusions

It is easy to speak of the levers of power, to imagine leaders pulling them and getting definite results. And surely if there were levers of power, they should exist in France, with its formal administrative hierarchies and its centralized political system. But Giscard's years as President of France show that the idea of levers of power is but illusion. His incumbency has been marked by small victories, important defeats, and, above all, uncertainties. Politics hardly ever supports a rationalist's view of life.

Organizing Power:
Giscard's First Cabinet

Despite having won the presidency for a term of seven years by a margin of barely 1 percent of the vote, Giscard's task was not to seek further popular support directly. It was, rather, to try to mobilize the complex powers of government, relating the bureaucracy and the parliament to his own purposes. Success in this enterprise would give him time and means enough to win sufficient electoral support in the presidential elections of 1981. Inability to do so convincingly would but hearten opposition to him on both left and right.

Having put the Interior Ministry in the hands of his old friend and campaign manager, Michel Poniatowski, and the Finance Ministry in those of Jean-Pierre Fourcade, a career civil servant without party affiliation, the new President turned to the key problem of relations with the National Assembly. What groups were to constitute his presidential majority in that body, and how was he to get them to act together?

Here partisan considerations had to count. In the Parliament now facing Giscard, though the Gaullists certainly no longer constituted a monolithic bloc delivering votes with faithful regularity to the occupant of the Palais Elysée, they nevertheless still did constitute the heart of any possible presidential majority. Giscard's own party, the Independent Republicans, on the other hand, having served as vehicle for Giscard's climb to the presidency, had already completed their principal mission, especially as they were far from being sufficiently numerous to make up a majority. So if Giscard did not quite turn his back on them (they got four portfolios out of approximately thirty-five) it was nevertheless to a Gaullist that he first accorded the premiership. And that Gaullist was none other than Jacques Chirac, leader of the rebellion of the forty-three Gaullists against Chaban-Delmas during the just concluded electoral campaign. Chirac had thus moved skillfully, taking the appropriate step at just the right moment in announcing his group's support for Giscard. Now he was ready to act as forger of the new and enlarged majority in the Assembly that was supposed to become the agent for "change without risk."

In order to make sure that no one could now misunderstand his intentions, Giscard again urged the abandonment of what he called the useless terms *left* and *right* in political discourse, declaring that current problems were susceptible, not to partisan solutions, but only to reason, and could therefore be dealt with effectively only on a case-by-case basis. Chirac, who had once been a visitor at Harvard Business School, was presumably entirely in agreement. But before getting into the substance of his policies, it will be helpful to know something of the style of Giscard's presidency.

Giscard's Presidential Style

"Citizen President"
Just as Louis Philippe came to be called the "citizen king" in the 1830s, so it may be said of President Giscard d'Estaing that he means to appear—in contrast to the autocratic style of President de Gaulle and the secretive one of President Pompidou—as the "citizen president." In contrast to his rather distant manner as Finance Minister, his presidential style has been marked by a studied openness and informality—informality so great, indeed, that it was briefly the subject of scandalous speculation about possible liaisons with ladies unknown during mysterious nocturnal disappearances from his official residence. The press's delight with these speculations was brought to a stop when Giscard took a well-publicized skiing vacation to the Alps with his wife and children in 1975. Since then, the President has frequently appeared in public places in Paris with members of his family—in restaurants, at the theater and the opera—to give the impression of a person who wants to share in at least the licit pleasures of ordinary mortals.

To emphasize his availability to the man in the street, he let it be known that he and *Madame la Présidente* would be happy to receive invitations to dinner from private households, with a view to learning more directly about the lives of ordinary French people. The small sample of citizens with whom he and Mrs. Giscard have dined have been more or less representative of the lower-middle classes, as he no doubt planned. But the repasts served have hardly been representative of his hosts' usual fare. Each has outdone the previous in providing a feast to wreck most family budgets for months, if not for years.

In politics the style of openness became equally notable. It has extended even to inviting the leaders of the left, including Mitterrand and the Secretary General of the Communist party, Georges Marchais, to meet with him personally at the Palais Elysée to discuss current problems, while guaranteeing the parliamentary representatives of this

"Burp.... I ate too much again. The next time I'm going to eat with someone who's out of work." (A comment on the sumptuous meals prepared for the Giscards at the homes of their hosts among the general public)

(Illustration by Kercetoux from "Le Canard enchainé")

same group a regular spot on the parliamentary calendar for its critical comments. At the same time, an equivalent of the British parliamentary question hour has been set up, which all Cabinet members must attend to answer questions from members of the Assembly. He has also moved to break up French Radio-Television into five regional public broadcasting corporations, thus mitigating the traditional central direction. It is clear that in all these procedural ways President Giscard has tried to be true to his liberal principles.

Policy Outputs

The policy outputs of this openness of style have, however, been very thin. Shortly after his election, President Giscard had declared that it was his intention to have France lead events, rather than be led by them. This hope has hardly been borne out since then. Like most political leaders everywhere, he has been more or less swept along by circumstances over whose genesis and evolution no one person, government, or nation has had effective control. Indeed, few have even begun to understand these circumstances, much less know what to do about them.

On the plus side of the ledger, Giscard's first year in office was marked by some new legislation, including a measure for legal abortion, paid for by national health insurance. Some of his campaign promises of higher social security pensions have been realized, though vitiated in part by a continuing high rate of inflation. On the whole, the legislature, with its presidential majority, has been less than enthusiastic about these and his more far-reaching proposals.

No doubt foreign relations with the United States are more cordial than they were when General de Gaulle used to embarrass Washington with some regularity. Though not yet formally back in NATO, France's military forces are now more closely integrated in defense planning, at a time when NATO's purposes seem ever more clouded with uncertainty. So far as Giscard's hopes of building Europe are concerned, the Common Market has, since the oil crisis, fallen into great disarray, with fewer hopes for unity than ever.

In domestic policy, Giscard's proposal to speed the "trickle down" from rich to poor by way of a capital gains tax has been abandoned, thanks to fierce opposition within the presidential majority itself. A similar fate has befallen a reform of regulations regarding investments and financial reporting, designed to provide government and public alike a better look into France's private, closely held corporations. Educational reforms were proposed that aimed at bringing about a closer integration of business planning and curricular programs at the university level, in an attempt to assure university graduates of more ready access to business employment. But these proposals have met strong opposition from faculty and students alike, who are afraid that Giscard means to put public higher education in the direct service of big business. Recent years have thus been marked by pale and scattered imitations of the student demonstrations of 1968.

Perhaps if these proposals were added all together and actually put into force, they might speed some changes in the distribution of burdens and benefits in French society. The most persuasive arguments for their implementation was put by a government spokesperson this way:

Historically, social change has come only at times of sharp upheaval in France, the turbulent mid-thirties, the Liberation, 1968, for example. Now we're trying to produce it coolly, step by step. It's that, or real strife.[1]

But this argument has not won the day, as the resignation in 1976 of Giscard's first Premier, Jacques Chirac, shows. Although his replacement, Raymond Barre, a nonpolitical economist handily won his parliamentary spurs in defeating a motion of no confidence inspired by the left, Chirac's surprise departure indicated serious trouble ahead for Giscard on what had been his strongest flank.

On the surface, the difference between Giscard and Chirac concerned the way of organizing the campaign for the 1978 legislative elections. The President's intention has always been to try to extend the presidential majority toward the center, thus to provide the executive with the widest possible range of support. Consequently, Giscard has never wanted to identify himself as an ardent partisan—either with the Independent Republicans or with the Gaullists. Chirac's position is very different. His political career has from its beginning been linked with the Gaullists, and he now stands as their undisputed leader. In his view, even if the center is not negligible in terms of numbers in French political life, it can exert no effective force apart from the right, with whom it will always throw in its lot when a confrontation with the left becomes inevitable. Thus Chirac's strategy is to wield the Gaullists as a hard-hitting tool in defense of business and strong economic activity. In so doing, he has taken aim at the main body of Giscard's presidential majority, dimming the latter's chances for reelection in 1981 and undercutting his limited strength today.

The long recession has strengthened Chirac's position. The center, never united, has declined in reformist convictions as the faltering economy has undermined confidence among its essentially managerial supporters. Those who control capital have in the meantime taken advantage of the situation to strengthen their predominant position in economic and financial life. The unity of the left has been stretched by strong Socialist gains at the Communists' expense in municipal contests and by-elections. Chirac is realistically assuming that in time of trouble French people will vote their pocketbooks, not their hearts. President Giscard is betting his political future on the hope that good sense and good feelings can still be brought to walk hand in hand.

Review

A review of Giscard d'Estaing's rise to the presidency, and his exercise of its powers, may help to distinguish ways in which his

[1] Flora Lewis, "Giscard Shaping French Reform Plans," *New York Times,* March 18, 1975, p. 2.

176

personal career illustrates features of French political life in general and the importance of more or less fortuitous circumstances that are inevitably a part of all life and history.

Background and Training

As with Macmillan, so it has been with Giscard. The right family background, the right education, the right kind of marriage, the right sort of money, and the early cultivation of political ambition with the encouragement and practical help of a family clan deeply and traditionally immersed in politics—all are clearly factors in Giscard's rise to power. Consideration of some of his closest political competitors would no doubt reveal many of the same factors present, though to a lesser degree. For Giscard seems to have enjoyed many of these contributing elements to a political career in double amounts—perhaps symbolized by the fact that he gained diplomas from not just one, but two, of the grandes écoles.

In contradistinction to the political career of Macmillan, however, Giscard's rise was meteoric. He spent barely three years in the desert as opposed to Macmillan's seventeen years on the back benches of Parliament, and three years, at that, which he was able to turn to the very good purpose of creating his own political party, while at the same time remaining free from the risk of being hurt by the events of May 1968. Indeed, the fortuitous and the planned in his career are hard to distinguish.

We need only recall that he began his political career under the Fourth Republic, was unscathed by its brusque collapse, came to the attention of General de Gaulle when all successful political ambitions had to be linked with the General's power, and then skillfully detached himself as the old man's power began to fail, without alienating the General's broad public. It is perhaps true that fortune never dealt such good cards to Giscard's competitors. But certainly no one played a strong hand better than did Giscard in his rise to the presidency.

Unique Characteristics

But in pointing to the way in which Giscard moved successfully from the Fourth to the Fifth Republic and then into the period after de Gaulle, we risk overlooking some of the very marked continuities in the French political system in the face of rapid, almost violent, changes. Perhaps the most important and enduring characteristic of all is the statist tradition. A dominant trait of French political culture has long been the apparently high value put on logic, rather than on experience, as the key to governmental policy. This trait is in fact a natural extension of the revolutionary impulse inspired by 1789. For a thoroughgoing revolution means far more than merely a change of rulers or even of the rules. It means that a society tries to leave behind its own accumulated experience, substituting for the rejected past a set of abstract or logical ideas that have not yet been tested or tempered by history. In such a society, the wisdom of the "elders of the tribe" is not only deemed insufficient, but in some measure is actually repudiated, to make way for a presumably purer intelligence, unfettered by the prejudices, injustices, and unhappinesses of the past. A revolution, therefore, puts a premium on youth and logic, while sending its ancestors, at least symbolically, to the guillotine.

Napoleon Bonaparte incorporated this revolutionary attitude into the French system of public administration during his reign. Thus the form of the revolution became incarnate in the institutions of the French state, which continues even today to recruit its members from youthful elites on the basis of competitive examinations, a practice reflecting the idea that governing is a matter for experts in abstractions.

But of course the substance of the revolution could not find a permanent home, either then or now. Indeed, the substance of the revolution is its spirit, which is surely no closer to being realized today than is its motto of "liberty, equality, fraternity." Old ways of thinking and doing things are still characteristic of France, and nowhere more so than in the lives of ordinary people in the provincial towns and cities. And this fact Giscard has fully understood, as is shown by his early moves to give himself at least the appearance of a person from the provinces: Mayor of Chamalières, municipal councilor of Rochefort-Montagne, elected representative from Puy-de-Dôme—all positions designed to balance and even blur somewhat the image of the *polytechnicien,* the *énarque* (as graduates of the National School of Administration [ENA] are not so affectionately called), the "computer on stilts" of the Finance Inspectorate. He has tried and, in considerable measure, succeeded in combining in one public image two of the basic continuities of French political life. He is the incarnation of the logic of the state, the purely rational, the abstract, the Parisian mind and, at one and the same time, the representative of the old verities of the small towns and rural regions, whose residents know that Paris is the center of the universe, but also know they have to get along as well as they can in their own little worlds. In the first realm, Giscard is brilliant. In the second, he is *sympathique.* It should have been a perfect political combination, had not events taken their usual random course.

Administrative Skills and Political Problems
Can a regime like Giscard's succeed merely by sticking with technical economics and

political pragmatism, as if such methods were politically neutral or as if economic solutions would eventually suffice for dealing with political problems?

This view would perhaps be unexceptionable if the desire of most people to take care of themselves were the only consideration in public policy. But for this to be true, we should have to be exclusively economic in our thinking and being. And we should have to live in a world with an inexhaustible supply of resources, more or less evenly distributed, so that every nation—in fact, every region within every nation—would have a fair chance at economic development and economic growth. On top of that, the benefits and burdens of capital accumulation, so essential to the processes of economic growth, would have to be shared in a fair way so that those means of production with the worst records—for environmental degradation, low wages, miserable and dangerous lives for workers, and shoddy, misrepresented goods accompanied by consumer confusion—were not also the most profitable, that is, the most likely to accumulate new capital the fastest. And, finally, we should have to be far more prescient about the processes and consequences of technological change than we have proved to be during the past three hundred years.

Obviously, none of these conditions is met today in any advanced industrial society. Yet there was enough hope of their practical realization during most of the so-called industrial and technological revolutions to bring about the development of political and economic systems throughout the North Atlantic world that resemble one another in many ways, in both their good points and bad. France is no exception in most of these respects.

Yet there is one feature of French life that is perhaps exceptional and may help identify another continuity of French politics. This feature is a long-standing political concern for a certain conception of human culture. Successive generations of French people have believed that their nation is not simply a kind of biological organism—a sort of weed—whose unalterable destiny is to expand as far as its resources and environment will allow and then to shrivel and die as the natural environment becomes exhausted. Rather, the nation is a certain idea whose destiny is in the hands of human beings, because they can unite around (and fight about) the ways in which this certain idea should find public expression. In short, however necessary economic thinking is to political life in France, it is quite insufficient in and of itself to define French political culture.

As for Giscard, his status as successor to de Gaulle reflects the double image that France has of herself. Most of his public reputation is based on the image of a clear-thinking economist, making the kind of judgments expected of a competent businessman. In this light, he is a catalyst of economic forces in a technological age. After thorough calculation of the interests and forces involved, he prudently distributes the weight of public power in such a way as neither to undermine existing stabilities nor to discourage future balances from coming into being. He is manager of a machine that for all its dynamism is still a machine and requires for its maintenance but a good social engineer. This is an image held not only by the public, but apparently even by himself. When asked on a television interview whether he thought history would classify him as a great President, he answered with an emphatic "no," as if to imply that France no longer needed great leadership, but only competent management.

And yet of all current heads of advanced industrial states, Giscard seems the one most publicly aware that the prospects for the in-

definite progress of such societies toward ever higher standards of living and a general upgrading of the condition of their poor may now be the greatest of all the great illusions of the past century. In a press conference of October 24, 1974, he said that "the crisis the world knows today will be a long one. It is not a passing difficulty. It is actually an awareness of permanent change." Its elements, he continued, were well known; they were population growth, growing shortages of raw materials and energy, growing scarcity of food, and increasingly grave disturbances of the world's monetary patterns, aggravated by the major financial deficits of the oil-importing nations. As for the increasing scarcities of raw materials for industrial production in Europe, he commented, "They are the revenge of the nineteenth century against the twentieth. . . . All the [economic signs] are pointing down."

If the crisis is not a passing one, if the coming changes are going to be permanent, what is to become of Giscard's political pragmatism, which he insists is based on ideas neither traditionally capitalist nor socialist? What is to become of his hopes—described in *French Democracy,* a book he wrote in 1976—"for a modern democratic society, liberal in structure, pluralist in its powers, advanced to a high degree of economic performance, social unification and cultural development"?[2] Will not coming events bring again to the fore that other conception of political values, which Rousseau so long ago identified as opposed to the economic viewpoint?

Perhaps in the back of his mind Giscard is aware of this. Perhaps he is not a sentimental fellow who was straightened out by engineering school, after all. Perhaps he is, rather, a modern Hamlet.

So although the rise of Valéry Giscard

2 *New York Times,* October 10, 1976, p. 14.

d'Estaing was one of almost uninterrupted personal and political success, his real testing time is at hand. Relatively easy victories in earlier political skirmishes have given him the not so enviable right to be held responsible for leading France at a time when the nation is ever more torn by conflicting centrifugal and centripetal tendencies.

Selected Bibliography

For a lively, synoptic view of French history since 1760—political, social, economic, and intellectual—see Gordon Wright, *France in Modern Times* (Chicago: Rand McNally, 1960). The book is excellent in its parts and as a whole.

For a different kind of history, more aimed at the special concerns of political scientists, see David Thomson, *Democracy in France Since 1870,* 5th ed. (New York: Oxford University Press, 1969). This is a classic analysis exploring the "special meaning, character, and working of democracy in France" during the course of the twentieth century.

For an interesting variety of highly interpretative essays dealing especially with the period after 1945, see Stanley Hoffman et al., *In Search of France* (Cambridge, Mass.: Harvard University Press, 1963). Six authors deal with various French traditions and institutions from the diverse perspectives of their own respective disciplines.

For a broad and up-to-date study by a major specialist of contemporary France, see Henry W. Ehrmann, *Politics in France,* 3d ed. (Boston: Little Brown, 1976). This presents an interweaving of sociological factors and political analysis, with especially interesting materials on the processes of political socialization through education and the media.

In an age when discussion of decentralization is the rage in all advanced industrial nations, Mark Kesselman's study of local politics in France, *The Ambiguous Consensus: A Study of Local Government* (New York: Alfred A. Knopf, 1967), is especially pertinent.

No bibliography on modern France, no matter how brief, would be adequate without mentioning Laurence Wylie, *Village in the Vaucluse* (New York: Harper & Row, 1964). This is still the best of the now numerous studies of French village life. The texture and grain of everyday life are found here.

In light of the world's present economic difficulties, it is perhaps too easy to write off the turbulence of the late 1960s as the product a time when young people had lost sight of the realities. This is to misunderstand the protest against consumerism, bureaucracy, and industrialism—a protest that is perhaps for the moment in abeyance because of unemployment, but remains no less important. In the case of France, in particular, the literature on the events of May 1968 is now so voluminous that interested students should refer to a recent bibliography: Laurence Wylie, Franklin Chu, and Mary Terrall, *France: The Events of May–June 1968, A Critical Bibliography* (Cambridge, Mass.: Harvard University, 1973), published under the auspices of the Council for West European Studies.

III

Willy Brandt:
Politician
and Statesman

Gerard Braunthal

Willy Brandt:
Short Biographical Sketch

On December 18, 1913, Willy Brandt, then named Herbert Frahm, was born in Lübeck, Germany. After joining various Social Democratic youth organizations, he was admitted into the Social Democratic party (SPD) in 1930, but left the party after just one year and joined the Socialist Workers party. In 1932, he completed formal schooling and received a high school certificate.

Hitler's rise to power in 1933 forced Brandt to flee to Norway, where he worked as a political journalist and headed the party coordination center until the Nazi invasion of 1940. During this time he traveled extensively in Europe, including trips to Germany and war-torn Spain. From 1940 to 1945 he lived in Swedish exile. His first marriage to Carlota Thorkildsen in 1941 lasted a few years; in 1948 he married Rut Hansen.

In 1944 Brandt rejoined the SPD, Stockholm branch; one year later he returned to postwar Germany as a Norwegian journalist. In 1947 he became press attaché with the Norwegian military mission in Berlin. The following year he started his political career in the SPD as di-

rector of the Berlin liaison office. From 1949 to 1957 (and again from 1969 to the present) he was one of the Deputies in the German Bundestag, and from 1950 to 1956 he was a member of the Berlin Chamber of Deputies, becoming its President in 1955. He served as Governing Mayor of Berlin from 1957 to 1966 and head of the Berlin SPD from 1958 to 1964.

Brandt's rise to national prominence was assured when in 1961 and 1965 he became the party's candidate for Chancellor. In 1962 he was elected Deputy Chairman of the SPD, and two years later Chairman—a post that he retains presently. From 1966 to 1969 Brandt served as Vice Chancellor and Foreign Minister in a coalition Cabinet in Bonn. In 1969, in the wake of an electoral victory for the SPD and its potential junior coalition partner, the Free Democratic party, Brandt became Chancellor. In 1972, another electoral victory assured his reappointment as Chancellor. Two years later, as a result of a spy scandal, he resigned the nation's highest political office. He has been the recipient of the Nobel Peace Prize and other top awards.

1

Introduction:
Germany – Land and People

The beautiful Hanseatic city of Lübeck in northern Germany was the birthplace of Willy Brandt. As a child, the future Chancellor of the Federal Republic of Germany must have been impressed by the charm of the old, high-gabled buildings and the seafaring atmosphere of the city, which had formerly belonged to the Hanseatic League, an association of cities that had engaged in trade with Scandinavia and Russia for many centuries. While Lübeck and his family were the immediate setting for Brandt's childhood and youth, his personal growth and attitudes were also shaped by broader historical forces and the national political, economic, and social configurations. Thus, before we begin the political biography of Brandt and see the interrelationships between the political systems in which he lived and his life, we must first consider Germany's geographic, demographic, socioeconomic, and historical settings as well as the contemporary political system of the Federal Republic.

Geographic and Demographic Characteristics

Germany lies in the heart of central Europe and occupies a territory that lacks natural obstacles on its frontiers, hence making military invasions in all directions relatively easy. The country has three major geographic regions: the northern German plain, the central German uplands, and a mixed region in the south—hills, valleys, lowlands, and the Bavarian Alps. Since 1949, the territory has been divided into two states, the Federal Republic of Germany (FRG, or West Germany) and the German Democratic Republic (GDR, or East Germany). Berlin, the capital of prewar Germany, also was divided. Located inside East Germany, more than one hundred miles from West Germany's border, West Berlin became a city-state of the Federal Republic, while East Berlin became the capital of the German Democratic Republic.

The demographic configuration of a country—in terms of age distribution, urban-rural balance, and sex ratios—affects not only voting behavior, but also the economic structure and the size of the military establishment. The total German population at the outbreak of World War II, primarily of German ethnic origin, totaled close to 70 million (including 10 million who lived in territories later ceded to the Soviet Union and Poland); by 1975 West Germany alone (including West Berlin) had an estimated 61.5 million, a gain of 18.5 million living in the same area. This gain was caused primarily by three groups: expellees and refugees immediately after the war, most of whom came

Germany

from the German-settled territories in Czechoslovakia and Poland (about 9 million); refugees from East Germany who escaped prior to the building of the Wall in 1961 (3 million); and foreign workers, many with their families (4 million). East Germany's population (including East Berlin) has stabilized at 17 million, a figure that is now hardly higher than that of 1939 because of the flight of a part of its population to West Germany. In the Federal Republic, the sexes are divided as 52 percent female and 48 percent male, a ratio caused partly by male attrition during wartime.

In both German states the population is predominantly urban. In the Federal Republic, one-fifth of the population resides in eleven large cities, and nearly one-half in small or medium-sized towns and cities, with a heavy concentration in the industrialized Ruhr region. In the German Democratic Republic, the pattern is nearly the same, although a proportionately greater number of people live in rural areas.

Religious Characteristics

Religious affiliations of a country's population often have an impact on its historical and political development. From 1871 to 1945, German Protestants outnumbered Catholics by a two-to-one ratio, although Catholics formed a majority in several regions, such as Bavaria, Silesia, and the Rhineland. Thus Protestants had a greater impact on national policy than Catholics, while educational and cultural policies of the constituent states varied depending on which religious group had a majority.

In the post–World War II period, the situation has changed dramatically. In East Germany the preponderance of Protestants is striking; only 11 percent of the population is Catholic. In West Germany the religious affiliation is more nearly balanced, with 45 percent Catholic, 49 percent Protestant, and 6 percent other or no denomination—only 0.1 percent is Jewish. As will be illustrated later, the religious distribution has had an impact on the strength of political parties and on public issues.

The Economic Base

The economic structure of a country as well as its trading pattern and financial strength provide clues to its capacity for growth, its potential for providing an adequate standard of living for its citizens, and its political stability. Once the devastation of war was cleared away in West Germany and foreign aid was channeled in through the Marshall Plan financed by the United States, the country used its natural resources (coal and iron ore being among the most important) and its high productivity to great advantage. In 1948, Ludwig Erhard, a high government official and future Minister of Economic Affairs, provided impetus to West German recovery by pursuing a free market policy with an accent on social welfare. He initiated a set of decontrols of the economic sector that set in motion the dormant productive capacities and the pent-up consumer demand for material goods. In order to stimulate the economy further, unions restrained their wage demands and employers invested in plants and modernization of facilities. As a result, total industrial production by the end of 1949 surpassed that of 1936, overseas markets were recaptured, and annual growth rates averaged 10 percent. In short, in the 1950s an economic miracle occurred that few other countries could match. Soon West Germany became the leading economic power in Western Europe.

One of the key components of this economic strength has been the country's trade. The Federal Republic ranks as the second most important trading country in the world, surpassed only by the United States, with much of its trade oriented toward the West and the Third World. West Germany imports primarily semifinished products, agricultural commodities, and raw materials, while its exports consist primarily of finished manufactured goods, including machines and machine tools, automobiles, chemicals, electrical and iron products. Yearly export surpluses have produced the highest favorable balance of payments in the world and a huge stock of gold and foreign exchange.

This economic prosperity and affluence suffered setbacks in the 1960s and 1970s in terms of unemployment and inflation, causing increased governmental assistance and regulation. In general, however, the average citizen—who owns an automobile, a refrigerator, a television set, and a washing machine —enjoys a comfortable standard of living.

Social Change
The legacy of Germany's past was bound to produce social changes in the Federal Republic. The impact of the war had acted as a powerful leveler of prewar class differences, although occupational and social mobility is not yet as pronounced as in the United States. A residue of class bias and tradition still inhibits most children of lower-income groups from seeking a higher education: as many as four out of five pupils leave school at the age of fourteen. Those who continue represent a disproportionately high percentage from middle-class families, whose parents encourage their children to seek a university education. Consequently, only 5 to 10 percent of university students hail from working-class families.

While education has remained a psychological barrier to advancement, an occupational shift has occurred, paralleling that found in the United States and other advanced industrial societies. The number of farmers and self-employed small entrepre-

neurs has plummeted (to 15 percent in 1972) and the number of blue-collar workers has declined gradually (to 45.3 percent), while the number of white-collar employees has increased swiftly (to 39.7 percent). The status and income of blue-collar workers, however, have increased in recent times, narrowing the social and income gap with the white-collar employees. Indeed, no longer is it uncommon to see a factory worker earning more money than a low-level civil servant or a clerical worker.

Limited social mobility has not meant the elimination of a rather blurred class system, but it has produced shifts among the elites in such institutional power centers as the government, the economy, and the churches. The political elite tends to be more heterogeneous than in earlier systems, with a chance for individuals from the lower and middle classes to rise into positions of power, especially when the Social Democrats are governing. The economic elite, too, has significant power in the world of politics. The influence of the churches has seen some decline, yet the Catholic church will still take a vigorous stand on issues, such as education and abortion, that are of importance to it.

Shifts also have taken place in the family and in the role of women. The paternalistic extended family of earlier decades is not yet a relic of the past, but it has been replaced increasingly by the nuclear family, especially in urban areas and among younger couples, in which a partnership between husband and wife is slowly developing. As a result of social awareness, the wife is playing a more important role in making decisions within the family; and as a result of legislation, she is not to be discriminated against in opportunities for employment or education, in divorce proceedings, or in the control of property. With an increase in the number of women entering the labor force, their role in society has become more significant, though their number in the political arena is as small as in the United States. While the women's liberation movement is only in its infancy (as compared to that in the United States), the heated controversy over legalizing abortion in the early 1970s raised the political consciousness of many women, especially after the Federal Constitutional Court in 1975 ruled a pro-abortion bill unconstitutional. In any case, the women's vote is crucial to all political parties, and issues of importance to women cannot be ignored by politicians.

A social problem that has remained unsolved has been the indifference shown by the bulk of the population to the millions of foreign workers and families in their midst. The Germans needed the workers to fill a labor shortage, especially in the unskilled, low-status jobs, but have treated them as outcasts and social undesirables. In the face of a persistent unemployment hitting Germans and foreigners alike in the mid-1970s, social tensions have correspondingly increased.

Yet despite tensions and problems characteristic of most advanced industrial states, the Federal Republic has witnessed a remarkable stability when compared to some earlier periods in German history. Whether such a stability, which ranges from the social and economic to the political spheres, can last in the face of serious problems encountered by some of Germany's neighbors remains to be seen. But in the meantime the average German citizen lives in a socially advanced state and enjoys a high standard of living—to the envy of many others.

2

German Government:
An Overview

Few other states can match the kaleidoscopic succession of political systems—empires, confederations, a Nazi Reich, republics—and the changing boundaries that characterize Germany. Its history is marked by violent power struggles among contending leaders and by a search for national cohesion among peoples who seek to maintain their ethnic roots, common culture, and language. The bulk of these people have lived between the Rhine and the Elbe rivers, but enough others settled in adjoining regions to produce political and military tensions with Germany's neighbors.

The Historical Legacy

After Rome's sovereignty over much of Europe collapsed in the mid–fifth century, political turmoil beset western and central Europe. While a succession of dynasties, be-ginning with Charlemagne in A.D. 800, reigned over this sprawling territory, actual power in the Holy Roman Empire was dispersed among a host of rulers governing small kingdoms, duchies, electorates, and principalities. The rulers were in constant conflict with the popes as well as among themselves—for example the Thirty Years' War, 1618–1648. When Napoleon swept through Germany in 1806, Prussia lost about half of its territory, most of the minor principalities were crushed, and sixteen territories in central Germany and the Rhineland were amalgamated into the short-lived Confederation of the Rhine.

Napoleon's defeat in 1815 produced new shifts in power and boundaries. The Congress of Vienna created a German Confederation of thirty-nine states, including an enlarged Prussia, to be ruled by Austria. Because of Prussia's challenge for supremacy and the inability of the representatives of the kings and princes to concur on vital external and internal security matters, the confederation remained shaky. Further difficulties arose with the 1848 revolution, one of several liberal national uprisings that swept Europe at the time. The German revolution was led by a new and growing liberal middle class that was still in a weak position because of the country's late industrialization. It was rebelling against the entrenched aristocracy and seeking to establish a national state and a democratic constitutional system. In May 1848 its representatives, predominantly intellectuals, first met as a National Assembly in Frankfort on the Main, and by March 1849 they produced a draft constitution embodying their aspirations for a more liberal order in which individual rights would be protected. But by the time they finished their deliberations, Prussian and Austrian reactionary forces regained strength and dissolved the National Assembly. Thus aborted the movement for national union and liberation—late in Germany when compared to the United States, Great Britain, and France.

It was not, paradoxically, liberal forces that eventually ended the territorial fragmentation of the confederation and established a national state. Credit must go instead to the conservative Prince Otto von Bismarck, whose skilled leadership as Chief Minister of Prussia led him to proclaim in 1871 the Second Reich, following the brief existence (1866–1871) of the North German Confederation and the military victory over France in 1871. National unification at last had been achieved, but not by democratic forces that could have taken credit for and been identified with the movement for self-determination.

The Second Empire

In the creation of a new state, the constitution may provide an important legitimizing framework for those exercising power. It may limit their powers, at least in theory, and it may guarantee and protect individual freedoms. But there was only tokenism, as far as such democratic objectives were concerned, in the 1871 constitution written by Bismarck. In reality, the German people remained under autocratic rule. Powers were vested primarily in the executive branch, headed by a hereditary Kaiser (Wilhelm I until 1888, Wilhelm II until 1918) who also happened to be King of Prussia. Although the Kaiser had such formal powers as the position of commander in chief of the armed forces and the right to declare war and to make foreign policy, the real executive power lay in the hands of Prussia's Chief Minister and national Chancellor (Bismarck until 1890, several successors until 1918). To ensure that the subversive ideas of liberal democracy would not triumph over authoritarian rule, the Iron Chancellor, as Bismarck was so aptly called, included in the constitution a provision that the Chancellor would be appointed by and responsible to the Kaiser, not to the legislature.

The Kaiser and Bismarck held supreme power not only in Prussia, but also in the Bundesrat (upper house of Parliament). Bismarck's control over the popularly elected Reichstag (lower house) was in theory less tight than over the Bundesrat, but in practice he held the upper hand. First, much domestic legislation emanated from the Prussian legislature controlling the bulk of the Reich territory, and not from the Reichstag. State legislative members were elected by a restrictive suffrage system skewed to produce only conservative majorities. Second, political parties represented in the Reichstag had little chance to block Bismarck's programs as he manipulated or bargained with them, and at times even attempted to suppress them (for example, the Catholic-dominated Center party from 1871 to 1875, and the Marxist-dominated Social Democratic party [SPD] from 1878 to 1890), in order to maintain political power. Despite such moves, the parties, including the middle-class-oriented National Liberals and the Prussian-dominated Conservatives, were not cowed. Indeed, the chief opposition party, the SPD, expanded its strength.

What kind of a party was the SPD—the political home of Willy Brandt? Founded in 1875, the product of an amalgamation of two socialist organizations created in the 1860s, this working-class party owed a debt to Karl Marx and other socialist veterans for its ideological and programmatic development. While the program was anticapitalist and revolutionary in content, espousing international proletarian solidarity and the class struggle of workers against the bourgeoisie, the party did not eschew working through Parliament to attain social reforms. At the turn of the century, a reformist wing, led by Eduard Bernstein and supported by the bulk of trade union leaders, sought to offer an alternative to the Marxist model. Influenced by the British Fabian approach to politics, Bernstein emphasized the evolutionary road to socialism through a program of gradual reforms and a rejection of revolution. He attempted to downplay the Marxist influence in the party, but could make only limited headway during the final years of the Second Empire. Despite the internal feud between radical and reformist wings, the well-organized party attracted an increasing number of members and voters. By 1912 it received close to one-third of the Reichstag seats, thanks to an increasingly articulate working-class movement that identified its interests primarily with the SPD. Yet that strength was insufficient to produce a political breakthrough.

Power was still concentrated in the hands of the conservative Chancellors, civil ser-

vants, and the army elite, who sought to preserve the status quo. The landed gentry and the rising industrial elite had assumed a principal role in the nation's affairs. They could easily identify with Bismarck and his successors, who enhanced Germany's international prestige and pursued a policy of national integration and nationalism, as reflected in the calls for German preparedness and unity. The industrialists may have been less enamored of Bismarck's ambitious social welfare program, even though it stole the thunder from socialist doctrine. But what all governing and economic elites had in common was a veneration for the state, authority, conservation of traditional values, and subordination of the individual to the state. They viewed the Reichstag as a body of legislators making sordid deals and the workers as a lower class threatening their interests. In short, they contributed to the costly delay in the emergence of a democratic ethos.

In spite of their calls for national unity, the governing elites failed to produce cohesion—southern and western Germany could not bow easily to Prussian hegemony, nor could the exploited industrial and agricultural working masses, sympathetic to the SPD, kowtow to a regime that had no sympathy for their aspirations. Thus in 1914, on the eve of World War I, Germany was governed by rulers who were unwilling to make concessions for the establishment of a parliamentary democracy or for greater personal freedoms.

The war, partly caused by Germany's expansionist goals, at first produced among the population a strong patriotic and nationalist fervor. Even the SPD, previously committed to international workers' solidarity, took on a nationalist stance and supported the war effort because it was afraid that its organization would be destroyed by the government and because it viewed the defeat of the reactionary tsarist regime in Russia as vital. After years of bloody fighting, a German victory did not materialize. Only when workers became increasingly restive and participated in political strikes and demonstrations did Chancellor Prince Max von Baden promise to establish a constitutional monarchy with limited executive powers. But by then it was too late.

Weimar Republic

Military defeats on the battlefronts and civil disturbances had their political consequences. In November 1918, in the wake of a mutiny among sailors, food riots in the cities, and demands for his abdication, Kaiser Wilhelm II fled the country, and the German High Command sued for peace. On November 9, Chancellor von Baden turned over constitutional authority to Friedrich Ebert of the SPD, who promptly proclaimed the establishment of a republic. Power was vested during this revolutionary transition period in a Council of People's Delegates, consisting of leaders of the Social Democratic and Independent Socialist parties—the latter having split off from the SPD during the war over dissatisfaction with the SPD's prowar stance. Workers' and soldiers' councils, patterned on the soviets in the Soviet Union, seized power at the local level, but soon most were in the hands of the SPD.

Characteristic of German history, no major uprising had occurred against the imperial state authority or against the established economic and social order. The major parties, including the socialists, had no blueprint ready to set up a regime that would swiftly produce fundamental changes in the country. They debated for years—without taking any action—whether or not industry should be nationalized, the Junker agricultural estates in East Prussia expropriated, and conservative army officers, civil servants, and

judges purged. Hence, the dominant economic and social forces of the Second Reich remained in a powerful position in the Weimar era.

A left minority of Independent Socialists and Spartacists (Communists) did demand fundamental reforms and the continued rule of the workers' and soldiers' councils. In a number of cities and regions they staged demonstrations, strikes, and uprisings to force concessions from those in power. But their efforts were in vain; the Reichswehr (army) was used to quell them in bloody reprisals. Fearful of Germany turning communist, the SPD leaders decided to establish swiftly a parliamentary regime.

In 1919, in the city of Weimar, a national assembly of members from the SPD, the Center party, the German Democratic Party, and conservative parties met to draft a constitution. The document was intended to lay the framework for a new democratic political order to replace the autocratic imperial system. The constitution's authors looked to certain features in the British parliamentary system for a workable model and blended into it progressive provisions to protect individual and social rights.

The President, popularly elected, was to be head of state with the usual powers that accompany this role in European parliamentary systems—such as receiving and accrediting diplomats, formally appointing the Chancellor, and countersigning laws. But the President's powers extended beyond those of the British monarch because Article 48 granted that office the right to suspend a number of constitutional guarantees and to rule by decree. The Chancellor once again was the chief political executive who with the Cabinet members formulated and executed government policy. Parliament consisted of a weak Reichsrat (upper house) and a strong Reichstag (lower house). The latter had to consent to the appointment of Chancellor and Cabinet members and could enact laws over the veto of the Reichsrat.

The constitution could have served as the foundation for an admirable democratic system, but too many upheavals soon shook the society into which it was introduced. Strong antidemocratic and nationalist forces labeled the SPD and other democratic parties responsible for the signing of the Versailles peace treaty. To these reactionary forces, the acceptance of the treaty ending World War I was so punitive and humiliating to Germany that it represented a stab in the back. With some telling effect, they denounced the SPD's lack of patriotism and won converts among many army and paramilitary units, whose loyalty to the republic was questionable at best. Some of the antidemocratic and nationalist forces also were responsible in 1920 for an attempted coup against the regime and for the assassinations of several democratic leaders in the early years of the republic. Their destructive efforts were paralleled by the French occupation of the Rhineland and the Allied extraction of large reparations payments. German government officials also had to combat a disastrous inflation and other economic dislocation.

From 1924 to 1929, Germany enjoyed a few precious years of relative economic and political stability. Although ten political parties produced shifting parliamentary majorities and frequent turnover of coalition Cabinets, enough Ministers remained in office to produce continuity in policies. An increasing popular commitment to the Weimar Republic seemed in evidence, but then in 1929 came the Great Depression.

The country was plunged into chaos as unemployment mounted to catastrophic proportions. Desperate voters turned to the National Socialists and Communists for a solution to their problems. Authoritarian conservative governments sought to maintain stability invoking the emergency provisions of Article 48, thereby further undermining the principle of parliamentary democracy. Their efforts to maintain stability were unsuccessful. On January 30, 1933, President Hindenburg, wary of political intrigues and fearful of a civil war, appointed as Chancellor the National Socialist leader Adolf Hitler, whose party had a strong, but not majority, representation in the Reichstag. The Weimar experiment in democracy, sparked by the SPD, had lasted less than fifteen years.

The Nazi Era

Without a bloody revolution, a new political system emerged swiftly from the ruins of the ill-fated parliamentary system. Once again, as in 1918, there was an orderly transfer of constitutional powers, but in 1933 few could forecast the catastrophe that would beset Germany and the world. True, Hitler's writings and his party's propaganda prior to 1933 gave clues to the direction his policy would take. There were ample references against the Jews and to the need for a virulent nationalism, a strong centralized government, the repeal of the Versailles treaty, and a build-up of the Reichswehr. Yet there were few clues that there would emerge a fascist system bent on the attempted annihilation of all political opponents and Jews at home and, eventually, on war abroad.

The German people did not have to wait long for many of these policies to surface. Soon after Hitler became Chancellor, he instituted a reign of terror against the left political parties. In March 1933, he intimidated all but the Social Democrats in the Reichstag in voting for an enabling act (an amendment to the constitution) that would provide him with powers to govern and legislate without the support of the Reichstag. He launched a policy of "coordination," in which all trade unions, all political parties other than the National Socialists, and all other democratic organizations were dissolved—or dissolved themselves. This policy facilitated the emergence of a totalitarian dictatorship in which the Nazi party, the leader, and the state became nearly synonymous, the rule of law was eliminated, and a system of terror, concentration camps, and executions of opponents was instituted. The annihilation of millions of Jews followed thereafter. Brave resistance groups emerged, but the efficient Gestapo wiped out most of them.

The Führer ensured himself Reichswehr support by becoming Commander in Chief, requiring the generals to swear an oath of loyalty to him personally, and promising them generous doses of armaments. Unlike Weimar leaders, he had no hesitation in purging civil servants, judges, professors, and other unreliable individuals from their posts.

He also ensured himself the support of the bulk of the population by swiftly reviving the economy through a program of public works, labor camps, and conscription, by creating a mammoth Labor Front providing recreation and cheap vacations to workers, and by placing a number of restrictions on big business, although also encouraging a concentration of industry. Thus he was able to govern without major difficulties through a massive propaganda effort and clever manipulation of the various social groups— indeed, with their active support.

This support also extended to Hitler's activist foreign policy that led to annexation of neighboring territories containing German-speaking peoples, such as Austria in 1938. Initially, the Western powers put up no resistance, but then Hitler overextended himself. In 1939, he launched a war against Poland in continuation of his piecemeal annexationist policy. In this instance, Great Britain and France reversed their appeasement policy and declared war on Germany.

World War II soon engulfed other states. At first Germany was victorious on the battlefield and occupied the bulk of the European continent. In 1941, it attacked the Soviet Union and declared war on the United States when the latter was attacked by Japan. The massive battles in Russia and Western Allied air attacks on German cities reversed the German tide. In May 1945, with defeat staring him in the face, Hitler committed suicide in a Berlin underground bunker. The Reich that Hitler had proclaimed would last "one thousand years" crumbled after twelve fateful years, having produced the most thorough break in German history. The damage that the Führer, his associates, and his millions of supporters had caused the world was incalculable.

Postwar Occupation and Reconstruction

During World War II, while the savage fighting was continuing but victory seemed in sight, the Allied powers (United States, Great Britain, France, and the Soviet Union) made plans for a postwar Germany. They decided to carve the country into occupation zones (causing the dismemberment of Prussia), to extract a more modest amount of reparations than that demanded after World War I, and to proceed with denazification and demilitarization. When a Nazi government leader surrendered unconditionally to the Allies in May 1945, power was transferred to the military victors. A few months after surrender, they created an Allied Control Authority for Germany responsible for dealing with matters of common concern to their four respective zones and empowered each zonal authority to act unilaterally within its own territory. The tasks of the Allied and zonal authorities were tremendous because the country lay in ruins, was short of food and other essentials, suffered a transportation breakdown, and had to cope with millions of refugees from the east.

Parallel to the efforts to rebuild the country came efforts to reshape basic institutions and processes in order to prevent a new Germany from embarking on ruinous policies. With varying degrees of success, the Allies sought to purge the Nazis from influential posts, permit the functioning of local government, democratize the administration of justice, reform the tax structure and public finance, and break up the industrial cartels.

Wartime Allied unity soon evaporated. The intention of the four powers to pursue a common political and economic policy was dashed when the Soviet Union and France, not forgetful of the invasion and destruction of their countries at the hands of a powerful German war machine, had increasing doubts about the wisdom of creating a united Germany. A further rift occurred when the Western Allies reacted negatively to the Soviet Union's imposition of a communist system on East Germany and East Berlin. (Berlin had been divided into four Allied-occupied sectors comparable to Germany's division into four zones.) The Western Allies also viewed Soviet reparations policy as too damaging and punitive to Germany.

The Soviets in turn were unhappy over the launching of the Marshall Plan to aid West Germany and Western Europe, over United States and British vetoes of German proposals to nationalize industry in the two western zones, and over the creation in 1947 of a bizonal economic authority in the West German territory. When the latter received executive and legislative functions in 1948, the Soviets viewed it correctly as a forerunner of a separate state. Their initial concern over a united German state had shifted to a fear of a potentially strong West German state that might be a more attractive model to the East German people than their own political sys-

tem. The Allied rift widened in 1948 when the Western powers introduced a currency reform in their zones in order to stimulate the economy and halt Soviet manipulation of occupation currency. In turn, the Russians imposed a blockade on West Berlin, necessitating in response a massive airlift of supplies to that beleaguered city. In short, Germany had become a battlefront in the emerging Cold War that supplanted the brief wartime honeymoon between the Western powers and the Soviet Union.

Before the rift widened, United States and British occupation authorities permitted a limited measure of self-government to the Germans, first at the local level and then at the state (*Land,* plural *Länder*) level. A more reluctant France did not grant such powers until 1948. In the three western zones, political parties were licensed to provide voters with a choice of rival candidates in local and Land elections. By 1948 it was clear to the Western Allies that a united Germany was not in the offing; a London conference that year confirmed their intention to permit the creation of a West German state whose territory would encompass the three zones. West German politicians, who would have preferred a united Germany, reluctantly gave their assent to this alternative. The Western Allies thereupon decided that a Parliamentary Council, whose members were to be elected by the Länder, would draft a Basic Law for the projected new state. For cosmetic purposes, the Basic Law was not to be called a constitution in order to give it the appearance of a temporary document that would be supplanted by a constitution of an eventual united Germany.

The Parliamentary Council was composed of an equal number of Christian Democrats and Social Democrats and a few minor party representatives. It had the task of drafting a Basic Law that would satisfy not only the often conflicting goals of its members but also those of the Western Allies. The members deliberated for eight months before they could agree on a document that would reconcile their views and prevent the mistakes of Weimar. In May 1949, the Western Allies and the Länder parliaments approved the Basic Law. In August, elections took place for the Federal Parliament. In September, the Federal Republic was born when its first government took office.

The Federal Republic

The Basic Law provided the constitutional framework for the political forces and institutions in West Germany. But as the new state matured, the political dynamics of the system evolved on their own. In the course of time a citizenry reluctant since 1945 to plunge once again into the political maelstrom gradually became more supportive of the new government and participated in the electoral process designed to give them an opportunity to do their civic duty. A changed pattern of German political culture and behavior became visible as the democratic ethos was emphasized in the schools and the media.

The Electoral System
Federal legislation provides for a mixture of Weimar's proportional representation and the Anglo-Saxon single-member constituency system. This unusual hybrid system was designed for election of Deputies to the Bundestag (lower house) in order to reduce the number of splinter parties, which had been a problem during the Weimar era. More specifically, the law stipulates that to receive Bundestag representation a party must either obtain a minimum of 5 percent of the total federal vote or win three seats in the districts. This provision has effectively

shut out many minor parties on the national scene.

How does the new system work? One-half of the seats are allotted to the single-member districts, the other half to parties that draw up slates of candidates in each of the ten regular Länder (as will be described, West Berlin has a special status). A voter casts two votes—one for his district candidate and another for the party slate. In the district, the candidate who receives a plurality of votes wins the election. At the Land level, the number of seats allotted to each party is determined by the percentage of the total votes it received under a complex system of proportional representation. A candidate may stand for election both in a district and on a party list as added insurance of gaining a Bundestag seat. If a candidate is not placed high on the list, election is unlikely unless he or she has won in the district or unless the party has received an avalanche of votes in the Land.

Political Parties
The Basic Law recognizes the right of political parties to organize and to function within the new system. This legitimization was intended to link the individual voter to the government and to prohibit parties that could undermine or destroy its democratic foundation. The Party Law of 1967 regulates the parties' internal structures, such as elections of officers, membership expulsion, and financing. As a result of this law and of court decisions, the parties receive government subsidies on a basis proportionate to the number of votes they received in the previous federal election. In addition, the parties also gain income from membership dues and from private organizations, such as corporations.

The parties, nearly all supportive of the governmental order, have provided political stability to the Federal Republic. No longer are the voters faced by a multiplicity of ideologically based parties (as in the Weimar period) or by a single party (as in the Nazi period), but normally by only two major parties and one minor party, although at the outset of the Federal Republic era quite a number of minor parties were competing for votes. As in Great Britain, ideological differences between the three parties are no longer sharply defined; rather, pragmatic differences on specific issues or, if these are unimportant, the personality profiles of candidates are emphasized.

In a review of each party, let us examine the Social Democratic party first, since Brandt has been one of its most illustrious leaders. The SPD was swiftly reconstituted after 1945; but not until 1972 could it gain a plurality of votes because its erstwhile area of greatest support, East Germany, was cut off. The party receives important backing not only from the industrial working class, but increasingly from government employees, clerical workers, and young voters. A typical voter would be a Protestant residing in an urban-industrial area who is sympathetic to the party's slightly left-of-center ideology. Membership in the party has had its ups and downs, but in recent years it has remained steady at close to 1 million.

The party's hierarchical organization differs little from other parties in West Germany or elsewhere. With few exceptions, policy is made by the top bodies and filters down to the local branches. The latter serve as centers to recruit members, collect dues, hold membership meetings, and participate in election campaigns. At the regional and subregional levels, candidates for high party office are selected, election campaigns are organized, and local and state problems are identified. According to SPD statute, the party's national convention, normally held every two years, is the highest authority. But policy decisions, especially those of an urgent

and unforeseen nature, can hardly be made by a convention that meets so infrequently. In practice, decisions are made by the smaller executive organs and ratified by the four hundred convention delegates, most of whom are paid party officials from the local and regional levels. During convention proceedings they will vote on reports of specialized party commissions (for example, property rights reform or abortion) and on hundreds of resolutions introduced by party organs and local branches. While resolutions from the base provide a tool for membership participation, they only give the appearance of participatory democracy. Controversial resolutions have little chance of passage or are shunted to the executive organs where they will be quietly shelved.

The de facto highest authority is the Presidium, or inner cabinet. Elected by the Executive Committee, these eleven senior party leaders, including SPD Cabinet Ministers since 1966, meet weekly to decide party organizational matters and the SPD position on domestic and foreign policy issues. These decisions are subsequently affirmed without much discussion by the Executive Committee. The latter consists of thirty-six members, all elected by the convention, including the Party Chairman, the two Deputy Chairmen, and the Treasurer.

Less important party organs are the Control Commission, handling grievances, and the Party Council, voting on Presidium and Executive Committee decisions. The council consists of a few Cabinet Ministers when the SPD is in power, regional party representatives, and deputies from the Land and national legislatures. Thus it serves as a coordinating mechanism between party and government.

Closely linked to the SPD organization is its *Fraktion,* the parliamentary group in the Bundestag. The Fraktion executive is well represented in the party organs, where it plays an important role in shaping policy. Deputies are encouraged to specialize in a substantive area in order to become experts in the Bundestag committees and on party boards.

A party with a mass membership is bound to be plagued by factional disputes reflecting ideological schisms within its disparate groups, and the SPD has been no exception. There are left and right wings whose representatives have frequently clashed in public, and a center group, led by Willy Brandt, which attempts to conciliate the warring wings. The left wing consists of the Young Socialists (Jusos), the party's articulate and often Marxist-oriented group of 300,000 members under thirty-five years of age. Typical of youth groups in other countries, the Young Socialists in recent years have taken the offensive against the right-wing leaders, calling their views pragmatic and devoid of ideology and accusing them of abandoning the goal of socialism. The Young Socialists have captured party branches in several cities and have gained about one-third of the seats on the party's Executive Committee.

The right wing, led presently by Chancellor Helmut Schmidt, believes that the SPD must not be an ideological party. Instead, it must serve as an integrative people's party appealing not only to the workers but to most segments of society. Whenever supported by the center group, the right wing is in control of all national policy-making bodies, including the Bundestag Fraktion. Its members are well-organized and vote in a bloc on issues. This faction receives important support from the powerful trade unions, although on occasion differences have arisen between them.

The second major party in the Federal Republic is the Christian Democratic Union (CDU). Prominent Catholic and Protestant lay leaders, noted figures in business, and nonsocialist trade union leaders founded the party after World War II. Many of the Catholic officials, such as Konrad Adenauer (the Federal Republic's first Chancellor), had belonged to the Center party of Weimar vintage—a Catholic party with only limited voter support. The CDU leaders were intent on establishing an interdenominational Christian movement based on a wide array of groups having a broad electoral appeal. They hoped to create a party with a strong counterweight to the more secular SPD. Their goal was not impractical because the times seemed ripe for a party that could bridge the traditional historical gap between Catholics and Protestants. Religious divisions were no longer acceptable to leaders who had suffered common persecution at the hands of the Nazis.

From 1945 on, the party grew into a nation-wide organization; in 1950 it held its first federal congress and adopted a constitution. Given its emphasis on a broad Christian movement, the CDU was bound to collect disparate groups—ranging from a Catholic trade union wing to conservatives in business—thereby increasing the difficulty of obtaining policy support from all groups. In the British zone, the party even adopted a Christian socialist program in 1947 that called for the nationalization of basic industries and labor's participation in management. But as the party gained a foothold in other parts of the Federal Republic, it abandoned the socialist goals and opted for a free enterprise system with a strong component of social welfare.

The conservative segment of the population supported not only this economic program but also Adenauer's call for European integration, backing of the Western alliance system, and opposition to socialism and communism. This popular support, facilitated by Adenauer's ability to hold the party's disparate groups together, provided the winning margin for the national electoral victories from 1949 to 1969. But by the late 1950s, Adenauer's prestige began to slip, and other party chiefs counseled him to retire.

In 1963, the eighty-seven-year-old Chancellor reluctantly stepped down from the post he held for fourteen years—although he remained Party Chairman until 1966. His Minister of Economic Affairs, Ludwig Erhard, who had been the architect of the government's social-market economy, succeeded him, but remained at the helm of government for only three years. Since 1966 the party has had a number of chairmen who have not possessed the magnetic personality of Adenauer; as a consequence the party, forced into parliamentary opposition after 1969, has had difficulties. It has failed to present a dynamic electoral appeal and to maintain internal cohesion and harmonious links to the Christian Social Union (CSU, the CDU's Bavarian affiliate). The slippage in electoral appeal in 1972, which was reversed in 1976, has also been caused by a shift in population from rural CDU/CSU strongholds to urban SPD strongholds, a continuing secularization of the population, and the CDU's failure to capture the support of enough young voters.

The party has a membership of about 630,000, drawing much of its backing from salaried employees, civil servants, the self-employed, and independent farmers. Local notables and professional politicians form the nucleus of four thousand CDU organizations at the village, town, and city levels. The chief governing body is the federal convention, whose delegates are party officials and Länder representatives. They elect the Party Chairman and four Deputy Chairmen, who are also the key members on the Federal Executive Committee and the Federal Committee. These two executive organs formulate policy in consultation with Fraktion lead-

ers. CDU chiefs must maintain close links to the Christian Social Union, which has remained a separate organization, but cooperates with the CDU in federal elections and in the Bundestag. Under the leadership of Franz Josef Strauss, the CSU has taken a more nationalist and conservative stance than the CDU. Intermittent friction and a loss of cohesion between the two parties has resulted.

The Free Democratic party (FDP) has remained the most important of the small parties, all others either perishing or being unable to gain seats in recent Bundestag elections. The FDP compares in ideology to the British Liberal party and the defunct French Radical Socialist party. Although attempting to pursue a traditional liberal policy dating back to the German liberalism of the nineteenth century, it constitutes only a remnant of an earlier strong political movement.

Founded in 1948, the party emphasizes the tenets of the free enterprise system, private property, and individualism (comparable to the CDU/CSU), but also anticlericalism (comparable to the SPD). This program attracts a scattering of Protestant white-collar employees, civil servants, the self-employed, owners and managers of businesses, farmers, and university students, but few unskilled workers. Thus its potential support is limited. While it is able to draw on both SPD and CDU clienteles, normally the larger two parties woo the same groups with more attractive programs or with the argument that votes for them will not be wasted. The gap between the two major parties has so narrowed that it leaves little room for a third. As a consequence, the FPD vote in federal elections has hovered between 6 and 13 percent.

The low vote has also been caused by factional and leadership struggles among its own left, center, and right wings, and by gyrations in and out of Cabinets. Intermittently, from 1949 to 1966 the FDP remained a loyal coalition ally of the CDU/CSU in the federal Cabinets, but from 1966 to 1969 it moved from junior coalition status to sole opposition party in the Bundestag. Since 1969 it has become once again the junior coalition partner, but in this instance with the SPD as the governing party. The FDP has been able to make this ideological shift in recent years when the liberal left and center wings eclipsed the nationalist-oriented right wing.

The FDP intends to remain an alternative or a swing party on the political spectrum and has reminded the nonsocialist voters that since 1969 it has been responsible for moderating socialist reform proposals in Cabinets led by the SPD. It has espoused the democratization of German society and the welfare state and has been supportive of a more flexible foreign policy.

The Federal Republic has not been spared the rise and fall of small extremist parties. Little attention would be paid to such fringe movements—which exist in the United States and other democratic states as well—were it not for the dangerous growth of extremist movements during the Weimar era, which ended in the rise of Nazism. To prevent a repetition, the Federal Constitutional Court outlawed the neo-Nazi Socialist Reich party in 1952 and the Communist party in 1956. More recently, the government has argued that it is healthier to let extremist parties surface than to prohibit them. Thus the Communist party has been able to function again, though it has not been able to muster even 1 percent of the vote owing to the party's close identification with Soviet communism—which has no appeal for the population.

A left-wing radical movement has been active on university campuses, where it has generated useful political discourse on issues that the established parties often try to sweep under the rug. But the movement has been unable to gather significant support among the general public.

On the other side of the political spectrum, a well-publicized National Democratic party emerged in 1964. This neo-fascist party received close to 10 percent of the vote in some Länder elections, but in the 1969 federal election it could not muster the 5 percent of the vote necessary for representation in the Bundestag. Its support came from the middle class, farmers, and soldiers who did not share in the economic prosperity or who feared a change in social status. The party was unable to survive the economic prosperity that filtered down to the masses once again by 1970.

The demise of the National Democratic party would seem to indicate that the bulk of the population has learned a lesson from the disastrous past and is willing to cast its lot primarily with the two major democratic parties. The commitment to a democratic system seems strong at the present time and has produced a remarkable political stability. But what percentage of the population would shift to parties with nondemocratic goals if a major economic depression were ever to break out cannot be predicted.

Pressure Groups

While political parties form one link between the public and governmental authorities, pressure groups form another. Seeking to maximize their power and to influence politics, such groups have built up an extensive network of channels to the most important decision makers at the federal and Länder levels and provide them with needed information, including statistical data. At the federal level, they will seek access to the centers of executive authority from the Chancellor on down to the lowest ranks of the civil service. If the matter calls for top-level discussion, a meeting with the Chancellor or a Minister will be sought, while an administrative ruling or the draft of a bill may be discussed with the civil servant in charge. With much of the initiative for legislation stemming from the executive, it becomes the chief target of the pressure groups.

Yet they cannot forget the legislative branch, which has a chance to introduce its own bills and to amend government bills. Indeed, much group time is spent not only in seeking passage of bills favorable to its cause, but also on preventing the enactment of injurious bills. The groups can exert direct leverage in the Bundestag, where their own officials may have won seats as Deputies. Such officials will then serve on committees that deal with their area of specialization and will speak up as experts in plenary session.

Pressure groups mobilize their members to vote for and provide financial support to a party sympathetic to their cause, while in return they expect patronage, nomination of their officials to the legislature, and favorable planks in the party platform. The groups are not always successful, because the parties must also heed the demands of competing groups and must not give the impression of being beholden to the pressure group fraternity. Hence the parties will emphasize their desire to serve the national interest rather than the special interest.

As powerful as their counterparts in the United States and other industrial nations, the West German economic groups are organized at local, regional, and national levels to enhance the interests of their members. The business community is well knit in three federal organizations. The Diet of German Industry and Commerce (which may be compared to the United States Chamber of Commerce) serves the regional interests of its members, analyzing economic developments, fostering vocational training, and advising government agencies that deal with business firms.

The Federation of German Employers' Associations serves employers as a coordinating and advisory center concerning labor and social policies. It may recommend basic wage policies to be followed by its constituent national associations—which comprise industry, banking, insurance, transportation, trade, crafts, and agriculture. It seeks to influence labor and social legislation, participates in government agencies handling social security and the labor market, and carries on an extensive public relations campaign.

The Federation of German Industry is composed of thirty-nine national associations representing the various branches of industry, such as mining, textiles, and food processing. It may be compared to the National Association of Manufacturers in the United States, both having a stake in national and state legislation affecting their clientele. Of the triumvirate of German business associations, the Federation of German Industry is the most powerful politically and financially, with close ties to the conservative political parties.

On the employee side, the German Trade Union Federation constitutes the chief organization, comparable to the AFL/CIO or the British Trades Union Congress. It represents sixteen national industrial unions with a membership of close to 7.5 million, or about one-third of the total labor force. Most of the members support the SPD, although a Catholic minority backs the CDU. The federation must compete with two rival union organizations for the support of white-collar employees and civil servants, but has no serious rival for the blue-collar workers.

In the agricultural sector, known as the Green Front, the most important organization is the German Farmers' Association. It gives support primarily to the conservative parties, is well represented in the Bundestag, and exerts a strong influence on the government. The farmers—and other groups—must pay attention not only to Bonn's legislative and administrative output but also to that of the European Economic Community in Brussels, as their welfare is affected increasingly by decisions made at the supranational level.

Social groups constitute another political force to be considered. Catholic and Protestant churches, as noted, take positions on social welfare, educational policy, and even foreign policy. The student movement has been vocal and persistent in its demand for educational and political reforms. The Army, however, has been more circumscribed in voicing its demands in the political arena, aware that its fateful involvement in German history recommends tact and discretion.

The catalogue of pressure groups would not be complete without citing a multitude of professional and civic organizations, not to speak of associations of war veterans, expellees, and those persecuted under the Nazi regime. Offering political cohesiveness and strength to their members, they also provide services, such as claims against the government.

As is true in the United States, Great Britain, and France, the degree of success that a pressure group will have in the body politic will depend on a range of factors, including its power and cohesiveness and the political complexion of the government.

Individual Rights and Courts

The Basic Law both provides the framework for parties and pressure groups that seek input into the political system and deals at length with individual rights and judicial and political institutions. What the Nazis had done to individuals was fresh in the minds of the drafters, who symbolically listed the protection of rights in the first nineteen articles. Freedom of speech, assembly, and association are guaranteed, unless the democratic order is threatened. In that case, the Federal Constitutional Court must assent to their suspension. National, religious, racial, and sexual discrimination is prohibited. Although the Basic Law can be amended by a two-thirds vote of both houses of Parliament, the democratic constitutional order and the provisions relating to human dignity cannot be amended.

Borrowing a leaf from the Constitution of the United States, the drafters created a Federal Constitutional Court, a body that does not exist in most parliamentary systems and that did not exist previously in Germany. The court must guard the rights of citizens, be the arbiter in federal-state conflicts, advise on the constitutionality of laws and decrees when so requested by Parliament, and act if it so desires on constitutional complaints received from private citizens. Given the court's powers and the parliamentary selection of its sixteen members (divided into two chambers), it has been thrust into the political limelight on a number of occasions when partisan or federal disputes have flared up.

In addition to the Constitutional Court, there exists an integrated and hierarchical system of courts that range from local and district courts to the Federal High Court and that handle civil and criminal cases. The Federal High Court deals with appeals and has original jurisdiction in treason or conspiracy cases. Administrative claims against government agencies are handled by separate administrative courts, while other specialized claims are handled by federal finance, labor, and social courts. Such a complex system of courts is serviced by more than thirteen thousand judges selected by examination for lifetime careers.

Federalism

One common characteristic of the Federal Republic and the United States is their federal system. Except for the Nazi period, in which the constituent Länder lost nearly all their powers, German history has been marked by strains between the central government and the Länder, or between the Länder themselves (especially when Prussia represented the dominant force). In 1949, the reconstituted SPD favored a strong central government in order to encourage national planning and reconstruction and to prevent regional dominance by the CDU/ CSU. But the Christian Democrats, supported by the Western Allies, insisted on the establishment of a federal system in which power would be diluted, rather than concentrated. They triumphed, and West Germany was once again carved up into a number of states.

At present, there are eleven Länder, including West Berlin, which has special status, and the Saar, which was amalgamated into the Federal Republic in 1957. With the territorial boundaries in many instances set artificially and not historically, and with massive postwar population transfers, the citizens' loyalty to the Länder has remained weak. While some regional particularism has developed (Bavaria can always be cited as an example), it has not been too damaging politically to the central government in Bonn, the capital city. Potential differences also have been eased by the fact that until 1969 the Christian Democrats controlled the central government and a majority of the Länder. The Social Democrats ruled primarily in the city-states of Berlin, Hamburg, and Bremen, and in the state of Hesse during the first fifteen years of the Federal Republic.

As in the United States Constitution, powers are divided between the central government and the Länder. The former has exclusive jurisdiction in such matters as foreign affairs, nationality, immigration, customs, and currency. Both have concurrent jurisdiction in civil and criminal law, labor law, public relief, and road traffic, but the central government has the right to legislate in matters the Länder cannot effectively administer. The Länder have residual powers of legislation in all fields—such as education, cultural affairs, and religion—that are not enumerated in the Basic Law. While constitutional provisions tend to be static, political realities show a definite trend toward centralization, with the Bonn government legislating increasingly often on complex issues requiring a national solution. Yet cooperation and coordination with the Länder are necessary because Bonn allows them to administer such laws. This is especially true for fiscal policy. The bulk of income tax receipts, for instance, are apportioned equally between the central and the state governments, with the small remainder granted to the cities and communities.

Coordination is necessary among the Länder too. Ministers of all states who handle the same subject matter confer with one another to seek common action, but often no easy solution is in sight due to political or ideological differences between them. Depending on the degree of accord, they will lobby individually or collectively for their objectives in Bonn through their special plenipotentiaries and their representatives in the upper house.

Each Land is governed by a Minister-President (comparable to a United States Governor), a cabinet made up of ministers in charge of state functions, and a unicameral legislature (Bavaria has two houses). All except one of the legislatures are elected for four-year terms. The political parties engage in intensive electoral campaigns in the Län-der, because they are seen as influencing national opinion.

A word must be said about West Berlin, the long-term political arena of Willy Brandt. Even though the city is a Land of the Federal Republic, comparable to the city-states of Hamburg and Bremen, it has a special status as a result of an Allied accord and does not come under some provisions of the Basic Law. For instance, its representatives in the Bonn Parliament have no voting rights in the plenary sessions. But the Bonn government insists that it has a right to stage official functions in West Berlin. Over East German protests, it has scheduled meetings of the Bundestag and assemblies to elect the West German president in the former capital city. The West German government has also funneled substantial financial assistance to West Berlin—the city that is seen as an outpost and showcase of the West and that requires subsidies for its industry and commerce. As will be detailed later, the city administration rests in the hands of a Governing Mayor, the Senate (cabinet), and the Chamber of Deputies.

Federal Parliament

As in the United States, the Bonn legislature consists of two houses, with the upper house representing the states and the lower house representing the people. Its functions are similar to those of Congress: it debates national issues, mediates and integrates group claims, legislates, controls the budgets, and seeks to check the executive. But there are significant differences between the American and German legislatures that can be traced to different historical and political circumstances and to the nature of the presidential and parliamentary systems.

In the Bundestag (lower house), whose term lasts a maximum of four years, the relatively disciplined and centralized parties play a role in the formulation of policy. The governing parties normally will give their consent to policy formulated in the executive branch, while the opposition party or parties act as critics. Chancellor and Ministers are Bundestag members; hence, they can explain and defend their policy to their fellow members.

A Council of Elders, composed of members of all parties in the house, organizes the work of the 496-member Bundestag. Its functions include selecting committee chairs and setting agenda schedules. The President of the Bundestag, an official of the governing party, is in charge of the plenary sessions. As in Congress, much of the painstaking legislative work is done in the nineteen standing committees, constituted on the basis of subject areas. Chairpersons are chosen not on seniority alone, but on their expertise or their power in the party, with the governing parties receiving a majority of such posts. Similarly, committee seats are distributed among the parties on a basis proportionate to their strength in the Bundestag. Although the committees do not have the power of their American counterparts, they do play a role in legislation introduced by the executive. Thus they tend to be more effective than the British parliamentary committees.

The Bundestag opposition has a chance to check the executive branch, especially over the budget, in parliamentary debate, and through the question hour, in which Ministers or their state secretaries are requested to provide information or defend their policy initiatives. The opposition can also attempt to topple the government through a constructive vote of no confidence, which means that it must be able to elect immediately a successor to the Chancellor who has been ousted. This provision, designed to enhance political stability, was included in the Basic Law in order to prevent frequent overthrows of the Chancellor without providing a replacement.

205

Normally, the opposition cannot win a vote of no confidence because it does not have a majority of seats in the Bundestag and because the governing parties (as well as the opposition) maintain party discipline over their Deputies. But if the governing parties have only a slim majority and there are abstentions or defections, then the opposition has a chance. This is precisely what happened to the Brandt government, which had the dubious distinction of being the first to be challenged by a vote of no confidence.

What kinds of occupations are likely for Bundestag Deputies? They are often civil servants on leave from governmental posts, party or union officials, managers in business, farmers, and lawyers. They often do not give up their occupations because the Bundestag remuneration is comparatively low. They probably have ties to pressure groups or are receptive to pleas for special consideration. But if there is a conflict with party directives, then chances are good that they abide by party discipline.

The Bundesrat (upper house) represents the interests of the Länder. Its approval is necessary for federal legislation and administrative decrees affecting the Länder; its concurrence, on other legislation. The Bundesrat's suspensive veto power is blunted by the Bundestag's power to override the veto by an equivalent majority. As a legislative body of the Länder, its forty-five members, which include four without a vote from West Berlin, are appointed by and are members of the Länder cabinets. Each Land, depending on its population, is represented in the Bundesrat by three to five members who must vote in a bloc on the basis of instructions from their cabinets. The votes tend to reflect Land and regional, rather than partisan, interests, especially if the Land is governed by a coalition of parties that disagree on a specific issue.

From 1949 to the present, the Christian Democrats have captured control of a majority of the populous states. Hence they have remained the numerically strongest party in the Bundesrat, despite the Social Democratic control of the Bundestag and the Bonn Cabinet since 1969. Not surprisingly, the Christian Democrats have attempted to make the Bundesrat coequal in power with the Bundestag in order to block government legislation. In 1974, the Constitutional Court ruled that the Bundestag had predominant legislative powers, thereby ending a few political deadlocks that had developed between the major parties.

The President

In Weimar, the head of state was given a generous dose of executive power to the eventual detriment of the democratic order. In order to avoid a repetition of history, the drafters of the Basic Law envisaged presidential powers to match those of the British monarch. The President is head of state and legally represents the Federal Republic to other states—accrediting ambassadors, receiving foreign diplomats, signing treaties and laws, and issuing pardons, although a Cabinet Minister must countersign these actions.

True, the President can propose the name of a Chancellor candidate; yet the choice is limited, because the candidate is expected to be the leader of the party capable of forming a Cabinet. The President appoints the Cabinet Ministers, but only on the Chancellor's recommendation. The President can dissolve the Bundestag, but only if there is a deadlock between it and the executive. And in spite of all these constraints on political power and authority, the President is expected to become a conciliator in case of a major crisis. There is a temptation to interfere in normal political affairs, but a tradition has developed that the incumbent is expected to remain nonpartisan and above politics.

The President is elected for five years, with a two-term limit, by a special convention consisting of all Bundestag members and an equal number of members elected by Land parliaments. This indirect election contrasts with the popular election of Weimar Presidents, who on occasion vied with the legislature in their claim to be representative of the people. While the Presidents of the Federal Republic have been shorn of political power, they have enjoyed wide support among all strata of the population as respected, impartial national leaders.

The Chancellor and the Cabinet

Executive power rests with the Chancellor, whose political role in the nation can be compared to that of the British Prime Minister. Normally, the Chancellor will be that leader of the party receiving the highest number of votes in a federal election who can form a coalition Cabinet able to muster a majority in the Bundestag. Once the President nominates him, the Bundestag must give its nominal consent by a simple majority of the total membership. After this election, the Chancellor selects Ministers who are then appointed by the President.

Chancellors play an important role in the executive branch. A constitutional provision stipulates that they shall determine and be responsible for general governmental policy guidelines. They are formally accountable to the Bundestag, which can dismiss them if it so inclined. But to provide the political stability lacking in the Weimar period, Chancellors can be ousted only on a so-called constructive vote of no confidence. If the opposition were to win such a vote, it would need a majority for its own candidate to replace the ousted Chancellor. This provision

requiring the legislature to come up immediately with another acceptable candidate was inserted into the Basic Law in order to forestall the frequent Cabinet upheavals typical of Weimar, when mutually hostile parties forced a Chancellor to resign without being able to agree upon a replacement.

The Chancellors in the Federal Republic can normally expect to remain in power as long as their party is numerically strong enough to keep forming coalition Cabinets every four years in the wake of federal elections. During that time they may be swept out of office if an internal party crisis erupts or if the coalition cabinet falls apart over policy differences. Or they may resign for political and personal reasons—as Brandt did. Adenauer can be cited as one Chancellor who reigned for fourteen years as his party kept rolling up pluralities in election after election. Indeed, Adenauer's position was so dominant that the period became known as the chancellor democracy. While his successors lacked the same authoritarian political style, the precedent he set of a strong chancellorship was not entirely lost on them.

The politics of coalition formation can be difficult, especially if the election results do not indicate which party is a clear winner. Delicate negotiations among the parties may last several weeks until the Chancellor candidate and the coalition partner concur on the allocation of ministries (how many each party will receive and who will occupy each post) and on the government program.

Once the Ministers are installed in office, they assume control of their ministries and represent its interests in the Cabinet. And serious disputes arising between ministries must be settled by interministerial conferences or by the Cabinet. Should the policy differences remain serious, the Chancellor may request a minister to resign or the Minister may decide to resign. While such possibilities for Cabinet turnover exist, in practice they have been rare. On occasion, Chancellors do reshuffle Cabinets, shifting a Minister from one post to another. In this game of musical chairs, some ministers will be assigned to the more prestigious ministries, such as foreign affairs, economics, finance, interior, and defense, while others will have to be content with the less prestigious, nonpolitical and technical ministries.

The Making of Laws

In parliamentary systems, the executive branch normally shapes the direction of domestic and foreign policy. Chances are good that it will be able to carry out its legislative objectives because it usually has majority support in the Bundestag. In West Germany, there are multiple sources for policy initiation in the executive: the Cabinet, a ministry, party planks, public or interest group pressure, economic crises, or the actions of foreign nations. Much of the government program can be mapped out in advance. In recent years, the Cabinet has prepared short-, medium-, and long-range policies based on data supplied by the planning staff in the chancellery. Coordination of proposed bills is made by the chancellery, which is charged with preparing the weekly agenda.

Once the Cabinet approves the draft of a bill, it is forwarded to the Bundesrat for an advisory opinion. The upper house has but a few weeks to consider the bill in committee and plenary sessions and then must return the bill to the Cabinet with proposals for amendment, if any, included in its report. The Cabinet must approve the bill once again either in its original or its revised form based on Bundesrat recommendations and the response of affected ministries. Soon thereafter the Bundestag deals with the bill.

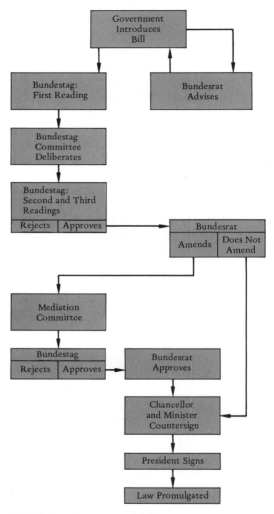

Legislative flow chart of bills

* The chart excludes the process for bills originating in the Bundestag or Bundesrat and bills needing the consent of the Bundesrat.

Prior to the first reading, the Fraktion (parliamentary group) of each party, representing all its Deputies, will meet to discuss it.

In plenary session the first reading of a major bill serves as a forum for debate on its substantive aspects; at this stage no amendments may be introduced. Once a bill is

208

assigned to one or more committees, deliberations may last for months, interspersed with a good deal of lobbying by ministries and private associations. After a committee vote is taken, a plenary session debates the bill in second reading. New amendments can be introduced, but normally the committee's recommendations will prevail with only minor changes voted by the Deputies. The third reading follows soon thereafter, allowing each party a final opportunity to explain its position on the general aspects of the bill.

Once the final vote is taken, the bill shuttles back to the Bundesrat for its reconsideration. If the Bundesrat accepts it as approved by the Bundestag, then it becomes law. If the Bundesrat does not accept a bill directly affecting the Länder, the bill is dead. On other bills, the Bundesrat can exert only a suspensive veto that can be overridden by the Bundestag. To encourage a compromise between the two chambers, a permanent mediation committee may or must be convened (depending on the nature of the bill).

While the executive branch is responsible for introducing most bills into the legislature, members of the Bundesrat or Bundestag may also introduce them directly into their respective chambers, but their chance of passage is slim.

The Administrative System
Most West German citizens have an ambivalent feeling toward state administration. They realize that, on the one hand, the bureaucrat makes the government wheels turn around; but, on the other hand, the bureaucrat also is responsible for issuing petty decrees that seem designed to compound the difficulties facing the already harried public. While the career service can proudly boast of its Prussian heritage of incorruptibility, efficiency, and impartiality, critics charge that it is not responsive to new societal needs. Numerous unsuccessful demands for reforms

at the Länder level would suggest that the system could stand improvement.

The higher civil servants in the ministries, recruited primarily from law schools, tend to be politically conservative and to follow strictly constitutional and legal norms. Once on the job, they are soon molded into experts who often look disdainfully at unpalatable political decisions made by the Ministers. Hence it is difficult for the politically responsible Ministers, especially if they are Social Democrats, to obtain their unstinted cooperation. But it should be emphasized that the bulk of the career servants work competently and loyally for every administration regardless of its political coloration.

The public service consists of the professional civil servants, salaried employees, and manual workers, ranked according to four grades. For the higher service, applicants must have earned a university degree, completed three years of training, and passed a state examination. Thereupon they are assured lifelong security, a generous pension scheme, and high social status. They can rise in a ministry to the top post of permanent state secretary, in charge of the bureaucracy. This post is more political in nature than its counterpart in Great Britain, for the state secretary may be called on to attend Cabinet meetings and to answer questions in Parliament. If a state secretary's partisan affiliation should clash with that of an incoming Minister, he or she could be reassigned to another ministry or even retired early. This problem arose in 1969 when Brandt formed a government. His removal of a number of senior civil servants produced a political outcry in the ranks of the opposition.

In 1967, the government created the new post of parliamentary state secretary. The holders of this position have not moved up through the civil service hierarchy but are political appointees directly responsible to the Minister. Their primary responsibility is

209

to maintain contact with Parliament; they, too, are empowered to answer questions directed to their ministry. After serving as such junior ministers, a number of them have been promoted to the rank of Minister.

Conclusion

This sketch of German political history and of the West German political institutions reveals sharp discontinuities and profound upheavals in the past, but remarkable stability in the present system—now more than a quarter of a century old. The Federal Republic has emerged as a truncated state whose democratic political system remains viable and whose economic strength is the envy of other democratic nations in Western Europe.

Chancellors and Ministers, who have formulated foreign and domestic policies, have remained relatively long in office. Only once, as we shall see, has the Bundestag been dissolved prematurely. And only once has a vote of no confidence been introduced in the Bundestag. The federal system has undergone strains, but has functioned fairly successfully. Minor political parties, numerous in 1949, have nearly disappeared, and the two-and-a-half-party system has emerged. Unlike the political situation in Great Britain, where one or the other major party can command a majority in Parliament, in the Federal Republic the major party has been forced (with but one exception) to invite another party to share in governance of the state because it could not muster 50 percent of the national vote. The resultant coalition Cabinets have had to hammer out acceptable government programs for which they then had to seek legislative approval.

While the political system has generated a broad consensus among the population,

economic and social problems have not been solved entirely and a feeling of malaise about future national and international developments lies just under the surface. For the West Germans, one source of malaise is the seemingly permanent Communist rule in East Germany.

German Democratic Republic

The establishment of a new state in West Germany in 1949 was paralleled in the Soviet zone of occupation, where a process of granting statehood to the East Germans also took place. A nonelected constituent assembly drafted a constitution, which was then accepted by Soviet authorities and in a referendum by 62 percent of the population. Thus, on October 7, 1949, the German Democratic Republic was created. This nation emerged as a typical people's democracy, or communist state, patterned on the model of the Soviet Union. According to a 1974 amendment to the constitution, the German Democratic Republic is a "socialist state of workers and farmers" and an "inseparable part of the socialist community of states" (meaning the communist bloc).

The Socialist Unity party emerged as a forced amalgamation of the Communist and Social Democratic parties, in which the latter plays no role. It has held the reins of power, while permitting a number of bourgeois parties to remain in nominal existence but without effective influence. Executive authority was originally vested in a President and a Council of Ministers, but in 1960 the presidency was abolished and replaced by a Council of State. The legislative organ, the People's Chamber, has no significant policy-making function, but merely approves without discussion those bills introduced by senior party and government leaders.

The creation of two German states in 1949 meant that the division of the country was no longer a temporary measure. It was the price that the German people, as the losers of World War II, had to pay; to them it was a heavy one. Their goal of reunification was shattered, although it has never been officially renounced. The Conference on Security and Cooperation in Europe provided in its 1975 accord for the possibility of border changes by peaceful agreement, but simultaneously it ratified Europe's territorial status quo—including the division of Germany.

This synopsis of the two German political systems merely opens the curtain for the entrance of our chief actor, Willy Brandt, who played an important role in both states.

Brandt's Early Years: From Childhood Through Exile

Willy Brandt was the prototype of a leader who steadily gained in influence and power as he matured and earned recognition from an ever widening circle of political actors. His ultimate road to success parallels that of many political leaders in other democratic countries, yet also reflects the specific stresses faced by German leaders, whose futures were so closely linked to the twists and turns of their country's political and socioeconomic environment. Brandt's social, religious, and educational background, his family, and his own personality provide important clues (but no more than that) to the kind of leader he would become once he was recruited into decision-making positions, to the handicaps he would have to overcome in order to be successful, and to his potential political attitudes and behavior.

Childhood and Politics

Willy Brandt was born in a Lübeck working-class suburb on December 18, 1913, as Herbert Ernst Karl Frahm. His mother was then a nineteen-year-old salesgirl in a consumers' cooperative grocery store, while his father was unknown to him. Since he was illegitimate, his mother gave him her family name. Brandt lived with his mother in a modest worker's apartment consisting of just one room and a kitchen. While his mother was working, he was cared for by a woman living near the shop. Perhaps because he was a loner, he had few playmates. These early handicaps and deprivations were offset by the close ties he developed with his maternal grandfather, Ludwig Frahm, who took on the role of the absent father.

When World War I ended, the five-year-old boy moved to the lodgings of Frahm and his new wife. Thereafter the mother visited her son once or twice a week after work, but the relationship apparently was not a very close one. (In the 1920s she married a brick-layer with whom she had one son.) However, the young boy adored his grandfather. A simple and honest man, Frahm had been a farm laborer on a large estate owned by a

Willy Brandt

(German Information Center)

that locale, it took courage to read such "subversive" literature; it took even more courage to be the first one to join the SPD and vote for it, especially when the estate's overseer checked upon the political views of each worker.

After World War I, young Brandt was undergoing a more overt political socialization process as he sat on his grandfather's knees and listened with awe to the visions of a socialist utopia, which included a classless society, and to the revolutionary workers' songs. He began to understand the philosophy of "we the poor—they the rich" that was at the root of the discontent among the working classes, especially when his grandfather was unemployed, out on strike, or unable to provide enough to eat.

In his memoirs Brandt vividly recalls an incident that occurred when he was eight or nine years old. During a strike at his grandfather's place of work, the boy stood outside a bakery staring at its merchandise. A plant director recognized him, took him into the bakery, and bought him some bread. Arriving home, the grandfather told him to return the bread at once to the bakery: "A striker accepts no gifts from his employer. We will not let ourselves be bribed by our enemy. We are no beggars, to whom one throws some alms. We ask for our right, not for gifts." Upon hearing this declamation of social warfare, young Brandt marched back to the bakery and told the salesclerk, "Here —we don't want it!" [1]

Most German socialists, while formally Protestant, tended to be anticlerical because the church was politically conservative. As was the custom, anticlerical families, such as the Frahms, nominally belonged to the church and baptized their children, but did

count in Mecklenburg. His own father had worked for the farm, too, incurring corporal punishment for minor infractions. Rebelling against this feudal setting, Frahm moved away to find a factory job. After the war, he became a truck driver for a Lübeck firm.

The Socialist Legacy
While still on the estate, Frahm had become a socialist and had familiarized himself with the writings of veteran socialist leaders. In

[1] Willy Brandt, *My Road to Berlin,* as told to Leo Lania (Garden City, N.Y.: Doubleday, 1960), p. 32.

not let them attend religion class in public school. Only in high school did Brandt, who considered himself a free thinker at the time, show an interest in the history of religion. In the course of his life he has been attracted to the ethos of Christianity and has had a "fluctuating" personal faith that "never quite fitted into established forms," as he put it.[2]

To the Frahm family the substitute religion was socialism. The party served not just as a political recruitment base, but also as a way of life from cradle to grave for its ideologically committed members. As Brandt noted later on, "I suppose I inherited a desire for social justice and political progress. That brought me into the workers' movement."[3] Brandt became a member of the children's section of the workers' sport organization, the youth branches of the party (Friends of the Children, Red Falcons), the workers' mandolin club, and the Socialist workers' youth organization.

At School

Normally the education of an individual is an important political socialization tool. In the instance of young Brandt, he rejected the conservative values taught by his teachers, many of whom had little commitment to the republic. He was a bright pupil in primary school, winning scholarships to a *Realschule* (high school) and then to the prestigious Johanneum *Realgymnasium* (university-preparatory high school), to which he transferred after one year in Realschule. At the Johanneum, Brandt was one of the few students from a working-class background.

Coming from wealthier and more polit-

ically conservative families, Brandt's peers often made life difficult for him. Consequently, either he isolated himself and withdrew into a dream world or else he defied his school occasionally by boldly appearing in a blue shirt and red bandanna, the uniform of the Socialist workers' youth organization. When he was singled out by one of his teachers to recite a poem in school on the solemn occasion of the founding of the 1871 Reich, he dared to show up in this attire; to Brandt's delight, the furious teacher sent him home immediately. Though Brandt was one of the top students in school, he often played truant because of his greater interest in the Socialist youth organizations.

Ties to a Mentor

From an interest in politics and the reading of books, Brandt developed an interest in political journalism, which was to become one of his main professions for two decades. While still at the Johanneum, he began to write short feature stories and essays for the Lübeck Social Democratic newspaper. Its editor was Julius Leber, a right-wing SPD leader and Reichstag Deputy, who became his political mentor and friend. In politics, ties with established politicians often mobilize young persons to make a commitment to a political career. This happened in the case of Brandt. Leber gave him self-confidence, self-esteem, and a boost to his ego by recognizing his skills.

Leber encouraged Brandt's political activities. The SPD editor was aware that Brandt, who had become a leader of the local SPD youth group, the Red Falcons, had leadership qualities that other young people recognized and esteemed. Brandt was developing a flair for public speaking, had the firmness of his convictions, and had an attractive personality and features. To him politics meant personal fulfillment and recognition by others of his abilities—characteristics shared by budding

[2] Klaus Harpprecht, *Willy Brandt: Portrait and Self-Portrait* (Los Angeles: Nash Publishing, 1971), p. 28.

[3] Terence Prittie, *Willy Brandt: Portrait of a Statesman* (New York: Schocken Books, 1974), p. 5.

political leaders in many countries. At the age of fifteen he headed the local Karl Marx group of the Socialist youth organization, and the following year he rose to district deputy chairman. In 1930, through Leber's sponsorship, the sixteen-year-old Brandt became a member of the SPD, although the party allowed only those eighteen or older to enroll.

In 1931, Leber's mentorship of Brandt came to a swift and unexpected end; rising political differences between them over the course of SPD policy could no longer be reconciled. The young, impatient, and radical Brandt, who in earlier years had not disagreed with the party's reformist policy, considered the SPD too soft and indecisive in meeting the pending Nazi danger even though the SPD paramilitary organization was already involved in anti-Nazi fights. He argued that the crisis demanded revolutionary measures, but the Social Democratic chiefs offered only resolutions. He viewed the party's reliance on parliamentary tactics in a period of political turmoil as a tactical blunder. Participating in heated arguments and street fights with young Nazis, Brandt had visions, unreal at the time, of a revolutionary breakthrough of the working class.

Into the Socialist Workers Party

The split between Brandt and Leber was symptomatic of a generational conflict between the dissident young members and the older cadres within the party over ideological versus pragmatic priorities. When the older group refused to change course, a small left-radical splinter group broke off from the SPD and created the Socialist Workers party (SAP). The new group stood ideologically midway between the SPD and the German Communist party (KPD). Thus it drew left-wing SPD dissidents and right-wing, anti-Stalinist Communist party members into its fold.

The SAP became an affiliate of an international union of radical Socialist parties. The SPD, on the other hand, was one of the key parties in the Labor and Socialist International (Second International), a group of reform Socialist and Social Democratic parties that sought to achieve socialism through evolutionary or parliamentary means; and the KPD was a member of the Third International (Comintern), a Moscow-inspired organization of Communist parties that sought to achieve socialism and then communism through revolutionary means.

Brandt and his party friends in Lübeck joined the SAP because they had high but illusionary hopes that the party would become a major political force in Germany and would spark a unity of the Social Democrats and Communists against the common enemy —the Nazis. The hope was in vain: not only was the SAP numerically too weak to produce such unity (it had only about twenty-five thousand members compared to more than a million SPD members), but the SPD and KPD had engaged in so many fratricidal feuds with each other since the 1920s that a reconciliation proved impossible. One can only speculate that if unity could have been achieved then, the Nazis might not have been able to assume power.

Brandt had to pay a price for his radical politics during this period of "political puberty," as he later called it. A sad Leber refused to let him continue to write for the SPD newspaper and withdrew an offer to pay for Brandt's future university education. While Brandt's dream of going on to a university in 1932 was shattered, he considered it more important to throw himself into the activities of the new party. Seeking a paying position at the same time to make ends meet, he found a job as clerk for a shipping firm.

For the SAP, Brandt worked as unpaid organizer, made speeches at its meetings, and soon became head of its youth section in

Lübeck. In July 1932, he and friends organized an anti-Nazi mass rally in the city. Leber, as keynote speaker, called for a fight to a finish against the Nazis (by then an SPD theme, too). In the wake of Nazi storm troop activities, Leber was arrested and imprisoned. He was released briefly in February 1933 and appeared at the final left mass rally held in Lübeck. That was the last time Brandt saw his mentor, who was to fall victim to the Nazis in 1944.

When Hitler assumed power, he outlawed the democratic parties. The left parties (SPD, KPD, SAP) made immediate plans to go underground in Germany and to establish coordination centers in neighboring countries. So in March 1933, the nineteen-year-old Brandt traveled to a secret SAP national meeting in Dresden under the pseudonym of Willy Brandt, a common name in Lübeck, chosen by him as a temporary safety measure to escape arrest. But the temporary name became permanent when the Nazi regime did not collapse as swiftly as most of its opponents had expected.

At the Dresden meeting, the SAP decided to establish secret headquarters in Berlin and centers in Paris, Prague, and Oslo. Speakers cited tales of arrests, torture, and murder of their comrades and of persecution of the Jews. The SAP central committee designated a top official to head the Oslo center, but on his way to Norway the Nazis arrested him. Thereupon the committee decided that Brandt should take over the center. The decision, crucial in terms of Brandt's future, provided him with a further chance to demonstrate leadership capabilities—but on a much broader basis than in Lübeck—and his first opportunity to meet socialists from other countries. He accepted this challenge and escaped Germany immediately, taking a fishing boat to a Danish island and from there making his way to Oslo.

Thus ended the first stage in Brandt's

political life. While thousands of members were active in the Lübeck SPD, few had a chance to rise into the limited number of leadership positions. Why then did Brandt and a few contemporaries rise in rank while the others did not? As for Brandt, the explanation may lie in the important mentor roles played by his grandfather and Leber and in the personal leadership qualities that he possessed.

In Exile

On his arrival in Oslo, Brandt immersed himself in Norwegian politics, unlike most émigrés, who restricted their political activities to the German scene. While he was busy as head of the small Oslo SAP bureau, the foreign headquarters of the SAP youth division, and the Refugee Federation that was established to help émigrés, he learned Norwegian, became a writer for many newspapers and union journals, made public speeches on foreign policy and Germany, and joined the Youth Federation of the Norwegian Labor party.

In his political work he kept in touch with the anti-Nazi underground in Germany by carrying on illegal correspondence (using invisible ink for writing messages between the lines of innocuous letters), smuggling illegal newspapers and pamphlets into Germany (in false-bottomed suitcases and empty fake books), and raising money for Nazi victims.

Brandt in his capacity as SAP leader began to travel abroad frequently to maintain contact with other émigré groups outside of Germany and to increase his visibility in Europe. In 1934, he participated in an International Conference of Revolutionary Youth in Belgium. Designed to create unity of action among the left youth organizations against fascism, the effort proved abortive. He received orders in 1936 from the Paris SAP headquarters to visit the underground SAP unit in Berlin for several months and then to make recommendations on future activities.

In 1937, Brandt spent four months in war-torn Spain as a political correspondent for Norwegian and Swedish newspapers and as an observer for SAP. He was disillusioned by the internecine disputes among left parties instigated increasingly by the Communists and feared that Spain might evolve into a Communist-party dictatorship, should the government win the civil war against General Franco's forces.

Brandt's exposure to Soviet tactics in Spain, as well as the reports filtering out of the Soviet Union about Stalin's purge trials in Moscow, made him more aware that the Soviet Union was not the promised land that he and his friends in the SAP may originally have hoped for. His disillusionment with Soviet communism coincided with an increasing appreciation of Scandinavian social democracy. Norwegian, Swedish, and Danish Social Democrats were in the vanguard of those introducing social welfare measures into their neocapitalist economic systems, narrowing the income gap between the poor and the wealthy, and minimizing class differences. They were intent on achieving socialism through gradual, reformist steps via the parliamentary route and hoped their party would serve as the means of integrating several diverse groups in their society. Brandt's gradual espousal of such a program meant he was beginning to abandon his views of the early 1930s, when he had supported the SAP ideology calling for a revolutionary class struggle against the capitalist elite.

Interlude in Norway
Brandt's political life cannot be separated easily from his private life; there were too many interlocking pieces. His ties to Lübeck

had become increasingly distant. In 1935 his grandfather had committed suicide for personal and political reasons. Shortly thereafter, Brandt had met his mother in Copenhagen, but for only a brief visit.

The period of gloom was punctuated in 1939 when Brandt, then twenty-six years old, fell in love again (his first lengthy affair had been with a German woman who had followed him to Norway). Carlota Thorkildsen was a Norwegian socialist intellectual who worked at a scientific institute in Oslo. In 1940 they had a daughter Ninja, and in 1941 they were married. The war had erupted by then, and Carlota provided for a time the stability that a restless and worried Brandt needed.

The marriage did not last: separated in 1943, they were divorced in 1947. In the meantime, Brandt met Rut Hansen. Having joined the Youth Federation of the Norwegian Labor party prior to the war, she became a member of the underground resistance during the war, was arrested, spent time in prison, and then fled to Sweden, where she worked in the press section of the Norwegian embassy until the end of the war. In 1948 she married Brandt.

The cycle of change in Brandt's personal life was paralleled in his political life. In April 1940, Nazi armies smashed into Norway. As an expatriate German who had been stateless since 1938 and was not yet a Norwegian citizen (he had applied for naturalization in 1939), he was in personal danger of being captured by the Gestapo, which was known to be looking for him. In this predicament Brandt fled Oslo. North of the city, he met a painter whom he had known and who lent him a Norwegian uniform. Brandt allowed himself to be taken prisoner with the painter's military unit, which was ready to surrender to the Germans. The plan worked well; the German troops in charge of the internment center had no suspicions of a man who spoke Norwegian so well. After four weeks in captivity, all soldiers of the unit, Brandt included, were released.

This short period of time in Norwegian uniform had haunting political consequences upon Brandt's later return to Germany. His opponents kept circulating a story that he had joined the Norwegian army and fired on the Germans. In 1963 the painter appeared in a Copenhagen court to testify that Brandt was never armed while briefly in his unit and that the soldiers, ready to surrender, had thrown away their weapons. The story did not die even then and produced other lawsuits in German courts.

The Swedish Experience

When Brandt was released from captivity in June 1940, he could not return to his home in Oslo because of the danger of a Gestapo arrest. After a few weeks in hiding, he decided to seek political asylum in Sweden. He made his new home in Stockholm, where he learned that the Norwegian government-in-exile had approved his application for Norwegian citizenship. During this period of second exile Brandt never became as involved with Sweden's politics as he had with Norway's, partly because the country was pursuing a neutralist policy while the Allies attempted to crush the Nazi war machine.

However, Brandt did plunge into work as soon as he was settled—primarily writing. In a great literary outburst, he wrote six books (some written in collaboration with another author), contributed to other books, and authored a series of articles on the Norwegian military campaign and several pamphlets for the Institute of Foreign Affairs in Stockholm. The books, reflecting a lucid mind and a grasp of political realities, dealt with wartime Norway, guerrilla warfare, and postwar aims for Germany and Europe. In

addition, he founded a one-man Swedish-Norwegian Press Agency, which produced copy for foreign newspapers about the anti-Nazi resistance movement in Norway.

Living in one of the most important left-wing exile centers in Europe, Brandt did not remain aloof from political discussions about the future of Germany and Europe. He met regularly with a group of more than twenty Social Democrats of many different nations, but primarily Sweden and Norway, who talked about ways to establish a new international order, to rebuild Europe (including Germany), to promote friendly relations with the Soviet Union, and to recreate the Labor and Socialist International. The group called itself the International Circle of Democratic Socialists, but was more affectionately known as the Little International. Brandt became honorary secretary of the group, whose members eventually founded the new Socialist International.

In Brandt's writings, memoranda, and talks with Allied diplomats in Stockholm—many of whom viewed him as a potential leader in postwar Germany—he emphasized the pending configuration of Germany and Europe. Several of his ideas on Germany matched Allied policy decisions, such as denazification, reeducation, and democratization, while a few forecasts, such as a revolution in Germany or the nationalization of cartels and banks, proved to be wrong. As to Europe, Brandt envisioned the eventual creation of a United States of Europe.

Brandt's assessment of the future reflected an internal process of "de-ideologization" or "deradicalization." In 1944 he and a number of other SAP members successfully petitioned the SPD executive committee in Stockholm for admission into the SPD exile party. There was a hint of opportunism in their stance: aware that the weak SAP would have difficulty in becoming a political force in Germany, they knew that their only chance to rise politically would be through the SPD.

May 8, 1945, marked the end of the war in Europe. Would those in exile return to Germany or remain in their adopted lands? Most of those who had been persecuted by the Germans and who could not forgive their crimes chose to remain (this group constituted about 70 percent of the exiles); those who were politically committed to aid in the reconstruction of a new Germany chose to return. Brandt postponed making a decision despite his earlier resolve to return to Germany. He did not want to leave his Norwegian friends in the lurch at a time when their war-ravaged land also had to be reconstructed.

Two days after hostilities ceased, he left Stockholm for Oslo in time to celebrate the downfall of the Nazi empire. Becoming a correspondent for Swedish newspapers, he shuttled frequently to Stockholm to help organize an aid program for exiles returning to Germany, to ship parcels to the hungry, and to organize vacations for German children in Scandinavia.

The Return of the Native

The desire to return to Germany, at least temporarily, proved irresistible to Brandt. In October 1945, he went to Nuremberg to cover the first stage of the war crimes trials of the top Nazi leaders as a correspondent for the Norwegian Labor party press.

Brandt's observations about war, fascism, and guilt are noteworthy because they reveal the inner thoughts of a man whose own emigration spared him from the Nazi horror. He rationalized the necessity for the Allied bombings, although the devastation of the country and the hunger of its peoples hit him hard. He agonized over the punishment meted out to the entire German population when a small segment had engaged in heroic

resistance against the Nazis. After witnessing acts of brutality against "poor devils" forced to expiate the Nazi regime, Brandt noted that such vengeance proved that the war had brutalized people in other nations too—Nazis could be found in non-German uniforms. Elaborating on this theme he wrote that fascism was not merely a German phenomenon. But it had received a German stamp and showed how power can be abused for evil purpose in a totalitarian-ruled country. In 1946 he published a book on this theme, provocatively entitled *Criminals and other Germans,* which proved to be controversial in later election campaigns.

Brandt supported the war crimes trials, but with reservations. Trying once again to plumb the moral issue of guilt, he asked rhetorically whether in any war only one party is guilty. No "grown" German could evade his or her share of responsibility, although such a position should not be identified with guilt. In his view, the worst Nazis had been those who were already Nazis when Hitler assumed power. He approved the denazification program, a "political de-lousing," but warned that the young had to be reoriented toward democracy. In conclusion, he noted that Germany's future lay in a united Europe.

While covering the Nuremberg trials, Brandt made valuable contacts with senior SPD leaders. Many of the leaders had come back from exile; others had remained in Germany, where few had escaped persecution. From conversations with them Brandt sensed that he would be welcomed back into the party as a member in exile and be given a responsible position. As an outsider, he needed the psychological reassurance that the party would actively recruit him for a position rather than passively accept him. In May 1946, he accepted their invitation to attend the first postwar SPD conference as a guest delegate of the Social Democratic exiles living in Scandinavia. It would give him the chance to watch the party and its leader, Kurt Schumacher, in action and to write about the proceedings as a journalist for the Scandinavian newspapers.

Brandt had met Schumacher earlier in 1946 and had mixed feelings about him. Brandt had respect for this man who, in spite of severe physical infirmities contracted during World War I and in Nazi concentration camps, had the will power to reconstruct the SPD into a new powerful party, the base for a democratic and socialist renovation of the country. And he admired Schumacher's resolve that the party in the western zones should not suffer the same fate as it had in the Soviet zone, where it was forcibly united with the Communist party. But Brandt considered Schumacher as too authoritarian in his attitude, too tenacious in clinging to wrong decisions, and too nationalistic in outlook. Schumacher and Brandt were not "kindred souls," the latter once noted.

Multiple Options
Brandt had arrived at the stage in his life where new career choices were opening up, indicating that those individuals who offered them were aware of his many talents. He would have to make a choice based on which position offered him the best prospect to fulfill his political ambitions. Although Schumacher did not yet offer Brandt any party position, in part because he mistrusted Brandt's flight into the SAP, other acquaintances apprised Brandt of opportunities to become Mayor of Lübeck, to head an American or British zonal news agency, to become press attaché in the Norwegian embassy in Paris or in the Norwegian military mission attached to the Allied Control Council in Berlin. Brandt accepted the latter offer because the post would put him in the cauldron of German political activity as a Norwegian and

would last only one year, giving him the necessary time and exposure to living in Germany to decide whether to make Norway or Germany his permanent home.

In October 1947, he finally opted for Germany when Schumacher offered him the post of special representative of the SPD in its Berlin liaison office. Brandt wrote to Halvard Lange, the Norwegian Foreign Minister who had been instrumental in his obtaining the position as press attaché, that it had been a hard choice to give up Norway, but the new job would give him a chance to help in putting Germany back into Europe.

This was true enough. Brandt certainly had a desire to serve the cause of Germany and Western Europe from pivotal Berlin, the center of the emerging Cold War confrontation in Europe. But he was also ambitious to climb the political ladder as high as possible. In Norway, as an outsider, it would have meant just a few rungs: "I could only have become a member of parliament with difficulty," he later said.[4] In Germany, as a native-born, the climb could be higher.

Brandt readily admits that the decision to remain in Germany was more difficult to accept for his future wife, who had joined him in Berlin in 1947 and also worked for the Norwegian mission. But Rut realized that Brandt would find the Berlin post to be more exciting and personally satisfying than anything Oslo could offer. Both decided not to sever all ties with her home country. When they married in 1948, a Norwegian Lutheran pastor officiated; when they took vacations, it was mostly at their Norwegian retreat. On the other hand, Brandt renounced his Norwegian citizenship and reacquired German

[4] Barbara L. Kellerman, "Willy Brandt: Portrait of the Leader as Young Politician" (Ph.D. diss., Yale University, 1975), p. 428.

nationality. He decided to make Willy Brandt his official name from then on. The name Frahm meant little to him: his grandfather was dead; his mother had changed her name when she married.

The change in citizenship symbolically ended Brandt's period of exile and three years of indecision about whether to make his political career in Norway or Germany. By opting for his home country, he consciously began a journey on the road that might carry him far, and as the mode of transportation he chose the Social Democratic party. The SPD was a much more powerful vehicle than the SAP ever had been or the Norwegian Labor party could ever become.

4

Brandt's Middle Years: Political Ascent in Berlin

There are many "ifs" in history. In Brandt's case, if he had not been able to launch his political career in Berlin—a city that would provide him with national and international visibility—his rise to the top in national politics might never have taken place. If Brandt had attempted to gain high office through the traditional career advancement within the party, he probably would not have made it to the top because he had not been loyal to the party for more than a decade. But Schumacher was willing to give Brandt an opportunity to redeem himself for his "sin" in becoming a leader of the SAP. Thus the fulfillment of career objectives depend often as much on chance, luck, and the people one knows as on personal qualifications.

Into the Maelstrom of Berlin Politics

In February 1948, Brandt started his new Berlin post. His duties consisted of meeting frequently with Allied officials to explain to them the SPD position on foreign policy matters and Berlin, attending sessions of the Berlin and the national SPD Executive Committees, and writing releases for the Berlin and the foreign press. As is true of political parties in Germany and elsewhere, Brandt soon was involved in political, ideological, and personal rivalries within the SPD. At the core of Brandt's difficulty was his relationship to the Berlin SPD Chairman, Franz Neumann, and to other local leaders who resented his arriving late on the scene while from 1945 to 1947 they had tenaciously fought the Communist attempt to produce a union of the Communist and Social Democratic parties in Berlin. Adherents of the traditional view that the party ought to be primarily a workers' party, a view still held then by the majority in the SPD, they also looked with misgivings at his advocacy of a people's party, comparable to the Scandinavian Social Democratic parties, and his belief that other social groups, such as the middle class, must be wooed in order to achieve a broader electoral base.

Brandt's new reformist outlook matched that of Ernst Reuter, the SPD member who became Mayor of West Berlin in late 1948—and Brandt's newest mentor. Reuter, an ex-Communist, had been active in the SPD during the Weimar era, emigrated to Turkey, and returned to Germany in 1946. As a department chief in the Berlin municipal administration and then Mayor, he distinguished himself during the trying 1948–1949 period, when the Soviets imposed a blockade on West Berlin to prevent the Western Allies from tying West Berlin too closely into the western zones, by counseling the populace to keep up its faith in freedom and independence. Reuter, Brandt, and other reform leaders became even more pro-West when the Western Allies conducted a massive airlift to supply the Berliners with food and other essentials.

Since Brandt's loyalty for Reuter did not sit well with Neumann and Schumacher, who considered Reuter a serious rival for power and too much of a pragmatist, new strains developed. Party Chairman Schumacher could not see how Brandt could represent him satisfactorily in the Berlin SPD organization and consequently tended to rely more on Neumann to be his spokesman in Berlin. In 1949, Brandt's job came to an end. These personal and ideological differences provided one reason; another was that the Western Allied officials transferred their base of operations to Bonn, the capital of the new Federal Republic.

Baptism into National Politics

Reuter and Brandt were the Berlin spokesmen for a reformist group within the SPD that was critical of the way Schumacher was running the party organization with its increasing bureaucratization, failure to recruit youth into the ranks, continued espousal of some Marxist views (especially nationalization of industry), reliance on the dwindling number of blue-collar workers as the main base for support, failure to present a modern image to the electorate, and dogmatic opposition to Chancellor Adenauer's foreign policy. Schumacher could not disregard the views of this important group because he had to allow a measure of internal democracy in the party; hence in 1949 he suggested that Brandt become a SPD candidate for the first parliamentary election. Brandt would be assured election since he would receive a safe seat in a northern German district. But Brandt declined the offer because he wanted to continue making West Berlin his political base; as events would show, that was a wise decision. The Berlin Chamber of Deputies (city council) selected him and seven others to represent the city as Deputies in the Bundestag in Bonn.

When the Bundestag convened in September, the CDU/CSU had just won the 1949 election by a narrow margin and had formed a coalition government with two smaller parties under Konrad Adenauer's chancellorship. The eight West Berlin Deputies (in later years increased to twenty-two) had a special status in the Bundestag because of Allied insistence that West Berlin continue under a special four-power status within the German body politic. Thus the Deputies could not be elected by the Berlin voters and received no voting rights in the plenary sessions of the Bundestag.

Brandt's apprenticeship training as a legislator was useful to him. He participated in Bundestag debates, became a member of the Committee on Foreign Affairs, and met Deputies from all parties. He established close contact with two SPD leaders who took a reformist position: Fritz Erler, the party's spokesman on defense affairs, and Herbert Wehner, an ex-Communist who also had been in Swedish exile and who was to become the de facto secretary-general of the party. For Brandt these contacts would prove very useful because the two men, Wehner especially, held many political strings in the central party headquarters in Bonn. With their support Brandt might have a chance to rise further in the party, but only if the reformist group were to gain strength at the expense of the traditionalist group.

At War with the Berlin Party Organization

The ambitious Brandt decided to wrest control of the Berlin SPD organization from Neumann in 1950. In an initial victory, party members in Brandt's district elected him district chairman, a post that provided him with a political base of operation and with membership on the Land executive committee. He was also selected editor-in-chief of the Berlin party newspaper, a job that he relinquished after one year, and was elected a member of the city's Chamber of Deputies. Brandt had finally made a breakthrough into the Berlin political arena, but he soon learned that the party regulars still considered him an upstart and an outsider. In 1952, with Reuter's encouragement, Brandt challenged Neumann for the Berlin SPD chairmanship. The timing was premature; two-thirds of the delegates at the Land conference cast their vote for Neumann.

In politics the professionals expect such reverses—it is part of a game with high stakes. Rare indeed would be a politician in any country who could score one success after another within a short span of time without patiently building a base of support, as Brandt learned the hard way. In his case, the struggle for leadership would last another six long years, but by then there would no longer be any doubt about the outcome, for a number of events fortuitously tilted the scale in his direction.

First was the death in August 1952 of Party Chairman Schumacher. His successor was Erich Ollenhauer, who remained in of-

fice for seven years. The new chairman did not have the same magnetic personality and forceful qualities of leadership as did his predecessor. Perhaps because he had been in exile (in Great Britain) and perhaps because he received some friendly letters from Brandt, their relationship was relatively smooth.

The second event was the spontaneous workers' uprising in the German Democratic Republic against the Communist regime in June 1953. When the workers protested poor working conditions and demanded more political liberties, Soviet army units stationed in the country crushed the uprising. As a Deputy, Brandt made an impassioned speech in the Bundestag supporting the workers, reminding them that they had not been forgotten by the West Germans, and calling on the Allies to solve the German reunification question. In the party newspaper, he advocated a more activist West German diplomacy and free elections in all sectors of Berlin as a model for both Germanys, predicting that no change in East German policy would take place as long as Walter Ulbricht, a hard-line Communist, was leader. This crisis was the first of several in the East bloc that Brandt skillfully used to make himself known in West Germany and later abroad as a spokesman of West Berlin deeply concerned about events behind the iron curtain countries.

Third in this series of events was the September 1953 federal election producing a Social Democratic party defeat at the hands of an Adenauer regime that had boasted of its positive record in the realms of domestic and foreign policy. For Brandt and other advocates of party reform, the poor election results confirmed their thesis that the party needed to modernize and bring its legislative proposals more in line with less ideologically committed popular views—although many government bills also received the SPD stamp of approval. The reformist group realized that much of the populace was tired of Marxist slogans and opposed to nationalization. It was tired, too, of the SPD's negative position on most foreign policy issues.

Finally, the fourth event was the death, soon after the election, of Brandt's mentor Ernst Reuter. In mourning him, Berliners turned out en masse to hear Brandt and others give simple and poignant eulogies. Brandt was beginning to endear himself to the Berlin populace as a man who knew how to speak to them in a clear and forthright manner.

While these gloomy events of 1952 and 1953 were in the long run to strengthen Brandt's hand, in the short run he could not capitalize on them as a means of gaining a swift victory over Neumann's Berlin machine. He was forced to do what many aspiring politicians have done in similar situations —that is, patiently build up grassroots support among party members and cadres. He addressed membership meetings, factory groups, and district functionary meetings in Berlin to convince his audiences that backing him meant a vote for party reform. This politicking, combined with Neumann's political blunders—such as making decisions without prior consultation with colleagues— paid off as an increasing number of rank-and-file working-class members and district executive committee members threw their support behind him. In the spring of 1954, Brandt once again became a candidate for Neumann's post, hoping that this time he had enough support from the voting delegates at the Land convention. He did not quite make it, losing by only two votes; as a consolation prize he became deputy chairman of the Berlin SPD organization, a post that would keep him in the limelight.

At the national party level, his record of success was equally mixed. In the fall of 1953 he became a member of the SPD Frak-

tion executive committee, but at the 1954 and 1956 party conventions he failed to win a seat on the party Executive Committee, then a body of twenty-five leaders who determined national policy. His defeat may be attributed primarily to his identification with the small reformist wing in the party and to his position on foreign policy issues, which still represented a minority view. In 1954 the United States Department of State, eager to see the more pro-West reformist wing of the SPD strengthened, invited Brandt, as a representative of West Berlin, and a few other SPD leaders to visit the country on a study tour. Brandt made political capital out of the trip since the West Berlin population was impressed by this visit to the country it considered the most loyal to its interests.

President of the Berlin Chamber of Deputies

From 1955 on, Brandt's rise to the top in Berlin politics began to accelerate because of a number of fortuitous circumstances and his embroilment in the Cold War. In January of that year, when a vacancy developed in the presidency of the Berlin Chamber of Deputies, the SPD Fraktion nominated Brandt to the post. Because the Fraktion represented the largest group in the legislative chamber, his election was assured. This victory put him one step ahead of any other candidate for the mayoralty whenever the incumbent should step down.

Brandt's prestige in Berlin increased further during the 1956 Hungarian uprising. On November 5, one day after Soviet tanks rolled into Budapest to quell the revolt that had toppled the communist regime, about one hundred thousand West Berliners attended a torchlight protest rally in front of their city hall. The crowd, furious at the Soviet action and feeling impotent to change the course of events in Hungary, shouted down the Christian Democratic speaker and

Franz Neumann, representing the SPD, both of whom spoke in platitudes. Although not scheduled to speak, Brandt seized the microphone and denounced the Soviet intervention. He calmed the crowd and eventually was able to disperse it peacefully.

The Berlin population was impressed by Brandt's performance in a crisis situation that could have had more serious consequences. Thus when the Social Democratic Mayor died in August 1957, there was a groundswell of popular feeling that Brandt should become the next Mayor. His candidacy was nurtured further by the United States embassy in Bonn, which reportedly suggested to an editor of a leading Berlin daily newspaper that Brandt, a staunch friend of the West and an anti-Communist, be built up as the ideal man. Other Berlin newspapers joined the chorus of praise for Brandt.

Neumann tried desperately to block Brandt's candidacy, but failed to produce an alternate candidate acceptable to the top party organs in Berlin. After the SPD endorsed Brandt's candidacy, the Chamber of Deputies in September 1957 officially elected Brandt as Governing Mayor—the highest political post in the city.

Governing Mayor of West Berlin

At forty-three, Brandt had at last reached the first major policy-making office in his career. When he assumed the new office, he had chalked up a decade of political activity in Berlin. Some other mayors have made it to the top more quickly, but it must be remembered that in German politics he was still a comparatively young man who had been an outsider. For most Berlin SPD leaders he was a representative of a minority wing that was struggling hard to become the majority wing in the party.

As the mayor of any large city can testify, the position is not an easy one. The responsibilities of the West Berlin Mayor exceed those of many others because of the city's pivotal location inside the German Democratic Republic and its fragile political status. Brandt had to spend several hours each working day on such administrative matters as answering correspondence and attending sessions of the Berlin Senate (the cabinet), while the district mayors and Brandt's assistants handled most of the day-by-day municipal problems. He also had to attend many official functions, make public speeches, open exhibitions, and meet with Allied officials, politicians, journalists, and foreign visitors.

Under Brandt's administration, progress was made in building more public housing, raising the citizens' standard of living, guaranteeing continued massive financial aid from the Bonn government, convincing business firms to remain in West Berlin despite Soviet threats to the city, and then assuring them of increased industrial orders from the Federal Republic. Critics, however, accused Brandt of spending too many days away from Berlin (about 25 percent of the time) and therefore neglecting the city's problems, including mounting frustration among radicalized students over the failure to reform schools. There was some truth in this criticism, although most of his time away from Berlin was spent in Bonn on official city or party business.

In addition to the normal duties of a Governing Mayor, Brandt consolidated his power in the SPD in January 1958 by wresting the chairmanship away from Neumann in another bitter feud. Brandt was also eager to increase his power at the national SPD level, where decisions are made concerning domestic and foreign policy positions that will influence the fate of the party in national elections. Four months after he became chairman of the Berlin SPD, he finally was elected, in his third try, a member of the national Executive Committee. He could take some satisfaction in Neumann's failure to be reelected to it. In the 1958 vote, the old guard in Bonn would have had difficulty keeping Brandt out again in view of his capture of the Berlin party machine and the mayoralty.

Brandt's election to a seat on the Executive Committee symbolized the increasing strength of the reform group in the party, especially after the party had suffered a third consecutive defeat in the federal election of 1957. Chairman Ollenhauer and his associates concurred with the reformists' earlier demand that the party must finally modernize its program if it ever expected to gain a plurality of votes in a federal election. At the November 1959 Bad Godesberg party convention, the bulk of the delegates, with only a small left wing opposed, adopted the program that had been drafted over a period of four years by a commission including top SPD leaders and experts. Brandt's role in the formulation of the program consisted of recommending minor reformulations; he was not one of its principal architects, although he could take credit for being one of the first reform leaders in the party. At the convention he did speak up for the program, which threw overboard the Marxist ballast of earlier programs and emphasized humanism, Christian ethics, and reformism. It endorsed the theory of free competition so far as is possible and planning only so far as is necessary, cooperation with the churches, rearmament, and a rapprochement among European states. It was designed to transform the SPD from a workers' into a peoples' party and to shield the party from conservative attacks against it as being pro-Marxist and pro-Communist. Acceptance of the program marked the end of the SPD commitment—more in theory than in practice—to Marxist ideology. This turning point in SPD history was not unique; other socialist parties in Western Europe adopted similar programs in order to boost their electoral opportunities. Brandt was swimming with the tide.

An Increase in Visibility

As Mayor of Berlin, Brandt was head of Land Berlin (one unlikely analogy: if New York City were to become the fifty-first state, the Mayor might also become Governor). In the latter capacity, Brandt had a seat in the upper house in Bonn. By sheer chance—an important ingredient in politics —he became Mayor just when the Berlin representative in the Bundesrat was to assume its presidency for one year. By further chance, the President of the Federal Republic was then frequently away from Bonn on state visits and speaking engagements, necessitating Brandt in his capacity as Bundesrat President and acting Federal President to stand in for the President on public occasions. The resultant publicity did Brandt no harm.

Brandt made numerous trips abroad in order to present the case of his city to other countries. This role of spokesman was especially important when in November 1958 Soviet Premier Khrushchev issued a six-month ultimatum demanding that West Berlin sever its ties with the Federal Republic and become an independent, demilitarized, and free city. Khrushchev threatened that if his demands were not met, the Soviet Union would sign a peace treaty with the German Democratic Republic granting it physical control of all Berlin, including Western rights of access to West Berlin. Brandt stated that West Berlin would never surrender; the Western Allies held fast; and through Allied diplomatic negotiations the crisis was ended.

In his speeches abroad prior to and after

this crisis, the Mayor hammered away at three themes that his city's continued existence depended on Western Allied support, that West Berlin should act as a link between the divided German states, and that it should promote human and cultural contacts between East and West. Since Brandt thrust himself into the front lines of the Cold War, he scored high as a good-will ambassador in the West, especially in the United States, where in February 1958 he spent two weeks being feted by President Eisenhower and other top officials, receiving an honorary degree from a university, and speaking before dozens of groups, to the press, and on television. One year later, in a return visit to the United States, he was the recipient of a triumphant ticker-tape parade arranged in his honor by the Mayor of New York City.

The trips to many parts of the world as spokesman for free Berlin produced another dividend for Brandt. The Federal President awarded him the Grand Cross of Merit of the Federal Republic, complete with star and sash, and told him, "Herr Brandt, we cannot very well send you off naked on your travels." [1]

The Mayor's increase in visibility at the national and international levels produced discomfiture in the ranks of the governing coalition in Bonn. Chancellor Adenauer took as little notice of Brandt as possible, regarding him as a potential threat to the CDU. On a visit to West Berlin in 1958, he canceled a private scheduled meeting with Brandt, who took the snub in stride. Brandt did not want a confrontation with Adenauer, since the foxy old man, as many labeled him, would have jumped at a chance to humble his much younger and less experienced political opponent. Ironically, while the two men feuded politically, their views on foreign

policy coincided to a great extent. Brandt assumed a tough anti-Soviet and highly pro-American stance and advocated a nonpartisan foreign policy. While Brandt's views clashed little with Adenauer's, many members of the SPD establishment, who for years had opposed the bulk of Adenauer's foreign policy objectives as too closely linked to the United States and too inflexible to achieve reunification, were distrustful of Brandt. Yet, as the 1961 national election neared, they became increasingly aware that the SPD would have to enhance its legitimacy as a prospective governing party by emphasizing the constructive role it played in concurring with the CDU/CSU on the bulk of domestic policy legislation and the host of capable experts and leaders in its midst who could become responsible government Ministers.

Chancellor Candidate: Round One

As in other democratic systems, German political parties must compete with each other for the support of the electorate in periodic national elections. Such electoral contests are crucial in determining which parties will form the governing coalition. Each party had to decide on their Chancellor candidates prior to the 1961 election. Adenauer was the choice of the CDU/CSU, and SPD Chairman Ollenhauer normally would have been that party's candidate once again. But recognizing his own limitations (colorlessness, lack of dynamism) and the mood of the party, he agreed not to stand. The field of likely candidates in the summer of 1960 increasingly narrowed to Brandt, especially when Wehner, initially hesitant, threw his support behind Brandt. If it had not been for Wehner's backing of Brandt, the latter's rise in the party was problematical. The two men never were personally close to each other, but both realized the advantage of a political linkage.

To the top party leaders, Brandt was not

[1] Heli Ihlefeld, *Willy Brandt: Anekdotisch* (Munich: Bechtle, 1968), p. 74.

the perfect candidate, but he had fewer liabilities than the others. The liabilities included Brandt's illegitimacy, his defection to the SAP, his exile, his wearing of a Norwegian uniform, his late reentry into the SPD, and his disagreements on a number of foreign policy positions. Some of these handicaps would not bother the average SPD member, but could bother the average German voter once the Christian Democrats made capital out of them.

Party leaders were willing to gamble that the important assets—his wide-ranging abilities, his highly visible and well-publicized activities in Germany and elsewhere, his impressive performance in the 1958 Berlin legislative election campaign, his attractive personality, and his appeal to youth—would outweigh the long list of liabilities. They viewed especially the 1958 Berlin election victory as a signal that the party could win if it were represented by a popular figure who knew how to tackle a foreign policy crisis. The party's highest organs nominated him on August 24, 1960, and the Hanover party convention endorsed his candidacy on November 25. In keeping with the new look of the party, conference delegates approved a party platform with an accent on tapping the energies of the younger generation, and they selected an election team of the party's notables as a backstop to the Chancellor candidate.

In the Federal Republic, the drama of electoral campaigns is not as long-playing as in the United States, although it may reach the same degree of excitement. Lacking are the American primaries; instead, each German party selects its candidates without involving the voters in the nomination stage. The selection process varies among the parties, but generally their leaders make the choices of candidates, and delegates at the district level must ratify the choices in secret ballot.

Brandt's campaign strategy, planned by a

"technical election commission" in which a number of young SPD academicians participated, was a replica of the 1958 Berlin campaign and had similarities to the 1960 Kennedy campaign. Indeed, Brandt had sent an SPD official to the United States to study the Kennedy and Nixon strategies. The commission planned the campaign in minute detail, down to the types of advertisements, the timetables for Brandt's speeches, and the commissioning of public opinion polls to see what issues to emphasize. It urged Brandt to make a barnstorming campaign across the country, unprecedented in scope in Germany, because he came across better at rallies than on television or radio, and it suggested emphasizing Brandt's political charm—and the personal charm of his wife.

The party, aware of the Germans' positive attitude toward the United States, had Brandt make still another trip to the United States in 1960 to see Kennedy, appear on "Meet the Press" on television, and make numerous personal appearances. Then, it made use of Kennedy's popularity in a pamphlet with photographs showing Brandt conversing with Kennedy; an accompanying caption read "Two statesmen who understand each other." The readers were told that both politicians were of the same generation and would be able to work well together on matters of foreign policy. Senator Hubert Humphrey was quoted as saying, "Brandt is my friend. All the people here like him. In the U.S.A. he certainly would be elected." [2] Nor was Mayor Richard Daley of Chicago forgotten; he was even willing to compare Brandt with Winston Churchill and Franklin D. Roosevelt.

The SPD election managers mapped out a three-stage campaign for their candidate.

[2] Harold K. Schellenger, Jr., *The SPD in the Bonn Republic: A Socialist Party Modernizes* (The Hague: Nijhoff, 1968), p. 180.

"For everyone something—'so help me God!'"

(Karl-Heinz Schönfeld)

Although tagged by some as the German Kennedy, Brandt needed a lot of bolstering—even in his own party. Therefore, the managers emphasized his role as a strong and experienced statesman ("Fighting Willy," according to one poster caption), the unity of the Germans, and noncontroversial domestic policy matters. Throughout the campaign, the popular Adenauer was mentioned as little as possible and never attacked personally.

The Berlin Wall

The party's intention to avoid dealing with foreign policy matters during the campaign collapsed when a new crisis erupted in Berlin several weeks before the September 1961 election. On August 13, East German authorities, concerned about a continuing exodus of their population to West Germany via West Berlin (in July alone, thirty thousand people had fled), sealed off the city by strings of barbed wire, antitank traps, and then a wall. When Brandt received news of this unexpected action, he flew back to Berlin immediately. He requested the Western commandants in Berlin to register strong protests at once with their counterpart in East Berlin, but not until two days later did they lodge ineffectual protests with Communist authorities.

Then the Mayor telegraphed a sharply worded letter to Kennedy, who had once told him to be in direct contact in a crisis situation, warning the President that inactivity and defensiveness might create among the West Germans a crisis of confidence vis-à-vis the Western powers. In conclusion, he wrote, "I consider the situation grave enough to write to you, Mr. President, with the ultimate frankness that is possible only between friends who trust each other utterly." [3]

[3] Harpprecht, *Willy Brandt,* pp. 202–203.

Upon receipt of the letter, the President, who earlier had been friendly to Brandt, was angry that the Berlin Mayor was using Kennedy's prestige during the campaign for his own ends. Kennedy reportedly told one of his aides, "That bastard in Berlin is trying to involve me in the upcoming German election." [4] Brandt, too, disappointed by the lack of an immediate Western response (which could have meant war if it had come in the form of Western tanks knocking down the wall), told one of his aides that Kennedy had "cooked our goose." These surprisingly negative feelings did not become public knowledge at the time; apparently, the two leaders resumed more fraternal relations thereafter.

Kennedy also received pleas to act from United States officials who were or had once been in Berlin. Thereupon he authorized the reinforcement of the American army garrison in Berlin and requested General Lucius Clay (former United States High Commissioner in Germany) and Vice President Lyndon Johnson to visit the city as symbolic gestures of support.

While there is no doubt that Brandt as Mayor responded correctly to the crisis by seeking diplomatic support for his city (although partially usurping the function of the West German Foreign Office), as Chancellor candidate he found it a ready-made opportunity to demonstrate to the voters that he was a statesman who stood above partisan politics. But the campaign took on bitter overtones with charges and countercharges, the CDU engaging in a bitter smear campaign against Brandt, including Adenauer's

reference to his illegitimacy ("Brandt, alias Frahm"). Others referred to Brandt's radical past "as a Communist agent," his flight from Germany in 1933 as an act of cowardice or lack of patriotism, and his donning a Norwegian uniform as an anti-German act. Despite a court injunction restraining one newspaper from printing unproven charges, they may have had an impact on the uncommitted swing voters who were already mistrustful of Brandt and his party.

On September 17 the election took place. While the SPD vote increased from 31.8 percent (in 1957) to 36.2 percent, and the CDU/CSU vote declined from 50.2 percent to 45.2 percent, the result was still disappointing to Brandt, who had hoped for a better showing. There were many reasons for the defeat. Adenauer was obviously still popular among a large segment of the electorate who were satisfied with the status quo and his policies and who regarded the SPD as a radical party. A number of voters were also repelled by the frantic SPD efforts to build an image of Brandt as a national statesman and questioned his qualifications shorn of the image. While the post-mortems were continuing, Adenauer, as leader of a party with the highest number of votes, formed a new coalition Cabinet with the Free Democratic party, and the SPD resumed its role of loyal opposition.

Another Interlude

Brandt returned to Berlin, true to his pledge that he would exchange the office of Mayor only for that of Chancellor. But the defeat produced a lengthy depression in him. He drank too much, earning him the nickname "Weinbrandt [brandy] Willy"; he would tell others that he had gotten as far as he would ever get and that younger men should step forward.

But Brandt snapped out of his personal

---

[4] Prittie, *Willy Brandt,* p. 146. Cf. also David Binder, "Willy Brandt: A German Life," *New York Times,* November 30, 1969; reprinted by FRG, Press and Information Office, p. 29.

despondency when other SPD leaders maintained their faith in him. In May 1962 they elected him as one of the two Deputy Chairmen of the party, while Wehner was re-elected to the other Deputy Chairman post. From then on the two men worked closely together—Wehner as the master strategist who worked well behind-the-scenes, making recommendations on party policies and candidacies, and Brandt as one of the leading

public figures and spokesmen of the party. Ollenhauer remained chairman, but died in December 1963. Since Wehner and other party leaders wanted Brandt to remain the standard-bearer at the next federal election, in 1964 they elected him Party Chairman. The chairmanship entailed presiding over the chief party organs, creating intraparty unity, directing the formulation of policy, and visiting party locals throughout Germany. These

Mayor Brandt and President John F. Kennedy, Berlin, 1963

(German Information Center)

matters were time-consuming, but Brandt gladly paid the price to finally win the coveted top position in the party.

Brandt, as chairman and Mayor, was buoyed by the party's smashing victory in the 1963 Berlin election. Seeking to produce a less hostile climate between West Berlin and the East, he entered negotiations with East German authorities and won concessions from them that permitted West Berliners to cross the Wall into East Berlin during restricted holiday periods and enabled East German old-age pensioners to visit relatives in West Berlin for several weeks at a time. In January 1963, Brandt also planned to meet with Nikita Khrushchev, then on a visit to East Berlin, to urge the Soviet Premier to pursue a constructive German policy. At the last minute Brandt was forced to cancel the meeting when the Berlin CDU threatened to pull out of the local coalition if he were to meet Khrushchev.

While Brandt made these diplomatic overtures to the East, he sought reinforcement from the West. Wanting to boost the morale of the West Berliners and to enhance his own political future, he invited Kennedy to visit Berlin on the latter's European summer tour of 1963. Kennedy in turn accepted the invitation in order to underline the United States' determination to provide continued support for the freedom of West Berlin. Upon arrival in Berlin, he spoke before a huge and wildly cheering crowd, and ended his speech with the famous remark, made in German, "I am a Berliner."

Not many months later, Kennedy was assassinated. President Johnson personally invited Brandt to join the many Presidents and heads of state who came to Washington to pay their last respects. After the funeral, the Kennedy family asked Brandt to join them for a visit; they talked about Berlin, and at the end Robert Kennedy told Brandt how much the President had loved the city.

Chancellor Candidate: Round Two

In 1965, another parliamentary election loomed on the horizon. The SPD was more optimistic than it had been four years earlier, partly because there had been trouble in CDU/CSU ranks. Chancellor Adenauer had resigned in 1963 due, among other reasons, to the *Spiegel* affair, in which Minister Franz Josef Strauss, CSU chief, had ordered the weekly magazine's publisher to be arrested for treason for having printed a damaging account of the West German army. Minister of Economic Affairs Ludwig Erhard, who had been the chief architect of the German economic miracle, had then become the new Chancellor. In 1965, the SPD also was optimistic about an electoral victory because public opinion polls indicated that an increasing number of young people and urban residents were leaning toward that party.

The SPD did not hesitate to put up Brandt again as its candidate for the Chancellor's position, mostly because it was a tradition not to switch candidates and because he still seemed to be the best candidate the party had. The 1965 campaign put less emphasis on creating a personality cult than did the earlier campaign, but Brandt once again stumped the country, making over five hundred speeches and granting many interviews to the media. When he appealed to artists and writers to support him, they organized a committee, gave speeches, wrote slogans ("The job of the citizen is to keep his mouth open" and, in a take-off on the Exxon slogan, "Put Willy in the Tank"), launched advertising campaigns, and raised substantial funds. Brandt was a strong campaigner, had excellent relations with the press, and drew large and enthusiastic audiences—he sensed victory was in the air.

Yet the election results did not confirm his optimism. While the SPD again gained in voters and in percentage points of votes cast—up from 36.2 in 1961 to 39.9 percent

*"As Party Chairman I concur with my esteemed
previous speaker, the Governing Mayor, as well
as with the now succeeding remarks of the
honored Chancellor candidate of the SPD."*

(Frankfurter Allgemeine Zeitung)

—the CDU/CSU and FDP easily maintained their majority. Thus Erhard formed
another Christian Democratic–Free Democratic coalition Cabinet, with the SPD again
as the sole opposition party in the Bundestag.
Its fifth straight defeat can be blamed on the
party's inability to present a program that
could have aroused the enthusiasm of the
uncommitted voters who were wary of "ex-
periments" and on its inability to challenge
effectively the record of the government.
Since most voters cluster in the center of the
political spectrum, it becomes difficult for
major competing and integrative parties in
the Federal Republic (and in the United
States and Great Britain) to present highly
differentiated profiles and programs. As a
result, the SPD and CDU/CSU, while still
slightly to the left and right of center, tend
to be candidate-oriented, rather than issue-
oriented, at election time.

Brandt was disappointed and depressed
about the 1965 election results. Blaming
himself for having let the party down twice
and being a born loser, he announced that
he would return to Berlin as Mayor and
never again run for the office of the Chancellor. He would remain chairman of the
party.

Brandt's psychological reaction to the defeat was understandable, although it is
doubtful that any other SPD candidate could
have produced an electoral victory under the
political circumstances. He returned to Berlin physically exhausted and withdrew into
himself. When the cumulative strain and
hard drive produced a cardiac attack in the
fall of 1966, Brandt thought he was on the
verge of death. As a consequence of this
experience, Brandt became more composed
and relaxed; he decided that the need to
justify his past and to seek constant public
approval, publicity, and image building, reflecting in part his own insecurity, would
have to be abandoned.

Indeed, his insecurity must have been
eased already by the 1966 party convention,
where he bounced back and made his reentry
into the world of politics. He was reelected
Party Chairman by a vote of 324 to 2, the
largest affirmative vote ever given a candidate
for the top post in the party. The delegates
were convinced that Brandt was their man
and should run again for Chancellor.

While that opportunity did not come for
several more years, Brandt and the party
suddenly were faced by the opportunity to
share political power in late 1966, when
Chancellor Erhard resigned because of difficulties with the United States and France
over financial matters, economic cooperation,
and the Common Market and because of a
national economic recession. On November

10, the CDU/CSU agreed on Kurt Georg Kiesinger, Minister-President of Baden-Württemberg, as their next Chancellor candidate. When he was unable to form another coalition Cabinet with the FDP, he turned to the SPD and suggested that together they form what came to be known as the Grand Coalition: he would be Chancellor, the two parties would share an equitable number of Cabinet seats, and the FDP, with only 8 percent of the seats, would be relegated to the opposition bench in the Bundestag. To an American student of politics raised in a presidential system where one party controls the executive branch, it must seem strange to hear about such coalition talks, especially between two parties that had been bitter foes at the national level for close to two decades. Yet it must be recalled that while publicly they sparred for power, at the parliamentary level they often concurred on legislative goals, especially on the bulk of bills devoid of a partisan character. Thus for the CDU/CSU, whose old-style political domination was no longer working well, bringing a reputable SPD into the government was no longer unthinkable. In short, in politics a tenuous marriage of convenience that benefits both partners happens on occasion. How long it will last before a divorce takes place is another question.

Indeed, the SPD was deeply split on the advisability of joining a cabinet with the CDU/CSU. The proponents won; they argued that the SPD had been in opposition for much too long and had to show the electorate that it was capable of sharing in the governing of the state. The opponents, primarily the party's left wing, were fearful that the maintenance of a socialist identity would be lost if the SPD joined the government and that democracy would be endangered if there was no effective parliamentary opposition to challenge a CDU/CSU–SPD government. Their views did not prevail. On December 1, 1966, the new Kiesinger-Brandt government was sworn in, marking the first SPD participation in a national government since 1930.

In Cabinet formations in the Federal Republic, a pattern has developed that applied to 1966, too. The Chancellor negotiates with his coalition partner on the number of ministries to be allocated to each party. Then follows the distribution of posts to specific individuals, keeping in mind that (as in the United States) some posts, such as Foreign Affairs and Finance, are more prestigious than others and that denominational, regional, and associational interests must be safeguarded. In 1966, the CDU/CSU received ten and the SPD nine Cabinet seats; among the SPD members was Brandt, who became Vice Chancellor and Foreign Minister, posts that were good springboards for the chancellorship.

Brandt's appointment closed the Berlin chapter in his political life and opened the Bonn chapter. While he had suffered numerous reverses, he had moved steadily up from the modest post of representative of the national party headquarters in Berlin in 1948 to Mayor of Berlin, to Party Chairman, and then to the second highest post in Germany in 1966—a track record that could be considered excellent for a young outsider who had to start his professional career in the postwar period against some heavy odds. His choice of pivotal Berlin paid off, as he gained swift visibility on the national and international scenes through skillful performance in his political duties and an increasing congruence between his attitudes and goals and those of the voters.

5

Brandt at the Top:
Political Ascent in Bonn

In 1966, the fifty-three-year-old Brandt had at last arrived on the national government scene, not yet as Chancellor but as Vice Chancellor and Foreign Minister. The latter position would give him a strong opportunity to help shape government policy. He knew that the SPD would have a good chance to assert itself by pushing hard for legislation reflecting its programmatic demands, particularly in the ministries it controlled. Of course, there would be the constraints of coalition bargaining and compromises in a Cabinet representing two parties, but Brandt stated, "In this government, the Chancellor never would try to impose a policy line on the Foreign Minister . . . which would not coincide with the latter's conviction, for then he and we would equally have a crisis of the coalition." [1]

Thus Chancellor Kiesinger became a skillful conciliator and conflict management specialist who had to be careful not to alienate the SPD for fear the coalition might break up. In order to reconcile coalition Cabinet policies with the preferences of the governing parties' Deputies, a small inner circle of CDU/CSU and SPD executive and legislative leaders met frequently.

Climbing to the Summit
as Foreign Minister

While the coalition was in power from 1966 to 1969, SPD policy initiation and output was expected to be high because the party was eager to show that it had the capacity to govern and that the programmatic demands made while it was in opposition could become responsible legislation. As soon as Brandt stepped into the Foreign Ministry post, he immersed himself fully into the work, in part because that was his habit and

[1] *Neue Zürcher Zeitung*, November 15, 1966.

236

in part because he wanted to demonstrate to the voters that he could be a competent Minister despite the litany of accusations against him. Indeed, while his emigrant status had hurt him politically during the campaigns for Chancellor, the connections he had made during his frequent travels, his ties to the international socialist community, and his knowledge of contemporary history, English, and the Scandinavian languages would now help him.

In a short time, he was able to master the intricacies of diplomacy and the ministerial bureaucracy, although administration and personnel policies were of limited interest to him. He made his mark in the post as a result of the imaginative and innovative strokes of his foreign policy, despite the fact that most ministry officials were conservative and that Kiesinger wanted to be his own Foreign Minister.

A parallel to the United States may be noted here. Whether chief executives share the decision-making process with their Secretaries of State (or their Foreign Ministers) depends on their interests and capabilities to shape foreign policy rather than on any specific constitutional provision. For instance, Chancellor Adenauer, immersed in foreign policy matters, appointed Foreign Ministers who were not expected to take the initiative or to challenge him.

Kiesinger did not have the same option to appoint a weak Foreign Minister. As a consequence, Brandt soon qualified as the best Foreign Minister the Federal Republic had had since 1949. One historian, Golo Mann, even claimed that Brandt was the best Foreign Minister the Germans had ever had. Foreign ministers of other countries considered him an ideal person to represent his country in the international arena because he had a clean anti-Nazi record, and, as former Berlin Mayor, had valuable experience in East-West negotiations. Thus he was able to

neutralize the widespread mistrust of the Federal Republic still so prevalent in other countries, especially at a time when Kiesinger was tainted by his membership in the Nazi party during the Hitler era. Brandt modestly stated that his calling card was not the worst one to present.

According to those who met him as Foreign Minister, he was always honest and reliable, intelligent and patient, instinctively right, helpful to others, and tough in negotiations. These were important qualities in the individual presiding over foreign policy, a realm of crucial importance to a country attempting to normalize relations with other countries.

The Grand Design

Although Brandt had originally supported Adenauer's foreign policy of dealing with Eastern Europe and the Soviet Union from a position of military strength, he later came to view it as outdated and counterproductive. It had perpetuated the Cold War and produced a hardening attitude on the part of Eastern European countries toward West Germany. It had isolated East Germany from much of the international community and produced a freeze in the relations between the two countries. Adenauer's view that the German Democratic Republic was a nonexistent state—it was labeled "the so-called GDR"—meant that no West German officials entered into any contacts with their East German counterparts. The Federal Republic could claim to represent all of Germany, Adenauer contended; thus, it would break off diplomatic relations with any nation that recognized the German Democratic Republic (with the exception of the Soviet Union, with which Adenauer had exchanged ambassadors in 1955, primarily in order to secure the release of thousands of prisoners of war). Because of this Hallstein Doctrine, so labeled after a high CDU official in the

Foreign Ministry, the Federal Republic did not enter into diplomatic relations with any Eastern European country other than Yugoslavia in the initial years. Third World states used the doctrine as a weapon to gain more foreign aid from the Federal Republic by promising never to recognize the German Democratic Republic.

Brandt sought to introduce an innovative policy toward the East, known as the *Ostpolitik* (Eastern policy), that would unfreeze the strained relations between West Germany and the Communist countries and would produce a policy of conciliation and detente rather than confrontation. This metamorphosis in policy was not a product of Brandt's sudden assumption of the Foreign Ministry post, but dated back to the early 1960s. At that time a number of West German intellectuals and Social Democratic youth leaders counseled a detente; President Kennedy initiated such a policy vis-à-vis the Soviet Union; and Chancellor Erhard's government adopted a slightly more flexible foreign policy stance. Brandt, then Mayor of West Berlin, engaged the brilliant Egon Bahr, his press secretary, to help him in the reformulation of policy, which led in divided Berlin to a limited number of concessions by East German authorities. As Foreign Minister, Brandt brought Bahr into the ministry as director of the policy planning staff to continue the work they had begun in Berlin, but on a broader scale.

Between 1966 and 1969, Brandt and Bahr launched their Ostpolitik, though they did not expect to conclude treaties with all Eastern states during this time span. The latter's memory of German invasions of their territory and of Hitler's racial policies that labeled the Slavs as a subhuman species still lingered. Moreover, the conservatives in the CDU/CSU were expected to block treaties considered as a potential sellout to the Communists. Yet there were indications that a new policy might succeed eventually, for the hard-liners in Eastern Europe and the Soviet Union were being challenged by pragmatic Communists who wanted to strengthen their countries' technological and economic structures by improving relations with Western states. The Soviet Union was engaged in a bitter struggle with the People's Republic of China and needed peaceful relations in Europe. Thus, the Federal Republic's interests matched those of Eastern countries, as both sought to increase trade and other contacts.

Brandt was eager to begin the laborious process of detente with Poland, one of the first victims of Nazi Germany's aggression. Previous CDU/CSU governments had failed to meet Poland's demand for recognition of its existing territory, especially the Oder-Neisse boundary bordering East Germany, which Allied powers at the 1945 Potsdam Conference had delineated subject to final determination at a peace conference. The division of Germany precluded the convening of such a conference; hence Brandt wanted to give assurance to Poland that the Federal Republic accepted the boundary. This would entail a de facto loss of about sixty-five thousand square miles of former German territory that Poland had occupied after the war (in partial compensation for Polish territory seized by the Soviet Union). His initiative was politically bold because many of the millions of expellees resettled in the Federal Republic still had not truly accepted the loss of their homeland even though they knew that there was no way back. In May 1969, Communist leader Wladyslaw Gomulka welcomed Brandt's intention to normalize relations, but by then difficulties within the Grand Coalition on foreign policy objectives prevented further action.

Brandt was more successful in reaching accords with several other Eastern countries.

238

In 1967 and 1968, he concluded agreements with Czechoslovakia on an exchange of goods and payments, as well as on trade missions with consular rights. He was able to establish close economic and cultural ties with Rumania in 1967, and the following year he signed an accord with Yugoslavia reestablishing diplomatic relations, which had been broken off when President Tito had recognized the German Democratic Republic a decade earlier. West German foreign officials also initiated discreet talks with Soviet, Hungarian, and Bulgarian authorities, but these feelers were interrupted by the Soviet military invasion of Czechoslovakia in August 1968, an invasion that sought to stop the political liberalization program instituted by Czech government officials. Thereafter, CDU/CSU ministers had increasing doubts about the usefulness of the Ostpolitik and put a brake on Brandt's efforts.

Prior to the invasion of Czechoslovakia, Brandt sought to improve relations with the German Democratic Republic through a policy of "regulated coexistence" designed to foster communication, trade, and cultural affairs. Except for an exchange of letters, no progress was made.

Brandt sought to improve relations not only with Eastern states, but with the West as well. He had to play a difficult juggling game between Great Britain, then seeking entry into the Common Market, and France, still attempting to keep Britain out; but he managed to improve relations with both countries, especially with France, where close ties had eroded during the Erhard administration. Without equivocation he backed the continued West German commitment to the NATO alliance, arguing that only a strong NATO could lead to detente.

While Brandt was busy making his mark on the foreign policy map, other SPD ministers contributed their share in achieving an impressive legislative record during the 1966–1969 era. The Minister of Economic Affairs persuaded his CDU/CSU cabinet colleagues to support Keynesian pump-priming measures to combat the recession rather than to seek a balanced budget. He pushed hard for stabilization of prices, wages, and profits, thereby running into difficulties with labor and business leaders. But the labor leaders, most of them Social Democrats, did not want to create political difficulties for the SPD, especially since the Minister's policies produced economic recovery within a relatively short period of time. The Minister of Transportation made progress in coordinating transport carriers, although running into some heavy opposition from the affected carriers. A major criminal law reform, the first in fifty years to focus on rehabilitation rather than punishment, was proposed by the Minister of Justice, while the Minister of Labor introduced bills on codetermination (labor's sharing decision-making power with management), profit-sharing, and compensation for sick workers.

Chancellor Candidate: Round Three
The Grand Coalition neared its end in 1969 as the four-year parliamentary term drew to a close. To no one's surprise, the SPD nominated Brandt for the third time to be their candidate for Chancellor. While he had been a two-time loser, the party still believed him to be their strongest candidate; besides, party tradition does not call for a change of standard-bearer in such a situation. Once nominated, Brandt and his colleagues had to work out an electoral strategy against the party with which they had been allied since late 1966. This was no easy task because much of the populace had difficulty attributing government policies to a specific party. Consequently the SPD decided to concentrate on the initial success of the Ostpolitik and economic stabilization and to accentuate in a "strategy of limited conflict" the few re-

maining differences, such as those in social policy, that still existed between them.

While the low-key campaign was in progress, the parties discussed future coalition alternatives, a perpetual necessity in a multiparty system in which it is extremely rare for one party to receive more than 50 percent of the vote in a parliamentary election. Brandt and most of his associates had little enthusiasm for renewing the strained alliance with the CDU/CSU, especially if the SPD would again have to take the second position in the Cabinet by receiving fewer votes than its rival. Brandt refused to visualize himself being Foreign Minister again. He became more interested in a coalition with the small Free Democratic party for three interrelated reasons. First, as leader of the strongest party, he could capture the chancellorship. Second, the foreign policy planks of the FDP matched those of the SPD. And finally, in March 1969 the FDP had helped to elect the SPD candidate for a five-year term as Federal President.

On September 28, the election took place. The results were at first little different from earlier elections, with the CDU/CSU again outpolling the SPD. The CDU/CSU vote dropped only slightly from 47.6 (in 1965) to 46.1 percent. The SPD vote increased from 39.3 to 42.7 percent, while the FPD suffered a massive loss of votes from 9.5 to 5.8 percent. The higher vote for the SPD was attributed primarily to its better showing in urban middle-class areas, encompassing white-collar workers and civil servants—an indication that the SPD had finally become more respectable and lost its Red taint.

Although the CDU/CSU emerged once more as the strongest party, it did not have an absolute majority of seats in the Bundestag and would have had to form a coalition Cabinet with another party. Kiesinger tried to form one, but failed. The SPD had ruled

out another Grand Coalition in advance, and a more liberal FDP was uninterested in allying itself again with the CDU/CSU, as it had done through most of the 1949–1966 era. The way was open for the SPD and FDP to form a ''social-liberal'' coalition government because together they had a majority, albeit slim, of 12 seats over the CDU/CSU in the 496-member Bundestag (SPD, 224 seats; FDP, 30; CDU/CSU, 242). Once the election results were in, Brandt did not take long to telephone Walter Scheel, FDP head, to propose a coalition of their two parties. Soon both leaders received support, although not unanimous, from their two parties.

To agree on a projected government program and the composition of the Cabinet, SPD leaders under Brandt's direction met with their FDP counterparts, after having informed Federal President Gustav Heinemann that they were ready to form a new government. Unlike the difficult bargaining process between the CDU/CSU and the SPD in 1966, this time a swift accord was reached on disputed domestic policy planks (to table them for the time being) and on the allocation of twelve Cabinet seats to the SPD, three to the FPD, and one to a Minister without party affiliation.

At the Summit as Chancellor

On October 21, 1969, the Bundestag elected Willy Brandt as Chancellor by a vote of 251 to 235 (with ten abstentions, invalid votes, and absences), constituting 3 more votes than the majority of 248 he needed in the 496-seat house. The SPD chairman was proud to be the first Chancellor of his party since 1930 and since the foundation of the Federal Republic. For him this was a moment of personal victory and triumph by the party, a fulfillment of a dream, but one that he surely never had in Lübeck. He could also take satisfaction that his Bundestag majority was 300 percent greater than that of Adenauer in 1949, a majority of one vote. At last, Brandt represented a party that had lost its sense of inferiority and had moved self-confidently and instinctively toward a position of power.

After the Bundestag vote, Brandt proceeded to call on President Heinemann to receive his letter of appointment. He thereupon told a television audience that he was satisfied, grateful for their confidence, and proud that he was enabled to move into the high office. In front of a reconvened Bundestag he was then sworn in as Chancellor. After the ceremony, while Brandt stepped outside and lit his favorite cigarillo, his companion, Mayor Klaus Schütz of Berlin, told him, "That is the way real revolutions take place." Schütz's phrase was too dramatic; the SPD certainly was not about to effectuate a peaceful revolution of the existing system. Rather it reflected a party leader's mood of euphoria celebrating the vincibility of the CDU/CSU—long overdue, from the SPD point of view.

On this triumphant day, Brandt exclaimed to journalists that "Hitler has now finally lost the war!" The implication of the statement was that Brandt and his party had never bowed to Hitler and had a spotless anti-Nazi record, unlike other leaders and parties in West Germany whose records were less clean. A flood of five thousand congratulatory messages poured in, while the British newspaper *Guardian* aptly wrote that for West Germany a nonconformist and a fighting Brandt represented a change after twenty years of respectable but unadventurous democracy. Indeed, Brandt's victory reflected a consensus for change among the majority of voters who were willing to support a government that promised more flexibility in foreign affairs and reforms in domestic affairs.

The Cabinet

On October 22, the day after Brandt's election, the Cabinet members received their letters of appointment from Heinemann and were sworn in by the Bundestag President. Walter Scheel of the FDP became Vice Chancellor and Minister of Foreign Affairs, taking over the post Brandt had just vacated.

Brandt's Cabinet represented a cross-section of the party elite, geographic areas, and occupational interests, ranging from trade union chiefs to a successful businessman, with a sprinkling of intellectuals in the middle. It was younger than its predecessors, with fifty being the average age and thirty-nine the youngest. Brandt also surrounded himself by a group of brilliant personal advisers and consultants, some of whom received positions in the chancellery and others who formed a circle of leading intellectuals and artists.

When Brandt assumed the mantle of the highest political office in the country, for which the Basic Law stipulates that its occupant determines and assumes responsibility for general governmental policy, he knew that the task would be difficult and time-consuming. Once again, as in his years as Mayor of Berlin, he could delegate much of the less important work to others, but that had limits too, especially since he remained Party Chairman. In one study of his calendar, a reporter calculated that in a four-week period Brandt had spent 152 hours in the chancellery and devoted 59 hours to party work, not to speak of evening meetings and trips to fulfill engagements outside of Bonn.

Although it was hard for Brandt to be in top form in the mornings, his normal working day started at home at 7 A.M. with a reading of the morning newspapers and a news summary compiled by the German News Agency. On the way to work in a chauffeur-driven Mercedes 300 SE, he studied telegrams received overnight from German ambassadors abroad. Normally at 8:30 A.M. he held a conference, nicknamed "morning prayers," with his advisers to discuss policy options and other immediate business. The rest of the day was filled with the normal administrative and political routine of a chief executive: holding conferences with government and party officials, taking care of correspondence, seeing official visitors, fielding questions at press conferences, and appearing at receptions. He attempted to keep as many evenings and weekends free as possible, but that proved difficult at best.

His style of leadership was reflected in his interpersonal relations with Cabinet colleagues. He was intent on instilling in them a spirit of teamwork and dedication to a common cause. By promoting solidarity and integration and by expressing confidence in their work, he expected to receive their confidence in turn. He prepared himself well for the Cabinet meetings by reading short memoranda on various agenda items prepared by the chancellery. Then he listened carefully and patiently to the opinions of the Cabinet members, letting the discussion on a major policy develop for hours, if necessary, without putting forward his own views except to point out possibilities of consensus. He attempted to find a common denominator of opinions, gradually weaving his own into the final decision. This nonauthoritarian technique of decision making reflected a subtle and often reluctant use of power except in crises, which he moved energetically and efficiently to solve.

The disadvantages of Brandt's leadership style sometimes caused legislative delays and occasional Cabinet resignations. In dealing with a number of temperamental Cabinet members—whose personality clashes were a frequent underlying cause of friction—Brandt was unwilling or incapable of dampening an emotional debate among them by pounding the table to restore order. Nor did he want to call for a vote too often for fear that it would destroy further the Cabinet's solidarity, which he prized above all.

While these problems recurred as long as Brandt was Chancellor, they were not grave enough to impede policy output appreciably. A revitalized chancellery made sure that the Cabinet and the ministries worked closely together on the basis of an intricate computerized information system that produced short-, medium-, and long-range plans for each governmental unit, with specific action dates and priorities. Gone was the relaxed atmosphere of Brandt's predecessors; it was replaced by a technocratic machine designed for maximum efficiency—even if it made enemies in the process, as it did. To provide for interparty coordination, an informal inner cabinet, consisting of a few SPD and FDP leaders, met on frequent occasions and invited the two heads of the SPD and FDP Fraktionen to join them whenever it was necessary to coordinate the executive and legislative machinery.

Any assessment of the Brandt administration must begin with foreign policy, for it assumed a greater importance and had a more dramatic impact on the German political scene than did domestic policy. The procedure by which foreign policy is made in West Germany parallels that of the system in the United States. As noted earlier, the Chancellor and the Cabinet are responsible for policy recommendations to the legislature, which then acts upon them. Normally, the executive introduces important foreign policy bills into the legislature and expects to see them passed without major amendments. The Chancellor, with the backing of the Cabinet, has the freedom to determine broad policy outlines and to engage in negotiations with other states, often concluding treaties that need parliamentary approval. But while the West German Chancellor can normally count on legislative support from a disciplined majority in the Bundestag, the United States President, faced by a Congress often dominated by the opposition party, may not achieve the desired objectives.

From 1969 to 1974, Brandt, Scheel, and Egon Bahr were the leading policy makers, receiving assistance from Foreign Ministry representatives abroad and at home and approval for their policies from Parliament.

Foreign Policy: Toward the West
Brandt's dream for Western Europe was for West Germany, one of its principal states, to promote more unity among the nationalist-oriented leadership. To this end, at a summit meeting of the European Economic Community (EEC, or Common Market) held in December 1969 at the Hague, he urged leaders from other member nations to act swiftly on approving applications for membership from Great Britain, Ireland, Norway, and Denmark. A negative decision, he warned, would retard European unity and would put the EEC at an economic and technological disadvantage vis-à-vis the major powers.

Brandt's speech signaled a change in the center of gravity within the EEC from France to West Germany and marked him as the strong man in Western Europe. French President Georges Pompidou, no match in the diplomatic game to his predecessor Charles de Gaulle, concurred with Brandt that talks for an enlarged EEC ought to begin in 1970. For years de Gaulle had fiercely resisted such a move for fear that France's strength in the EEC would be dissipated, but Pompidou calculated that Brit-

ain's membership in the EEC could act as a check on the increasingly assertive Federal Republic.

The British government welcomed Brandt's positive stance on its entry into the EEC and appreciated his tact in not antagonizing the French on this contested issue. In two official visits to Britain (March 1970 and April 1972) the Chancellor was feted as the man who had finally overcome European stagnation. He was invited to speak before a joint assembly of both Houses of Parliament and to visit the Queen at Windsor Palace—honors tendered to very few—and he was given an honorary doctorate at Oxford University, becoming the first German public official to receive one in the twentieth century. Brandt's triumphal visits in Great Britain helped to dissipate the anti-German feeling that had clung there longer than in almost any other European country. Not only in Britain, but elsewhere in Europe, Brandt was viewed as a representative of a more mature German state, incorporating its dynamism, energy, and self-confidence.

West German relations with the United States remained amicable. Brandt spoke up repeatedly for the maintenance of NATO strength and the continued full United States military presence in the Federal Republic. Richard Nixon had pledged not to cut back troop strength in West Germany on a unilateral basis. Meeting in April 1970 and June 1971 in Washington, with Brandt assuming the role of an equal partner, rather than a supplicant (as earlier Chancellors had done), the two leaders discussed such questions as troop commitment, EEC–United States trade, and the Ostpolitik. Hence Brandt was not displeased when Nixon was reelected President in 1972, even though he did not share Nixon's conservative economic ideology.

In June 1972, on the occasion of the twenty-fifth anniversary of the Marshall

Plan, Brandt announced to a Harvard University assembly that the Bundestag had authorized a George Marshall Memorial Fund to promote European–United States research projects dealing with the problems of highly industrialized nations. The fund was designed as a token repayment for the massive aid Germany had received after the war.

Foreign Policy: Toward the East

The Chancellor was viewed as a European statesman not only by Western leaders but by Eastern leaders as well, the latter being more interested in his Ostpolitik. Increasing the momentum that he had generated during his term as Foreign Minister, he sought to conclude accords with the Soviet Union and the Eastern European states that would provide for a mutual renunciation of the use or threat of force in order to dispel their fear of a renewal of German aggression and to establish closer political, economic, and cultural relations with them. Brandt took some risk in this policy, especially since he had only a small majority in the Bundestag. But he thought it was worth the gamble.

First on the Chancellor's agenda was a further normalization of relations with the Soviet Union, with which the Federal Republic had established diplomatic ties in 1955. In January 1970, Brandt appointed Egon Bahr as special envoy to head the negotiations in Moscow. After only two months Bahr reached agreement with the Soviets on the details of the accord. It affirmed the intent of the signatory states to maintain peace and achieve detente in Europe, to settle their disputes exclusively by peaceful means and not to resort to the use or threat of force, and to agree on the inviolability of the frontiers of all European states, especially that between the two Germanys and the Oder-Neisse line.

The Soviet interest in signing the treaty so swiftly stemmed from the fear of a militarily powerful Germany and the desire to have the Federal Republic accept the status quo in Central Europe. (These same reasons caused the Soviet Union to press for the signing of the Conference on Security and Cooperation in Europe treaty in August 1975.) In Moscow on August 12, 1970, Brandt and Soviet Premier Aleksei Kosygin, amid pomp and circumstance, signed the historic treaty, a cornerstone of Brandt's Ostpolitik because it was expected to facilitate the conclusion of accords with other Eastern states. Yet the treaty also represented a renunciation of West Germany's most cherished foreign policy illusion, reunification. In a television address from Moscow, however, Brandt said nothing had been given away that had not been lost a long time earlier.

In February 1970, West German negotiators began talks in Warsaw parallel to those in Moscow; these were concluded on November 19, when Scheel and Polish Foreign Minister Stefan Jedrychowski affixed their names to another important treaty. Because Brandt had expressed willingness to accept the Oder-Neisse line during his years as Foreign Minister, the treaty included such a provision, as well as others similar to those of the Moscow accord.

On December 7, Brandt and Prime Minister Josef Cyrankiewicz, as the political chief executives, formally signed the historic treaty in Warsaw. After the ceremony, Brandt once again reminded the Germans about Poland's sufferings inflicted by the Nazi armies and about the Auschwitz concentration camp where hell on earth was possible. On a tour of Warsaw, he stopped at the monument for the five hundred thousand Jews who had perished in the Ghetto in 1943, and deeply moved during the brief ceremony, he spontaneously sank down on his knees. This gesture of shame and atonement for the past caused a flurry of criticism in the Federal

Republic among the Chancellor's conservative and nationalist opponents who viewed it as exaggerated and theatrical. But Brandt later said that most Germans understood what he wanted to say without words; he had not planned the action in advance and was not ashamed of it. To run away from the nation's history and to cut oneself out of a chain of generations is impossible if one wants to be an equal part of the family of nations, Brandt averred on another occasion. Symbolizing the desire to take full responsibility for the crimes of the Third Reich, his gesture to atone for the past in Warsaw— and not in Germany—probably did more to soothe anti-German feeling in formerly occupied countries than any number of speeches given on the same subject in the Federal Republic could have done.

Like all laws in the Federal Republic, the signing of the Moscow and Warsaw accords needed West German parliamentary approval. The procedural aspects provide us a graphic picture of how a bill becomes law in the Federal Republic (described in general terms in chapter 2). Once the Cabinet forwarded the text of the accords to the Bundesrat, in which the CDU/CSU had a majority, that body not unexpectedly defeated the treaties by a vote of 21 to 20. But the government was not too concerned because the Bundestag had the power to override the Bundesrat. In February 1972 the Bundestag debated the treaties in the initial first reading for twenty-five hours, attesting to their controversial nature. The CDU/CSU leadership claimed that the treaties represented a disguised capitulation to the Communist powers, an illusion that relations with Moscow and Warsaw could be im-

"Ach! Everybody loves Germany NOW!"

(London Daily Express)

Brandt kneeling in Warsaw (*Homage without words*)

(German Information Center)

proved, a reduction of West German security, and a deepening of the division of Germany. In reply, Brandt and other government supporters reiterated their well-known views. Thereupon, the treaties were submitted to the Committee on Foreign Affairs for its perusal and recommendation and then to the Bundestag plenary sessions for a final debate in second and third readings. CDU leader Rainer Barzel recommended that his Deputies abstain during the voting because they failed to reach a consensus on the merits of the treaty, while CSU leader Franz Josef Strauss recommended to his Deputies from Bavaria that they vote against the treaties. Brandt managed to get Bundestag approval (248 SPD and FDP for,

10 CSU against, and 238 CDU abstentions on the Moscow treaty; a slightly different vote on the Warsaw treaty), but only because of Barzel's decision. A negative CDU vote would have resulted in a tie because a number of SPD and FDP Deputies had permanently defected to the CDU/CSU over their dissatisfaction with Brandt's Ostpolitik. Since the Bundestag vote overrode the negative Bundesrat vote, the treaties soon received the Federal President's signature and were officially announced as law.

West German relations with the Soviet Union and Poland did improve thereafter. On July 5, 1972, West Germany signed a long-term trade accord with the Soviet Union, freeing many goods imported from the Soviet Union from trade restrictions. In September 1972, Poland established diplomatic relations with the Federal Republic, thereby allowing thousands of ethnic Germans to resettle in Germany. (In 1975 a new accord permitted most of those still in Poland to finally resettle.)

Brandt and Scheel viewed the two treaties as curtain openers for others. Their emissaries started negotiations with Czech leaders, who were still haunted by painful war memories and the 1938 Munich Accord, in which Hitler forced the dismemberment of Czechoslovakia. West German emissaries also opened negotiations with Hungarian and Bulgarian officials. In late 1973, after protracted negotiations over a disputed Berlin provision, the Federal Republic reached accords to establish diplomatic relations with these three countries. In the meantime, in October 1972, it began diplomatic relations with the People's Republic of China.

Ties with the German Democratic Republic

While these negotiations with Moscow and other Communist capitals proceeded swiftly or at a tortoise pace, the Chancellor was eager above all to normalize relations with East Germany. On October 29, 1969, soon after assuming office, he acknowledged in a policy statement that a final settlement of the German question could be made only at a European peace conference, but that in the meantime any further alienation of the Federal Republic and the German Democratic Republic within one German nation must be prevented at all costs. He proposed the development of a "regulated coexistence" between the two states and admitted that reunification as an immediate foreign policy goal would have to be abandoned.

The spirit of cooperation was not yet reciprocated. In December 1969, Walter Ulbricht, then East German head of state and party, submitted a counterproposal calling for full diplomatic relations between the two nations, for he was eager to enhance the status of East Germany in the international community. But to Brandt an exchange of ambassadors ran counter to his thesis that the two states did not have alien populations. While Brandt rejected the counterproposal, he agreed to meet in March 1970 with Prime Minister Willi Stoph in Erfurt, East Germany, to discuss other questions of mutual concern. It was an important occasion since no such meeting had taken place between feuding German leaders in the two decades since the formation of their states. But the discussions reached an impasse, not broken at their next meeting on May 21 in Kassel, West Germany.

Secret diplomacy between Bahr and his counterpart did begin. In September 1971 and May 1972 they concluded postal and transportation agreements to improve communications and to ease the entry of West Germans into East Berlin and East Germany, while conversely permitting East Germans to travel to the Federal Republic on urgent family matters. On November 8, 1972, they initialed the Basic Intra-German Treaty. Its

provisions are similar to those in the Moscow and Warsaw treaties (renunciation of force, territorial integrity, cooperation in nonpolitical fields), but it does not call for full diplomatic exchange of ambassadors and recognition—a victory for Brandt. Instead it provides for an exchange of permanent representatives with the title of Plenipotentiary Minister. The German Democratic Republic promised to ease the problems of families separated by the border, to open new crossing points, and to release political prisoners to the Federal Republic.

The treaty in effect signaled the Federal Republic's de facto recognition of the German Democratic Republic, a minimum goal long sought by the latter, in return for humanitarian improvements. It also produced full diplomatic exchanges by East Germany with many other states, including the Western Allies. While the treaty, which came into force on June 21, 1973, has not solved the question of reunification, it has created the basis for a detente in Germany and Europe by ensuring that the German question will not continue to provide a source of constant tension between East and West. West German public opinion polls showed that a majority of respondents were supportive of the treaty, which was an important factor in enhancing the image of the Brandt administration.

The Berlin Problem
The final item on Brandt's agenda was to gain Soviet approval for an Allied accord on Berlin, a city that is still under their supreme control. To speed up negotiations among them, Brandt insisted that the Moscow and Warsaw treaties would be submitted to Parliament for ratification only after the Allies reached an accord on Berlin. This diplomatic finesse was to pay off; by September 3, 1971, the four Allies signed the Quadripartite Agreement. It reaffirms West

Berlin's ties to the Federal Republic, although recognizing that the city is not a constituent part of West Germany; it guarantees Western access rights by air, land, and water to West Berlin, which in the past had always been vaguely agreed to and never formalized; it provides West Berliners with an opportunity to visit East Berlin and East Germany for the first time since the Wall was put up in 1961; it gives the Soviets the right to establish a consulate-general in West Berlin; and it recognizes the right of West German consular authorities to represent West Berliners in Eastern Europe. The treaty, which went into effect in June 1972, represented a compromise between the Western Allies and the Soviet Union, but for Brandt it marked another milestone in his quest for a normalization of relations and detente between East and West.

A Bestowal of Honors
The success of Brandt's Ostpolitik was recognized in Germany and abroad and was accompanied by a number of honors. In December 1970, the Chancellor received the Freedom of the City of Berlin award, while in January 1971, *Time* magazine named him Man of the Year. That October he won the 1971 Nobel Peace Prize, the highest international honor for the promotion of world peace. The citation spoke of his moves to extend "his hand for a policy of reconciliation between old enemies," which ought to contribute to a strengthening of peace in Europe and the world. His journey to Oslo to accept the award brought back memories of the exile years; Scandinavian friends sat in the audience, reminding Brandt that the German pacifist Carl von Ossietzky had received the same prize in 1936 partly because of Brandt's efforts in Scandinavia. In his address, he stressed his country's desire for peace, the need to solve Germany's division, the need for European unity, and the need to

help poorer countries. The Nobel Prize boosted his popularity and made it easier for him to complete the Ostpolitik edifice.

In February 1972, Brandt's native Lübeck bestowed on him the Freedom of the City award. To Brandt this award may have been as treasured as the Nobel Prize, for it symbolized the story of a young Lübeck boy who had made it in the world.

Domestic Policy: Small Steps
While Brandt's fame spread with each new victory in his foreign policy, he also attempted to become the Chancellor of domestic reforms, knowing that he could not neglect domestic policy issues. What was his vision of the future? He viewed Germany as a progressive social welfare state in further need of reforms because some programs and concepts still rested on those of the nineteenth century. A need existed to create not only a perfect welfare state, but also a society in which the rights of the individual and the collectivity would have the proper mix. While maximizing the freedom of the individual, the state would have to institute further controls over the economy in such areas as pollution, overcrowding of cities, and transportation. Brandt was, of course, aware that constraints on his ability to shape domestic policy were inevitable, given the nature of German federalism, in which the Länder have powers in such fields as education and cultural affairs, and given the nature of coalition Cabinet bargaining.

As promised in the 1969 government declaration, the Chancellor sought to introduce reforms that were based on earlier policies or on new ones developed from the programs of the social-liberal coalition. He acknowledged that the conservative governments had initiated useful domestic policy legislation, especially that which the SPD had supported, but there was a need to speed up. He sought to allay the fears of powerful industrial and agricultural associations and of the middle-of-the-road voters that his government would embark on radical reforms producing deep economic and societal alterations in the system. He insisted that his government would propose only mild reforms and was not an enemy of the business community; on the contrary, it wanted to encourage industry to produce to its maximum capacity. Yet the social responsibility of business would have to be increased in the fields of environmental protection, accident prevention, codetermination (in which workers' representatives would have equal representation with management officials on the boards of directors of corporations), and workers' capital accumulation based on their sharing in some corporate profits. The capitalist system based on private profits must be linked to such social responsibilities if the democratic system was to be protected from radical groups intent on crushing it.

Brandt also welcomed the support of the numerically powerful trade unions, primarily oriented toward social democracy, in their adherence to the democratic order. Even though they represented an important interest group that produced votes for the SPD, their interests were of necessity more narrow-gauged than those of the government, and occasional clashes were bound to occur.

During Brandt's first administration (1969–1972), fiscal constraints soon dampened the reform euphoria of the Ministers. The Cabinet was caught in the familiar bind in which the public demanded more schools, hospitals, and road improvements, but did not want to see taxes increased. The Chancellor was discouraged that private consumption ranged higher in the public's priority than did tax increases that would finance improvements for the general welfare—a problem not restricted to the Federal Republic. Discreetly he sought to increase the proportion of public investment as a percentage of the gross social product at the expense of private investment.

Brandt had only limited success in producing a tax reform that would retain enough revenue and at the same time provide tax relief for low-income groups. The Parliament enacted a modest capital accumulation law that aided such groups and increased by 2 percent the levy on the wealthy. The SPD would have preferred a steeper increase on high-income groups, but the more business-oriented FDP vetoed any such proposals in the Cabinet.

Both parties did enact a battery of less controversial social legislation providing health insurance for white-collar employees, extending the coverage of those entitled to family allowances for children, and raising the level of retirement pay for pensioners and disabled veterans. The Cabinet also sent to Parliament bills dealing with codetermination, city planning, reform of rents, cartels, education, and justice, but many of them could not be enacted into law prior to parliamentary adjournment in 1972. Indeed, in 1971 the reform program, which had been meticulously coordinated by the chancellery's computer and the planning-staff brains behind it, ran into financial roadblocks that had not been foreseen a year earlier. Of the 455 reform bills promised in the legislative period, many fell by the wayside; others were so minor in nature, often containing just a change in wording, that the government was criticized for giving the impression that the 455 bills were all substantive ones. The government undoubtedly was guilty of an oversell campaign in its promise of a host of reforms; however, the head of the chancellery argued that the government had not promised too much, but the mass media had nurtured high expectations of miracles among the public. Regardless of who was to blame, the public expected, for instance, wide-ranging educational reforms after the government announced its goals: a long-range target of 3 million places in kindergartens against the existing 1 million places and an increase of the university student body from 550,000 to 650,000 by 1975. But a creeping inflation in which the cost of living rose by 4 percent in 1971, twice the average of the previous three years, made such reforms impossible at the time. It also led to more feuds within the Cabinet and the resignation of the Minister of Finance. His place was taken by Minister of Economic Affairs Karl Schiller, who also retained his own ministry, thereby becoming a "super-minister" to the discomfort of other Cabinet members, who cordially disliked him. Economic difficulties also contributed to setbacks for the SPD in Land elections during these years.

The Youth Rebellion

While Brandt's reform plans ran into some choppy waters, he did not have clear sailing in his party, either. As we noted earlier, the SPD is not made up of a monolithic bloc, but harbors loosely-knit radical, centrist, and conservative wings. Within the radical wing may be found "old Marxists" and the Marxist-oriented Young Socialists (Jusos). Typical of youth groups in other countries, the ideologically attuned Jusos took the offensive against the pragmatic, de-ideologized, and integrationist views of older party leaders, who were to be found primarily in the centrist and conservative wings and who as Cabinet members formed a part of the ruling elite. Brandt was a member of the centrist group that attempted to bridge the gulf between the radical and conservative wings. While sympathetic to some Juso objectives, Brandt had become less ideologically committed, emphasizing the SPD's becoming a catchall party that would draw broad support from a wide range of groups. But the

Jusos considered such a position somewhat of a sell-out and accused the Ministers in the Cabinet of de-emphasizing workers' interests and of abandoning the goal of socialism.

At the 1970 party convention, the Jusos demanded that the party become more socialist in orientation and make inner democratic reforms. Their demands met with little success, although Brandt called a special convention in November 1971 to discuss their governmental proposals, including a radical program of tax reform. The Chancellor and other SPD Ministers argued that their proposals would not be supported by the FDP, would be too costly, and would be detrimental to the SPD image of being a moderate party.

Despite Brandt's negative stance toward many Juso demands, he takes a relaxed view of the radical youth—after all, he was one himself at an earlier stage of his career. He regards it as natural for the young to go through a transient radical phase and believes they have ideas to contribute that may be as important as those of their seniors. No age group holds the truth exclusively. Brandt feels that anyone who has not been a radical before age twenty will never make a good Social Democrat. The party must remain open to the worries and the demands of the young, for otherwise "our feet would fall asleep."

In his own family, Brandt had to cope with a similar generational conflict with his son Peter, who was born in 1948. (Brandt and his wife also have two other sons: Lars, born in 1951, and Mathias, born in 1961.) Peter, then a university student, was arrested and fined twice for participating in political demonstrations in the 1960s. He took a Marxist stance, further to the left than the position his father had once espoused. Father and son have since given up trying to convince each other that their position is the correct one.

In a Political Crisis

While the Chancellor was beset by these multiple problems, it was his successful Ostpolitik that produced a major backlash. When the SPD and FDP formed a government in 1969, they had a majority of only twelve votes in the Bundestag. After several conservative Deputies critical of the Ostpolitik defected and crossed over to the CDU/CSU (an infrequent practice in the Federal Republic), Brandt's delicate majority evaporated quickly. By the time the Bundestag debated the Moscow and Warsaw treaties in the spring of 1972, the government could count on a majority of one vote at the most. Since such an impasse would destroy its ability to push its legislation through the Bundestag, the Basic Law provides two alternatives; either the executive dissolves the Bundestag upon a loss of a vote of confidence, followed by new elections, or the incumbent Chancellor is immediately displaced by a challenger if the latter can muster a majority in the Bundestag. This second alternative is the constructive vote of no confidence, intended to prevent a political vacuum and to enhance political stability.

The CDU/CSU decided to follow the second course, and on April 27, 1972, for the first time in the history of the Federal Republic, it introduced a no-confidence vote. The party could muster only 247 votes for its candidate, Rainer Barzel, head of the CDU, and thus fell 2 votes short of the majority needed to topple Brandt. If three members had not abstained, Barzel might have won. But he, too, would have had such a slim majority that he could not have governed for long.

Despite the April 27 victory, Brandt saw another SPD deputy defect to the enemy ranks soon thereafter. Hence, after consulting with the CDU/CSU, Brandt opted for the first constitutional alternative. Even though the four-year Bundestag term did not

Brandt, his wife, and son Mathias in 1972

(German Information Center)

expire until 1973, he called for a new election in the hope that the SPD/FDP majority would be increased. Under a constitutional provision, he would first have to lose a vote of confidence, which he did on September 22 by letting all Cabinet members deliberately abstain from voting, thereby producing a CDU/CSU majority against a motion of confidence introduced by the remaining SPD and FDP deputies, who voted for it. President Heinemann immediately announced the dissolution of the Bundestag and scheduled the election for November 19.

Brandt hoped that the SPD and FDP would score another victory in the election, but he could not be certain in the light of economic problems, intraparty dissension, and the dramatic resignation of Minister Schiller in July over long-standing disputes with his Cabinet colleagues concerning economic and financial policies. Brandt's critics in the SPD accused the Chancellor of indecision in keeping the Minister too long in his post, but Brandt had an aversion for getting rid of associates (he had once said about another official, "I can't just put him on the street") and feared that Schiller's resignation, in view of his popularity as Minister of Economic Affairs during the coalition years, could have damaging consequences at election time. The Chancellor appointed Helmut Schmidt, then Defense Minister, as replacement for Schiller, thereby grooming Schmidt as a future Chancellor candidate by familiarizing him with the work of key ministries.

The campaign lasted the few weeks that are customary in Europe and was a relatively sober one. In October, the SPD convened a special convention to agree on an election platform, which in turn would become the basis of discussion for a new government program should it win. The party made a determined effort to capture the maximum of votes by capitalizing on Brandt's personal popularity. He toured the country, attracted large crowds, and made numerous speeches in which he defended the government record in the foreign and domestic spheres and assailed the CDU's domination by its small Bavarian ally, the CSU, led by the archconservative Franz Josef Strauss, "the last Prussian from Bavaria." The SPD revived the 1961 personality cult with the slogans "Vote for Willy—who else is there?" and "Willy must stay!"

The CDU counterstrategy was to present their Chancellor candidate Barzel as a member of a team whose task it was to assail the Ostpolitik and inflation. The FDP sought support on the premise that the nation needed to sustain a third national party capable of maintaining a check on the two major parties. The November election represented a smashing victory for the SPD and FDP. For the first time in West German history, the SPD captured more votes (45.9 percent) than the CDU/CSU (44.8 percent), while the FDP received 8.4 percent. The coalition partners had a safe majority of 46 seats when they received 271 seats in the Bundestag to 225 for the CDU/CSU.

Brandt could take much credit for the SPD victory. He was able to gain votes from many women, Catholic workers, and farmers who had not previously voted for the SPD and from newly enfranchised youth (the voting age had been reduced from twenty-one to eighteen). The foreign press, including newspapers in the Communist countries, hailed his victory as further proof that the Cold War was ebbing. The London tabloid *Daily Mirror* ran the headline, "Wunderbar Willy Back in Triumph," while other newspapers labeled Brandt "the strong man in Europe."

The Second Term
On December 14, 1972, Brandt was sworn in for his second term as Chancellor; the following day his Cabinet was sworn in, consisting of thirteen SPD and five FDP members, with few changes from the previous era. There was some grumbling in SPD circles about the high FDP representation, but the FDP had driven a hard bargain during the delicate negotiations about Cabinet membership, insisting on certain ministries as the price for participation.

Brandt delivered to the Bundestag the official Policy Statement (comparable to the presidential State of the Union message in the United States) on January 18, 1973. It was a cautiously worded document that promised to speed up domestic reforms and to raise the quality of life of the citizenry, but the promise was going to be difficult to fulfil. Brandt's optimism engendered by the SPD electoral victory soon dissipated. Although he had reached accord with the FDP Ministers on an action agenda for domestic legislation that had been delayed in his first administration, conservative FDP deputies in 1973 and 1974 were not eager to proceed swiftly on tax, land, and education reforms or on capital asset formation and codetermination. In addition, inflationary prices led in August 1973 to wildcat strikes by metal workers, who saw their wages trailing prices. Brandt condemned the strikes and urged the workers to let the union settle their grievances.

The Chancellor's difficulties were compounded by snags in his Ostpolitik. The German Democratic Republic took an increasingly tough stance concerning inter-German relations. For instance, it raised the minimum amount of currency that visitors had to exchange upon entering its territory. As noted, Czechoslovakia, Bulgaria, and Hungary delayed signing accords with West Germany because of a disputed Berlin provision. SPD Fraktion leader and Deputy Chairman Herbert Wehner, who was the principal strategist of the party, became increasingly frustrated with the tough stance Brandt and Scheel took toward the three countries and urged the two leaders to quietly make concessions. But when Brandt and Scheel did not, Wehner, while on a visit in Moscow, publicly stated that the West German government had pushed too hard for concessions from the East. This statement caused a bombshell in Bonn. The Chancellor rushed back from a trip to the United States one day early to meet with Wehner and try to undo the political damage caused by his remark. While publicly professing that all was well, Brandt never forgave Wehner for

undercutting his authority and for having criticized him publicly—in Moscow, to boot. Brandt viewed Wehner's remark as a breach of party practice; criticism of official policy must not be voiced publicly, but should be made behind closed doors. Wehner, on the other hand, felt that only a dramatic statement would change foreign policy, make Brandt a more forceful leader (Wehner reportedly once said, "What is missing in the government is a head"), and cut the FDP down to size because it had wrung too many concessions from the SPD in the government program. Through this tactic Wehner sought to bring his dream of an SPD ruling alone, without having to dilute its program to maintain a coalition, one step closer to fruition. But while this long-range objective may have been laudatory from the SPD point of view, it undercut Brandt's relationship with the FDP and produced an image to the electorate of SPD leaders feuding among themselves. The image was real enough—Brandt and Wehner were hardly on speaking terms by then.

The mounting difficulties exacted a toll on Brandt's government and party leadership and on his emotional state. As a result of having made his mark in foreign policy during the first administration and of being less interested in domestic policy, he seemed bored and lapsed into another stage of listlessness, moodiness, and depression. He said to an old friend, "What do they [the critics] want of me? Don't they see that I have yielded my milk?" [2] Magazines had a field day. On an earlier occasion the weekly *Stern* had written, "Brandt is acting like the aging Emperor Napoleon, who issued orders only in writing, habitually tossing the scraps of paper out of the speeding coach." [3] Now, in issuing a mock report card on Brandt, it

[2] *Newsweek,* February 4, 1974.
[3] Quoted in *Newsweek,* January 29, 1973.

said that the Chancellor "avoids decisions and is frequently withdrawn, but he carries his halo with dignity." [4] In a January 1974 poll, only 41 percent of respondents claimed to be satisfied with his leadership, although 60 percent regarded him with high esteem.

As in earlier periods of frustration, Brandt's inner core of toughness and resilience, combined with encouragement from his wife and friends, produced after some months a new mood of determination and optimism. There were, after all, positive achievements to register during the period of reversals. In June 1973, Brandt paid a state visit to Israel, the first German head of government to be invited to this country with bitter memories of the Nazi past. In September, both Germanys were admitted as new members into the United Nations. Brandt traveled to New York for a major address there on the need to renounce force in international relations, to eliminate poverty and hunger, and to recognize human rights as important ingredients of world peace. The Federal Republic resumed diplomatic relations in December with Czechoslovakia, Bulgaria, and Hungary, having shelved the disputed Berlin question. In January 1974, the Chancellor delivered a strong Policy Statement to the Bundestag in which he announced that the coalition parties had reached an accord to push the long-delayed codetermination and capital assets bills through the legislature, and in April he went on a much lauded trip to Egypt to talk with President Sadat about the Middle East situation.

Yet Brandt's determination to weather the storm failed. The Public Service Workers Union called its members out on strike against the government in February 1974 over a wage dispute that the Chancellor set-

tled only with difficulty. In March the SPD suffered serious reverses in Land elections in Hamburg and municipal elections in Rhineland-Palatinate because of a general fear among middle-class voters of the short-lived energy crisis, inflation, Juso attempts to shape government policy, and left terrorism. Voters who had only recently cast their ballots for the SPD and who were sympathetic to its moderate goals were worried that Brandt was not a strong enough leader to cope with the new problems. Once again these voters switched back to the CDU/CSU—at least for the time being.

During this time of stress, Brandt's attempt to maintain a fragile unity in the SPD suffered another serious blow. "Crown prince" Helmut Schmidt, then Finance Minister and Party Deputy Chairman, publicly assailed Brandt on television for his "weak" leadership. This was not the first time that the Minister, ambitious to become Chancellor, had criticized Brandt's leadership style. Privately, Schmidt also urged Brandt to make a major Cabinet reshuffle in the light of the pending selection on May 15 of a new Federal President. Brandt, who already was disappointed that Heinemann would not stay in office for another term so that the Brandt-Scheel team could continue governing, was furious that Schmidt did not maintain party loyalty and that he seemed ready to stage a putsch against Brandt. The Chancellor told the SPD Executive Committee that no one in the SPD would bind him to a specific Cabinet reshuffle, but he knew that a reshuffle was imminent: Foreign Minister Scheel had agreed to become the candidate of the SPD-FDP for Federal President, thus creating a vacancy in the Cabinet. Scheel, incidentally, agreed to become the candidate only because Brandt refused to run for a primarily ceremonial and nonpolitical post.

Remarkable about the Schmidt assault on

[4] Ibid., February 4, 1974.

Brandt was not so much the rivalry for political power, which would be the normal characteristic of party aspirants who challenge the incumbent in office, but the open nature of the challenge. It caused a debilitating effect on party cohesion and showed the voters that the SPD leadership troika (Brandt, Wehner, and Schmidt) was hardly on speaking terms. If a party is incapable of governing itself, the perplexed voters may have asked, can it govern the nation? Many of them provided the answer by casting their ballots in the Land elections for other parties. The question of why Brandt did not attempt to oust Wehner and Schmidt after they had challenged his authority must also be posed. To

put it briefly, Brandt was averse to such an attempt because it ran counter to his penchant for compromise and because he still viewed Wehner as a valuable party strategist and Schmidt as a strong Chancellor candidate should he, Brandt, decide to resign.

The Guillaume Affair
In April 1974, the last bombshell of Brandt's second administration burst on Bonn. Banner headlines proclaimed the news that an East German spy had been uncovered working in the chancellery as a personal aide to Brandt. The short, rotund, and colorless spy, Günter Guillaume, had for eighteen years been an agent of the German Democratic

The SPD troika: Helmut Schmidt, Willy Brandt, and Herbert Wehner

(German Information Center)

Republic. He came under suspicion of being an agent in the spring of 1973 after having received an earlier security clearance. Intelligence recommended to Brandt to leave Guillaume in his post so his accomplices could be uncovered. Brandt agreed. To make matters worse, he took Guillaume on his Norwegian summer vacation as an aide charged with handling dispatches coming in from Bonn, including highly classified NATO documents. Brandt apparently felt that the intelligence branch was mistaken (it had happened before that suspects were not agents), but the damage had been done.

Not uncovering any accomplices, intelligence decided on April 24, 1974, to arrest Guillaume and his wife, who also was implicated in spying for the East Germans. During their 1975 trial they were charged with treason, espionage, and breach of state secrets, and Guillaume admitted that he had been a spy. Upon conviction, he was sentenced to thirteen years imprisonment; his wife, to eight years. While spying in both Germanys is a daily fact of life, the East German secret service had never before been able to place one of its agents so high in Bonn's executive branch. This was a heavy blow to Brandt's administration.

The Chancellor's decision to resign was caused not only by the Guillaume affair and the adverse political and economic factors that had plagued him since his reelection in 1972, but also by revelations about his personal life. Soon after the arrest of Guillaume, reports surfaced that the secret service had information about Brandt's casual affairs with women, especially on his election campaign train trips, which Guillaume also knew about and might testify to in court. When the tabloid press played up these reports and when politically conservative officials of the secret service reportedly passed this information on to the CDU/CSU, Brandt's intention

to resign as Chancellor—which he may have been toying with for some time—was strengthened.

Brandt admitted the veracity of the reports about his private affairs in a television address after his resignation. He had quit partly because there were indications his private life would be drawn into the case. But he also contended that it was grotesque to maintain that the Chancellor could be blackmailed. In a letter to all SPD members, he wrote that "I am no plaster saint and have never said that I am free of human frailties. But I shall not allow myself to be brought down by the abominable methods with which certain opponents—not for the first time—want to destroy me now." [5]

Even with the lurid revelations about Brandt's private life splashed in the tabloid press, he need not have resigned, for dalliances by government officials are taken in stride by the German population. Brandt could have asked other high government officials to take the blame for the Guillaume affair and to resign. While this action would have been the easy way out, Brandt viewed such a move as dishonest and unworthy. Rather, the upright course was to take all the blame on himself and resign. During those traumatic days of crisis, Brandt became despondent and, according to one unconfirmed report, even fleetingly considered committing suicide. But this mood of depression eventually passed.

Resignation
In systems with political stability, top national leaders rarely resign. They may take such an extreme step if there are insurmountable policy disputes within the government, if they lose the confidence of their own party, or if a major scandal for which they assume

[5] SPD, *Auslandsbrief,* May 13, 1974.

responsibility rocks the country. If a successor is swiftly chosen, then the political turmoil may be minimized.

In the case of Brandt, the Guillaume scandal and news of his private affairs precipitated his resignation. A detailed account of the procedural aspects of his stepping down from the chancellorship will give us an added glimpse of the West German political system.

On Saturday, May 4, 1974, ten days after Guillaume's arrest, the Chancellor consulted Wehner and two other party leaders about his decision to resign. While the latter two attempted to dissuade him, Wehner was non-committal. If he had urged Brandt to stay on, perhaps the Chancellor might have changed his mind. On Sunday, May 5, Brandt met again with a few senior party leaders, informed them of his irrevocable decision to quit, and suggested that Schmidt succeed him as Chancellor. That evening Brandt composed the brief resignation letter addressed to President Heinemann in which he accepted the political responsibility for negligence in connection with the Guillaume espionage affair and announced his resignation as Chancellor. In the letter he requested an immediate acceptance of his resignation and the appointment of Scheel as acting Chancellor. Brandt showed the letter to a few party friends and to Scheel, who urgently asked him not to resign, but by then Brandt had made up his mind. On Monday evening, May 6, Brandt called government and opposition leaders to his office to explain the decision to them, while the head of the chancellery carried Brandt's letter to Heinemann, who happened to be in Hamburg.

At midnight, radio listeners heard the first dramatic, and to them unexpected, announcement that Brandt had tendered his resignation to the President. Soon thereafter, in the early morning hours of Tuesday, May

7, several hundred shocked sympathizers appeared before Brandt's private residence in Bonn, and later that day tens of thousands demonstrated in major cities as an expression of sympathy and support for him. In the meantime, that morning, the SPD Presidium and then the Executive Committee met in separate sessions to endorse Brandt's proposal that Schmidt be his successor. Then Brandt proceeded to a meeting of the Fraktion, where to a wildly cheering gathering of deputies he said, "My resignation is a result of my experience in office, my respect for the unwritten rules of democracy, and is to prevent my personal and political integrity from being destroyed." [6] Brandt indicated by this statement that West Germany's institutions were more important than any individual, that the nation's interest was broader than his own personal interest, and that for him there were other things more important than holding public office.

At 2 P.M., May 7, 1974, Brandt's resignation became effective as Heinemann, back from Hamburg, officially relieved the sixty-year-old Chancellor of his duties and in the name of the German people thanked him for his services. Acting Chancellor Scheel had met with the Cabinet members earlier that day and informed them that their resignations would take effect at the same time as that of Brandt, but that, according to constitutional provision, they would be requested to remain in their posts on a caretaker basis until a new Chancellor was chosen.

The reaction in Germany and abroad to Brandt's resignation was one of dismay, consternation, and surprise, but on the whole it was highly sympathetic. There were many people who felt that he need not have resigned, but admired the importance he had placed on morality in politics. One aide

[6] *New York Times,* May 8, 1974.

said, "If he had stayed on, he felt, he would simply be another Nixon. He wanted to show that he at least was an honest leader. Think what people will say of him now." [7] Another noted that there was still one leader of integrity in the Western world, but that he had been betrayed by foes and friends alike. Foreign leaders lauded him as the "peace Chancellor" who had done so much to produce a detente in Europe, but were concerned whether Brandt's successor would continue his Westpolitik and Ostpolitik. The CDU/CSU denounced his failure to control inflation and left-wing extremism and called for a new federal election to deal with the "crisis of the state." But the party knew without saying so publicly that no such election would take place because the governing parties would support the SPD nominee by a wide margin.

[7] Ibid.

Brandt's resignation abruptly ended at the political summit a career that had seemed so auspicious at the beginning. The political ascendancy of Brandt in Bonn was marked by two phases. In the first, from 1966 to 1969, he was a successful Foreign Minister who launched an imaginative Ostpolitik that had favorable repercussions on the European scene and eased the Cold War confrontation between East and West. In the second, from 1969 to 1974, he was a Chancellor who achieved further dramatic breakthroughs in foreign policy but less spectacular ones in domestic policy. While the 1972 election proved a personal victory for Brandt, and observers forecast another four-year term for him as Chancellor, the mounting difficulties in 1973 and 1974 were of such dimensions that he felt he had no other choice than to resign, although he announced that he would remain chairman of the SPD, a post of national visibility.

6

Assessment
and Conclusions

Brandt's Successor
In a stable democratic system, political succession from one leader to the next normally poses few problems in the expected orderly transfer of power. In the case of West Germany, resignation provides a Chancellor with an opportunity to recommend to the top party organs who the successor ought to be. Such a procedure prevents a mad scramble for power among rival contestants and ensures a continuity in foreign and domestic policies, although the priorities and accents will undoubtedly reflect the predispositions and doctrine of the successor.

In 1974, Brandt's successor was the fifty-five-year-old Helmut Schmidt. His background and political style differed considerably from those of Brandt, yet for nearly two decades the two leaders had managed to work together, except for occasional disputes. Ideologically they did not always agree, for Schmidt stood on the political right within the party. The new Chancellor was acknowledged to be a skilled and pragmatic leader who had imagination, authority, and vigor, but no patience with less capable or indecisive persons.

On May 16, 1974, Schmidt was sworn in as West Germany's fifth postwar Chancellor. The SPD-FDP cabinet contained few new faces, but the accent was on technocrats and pragmatists rather than intellectuals. On May 17, Schmidt issued the government's Policy Statement in which he pledged to continue Brandt's social-liberal coalition programs. Praising Brandt's determination to win for Germany a position of respect in the international community and his efforts in aiding the world to take "a big step" toward peace, he also noted that Brandt's domestic reform program from 1969 to 1974 had achieved more gains than any previous program for a comparable period.

At the Helm as Party Chairman
While Schmidt took quick command of the top post, Brandt was not disposed to stay on the political sidelines after his resignation as

Chancellor. Unlike many leaders who simply fade from public attention once they are no longer in office, Brandt remained Party Chairman. (At the 1977 party convention, he was reelected.) The collective leadership of Schmidt and Brandt was almost unprecedented in postwar Germany, since normally the Chancellor is simultaneously Party Chairman. The advantage of one person holding both posts is that party and government policy are fused more effectively than with two persons, but the disadvantage is that the workload increases correspondingly. Schmidt claimed that he could not handle both jobs satisfactorily and that, in any case, Brandt's political strength, personal attractiveness, and skill in integrating warring factions in

the party made him the ideal chairman. Schmidt did not say publicly that SPD members were still shocked by Brandt's resignation and had a loyalty and sympathy for Brandt that he himself did not command. But this was general knowledge in Germany.

Schmidt and Brandt arrived at a modus vivendi in dividing their spheres of operations; the Chancellor would handle the day-to-day governmental affairs, while the Party Chairman would deal with party affairs. Brandt requested party members to support Schmidt fully and remained a Bundestag deputy, which gave him an additional platform to express his views.

Despite public expressions of a team effort between Brandt and Schmidt, their personal

The pilot quits the government ship—the party ship needs him. (The boat is labeled "Federal Government")

(Illustration by Adalbert Wiemers published in *Vorwärts*, 5/9/74)

BUNDESREGIERUNG

A. WIEMERS
NACH "PUNCH"

relations remained as cool as ever. Schmidt was unperturbed by the antagonism he aroused in left party circles over sharp remarks he made publicly against the Jusos and over his anti-left course. He felt that his more conservative course had the better pay-off in mustering support among the floating voters at election time than any pro-left policy. While Schmidt's relations with the Jusos reached an all-time low after his verbal assaults, Brandt was instrumental in 1975 in arranging an uneasy truce between them. Aware that any counterattack against Schmidt would cause a backlash against the party in 1975 Land and 1976 federal elections, the Jusos preferred to hold their fire against a Chancellor whose popularity among the citizens was greater than among party members. Their strategy was correct. Schmidt's coalition government won another parliamentary term in the October 1976 federal election.

Brandt, as Party Chairman, sought to revitalize the party base. In a series of working sessions, he met with nearly all the ten thousand local party functionaries throughout the Federal Republic, seeking to hear their complaints and attempting to instill a sense of optimism about the party's future and to produce greater internal consensus. In the 1976 election, he campaigned vigorously for the party ticket.

Brandt also sought to maintain his image as an international statesman. As a result of the many acquaintances he made abroad while Chancellor, he received a host of invitations from foreign countries. He paid visits to Western European countries, Mexico, Venezuela, the United States, and the Soviet Union. There were warm receptions not usually accorded a party leader without a public office that enhanced his standing in the SPD. On the other hand, he had lost his charismatic appeal and his godfather image among most of the West German public; out of public office, Brandt just could not main-

tain the momentum or determine policy that produced the accolades of the past. Although he played an influential advisory role in foreign affairs, made a number of speeches reflecting a visionary spirit, and was mentioned as a possible candidate for the post of United Nations Secretary-General, he knew that his chances of ever becoming Chancellor again were extremely slim. When an American reporter asked him in 1975 whether he would like to be Chancellor once more, Brandt answered that he had enough to do as Party Chairman. Yet, in November 1976, he was elected president of the Socialist International, a prestigious position. In March 1977, he accepted the chairmanship of an international commission for Third World development problems offered to him by World Bank President Robert McNamara.

Assessment of Leadership

In conclusion, we must assess how Brandt's career as a political leader compared to that of other German leaders, what motivated him to seek such a career, and how his personality and leadership style contributed to the impressive record he achieved as Chancellor.

A study of German political leadership would have to range from the earliest tribes to the present truncated nation. Presenting a number of types of leaders, from the most autocratic to the most democratic, it would demonstrate that at any one time in history the political culture and socialization process do not necessarily produce one kind of leader or one type of leadership style. For instance, in the era of the Federal Republic, the five Chancellors thus far have had different styles of governing the country, reflecting different personalities and skills and adapting to different national problems. They have conceived of the powers of their office in different ways and have had different degrees of success in reaching their political objectives. Konrad Adenauer was the prototype of a powerful Chancellor who dominated his Cabinet through strong willpower, ruled the party with an iron fist, and received effective support from a majority of the voters for close to a decade and a half, although in the last few years his authority declined and party officials sought ways of easing him out of office. Ludwig Erhard lacked the power and political skill of his predecessor; consequently he delegated authority to other Cabinet members and decided conflicts among them by majority vote. Kurt Georg Kiesinger also lacked Adenauer's authoritarian style and sought to reach governmental objectives by seeking a consensus between the major coalition partners.

These three models of leadership were not appropriate for Brandt to emulate, but even if he had wanted to, his personality, social background, and political objectives differed from theirs. He had to make his own imprint on the various leadership positions he held in his checkered career. Focusing this study on Brandt gives clues to the role one leader can perform in a political system.

While Brandt's background differed considerably from that of his CDU predecessors, he shared a number of characteristics with other SPD leaders. Most were men from working-class parents who resided in Protestant urban areas, had held office in the SPD prior to 1933, been organization careerists or party journalists, remained politically active if in exile, and ascended rapidly through the party hierarchy into important leadership positions. If Brandt's background resembled that of other SPD officials, his specific life experiences did not; these would have an impact on the kind of leadership roles that he would perform.

The Political Career

We must recall that Brandt came from a modest working-class background in which his grandfather and Julius Leber played important political socializing roles during his childhood years. His selection for office in socialist youth groups showed early leadership potential. He demonstrated a spirit of independence by breaking with the SPD and joining the SAP, fleeing from Germany to Scandinavia, and participating in exile politics. He showed courage by his trips into Nazi Germany and civil war–wracked Spain. The exile years proved to Brandt that the radical ideology of the SAP was out of tune with the times and that a moderate reformist Social Democracy was a more satisfactory and practical alternative. At the end of the war, Brandt had difficulty deciding on a career objective and domicile but finally chose Germany where his chances for moving to the top were less limited than in Norway. The gamble paid off after he settled on embattled Berlin as his base of operations. Against heavy odds—being an outsider, young, reform-oriented, and not a disciple of party chairman Kurt Schumacher—Brandt in 1957 became Mayor of West Berlin, and in 1961 and 1965 the party's candidate for Chancellor.

One year later Brandt unexpectedly became Vice-Chancellor and Foreign Minister in a Grand Coalition that lasted until 1969. He was able to launch his policy of detente with the Communist states that would eventually bring him the Nobel Peace Prize and fame throughout the world. In 1969, the SPD and FDP formed a coalition with Brandt as Chancellor. At the age of fifty-five, his dream of reaching the highest political office in the Federal Republic was consummated. It had taken him twenty-one years to make it to the top from his first position as Berlin liaison official, a time sequence that corresponds exactly to that of the rise of

West German elites. His age upon entering the chancellorship also corresponds to that of a majority of the elites.

Undoubtedly, his rise to the top would not have been possible if the German population had remained set in its traditional ways and had continued to support the CDU/CSU governments for fear of "rocking the boat." In that case, Brandt, despite his recognized capacity for leadership, would have remained merely another middle-level politician. But the population from the sixties on was changing its life style, becoming less class-conscious, more affluent and upwardly mobile. Its immediate economic needs met by a flourishing economic system, the population had more leisure to pursue its own private desires and felt secure enough to be less dogmatic in its political attitudes. It no longer saw the SPD as a threat to its hard-won materialistic acquisitions; more progressive and democratically-inclined, it was willing to gamble on the SPD as a viable alternative to the CDU/CSU.

What was Brandt's role as Chancellor? He chalked up one success after another in reaching his foreign policy objectives of producing a stronger Western community and a normalization of relations with the East. Confronted by inflation and discords on domestic policy objectives with the junior coalition party, toward the end Brandt was also plagued by intraparty dissent, losses in state elections, personal weariness, an erosion of support from close associates, the Guillaume spy scandal, and allegations about his personal life. By May 1974, Brandt felt the only honorable way out of these cumulative difficulties was to tender his resignation as Chancellor but to remain party chairman.

Motivation
Why did Brandt want to become a leader? Some clues can be found in Brandt's personality, although Brandt is probably correct when he warns others not to try to delve into his unconscious because he himself has had difficulty sorting out one reason from another. Since other leaders have been motivated by such goals as prestige, popularity, fame, money, and the psychological lures of power, excitement, and camaraderie, we may assume that Brandt was motivated by most of these as well.

Power or the capacity to influence others as a way of gaining achievement, respect, or security is of course a crucial reason. The sociologist Harold Lasswell has noted that individuals may seek political power when a severe deprivation occurs in childhood, when disturbed times prevent the completion of a regular education, or when an individual chooses a profession such as political journalism that can be an avenue to political power. Such persons often emerge as reformers and innovators who attempt to create new leadership roles that fit their political style. These characterizations hold true for Brandt—who had no father at home, who seemed to have a low estimate of himself and his intellectual capabilities, and who had no university education but instead became a political journalist. The ease with which he gained a number of leadership posts in his young adulthood were compelling reasons for him to be more than a nominal member in the political organizations he joined. If others thought he had the capacity for good leadership, then there was no reason for him to decline such honors. Hence we can explain why after the war he chose to join the SPD and settle in Berlin, where upward mobility was possible but where he also would have to overcome the liabilities of the past.

Personality Profile
To study personality is important because it is a crucial variable in leadership recruitment and performance in office. It furnishes indicators as to the person's motivations,

values, attitudes, emotions, and political behavior. In the case of Brandt, it is true that
the offices in which he gained incumbency
prescribed certain functions to be performed
that individuals with different personal
characteristics could manage. Yet they also
gave Brandt an opportunity to put his stamp
of leadership on them.

As political scientist Barbara Kellerman
suggests, it is difficult to grasp Brandt's personality because it seems so contradictory.
There was a need for him to make himself
distinct from others, as seen in his break
with Julius Leber, in his plunge into Norwegian politics when most German émigrés
remained aloof, and in his attachment to
Norway while a German citizen; on the
other hand, he also sought to be a loyal
member of SAP and SPD groups. These
contrasting outsider and insider roles reflected other shifts in his professional career
and personal life. He had many friends, but
few close ones, and they tended to be outsiders like Brandt himself. While this may
have been an asset in keeping a distance
from others while serving as Mayor, Foreign
Minister, or Chancellor, it was also a lia-
bility: he was unable to retain the support
of Wehner and Schmidt in the crucial 1973–
1974 period.

Average West German citizens did not
find Brandt such a complex person, but instinctively empathized with Brandt's values
and goals of humanitarianism and idealism
and his search for freedom, justice, and
peace. They understood Brandt's speeches,
delivered with clarity and simplicity. They
appreciated Brandt's occasional sallies to a
bar in order to drink a beer with the workers. They viewed Brandt as a man of the
people who had personal integrity, charm,
and sympathy for weaker persons and who
was fair, generous, and compassionate.
Brandt's intelligence, keen analytical mind
and outstanding memory, reserve and mod-

esty, endurance and energy, self-control and
persistence—all were considered valuable
traits by his colleagues, who appreciated
Brandt's leadership style. He disliked authoritarian or coercive rule, used power
sparingly, refused to manipulate people,
searched for consensus among colleagues,
and carefully weighed alternatives before
making important decisions.

These attractive—and for many people
charismatic—traits easily compensated for
the fact that Brandt was not the most brilliant writer, intellectual, or orator in public
life (although in later years he became a
polished speaker) and that he was at times
moody, depressed, incommunicative, and
brooding. Thus, after the 1961 and 1965
electoral defeats, he needed to be left alone
to work out his own feelings and to tackle
his inner loneliness. On other occasions, his
trust in people was misplaced; some whom
he considered friends turned against him.
Moreover, the charges by his political enemies about his past hurt him, until he
finally built up a shell around himself to
ward off their verbal attacks. More serious
in terms of his eventual downfall as Chancellor was the fact that some of his attractive
personality characteristics also proved his
undoing. For instance, his spare use of
power meant that he could not settle intraparty disputes, rally the party behind him,
make personnel changes, and deal effectively
with all political and economic crises. Nevertheless, despite Brandt's resignation, a
major political defeat, he was still liked by
both heads of state and the people in the
street, a tribute that not every politician
leaving office receives.

While Brandt exhibited strengths and
weaknesses on the domestic scene, his appeal
in other countries has been great. Those
who have known him well, foreign leaders
and journalists on both sides of the iron
curtain, praise him highly as a German and

European statesman. Typical of the praise is that of a French journalist who said that Brandt is a man whom one likes to shake hands with (a compliment seldom heard in France) and of an American journalist who said that Brandt had "a puff of Abraham Lincoln." Brandt's receptions abroad have invariably ranged from warm to enthusiastic, reflecting a recognition of his attractive personality and effective foreign policies.

In international public opinion polls, he was consistently named as one of the ten most admired men in the world, while Eastern European polls ranked him as the most popular foreign personality by a wide margin. In France, 34 percent of the respondents had seen him on television and lauded his knowledge about France, with some comparing him to the handsome French movie actor, Jean Gabin. In Britain, a majority could identify him by name, liked him, and wished he were their leader. One said, "He seems a sturdy kind of chappy," and another called Brandt "the only German I have ever liked. I like his manner, he is mild, no shouting and screaming." [1] This poll indicates that the negative stereotypes about the Germans and Germany have gradually receded and been replaced by more neutral attitudes, caused by the passage of time and the positive responses Brandt has evoked abroad.

The Record
Brandt's personality and leadership style are important ingredients in the complex process of policy formulation in which he was but one political actor, albeit an important one. His performance and record in office must be assessed in the broader context of the constraints of coalition politics, the strength of the opposition, interest groups, the communications media, public opinion, the economic and social setting, and the international community. From this point of view, Brandt as a national leader made a significant impact on the course of West German history.

He proved to the people that the SPD could become a responsible governing party and that a man with his social background could make it to the top. He shored up the people's confidence in the stability of the country's political and economic institutions when his party came to power. The fear of conservatives that a radical restructuring of the existing order would take place proved false. While Brandt's domestic policy output had its successes and failures in effectuating moderate social reforms, his bold foreign policy initiatives opened up a new chapter in West German history. Despite a precarious parliamentary majority, he scored one success after another in producing a rapprochement and detente in the Cold War with Eastern states. Thereby he significantly increased West Germany's stature in international politics.

Selected Bibliography

The following books on German politics represent only a small sample of the numerous works that may be of interest to a student who would like to pursue this subject matter. Most of the works cited in notes are not listed here.

For a general survey of West and East German politics, see Arnold J. Heidenheimer and Donald P. Kommers, *The Governments of Germany* (New York: Thomas Y. Crowell, 1975). Among recent works on West German politics, see Lewis J. Edinger, *Politics in West Germany* (Boston: Little, Brown, 1977). A compre-

[1] Manfred Koch, "Willy Brandt und das Ansehen der Bundesrepublik im Ausland," in *Was hält die Welt von Willy Brandt?* (Hamburg: Hoffmann and Campe, 1972), pp. 149–166.

hensive survey of parliament may be found in Gerhard Loewenberg, *Parliament in the German Political System* (Ithaca, N.Y.: Cornell University Press, 1966), and of law making in Gerard Braunthal, *The West German Legislative Process* (Ithaca, N.Y.: Cornell University Press, 1972).

For a study of a typical electoral campaign, see Uwe Kitzinger, *German Electoral Politics* (Oxford: Clarendon Press, 1960). Two authors focus on the SPD: Douglas A. Chalmers, *The Social Democratic Party of Germany* (New Haven: Yale University Press, 1964), and Harold K. Schellenger, *The S.P.D. in the Bonn Republic: A Socialist Party Modernizes* (The Hague: Nijhoff, 1968). A political biography of the first postwar SPD leader may be found in Lewis J. Edinger, *Kurt Schumacher: A Study in Personality and Political Behavior* (Stanford,

Calif.: Stanford University Press, 1965). For Brandt, see Terence Prittie, *Willy Brandt: Portrait of a Statesman* (New York: Schocken Books, 1974), and David Binder, *The Other German: Willy Brandt's Life and Times* (Washington, D.C.: New Republic Book Co., 1975).

Social and economic movements are dealt with in Ralf Dahrendorf, *Society and Democracy in Germany* (Garden City, N.Y.: Doubleday, 1967), and Gerard Braunthal, *The Federation of German Industry in Politics* (Ithaca, N.Y.: Cornell University Press, 1965). For a review of foreign policy, see Wolfram Hanrieder, *The Stable Crisis: Two Decades of German Foreign Policy* (New York: Harper & Row, 1970), and Karl Kaiser, *German Foreign Policy in Transition* (New York: Oxford University Press, 1968).

IV

Nikita Khrushchev and Soviet Politics: Reform or Revisionism

Karl W. Ryavec

Nikita Khrushchev
Short Biographical Sketch

Nikita Sergeyevich Khrushchev was born April 17, 1894, the only child of a peasant family. Receiving little schooling, he worked first in agriculture and then as an apprentice mechanic in the coal mines of Yusovka. Khrushchev married in 1915, and his first child, a son, was born in 1916. His first wife died shortly after the birth of their daughter in 1918.

Although he did not serve in World War I, Khrushchev joined the Red Army in 1918. Soon after, he joined the Communist party and became party secretary of his regiment when the civil war ended.

At age twenty-eight Khrushchev enrolled in a workers' faculty for basic education and served as secretary of the school's party cell. Within three years he had become party secretary, the chief political figure, of Marinka County and part of Stalin's faction. In 1927, with the fall of Trotsky, Khrushchev became head of the regional organization, and in 1929 he was given the top party job in Kiev, the major city of the Ukraine. His rise was swift: First Secretary of the Moscow district, 1931; First Secretary of Moscow City and member of the Central Com-

mittee, 1934; and full member of the Politburo, 1939.

Khrushchev returned to the Ukraine in 1938 to rebuild the purge-torn party. Through World War II he performed vital party political work in the army, and after the Allied victory he again returned to the Ukraine and worked to reconstitute its war-ravaged economy.

Having survived an attempted ouster, Khrushchev was reappointed party leader both of Moscow and its region in 1949. He rose to the position of First Secretary of the entire Communist party after Stalin's death in 1953 and became Chairman of the Council of Ministers in 1955.

In 1956, Khrushchev put the Soviet Union on a new course, denouncing Stalinism and promulgating major revisions in Soviet Marxism. He weathered the Stalinist opposition in mid-1957, holding the two top positions until his own followers removed him on October 14, 1964. Afterwards he lived in enforced retirement and semi-isolation until his death on September 11, 1971. He was survived by his second wife and three children.

1

Introduction:
The Soviet Union – Land and People

The System Tested

On March 5, 1953, a man with the pseudonym Stalin (man of steel) died. He had been the absolute and terrible ruler of the Soviet Union since at least 1934. The effect of his death was psychologically shattering in his own country, but—to the surprise of even his close associates—the rigidly centralized, crudely industrialized, and effectively dictatorial political system of which he had been the master builder survived his death, a powerful and effective tribute to his political genius, perverse as it may have been.

The all-pervasive fear induced by Stalin's rigid and stern dictatorship is suggested in a poem by a Soviet poet:

> One day I was walking down Arbat Street
> And God drove by in five great motor cars,
> The guards in their greatcoats,
> Lined up, stood all a-tremble,
> Hunched nearly hump-backed with fear.

> · · ·

> We all lived near to God
> Almost next door to God.[1]

Another poet refers to Stalin as the man who was able to say to the sun, "Don't move!" and to the earth, "Hands up!" and who was able "to freeze all things." [2]

The great power of the central government under Stalin was symbolized at his funeral by the refusal of a police officer to move some trucks against which spectators were being crushed to death by the press of the crowd. "I can't do it! I have no instructions," the officer kept shouting. The man they were burying was not innocent of this disaster, wrote another poet: "no instruc-

[1] Boris Slutsky, "God," in "Poems of Various Years," *Literaturnaya gazeta,* November 24, 1962, p. 2, translated in *Current Digest of the Soviet Press* 14, no. 48 (December 26, 1962): 19.
[2] Leonid Martynov, "Cold," in George Reavey, ed., *The New Russian Poets* (New York: October House, 1966), p. 21.

tions" was typical of Stalin's Russia.[3] In a way, Stalin had survived his own death—but for how long could he haunt the country? This was one of the questions that Nikita Khrushchev, his successor, could not avoid facing. It is to his credit as a human being and a politician that he tried to answer it.

Within two weeks of Stalin's death this rotund ex-peasant from the Ukraine, then fifty-eight years old, acquired the most important share of Stalin's former duties, those of chief administrator of the Communist party, or First Secretary of the Central Committee. (The term used for Stalin's position, General Secretary, was returned to use by Leonid Brezhnev, Khrushchev's successor, in 1966.) By the middle of 1957, Khrushchev emerged as the preeminent and seemingly sole ruler of the Soviet Union, having eliminated all those then opposed to him from the Politburo, the highest policy-making body of the party. It was clear that as a politician he had outmatched all others at the top levels of Soviet government. What was the nature of the country that Khrushchev came to rule?

The Setting
Some topics that recur continually when Russia is discussed are: space, distance, and cold; a large population with many ethnic groups; direction by the central government in social, economic, and political matters; a despotic political tradition; a brilliant artistic legacy; shortages of food and consumer goods; a large and modern military force; repression and censorship; Marxism, Communism, and the Communist party; rapid economic growth; bureaucratic inefficiency; the Kremlin and parades in Red

[3] Yevgeny Yevtushenko, "A Voice of the Post-Stalin Generation," in *Political Science News/* Houghton Mifflin (September 1971), p. 3.

Square. These are, of course, only impressions distorted through the prisms of distance, the Cold War, and the lack of familiarity bred by Russia's relative isolation from Western Europe and America through much of history. Yet even such rough images do contain some of the outstanding features of the Soviet scene. This view can be refined by looking more closely at the major factors that underlie Soviet politics.

Geography

The Politics of the Land
The land is a central political fact. More than once the population has shown that it has a deep and abiding loyalty to the land that works to the advantage of any existing political system. During World War II, despite the earlier arrests and deaths of millions and the imposition of a harsh and omnipresent tyranny, the Soviet soldiers eventually stood firm against the Nazi invaders and their allies and, with British and American aid, pushed the Nazis back to flaming defeat.

The defense of the motherland is still a central symbol in Soviet political life and might be considered the great shared or common experience that has psychologically bound older Soviet citizens, particularly the Russians, to the political system as it is. The large military, backed by the political allies that this attitude engenders, is a force in its own right. Khrushchev lost the crucial support of conservative politicians and military officers when he began to reduce the size of the armed forces and to alter their structure and tactics.

More tangible qualities relating to geography are the vastness of the Soviet Union and its northern location. It is now smaller than

it was before the revolution, because the Soviet Union did not retake Finland, formerly a part of the Russian Empire, despite an attempt to do so in 1939. Nevertheless, it is the largest political entity in the world and has always posed formidable challenges of communications and control for its political leadership. The Soviet Union's large territory leads to problems of security because of the lack of defensible borders or natural boundaries (except perhaps in the south and the southeast) and the inclusion of many minority groups.

Geographical contact with eleven other countries produces tensions and difficulties of many kinds—territorial disputes, for one thing. The Soviet Union refuses to negotiate with China over territorial issues, probably fearing that any negotiation will cast in doubt all its borders. Other boundary disputes exist with Japan and even with Rumania. New disputes may arise in the future, possibly with Poland, whose boundary was moved westward at the end of World War II. The Soviet Union has also entered into dispute with Norway over their relative rights on the mineral-rich island of Spitzbergen in the Arctic Ocean. This nation suffers from an age-old problem of the growing power: finding a natural and secure place to stop expanding.

Geographically, expansion has also brought with it the potentially explosive "nationalities question." The country lacks the stability arising from a relatively homogeneous population, as in France, Germany, or Sweden. The Russians are only a bare majority, if that, of the total Soviet population. In addition, the minorities in the border areas of the Soviet Union also live on the other side of the border in several areas, notably in the southwest (Rumanians), the southeast (Azerbaidzhani Turks, Kirghiz and Tadzhiks, whose religious background has been Moslem, not Christian), and in the northeast (Mongols). As a result, some of the people in the borderlands can identify with other countries, particularly in terms of racial differences between themselves and the Russians. The ethnic difference is also a linguistic one; most of the ethnic groups use their own languages, not only at home, but in the schools and in all aspects of daily life as well. Interethnic tensions exist, so much so that even the censored press reports on them and Soviet sociologists study them at length.

The Land Itself

The Union of Soviet Socialist Republics constitutes one-sixth of the earth, more than 8.5 million square miles in area (two and one-half times the size of the United States of America, including Alaska) and stretches over eleven time zones. It is about 3,000 miles from north to south, extends about 6,000 miles in length, and has a 35,000-mile border that touches eleven countries. The train ride from Moscow to Vladivostok, located on the Pacific Ocean, takes eight to ten days.

It is no wonder that the administration of the tsarist and Soviet governments has tended to be rigid and inflexible. A flexible administration that changed to match local conditions might break up into movements of ethnic or regional resistance, thus threatening the existence of the political system. Whatever decentralization either the tsarist or the Soviet government has allowed has been of essentially low-level economic or minor societal significance, for example, road maintenance, public health inspection, and handicrafts production. The political and ideological sphere as well as most economic questions have always been lodged securely in the central government.

One central fact of its location cannot be

overemphasized. Since the southern borders of the Soviet Union lie approximately along the latitudes of the northernmost states of the United States, most of the Soviet Union is subject to harshly cold weather. Almost all of the country has three months or more each year with average mean temperatures below freezing. (Such conditions occur in only one-third of the United States.) Another factor comes into play here: only 15 percent of the land is arable. When these facts are combined with the relatively large population (about 250 million people) and the presence of limitations on the initiative and energies of farmers (collectivization of agricultural efforts), the possibility of agricultural surpluses year after year—common to Canada and the United States—is ruled out. The Soviet land can and does produce enough food, but not every year. Crop failures occur every three years or so. As a result, any government must be deeply concerned with agriculture and must be prepared to provide a minimum amount of food for the inhabitants, with purchases abroad becoming crucially important. Thus a national system of food acquisition and distribution (a form of rationing) exists, and the harvest becomes a politicized national effort, with even university students mobilized to bring in the food and other agricultural products, such as cotton and flax.

The country as a whole can be divided into four climatic and topographic zones. However, in European Russia, the area west of the Ural mountain range, there are essentially only two zones, the forested north and the south of "black soil," long devoted to agriculture. The agricultural area in the southwest, particularly that in the Ukraine, is the traditional breadbasket of Russia. East of the Ural Mountains, in Asiatic Russia, there is little good cropland. Although the

climates in the northeastern and southwestern United States can be found in the Soviet Union, those of the northeastern Soviet Union and the southeastern United States are peculiar to their respective countries.

During the last two decades the Soviet government has made strenuous efforts to derive more from its agricultural efforts. Khrushchev put vast tracts under the plow (the so-called Virgin Lands campaign) and increased the number of party members on the farms, while Brezhnev has provided more machinery and specialists to the farms and finally, in 1965, brought to the peasants the benefits of social security for the first time. These recent actions complement the long-standing effort to change the face of the land through canals, huge dams, and irrigation projects, the latest form of which has used atomic explosions to move mountains. Despite these efforts, some of them grandiose, the land is still a barrier to the realization of the state planners' dreams, though recent advances, such as an increase in chemical fertilizer output, will have some positive effect.

In natural resources the Soviet Union is the wealthiest of countries, lacking only tin and natural rubber. Everything else is present but, ironically, in many cases still locked within the earth, sometimes under a sheet of permafrost. The Soviet Union has become an exporter of oil in recent years and has benefited from the higher prices that commodity now brings. (Whether it will still be able to export oil when its automobiles are much more numerous, say in 1980 or 1985, is still unknown.) Generally stated, the country was bountifully supplied in resources for the massive and rapid industrialization drive that Stalin forcefully pushed forward from the late 1920s on, but in recent years the continued expansion of heavy and light industry has created a need to develop new mines and wells, a need the country seems unable to meet without massive foreign aid. The Soviet state has still not fully conquered the land and now faces pollution problems of its own creation.

In addition to resources, it is only realistic to speak of natural "anti-resources"—those factors that hinder development. All countries have them, but the Soviet Union may have more than its fair share. In addition to severe cold, permafrost (which affects half the country), and the resulting swampy situation in the summer, there must be added poor soils, mountainous terrain (a quarter of the country, mainly in the east), arid and drought-prone areas, and distance from open seas. As a British geographer put it, "The burden of anti-resources is not entirely a physical one, but also human and psychological. . . . The Russians . . . in a sense, are constantly at war" with their environment.[4] The state's great reach and power is a way to try to control the effects of this problem.

No discussion of the Soviet land is complete without mention of the seemingly unimportant, but historically crucial, fact that the rivers of European Russia generally flow either north or south—not east and west, out of and into Europe proper. The easiest and cheapest means of travel, communication, and trade were determined by this direction of flow. Thus, medieval Russia took its culture, its alphabet, and its political forms, style, and, to some extent, content not from the legalistic Germano-Roman West but from the despotic Byzantine Empire centered upon Constantinople (now Istanbul, Turkey). A major borrowing was the concept of Caesaro-papism, or

[4] W. H. Parker, *The Super-Powers* (New York: Wiley, 1972), p. 98.

the merging of political and religious authority in a single ruler.

The difference of source of political principles and style may not have been so important in itself (though most scholars assume it was); but from that moment on, the West was confirmed in Russian eyes as an outsider, an alien that was seen to be fundamentally different in terms of values and politics. This general view of the West has never yet been overcome. The Bolsheviks carried on the tradition.

Population

The Nationalities or Ethnic Groups

An outstanding characteristic of the human side of the Soviet Union is its ethnic diversity, which even includes one racial difference—between Europeans and Asians. There are approximately two hundred ethnic and linguistic groups with the major group, the Great Russians, comprising at the most a bare majority (officially 53.4 percent of the population in 1970, but probably less, perhaps even a minority). Although peoples speaking Slavic languages, including the Great Russians, make up almost 75 percent of the total population, there have long been tensions between the Great Russians and the second largest Slavic ethnic group, the Ukrainians (at least 16.9 percent of the population in 1970). Several of the more prominent dissidents have been Ukrainians who have protested the effects of Russian culture on their land. Formerly under Polish rule, the Ukrainians have been closer to Western European patterns of life than to the Russian. And during the Russian Civil War of 1917–1920 the Ukraine was a separate state until conquered by the Red Army, a

Bolshevik creation that acted as a new Russian army. Some foreign residents in the Soviet Union speculate that at present the upwardly mobile and educated Ukrainians are favored in an attempt to transform Russian preeminence into a general Slavic dominance. (The origins of this arrangement probably lie in the political activities of Khrushchev in the Ukraine during the 1930s and 1940s.)

It remains to be seen whether the change-oriented processes of industrial society are enough to extinguish ethnic identity. Certainly the highly praised, but somewhat

Major ethnic groups in the Soviet Union

(Source: U.S. Senate, Committee on the Judiciary, *The Soviet Empire* [Washington, D.C.: Government Printing Office, 1965], Map No. 6)

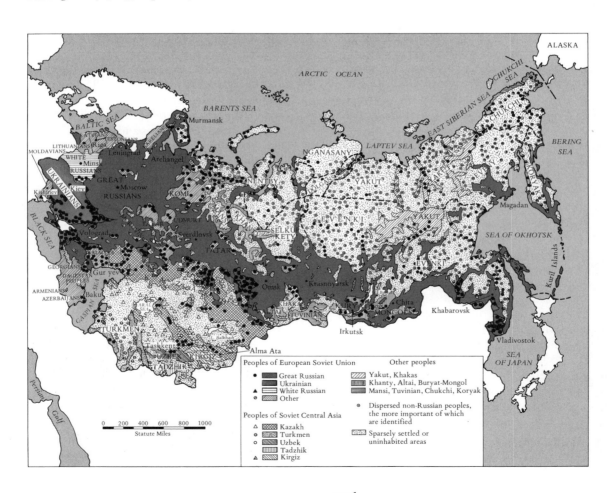

mythical, American melting pot has not done so. Several ethnic groups in the Soviet Union have generated political tensions. Those of the Jews and the Volga Germans are well known, partly because some have been allowed to emigrate. In the European Soviet Union the three formerly independent peoples in the northwest, Estonians, Latvians, and Lithuanians, have exhibited dissatisfactions. So have the Georgians, a Caucasian people in the south with an ancient cultural history, and some of the Asian peoples in the southeast, for example, the Uzbeks and Tadzhiks. These Russian–minority group relationships have actually resulted in rioting, bombings, the use of troops, and large-scale changes in local leadership within recent years. The entire stories are not yet known, but enough has come into the open to indicate that the Soviet state, despite all its means of control and coercion, has had to contend with the interethnic conflict lately so visible elsewhere. Since most of these people occupy territories that have been their historic homelands, and at times independent nation-states, it is difficult to extinguish feelings of distinctiveness and separateness, although the Soviet state and Communist party have tried to do this to a degree.

Native cultures have remained intact for several reasons. One is that Russian has become only a *lingua franca*, or secondary common language, not a primary Soviet national language. Unlike the United States, where the children of many immigrants lost the use of their parents' native languages, Soviet young people often continue to use their parents' language as their major language, Russian being a second language learned only in school. However, if one wants to rise socially or politically, Russian has to be learned well and so is becoming the major language of those who desire upward mobility.

Despite their efforts to create a single,

Russianized national culture, the party and the state have been limited by the vitality of many of the national cultures and, significantly, by their own official policy, which Stalin labeled as "national in form and socialist in content." All expressions of the native cultures are to strengthen, not to detract from, the Soviet social and political order—and, specifically, the image of unity among the nationalities. The effect of this policy is that Russian culture is presented in local areas, languages, and artistic forms as determined and censored in Moscow. This has been a major source of dissatisfaction among minority intellectuals, who find it difficult to be published. The policy of national in form and socialist in content restricts the creation of a single new Soviet culture even in the limited sense in which it is allowed to operate. The use of the native languages in schools and even universities is lodging them in the social fabric for the future. As a result, little overt Russianization is taking place.

Russian preeminence is also threatened, both socially and politically, by the higher birth rates of several other peoples. For example, the average size of Russian families, 3.6 persons, is exceeded by that of ten other major nationalities (not counting small nationalities), the largest being the Tadzhik family, which averages 5.2 persons.[5] There is no sign of this gap decreasing. Another irritant is the higher educational level of some of the minorities as compared with the Russians and the resulting realization by these minorities that they are being ruled by people generally less educated than they.

One test of Russian influence in any area

[5] This and other demographic data are drawn from tables based on Soviet data in David Lane, *Politics and Society in the USSR* (New York: Random House, 1971); and Ellen Mickiewicz, ed., *Handbook of Soviet Social Science Data* (New York: Free Press, 1973).

is their percentage of the population. In some areas (for example, Latvia and Kazakhstan) transplanted Russians will probably soon overwhelm the native peoples by outnumbering them. Other nationalities, notably the Georgians and the Armenians, have relatively few Russians resident in their homelands and will probably retain a clear sense of ethnic identity. Intermarriage across ethnic lines occurs between whites, but racial intermarriage is not frequent and is burdened with difficulties such as prejudice and familial opposition on both sides.

The political effect of these ethnically based cultural differences is a weakening of the possible supports of the Soviet political culture. In consequence, the government and the Communist party must try to make up for the lack of a major single set of supportive political attitudes within the society. Governmental outputs have to create supportive societal inputs artificially. This is a process in which Leninist political systems excel.

A Demographic Outline

In 1970 the total Soviet population was 242 million. This is 18 percent greater than that of the United States in the same year (203 million), but the gap seems to be closing. The difference in population sizes was even larger (45 percent) in 1940. The Soviet Union's population, previously reduced severely by civil war, famine, and the great "blood" purges, will grow, but projections are difficult to make because the government pursues contradictory policies. There is an official rhetoric favoring larger families that is supported by maternity benefits, child allowances, and awards for large families. However, partly since abortion is legal and free and contraceptives are available, no great growth is taking place except among the rural population. Growth from immigration is negligible, although there has been some flight of Asians into the Soviet Union from China and a return of Armenians from Turkey and the Middle East. (For some minorities life in the Soviet Union can be better than in certain neighboring countries.)

A notable feature of the Soviet population profile is the larger numbers of women in several, particularly the older, age groups. Even overall, there are more women than men: in 1970, 54 percent of the population was female. This situation, a result of World War II, has led to certain strains in the social fabric.

A look at the density of settlement of the country shows that its population is not packed closely together, resulting in part from the country's large size. The United States is more densely populated. The Soviet population is not evenly distributed, however; 70 percent lives west of the Ural Mountains, that is, in the European Soviet Union. And, although government policy has long been to people the broad expanse of Siberia, the persons who are sent there return in droves whenever possible to the European part, where the living is a bit easier. Indeed, the actual movement of the Soviet population is generally southward, to the warmer climate of the Black Sea, the Caucasus, and central Asia. This is producing difficulties for the economy since the major new sources of raw materials and energy are in the east, in Siberia.

No other modern industrialized country has such a high percentage of its population living in rural areas, 44 percent. Also, there is nothing resembling American suburbs in the Soviet Union. Densely built cities extend right up to the countryside or to old villages of traditional hand-decorated log cabins. Soviet citizens have had neither the automobiles (fewer than 2 percent of Soviet citizens own cars) nor the building materials that allow the creation of extended urban aggregations. Soviet cities are compact and isolated in the large land mass.

Although city life is attractive to Soviet citizens, movement into them is restricted by government regulation, including the need to have a job in order to be granted the required residence permit. Peasants find these permits are difficult to obtain. Because they lack the internal passport required to travel even within the country, peasants still tend to be bound to the land. The largest and most important Soviet cities are distinctive in being under central government regulation, but then this is only a continuation of Russian tradition. Cities there have never been primarily autonomous centers of commercial activity as in western Europe, but have been basically government administrative centers.

Society

Ideals and Ideas

Is Soviet society unique, or is it essentially like the other industrialized societies of Europe? Certainly Lenin and the other founders of this state assumed that a new, improved, and liberating form of social organization would be created by the revolution. And many observers opposed to Marxism-Leninism agreed that Soviet society was new, but said instead that the new society was no improvement, economic domination having been strengthened by a new and stronger political domination by the Leninist party.

The most critical view of the claims of the Soviets is the totalitarian model or perspective that was applied mainly to the years of Stalin's harshest rule, 1935–1953. Its central thesis is that society, culture, and the economy are all effectively under the control of the political sphere, itself controlled by a dictator or by the Communist party's top leaders. The totalitarian model holds that what was new and distinctive about totalitarian dictatorship was its use of technology to mobilize all of society for political ends. This perspective has been much criticized in recent years for assuming that the dictatorship was highly effective and for neglecting that even dictatorships have some—at times substantial—popular support. Perhaps the totalitarian model would have been more realistic if it had emphasized totalitarian intent or goals as the distinctive characteristic of certain powerful mobilization regimes and had not stated that such regimes were all-powerful, an assertion easily proved to be false.

The official Soviet model of society ought to be discussed first. The acceptance of inequalities of income and therefore of status and even of power distinguishes Soviet from some other types of socialism, notably Chinese, in which egalitarianism receives great stress. Nevertheless, the Soviet position is that its type of socialism is, in Marxist terms, a qualitative improvement over earlier societies and a more realistic way of organizing society at present than by stressing equality as an immediate goal. Progress toward real equality of income, status, and power is said to be occurring, but its attainment is now left to the unspecified future. Khrushchev daringly brought the issue to the forefront, predicting that the Soviet Union would begin to enter communism in the 1980s. His successors no longer make the claim; their official formulation for the present stage is "developed socialist society."

The Soviet leaders have not been allowed to monopolize Marx and his vision. Certain brilliant political figures have maintained Marxism as a sharp tool of critical sociopolitical analysis and have used it to carve away at the edifices of Soviet society to reveal, they say, concealed processes of exploitation similar to those of capitalist society. Three such thinkers deserve mention: Leon Trotsky, who brought about the Revolution of November 1917 at Lenin's order and led the new Red Army during the civil war; Mao Tse-tung, who successfully adapted Marxism to China with its small proletariat but large peasantry; and Milovan Djilas, once the second figure in Yugoslav Marxism, who gave it all up when he saw what had been created in Marx's name.

After Trotsky was eliminated from the succession struggle by Stalin after Lenin's death and was forcibly expelled from the Soviet Union in 1929, he put together an explanation of what he thought had happened to Marxism in the Soviet Union. In *The Revolution Betrayed* (1936) he argued that Soviet Marxism had become mired part way in the movement to socialism because the working class had not come to power. The society was ruled by a new bureaucratic elite that had emerged unchanged out of the old Russian society to capture the Communist party and to use it to mask the aggrandizement of power for its own wants. True, property had been nationalized; but, crucial in Marxism, it had been given not to the proletariat but to a clique falsely ruling in the name of Marx and the proletariat.

According to Mao, the Revolution of 1917 has gone soft. Consumerism for both the elite and the masses has come to be the general goal of Soviet society. In addition, in its forms and operations the party has become a typical hierarchically ordered bureaucracy that is divorced from the masses and from the true Marxist goal of pursuing the revolution to communism. It is mesmerized by material production and the demands of mere industrial management. In foreign affairs, the leaders of the Soviet Union are, in effect, new tsars who act in a typically Russian imperial fashion toward

weaker countries, including Marxist ones such as Czechoslovakia and China.

Djilas's analysis, presented in his book *The New Class* (1956), applies basic Marxist assumptions and views to the questions of who rules in the Soviet Union and what sort of group it is. Djilas asks a question fundamental to the Marxist analysis of power: Who owns the means of production (factories and resources) in Leninist societies? The Leninist party does, he answers, for only it can sell the means of production. Accordingly, since communism has not been attained, the party is the ruling class and therefore the exploiting class as well.

Other models of Soviet society worth mentioning are the developmental and the industrial. The developmental model holds that the Soviet society was the first to be consciously preoccupied with rapidly attaining definite economic growth and general societal change and modernization. Thus, the Soviet Union is a former underdeveloped country that has been trying to attain goals common to many other such countries—to educate a population, to create a national health service, to integrate nationalities, and to organize popular loyalties around a new national image. This model views the Soviet Union and, say, India as engaged in the same process, although on different points along the way to development.

The industrial model holds that the Soviet Union is now industrialized and is essentially like other societies in terms of social groupings, processes, issues, and problems. Its major assumptions are that industrialization necessarily breeds a certain kind of complex, differentiated society and that in all such societies people occupying the same social roles are similar. Industrial managers, military officers, scientists, politicians, and workers do not differ in any fundamental way in different industrialized societies. At times the model is pushed further, to the idea of convergence; that is, all industrial societies will converge or become alike.

Some essential information about Soviet society will enable readers to judge which, if any, of these models of society fits the realities of Soviet life. Perhaps a combination of models will be most accurate.

Social Classes

Soviet socialism is mainly of an economic variety—and only to a degree. Workers are not paid equally, and one of Marx's main conditions for a classless society, the absence of a division of labor, has not been attained. The official position of the party is that two classes exist, the workers and the peasants. No doubt a third exists as well, the white-collar, non-manual-labor working class, known as the *intelligentsia* in Soviet terminology, but officially considered a stratum, or part, of the blue-collar working class. (Official Soviet social categories lack precision. For example, the peasants on state farms are counted as workers.)

When the Soviet Union was proclaimed a socialist society in 1936, it was meant that no antagonistic classes remained. The former capitalist and aristocratic ruling classes had been eliminated. However, economic inequality remains. People are paid according to their work and unequally so, since not all work is considered of equal worth for the needs of continuing industrialization (and thus developing socialism), though the difference between the highest and lowest paid is not as great as in many other societies.

What of social inequality and the existence of stratification? Although the Soviet middle class does not own the land or the factories, it nevertheless receives a better education than the workers and the peasants, generally earns more, receives more and better special nonmonetary payments such as better apartments, dominates the member-ship of the single political party (never primarily a workers' party), and in general possesses better life chances or opportunities. And, since income and inheritance taxes are small and not progressive, the middle class can pass on its privileges and possessions to its children, thus perpetuating its special position.

Political power cannot be inherited, however. The children of politicians very rarely enter politics. They tend to show up, when they are noticed by outsiders, in interesting state, not party, jobs. Brezhnev's daughter, for example, is an American specialist in the Institute for the Study of the USA and Canada, a research arm of the Academy of Sciences. A son of Andrei Gromyko, the Foreign Minister and a member of the Politburo, is a functionary in the Foreign Ministry. Obviously something akin to nepotism is at work. But political power must be earned, and, given the rough-and-tumble nature of Soviet politics, it seems that, as in the past and in the case of Khrushchev, future Soviet politicians will come disproportionately from the lower classes, thus tending to make the system seem more egalitarian than it is (through a sort of Soviet version of the American log cabin or humble background political myth).

Thus, Soviet society is not different in operation or general structure from societies where socialism has not been adopted. As time goes on, it is likely that Soviet society will become less and less changeable and will have rather permanent class subdivisions with the members of these and their children being frozen into them. The likelihood of social mobility, high in the past, is already gone. And, since the new middle class has a disproportionate access to education—including the special schools teaching such important skills as languages, mathematics, and sciences—it has a powerful hold on a major channel for upward social mobility.

The universities, the most prestigious institutions of higher education, are still the preserves of the middle class, the less prestigious specialized and technical schools bearing the weight of whatever favoritism exists for lower-class applicants. Non-middle-class students find the economics of life in Soviet higher educational institutions difficult. After passing rigorous competitive examinations, which are oral as well as written and which often stretch over a whole summer, students receive a free education, and grants are provided as well. But additional funds, which usually come from parents, are required to meet expenses. Most non-middle-class students are relegated to night and correspondence courses for the acquisition of higher education. The Soviet pattern for higher education is still fundamentally of a normal European type, although the pattern has been modified somewhat through emphasis on technological and scientific training combined with the economic and political priorities of the party. Khrushchev was never allowed to implement his radical plan of making all high school graduates work in factories for two years prior to beginning higher education.

The amount of social differentiation or stratification existing in the Soviet Union is even greater than indicated above. For example, Soviet sociologists divide the non-manual-labor intelligentsia class into eight main groups and the working class into three groups. Even the peasantry is divided three ways. The criteria used for these divisions are mainly education and job skills. It is obvious that sociologically this nation has a complex society fundamentally not unlike those of other industrialized countries. Along with this differentiation by education and skills goes a differentiation by income and by the power of claiming the products or outputs of society. It would be only logical to add another stratum at the bottom of

Soviet (and indeed any) society: prisoners, both criminal and political, and those subjected to various forms of harassment. The intense amount of politicization affecting Soviet society actually determines another criterion of social standing. The holding of dissenting views, for example, is certain to bring loss of employment and rapid descent to the bottom social rung.

The Soviet government instituted a minimum wage in 1965 (now about 65 rubles per month) and has begun paying income supplements to the lowest paid, but in general has only slightly narrowed the gap between the highest and lowest paid. This gap varies by industry from a ratio of thirteen to one to about five to one, with collective farmers tending to earn less than even the lowest paid industrial worker. Some figures in American dollars may be of use. In 1960 a government Minister earned from $700 to $3,500 per month; a research scientist from $880 to $1,650; an industrial manager from $330 to $1,100; an engineer from $110 to $330; a high school teacher from $94 to $165; and an unskilled worker from $30 to $55 per month. The need for a minimum wage was clear.[6]

Women are generally not paid as much as men, because they are employed mainly in low-paying occupations, for example, education and health. While the average monthly wage in 1968 was 113 rubles (about 150 now), that in education was 103 rubles and in health only 90. In addition, women working in industry tend to be either clerical staff or unskilled workers, often engaged in heavy manual labor.

Despite the relatively small gap between highest and lowest salaries in the Soviet

6 From Nicholas De Witt, *Education and Professional Manpower in the USSR* (Washington, D.C.: National Science Foundation, 1961); cited by Lane, *Politics and Society*, pp. 399–400.

Union as compared to other industrialized societies, such as the United States or Britain, it is clear that these Soviet income differentials relate to meaningful and noticeable differences in social standing. And since influence and power relate closely to job held and especially to party membership and ranking within the party, a meaningful differentiation among Soviet citizens relates not only to income but also to what might be called political standing. For example, although Soviet political leaders are not well paid in monetary terms, they can use their political power to draw material benefits from the state treasury. Brezhnev uses a state game preserve for hunting and occasional residence. Thus, Soviet society is differentiated both in accordance with income, as in the West, and in accordance with commitment to the ruling political grouping, the Communist party. This shows up as well in the relatively high status and influence of the military. In 1967, 93 percent of military officers were party or party youth group members, a significant linking of political and military power.

The existence of stratification by income and prestige results in a scramble for jobs highest in these qualities. Soviet sociologists have polled citizens and found that the relative desirability of jobs is about the same as in capitalist countries.

If upward social mobility becomes more uncommon, political support for the system may come to rest much more on the middle class than it does now, a result with uncertain effects. Although, "compared to western societies, social promotion is probably relatively easier, there can be no doubt that in the USSR the social position of parents plays a most important role in determining the education and, therefore, the subsequent social standing of children."[7] Khrushchev

once criticized this condition, saying, "A person is admitted to a higher educational establishment not because he is well prepared, but because he has an influential papa and mama."[8] The inability or unwillingness of the government to create equality, despite a current policy of encouraging admission of students of poor parents into higher education, can lead only to a more definite stratification of Soviet society.

The Family and the Individual
The primary social units in the Soviet Union are the individual and the family as anywhere else. There, as in most industrial countries, the extended family of rural life is well on the way to extinction and the nuclear family is weakening as well. Of course, the Soviet state has always had claims on the family's members that are stronger than in most other societies. Besides being compelled to attend school, children also must spend time in official youth movements and are subject to work assignments during vacations and to compulsory initial job placement upon completing schooling. Under the Constitution of the Soviet Union, males are subject to the military draft as well unless they are part of the relatively few who complete higher education. The latter are subject to compulsory job assignment for only a brief term.

Women tend to work, partly because they are encouraged to by the state system of paid maternity leave and nursery schools for young children over age two and partly because they wish to increase the family's earnings. Also important in encouraging women to work is the long-standing state pressure to give women equality with men. However, this has not been highly successful. Soviet women do the shopping, cooking, and cleaning in addition to their work outside the

[7] Lane, *Politics and Society*, p. 415.

[8] *Pravda,* April 19, 1958.

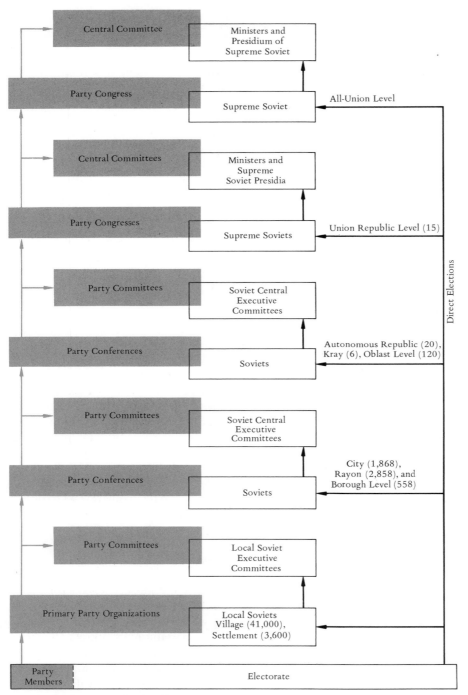

Interlocking party and state structures

(Roy Macridis, Robert E. Ward, *Modern Political Systems: Europe,* © 1968, p. 570. Reproduced by permission of Prentice-Hall, Inc., Englewood Cliffs, New Jersey)

family. The men dominate, although not totally.

The state has supported the continuation of the family as a basic social unit for the past forty-odd years, while the loose, often temporary unions characteristic of the period right after the revolution no longer have official approval. Although divorce exists—and at a relatively high rate in urban areas—marriage and the family are surviving as institutions, and with the legal support of the state. The family has become more supportive than critical of the goals of the Soviet regime and, in any case, now lacks the strength and cohesion to stand in its way.

The individual in Soviet society has one central obligation, work. This almost always means working for the state, since private employment of persons who are not direct relatives is unlawful, and most legal forms of self-employment are low-status or low-paying, for example, shoe repairing or tailoring. Occupations that are often free professions abroad are not so in the Soviet Union. Doctors work directly for state agencies, and lawyers practice within collectives. But an important exception to collectivity exists. Peasants who work on collective farms (not state farms) are allowed to sell for profit on the free market whatever they raise on their small private plots. These gardens provide most of the country's eggs, dairy products, and fruit.

Refusal to work is punishable under the so-called anti-parasite laws. Being financially successful in an illegal capitalist enterprise makes one liable to the death penalty, which is carried out in cases of large-scale economic crimes. (One such case involved the manufacture of plastic shopping bags.) Except for the broadly defined crime of treason, which is also punishable by death, the maximum penalty is fourteen years in most other cases of crime. In recent years oppositional political writing or activity has brought not only sentences to prison and the labor camps but also the terrors of the special mental institutions controlled by the security police.

The individual who works well and does not oppose the system finds that his main problems are either personal or economic, or they entail the particular irritant of waiting in lines and dealing with a typical Russian type: the petty bureaucrat become minor tyrant. One wide-scale release from the boredom of a society where entertainment is made to support state goals and where conspicuous consumption is made difficult is drunkenness. According to Soviet sources, it is involved in a large proportion of crimes. The cost of food is high (taking about half the average family's income), as is the price of clothing (taking most of the rest of the budget). The cost of housing is minimal, only 4 or 5 percent of one's income, but household appliances have only just become widely available. Medical and dental care are provided free by the state, and old age pensions are granted to men aged sixty and women aged fifty-five. Unemployment is usually only a short-term problem. The Soviet Union has a labor shortage, though increasing automation may change this.

One may ask what the lack of political freedoms means to people who have never had them and who have also been taught, or socialized, to fulfill the role of faithful, laboring subjects to a government that they never selected. Such freedoms may not be natural desires in all situations, particularly when the right to form associations separate from the government, an important practice that teaches and encourages political participation in the West, is denied in the Soviet Union. Also lacking is free association for economic purposes, another fundamental stimulus to political activity. Thus, Soviet politics is one involving only elites, the few, and not the masses.

The Economy

The Essentials

Abundant natural resources provide the fundamental support of the Soviet economy, as only a few raw materials and, occasionally, food must be imported. The daring and magnitude of Soviet economic operations are partly a function of the bounty of nature.

The economy is the central concern of the party as a political organization, and economic growth may be the central goal of the political system, the operational core of Soviet ideology in fact, though not in theory. Accordingly, the most common form of higher education in the Soviet Union is one or another kind of engineering, and the majority of the members of the party Politburo (its highest body) are engineers. Brezhnev, the leading member, is a metallurgical engineer. And, even though Khrushchev was not a graduate engineer, he continually had to deal with general economic and engineering issues and to make far-reaching decisions concerning them. This intimate economic and technological involvement of the political leadership heavily conditions its membership, organization, work, and thinking. One senior scholar of Soviet politics dubs the nation "U.S.S.R., Incorporated" and likens the society to a vast company town. Soviet leaders seem to show an easy familiarity in dealing with top-level Western corporate executives, but try to avoid meeting Western labor leaders, with whom they have a longstanding conflict based on the early Soviet suppression of genuine unions. There is probably no other political leadership in the world so molded by engineering and economic considerations. The typical American politician is a lawyer, while the typical British political leader is a generalist trained either in the classics or in economics.

Certain fundamentals of the Soviet economy make it quite different from other nationalized economies, including even some Leninist states of eastern central Europe. First, the state owns the means of production (factories, machinery, and power plants) and all the land. (In Poland and Yugoslavia private land ownership exists.) Second, the state operates the productive economic institutions directly. In contrast, nationalized industries in Britain are run by public corporations organizationally apart from the government and also apart from day-to-day politics, and in Yugoslavia the workers' councils exercise self-management of a sort, along with managerial and white-collar employees. In the United States, the Soviet pattern of political connection with industry would mean that a federal regulatory agency such as the Civil Aeronautics Board would actually operate all the nation's airlines as one mammoth corporation. More than 90 percent of industrial production in the Soviet Union is produced by plants under the control of government ministries with headquarters in Moscow and the republic capitals.

A third distinctive feature of the Soviet economy is its strong orientation toward the needs of national security and strategy. This is an intensification of the guiding economic principles and patterns of tsarist Russia that also served state ends to a great extent (a general orientation borrowed from imperial Germany and also found in imperial Japan). It is a permanent "war economy" similar to that of the United States during World War II, when nothing was produced that was not a priority item, when most commodities were rationed, and when the government specified items to be produced in terms of amount and structural detail. Soviet plants manufacturing defense materiel employ the best workers, pay the highest wages, receive the most talented specialists, utilize the most modern innovative technology, and consequently produce good weapons systems. The remainder of the industry in group A (heavy industry) receives second priority. Even so, the Soviet Union does fairly well. For example, it exports complete steel plants and the machinery for hydroelectric dams to much of the world, and a few examples of its technology have been purchased for use in United States industry. Sadly for light industry and the consumer, the high standards and new technology of the heavy industrial sector are not generally applied to the design, manufacture, and distribution of consumer goods. Whatever is used in defense industry is classified and, for this reason but also due to bureaucratic compartmentalization, does not spin off into the consumption sector (group B industry). A current attempt to reduce this problem involves defense and heavy industries themselves producing appliances.

Clearly the Soviet Union has a limited, or conservative, defense-oriented type of socialism. Accordingly, some Marxist critics have labeled its system state socialism, or even state capitalism, since there has occurred no fundamental political revolution granting the working class a voice in economic decision making. One explanation suggested for this is based on international affairs: the Soviet Union was long considered a pariah among nations and thus defensively concentrated on heavy industrial and weapons production. Others stress the tsarist heritage of centralized operation of the economy by the state bureaucracy for strategic ends. Still others emphasize Stalin's acquisition of political support; the rapid industrialization he began required the creation of millions of new white-collar jobs. Certainly Stalin tied these forces together to his own political advantage when, in 1931, he cited the dismal record of defeats in Russian history and the need to create rapidly

the industrial base that would forestall other defeats.

The Soviet Union, then, has long engaged in a process of catching up with the West without undergoing Westernization in the cultural or political sense. It amounts to an attempt to "turn Marx upside down" by not allowing economic development to have the usual social and political effects. This is a policy many authoritarian governments have tried to follow, for example, imperial China with its "self-strengthening movement" and Shah Pahlavi's Iran today. It is still too early to say whether it will fully work for the Soviets.

The Command Economy
This command economy has been successful in terms of gross output of certain standard industrial products incorporating basic technology of the time. However, although it has met military goals, at least in terms of quantity, it has harbored economic irrationalities. Even by the early 1930s much of industry was operating at a loss. And by the 1960s, if not earlier, this Stalinist approach was causing technological irrationalities as well as economic ones. New technology was not being adopted, and industry continued to produce the same standardized items that had been made thirty years earlier, though in greater numbers. The Soviets tended to rely on quantity, not quality. Even some weapons used old technology discarded elsewhere, as analysis of the Soviet interceptor, the MIG 25, has shown. (A MIG 25 was flown to Japan by a defecting Soviet pilot in 1976.) The growth rate, long the chief claim to fame of Soviet planners, began to slow, even in the 1950s. From the highs of above 10 percent it slipped to 6 percent and in some years to only 2 to 3 percent. (These rates apply only to heavy industry. Light in-

dustry and the service sector were developing hardly at all.)

Top Soviet economists expressed alarm at this decline.[9] Khrushchev strived mightily to reform the economy through diversification, but achieved no lasting success. His successors, notably Premier Kosygin, took up the task anew with greater care. In 1965, Kosygin introduced a new reform of the economy with these words: "The forms of management, planning, and incentive now in effect in industry no longer conform to present-day technical-economic conditions and to the level of development of productive forces."[10] The reform was innovational in content and intent. A producing enterprise no longer fulfills its plan by merely producing the number of products specified in the plan; instead, it must sell those products (that is, produce them of a quality acceptable to buyers), must make a profit for the state, and must pay interest on funds lent it (no longer given it) by the state. (This concept often goes under the name "Libermanism," after the economist who first suggested it in the 1950s.)

But the new system has still not produced outstandingly different results. It remains a command economy, though a revised one, which, ironically, cannot command forth what the leaders want: modern and high-quality products in vast array. There are several reasons for this: the rigid state bureaucracy refuses to allow the producing enterprises to make the requisite decisions, the industrial managers both fear and fail to understand the new freedoms granted them, and the Communist party continues to supervise industrial operations closely. After all, if it were to give up its major field of activity, it would eventually become a mere ideological force and thus lose its political dominance. Thus, the reform of 1965 itself awaits reform.

[9] *Novyi mir* 11 (November 1968): 276; cited in Karl W. Ryavec, *Implementation of Soviet Economic Reforms* (New York: Praeger, 1975), p. 18.
[10] *Pravda,* September 28, 1965, p. 2.

2

Soviet Government:
An Overview

The Mark of the Past

History, Henry Ford said, is "bunk." But perhaps history is politics' past tense. No nation is able to escape from its traditions in its politics. They seem to provide parameters or limits beyond which the political system never goes, unless perhaps military conquest or actual collapse allows another start. But the new start offered to Russia by the events of 1917 seems to have been only a brief interlude of apparent change. The result is only a new layering of politics; the new is simply sandwiched in among the old, and the political system creeps on to its unknown destination.

Soviet politics shares several features with the tsarist political system: a single official political ideology or perspective, the tenets of which are religiously taught and enforced; a centralized government, typical of continental Europe, holding much political decision making to itself; a large state bureaucracy that overawes the citizens even in their daily lives and has political power in its own right; a population of subject-participants who have been taught and conditioned to accept a political role limited to providing support for the system (a heritage of serfdom); and a complete lack of interest groups with a power base outside the party and government. As one scholar, a resident of the Soviet Union for several years, says, participation does not occur on an individual or independent group basis, but "within a framework of values, directives, and controls emanating from a ramified national bureaucracy subject to the commands of the Moscow Politburo [of the Communist party]." He goes on to characterize the dominant political culture as "partisan, elitist, and subject-participatory." [1]

Russian governments have never recognized the independent existence of definite

[1] Frederick C. Barghoorn, *Politics in the USSR*, 2d ed. (Boston: Little, Brown, 1972).

spheres of nonpolitical activity, and thus society has never remained independent of government. All matters, even cultural ones, can be dealt with as political matters by the government, an attitude usually attributed to the formative influences of the political philosophy and style of the Eastern Roman Empire (Byzantium). There the Emperor was both religious and political overlord. Religion and politics were not separated, as often occurred in Europe because of the prolonged and inconclusive struggles between church and state. And since the Russians are politically dominant, the Soviet Union, too, has been shaped by this political tradition.

Another feature common to both the tsarist and proletarian dictatorships is a political police, the existence of which suggests both a strength and weakness in the Russo-Soviet political tradition. Far more than a police force, it is an active guarantor of the political system through the pervasiveness, intensity, and efficiency of its operations. Tsarist repression gave birth to its revolutionary imitator and rival when Lenin recreated the secret police in 1917 as the *Cheka* (Extraordinary Commission for Fighting Counterrevolution and Sabotage). It had not been out of existence for even a year.

In foreign affairs there is a continuity as well, for the Soviet Union occupies substantially the same territory as tsarist Russia. Here the continuity consists of an uneasy combination of isolation and involvement. Because the Soviet Union has long been in the common European situation of great power politics, its involvement in international affairs has been unavoidable. The ease of invasion of the Russian heartland, a plain with no formidable obstacles, led to a long series of wars. This created such a high degree of defensiveness among Russians that it often cannot be distinguished from

aggressiveness by an outsider. To a Russian, however, that attitude is the only realistic one to hold. The Russo-Soviet state was built upon both the long-drawn-out conquest of the ancestors of half the present inhabitants and the defeat of several neighboring states. Defense became offense, and after a war Russia often became larger than it had been before, as a result of overrunning the previous border and establishing a new one beyond.

Ironically, at times the state was enlarging by what might be called absent-mindedness; a Russian general (sometimes a German mercenary) would seize a khanate or a minor kingdom on his own initiative and then announce it to Moscow after the fact. This sort of expansion worried the foreign offices of other states, particularly Britain, whose leadership thought it saw a master plan being worked out. Naturally, the British explanation was couched in British terms —a drive to the sea or to "warm water" (as if Russians were a race of lemmings). Ever since Catherine's time (1762–1796) Russia's growth has brought it periodically into the thick of international strife, although conflict with the United States came only after 1945. But, whereas tsarist Russia was a major power only within three bordering regions—central Europe, the Middle East, and northern Asia—the Soviet Union is a world power affecting developments also in Africa, Latin America, and even the United States. (Witness the effects on the United States economy of Soviet military power and economic needs, for example, grain, technology, and computers.)

The Present Political Situation and Institutions
Differences exist between the Russian and the Soviet political systems, of course. For one thing, the topmost political elite now has low-status origins (mainly peasant).

However, it is still small and is itself dominated by only a few men. The ideology is ostensibly progressive and oriented to change, in contrast to the former one of autocracy and orthodoxy, but still only one general political point of view is allowed. The power of the centralized state is not limited or attenuated by local government, and the state bureaucracy, originally patterned partly after the Prussian, still is not run with as much rationality, effectiveness, and legality as was its model.

Although the society is now more egalitarian in outward appearance and somewhat so in terms of income, definite differences of status and power exist. And, as before, no "island of separateness" has a legitimate political role or is allowed to express a political position publicly. Participation by the population is still mobilized and regulated by the party and its youth organizations. Elections take place every year, but the ballots offer no choice and elect only state legislators, not the real rulers, the Communist party elite. Significantly, the legislators always pass unanimously into law the bills put before them by the legislative leaders, who are high party officials. In any case, these formal laws are "few and vague." [2] Most of the regulations by which Soviet citizens live, as under the Tsar, are decrees issued by the state and party bureaucracies that are binding even on the courts. Ironically, the censorship is more far-reaching and effective than previously. As a result of this and other limitations put on political activities by the party, the social factors that often influence political behavior elsewhere have not affected the Soviet system. Besides the regular army and the centrally controlled police, some form of paramilitary special police still exists (as in France, Italy, and Spain). The Soviet approach to governing a large territory has been to disperse throughout it representatives of the central government who can meet expressions of dissent with overwhelming force. In 1945 the approach was transferred to much of Eastern Europe, too, but there it has since been modified. This pattern of centralized political surveillance is matched by the similarly centralized system of bureaucratic regulation and economic planning and operation.

The real government is the bureaucratized apparatus of the Communist party of the Soviet Union (CPSU). This party, the vital core of the Soviet political system, is really a change-oriented, partly militarized political bureaucracy with a mass following, a command of the instruments of violence, and a monopoly of the channels of political activity. Early in this century Lenin came to the elitist conclusion that the working class was not revolutionary, being only reformist and seeking higher wages alone, and that the goal of revolution required the proletariat to be led by a vanguard of professional revolutionaries.

Despite the changes attempted by Khrushchev and the improved living standards in the Soviet Union, certain key features of the Leninist-Stalinist political pattern remain. Fundamentally, the political decision makers at the head of the party are able to control and even manufacture support for themselves. They dominate inputs (demands and supports) as well as outputs (decisions and policies). More specifically, the bulk of major decision making takes place secretly in small groups dominated by officials of the party.[3] No effective legal restraints exist upon the will of the party, and public issues, those discussed in the

---

[2] Derek J. R. Scott, *Russian Political Institutions*, 3d ed. (New York: Praeger, 1966), p. 121.

[3] This list is adapted from a paper by Alexander Groth, "The CPSU: Institutional Legacy and the Prospects for Modernization" (May 1974).

mass media, are determined by the party leadership. Groups independent of the party are forbidden to act politically. So there is no legitimate way to present views to the leadership or to the public except through party channels.

Despite these great powers of the party and their withering effect on potential opposition, it is not all-powerful. Besides natural and technical limits to its will, the party faces inherent mass dissatisfaction in the populace. Although organized opposition is out of the question, the Soviet citizen is adept at the slowdown and the withholding of honest support. In recent years people have even been known to riot and burn down local party headquarters when their sense of fair play has been violated. Examples have included rioting over high food prices in Novocherkassk in 1962, striking in Odessa over the shipment of scarce butter to Cuba (the strikers' slogan was "Cuba yes, but butter no"), storming of party headquarters in a city in the Ukraine in 1973 over the callous treatment of people arrested for drunkenness, and rioting against Russian influence in Lithuania in 1972. In the case of Novocherkassk the troops of the KGB fired on the crowd, and in Lithuania army paratroopers were used. In 1968 some Soviet citizens actually demonstrated briefly in Moscow's Red Square against the invasion of Czechoslovakia. There is one reported instance of an assassination attempt on Brezhnev's life by an army officer, while rumors of political clubs of independent orientation among the crews of Soviet nuclear submarines and of mutinies on warships may have some basis.

The political system seems, then, to have little automatic support in some situations although it does not face an effective opposition. What is forestalled is not protest, but organized, large-scale, effective protest. The key limitation on protest is not the security police or the army but rather the party's monopoly of communications. Since protest is not publicly reported, like-minded people hear of it, if at all, only through the rumor mill and from foreign broadcasts. By then the news is old and provides only another dulling instance of the regime's continuing success. The independently produced political commentary and criticism of *samizdat* (self-publication) does not make up for this.

The Soviet political system has thus far been that rarity, the politically effective authoritarianism. If it changes, this will occur most probably not through mass violence but from within and, if Russian history is still pertinent, from above. Khrushchev tried to institute changes that might ultimately have been of significance. His successors seem ruled by the quest for strengthening the system overall while leaving politics stable, a difficult task in the long run.

The formal government is legally a federalism with autonomy for national minorities, but the key institutions of actual rule are centralized and act rather uniformly throughout the land. The party, unlike the government, is not organized on an ethnic basis, nor is most of the economy. Local soviets, or legislatures, control only 10 percent of the economy. Local government concentrates on nonpolitical issues similar to those dealt with by local government in late tsarist times, that is, transportation, housing, and public health. The central government and party elite control the lion's share of decision making.

The governmental arrangements have yielded to the symbols, though not the substance, of liberal democracy. There exists a constitution that is democratic in text and provides for the popular election of legislators. In fact, citizens vote for one or another level of soviet every year. The liberal democratic example is so strong that the top party leaders are elected members of the national legislature, though they derive their power not from either elections or their governmental positions but from their support within the core of the party, its apparatus (known as the *apparat*).

Why, then, does this dual structure of government exist? Historical reasons supply a partial explanation. The Bolsheviks originally came to power in November 1917 through manipulation of the soviets, then popular gatherings of elected delegates of workers, peasants, and soldiers. Their rivals, many of them socialists, walked out in protest at the Bolsheviks' takeover, leaving them in absolute control of a legitimized symbol of people's power. Lenin then established a new, purely Bolshevik government within what was now a mere husk of democracy. Once established, this indirect rule has had certain advantages for the party. For one, the party never seems at fault for governmental errors and failures; instead the state bureaucracy of the soviets is blamed. Second, the top party *apparatchiki* can devote themselves to long-term policy making, while lower levels of the party organization can check on the state bureaucrats' general performance periodically (an activity known as *kontrol* [supervision]). Actual party control is not lacking if it is needed. The party apparatus has the power of appointing and removing key governmental administrators (the power of *nomenklatura*) and exerts an indirect control through its ordinary members in primary party organizations existing throughout the state bureaucracy. Permanent involvement in direct administration by the party would lay it open to additional criticism for administrative and economic failures.

Despite Lenin's dislike of federalism, the existence of many nationalities made it pru-

dent that the Bolsheviks structure the new Soviet government in such a manner, with the criteria for each regional unit of the federation being nationality (ethnicity) and language. When Stalin spoke on the present constitution prior to its adoption in 1936, he devoted great attention to the interconnection between the national question and government, saying, "But in addition to common interests, the nationalities of the U.S.S.R. have *their special, specific* interests connected with their specific national characteristics. Can these specific interests be ignored? No, they cannot." [4] Because of the continued existence of national feelings, the federal form of the Soviet state survives.

Soviet federalism takes the form of a five-tiered structure of government as determined by compact ethnic settlement. Each level has its own soviet elected by the voters and its own administrative network to carry out lesser governmental tasks. The five main levels consist of the all-union; the union republic (15); the *oblast* or province (approximately 5,600), including many smaller cities; and the local or village (approximately 60,000). More than 2 million persons are elected members, or deputies, of the lower three levels of soviets. All soviets are unicameral, with electoral districts established on the basis of population, except for the Supreme Soviet, which is bicameral. One of its chambers, the Council of Nationalities, contains delegates from the ethnic areas of the Soviet Union, with representation from each area determined by its general size.

The government flows out of the Supreme Soviet, whose Chairman is always a member

[4] J. V. Stalin, *On the Draft Constitution of the USSR* (Moscow: Co-Operative Publishing Society of Foreign Workers in the U.S.S.R., 1936), p. 38. Emphasis in original.

of the Party Political Bureau (Politburo).
The administrative units of the government,
the ministries, are headed by a Council of
Ministers legally subordinate to the Supreme
Soviet and its Presidium. The Chairman of
the Council of Ministers, or the Premier, is
also a member of the Politburo. This post
is now held by Aleksei Kosygin and not by
the party's General Secretary, as was the case
in Stalin's and part of Khrushchev's time.
A Supreme Court exists, but it has no
constitutional role.

The government does not act independently of the party at any level. The Leninist
tradition of discipline ensures that the party
members who constitute the majority of the
elected Deputies of the soviets at the top
three levels vote the party line. (Party
membership in county and village soviets
can be low.) There has been no instance of
significant disagreement between soviets at
different levels nor have the two chambers of
the Supreme Soviet ever passed even different versions of a law. Besides the limitations
imposed by a Leninist party, local government is restricted in its range of activity by
its subordination to higher level soviets.
All-union laws always prevail over those of
lower levels, and the Presidium of the Supreme Soviet may set aside decisions and
orders of the councils of ministers of the
federal units. Limitations on lower-level and
regional governments are such that the very
existence of federalism comes into question.
Perhaps it is best to think of the Soviet
Union as a centralized or unitary state with
some structural diversity of administrative
units.

The Constitution of 1936, replete with
rights for citizens and the federation's units,
was presented as offering a degree of real
democracy not existing elsewhere. Perhaps
Stalin's call for "stability of laws" was the
true basis of the constitution, for it fulfills
the necessary function of stating what the

formal governmental structure is. But
despite the constitution's granting the right
of secession to the union republics and
establishing the requirement for arrests to
be sanctioned by a court, Soviet history contains much that belies such provisions.
Nevertheless, the existence of elections and
the principle of democracy, however restricted, provide an institutional basis for
future democratic political development if
the Leninist party were to change its role and
activities. For example, the idea of allowing
voters to have a choice in elections was
raised in the 1960s, but dashed by the post-
Khrushchev leadership. It may arise again,
although the draft of the new constitution
announced in May 1977 did not offer more
civil rights.

The Party: The Core of Politics
Lenin rejected the views of the majority
branch of the Russian Marxists, the so-called
Mensheviks, on the nature of the Russian
Social Democratic Labor party. They wanted
an open and democratic party of cobelievers,
which to Lenin was an unrealistic and almost
morally reprehensible goal. He instead
wanted a closed, cohesive club of coconspir-
ators who would faithfully devote all their
time to the revolution and would unquestionably accept the dictates of the central
committee (Lenin and a few others) in
bringing about the revolution through force.
He tried to stifle spontaneity, always suspected by Bolsheviks, and to operate on the
basis of central planning and consciousness.
Rosa Luxemburg, a leader of the Polish
socialists allied with the Bolsheviks, and
several others charged that Lenin had confused the idea of a political party with that
of pure organization itself. Only because of
the defection of certain minority Marxists
in 1903 was Lenin's group brought temporarily into the majority position in the
Russian Marxist movement and henceforth

known as the *Bolsheviki* (people of the majority).[5]

Once the removal of power from a socialist government had been engineered in a coup d'état (not a revolution in any sense) by troops mostly thinking that they were following the wishes of the Congress of Soviets, Lenin's original conception of the movement as a cadre party had to be modified. This modification, however, was never allowed to go so far as to make the Bolshevik party (now called the Communist party) similar to a Western democratic political party, which counts as members those who do not accept party discipline and only support, vote for, or contribute to it.

Victory required administrators to govern and large numbers of members to radiate the party's will throughout society. Instead of revolutionaries, executives were needed to run the enlarged party and to supervise the activities of the state apparatus and Red Army, both of which were still filled with holdovers from the tsarist regime. (Perhaps thirty thousand former tsarist officers were signed on to help the Bolsheviks win the civil war, while a comparable number of tsarist officials remained in the civil service.) Dilution of the party occurred through enlarging it from a network of revolutionaries to a big organization of victors and careerists who joined simply because it had won and through adding tens of thousands of ordinary persons who were to provide the eyes and ears the party needed for its supervision

Social Background of Party Members and Candidates

| | % of Party Members and Candidates | | | % of Total Population |
	1961	1964	1968	1964 [a]
Manual workers	35.0	37.3	38.8	75.1 [b]
Non-manual workers or employees	47.7	46.2	45.4	
Peasants on collective farms	17.3	16.5	15.8	24.9
Total	100.0	100.0	100.0	100.0

Source: "KPSS v tsifrakh," *Partiynaya zhizn'*, no. 10 (May 1965), p. 11; 1964 figures, Leonid Brezhnev, quoted in *Pravda*, March 30, 1966; 1968 figures, *Partiynaya zhizn'*, no. 7 (April 1968), p. 27.
[a] "Klassovy sostav naseleniva SSSR," *SSSR v tsifrakh v 1964g* (Moscow, 1965), p. 12.
[b] Workers accounted for approximately 55 percent and employees for 20 percent of the population. Manual workers here include agricultural workers on state farms.

of society. The Marxist-Leninist ideology became the justification for their actions in their quest for power and privilege.

Lenin coped with the problems of success and size by abolishing the right of party members to form groups of like-minded persons. This occurred at about the same time that party members cruelly suppressed the first rebellion against Soviet rule, that of the soldiers and sailors of the fortress of Kronstadt, near Leningrad, who had become sadly disillusioned by Bolshevik treatment of other socialists and of peasants. Another device adopted by Lenin was the purge, which initially involved only the periodic review of party members' records in order to ascertain who should be kept and who expelled. In order to carry out this task and to keep the party records, an office called the

[5] The Marxists, even if all factions were added together, never were the largest revolutionary group. This was, instead, the Socialist Revolutionary party, a group that was based in the peasantry and used the greatest violence against the tsarist regime. This party won a majority of seats in the Constituent Assembly in free elections held after the revolution, but the Bolsheviks dispersed the assembly and prevented it from setting up a democratic government.

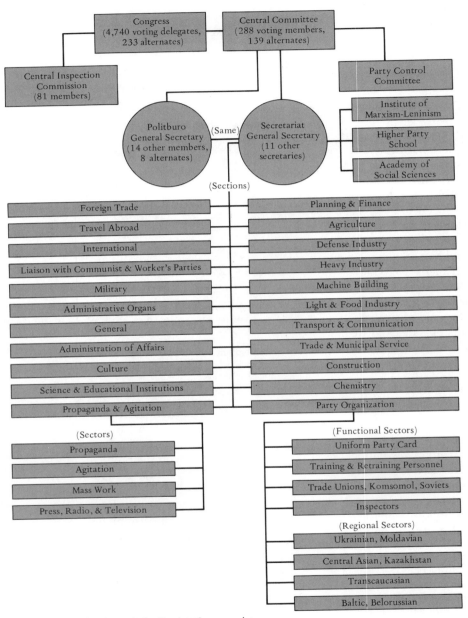

Central organization of the Soviet Communist Party

(John Armstrong, *Ideology, Politics, and Government in the Soviet Union*, 3rd ed., © 1974, p. 78. Reproduced by permission of Praeger Publishers, Inc., New York, N.Y.)

Secretariat was established. Upon the death of the first holder of the office, the post went by default to Joseph Stalin, the only one near the top ranks who wanted what many party leaders thought was a dull, apolitical job.

Stalin quickly proved them wrong. He learned that the devices of the demotion, the promotion, and the transfer, all carried out through the shuffling of papers, could be used to place party members who supported him in key positions throughout the land. The office under Stalin became preeminently political. Ironically, the party at large feared the "man on horseback," the Red Napoleon, who could be only Leon Trotsky, the leader of the Red Army. But by 1924, Stalin had isolated Trotsky bureaucratically within the army, having even appointed Trotsky's first deputy. Although he was to show some fight in the next few years, Trotsky was effectively powerless. In 1927 he was defeated in politics and just two years later was forcibly put aboard a ship for exile and eventual death by assassination.

It was clear by then that it was not the workers of the world who were on the march, but the Red bureaucrats. The essential nature of Soviet politics had emerged. The key people were party professionals, the apparatchiki, who ran the party and all other organizations and permanent groupings through the party's rank-and-file members in them. Chief among these was Stalin, the arch-apparatchik, who stayed above the struggle among these party executives. It was into this world that Nikita Sergeyevich (son of Sergei) Khrushchev came as a young man and began to make his way to the top.

3

Khrushchev's Early Years: Entry into Politics and the Party

Fragments from a Childhood and Adolescence

Here fact and fancy must both be sifted and weighed, but, unfortunately, a clear separation is impossible. When Khrushchev became the leader of the Soviet Union, he acquired a power denied most people, including most politicians: the power to rewrite history. Khrushchev made several conflicting statements about his childhood and youth, behavior typical of this man. Dissimulation probably stood him in good stead during those long, difficult years when he stood near Stalin, for political power in the Soviet Union did not then protect one from arrest and death.

Khrushchev begins his memoirs not with his early years, but with his return to his workplace after the Bolshevik Revolution and the civil war, when he was twenty-eight years of age.[1] His youth is not a completely

blank page, however, because he made several public statements about his early years. Along with official Soviet biographical data, these have been carefully examined by scholars, but they have not been able to resolve all inconsistencies.[2]

It is known that Nikita Sergeyevich Khrushchev was born on April 17, 1894, in Kalinovka, a village in the province of Kursk located in the southern Russian part of the empire. The location was later to be

[1] Unfortunately, Khrushchev's memoirs were edited at least twice, once by members of his family, who protectively deleted certain statements from the tapes, and again by the editor-translator. The tapes on which the two-volume memoirs are based are now at Columbia University. They have been published as *Khrushchev Remembers,* Strobe Talbott, trans. and ed., 2 vols. (Boston: Little, Brown, 1970–1974).

[2] The biographies of Khrushchev upon which this chapter is based are Edward Crankshaw, *Khrushchev: A Career* (New York: Viking, 1966) [which is based partly on Pistrak]; George Paloczi-Horvath, *Khrushchev: The Road to Power* (London: Secker and Warburg, 1960); and Lazar Pistrak, *The Grand Tactician* (New York: Praeger, 1961).

Nikita Khrushchev

(Life Magazine Collection)

important for him, because the population of that area was one-fifth Ukrainian. As a result, Khrushchev could speak and understand the language of the second most numerous ethnic group in the Soviet Union, an ability he was to put to good use in his career. (Brezhnev, Khrushchev's successor, has the same important advantage, being born a Russian and raised in the Ukraine.) Also important was the diversified character of the economy there, a mixture of agriculture and industry. Khrushchev gained work experience in the two major sectors of the economy.

He seems to have been an only child. His

grandfather had been a serf (freed in 1861) —in effect, a slave. Of his mother only her name and year of death are known (but she lived until 1945 and thus had ample time to be an influence on her son). His father began life as a peasant, but became a coal miner while Nikita was still a boy. The family's life had not been economically improved by freedom since it had not brought enough land. Khrushchev once said of this period: "Life did not pamper me. . . . I began working when I learned to walk. Till the age of fifteen I tended calves, then sheep, and then the landlord's cows." [3] He also reported that his father made him quit school when he could count to thirty, saying that he would never have more than thirty rubles anyway.

In 1909, at the age of fifteen, Khrushchev was abruptly thrust into confrontation with Western capitalism. His father got him a job as a beginning mechanic at a mine in a town founded only forty years earlier by a British entrepreneur, John Hughes. Called Yusovka after its founder, (later Stalino and now Donetsk), it was in the center of the Donets basin, the major iron and steel area of the Russian Empire. Yusovka was divided literally into classes, the English colony of the management personnel and the "dog town" (*sobachevka*) of the workers. Khrushchev then saw at first hand the "two nations" that the industrial revolution had created and that Harold Macmillan and many others were later to decry in Britain. Although there is no record of Khrushchev having been driven to radical, or even union, activity in Yusovka, he must have had definite views on capitalism and foreigners.

Here, young Khrushchev for the first time saw East meeting West—the contrast between West-

[3] From his remarks in New York in 1959, quoted in Pistrak, *Grand Tactician,* p. 4.

ern technological know-how and civilization and Eastern technical backwardness and primitive life. Khrushchev's . . . urge to "catch up and overtake" the West was perhaps born in this atmosphere of sharp contrast.[4]

He was participating in the formation of a Russian working class, which—despite Lenin's statements that Russia was in the capitalist stage of development—in reality was still only a small minority of the population. Perhaps Khrushchev was satisfied with his station in life because he had already achieved some upward mobility in comparison to his father's social position.

In 1914, when World War I broke out, he was twenty years old. Significantly, Khrushchev did not serve in the international contest that brought down the tsarist system. He was probably deferred because his specialty was considered essential. But his deferment also implies that he was not a political activist, for troublemakers were frequently drafted to get them under government control. Perhaps, too, he had other concerns; it seems he was married around 1915 and that two children were born, a son in 1916 and a daughter in 1918.[5] His first wife died during the famine after World War I.

There is no record of Khrushchev's becoming involved in the strikes that proliferated toward the middle of the war when the effects of backward Russia fighting the world's most industrialized power of the time came to be felt—inflation, shortages, the land farmed by women and old people. But despite the difficulties caused by Russia's staying in the war, its military role was crucial for the allies, particularly the French, since it drew some German troops eastward.

Most historians agree that it was the pro-

longation of World War I that literally tore Russia to pieces and made a general political crisis inevitable. Russia's inefficient bureaucracy and backward-looking ruling class could not deal adequately with the complex tasks of waging a modern general war. Anti-German nationalism wore very thin after two years of enervating war. The political institutions were old and creaky, never having undergone thorough reform, while the social props of the regime were weak as well. The uneducated clergy, which never stood up against the government, was not respected. The landowning class, the regime's natural eyes and ears in the vast countryside, was much smaller and weaker after the freeing of the serfs some fifty years previously; the army was swollen by peasant draftees who wanted to sow seeds, not to make war; and the Russian bureaucracy somehow could never function like the Prussian bureaucracy on which it had been modeled. The masses of peasants had at most a passive attitude of subjects, not one of political participants, since most of them felt the government of French-speaking aristocrats in Moscow was not their government. The Tsar was a "little father" to many peasants, yet he was far away. This attitude of puzzled detachment is exemplified well by the question put to an English scholar by a Russian peasant in 1914: "The Tsar and the Kaiser are at war, they say. Tell me, is this my war, too?"

As a political system Russia had very little of the social support essential to survival under stress (a problem for the Bolsheviks as well). Without war Russia probably would have continued the slow but significant industrial and social development that was already occurring, and it might have become a quasi-democracy with a limited monarchy. Illiteracy was being eliminated, social mobility was occurring (some of the top bureaucrats and generals in 1914 were

[4] Ibid., p. 6.
[5] Paloczi-Horvath, *Khrushchev*, pp. 9–10.

former peasants), and industry was being built. Russia was beginning to reap the advantage of backwardness, that is, the ability to adopt the most modern machinery and methods. (The southern Russian steel industry in 1910 was the most modern in the whole world.)

Why, then, did the government stay in the war at the risk of a general political failure? There seem to have been three reasons: first, a belief that commitments must be honored; second, a fear of reprisals by the French and British; third, a desire to reap the rewards of victory, aid promised by the Western allies as well as the realization of an old dream of the Tsars, the acquisition of Constantinople (now Istanbul) and the outlet of the Black Sea. Russia would then be a major Mediterranean power, and perhaps even an Atlantic and a world power, a goal the Soviet Union has achieved only recently.

By March 1917 the shaky Russian house of cards collapsed in all directions and the February Revolution resulted. (It was so named because Russia then used a different calendar than the West.) Russian women asking for bread set in motion the demonstrations against which the Russian government at first decided not to contend, thinking these were only more of the usual protests and thus, in effect, abdicating power to the people in the streets. This was one of the most nearly bloodless downfalls of an empire in history: only a few policemen were hurt in the government's belated attempt to stem the human tide sweeping over Petrograd.[6]

The immediate political successors to the tsarist government were mainly three: a Provisional Government of members of the

former parliament, a federation of soviets representing the workers and the soldiers, and the officers and soldiers who elected to remain in the war. Of course, the picture was soon much more complex, with the empire falling apart into new nations and an almost endless variety of political splinter groups.

Adulthood, Civil War, and a Political Start

While all this was happening, Khrushchev had run back to his old village of Kalinovka to pace off his share of the land that the peasants were then seizing. Obviously, he was still essentially a peasant with a private ownership mentality. This does not mean that he had no political thoughts, only that he made certain his own interests were protected. If he was in some political movement, it almost certainly was not the Bolshevik party, which had no support in rural areas at that time. Possibly he was connected with one of its rivals, perhaps the Socialist Revolutionaries, because they had a land program that worked to the peasants' interest, something Lenin and the Bolsheviks acquired only by borrowing from them.

Russia was not able to settle down to peaceful reconstruction because there was no effective successor government. The Germans pressed on eastward into Russia and the Ukraine. The dual power of the Provisional Government and the soviets was really a nonpower, the two partners maintaining only an uneasy truce. Even though the Provisional Government came to be led by socialists by mid-1917, it stayed in the war, thinking about foreign affairs much as its predecessor had. Consequently, under the leadership of Lenin, who had returned to Russia in April after many years of exile

[6] St. Petersburg (*Sankt-Peterburg*), Petrograd, and Leningrad are all names for the same city at different times. It is now Leningrad (Lenin's city).

in Switzerland, the Bolsheviks found more and more support, at least in the army and among workers and some minority ethnic groups. Their slogan of "bread, land, and peace" fell on fertile ground, and Lenin's energetic image seemed to promise effective problem-solving action.

In October, after an unsuccessful attempt by an army general to take over Petrograd, Lenin ordered his organization to seize power. The Provisional Government was tarnished by ineffectuality and possible complicity in the attempted military coup; and Trotsky, having recently associated himself with Lenin and the Bolsheviks, now was chairman of the committee of the soviets that dealt with military matters. Since "power lay in the streets," Trotsky issued an order (upon Lenin's initiative) in his soviet capacity to assume control of key installations and disperse the Provisional Government. The coup was more comedy than heroic act. The famous cruiser Aurora, now a floating patriotic museum in Leningrad, was only firing blanks. Lenin showed what Stalin was later to prove repeatedly: people can be politically controlled through manipulation of the organizations to which they belong. The popular soviets became, in Stalin's words, a "transmission belt" for achieving purely Bolshevik aims, and the Red Guards of the soviets did not all know they were acting for the Bolsheviks.

That distinctive Leninist concentration on military force and violence paid off handsomely. By the next morning, November 8, Lenin was master of Petrograd and its environs. At Lenin's announcement of the coup from the rostrum of the Congress of Soviets, most of the other delegates to the congress walked out in protest, a political mistake of lasting significance. Lenin and the Bolsheviks were thus handed the major legitimate organ of people's power, the

name and image of the soviet. Accordingly, Lenin then and there set up a new Soviet government—composed of People's Commissars, all of whom were Bolsheviks, and headed by himself—and announced fatefully, "We shall now proceed to construct the socialist order." Although it was no longer representative of the country, it had a representative image because of the revolutionary history of soviets in Russia.[7]

But victory in the capital city did not mean the country fell into the Bolsheviks' lap. The vast Russian land was in the hands of a myriad of groups. Beside the Whites, tsarist officer corps and loyal enlisted men in several regional armies, and the Reds or Bolsheviks in the main urban centers, there were the Greens (peasant revolutionaries), the Yellows (Ukrainian nationalists), the Czech prisoners-of-war who held the Trans-Siberian railway, and various ethnic independence movements, such as the Finnish, the Latvian, and the Georgian. Later, the armed forces of Britain, France, Italy, Rumania, Japan, and the United States intervened on the side of the Whites, but did not do more than skirmish with the Bolsheviks. These interventionists landed initially to maintain an eastern front and to keep war materiel sent to the tsarist government out of the hands of the Germans and their seeming agents, the Bolsheviks; only later did they drift into an ineffectual effort to oppose Bolshevism.

In the great civil war that began in earnest in the spring of 1918 the Bolsheviks had some important advantages. They manipulated the only institution with popular legitimacy, the soviets. The top aristocracy had

[7] Again, because a different calendar was in use in Russia at that time, this coup has come to be designated as the October Revolution in the history books.

given in to its non-Russian nature and had fled to the salons of Paris, to be joined in a short time by hundreds of thousands of others. The royal family was captured and eventually executed. Strategically, the Bolsheviks held the classic central position crucial for war and sat astride most of Russia's industry, railways, and communications. They lacked food, however, and during the civil war they simply took it from the peasants by force as part of what Lenin euphemistically called "war communism." In reality a policy of theft, war communism was the direct opposite of the principle followed by the Chinese Communists after 1935 and the Yugoslav Communists later, who made the peasants their allies.

Now the fates of the Bolsheviks and of Khrushchev were joined. He entered the Bolshevik party in 1918, at age twenty-four, through enlistment in the new Red Army. How did Khrushchev come to join? This has never been explained. Perhaps he was forced to join by a band of Red Army men, not an uncommon practice. One joined up or was shot as a class enemy; sometimes "recruits" knew nothing of the ideology of the group they were joining. Maybe he wanted to protect his now motherless children and took a way open to ensure their safety at the moment. In any case, Khrushchev took part in the civil war in the Ukraine on what turned out to be the winning side. The civil war was a process of violent brutalization of its participants and the destruction of human relationships, even the family, a struggle more inhumane than anything yet seen in Europe, except perhaps the Thirty Years' War (1618–1648).

Luckily for the Bolsheviks, everyone was ready for some sort of order after the civil war; it mattered little who imposed it. The Bolsheviks won not because they had the support of the peasants but because they

were an unknown quantity, and the peasants thought the Whites would take back the land. The war ended with the Bolsheviks and the peasants, still the majority of the population, in uneasy truce. The countryside had been conquered by the city, in total opposition to the Chinese and Yugoslav revolutionary processes. As a result, the millions of peasants (about 90 percent of the population) were potential, if not actual, enemies of the new system.

Though different in terms of attitude toward the peasantry, the Chinese, Soviet, and Yugoslav Marxist revolutionary takeovers did have one thing in common: the militarization of the party. At the end of the civil war, half the Soviet Communist party membership was in the army. Indeed, Khrushchev entered the party through enlistment in its army. Marxism in power has usually had some of the style and habits of the soldier, and in Soviet Russia, as in the former regime, the political and military elites were close in some respects. The party-army was able to reconstitute most of the Russian Empire, its divisions substituting for revolutionary fervor and persuasion in the case of more than one ethnic group. The example for the future militaristic expansions (of 1940 and 1945–1948) had been set.

Khrushchev does not seem to have made a name for himself in the Red Army during the civil war although he became part of the network of party controls in the military, his first distinctly political work. But, despite his service in the army for at least three years, partly in the key post of party secretary of a regiment, he was out of politics for a short time after he left the army and returned to Yusovka and the mines.

Whatever the reason for Khrushchev's briefly leading a nonpolitical life in 1922, he did not stay out of politics long. Perhaps he found he could not leave it behind; it might have become very meaningful or important to him. The revolution was to continue; Stalin was to see to that. If Khrushchev had not rejoined politics as a participant, he might have been one among the anonymous millions crushed by it. (Years later, during his trip to the United States, Khrushchev met Samuel Goldwyn, the movie czar, who told Khrushchev he had left Russia. Khrushchev answered, "I don't blame you. Things were terrible.") Khrushchev never had a chance to leave, only to try to survive. Or maybe the growth of the state and party bureaucracies necessitated his re-recruitment. All political systems must recruit people into active political roles in order to maintain ties with the population and to provide a testing and training ground for future leaders. The great revolutionaries such as Lenin and Trotsky had recruited themselves. Not so for Khrushchev: he was being invited in by a system whose basic rules had already been forcibly laid down. He was, therefore, a new type of revolutionary, one on the payroll of the revolutionary state. He never even met its creator, Lenin. Although he was to affect the new system, it was also to affect him. As he said years later, "The Party made me everything that I am." He became a part of the party and remained a part of it for more than forty years, until 1964 and later.

Whatever happened to bring him back into the party, he soon was working for it in the mines of Yusovka, where he had started industrial life a dozen or so years before. But this time Khrushchev had changed social classes, having become part of management. Accordingly, he worked to get the workers to produce or, as the Soviet sources put it, "mobilized the miners to restore coal production." Now a member, although only a lowly member, of the new ruling class, he became a secretary of a primary party organ-ization and thus Moscow's eyes and ears among coal miners. As such, he was doing basic-level work for the party apparat: checking on the fulfillment of both party and state mine administration decisions (the work of kontrol), rewarding those who worked well and punishing those who did not, exhorting the miners to produce more (an offshoot of agitational-propaganda work), and no doubt making certain he and his mines looked better than other party secretaries and their mines, thereby preparing the way for his promotion into the full-time party apparat itself.

On the First Rungs
of the Ladder of Success

By moving back into party work, however it was managed, Khrushchev had made himself politically available. But the lack of an education stood in his way. Marxism, a protest against industrialization, was becoming in Soviet Russia—a peasant country—an ideology of industrialization; in so doing, it was recreating some of the very conditions of early industrialized England against which Marx, horrified, had railed in righteous anger. Those who were to push and guide this process had to have an education, for otherwise it would not have been possible for the party to supplant the old intelligentsia. In late 1922, Khrushchev enrolled in a local workers' faculty in order to obtain, in a few years, the content of both late elementary and secondary education. He continued in politics as a sort of elder student leader, that is, as secretary of the school's party cell. He was thus part of another control network of the Communist party, that in the schools. In order to change Soviet society, the party leadership had to have its people everywhere, not just behind

304

bureaucrats' desks. The party in the Soviet Union has not been content with conventional dictatorship such as exists in Latin America or in Spain; instead, it gains active control of society itself.

The following year, Khrushchev was promoted and became the major party figure in the school, mobilizing students for manual work and for political agitation and other "social work" among workers. Now Khrushchev had to become a public speaker. It is hard to imagine that he did not take to this naturally, for in his later years, as the party's leader, Khrushchev spoke to large masses of people with a vigor and directness that prompted some Americans to say that he would have made a good American politician on the tactical and public-speaking level. Soon after Khrushchev was graduated in 1925, he was thrust into greater political responsibility, becoming the party secretary in the raion (or county) of Marinka, located in his home area, the oblast (or region) of Stalino. Thus he began the life of a local political leader. Here he was politically responsible for the effects of the party's policies in the district.

The lack of successful rebellions and the

Khrushchev (first row, second from left) with his colleagues in the Donbass in the early 1920s

(Life Magazine Collection)

ability of the party to send out its chosen leaders showed that it had made itself master of the Tsar's former empire. But could it do more with these vast lands and the peasants than had the former system? Khrushchev and the thousands of men like him were the party's main hope for carrying the revolution forward. Here Khrushchev showed his talent for getting around to talk to people and seeing things firsthand year-round, traveling about in a sleigh during the winters.

At this time the continuation of the revolution was in question. Lenin, founder of the regime, had died in early 1924, not having designated a successor. Indeed, he had left behind a testament critical of his likely successors, particularly Stalin. Lenin's heirs were divided among themselves as to what policies to follow. Some, like Nikolai Bukharin, wanted to take no new direction, but to stay within the bounds of the moderate policy toward Soviet society, including peasants and small-scale capitalists, that Lenin had embarked upon in 1921. Known as New Economic Policy (NEP), it was a halt to revolution and even a retreat. The party and the new state held the commanding heights of big industry and banking and monopolized political power, but allowed small-scale capitalism and private ownership in land to remain and develop. Bukharin and those in the right wing of the party wanted to continue this policy indefinitely. On the left, Trotsky, the maker of the revolution, was unsympathetic to NEP and favored domestic radicalization and active support of the spread of socialism abroad, particularly in Germany, China, and the European overseas colonies. Stalin seemed to be the reasonable moderate of the time, minding the party office and getting the humdrum, nonideological work done.

It then seemed to many that either the right or left wing would win, not the centrist faction and chief party administrator Stalin. Such people were basing their views on appearances. Both the left and right wings had brilliant leaders, flamboyant speakers, and powerful images. But Stalin controlled the party's offices, communications, and personnel records and the "intake valve" of the party's recruitment activities. He also had the power of expulsion; he could promote, demote, and transfer (to a village of log cabins or to Moscow). It is not surprising that Khrushchev aligned himself with Stalin's machine.

Stalin's policies were the only ones that the new, rough entrants into what had been Lenin's party could support with a reasonable expectation of reward. By 1924 or 1925, it was Stalin's party. It is surprising his "intellectual" opponents could not see this, but perhaps it was obvious only from below, by the people on the make. In addition, the new Red organization men were comfortable with Stalin. Mostly people of peasant and working-class backgrounds from the interior of Russia, they had never been abroad, knew no foreign languages as a rule, and thereby saw no reason to meddle in distant lands. For them, Stalin's slogan "socialism in one country" translated into the common-sense idea of "USSR first." In addition, they understood, as did Stalin, the primitive politics of the situation. Unless the new petty capitalists were stopped and the millions of peasants put under control, the party dictatorship could not last. Hence they supported the leftist course Stalin took in 1928 (after the left had been safely beaten) by dispossessing the peasants of their land through forced collectivization and beginning a huge program of further industrialization under state and party control. Here jobs were being made for them as the peasantry melted to a more controllable size in the red heat of "primitive socialist accumulation."

Accordingly, Khrushchev voiced the Stalinist line at the party conferences and congresses to which he was sent as a delegate during the 1920s. It is likely Khrushchev added his voice to those shouting down the oppositionists. The Stalin faction's argument against intraparty democracy was childishly simple: it might spread. Lev Kamenev, once one of Lenin's chief lieutenants, sided with Stalin against Trotsky (Stalin's major rival), and shouted: "Today one says: democracy within the Party; tomorrow one will say: democracy in the trade unions; the day after tomorrow, the workers may say: give us the same kind of democracy you introduced for yourselves."[8]

Khrushchev's later anti-Stalinist speeches must be read against the background of his early support of Stalin. He never publicly criticized Stalin for anything he did during the 1920s, only for certain activities of later decades; to do so would have cast doubt on Khrushchev's own political origins. It is not surprising that Khrushchev later moved decisively and strongly against his opponents on several occasions, for he had learned much during his political apprenticeship.

Khrushchev rose steadily in the party hierarchy, becoming in 1927 (the year of Trotsky's defeat) the head of the Organizational Department of the Stalino Party Committee. Next he moved on to a top-level party job in Kiev, a major city in the Ukraine. Here, in 1929, he took part in organizing the "socialist-competition" movement, a new, nationwide speed-up system for workers. Later in 1929, Khrushchev was transferred to Moscow. Although still a minor actor, he was now to be at center stage, the point from which the Soviet world, including its hireling parties and secret agents abroad, was being manipulated by the leader. Within a few years Khrushchev was to become one of Stalin's ruthless assistants. At this point, he could only go forward; going back was impossible, an instant mark not only of weakness but also of treason, in its Soviet definition. He was approaching the power for which he had trained.

[8] *Pravda,* January 15, 1924, p. 5; quoted in Pistrak, *Grand Tactician,* p. 18.

Khrushchev's Middle Years:
At the Center

Moscow, More Schooling, and Political Takeoff

Khrushchev was thirty-five when he arrived in Moscow, the historic center of Russia, in the fall of 1929. Remarkably, he became a full member of the highest body of the party, the Politburo, in less than ten years after his arrival.

Moscow, the well-situated point from which the regathering of the Russian lands from the Mongol khans had been begun and completed, has had a specific symbolic meaning to the people, signifying an inward-looking orientation. Leningrad, situated on the Gulf of Finland has always been a "window on the West." In this city, which was the capital during the eighteenth and nineteenth centuries, politics has been, and remains, more rationalistic than in Moscow. However, the political factions based on Leningrad have never been able to win. Khrushchev was to be with the Muscovites when they triumphed over Leningrad again through the murder of the party boss of Leningrad in late 1934.

Khrushchev was sent to Moscow on the basis of merit, but it was a politically based merit. Although hard work had been involved, it was hardly politically neutral. His activities in the Ukraine had come to the attention of Lazar Kaganovich, one of Stalin's closest associates who discovered a few other up-and-coming politicos. One of these, Georgi Malenkov, was to be Khrushchev's major rival immediately after Stalin's death, while another, Nikolai Bulganin, was later to co-rule the Soviet Union with Khrushchev.

Political success in the Soviet Union, as in many political systems, depends heavily upon the young political aspirant's being discovered by a successful political figure at a higher level who co-opts him or her into political activity. (In Britain, most Members of Parliament entered politics because they were invited.) Of course, aspirants can make themselves available, but cooperation or invitation into politics by established figures is still the main or only way into meaningful political activity in most systems. (The American practice of "self-co-optation" through winning primaries or local-level elections is almost unique.)

But single parties are still made up of human beings, obviously, and each individual human gets along better with some people than with others. So major political factions operate within the one Soviet party despite Lenin's prohibition of them. During the 1930s and 1940s these factions were to a large degree the creations of individual members of Stalin's Politburo, like Kaganovich.

Khrushchev then began to put together his own faction. Stalin made the major decisions, but kept himself effectively insulated from the struggles among his lieutenants' factions or cliques through his personal control of the security police and other key institutions. These lieutenants could destroy each other, but they could never reach Stalin, who was above the struggle. What spurred the continuing conflict was the certainty of imprisonment under terrible conditions for failure or displeasing Stalin and the possibility of great (though always second-ranking) power for success and pleasing the leader.

Khrushchev and Kaganovich formed a patron-client relationship in which Khrushchev's political future was hitched to that of Kaganovich. To see what sort of impression Khrushchev might have made, a brief look at Kaganovich is useful, for likes tend to choose likes. Lacking any clearly identifiable position of his own, Kaganovich was first of all Stalin's unthinking right arm and remained so even after Stalin had Kaganovich's two brothers executed. (This behavior, reminiscent of Ivan the Terrible, gave

Stalin a certain advantage—unpredictability. Because even his closest associates could never second-guess him, they were always his servants psychologically as well as physically.) Khrushchev later defended himself for not opposing Stalin, giving the example of Stalin having someone Khrushchev was defending shot the very morning Khrushchev took up the man's case. Secondly, Kaganovich was of lower-middle-class origin, but uneducated, like Khrushchev, and had been in the party prior to the revolution. (Stalin favored those who, like him, did not have great intellectual attainments to their credit and opposed those who could outshine him intellectually.) One old Bolshevik saw Kaganovich as a

very outstanding man . . . extremely industrious, with an excellent memory and organizational talents. It is a pity that . . . one cannot rely on his word. . . . Maybe circumstances are to blame . . . : he began his Party career at a time when perfidy was very much in demand. . . . But . . . was he not one of those who most of all contributed to the increase of that demand?[1]

He was Stalin's long-time master troubleshooter who dealt with several problem areas at the same time: purges, selection of new cadres, collectivization of peasants, and even subway building. Kaganovich was doing so much that he needed helpers, and Khrushchev came to Moscow as one of them. His job was to help purge Stalin's opponents from the Stalin Industrial Academy in Moscow.

Khrushchev entered Moscow as a political student-informer-agent in a key new educational institution set up to train future Red managerial personnel. Stalin wanted

[1] *Sotsialisticheskii vestnik,* no. 6–7 (1930): 18 [a journal of émigré Russian socialists]; quoted in Pistrak, *Grand Tactician,* p. 54.

their Redness, or Bolshevik commitment, to be of one hue only. Since most students in Moscow supported the intraparty opposition led by outstanding figures such as Trotsky and Bukharin, Khrushchev's task was to separate the Stalinists from the oppositionists and to decide which among the latter students were to be expelled and purged from the party. Although the great purges had not yet begun, Stalin had already created his own apparatus to carry them out.

Purges are only noticeable high points in what actually is a continuing process. Expulsions from the party never end; they are only greater in some periods than in others and are sometimes obscured by recruitment. (In the late 1960s and early 1970s the annual rate of expulsions was between thirty and forty thousand members. Recently the party has been engaged in a nonviolent purge called an "exchange of party documents.") The reason given for this is the need to maintain the party's purity. Certainly, careerism —joining for selfish reasons—is a problem, but since the purge is run by people whose own careers are heavily involved in the outcome, some careerists are bound to remain in the organization after its completion. When Khrushchev took up his new job, purges did not generally result in the deaths of party members. That was to come in only a few years, however, and Khrushchev knowingly or unknowingly was doing his part to bring that dark and bloody period closer.

Khrushchev arrived in the capital when the Soviet Union had been authoritatively set on a course from which no deviation was possible. The stakes were the highest. Stalin might win over his rivals, collectivize the peasants and reduce their number, and, using the labors of peasants torn from their farms, build a great industry that would overawe all of Europe. Alternatively, the system might be ripped asunder by his failure. Having thrust Soviet Russia forward

into the unknown, Stalin sought men who could maintain and even intensify this effort. Kaganovich was one such man and Khrushchev another. These men found each other and gathered together for the great push to "build a second America" (an actual slogan of the time). Strong measures were being taken. The peasants who did not become urban workers entered upon a new period of serfdom, being forced to give up their land, to farm collectively, and to pay the state a definite share of their produce. (They could pay themselves only from what remained, if anything). All available resources were invested in new industry that would make mainly machines that make more machines, and political repression was heightened. A system of payment not by hourly wage rates but by piecework (long opposed by unions in the West) was introduced. The grip was fastened on! Khrushchev's mission was to use it to make society produce.

Why did the Soviet people allow this to happen? Society had been atomized by the cruelties of the civil war, and all individuals were politically alone. Also, the effects of serfdom and autocracy may have tended toward the passive, though unwilling, acceptance of the new despotism. Stalin's new party-controlled "transmission belts," or mass organizations, limited whatever recreation of society had been haltingly taking place during the short NEP. The continuation of the process of forming a society apart from government would have to await his death. Then Khrushchev would have a new role.

Khrushchev put his stay in the academy to his own political uses. Once again a "student," he carried on what the official biographies term "an active struggle against the Right" and other "traitors." Early in 1930, through the manipulated elections that Stalin's followers brought to a high art, he was elected secretary of the party cell of the academy. A stronger attack was called for, which soon gained Khrushchev praise for his "organizational abilities" in the struggle with the opposition. This experience in re-making party organizations was to be of use to him later in his role of party boss of the Ukraine and most of all after Stalin's death, when he fought for personal control of the Soviet system.

His work at the academy took him into a delicate, dangerous, and shadowy intrigue. Stalin's second wife, Nadezhda Alliluyeva, was an active member of his party cell. Then about twenty-nine years old, she was beginning to express opposition to her husband's policies, particularly those toward the peasantry.[2] Her presence was a curious and risky bit of luck for Khrushchev. It seems he hedged his bets by not taking overt action but instead by informing on her through Kaganovich, his mentor. Thus he could always claim to have done something without ever having taken actual, and very risky, action. For reasons unknown, his maneuvering was successful. His activities were favorably noted in the Central Committee itself; he began to imitate Kaganovich by building up his own coterie of clients, or followers, at the academy; and he was promoted in early 1931 to party boss of a prestigious district of Moscow (the same district that Brezhnev, once Khrushchev's client, now represents in the Supreme Soviet). He had survived another trial. Nadezhda Alliluyeva survived only for a time, however. In November 1932, she reportedly committed suicide after a political argument with Stalin. Khrushchev has said of this, "However she died, it was because of something Stalin did."[3]

Whether Khrushchev's actions contributed to her death remains a mystery.

Nadezhda (Nadya) had undoubtedly been important to Khrushchev, for he himself said years later that his promotions at this time were due more to Stalin's wife and to Stalin than to Kaganovich: "She sang my praises to Stalin, and Stalin told Kaganovich to help me along." More than that, Khrushchev said she literally saved his life, saved him from the death that awaited most of his friends and classmates at the academy. Khrushchev mused, "Why did I escape the fate which they suffered? I think part of the answer is that Nadya's reports helped determine Stalin's attitude toward me. I call it my lottery ticket. . . . It was because of her that Stalin trusted me."[4] He may well have been right.

As he progressed upward from office to office in Moscow, Khrushchev began to be Stalin's guest at parties and, by the time he was made First Secretary of Moscow in 1934, he was a regular dinner guest. By then Nadya was dead, but his luck held nevertheless. Obviously, he made his own luck as he went along. Two stories tell the tale. The first concerns Khrushchev's major role in the building of the Moscow subway system, or *metro*, a grandiose project that was pushed at a frenetic pace with great disregard for safety in order to have a beautiful monument to the Soviet revolution ready in time for its seventeenth anniversary. Khrushchev, with no experience in construction, acted as chief foreman and even as engineer when technical difficulties stalled the digging. A book published to commemorate Khrushchev's role says that

all engineers . . . and shock workers . . . know Nikita Sergeyevich . . . he visits the construction

---

[2] A. S. Alliluyeva, *Vospominania* [Recollections] (Moscow, 1946), p. 153; quoted in Pistrak, *Grand Tactician*, p. 64.
[3] *Khrushchev Remembers*, 1: 291.

[4] Ibid., 1: 44.

311

sites every day, gives instructions daily, checks, criticizes, encourages, advises one or the other shaft chief, one or the other Party organizer, on concrete urgent questions.[5]

Once, in a scene reminiscent of the Great Leap Forward in Mao's China, Khrushchev ordered the crew of a Soviet-made mud shield to dig forward faster than the imported English shield (which was itself being pushed forward at three times its designed rate). Serious accidents occurred, but they did not slow down the politicized schedule. Leaders and led were locked together in a purposive drama of transformation, arduous, grueling, and cruel, but inspiring nevertheless. Here he was learning what was to become a permanent and fundamental part of his political style: "the stimulation of initiative through inspirational leadership." [6] He brought to industrial society the style of an earlier age. Although he was a party bureaucrat, he could act as a village elder. He was not a grey, blurred "clerk" of the system, as is his successor, Brezhnev.

The second story that humorously illustrates Khrushchev's direct involvement in people's lives is that of the "toilet affair." One day in 1934, Khrushchev got an unexpected personal telephone call from Stalin, who brought up a basic problem. "Comrade Khrushchev," he said, "rumors have reached me that you've let a very unfavorable situation develop in Moscow as regards public toilets. Apparently people hunt around desperately and can't find anywhere to relieve themselves. This won't do. . . . do something to improve these conditions."

Khrushchev recounts that "Bulganin and I began to work feverishly. We personally inspected buildings and courtyards. We also booted the militia [uniformed police] off their behinds and got them to help." [7]

Khrushchev told this story seriously and implied he considered it as an important accomplishment. He had become an integral part of the transformational process directed by Stalin and was to serve well his two masters, the goal of Soviet industrial socialism and Stalin, its designer, through the next four perilous years. This was the period of the great terror, or the blood purges, when Stalin added much of the party itself and many new Soviet institutions to his enemies list. The end result was the elimination of even the possibility of organized opposition, the magnification of his control over society and the establishment of his undisputed sway over even the political elite.

During this period Khrushchev both accumulated his own following of clients from a larger and larger area and inspired his own personality cult on Stalin's example. Stalin made him the First Secretary of the Moscow City Party Committee and a member of the Central Committee in 1934, and in 1935 he became First Secretary of the Moscow Province Committee as well. Khrushchev got the job of his former patron, Kaganovich, who was shifted to work in the governmental apparatus, a move that eventually weakened Kaganovich's political position irreparably. Under Stalin it did not matter much in which of the system's supporting organizations one served. But after Stalin's death, Khrushchev's revitalization of the party made it once again the master political organization.

In 1938, Khrushchev was made a candidate, or second-echelon, member of the Politburo, and just one year later he went as high as one could go in Stalin's lifetime, to full

[5] *Istoria metro Moskvy* [History of the Moscow Subway] (Moscow, 1935), 1: 38–39; quoted in Pistrak, *Grand Tactician,* p. 88.

[6] George W. Breslauer, "Transformation and Adaptation in the Soviet Union since Stalin," in Karl W. Ryavec, ed., *Adaptation and Continuity: The Soviet Communist Party Today,* forthcoming.

[7] *Khrushchev Remembers,* 1: 62–63.

membership in the Politburo. He did not attain these heights on the basis of merit alone, for that was never enough in Stalin's time. Khrushchev was one of the first men to use terms like *vozhd* (chief, führer) and *genius* for Stalin. He also was early in putting the term *enemy of the people* into use during the great purges, a series of events from which he profited and in which he may have been actively involved. "From 1938 onwards he . . . was . . . an important part of the terror machine," claimed one biographer.[8]

He came to employ a large staff of experts that kept him informed on all aspects of Soviet life and maintained ties with his growing following within the apparatus and in governmental agencies. He began, too, to enjoy the material perquisites of power in the Soviet Union, the large apartments, country homes (*dachas*), and chauffeured cars. Khrushchev even changed history in his own interest: the official "short course" history of the party stated falsely that at the time of the revolution Khrushchev had been one of the party leaders, while the truth is that he had not yet even joined the party. He achieved this eminence on the bodies of those who had been the real revolutionaries in 1917 and as a result of the deaths of millions of others, some of whom were forced to confess that they were foreign spies. Khrushchev said of the victims:

By lifting their hand against Comrade Stalin, they lifted it against the best humanity possesses. For Stalin is our hope, he is the beacon which guides all progressive humanity. Stalin is our banner. Stalin is our victory![9]

The Bolshevik party had been transformed by 1937. Its leading members now were Stalin, his security chief of the mo-

ment, his old cronies, and various new men such as Kaganovich. The rest were people who were paid off with jobs and other patronage. After his retirement Khrushchev said of this period:

Since . . . every promotion or transfer of Party personnel had to be made in accordance with directives from the NKVD, the Party lost its guiding role. . . .

All you had to do was submit a report denouncing him [anyone] as an enemy of the people; the local Party organization would glance at your report, beat its breast in righteous indignation, and have the man taken care of.

In those days we still had absolute faith in Stalin. . . . We thought we lacked Stalin's deep understanding of the political struggle and were therefore unable to discern enemies in our midst the way Stalin could.[10]

After all, Khrushchev and his coworkers were unlettered men who had been quickly lifted high out of the mud of backward villages in an authoritarian society. What Stalin was developing looked better in their eyes than what had been. Why should they have protested? It would have been completely out of character.

Back to the Ukraine

Khrushchev returned to the country's breadbasket in January 1938 as a powerful political figure with a small organization of his own men. He was the new First Secretary of the second largest Soviet republic and came with the ability to understand the language. He claimed later that he had been "reluctant" to accept the position, but had

[8] Crankshaw, *Khrushchev: A Career*, p. 115.
[9] Paloczi-Horvath, *Khrushchev*, p. 89.

[10] *Khrushchev Remembers*, 1: 82, 83, 93.

been forcefully told by Stalin, "No more argument. You're going to the Ukraine." [11]

Unable to refuse Stalin's offer, Khrushchev was soon embarked on a sea of risks. He was leaving the center of intrigue and losing the chance to see Stalin daily. He was also letting himself be held accountable for everything that occurred in the second most important part of the country. The two risks could explode together and almost did. Lavrenti Beria, Stalin's last security police chief, kept a so-called black file of derogatory material on all leading personalities. Very soon after Khrushchev got to the Ukraine, Beria had one of his supporters arrested and tortured in hopes he would denounce Khrushchev as part of a conspiracy. However, somehow Beria was unable to carry through; Khrushchev's man was released, but returned "beaten up, crippled in body and spirit." [12] Beria might try again at any time.

Advantages did exist for Khrushchev because, as he said, the party in the Ukraine had been "demolished" during the purges, and he was able to reconstitute it to his own liking. Enlarging his following and establishing another territorial base for himself in addition to Moscow, he created a personality cult of his own: "In a word . . . Khrushchev in Kiev did as well as, if not better than, Stalin in Moscow. By 1940 he had an instrument exactly suited to his will." [13] While plucking advantage out of risk, Khrushchev was allowed a means of carrying out Stalin's will and also of continuing that murderous rivalry among the lieutenants that protected Stalin. Khrushchev had to, and now could, counter the clique from the Caucasus and elsewhere.

Khrushchev unleased another characteris-

tic burst of energy, visiting factories, farms, military units, and schools, meeting their leading people, and inquiring into their work. He even took a deeply personal role in improving tank production by pressing for introduction of the ideas of scientists that he discovered. He issued orders and advice in torrents and made his imprint. Soon the Ukraine was his, and not long after it was actually enlarged, giving him greater scope and power.

The Western Ukraine, then a part of Poland (known as Galicia), was annexed as a major Soviet gain resulting from the pact with Nazi Germany concluded in August 1939. Stalin in effect rejected the possibility of an alliance with Britain, which had a negotiating team in Moscow at the time. Perhaps only another dictatorship could give the USSR half of Poland as a buffer zone, the rest of the Ukrainians, and a breathing spell as well for war preparations.

The Ukrainians had lost a foreign example of a milder form of rule, and all were now together under Stalin. It fell to Khrushchev to Sovietize a large part of the new territory. This work gave him thousands of new party and state positions to fill as he saw fit, a real boost to his already greatly increased power. Again he was lucky, for his new Soviet "citizens," who had last seen Russians in tsarist uniforms, failed in their attempt to kill him with a bomb.

The Western Ukraine, containing 8 million people, required extensive Sovietizing: "All former state and local government officials, industrialists, merchants, landowners, bank employees, teachers, lawyers, judges, were summarily arrested and in most cases were deported together with their families [to Siberia and the camps]." [14] Polish and Ukrainian communists were treated badly, as were, of course, socialists. The Western

[11] Ibid., 1: 106.
[12] Ibid., 1: 108.
[13] Crankshaw, *Khrushchev: A Career*, p. 122.

[14] Paloczi-Horvath, *Khrushchev*, p. 99.

Ukraine was then overrun by Khrushchev's appointees. The same process was repeated, but on a smaller scale, in mid-1940 when the Soviet Union annexed territory from Rumania after threatening it with an ultimatum. This land also was given to the Ukraine. With additional land Khrushchev gained additional political influence.

War

On June 22, 1941, Stalin's hopes were shattered when his allies, the Germans, attacked the Soviet Union. At first there were massive defections to the Germans by Soviet troops, particularly Western Ukrainians. Stalin retired from command and probably from Moscow for two weeks under the shock; some say he suffered a nervous breakdown. Stalin seems to have believed the German system superior to his own and to have sat transfixed, "paralyzed by his fear of Hitler, like a rabbit in front of a boa constrictor." [15] He is supposed to have said at the time that he had been left a real country by Lenin, but he had botched it so badly that nothing good was left. Khrushchev claimed in his memoirs that he had warned Stalin that the Germans would attack, but, one biographer asserts, "there is no evidence at all that in those days Khrushchev took an active interest in foreign affairs." [16] Khrushchev himself admitted that Stalin never consulted him or even told him anything about foreign policy.

Why did the Nazi government turn against its ally? The rapid German conquest of France—due in part to Russia's not being on its side, as in World War I—had freed Germany for new adventures in the east.

And the failure of the Russian attack on small Finland in 1939 had shown how ineffectual the Soviet military was. Khrushchev speaks of the Soviet soldiers as "poor fellows" who "were ripped to shreds" by the Finns: "I'd say we lost as many as a million lives. . . . In short, our miserable conduct of the Finnish campaign encouraged Hitler in his plans for the blitzkrieg." [17] The purges of the Soviet military during the 1930s had cut deep. Finally, Stalin had rejected all warnings of German plans, whether from the British, the Americans, German deserters, or even his own intelligence. He had trusted the fellow dictator above others.

But due to a combination of ineffectual pseudogeneralship by Hitler and eventual dogged resistance, particularly by Russians, the invaders were brought to a standstill. By mid-1943 the tide had turned. Showing a new confidence, the Soviet leadership returned to its ideologically based prewar hostility against its recent allies, Britain and the United States. Stalin's plans had turned out well after all, but for reasons he had not taken into account. Japan's attack on Pearl Harbor had brought the United States into the war on the Soviet side, and the Russians (not all the ethnic groups by any means) had stood by the government's side in order to defend Russia from the latest Germanic depredations. Stalin even had encouraged traditional Russian nationalism by reconstituting the Orthodox church and using tsarist symbols, even to the extent of renaming units for saints and holding mass prayers at historic monuments for troops moving to the front. Holy Russia rose to defend Marxism. This important shift in policy raised high hopes among the Soviet population that once the war was over, the regime would relent in its drive to achieve communism. The hopes were to be disappointed.

---

[15] *Khrushchev Remembers,* 1: 169.
[16] Crankshaw, *Khrushchev: A Career,* p. 130.

[17] *Khrushchev Remembers,* 1: 153, 155, 156.

During the war Khrushchev increased his influence greatly through his work with the military. Indeed, the war was a time when the party and the military came again to terms with one another as their members risked all together, and Khrushchev played a large role in this process. Given general's rank and attached to the army command in the Ukraine, he made certain Stalin's orders were carried out (sometimes trying to reason with Stalin or his underlings when a particularly stupid or costly order was issued) and checked on the loyalty of the military leaders. Although tension was inherent in his role, he came to develop close ties with some of the generals and marshals. Khrushchev was also instrumental in establishing

a guerrilla movement behind enemy lines and keeping it supplied. Despite the lack of military preparedness and corruption by power at the top, the party was reformed and met the challenge of the invader—but mostly on the bases of Russian patriotism and traditional defense of the land. Khrushchev was a major figure in this successful effort, though not without perpetrating some military blunders on his own. He developed further as a leader during the war and now could not avoid seeing humanity suffer, something he either missed or shielded himself from during the purges.

At the end, when the blackened ruins of Berlin had been seized, the Soviet Union, Stalin, and Khrushchev were in a qualita-

Khrushchev in the Ukraine, at the time of liberation, 1943

(Life Magazine Collection)

tively different position than before. They
had endured the ultimate test of politics and
survived. The Soviet Union stood out as
the major European power. Germany and
Japan were utterly defeated. France was
only a freed prisoner. Britain only seemed
a victor, having been impoverished and
gravely weakened. China was not yet reconstituted and remained on the verge of civil
war. Only the United States, which had provided the Soviets with about 10 billion dollars worth of food, clothing, and armaments,
was a major world power. The Soviet
Union, which previously had been kept
within the borders of the tsarist empire, was
now to expand beyond them, a fact that in
itself justified the regime to many in the
Soviet elite and the middle class. Keeping
the territories it had seized while allied with
Nazi Germany, the Soviet Union added
those it had occupied in driving the Germans
back, including part of Germany itself. The
attempts to gain a United Nations trustee-
ship in Africa, take parts of Iran and Turkey, and acquire a role in the occupation of
Italy and Japan were frustrated by the United
States, but this was only a minor setback.
The Soviet Union was coming to have a new,
global role that was to be limited only temporarily by American power, the exigencies
of reconstruction, and the situation in the
underdeveloped world. Was a destiny being
fulfilled? If so, was that destiny Marxism's
or Russia's? Khrushchev would be very busy
with foreign affairs one day.

The last time a Russian army had poured
into Europe—in 1815 to crush Napoleon—
it had been only an equal in a broad coalition of powers. This time, in 1945, it was
the strongest European power on the winning
side, and it also had erased seven hundred
years of German history. Khrushchev and
the Soviet people knew that they had made,
at horrendous cost, an historic breakthrough.

The cost sanctified the victory and the system
that had achieved it for them. But at the
end of the war the gains had to be consolidated, the destruction of war cleared away,
the economy rebuilt, and the people's livelihood restored. This gave Khrushchev much
to do.

Postwar Reconstruction and Recompression

Stalin had repeatedly told his wartime allies
that only democratic governments would be
allowed to exist in eastern central Europe.
The allies agreed, also wanting democratic
governments there. Stalin's definition of
democracy differed from theirs, however.
These new "people's democracies" were to
be made part and parcel of the enlarged
Soviet system economically, politically, and
even culturally. (Khrushchev was to have
to deal with the Eastern European problems
that resulted more than once.) The postwar
repression in Eastern Europe was accompanied by a similar one at home.

In the Soviet Union the implicit wartime
compact between regime and people broke
down soon after the war. The party was
purged of many of the soldiers who had
been invited to join only a few short years
previously. The leadership had a paranoid
fear of all who had even seen the hated
West. Soldiers who had been captured by
the Germans were often imprisoned as traitors (since anyone who had been associated
with Germans must be a traitor). Even
those who had had to communicate with foreigners as part of their work were suspect
and often were arrested and sent to the
camps. Soviet society, so lately given hope
of relaxation, was being forcibly pressed
back into the Stalinist mold.

Khrushchev played an important role in this political-economic reconstruction. Again his major base of operations was the Ukraine, where he even had to wage a bitter counter-revolutionary war against hundreds of thousands of anti-Soviet guerrillas.[18] In this effort he acted more as a general than as a party secretary, though the merger of the two roles shows how powerful a party apparatchik can become. Armed popular resistance to Soviet rule continued into 1948 in both the Ukraine and Poland. The Soviet Union could not grant a special status to the Ukraine while it was Sovietizing eastern central Europe and facing the onset of the probably inevitable Cold War. Even the eventual Soviet victories over Ukrainian and Eastern European popular sentiments did not bring a domestic relaxation, and the atmosphere became even tenser and more heated with the launching of a campaign against what was called cosmopolitanism, or Western culture. This campaign was known as the *Zhdanovshchina,* after Andrei Zhdanov, one of Stalin's "counter-heirs" who had been sent to the Leningrad area to do what Khrushchev was doing in the southwest. Zhdanov was engaged in a power struggle with Khrushchev's opponent, Georgi Malenkov, but he was by no means Khrushchev's ally.

Some think that if Zhdanov had not died in mid-1948, both Malenkov and Khrushchev would have lost out in the struggle for Stalin's post. Zhdanov was "Stalin's natural heir" by virtue of his toughness and cleverness in carrying through a politics of Stalinist principle.

Zhdanov passionately believed that the Soviet people had to be saved from the corruption of the West . . . , that there must be a fight to the finish with the United States over . . . Europe, and all his actions were informed by a savage

rejection of Western influence and by an equally savage belief in Russian messianism [perfectionism] expressed in Marxist terms.[19]

He represented the total rejection of the "corrupt" West that periodically figures in Russian and Soviet politics of both left and right. Khrushchev was not immune to this feeling. Under Zhdanov a strident campaign against Jews and foreigners was begun, and history was rewritten to suit nationalist goals. Supposedly, Russians had invented the telephone and countless other things besides. The campaign had a political logic: Russians had to be told their victory was neither a fluke nor a result of American aid.

Khrushchev did not yet clearly represent a definite set of ideas, policies, or principles, although he seemed to represent a particular style or approach to problems. He and his people stood out because they got outside party offices, saw actual economic and social processes in operation, and reacted to them pragmatically. But the furthest Khrushchev then went toward a new departure were his two minor ideas for further communizing agriculture: working the land by big brigades instead of links, or small groups, and replacing the traditional peasant villages by "agrotowns" of apartment houses away from the farmland. This Maoist-type vision was the first of the "harebrained" schemes that were ultimately to contribute to his political downfall.

Khrushchev was now out of Moscow in the field, extraordinarily busy with suppressing guerrilla warfare and encouraging economic and political reconstruction. People in the Ukraine were dressed in rags, living in holes in the ground. The party had been decimated during the war, and the cities had

[18] Paloczi-Horvath, *Khrushchev,* p. 108.

[19] Crankshaw, *Khrushchev: A Career,* pp. 160–161.

been completely destroyed. Khrushchev found that "the whole cruel business of sovietization had to be gone through a second time." [20] This left him at the mercy of intrigues at the center. One of his competitors was Andrei Andreyev, who was in overall charge of agriculture (naturally one of Khrushchev's major concerns in the Ukraine) and was also a member of the Politburo and the national Party Secretariat. "Dim but tough," Andreyev came to be Khrushchev's major critic at Stalin's elbow.

Khrushchev's opponents were given their chance by that periodic enemy of agriculture, drought. The worst one since 1890 occurred in the Ukraine in 1946, resulting in a famine of classic dimensions. Once more Ukrainians were starving. Obviously, Khrushchev was vulnerable. Andreyev announced to the Central Committee that unspecified "serious failures" had occurred in Ukrainian agriculture. Khrushchev was relieved as First Secretary of the Party in the Ukraine by Kaganovich, his former patron. It must have been both galling and frightening to Khrushchev to have become a potential sacrifice to the rain gods of Bolshevism.

But Khrushchev survived the threat. Although he dropped completely out of sight for six months, usually a sure sign of complete political failure, he surprisingly reemerged with his old job as Ukrainian First Secretary at the end of 1947. Kaganovich was recalled to Moscow. This must have been a period of feverish behind-the-scenes activity for Khrushchev, reestablishing his special relationship with Kaganovich and somehow regaining Stalin's favor. His considerable body of supporters had to fight back for him or lose out themselves. They may have split some of the anti-Khrushchev people away from Malenkov. Perhaps Stalin felt Khrushchev was an indispensable coun-

terpoise to Malenkov and Andreyev, who were constantly intriguing around him in the Kremlin, and so recalled Khrushchev from the shadows. Obviously, Khrushchev had become a consummate politician to have pulled victory from what was usually certain defeat.

As soon as Khrushchev regained his viceroy-like position, he purged those whom Malenkov and Andreyev had inserted into the Ukrainian party apparatus during his enforced absence and reinstalled his own followers. Purge followed purge. He rebuilt his power base quickly, and in December 1949 he left the Ukrainian first secretaryship for good, being called to Moscow as the boss of both the Moscow city and regional party organizations and, much more important, with a secretaryship of the national party Secretariat.

Ostensibly the Secretariat is only the staff of the Central Committee, but since the early 1920s it has been the main agency used by the leader or the Politburo for running the party, the government, and society as well. When the majority of the members of the Politburo are Secretariat members, the Secretariat rules. When the majority of the Politburo's members are not on the Secretariat, the Politburo has pride of place and is most powerful, while the Secretariat then serves as its controlling linkage with the rest of the party, the government departments (the ministries), and societal groupings and social processes.

Khrushchev may have been called to Moscow to restore the balance among the leaders that was destroyed by Zhdanov's death and the resulting "Leningrad affair," when Zhdanov's supporters were purged and hundreds were executed. (Kosygin, the present Premier, was one of those then purged.) Malenkov seems to have been behind this. Khrushchev returned to Moscow as a counterweight to Malenkov and in the bargain got

[20] Ibid., p. 151.

the job of his former competitor, Andreyev. Khrushchev was now in overall charge of agriculture in the Soviet Union as well as having several top party posts. The men who mattered now were, first, Stalin; second, V. M. Molotov, the old Bolshevik who was his long-time associate; then Malenkov, the boss of the party apparatus; and finally Beria, the police chief who also was in charge of Soviet nuclear weapons development. Khrushchev was now clearly in the inner circle, having amassed considerable support in the Moscow area, in the Ukraine, and among the top military. As his reappearance from disgrace and his long-time rule of the Ukraine proved, he had considerable political capability and administrative experience. Khrushchev had already shown he could succeed Stalin because he had established himself as "a human being of a certain boldness and certain independence of mind, a man who had broken out of the tight, self-regarding circle of the higher Party leadership and could go among the people and show a certain awareness of the country's needs." [21]

Stalin's Last Play

Doubtless Khrushchev might still have been consigned to political oblivion and even death. In the last year of his life, Stalin was hatching a grand scheme of the sort only he could dream up and dare to execute. Put most simply, he was planning to put all of Soviet society, including the party leadership, once again through the mill of a great blood terror. Suddenly, in January 1953, only a

few months after the Politburo had been renamed the Presidium and expanded to a size that precluded unified action, a group of physicians who had been the doctors for Stalin and the Politburo were arrested. This "terrorist" group of nine, seven of them Jews, was charged with being in the employ of Zionist organizations and United States intelligence and with plotting the deaths of the leadership. According to Khrushchev's "secret speech" denouncing Stalin three years later, "Stalin evidently had plans to finish off the old members of the Politburo" who were to be charged with complicity in the plot.[22] Whether Khrushchev would have been so charged is not known. Certainly Beria was a target, for the Soviet press accused the Ministry of State Security of "lack of vigilance." Some think that Malenkov and Khrushchev were meant to survive and that among the leaders Molotov, Beria, K. E. Voroshilov, Kaganovich, and maybe Anastas Mikoyan were to be liquidated.[23] Exactly what Stalin was trying to prove no one can say.

Stalin wanted a confession fast and ordered the doctors beaten. Some did "confess," and two died under torture. In the midst of this grandiose attempt, Stalin died on March 5, 1953, at age seventy-three, and the members of the Soviet leadership were freed from a burden that had weighed on some of them for three decades. Khrushchev had felt it for more than twenty years. He was not totally free, however. Although Stalin had been a threat to him, he had also been a protector. Khrushchev now had to depend on himself alone, for his rivals were very much alive.

---

21 Ibid., p. 171.

22 Quoted in ibid., p. 186.
23 Paloczi-Horvath, *Khrushchev,* p. 128.

5

Khrushchev at the Top: Chance and Challenge in Moscow

At first Stalin's successors seemed to stick together, calling for "the prevention of any kind of disorder and panic," even trying absurdly to fit themselves always into the same limousine so no one could ride ahead of the others.

Maybe they had come together at the last moment to save themselves from the tyrant's paranoid scheme. Political maneuverings of some sort began before Stalin was dead, indicating a possibility that his death was contrived or hastened by his intended victims. The general who served as chief of Kremlin security had died suddenly a few weeks earlier. Khrushchev claimed Beria had been speaking "disrespectfully and even insultingly about Stalin" for quite a while and had been trying to trick him into making an anti-Stalin statement: "However, I was familiar with Beria's treachery, so I listened but never said anything. I never closed my ears, but I never opened my mouth either."[1] But Sta-

lin's daughter Svetlana accepts his death as a natural one.

After Stalin's death, intrigue was incessant. Now a combination began to develop against Beria, the man feared most by the others because of his control of the security police.

The Succession Struggle: One Leader or Many

Fears of Beria were not without reason, because he had Moscow under his personal control before Stalin's death had been announced. His paramilitary police had sealed off the city; the army was neutralized; and the military commanders of the Moscow military district, the city garrison, and the Kremlin were all placed under arrest. Beria could have taken over then and there, but he chose to make himself popular through amnesties and the abolition of the most infa-

[1] *Khrushchev Remembers,* 1: 314.

mous forced labor camps. His police powers made him a serious threat to his colleagues. Although Beria may not have been an active conspirator against his colleagues, "all his actions justified his enemies in describing him as such." [2] He corresponded with his underlings in a personal code and was most uncooperative toward Khrushchev and the others. Once Stalin's private secretary and his staff had been removed, a plot against Beria was developed. Khrushchev said he told Bulganin of the threat Beria posed and urged that he be removed "absolutely no matter what!" [3]

But Beria was not confronted immediately. The first order of business for the top men was to eliminate those new politicos recently brought into the limelight, an action accomplished with Beria's security police troops acting as a guard. Five members of the Secretariat and twenty-two members of the enlarged Presidium (formerly the Politburo) were summarily removed. Brezhnev (a Khrushchev man not liked by Malenkov) and Kosygin, now in the Politburo, were among those downgraded. The new, smaller ruling group was ostensibly led by Malenkov as both Premier and the preeminent Party Secretary. (An altered photograph appeared in the Soviet press showing Stalin, Mao, and Malenkov together.) Beria was second, whereas Khrushchev was fourth or fifth in the Presidium and second in the Party Secretariat. The new leaders tried to appease the Soviet population by granting an amnesty to many in the prison camps, the army by giving Marshal Georgi Zhukov an important post, and the West by stressing peace and peaceful coexistence. (Soon some movement in drawing the Korean War to an end was apparent.)

[2] Victor Alexandrov, *Khrushchev of the Ukraine* (London: Gollancz, 1957), p. 111.
[3] *Khrushchev Remembers*, 1: 319.

Malenkov was able to dominate both party and state for only about two weeks. By mid-March he resigned his post as First Secretary of the Party. This was obviously a forced resignation, though it is possible Malenkov thought that, based on Stalin's last years, the state premiership was the more important office and so retained it. The resignation allowed Khrushchev to move up to First Secretary in fact although he was not formally given that title for several months.

At fifty-nine, Khrushchev now had the main political position in the country, but he faced three problems in trying to convert it into effective power. First, it seemed that the state bureaucracy had become supreme and that the party had been relegated to a subordinate, perhaps ceremonial, status. Therefore, Khrushchev had to reestablish the party as the prime political instrument. Second, then, he had to begin appointing his own people to party posts and to restore the party's spirit as the prime activist force in politics. Third, Beria stood in his way. But since he was in the way of everyone else at the top as well, it was possible to put together a clique to remove him. Beria perhaps did not realize that his power existed only before a combination could be called forth against him and that he lacked any basis of support outside the security police despite some belated efforts to gain popularity. Stalin's former engine of mass torture and death had no legitimacy. Thus, every day that passed saw more of both the aggrieved and the fearful arraying against Beria. Khrushchev won Malenkov and most of the Presidium's members to his side although, to hear Khrushchev tell it, Malenkov was always a waverer and Mikoyan, a native of the Caucasus as was Beria, was on the best of terms with him. The old Bolshevik Molotov, who had been in Petrograd in 1917 even before Stalin and Lenin, knew all that had ever happened in Soviet politics and accordingly took a realistic view of the situation. Removal of Beria from his posts was not enough, he said; "I think we must, so to say, resort to more extreme measures." [4]

Their chance came with the workers' riots in East Germany in June 1953. The secret policeman Beria was more liberal than his colleagues and had relaxed controls in the Soviet satellites of Eastern Europe and in the nationality areas of the Soviet Union. The riots, really a rebellion, made Beria appear indecisive. At this point Khrushchev, cashing in on his good relationship with the military, brought Marshal Zhukov and a number of other high-ranking military men into the plot. They were most willing to even the old scores dating from the 1930s and to make certain that the satellites for which they had fought a bitter war remained a Soviet buffer zone. Accordingly, at a Presidium meeting in the Kremlin, Beria was denounced by the other members, Khrushchev first. At the appropriate moment they called in the military men who seized Beria and spirited him out past his own bewildered guards and to a military base. He and six lieutenants were shot sometime between late June and mid-July 1953, although the execution was not announced until December. Ironically, one of the charges against him was that he might have been a British agent in the Caucasus during the civil war. Now the Soviet political elite was truly free for the first time in twenty years or more.

This continuing problem with Germany was to have a hand in unseating Khrushchev as well, eleven years later. The possibility of losing East Germany and of its recombining with West Germany raises in Soviet minds, particularly those of the military, the specter of a real rival to the Soviet Union in Europe. The present Soviet elite has worked

[4] Ibid., 1: 333.

hard to avoid this possibility in its recent treaties with the West settling the borders in Europe (the Helsinki Accords).

Implications for the Security Police and the Military

Since 1954 the security police (now the KGB) has been firmly under the party's control, although this has not rendered it weak. The Soviet masses as well as dissident intellectuals still have good reason to fear it, but the political leadership does not. It is still a formidable espionage force abroad and even conducts some diplomatic activities. Since Beria's removal, top positions in the security police are generally reserved to persons in the party apparatus, the last two heads of the police having been former leaders in the main party youth organization, the *Komsomol* (Communist Union of Youth). This policy is designed to prevent purely police types from ever again rivaling the party apparatus. (The recent downgrading of Alexander Shelepin, a politician who formerly supervised the police, indicates that these new party supervisors of the security forces are also unable to maintain their political positions.) A definite change in Soviet politics is reflected, and Khrushchev deserves a real share of the responsibility for achieving it.

Although Khrushchev weakened the security police, he made the military leadership more important politically. Perhaps he had no alternative: when one uses organizational instruments of violence against each other, there are few choices. Luckily for Khrushchev then and the party later, although there is a tsarist-Soviet tradition of honoring the military life and military leaders, the military as a social grouping has tended not to take a leadership role in politics in its own right. It lacks its own socioeconomic base, unlike the Latin American military. Instead it has been, beginning in the Khrushchev years, a major organized claimant on the economy and has pressured the leadership to uphold and strengthen the Soviet position abroad. Nevertheless, when Khrushchev and the others called in armed marshals and generals to seize Beria, they were changing Soviet politics. A new group was now entering the political arena and would enter again in 1957, also at Khrushchev's call. By 1964 the military could decide on its own whether to enter politics or not, and on whose side. In that year they "entered" politics by standing aside while Khrushchev was himself removed. Khrushchev eliminated one monster, but built up what might someday be another. Such are the unavoidable risks at the top. It is to his credit as a politician that he acted and did not shrink from taking risks.

The Next Move: The Removal of Malenkov

The blow at Beria was defensive. Now Khrushchev moved to the offensive—against Stalin's designated heir, Malenkov. A roly-poly man of middle-class origins, he had played a key role as head of the Secretariat's Cadres Administration in manipulating the party records for Stalin and had thus facilitated the purging of old Bolsheviks and top party cadres during the 1930s. Accordingly, Malenkov, too, had many enemies within the party and the military.

Khrushchev had been demanding and cruel toward the population, but had a somewhat better record of behavior vis-à-vis his fellow apparatchiks. Perhaps he did not believe in killing his opponents, but possibly he acted differently because he lacked Stalin's power. At any rate, though he had killed for Stalin, he did not kill for himself. This may not seem a great distinction, but it nevertheless was significant in Russo-Soviet history. He did try later to have those opposed to

him expelled from the party, but was usually frustrated by his colleagues, probably because they did not really believe Khrushchev could be trusted to refrain from acting as Stalin had. It will never be known whether they were right.

He came by his crudity and toughness naturally. Peasant life may have made him suspicious of others, secretive of motive and action, willing to resort to violence—but mainly when it was necessary to defend himself or to realize some goal that he felt justified force. He did not believe in hurting people physically without its serving or seeming to serve some overriding purpose. One of his biographers suggests that he had been affected by the rough-and-tumble Ukrainian Cossack political tradition in which public opinion played a role.[5] Thus he was not committed to unchanging totalitarian despotism of the Stalinist variety and displayed a certain flexibility. Though somewhat humanistic, it did not, however encompass liberal—much less participatory—democracy.

Malenkov made himself even more vulnerable by taking a position that has arisen at intervals in the history of the Bolshevik party, but has never been generally accepted within the movement's leadership: the position that socialism in the Soviet Union had been fundamentally built. Thus Malenkov announced that the country would now develop "the light and food industries at the same rate as heavy industry."[6] This was a policy of the profoundest importance. If it could be held to, it meant that material, financial, and human investment could now be reduced for heavy industry (and, by implication, for weaponry) and more resources devoted instead to consumer goods and light

---

[5] Alexandrov, *Khrushchev of the Ukraine*, p. 139.
[6] Quoted in Paloczi-Horvath, *Khrushchev*, p. 155.

industry. Taken on top of his earlier statements that a nuclear war would end civilization, this stand deeply disturbed ideologues, conservatives, Russian nationalists, and the military. The fact that the Malenkov New Course, as the policy was called, led to another loosening of controls in Eastern Europe was also of concern to them. Their concerns were not unjustified. The Soviet Union still did not match the United States militarily, and nationalistic, anti-Soviet feelings had been revived in the satellites, leading to the Hungarian Revolution and the political changes in Poland of 1956.

What was at stake was not only ideological orthodoxy, but jobs and power. Any shift in investment meant that patronage would no longer be available in the areas of the economy formerly favored, that tens of thousands of new jobs would be created in new sectors, and that Malenkov would create and fill them. Jobs would be lost, too, with the military being a possible target for a massive reduction in force.

Malenkov was trying to appear to the common people to be dominant over the established institutions of power: the party apparatus led by Khrushchev, the military, the state planning apparatus, and the managers of heavy industry. All had been committed to the unthinking production of more and more metal, heavy machinery, and weapons for a quarter century. They stood to lose personnel, funds, prestige, and thus power.

Malenkov could have won if the Soviet constitution had been observed, for he had the approval of the Supreme Soviet, the national legislature, and perhaps of the people as well. He might also have won if he had been willing to force an open clash or stage a coup, using the mechanisms of power in the state that he commanded against his opposition. However, this latter

sort of move might also have failed. Stalin had casehardened Soviet society and politics against easy or rapid reform. Khrushchev knew this, was the better politician, and seems to have taken Malenkov's measure as a man long before. Khrushchev claimed that Malenkov had never been more than an "errand boy" and "clerk" and cited Stalin as saying that Malenkov "has no capacity at all for independent thought or initiative." [7] Malenkov the bureaucrat had been too long a shuffler of papers, dependent on formal state institutions, allowing Khrushchev the politician to put together a coalition against him. The politician won over the bureaucrat. Whether Khrushchev already knew he would soon adopt Malenkov's position is an open question. If he did, he had determined that he, and no one else, would carry the idea of reform forward to victory. Khrushchev charged that Malenkov's policy would weaken the Soviet Union before the West, cast doubt on the main achievements of Soviet history, destroy the party, and raise the danger of a new Stalin. Malenkov had spoken of basic change too early. Khrushchev was now to try. He, like Stalin and Lenin earlier, was to steal the ideas of his opponents and use them for his own political needs.

In February 1955, Malenkov was removed from the premiership by a coalition of Khrushchev's followers and Stalinist types such as Molotov. In his resignation, he engaged in the self-criticism required of the fallen in Leninist regimes. One is often not allowed to creep out of power, but must attack one's own position as well, thus discouraging supporters and discrediting oneself historically. Although he had been one of the top five rulers during the war, he cited his "lack of experience in State work" and even had to

[7] *Khrushchev Remembers,* 1: 323.

take the blame for Khrushchev's failures in agriculture. Khrushchev's political sense of humor had other elements; Malenkov was demoted to Minister of Power Stations. However, he remained on the Council of Ministers and the Party Presidium. Stalinism no longer operated fully, and Soviet politics had advanced to the level of Britain's in 1688: political changes no longer involved deaths of leading personalities. This significant alteration in politics has held to this day, and Khrushchev was heavily responsible for it.

Bulganin, Khrushchev's associate, became Premier, and the primacy of heavy industry in economic policy and of the party in politics was reaffirmed. Khrushchev was now a more powerful First Secretary of the party.

An Attempt at Reform
Khrushchev had long been a realist and, as such, he was a potential reformer. While he had seemed to go against Malenkov's policy totally, it is most likely that he opposed it only in part. He wanted to improve living standards of the population and also to develop Soviet military power. But he was not going to risk a war by harassing the West as would the dogmatist Molotov. Thus, he was hacking out his own position and his own way of giving it effect. In one writer's opinion,

Khrushchev's plan was to postpone Malenkov's measures until equality with or superiority over the West in . . . weapons and means of delivery was achieved, and to prepare the ground for an offensive by a means unknown as yet in . . . Soviet foreign policy, namely personal diplomacy and attacks on the psychology of the world public with waves of intensive propaganda on "peaceful coexistence" coupled with rocket rattling threats.[8]

[8] Pistrak, *Grand Tactician*, p. 252.

In his characteristic style, Khrushchev had already set in motion massive domestic changes. A year before Malenkov was removed, he had launched the grandiose Virgin Lands campaign, putting into cultivation for the first time an area in central Asia and southwestern Siberia that equalled all of the cropland in Britain, France, and Spain. The thinking and approach were typical of Khrushchev. He often attempted to deal with a problem or issue by avoiding the direct approach; instead he would try to take a bold leap beyond it to a new situation that would make the original problem or issue seem insignificant. He would often try this using a minimum of resources, thus disturbing no entrenched interest. (This same sort of inexpensive short cut was taken in Cuba during 1962.) Therefore he used the Young Communist League (Komsomol) to mobilize volunteers in the country's high schools for an expedition to open up huge tracts of farmland in the east without any real provision of machinery or housing. This combination of new blood, new land, and suffering was successful in enlarging the food supply for a few years, until the lack of fertilizer and the dust bowl conditions caused by turning over the semiarid steppe put an end to his dream of a cheap solution of the food problem. But by then he was more powerful and no longer an easy target. He had bought time and further nurtured his successor, Leonid Brezhnev, who was given a chance to run a large-scale operation on his own. (Brezhnev was in charge of the Virgin Lands program in its early successful phase.)

The Virgin Lands put Khrushchev in a spotlight that he never left until his removal ten years later, in 1964. He began traveling all over the Soviet Union, to Eastern Europe and China, and soon outside the Leninist world to India and Britain. Having appointed supporters to key positions across

Khrushchev examining grain at harvest time

(Life Magazine Collection)

the country, he began to place his own people even in diplomatic posts abroad. In 1955 it was clear that Khrushchev had his clients and allies high within the state apparatus that had been so recently run by Malenkov and within the military high command, too. The Party Secretariat had become an actual government within a government. Of the eleven new Marshals appointed a month after Malenkov's fall, the majority had been associated with Khrushchev during the war.

Khrushchev's progress became a more varied and broader process because he began to operate in a dimension new to him, foreign policy and international affairs. "For a decade to come the Khrushchev story was to be the story . . . to a very large degree, of the world." [9]

Khrushchev, the Soviet Union, and the World

Although Khrushchev still refused to admit openly that the struggle between the West and the Soviet Union had to change in character because of the threat of nuclear weaponry, he in fact began to act on that basis in 1955. This does not mean he gave up the anti-Western struggle (whether it is seen as offensive or defensive in nature is a matter of perspective); instead, he found a way to oppose the West and try to weaken it without direct confrontation. Khrushchev rediscovered the Third World, or the underdeveloped countries, so many of which either had been colonies until just recently or were in some stage of the national liberation effort. He rediscovered what Lenin and Trotsky had thought they saw and what even Stalin in his last days had come to see: that the economically developed, capitalist countries could be weakened indirectly, by either wearing them down in colonial guerrilla wars or denying them the raw materials of the Third World countries. The goal was to push the influence of the West back to its source and keep it there.

Khrushchev and Bulganin plunged into this new territory with shirt sleeves rolled up, appearing as anti-capitalist proletarians offering both example and aid. And so began a new form of the Soviet competition with the now weak colonial powers and their supporting ally, the United States. This

[9] Crankshaw, *Khrushchev: A Career,* p. 202.

327

competition was taken by Khrushchev directly to London, once the seat of a great empire rivaling Russia's own, and onto the international stage itself at the summit conference of 1955 at Geneva. Here he got his first look at Western politicians, but even though he could have spoken as the real leader of the Soviet Union, he chose to let Bulganin and Molotov do the talking. He was shocked to find Secretary of State Dulles writing notes that President Eisenhower read "like a dutiful schoolboy taking his lead from his teacher." He thought Eisenhower a "good man, but he wasn't very tough." [10] In London, to which he came on a cruiser to impress the navy-oriented British, he saw his first crowds of people able to vent their opposition to him and his system. "What is that 'oo-oo' sound they make?" he asked of Sir William Hayter, the British Ambassador accompanying him. "It is 'boo-boo,' sir," Hayter replied. Khrushchev's visit to Oxford University must have been an incongruous sight in itself. Fun-loving British students gave him a start, as they kept popping out from behind corners, dressed as Stalin. By the time he got to the United States a few years later, he had a series of caustic replies ready for expressions of anti-Soviet feelings.

The Soviet indirect approach and challenge inevitably became direct, the first major crisis arising in connection with Egypt and the Suez Canal in 1956. The combined armies of Britain, France, and Israel invaded Egypt, which enlisted the Soviet Union to act as its protector and to issue an ultimatum to the invaders. For this and other reasons, including the United States' undermining the offensive through naval interference and a refusal to support British currency, the invasion was ended. (The Soviet Union's brutal suppression of the Hungarians' bid

for independence during this same week was obscured by the Suez Crisis.)

At the same time as the Soviet Union began to export arms and other aid to the Third World in return for influence and limitations on the West, it made some small, but strategic, withdrawals in Europe. In 1955, Soviet troops were withdrawn from Austria, which was allowed to become an independent state again, though permanently a neutral one. Finland was given back some territory. And Khrushchev humbled himself by traveling to Yugoslavia and apologizing to Tito for Stalin's ostracism of that country. These retreats show that the Soviet Union had abandoned much of its ideological bent for revolution, but had instead opted for increased influence and power through the indirect methods given so much drive by Khrushchev.

Of course, these new foreign commitments, including those made to China, put a heavier strain on the Soviet economy and on the individual Soviet citizen-subject. After the Hungarian Revolution of 1956 a "new deal" had to be given to the Eastern European countries, at least economically, thus adding to the already burdened Soviet economy. The Soviet Union became an active participant in a new stage of the Cold War, one that involved both economics and propaganda. It seemed at first to be a less dangerous stage, but the increased points of Soviet involvement led to more crises than had Stalin's rigid isolationism. Khrushchev was risking not only his own future but that of the world.

The Secret Speech and the Anti-Party Group

In 1956, when Khrushchev was sixty-two years old and at an age when many people think of retirement, he took steps to implement his dream of liberating Soviet productive forces from the ancient tsarist-Stalinist

[10] *Khrushchev Remembers,* 1: 397.

deep freeze. But it was a ticklish process to bring this about without simultaneously unleashing a torrent of political rebellion and change as well. He did not want political liberation, something he scorned, perhaps from lack of experience with it. Rather, his aim was one that any dictatorship may reluctantly find to be necessary: increasing productivity and efficiency without letting the aggrieved members of the population take revenge for what the dictatorship had done to them or their relatives. Despite the risk, Khrushchev struck at exactly the main impediment, the adulation or cult of Stalin still enveloping Soviet society like a shroud. This sentiment had created tens of thousands of "little Stalins" who held back progress by freezing all into the limited Stalinist pattern. It appears he struck belatedly, but with full force nevertheless, when it became apparent that others (Mikoyan among them, according to some observers) were to begin to criticize Stalin. The occasion was the Twentieth Party Congress of February 1956. Khrushchev beat his competition to the punch by delivering an hours-long speech to the thousands of assembled party delegates from all over the Soviet Union in which he detailed Stalin's crimes, stupidities, crudities, and errors. The effect was shattering; the party could never be the same again. He had given the party and Soviet politics a new start, but one still within the authoritarian bounds of Leninism, a neat achievement. He also introduced other ideological shifts at the congress. War was declared not to be inevitable and socialism was said to be attainable by various roads, including the peaceful, electoral way.

But a blow at Stalin's ghost, however powerful its psychological effect, did not immediately make the economy more productive, efficient, or responsive to needs. Therefore, Khrushchev had to become an administrative reformer as well, attempting

to decentralize and to move some decision-making authority downward, nearer to the places of work. This was only logical, since much knowledge concerning work exists at the workplace. But the plan had a political purpose as well—to weaken the state bureaucracy, still filled with Malenkov's people. All this was to be accomplished in a typically Khrushchevian "package." Most government Ministries were to be disbanded, their personnel literally ousted from Moscow to the provinces, where they were to work in new Councils of the National Economy (*Sovnarkhozy*) closer to production. The plan meant the strengthening of the party as the overall coordinator in economics as well as politics, especially at the provincial, or oblast, level.

Malenkov, still in the Presidium and Council of Ministers, saw this, correctly, as a kind of coup and mustered a numerical majority against Khrushchev within the Presidium. In mid-1957, Khrushchev was outvoted seven to four, mainly on this issue of economic organization; some of his previous supporters now opposed him, though his main opponents were three, Malenkov, Molotov, and Kaganovich, his former mentor. Another man might have conceded defeat, but not Khrushchev. He is supposed to have quipped to his opposition, now a majority arrayed against him, "in politics two and two does not necessarily equal four." Khrushchev responded by again calling on the military, this time not to intervene directly, but to provide the members of the Party Central Committee with military aircraft for their travel to Moscow. His intermediary was Marshal Zhukov, the "Soviet Eisenhower" whom Khrushchev had brought back from obscurity. Khrushchev also used the military's communications system for calling a Central Committee meeting. As First Secretary it was his prerogative to do so, and naturally that body would favor him, since he had packed it with his people for years. A novel event occurred; Khrushchev's supporters in the Central Committee began pounding on the doors of the Presidium's meeting room. Khrushchev's opponents, some with guns drawn, realized they were outnumbered by his supporters and gave up. They lost their political positions and were labeled the anti-party group. So passed the chance for a restoration of Stalinism.

First Among Equals

Khrushchev was not clearly "number one." He immediately packed the Presidium as well with his own people, among them future leaders such as Kosygin. Mikoyan, who had changed sides correctly so often, did so again and remained a member. But Khrushchev had had to pay for support. Marshal Zhukov, as Minister of Defense, became the first genuine military man to enter the Presidium. (He was removed only a few months later, when Khrushchev felt stronger, for the Bonapartist danger was too great to be allowed for long. The flavor of Soviet politics is conveyed well by the story that Khrushchev had decided to move against Zhukov before he became a member of the Presidium, indeed, "as soon as he agreed to help me.") Now Khrushchev proceeded to implement his reforms without opposition.

But although the way to the realization of his plans seemed clear, Khrushchev had altered Soviet politics in a fundamental way. The leader's authority no longer rested only on terror, the camps, and the security police, but instead depended on a social compact of sorts, a contract with the Soviet people for a better tomorrow. Khrushchev soon made it plain, however, that this compact was not with all the people, only those he

needed. Particularly, it was not with independent-minded intellectuals. A poet defending abstract artists had said, "Some of the formalistic tendencies in their art will be straightened out in time," to which he replied, "The hunchbacked are straightened out by the grave." [11]

He had enlarged the arena of power in the Soviet Union, a historic act, and had shown that the leaders of the party could be toppled, an example that Brezhnev and others of Khrushchev's men were to use against him in 1964. Twice the army had been brought into high politics. What besides a now eroded tradition would keep them out at some time when Khrushchev did not want them in? As it was, he had to make concessions to the military. The Ministries in charge of defense production had not been decentralized, thus leaving some top state bureaucrats in Moscow and in the thick of major decision making. More important, a Soviet military-industrial complex stayed in existence, conscious of its untouchability and convinced of its power. It was to be in Khrushchev's way when he attempted further reform.

The Central Committee also received a real political role, serving as a sort of court to decide whether the Presidium (Politburo) had made the correct decision regarding the Khrushchev faction. This was a role it had lacked since 1927, if not earlier. Since that time, the Central Committee had been mainly an honorific body that included top apparatchiki, state bureaucrats, Ambassadors to key countries, and a few outstanding (but tame) writers and artists and that met for only a few days, two or three times a year, to give formal and unoriginal confirmation to the party leaders' own decisions. It now came to have a role in leadership selection and, therefore, in policy making as well

[11] Crankshaw, *Khrushchev: A Career*, p. 255.

330

when the top leadership was not in agreement. Since the Soviet system lacks a constitutional formula for solving the major question of political leadership succession, the question always has to be solved politically by finding a consensus. When that agreement cannot be found within the top leadership, the Central Committee of (now) 425 full and candidate members takes a hand in it.

Khrushchev was forced to compromise in several ways; he was unable to expel his opponents of 1957 from the party for four years; he had to shelve outright anti-Stalinism (and to say that "Stalin's merits outweighed his faults," particularly prior to the purges of the 1930s); he had to reaffirm the traditional dominance of heavy over light industry; and he had to contend with Frol Kozlov, a conservative and later an opponent, within the Presidium. This latter limitation of the party's chief leader was new.

In a curious way, then, Khrushchev began a significant broadening of the Soviet power elite and, by not killing his opponents, he created a potential opposition party of outs who someday might ally with part of the Central Committee to become ins. Perhaps a Soviet democracy can slowly evolve this way over the decades, once the rigid Bolshevist commitment to a single way of doing things loosens.

Khrushchev eroded this idea of Bolshevik uniqueness to a degree. At the Twentieth Party Congress he said that there were various ways to socialism, including the nonrevolutionary or parliamentary way, that war is no longer "fatalistically inevitable," and that with the aid of the underdeveloped countries the Soviet Union could outmatch, or at least be secure from, the West. He also considered it possible to shift the economy to emphasize more light industry, consumer goods, and agriculture. All this tended to relativize the ideology and to favor pragmatic, limited solutions.

New Political Facts of Life
But Khrushchev was not allowed to follow through with the implications of these stands. The dogmatists, or Stalinists, may have been displaced from the Presidium, but the conservatives—among them Russian nationalists, people committed to heavy industry and weapons production, and the military—were so numerous in positions of responsibility everywhere that Khrushchev's attempt at change and reform was a labor like that of Sisyphus, the unfortunate mythological hero condemned to rolling a boulder up a hill forever. So throughout Khrushchev's remaining years Soviet politics was a clash between conservatives and reformers, or modernizers, with Khrushchev then leading the latter. Although they were not organized into any overt interest or pressure groups (still an impossibility under Soviet conditions), these reformers and conservatives existed as what could be called communities of viewpoint throughout Soviet society and made their preferences known informally to one another and within the party to some effect. The terms *left* and *right* cannot have much meaning in Soviet politics since these terms have their own meanings for Marxists and since all important factions in the party are agreed on "the preservation of the vitality of the party dictatorship." [12] Liberals and radicals of all kinds do exist, but they are frozen out of politics and operate mostly in the realms of culture, philosophy, and rare, fruitless demonstrations. No grouping in the party seems to espouse such causes.

Khrushchev was to find that it is meaningless to triumph over dogmatists in the Soviet

[12] Carl A. Linden, *Khrushchev and the Soviet Leadership: 1957–1964* (Baltimore: Johns Hopkins University Press, 1966), p. 19.

Union unless they are beaten abroad as well, hence a drive against Mao Tse-tung and the Chinese position (plus tiny Albania, a Chinese ally in Europe) became unavoidable. The Chinese, in turn, were to use the old Marxist epithet *revisionist* for Khrushchev (a term implying erroneous change of some kind) and to say he was a rightist revisionist.

Khrushchev continually searched for new issues that would serve two goals: first, to dramatize both the country's problems and his attempts at solution; and second, to gather new combinations of supporters and array them against his opponents who remained in the party and those who limited his freedom of maneuver and action. For a few years he seemed to be successful, acting as if he were the uncontested and unlimited single leader of the Soviet Union. He was trying to make that victorious across-the-board definition of issues that would bring him overwhelming support and allow him to break completely free of his fetters. Thus freed, he would make the Soviet economy a balanced one, limit the power of the state bureaucracy, and reestablish a degree of democracy within the party. It was a brave attempt, a grand show by a grand showman, but one doomed to failure by the new complexity of Soviet society. It was now too complex and too well structured to be easily controlled or changed, for no leader was trusted not to become a Stalin. Khrushchev's own supporters applied this lesson continually. He could try to move mountains, but ultimately he would be denied the power. The Soviet Union, leaders and led alike, was in a conspiracy for peace and quiet against Khrushchev, a position known in game theory as the "coercive power of the weak."

In Search of a Breakthrough
The First Secretary strengthened himself after ousting the anti-party group in mid-

1957 by swamping the Presidium with his followers from the Party Secretariat and, in 1958, by taking Stalin's other title of Premier (technically Chairman of the Council of Ministers). Now the party and state were again joined under one leader, a feat Brezhnev has never accomplished, though he has had more than a decade in which to do so. Under cover of these symbolic acts of apparent victory Khrushchev covertly took up the old Bukharin-Malenkov position; that is, since heavy industry has been built, now light industry and consumer goods can be emphasized. Cleverly, he presented it not in those terms but under a new formula, designating chemicals as the "decisive" branch of heavy industry. Thus "heavy industry" became only terminology and was redefined as the basis for increased food and consumer goods production. Along with this reformulation there appeared, but in muted terms, an old Leninist idea that had not been broached for decades; the acquisition of financial credits and technical aid from the capitalist West. Was not the West on the retreat because of the loss of colonies and the Soviet space achievements? (Sputnik had been put into orbit in the fall of 1957 to great dismay and soul-searching in the United States and to overconfidence in communism's military capabilities in China.)

In early 1959 Khrushchev called an Extraordinary, or irregularly scheduled, Party Congress, partly to have himself confirmed as the preeminent leader. (Some intellectuals in the opposition saw this as the creation of another Stalin and consequently were quite concerned.) Khrushchev also reopened the attack on the anti-party group, but was blocked from success in this effort by other senior members of the Presidium, notably Mikoyan, Mikhail Suslov, and Kosygin, later to become Premier after Khrushchev's removal. The most Khrushchev could do was to reveal that Bulganin had opposed him in 1957 and then to remove him from the Presidium (though he remained in the Central Committee). Kosygin was for economic, but not political, reform. Announcing that the anti-party matter was finished and required no further discussion or action, he significantly offered none of the usual praise of Khrushchev and indeed hardly mentioned him.

The foreign policy arena during 1957–1959 was also one of difficulties for Khrushchev. He was able to make neither the Americans nor the Chinese Communists yield in their respective positions. (The Sino-Soviet conflict was still shrouded from the outside world.) Although Khrushchev had been claiming that dogmatism, or Chinese-style revolutionary drive, was the main danger to the international communist movement, the 1957 meeting of the twelve ruling Leninist parties declared, under Chinese pressure, that revisionism was the main threat. This line lasted until after 1960 and served as a symbolic slap in the face to Khrushchev. In 1958 he worsened the relationship with China by not providing any concrete support for its attempts to seize certain islands held by the Chinese Nationalists with active United States aid. Khrushchev never was moved by the Chinese position that the "paper tiger" ought to be pushed a bit harder by the Soviet Union and was supposed to have said, "Ah, but the paper tiger has nuclear teeth." Any confrontation with the United States would have endangered the Soviet Union, not China, most of all. Mao and Khrushchev are said (by Eastern European Communists) to have gotten along poorly as individuals. The poet-philosopher Mao considered Khrushchev to be crude and uneducated, while Khrushchev thought Mao to be a mad risk-taker—and with Soviet, not Chinese, wealth and soldiers. The Soviet engineering-bureaucratic approach to issues and problems

could not have gone well with the Chinese guerrilla war–psychological approach. Regarding the way to combat the main enemy, the United States, the Chinese thought it could be pressured onto the defensive whereas the Soviets counted its bombs and bombers and doubted this.

Khrushchev did try to pressure the United States, but to mutually beneficial concessions, not to great loss of prestige or defeat. One persistent device he used in this quest was threatening to change the German situation fundamentally by signing a peace treaty with the Soviet-backed East Germans on his own. This would have ended the possibility of German reunification, at least in the short term, and given East Germany control over the Soviet sector of Berlin. He hoped by these threats to force the United States to the bargaining table, where a detente situation crucial for his domestic policies of reform could be created and where perhaps the United States would agree to a situation in the western sectors of Berlin that might eventually allow that city to be controlled by East Germany. He was to get a summit meeting with Eisenhower in 1959, which fostered, though only briefly, a better American-Soviet atmosphere (the "spirit of Camp David"), but which foundered as a result of the U-2 (May 1960) and Bay of Pigs incidents (April 1961).[13]

In 1959, Khrushchev also launched a series of ideological formulations and domestic innovations that gave his programs intellectual and organizational bases. Striking out ideologically at the Chinese by defining communism as a stage of material abundance, he thus denigrated the then current Chinese Great Leap Forward and its new communes as representing still a low

13 On April 17, 1961, an amateurish invasion of Cuba by about 1,500 CIA-trained Cuban refugees was attempted and failed.

standard of living and declared that all socialist states would enter communism simultaneously. This also undercut Chinese pretensions to leadership of the international communist movement that were becoming based more and more on Mao's position and thought. Domestically, Khrushchev began a further attack on the state apparatus by speaking of the approaching "withering away" of the state, a long-standing standard and crucial Marxist goal, and instituted new public nonbureaucratic organizations, such as the "people's militia" and "comrades' courts" to deal with public order and minor crimes. The essential element in these organizations was their use of ordinary citizens to perform certain functions usually carried out by the government bureaucracy. (They still exist, but are no longer presented as patterns for the future.) While constituting a Soviet challenge to Chinese pretensions of originality, such bodies also provided a potential means of introducing more citizen participation in processes formerly reserved to formal state agencies independent of popular desires. This, then, was a blow at the bureaucratic capriciousness and rigidity so long typical of Russian government.

By 1960, Khrushchev decided to attack the Chinese issue head on and to master it, criticizing the Chinese at the Rumanian Party Congress and, more important, taking a decisive harsh step. He abruptly withdrew thousands of Soviet technicians from China and thereby dealt a severe blow to Chinese economic development. The Soviet specialists in China actually burned the blueprints of the projects on which they were engaged. (He had also reneged on his earlier promises to give the Chinese one or more nuclear weapons and to create a joint Sino-Soviet naval command in the Pacific.) Khrushchev decided that he was no longer going to be used by the Chinese and that he would make them come around to a subordinate position.

Although the Sino-Soviet dispute was not yet believed in by those outside what was then called the communist bloc, its continuation was inevitable. It came fully into the open in October 1961 at the Twenty-Second Congress of the CPSU. From that moment the international communist movement no longer existed as a unified force, falling instead into a quarrelsome state reminiscent of struggles among schismatics and heretics within medieval Christianity. As then, the main struggle came to be that against other believers, not the "infidel" (the capitalist United States).

Khrushchev was attempting too much. Some of his associates, notably Kozlov, did not want the drive against China to be pursued. (Kozlov criticized Yugoslav revisionism instead.) Also, foreign Communist parties did not favor, and still resist, the Soviet idea of an international Communist conference that would declare China non-Communist. If this were allowed to happen to the Chinese, why could it not occur as well to the French or Italian Communists or to any foreign Communist party disliked by the Soviet leadership of the moment? The Eastern European Communists would be particularly affected.

Hopes of a detente with the Americans were similarly dashed. Here the hindrance was the U-2 flight of May Day 1960, a routine CIA-sponsored overflight of the Soviet Union from Pakistan to Norway, which this time was shot down. Khrushchev was gravely undermined domestically by this event, but he cleverly tried to make it into a victory of sorts by offering President Eisenhower, the man who had taught him the English words *my friend,* the opportunity to disavow the action or blame the CIA for it. This Eisenhower refused to do, accepting responsibility instead in American constitutional terms. Khrushchev then was forced to save himself by thundering in a warlike

Khrushchev at the United Nations, 1960

(Keystone Press)

manner and taking a beefy Soviet marshal with him to the already doomed summit meeting in Paris, which obviously could not continue after its formal opening meeting. The great hope of a Soviet-American basic agreement in 1960 was shattered.

The Struggle for Survival

From then until his fall in 1964 Khrushchev was fighting a battle for survival that has become clearly visible only in retrospect. His posturing and sloganeering made him only appear strong, as he was trying to overcome his opponents at home and abroad with words. His growing domestic problem was that more and more of his associates, and at times even his own protégés, were becoming his opponents.

He was trying to move too fast with too little and risking too much in the process. It seemed during the Cuban Missile Crisis of October 1962 that he was risking the Soviet Union itself. His colleagues, organization men all, thought this not only unwise and dangerous, but embarrassing as well, particularly when the Chinese charged him with "adventurism" and "capitulationism." (At about the same time the Chinese had won a conflict, having driven the Indian army back in the Himalayas and taking many prisoners. They tried to expose the meaninglessness of Soviet foreign commitments by invoking the Sino-Soviet treaty of 1950, knowing they would receive no response.)

During this post-U-2 period Khrushchev lost some of his preeminence. He was still first, but not by as great a degree as before. The conservative Frol Kozlov took over the number-two post in the Secretariat, and he and Suslov, the chief ideologue, pressured Khrushchev to take a harder line on culture and art and to be more restrained toward the Chinese. His protégé Brezhnev was shifted from the Secretariat to the honorific post of chief of state (Chairman of the Presidium of the Supreme Soviet), in which he could do nothing in the party. In early 1961 the Central Committee refused to adopt Khrushchev's programs on agriculture and consumer goods in their entirety. Khrushchev retaliated, but only verbally, by lashing out against those who rigidly advocated the production of more and more metal. He struck out at the conservatives by proclaiming the Soviet state a "state of the whole people," a far cry from the "dictatorship of the proletariat," and began, in effect, to treat the party the same way. The party almost doubled in membership under Khrushchev, who opened its gates to 5 million new members, many of whom were reformers. (But these new entrants, too low in seniority and status, could not yet help Khrushchev.) He also had a new party program written, but it did not say, as he had wanted, that the state was withering away. Suslov claimed this result could be possible only when a communist society

335

existed in the Soviet Union and when socialism had won a world victory; that is, when capitalism no longer existed.

By mid-1961 Khrushchev saw his military programs restricted and even turned around. The troop cuts he had ordered the previous year were suspended (though the military had been greatly reduced in size), the military budget was increased by one-third, and nuclear testing was resumed. Though still in command, Khrushchev had to act against his own policies in order to stay there. He was wielding the levers of power and making the main pronouncements, but he was expending a lot of effort in staying ahead of his opposing colleagues and in buying time for new ideas and new departures that might regain the initiative for him. The daring move that he and the East German leadership had made in East Berlin—constructing the Wall—had only locked in the East German subjects, a stabilizing measure to be sure, but the Western allies were still ensconced in West Berlin, 110 miles inside East Germany. His saber-rattling and tough talking had not been enough. At the Twenty-Second Congress in the fall of 1961 some of his supporters left the Party Presidium and Secretariat. As a result, his opposing colleagues were able to match him. He still held the symbols and levers of supreme power, but his support at the top was wearing thin.

In September and October 1962, Khrushchev went forth against the conservatives once again, this time with a new combination of original domestic and foreign policy initiatives. Again there was the typical Khrushchevian style: the sudden and bold stroke, the use of limited resources for great goals, and the indirect attack around the target to its rear. Domestically, the new initiative involved a novel attack on Stalinism, the use of anti-Stalin literature. Khrushchev personally read Alexander Solzhenitsyn's

prison-camp novel, *One Day in the Life of Ivan Denisovich,* then ordered both this book and Yevgeny Yevtushenko's poem, "Stalin's Heirs," to be published. With the poem and the novel "Khrushchev raised the threat of a purge of those in the leadership who had obstructed his purposes." [14] These may have included Suslov and Kozlov, who reportedly had opposed the publication. (As Khrushchev's prosecutor before the Central Committee in October 1964, Suslov made this act one of the charges.)

Khrushchev also conveniently rediscovered and had published a major article by Lenin that stressed the supremacy of "economic organizers" (read "Khrushchev and company") over "political agitators" (read "Suslov, Kozlov, and their group"). On this basis he restructured the local levels of the party along the lines of production and created separate hierarchies in the party for active control of agriculture and industry. This had the result of creating a number of new party secretaries who, he no doubt assumed, would be grateful to him for their promotion.

The most daring part of the plan was the emplacement of strategic missiles in Cuba to force the United States, which he assumed would act "reasonably," to come to a deal on Berlin. About the attempted American invasion of Cuba Khrushchev said:

The Americans miscalculated. They did not plan well. They overestimated the strength of the counterrevolutionaries. They thought that the invasion would trigger an uprising. . . . But that was wishful thinking. Castro handled the situation brilliantly.[15]

But after the United States revealed that it knew of Soviet actions and intentions in

[14] Linden, *Khrushchev and the Soviet Leadership,* p. 147.
[15] *Khrushchev Remembers,* 2: 509.

Cuba and began to counteract them, Khrushchev quickly sent a long, rambling message to President Kennedy pleading for "reason" and some mutually agreeable arrangement to avert a violent confrontation and to end the crisis. This first letter, delivered by the top representative of the Soviet intelligence service in the United States (who was serving as a delegate to the United Nations with diplomatic immunity), was the one to which President Kennedy replied. The second more demanding letter, written by the diplomatic apparatus (perhaps with encouragement from Khru-

shchev's conservative associates), was ignored. This willingness of Khrushchev to compromise shows well his realism, pragmatism, and limited aims. He later praised President Kennedy for being "intelligent" and "sober-minded" and for allowing them to find a "common ground and common language" to avert war. As it was, Khrushchev did not let the Soviet Union go away from the Cuban Missile Crisis without some gains. The United States agreed to a Soviet request for a specific promise that it would not intervene militarily in Cuba.

In his typical forceful and picturesque

Khrushchev with President John F. Kennedy at Vienna in 1961

(Keystone Press)

style, Khrushchev later justified Soviet actions and achievements as contributing to peace:

Our intention was to install the missiles not to wage war against the US, but to prevent the US from invading Cuba [again] and thus starting a [world] war.

It would have been preposterous for us to unleash a war against the United States from Cuba. Cuba was 11,000 kilometers [6,820 miles] from the Soviet Union. Our air and sea communications with Cuba were . . . precarious. . . .

For the first time in history, the Americans pledged publicly not to invade one of their neighbors and not to interfere in its internal affairs. . . . The American imperialist beast was forced to swallow a hedgehog, quills and all. And that hedgehog is still in its stomach, undigested.[16]

The United States and the Soviet Union had faced each other, mutually taken stock of the other, and jointly made concessions. The former purely antagonistic relationship was coming to have some elements of respect and mutual aims on the basis of which a better relationship might be built. By mid-1963 the two nations agreed to limit their testing of nuclear weapons and to establish an emergency communication system, the hot line. Since then, more than 110 agreements have come to be signed by the two. The Cuban crisis may have been the crest of the "fever chart" of their relationship.

Despite Khrushchev's claim that his action in and toward Cuba had limited the United States, the outcome was perceived and treated as a Soviet defeat by his associates in the Politburo. The military budget

was increased; opposition to Khrushchev's view of the party as an agency of economic administration was intensified; *Pravda* said that revisionism was the main danger; and, most pointedly, some praise of Stalin began to appear. Khrushchev began to sound tougher, going out of his way to display his temper crudely on artistic and literary innovations in early December 1962. He probably survived because his opposition was not yet ready to displace him and because too rapid a removal would have embarrassed the Soviet Union still further. A decent interval had to be allowed to pass.

In order to avert his political demise in 1963, Khrushchev reverted to a typical ploy: the campaign. Again he launched a massive drive, bolstered by loud ballyhoo in the media, to shift the economy's center of gravity toward chemical production, light industry, agriculture, and the consumer. He even was lucky and regained some initiative due to the serious illness of Kozlov, his conservative archrival of the time, and to the Chinese demands for rectification of the borders, which enabled him to draw on Russian nationalism. But the situation was fluid, and at the end of April he even said publicly that he could not hold his job indefinitely. In June he was able to get his two supporters, Brezhnev and Nikolai Podgorny, into the Secretariat. But in hindsight it is apparent that this move gave his opponents an acceptable alternative to him, namely Brezhnev as "first among equals" within a collective leadership. It is not known how Brezhnev came into the opposition as Khrushchev's successor; perhaps he was tempted by the opposition's offer of the first secretaryship.

A trap was being constructed both by Khrushchev's conservative opponents and by Khrushchev himself as he maneuvered more and more erratically within a less and less

16 Ibid., 2: 511–512.

Khrushchev and Fidel Castro at Lake Ritsa in the Caucasus in 1963 after the Cuban missile crisis

(Life Magazine Collection)

open political arena. In October 1964 the trap was sprung with smooth and consummate effectiveness.

Failure and Fall

Unfortunately, not enough is known about the machinations preceding Khrushchev's removal to talk about the plot in detail. No doubt there were only a few main conspirators, in complete agreement and mostly in

the Presidium and Secretariat. A bit more is known about what happened after the removal process was underway, because the Central Committee was called into session and the enlargement of the number of persons involved made leaks possible. (Khrushchev says nothing about his removal in his memoirs. Perhaps he or his family considered the topic too dangerous, since those who removed him were still in power.)

On the morning of October 12, 1964, while on vacation, Khrushchev was having a conversation with the French Minister for Atomic Energy at Khrushchev's Black Sea villa when an official rushed in to Khrushchev. After a few moments of urgent conversation between the two, the interview was abruptly ended, Khrushchev explaining that the Central Committee was meeting in Moscow and that he had to attend. Obviously, someone other than Khrushchev had called that meeting and had borrowed a leaf from Khrushchev's book of political maneuverings in calling it. The Central Committee, used by him to legitimate himself, was now being used against him. Clearly, he had lost great support within the political elite.

According to one account based on conversations with Western and Eastern European Communists, Mikoyan had been delegated by the Presidium to try to get Khrushchev to relent in his drive for reform, but Khrushchev would not.[17] Supposedly, after hearing Mikoyan's report on October 12, the active stage of the plot was put into effect. More likely, the plot was well underway, and Khrushchev's few friends in the leadership were being given one last chance

[17] Martin Page and David Burg, *Unpersoned: The Fall of Nikita Sergeyevitch Khrushchev* (London: Chapman & Hall, 1966).

to persuade him to slow down. Significantly, his friends did not warn him of the plot. Thus, it appears that everyone of consequence except Khrushchev was in on it. He had alienated everyone else who counted and wound up alone. By outdistancing Russian politics, he had broken Lenin's key rule never to get too far ahead of one's political base.

As soon as Khrushchev arrived at a nearby airport for the flight to Moscow, he found that his usual pilot and crew had been replaced by others; the same thing had happened to his driver in Moscow. The security police were no longer in his employ. He must have had a sinking feeling as he was driven to the Kremlin. Nevertheless, he had survived too much to be paralyzed and chose instead to fight. But when he arrived in his office in the Kremlin, he found that his situation was desperate. He dialed certain telephone numbers, but was answered by unfamiliar voices. The numbers had actually been changed, and recently, for he had been on vacation only about two weeks. He was in a Kafkaesque maze from which there might be no way out.

He then moved into the Presidium's meeting room, but Brezhnev was sitting at the head of the table, in Khrushchev's place, and did not give it up, instead motioning him to another chair. Khrushchev was told that the Presidium had just voted to accept his resignation and that if he agreed, he would be given a magnificent public farewell and an honorable retirement. He had only to confirm Brezhnev as his successor in public. Khrushchev refused and demanded the chance to put his case before the Central Committee. This he was allowed to do, but to no avail.

Suslov served as prosecutor, reportedly detailing the case against Khrushchev in a speech lasting five hours. (The summary is said to be forty pages long.) He presented

twenty-nine different charges against Khrushchev, the primary one being that he had disrupted the functioning of the party apparatus. (Though he had rebuilt it, it destroyed him.) His giving the party apparatus definite economic and administrative functions was most unpopular within it: the apparatchiks wanted overall control, not the drudgery of detailed administration. Suslov also accused him of having undermined the authority of the Central Committe by having listened to experts he had invited and having slighted the actual members, the largest group of whom were party apparatchiki. He was charged with being impulsively dictatorial and of having "repeatedly transgressed and violated the principle of collective leadership." The military-industrial complex got in its licks as well with the charge that Khrushchev had weakened and disorganized heavy and military industry by his stress on light industry and his administrative reorganizations. His foreign policy came in for severe criticism, particularly his aggravation of the relationship with China and his dangerous risk taking regarding the United States and Cuba. Lastly, he was condemned for his public behavior—for example, his shoe-banging incident at the United Nations in 1960—and for nepotism in putting members of his family in positions of significance (one son-in-law, A. I. Adzhubey, was editor of *Izvestiia,* the main government newspaper).

Khrushchev's defense lasted about an hour but was vituperative and abusive in his rich, peasant style. Perhaps it cost him support, but when the vote came, not all were against him. Possibly one-third of the members voted in his favor, and some abstained on the motion to "accept his request to be relieved of his duties, in view of his advanced age and the deterioration of his health." Khrushchev was no longer First Secretary of the CPSU and Chairman of the

Council of Ministers. (This last was unconstitutional, for the Supreme Soviet never relieved him of his government position.) He left the ordeal as another defeated, common Soviet subject and was sped off in the darkness to obscurity.

His removal occurred on the same day as the British general election and the testing of the first Chinese nuclear explosion. Pollsters say if either the removal or the explosion had come one day earlier, the British people might have been sufficiently concerned to have reelected the Conservative party, not the Labour party. Perhaps the Chinese nuclear test showed that Khrushchev had been more right than wrong about China. A new threat had arisen for the Soviet Union.

A few ironic notes can be mentioned. President de Gaulle, when he was told the news, said, "Poor Khrushchev, he has gone," and added with a bow to the visiting delegate from the Pope, "Sic transit gloria mundi." (So passes the glory of the world.)[18] The Soviet press, with its major editors changed, gave his passing only a single line. His picture was removed from all public places and pictures of the three leading lights in the new collective leadership (plus those of Marx and Lenin, of course) were put in its place. A Western newsman, asking one of the old women at work on the new pictures when the leadership change had been decided, received the tired, listless reply, "At night. They always do it at night."

[18] Martin Page, *The Day Khrushchev Fell* (New York: Hawthorn Books, 1965), p. 125.

6

Assessment
and Conclusions

Since Suslov's denunciation was the impassioned argument of a puritanical prosecutor, it cannot be considered a judgment, much less a balanced one, of the work of a man who took the Soviet Union through some of its stormiest years. Certainly the Soviet Union was much more powerful by any method of measurement in 1964 than in 1953. Therefore, Khrushchev must have served some Soviet interests well.

He cannot be judged an incompetent or even an average statesman. At the least he deserves to be called an above-average Russian political leader (even when compared with the Tsars), though he was not an outstanding success. Again a story about de Gaulle is appropriate. The French President was once asked by what standards Khrushchev could be called successful. De Gaulle replied, "In one of two ways. If he makes a successful peace or wages a successful war." Clearly, he shrank from the second and did not engage in a losing war, as many Tsars

had. Accordingly, he kept the peace and was therefore somewhat a success. The Soviet Union maintained its position during his supremacy, unless the rise of a hostile China and a polycentric international communist movement are counted against him. But that began before his time, and a return of China to greatness was inevitable. Further, given the ethnocentric Chinese view of the world and the self-esteem of its Communist leaders, it is doubtful that he could have maintained China's friendship without having gone to war against the United States in alliance with it, an action that would have resulted in a nuclear holocaust. Undoubtedly he worked without tiring and even with some flair in the interest of Soviet communism, lost nothing and gave nothing away (unless the independence of Austria is counted) and even made some gains. Most of his colleagues had nothing personal to complain about, Khrushchev having made them what they were (except perhaps Kosygin and

Suslov). Of course, by 1964 the first flush of gratitude had worn off and former clients had come to wield some power on their own, to feel comfortable with it, and perhaps to want still more. But what prompted them to move against their sponsor when they did?

Precipitating Reasons for the Coup
By late summer of 1964 it was obvious that Khrushchev was bringing matters to a head. Certain issues were being brought forcefully into the open and their resolution was being pushed just as forcefully—and by Khrushchev. His associates would have felt threatened by what looked like a radical reorientation of Soviet foreign policy and some definite change in the status of the peasants and hence in their political significance. What was involved was peace with Germany, an irrevocable break with China, and a somewhat freer situation for the Soviet peasant. This was too much for his bureaucratic associates.

Khrushchev moved toward an accommodation with the Federal Republic of Germany by sending his son-in-law to its capital in August and by planning to visit it himself later in the year. The "establishment" of Soviet politics, the military-industrial-ideological elite, was not ready for this. Their memories of the war, understandably, may have been too vivid. In any case, Germany was then still ruled by a Christian Democratic, not a Socialist, government, and Willy Brandt was not yet Chancellor. Khrushchev's vision was not met by a visible, trustworthy, comparable vision from the West. It was too early for bureaucrats, who usually have limited vision. They needed time to think. Khrushchev, on the other hand, had never been a bureaucrat. "He was preparing the great coup which would convince American opinion of his good intentions and cut the ground from under Senator

Goldwater's feet. . . . He was getting ready to sell Comrade Ulbricht down the river." [1]

As for China, Khrushchev was moving relentlessly to a December meeting of the world's Communist parties whose function it would be to read China out of the international communist movement. If the assembled parties refused to do it, the Soviet Union would be greatly embarrassed and therefore weakened. If they performed according to plan, the break would stand and there would be hardly any hope for reconciliation. Whatever happened, the Chinese price for friendship would be higher. That the Soviet Union is better off with the present situation is hard to argue. China is at present encouraging the NATO countries and the United States to be firmer with the Soviet Union and is competing against the Soviet Union everywhere and in any way it can, even in Africa. But again, organization men abhor any decisive position or action.

This former peasant's intentions regarding agriculture are less easy to state; this had been his bailiwick for decades. It stands to reason he was going to do something radical with agriculture and the problems it posed for the Soviet economy. The Poles and Yugoslavs had abolished collectivization by then, thereby greatly increasing their food production. (Poland even exports food for profit and is able to feed her people, something the mighty Soviet Union cannot do.) So he had a socialist precedent.

The Basic Vulnerability
These moves of the First Secretary were too radical for the established interests of Soviet society and therefore could not be imple-

---

[1] Crankshaw, *Khrushchev: A Career*, p. 286. Goldwater was then the Republican candidate for President of the United States; Ulbricht was the leader of East Germany.

343

mented by someone without Stalin's powers. Here was a fundamental limitation turned vulnerability that Khrushchev had brought upon himself by his secret speech eight years before. By relativizing Stalin he had relativized himself. (The Chinese knew that de-Stalinization implied de-Maoization, a weakening process that their political system was too new to withstand without raising the danger of fragmentation.) In addition, he had put himself within the main processes of Soviet politics and not, as Stalin had, above and insulated from them. Stalin's errors could always be blamed upon others, his executors or counter-heirs. Khrushchev's failures were clearly his own. Thus he was effectively responsible, a fact brought home to him by his own men in October 1964. He had never set up his personal terror apparatus or institutionalized a new cult of personality, yet despite his great efforts, Soviet political institutions remained Stalinistic in the main. In addition, having trustingly left much of the work of daily and detailed administration to his colleagues on the Politburo, he could be removed without having to remove a part of the political system as well. Thus his fate need not have affected the Soviet system in any structural way. And it did not, although the leadership now acts with a different style and has put aside the hope, often raised by Khrushchev, that some decisive change to a new political system is imminent. What this bottling up of hope means politically is too early to tell.

Specific Vulnerabilities

These particular weaknesses in Khrushchev's position can be summed up as a matter of too much, too fast. Although Khrushchev was able to overcome the limitations of his origins and his dark deeds for Stalin, his own men could not. They are only products of the bureaucratized society and party that Stalin had built. Many of them joined the party during the worst excesses of Stalin's rule, while Khrushchev dated from an earlier, freer age and no doubt was, as he once said, a "free cossack" to a degree.[2] He had a restless imagination, while his successors are only cautious bureaucrats (though not cautious enough to hinder the increase in the power of the Soviet Union).

Khrushchev had a string of unsuccessful attempts at change and even some outright failures behind him. The economy had begun to suffer from an endemic low rate of growth after the boom of the Stalin period. This should not have been a surprise; the bigger an economy, the more investment is required solely for maintenance. Not much is left over for growth. His attempt at solution, turning the party into an active, day-to-day controller of economic details, was most unpopular with the apparatchiki. This bifurcation of the party apparatus into industrial and agricultural sectors was repealed immediately after his ouster. His related widespread use of nonparty experts in decision making was so unpopular that Suslov used it as a specific charge against him. His successors labeled him a "harebrained schemer."

His style of intermittent rapid moves with a few resources had given him a string of defeats in both domestic and foreign affairs and had united both conservatives and modernizers against him. In addition, certain elements of his personal style, such as his shoe-banging act at the United Nations, were considered unseemly and uncultured by the new Soviet white-collar class.

[2] In tsarist Russia the Cossacks lived their own way of life apart from Russian society. In American terms their communities were a series of permanent cowboy settlements. An excellent and entertaining literary treatment is Leo Tolstoy, *The Cossacks.* The Soviet regime destroyed this unique form of social organization, but now, ironically, is building "typical Cossack settlements" as tourist attractions for foreigners.

In foreign affairs he had brought the conflict with the Chinese comrades to an embarrassing level and that with the Americans to a dangerous point of near explosion. And this risky behavior had brought the Soviet Union neither reconciliation with China nor a beneficial arrangement with the United States. On top of this, in August 1964 the new American President, Lyndon Johnson, sent the United States Air Force to attack openly North Vietnam, an ideological ally of the Soviet Union. It looked to Communists as if the United States had begun a policy of rolling back Communist gains. This and Khrushchev's attempt to reach out to the former enemy, the Germans, in the same month was clearly too much for the Soviet military and their allies within the party. Khrushchev's behavior could have seemed potentially treasonous.

The poor harvest of 1963 hit Khrushchev in his area of special responsibility, agriculture, and made his speech making in favor of increased corn production look patently ineffectual and ridiculous. (He had acquired the nickname of *kukoruznik,* "corn-nik," for his efforts.) Certainly Khrushchev had indulged in desperate acts in agricultural policy, including planting precious fallow land and letting charlatans such as Lysenko ruin research. The charges of "harebrained scheming" were not without foundation, yet Khrushchev's stature is not much reduced by his failures.

*Achievement, Legacy, and
Significance*
A former British Ambassador to the Soviet Union, Sir William Hayter, suggests why this is so:

He was an outsize personality in an outsize job. The deliberately faceless men who overthrew him and now wield his power are less interesting, though we may feel safer with them. With Khrushchev we never knew where we were, but we were seldom bored.[3]

He goes on to say that Khrushchev's character "constantly eludes our grasp." This is still true, more than ten years after Hayter made these remarks. The Soviet leader played so many roles well:

The rough young peasant and the dedicated apparatchik, the vicious exponent of Stalinist terror and the posthumous demolisher of Stalin, the man of peace and the butcher of Hungary, the co-exister and the rocket-rattler, patient and choleric, deceitful and frank.[4]

Ironically, Hayter guessed correctly in 1966 that even if Khrushchev's memoirs were published, the truth might not be known since Khrushchev was an actor of great skill. He had to be to survive so many years in Stalin's entourage and then beat both his secret police chief and the latter-day Stalinists. He lost out only to his own followers. When he finally came to trust others, they turned against him.

Khrushchev's achievement lies in the fact that although he was a product and a builder of Stalinism, he saw and acted beyond it, partly for his own political reasons, to be sure, but partly for humanity's sake as well. This "rough peasant" left behind him an "impressive body of theoretical revisions and innovations in Soviet doctrine" raising the promise of a non-Stalinist path for his country that the present gray bureaucrats can never totally erase.[5] In international affairs he proclaimed the noninevitability of war,

[3] Sir William Hayter, "Showman in the Kremlin," *The Observer* (London), September 25, 1966.
[4] Ibid.
[5] Linden, *Khrushchev and the Soviet Leadership,* p. 215.

345

the peaceful transition to socialism, and the end of capitalist encirclement. In domestic politics he spoke of the waning of the class struggle and of the end of a need for Stalinist repression, the withering away of the state, a party and state of the whole people, and the transition to a higher phase of socialism. All this made possible a political relaxation out of which a real liberalization may someday grow if a less restrictive leadership comes into being and Soviet society realizes that it can exist independent of party guidance. When that day arrives, the Soviet Union has a firm political legacy from Khrushchev with which it can begin again. His thoughts and actions live on as political alternatives.

Khrushchev and the Soviet Political Pattern

Since Khrushchev was one of only four Soviet political leaders to date, a brief comparison illustrates both his own political qualities and those of the top Soviet political leadership. In what ways was Khrushchev similar to and different from Lenin, Stalin, and Brezhnev?

Some important indicators of similarity and difference are social origin, education, political beginnings and career experience, style, policies and actions, accomplishments, and ending of political career.

In social and ethnic origin he was closest to Brezhnev, a Russian of working-class background from the Ukraine. Lenin was of upper-middle-class (technically low-aristocratic) family background and a Russian, whereas Stalin was a Georgian (not a Slav), though his background was lower class. In the future, top Soviet political leaders will most likely be Russian, but it may be increasingly rare for them to be of peasant or working-class background, given the current

importance of the white-collar or middle class.

As for education and early work, Khrushchev, with his incomplete schooling, was more like Stalin than like Lenin or Brezhnev. But there was an important difference between Khrushchev and Stalin that made Khrushchev and Brezhnev somewhat similar. Whereas Stalin had a religious and theological education, both Khrushchev and Brezhnev worked with machinery in industry, though only the latter had a higher education. Lenin was trained in the law, but worked as a professional revolutionary, an employment category of relatively recent historical origin.

Lenin and Stalin entered politics as professional revolutionaries, though of very different kinds, prior to the Bolshevik Revolution. Khrushchev entered politics after the revolution, but still took grave risks during the civil war. Brezhnev joined the party long after it had become the victorious and prime apparatus of power. His most risky test was World War II, a period of trial he and Khrushchev shared and in which they became associated politically. Brezhnev is clearly a product of the Soviet system, especially of its Stalinist phase. He is a party functionary or bureaucrat whose life has been mainly conditioned by the type of struggle characteristic of all large organizations. Politics for Khrushchev and his two predecessors was more free and open-ended since the party and other large organizations of Soviet politics were not clearly structured until Stalin's later years. Thus, Lenin, Stalin, and Khrushchev had more options domestically than Brezhnev has. They built the Soviet political edifice; Brezhnev can only strengthen it, not change it. No doubt politics solidified under Khrushchev and came to be less and less alterable by him.

Partly since he was a product of a time of

political creation, Khrushchev's style and policies were oriented toward creation and
change, as were those of Lenin and Stalin.
Brezhnev is forced to try to perfect what
already exists. Obviously, any attempt at
real change would affect large established interests and would endanger the bases of
support of the political elite. Perhaps Khrushchev did not understand this danger because it had not existed in his early political
career.

Accordingly, the accomplishments of
Brezhnev have derived from the use and
manipulation of existing political processes
and forces. Khrushchev and his predecessors
called new ones into existence for their own
benefit. At the end of Khrushchev's career
he could no longer perform this creative feat
of politics, as political instability came to be
desired by fewer and fewer politicians and
interest groups. A new and rather stable Soviet society came into existence, one not
highly amenable to political manipulation.
So Khrushchev was the only one of the four
removed from office. Lenin and Stalin both
died while politically dominant. Khrushchev
died a political nonentity. The Soviet press
noted his 1971 death in a mere four or five
lines, calling him only a "pensioner." Again
Soviet history was changed to suit the rulers.
Khrushchev had violated a new rule of Soviet politics: no one can now be an absolute
political leader like Lenin or Stalin. Brezhnev is only "first among equals," while
Khrushchev was the last of his kind.

Ironically, some of Khrushchev's main
opponents outlived him. Even his patron
Kaganovich was alive in early 1976, as were
Molotov and Malenkov. But they too were
"nonpersons," only Molotov receiving mention (a scant reference) in the newest edition
of the main Soviet encyclopedia. Soviet politics seems to allow giants no longer. A big
question for the system's future is whether

Khrushchev in retirement

(*Life Magazine Collection*)

rule by party committees, however expert, is
a viable substitute for participation and influence by larger groupings of Soviet citizens.

Selected Bibliography

The major political history of the Soviet Union
remains Merle Fainsod, *How Russia is Ruled,*
rev. ed. (Cambridge, Mass.: Harvard Univer-

347

sity Press, 1963). The best history of the party in English is Leonard Schapiro, *The Communist Party of the Soviet Union,* 2d ed. (New York: Vintage Books, 1971).

A thorough discussion of the party's membership is T. H. Rigby, *Communist Party Membership in the U.S.S.R.: 1917–1967* (New York: Columbia University Press, 1968). For a description of party activities drawn from actual party documents, see Merle Fainsod, ed., *Smolensk Under Soviet Rule* (Cambridge, Mass.: Harvard University Press, 1958). A detailed study of party operations in industry is in Jerry F. Hough, *The Soviet Prefects: The Local Party Organs in Industrial Decision-Making* (Cambridge, Mass.: Harvard University Press, 1969).

The role of various groupings in politics is analyzed in H. Gordon Skilling and Franklyn Griffiths, eds., *Interest Groups in Soviet Politics* (Princeton, N.J.: Princeton University Press, 1971). For a wide-ranging presentation on opposition, see Rudolf L. Tökes, ed., *Dissent in the USSR* (Baltimore and London: Johns Hopkins University Press, 1975).

A study comparing American and Soviet politics is Z. K. Brzezinski and S. P. Huntington, *Political Power: USA/USSR* (New York: Viking Press, 1964). For comparative sociological discussion, see Paul Hollander, *Soviet and American Society* (New York: Oxford University Press, 1973).

A well-documented sociopolitical analysis is David Lane, *Politics and Society in the USSR* (New York: Random House, 1971). A well-written short text on Soviet politics is John N.

Hazard, *The Soviet System of Government,* 5th ed. (Chicago: University of Chicago Press, 1978).

A straightforward text on the economy is Marshall I. Goldman, *The Soviet Economy* (Englewood Cliffs, N.J.: Prentice-Hall, 1968). A good history of the Soviet Union is Donald Treadgold, *Twentieth Century Russia* (Chicago: Rand McNally, 1964).

Khrushchev's memoirs are available as *Khrushchev Remembers,* 2 vols. (Boston: Little, Brown, 1970–1974). Two prominent dissidents, Roy Medvedev, and Zhores Medvedev, have recently written a biography stressing Khrushchev's drive for innovation, *Khrushchev: The Years in Power* (New York: Columbia University Press, 1976). A highly readable biography is Edward Crankshaw, *Khrushchev: A Career* (New York: Viking Press, 1966).

Khrushchev's political goals and difficulties are presented in Carl A. Linden, *Khrushchev and the Soviet Leadership: 1957–1964* (Baltimore: Johns Hopkins University Press, 1966). Khrushchev's long-term significance is evaluated and underscored in a recent essay by George W. Breslauer, "Khrushchev Reconsidered," *Problems of Communism* 25, no. 5 (September–October 1976): 18–33.

For an informative and entertaining discussion of present-day life in the Soviet Union, see Hedrick Smith, *The Russians* (New York: Quadrangle, 1976). A powerful novel of political relevance is Alexander I. Solzhenitsyn, *The Cancer Ward* (New York: Dial Press, 1968).

V

Fidel Castro and the Cuban Revolution

Harvey F. Kline

Fidel Castro
Short Biographical Sketch

Fidel Castro Ruz was born on August 13, 1926, in Birán, Mayarí township, in Oriente Province of Cuba. He studied at LaSalle School of the Marianist brothers and Colegio Dolores of the Jesuits in nearby Santiago, completing his secondary education at the fashionable and expensive Colegio Belén, a Jesuit preparatory school in Havana, and graduating in 1945. From that year until 1950, he studied law at the Universidad de Havana, graduating with a Doctor of Laws degree.

While in private law practice from 1950 to 1953, Castro continued a career in national politics that had begun during his university years. In 1952 he was a candidate for the lower house of the national congress, as a member of the Orthodox party. His candidacy was ended by the military coup d'état of Fulgencio Batista in March 1952.

Fidel Castro led an armed attack against the Moncada army barracks in Santiago on July 26, 1953, with the aim of ending the Batista dictatorship. After failure and subsequent capture, he was sentenced to prison on the Isle of Pines and incarcerated until May 1955.

From mid-1955 until the end of 1956, Castro prepared a guerrilla warfare plan while in exile in Mexico. The war, originating in Oriente Province, lasted from December 1956 until January 1959, when Batista fled the island.

Since January 1959, Fidel Castro has been the "maximum leader" of Cuba and has led the country to socialism and, later, to communism.

Married in October 1948, he and his wife, Mirta, had a son in 1949. He was divorced from his wife in 1954 and has never remarried.

1

Introduction:
Cuba – Land and People

The island of Cuba has occupied a prominent place in world headlines since the coming to power of Fidel Castro in 1959. This importance is due to its proximity to the United States and what that has meant historically. One could speculate that a bearded leader bringing a social and economic revolution to a small island far removed from the United States, both geographically and economically, would have had entirely different international repercussions.

Geography
Cuba is a small island in territory, 44,218 square miles, roughly the size of Pennsylvania. It includes some very rough terrain, as about 25 percent of it is mountainous. There are three major mountain ranges, one each in the eastern, central, and western parts of the island. The other three-quarters of Cuba is composed of gentle slopes, suitable for agriculture.

Located at the northern part of the Caribbean Ocean, Cuba is only ninety miles from Florida and close to the Mississippi delta and, indeed, occupies a strategic position between the continental United States, Central America, and the Panama Canal. For this reason, the island has always been seen as important for the defense of the United States, which has considered its annexation at various times in history.

The tropic location of Cuba, along with its soils, makes it ideal for the cultivation of sugar cane. The temperatures are warm, with a mean temperature of seventy-seven degrees in the winter months and of eighty in the summer. This temperature is fairly uniform for the island, although there are cooler places at the higher elevations of the mountains.

Yet another characteristic of the island is its relative homogeneity. Surely not all parts of the national territory are exactly alike. Nevertheless, as compared to the other countries considered in this book, Cuba is a homogeneous country with too few geographic barriers to allow much political regionalism.

Its small size makes integration of the nation relatively easy.

People

Cuba is a fairly densely populated country, having today a population of 9.25 million and a low population growth rate of slightly less than 2 percent a year. Only Haiti, the Dominican Republic, and El Salvador have denser populations in Latin America.

The people of Cuba have a variety of ethnic backgrounds, reflecting European and African migrations to the island, the Amerindian population (which was slight and soon decimated by disease), and a very small Asian element. The two predominant racial strains—white and black—have intermarried, leading to the *mestizo* group, as it is called in Cuba.

It is difficult, if not impossible, to state the exact racial make-up of the Cuban people. The national census of 1953 concluded that whites made up 77.8 percent of the population, while blacks were only 12.4 percent, the rest being mixed. However, these figures were based on the impressions of the census takers. Racial breakdowns are not considered important by the revolutionary government, as all racial discrimination has, in theory, been ended. Nevertheless, a general figure

Cuba

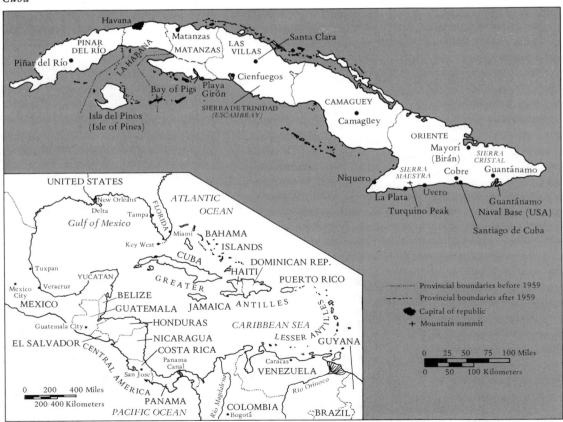

for racial composition today would be about one third each for blacks, whites, and mestizos.

Race relations in Latin America have generally been different from those in the United States. In the Latin countries, prejudice has tended to be based on appearance of an individual, rather than his or her background. Hence an individual who appears white, although he might have some background in nonwhite groups, is treated as a white. The result in Latin American countries is that there is a white-nonwhite continuum, rather than neat categories.

Cuba never followed the Latin American pattern of race relations completely. Due to the great influence of citizens of the United States in Cuba, racial prejudice was more like that of the North American country. Blacks were discriminated against, not being allowed in certain social clubs and exclusive groups, and there were even some public facilities that did not serve potential black patrons.

In sum, before the revolution nonwhites tended to have lower-paying jobs, less education, and less social status. Race correlated quite strongly with class. This is not to say that there were no exceptions; a notable one was President Fulgencio Batista, a man of mixed blood. Even so, Batista was not accepted by the social elite of Havana and, indeed, was rejected for membership in one yacht club while he held the post of chief executive.

The people of Cuba have predominantly been urban dwellers, although the economic wealth of the country has been rural. Before the Revolution of 1959, about 60 percent of the Cuban people lived in urban centers, the largest being the national capital of Havana, with about a million inhabitants, followed by Santiago de Cuba, with about one-quarter of a million. As in the rest of Latin America, the cities have been the political, commercial, educational, and industrial centers. Before the Cuban Revolution, and still today, there was more wealth in the cities, and clearly they are the preferred places to live.

Social Relationships

Before the Cuban Revolution, there were strict class lines on the island. A number of factors went into one's social position—race, wealth, and education—but most basically, social stratification was based on occupation. The great dichotomy in Cuba, as in most of Latin America, was between those with manual occupations and those with non-manual or mental work. Numerous examples could be given of individuals who had non-manual occupations and, therefore, higher social status than others who made more money, but had manual occupations. Hence, in broad terms there were only two social classes, although there were various gradations within each due to the other factors of income and race.

Upward mobility in such a class system was based primarily on education, but in Cuba before the revolution this possibility was limited. Educational institutions, particularly at the post-elementary level, tended to be private and church-run. One had to have money to pay for books, fees, and room and board; and, further, there was the negative cost of not having income from working during the school years. This system effectively excluded the sons and daughters of the working class, whether rural or urban, from more than several years of education. Marriage, generally speaking, was not an effective method of social mobility, as sons and daughters of the middle and upper groups had little contact with those of the working class and even less desire to form a union with their social inferiors.

The pre-1959 class system has largely disappeared. Many of the top group left the island, and education has been made much more available for all. This was one of the first policies of Fidel Castro after he came to power.

Women, just as nonwhites and manual laborers, were in clearly secondary positions before the Cuban Revolution. This was the result of the general cultural characteristic of male dominance, or *machismo*. Women were pampered, sheltered, and made subordinate to men. Men were expected to display marital infidelity; women were to be faithful. Wives stayed in the home, reared children, and attended mass. This was another of the social relations that the Castro government is now trying to change.

The Economy

Cuba is a relatively poor country. In 1956 the per capita gross domestic product was only $415, as compared to about $700 in 1974. In the period before Castro, Cuba was, like most underdeveloped countries, also characterized by extreme variations of income, with a few very rich people, a small middle-income sector, and a large number of very poor people. One of the chief policies of the Castro government has been to lessen those great disparities.

Compared to the rest of Latin America, Cuba had a fairly developed economy in 1958. The island ranked fourth in per capita income, fifth in manufacturing output, and at the very top in such elements of economic infrastructure as transportation and communication. Nevertheless, Cubans tended to compare themselves with the United States. When they did so, they saw that the island was poorer than this nation's poorest state, Mississippi.

The key to the Cuban economy was, and still is today, sugar. Its cultivation occupied about one-quarter of the labor force and one-half of the cultivated lands before the revolution, while 80 percent of Cuban exports were in the form of sugar. This has not changed greatly.

Before the revolution there were three important consequences of the sugar economy. First, it gave a precarious position to the Cuban economy, booming when sugar prices were up and desperately sagging when the prices were down. Since each one-cent variation in the price of sugar on the international market typically meant a difference of about $60 million to the Cuban economy, the entire economic system depended on world prices, something largely out of the control of the Cubans themselves. However, Cuba did have comparative advantage in the production of sugar, since there are few places in the world with better soil and climate for the crop.

Second, the sugar economy led to a rural proletariat in the Cuban countryside. The Cuban peasants (*guajiros*) were wage-laborers, rather than the more traditional peasants of much of Latin America. The latter have been either squatters, illegally occupying unused land, or workers on *haciendas,* large family farms, in which a *patrón* took care of their needs in return for their work. Needless to say, both squatters and hacienda dwellers existed in Cuba, but no other Latin American country has been so characterized by large numbers of rural wage-laborers. Furthermore, the Cuban sugar worker had a precarious existence. Sugar is a crop that requires relatively intensive work during planting (even though it is a perennial and lasts about eight years) and very intensive work during the harvest. Thus, most Cuban sugar workers had full-time employment for four or five months of the year. At the time of the harvest, the Cuban working force was not even large enough; cutters were brought in from other countries of the Caribbean. During the other months, the Cuban sugar worker had to live on the money accumulated during the harvest or, failing that, go into debt to the company store.

Third, the sugar economy was concentrated in a few hands, primarily foreign. The cane is most economically grown on large plots of land; it simply cannot be done as efficiently on small, family-sized farms. The large sugar plantation was centered around the mill, or *central*. These large mills tended to be few in number, about 160 for the entire country, and the largest were owned by United States economic interests.

There were other agricultural ventures in Cuba before the revolution, but none were nearly as important as sugar. Cuba has long been known for its tobacco, which tended to be grown on smaller plantations. Also there was production of coffee, cocoa, rice, and livestock. The coffee was grown in the hilly regions not suited to sugar. Livestock occupied much space and were raised with

about the same density per acre as in the southwestern United States, although the Cuban land and vegetation favored a much denser livestock industry.

A small amount of industry grew up on the island, particularly after World War II. Much of it was consumer goods, but Cuba was far from self-sufficient even in such things. Most of the heavier industry—including chemicals, rubber, and pharmaceuticals—was owned by United States companies, as was the small amount of mining, especially in copper and nickel.

This was the nature of the economy of Cuba during the childhood and adolescence of Fidel Castro. Many Cubans were not at all pleased with such a situation. When he came to power, Fidel Castro turned immediately to attempts to change the economic basis of the island.

2

Cuban Government:
An Overview

The first week of January 1959, a thirty-two-year-old bearded revolutionary came to power in Cuba, after a two-year guerrilla war. Few people expected that Fidel Castro would change Cuba dramatically. Yet in the years that followed, he personally led his nation away from private enterprise to socialism and, finally, to communism. Cuba is quite different today than it was in 1959; a return to the *status quo ante bellum* would probably be impossible.

The Cuban Revolution can be divided into two stages. The first, 1959–1970, can be called the *charismatic stage*. At various times during that period, Fidel Castro promised to become less dominant and to delegate authority; at other times, groups tried to take more power and to reduce his control. Yet power remained in the hands of the maximum leader, and the erstwhile pretenders were rudely awakened to the realities of personal leadership on the island. During the charismatic stage, Fidel Castro could take credit for many of the good things that had

happened in the country—but he also had to accept responsibility for those policies that were bad for the Cuban people.

The second stage of the Cuban Revolution, the years since 1970, can be termed the *institutionalized* one. Fidel Castro is still the most powerful individual in Cuban government and the chief policy maker. Nevertheless, due to domestic failures and international pressures, this leader decided on a set of procedures that would institutionalize the revolution. These included a procedure for choosing the chief executive; rule making bodies at the local, regional, and national levels; and an increased emphasis on the Communist party.

The Charismatic Stage

Fidel Castro, initially and to some extent to this day, is one of those relatively few individuals in history who derive their authority and legitimacy from their own characteristics and accomplishments. Most political leaders receive their legitimacy from being born with certain rights (as in a monarchy) or from being chosen in a prescribed manner such as an election (as in a liberal democracy). But Castro was and is accepted because he has charisma, literally "the gift of grace." It is mystical and, some would say, God-given. Having this characteristic in the last quarter of a century, Castro is in the select company of such individuals as Mao Tse-tung, Charles de Gaulle, and Jawaharlal Nehru.

Charisma has five important qualities. The first is that charismatic leaders are the creation of their followers. One does not become charismatic simply by deciding to do so; rather, this is a characteristic bestowed on leaders by their followers. In the case of Castro, this almost superhuman quality grew out of the impossible things that he was able to do. By defeating the Batista regime with only a small band, he performed the impossible. He became a legend before his thirty-third birthday and has been the maximum leader of Cuba ever since.

At times charismatic leaders are given almost religious characteristics by their followers. In the early years of the Cuban Revolution, it was reported that many Cuban families had pictures of Castro, with his band of "disciples" around him and the slight hint of a halo around his head. Other reports tell of Cubans who fingered rosary beads or genuflected when Castro made a visit to a particular area. The most dramatic statement of this nearly religious nature of Castro's attraction was made by a Cuban Presbyterian minister who wrote in 1960, "It is my conviction which I state now with full responsibility for what I am saying, that Fidel Castro is an instrument in the hands of

God for the establishment of his reign among men." [1]

A second quality of charismatic leaders is the extent of their contact with the people, which in the case of Castro has been constant and almost complete. He has traveled throughout the country, meeting the people and discussing the problems of the country and the area. Many commentators have described these meetings as very friendly ones, with a give-and-take between leader and follower and much good humor. Cubans have been known to make such comments as "You're getting fat now that you're in power," which indicates that, although charisma gives an individual certain almost supernatural qualities, Castro is still an approachable figure. Further, revolutionary Cuba is such that nearly all inhabitants of the island can come in contact with Castro in one way or another. The public rallies with speeches by Castro that are now famous have brought large numbers of Cubans together, attracting at one time in the early 1960s nearly 1 million of the approximately 7 million people on the island to a plaza in Havana. Another method of contact is through television. The Cuban Revolution has been called the first revolution by television. Even before the Castro Revolution, Cuba had the most receivers per capita for that medium in Latin America (and a higher level than in most European countries.)

A third characteristic of charismatic authority is that the leaders regard themselves as elected from above to fulfill a mission. Fidel Castro—even before his conversion to communism—perceived the revolution as part of a greater historical movement against tyranny and oppression. Therefore, the Cuban Revolution and its leader are seen to be protected and blessed in their role as part

[1] Rafael Cepeda, "Fidel Castro y el Reino de Dios," *Bohemia*, July 17, 1960, p. 110.

of the larger historical movement. Likewise, since the leader is acting in concert with larger historical forces not always visible to more ordinary men, he alone retains the right to determine correct behavior in the service of the revolution.

Fourth, the behavior of the leader in power in a charismatic situation is antibureaucratic. Castro has consistently been highly disdainful of and uninterested in the routine processes of public administration. In the 1960s, he resisted any attempt to institutionalize his revolution and defeated those who attempted such a process, but at the same time used these events to the benefit of his own noninstitutional leadership.

The final characteristic of charismatic authority is its instability over time. In the short run, people may follow charismatic leaders regardless of how well they govern, particularly if there is an outside threat. In the longer run, leaders must deliver some beneficial outputs of government. Further, even when the leader is as antibureaucratic as Castro is, there is still some routinization through a new revolutionary tradition. Finally, charisma is unstable simply because the leaders are human and die. Charisma cannot be passed on to the next generation, so leaders must find some way to make their revolutions "immortal," most likely through some sort of institutionalization.

*Relationship with the People:
Egalitarianism and Elitism*
Although the basis of his legitimacy is charismatic, it is the mixture of egalitarianism and elitism that Castro displays that makes

Castro talking with workers

(Lee Lockwood/Black Star)

360

his government unique. Although the two elements are seemingly contradictory, they are combined by the leader in a consistent fashion.

After 1959, Fidel Castro continued to differentiate himself from previous Cuban political leaders by adopting a highly egalitarian, populist style of government. He tried to preserve the egalitarian mystique of his revolution by such actions as continuing to wear his army fatigues and his beard and maintaining his informal bearing. In consequence, the masses at large identified themselves with their new leader, both as a charismatic hero and as a genuinely popular hero. This popularity was not ended immediately, if at all, by the hard times the revolution fell on in the 1960s.

However, all was not just style. Fidel Castro and his circle of followers believed that a more meaningful "direct democracy" had been established. Rather than a formal democracy based on elections, the *fidelistas* argued that they had a democracy based on face-to-face contacts. Castro traveled the country, talked to the people about their problems, and tried to solve those which he deemed needy of solution. Hence Cuba, according to the true believers, had become a democracy in two senses. Cuba was a democracy because Castro was the people's choice: he would have won any election staged during the early years of the revolution. But equally important, Cuba was a democracy in the sense that it was taking care of the true needs of the people. This could be done, they would argue, because of the small size of the island.

Nevertheless, this does not mean that Castro's brand of democracy is one that gives the people what they say they want. It is elitist in the sense that the political leader decides what is in the true interests of the people. This was not new to Cuba with the Castro government, as the Latin American tradition is one in which the common good is not seen as the result of the bargaining of the interest groups of the society. Rather, the tradition is that there is an objective common good, which is greater than the sum of the individual interests and which the good leader can and should strive to bring to the people. As Castro himself stated,

The leaders in a revolutionary process are not infallible receptacles of what the people think. One must find out how the people think and sometimes combat certain opinions, certain ideas, certain points of view which, in the judgment of the leaders, are mistaken. One cannot conceive of the leader as a simple carrier of ideas, a simple collector of opinions and impressions. He has to be also a creator of opinions, a creator of points of view; he has to *influence* the masses.[2]

In theory and in practice, then, *fidelismo* is premised on the belief that the leadership of a select core of intellectually superior and proven revolutionaries has to lead the masses, who are intrinsically nonrevolutionary. Beginning in 1959, the fidelista governing formula was one in which basic policies were set from above by Castro and his circle of trusted advisers. In turn, the masses below were mobilized by the regime's revolutionary organizations, in compliance with the directives from above. So there was much political activity of the masses, a lot of it spontaneous or voluntary, but it was always in compliance with the directives and tasks determined by the leadership. Revolutionary Cuba thus had developed a system of mass mobilization in which decision making was highly centralized.

[2] Lee Lockwood, *Castro's Cuba, Cuba's Fidel* (New York: Vintage Books, 1969), p. 150.

Decision Making

In the first decade of the revolution, this centralization was in the hands of a very few people, and especially those of Castro himself. He tended to make not only the major decisions, but also a number of minor ones. Indeed, he was criticized by foreign supporters of the revolution for acting as if he personally had to make all the decisions. Surely the gamut of decisions made by Castro personally was impressive, including the exact route of highways, the best use of a plot of land, artificial insemination techniques, designs of fishing boats, strains of sugar cane to be used, and many others. On occasion he was known to make impromptu policy decisions while talking on national television. On other occasions he imposed his views by personal fiat even though his technical advisers counseled other courses.

No modern leader, even Fidel Castro, can make all decisions alone. Advisers, both political and technical, are necessary. In the case of Cuba, the leadership circle that surrounded Castro in the 1960s consisted primarily of his ex-guerrilla comrades from the mountain days, who tended to react still as soldiers obeying their commander. Therefore, there was a lack of criticism and debate in the inner circle.

This does not mean that the inner circle was completely homogeneous. There were subgroups with differing backgrounds, ages, and probably functional interests. Occasionally, the disputes within the leadership group became public; at other times individuals and even groups enjoyed sufficient latitude to coalesce around a policy position and to voice their opinions independently of Castro. But in the long run, any coalition without him was unstable. If such a coalition was perceived by Castro as an opposing faction, it was expelled from the inner circle. At other times, he played off opposing groups to his own advantage, but in the end he always was pivotal to the outcome of internal power struggles and policy disputes. Any coalition ultimately had to group around Castro if its position were to prevail within the regime.

One of the results of this kind of centralized decision making was that personal access to the leader was essential. Given the lack of institutionalization of decision making and the informality that Castro and his inner circle showed, there simply were no normal channels to reach the leader. He might have been in Havana, in the Soviet Union, or in an extremely remote part of the island, checking on the progress of the agrarian reform or the educational program or anything else. Furthermore, it was quite possible that no one would know when he would be back in the capital. This informal nature of Castro's government would not have been so important if power had been delegated to ministers and heads of departments. But the fact is that such delegation had not been made—and for that matter the ministers and heads might have been acting in the same informal way.

In sum, the decision-making process in Cuba in the pre-1970 period could be categorized as the Moncada complex or the Sierra Maestra complex. All decision making shared the four characteristics of those two armed experiences discussed in chapter 4. First, maximum, if not unfeasible, objectives were staked out. Second, there was a belief in the subjective factors (will and determination of dedicated revolutionaries) in spite of the objective problems. Third, the decision making continued to depend on the penchant for revolutionary action and elitism. And finally, there was a disdain for political organization. Castro dominated all major decisions, and projects were undertaken as if they were military adventures, often without adequate preparation.

This system did give the Cuban government much flexibility in meeting its problems. Many Cubans, including the leaders, saw this system as a positive feature of the period. Castro talked about his personal power in the following way:

I don't experience any personal satisfaction whatsoever when I read or hear some of those flattering qualities which are attributed to me in the press. I have never spent a single second of pleasure over such things. I can tell you in all sincerity that they have no importance to me. And I think this is a positive thing. Because, as a general rule, power corrupts men. It makes them egotistical; it makes them selfish. Fortunately, this has never happened to me, and I don't think it will. Very honestly, I can say that nothing satisfies me more than seeing that every day things depend less and less on me, and more and more upon a collective spirit grouped in the institutions.[3]

The Uses of Institutions

In spite of Fidel Castro's protestations, the evidence was to the contrary before 1970: institutions had no more significant power— and the leader no less—than before. Castro feared that institutionalization and bureaucratization of the revolution would take the impetus away from the original goals of that movement and that there would be a new class, a new oligarchy, governing in its own interests. Castro also believed that he, better than anyone else, knew best what the interests of Cuba were, a feeling shared by many of his followers. Finally, he fully recognized that the institutionalization and bureaucratization of the revolution would limit him personally both in freedom of spontaneous informal action and in power.

In the first two years of the revolutionary government, there was no formal organiza-

[3] Ibid., p. 186.

tion of Castro's supporters. Rather, there was an uneasy alliance of his guerrilla movement members, along with increasingly large numbers of the pre-Castro communist party, the Popular Socialist party (PSP). In 1961 the two groups were merged into the Integrated Revolutionary Organization (ORI). In the following two years, the old PSP members became more and more powerful, until they were stripped of authority and the ORI was replaced by the more fidelista-dominated United Party of the Socialist Revolution (PURS) in 1963. PURS lasted but two years until 1965, when it was replaced by the Cuban Communist party (PCC).

On paper, it appeared that Castro had lost power with the creation of the PCC; however, the contrary was the case. Although the PCC followed closely the Soviet model of the party, an examination of the composition of the various levels shows that the founding of the PCC actually guaranteed the continued supremacy of personal rule over institutionalized authority. Indeed, it signified the further extension of Castro's personal authority through organizational means. At the apex of the party were a hundred-member Central Committee, an eight-person Politburo, and a six-member Party Secretariat. Although some ex-PSP members were in the Central Committee, most of its members had military titles, indicating that they were former guerrilla fighters with Castro. The Politburo was entirely of fidelista background. The ex-PSP leadership was allowed representation in the Party Secretariat, but the latter's functions were placed under control of one of Fidel's most trusted subordinates, Armando Hart, who was named Organizational Secretary of the PCC. Castro was named First Secretary of the Cuban Communist party. The party (as well as the police, the armed forces, and the mass organizations) has been led exclusively by the fidelistas who have demonstrated personal commitment to Fidel Castro.

The two best instances showing that Castro did not let the party institutionalization detract from his power involve the same man, Aníbal Escalante, who had been a member of the PSP before the Castro Revolution. With the organization of the ORI in 1961, he became the Secretary (or, in effect, its head), and during the following year the PSP became increasingly powerful, led by Escalante. On March 26, 1962, Castro addressed the nation on television and passionately denounced the leader. According to Castro, Escalante had forced Cuba into a sectarian straitjacket, and so had many of his subordinates in the provinces. All of them were displaying an incredible degree of arrogance, since the PSP had been very late in supporting the guerrilla war. Escalante and his followers were becoming an independent power source in the revolution, something Castro was not willing to tolerate. The Escalante clique was removed from party office.

Escalante spent the next few years in Eastern Europe, in a relatively unimportant post for the Cuban government. Toward the end of 1965, he returned to Cuba and began to hold meetings with former PSP disciples or like-minded dissidents who were critical of the fidelista line in foreign and domestic policy, although not critical of the revolution itself. They were pro-Soviet in their orientation and loyalty. Later, the Escalante group established contacts with Soviet bloc embassy officials, journalists, and other representatives.

In late 1967, in the second Escalante affair, he and thirty-four other individuals were arrested, tried by the Central Committee of the PCC, and sentenced to from two to fifteen years on charges of having operated as a subversive "microfaction" within the regime. The principal charges against the group were that it had actively opposed Cas-

tro's foreign and domestic policies and that, through its contacts with Soviet and Eastern European representatives, it had conspired against his leadership by advocating a reduction of Soviet bloc support to Cuba in order to force his ouster and replacement by more reliable old-line Communist leaders. These clearly were activities that Castro could not countenance.

Both cases show quite clearly that in the 1960s Fidel Castro was not limited in his freedom of action and power by the many organizations that appeared in revolutionary Cuba. The nation did not develop into a bureaucratic communist system of the Soviet mold despite its formal adherence to Marxism-Leninism and its creation of a ruling Communist party in theory. Instead, the Cuban regime remained distinctively fidelista in character, combining personal rule by a charismatic leader with a socialist reordering of Cuba's economy, society, and polity. Castro's initial charismatic authority was strengthened as he gained personal control over the pivotal organs of political power and decision-making. At various times, he occupied all of the following posts, indeed, four and five simultaneously: Commander in Chief of the Armed Forces, Prime Minister of the Revolutionary Government, President of the National Institute of Agrarian Reform, First Secretary of the Cuban Communist party (and therefore ranking member of the Politburo and Secretariat of the party), and head of the high-level Economic Group for Special Plans.

Castro's distrust of organization included not only that which affected his power directly, but also lower-level bureaucracy that might decrease his power indirectly and corrupt the revolution. In 1967 he attacked civil servants, many of whom he had chosen personally. His antibureaucracy attack blamed European socialist countries for imposing upon Cuba "certain administrative systems and certain forms of organization heavily infected with bureaucratism."

At that time, there were in Havana alone some seventy-four thousand administrative clerks earning a total of more than 140 million pesos a year. While it could seriously be argued that that was too much, the solution of the Cuban leadership was to control this bureaucratization by increasing the power of the executive and by instructing its representatives to "discuss and examine" the views and suggestions of the rank and file. In short, the "debureaucratization" campaign led to more power and responsibility at the top of the structure, in the hands of Castro and his inner circle.

Institutionalization
in the 1970s

The year 1970 seems to be a turning point in the Cuban Revolution, although both the time for proper perspective and the empirical studies of the changes are lacking. That year was important because Fidel Castro dramatically failed for the first time in his post-1959 political career, specifically in the highly touted sugar harvest. Apparently, what followed in the 1970s was a change in the nature of Fidel Castro's personal power, from that Sierra Maestra style of the 1960s to a more institutionalized system. This institutionalization came about in both the political structure and the Communist party.

In November 1972 there was a reorganization of the top Cuban government apparatus resulting in the establishment of an Executive Committee that held power above the Council of Ministers and was composed of ten Deputy Prime Ministers with direct control over several agencies or Ministries. Not surprisingly, Fidel Castro became the President of the new Executive Committee and

retained the premiership of the Council of Ministers. He also maintained his control over several Ministries and agencies, especially armed forces and security, surely two that any leader would like to control. However, there was more delegation of authority than before.

In 1976, after a year of discussion of drafts within Cuba, a new constitution was adopted. This new constitution envisions delegation of authority in Havana, more democracy in the choice of leaders, and a certain decentralization of power away from Havana.

The basic unit of the new governing system is the Municipal Assembly of Peoples' Power, one for each of the municipalities in Cuba. The Municipal Assemblies are chosen for two-and-one-half-year terms in free elections, with all (except criminals) over age sixteen voting. They are in charge of all matters that are purely municipal in nature, within the broad guidelines of national policy. They do not, however, have authority over national functions that are carried out within their geographic domains, such as sugar production.

The Municipal Assemblies elect delegates to Provincial Assemblies of Peoples' Power on the basis of population. These delegates, along with the presidents of the Municipal Assemblies who are ex officio members, serve for two-and-one-half-year terms and have authority over all matters that are provincial in scope.

The Municipal Assemblies also elect the members of the National Assembly of Peoples' Power for five-year terms. The National Assembly is the law-making body of national scope. From among its members, it also elects a Council of State, composed of a President, one First Vice President, five Vice Presidents, and twenty-three members. The President of the Council of State, thus elected, is at one time both the Head of State and the Head of Government. The duties of the Council of State include bringing legislative projects to the National Assembly and serving as an interim law-making group between sessions of the assembly.

The highest ranking executive branch of the new system is the Council of Ministers. It "constitutes the Government of the Republic" and is composed of the Head of State and the Head of Government (that is, the President of the Council of State), the First Vice President and five Vice Presidents from the Council of State, the President of the Central Planning Board, the other Ministers, and "others that the law determines."

The system produces notable contrasts with the Soviet system. As in the Soviet Union, it is not necessary to be a member of the Communist party to be elected to these governmental assemblies. However, apparently there will be multiple candidates at the Municipal Assembly level, thus necessitating an electoral system more in keeping with that of France; if a candidate does not obtain an absolute majority (50 percent plus one) on the first ballot, there is a second ballot among the top vote-getters. Also in contrast to the Soviet Union, only the municipal level in Cuba is elected by the people directly, other levels being elected by the Municipal Assemblies.

Further, the Cuban system, unlike the Soviet, explicitly combines the Head of State and the Head of Government into one individual. Since the new Cuban Constitution mentions the contributions of Castro, by name, in its preamble, this perhaps is no accident.

As a prelude to this new system, the people in the provincial capital of Matanzas elected the first Municipal Assembly of Peoples' Power in 1974. These elections were secret and voluntary, and the experiment was apparently a success.

Organization of the Cuban national government, as stated in the 1976 Constitution

* By constitutional provision, individuals chosen by the National Assembly for the posts of President and Vice-President of the Council of State hold the same positions on the Council of Ministers.

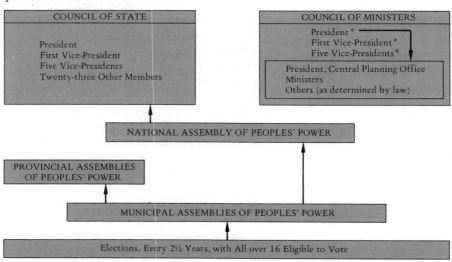

At the same time, the attempt is being made to vitalize the Cuban Communist party, which during the 1960s was the smallest and least powerful of any communist country. In December 1975 the PCC held its first national party congress, adopting a program in keeping with the new constitution. Concurrently, the attempt is being made to expand PCC membership in size, while at the same time training its members more effectively for its chief function as the vanguard organization: political guidance.

Cuba is apparently in a stage of transition from charismatic to institutionalized power. What this means for the personal power of Fidel Castro is not at all clear. Surely he is still the most powerful person in Cuba, and visitors are still impressed with his great knowledge of many policy fields. If the experience of the 1960s is any key, one might argue that Castro will be able to use this institutionalization to enhance his power.

The evidence is sketchy. When asked in 1974 if the Politburo had ever rejected any proposal of his, Castro responded with a big smile, "It could happen." [4] Yet scholars disagree. One recently concluded that "the Cuban Revolution is over," meaning that Cuba was no longer different than the countries of Eastern Europe.[5] Another less dramatically concluded that "the romanticism of the 1960s has apparently come to an end." [6] Charisma has given way to pragmatism, delegation of power, technocracy, and revitalization of the Communist party.

Castro has more formal power than ever before, since his late-1976 election as President of the Council of State. For the first time, he is both Head of State and Head of Government; moreover, he is still First Secretary of the PCC. Probably he no longer makes dramatic decisions without consulting and listening to his experts among the technocrats; perhaps there is more "collegial leadership" within the Council of State and the Council of Ministers, although he heads both. Castro was fifty years old in 1976; he is likely to be at least "first among equals" for a long time to come.

[4] Frank Mankiewicz and Kirby Jones, *With Fidel: A Portrait of Castro and Cuba* (Chicago: Playboy Press, 1975), p. 240.

[5] Maurice Halperin, *The Rise and Decline of Fidel Castro* (Berkeley: University of California Press, 1972), p. vi.
[6] Carmelo Mesa Lago, *Cuba in the 1970s* (Albuquerque: University of New Mexico Press, 1974), p. ix.

3

Castro's Early Years: Childhood and Youth in Prerevolutionary Cuba

Fidel Castro Ruz was born on August 13, 1926, on his father's ranch near the town of Birán, Mayarí township, in Oriente, the easternmost province of Cuba. The area was a poor one, with an inequitable distribution of wealth. In 1953, a national census reported that only 1 percent of the inhabitants of the area had attended college and only approximately 40 percent had attended even the first grade. Yet Fidel was born into wealth. His father raised sugar cane, which was sold to the nearby sugar refinery of the United Fruit Company, and employed some 500 workers, most of whom were black.

The Cuba Fidel grew up in was very different from that of today. Before turning to his personal life, we must consider the nature of his native land at the time of his birth.

Cuban History

Of all the countries colonized by Spain in the sixteenth and seventeenth centuries, Cuba was the last to obtain its independence. This short national history is important in understanding the Castro Revolution.

The Spanish Period

Christopher Columbus landed on the island during his first voyage in 1492, and just a few years later a colony was established, beginning a colonial period that lasted until 1898. The island was an important center of Spanish colonialism only for a brief period in the sixteenth century. Interest soon turned to the mainland, especially to the precious metals of Mexico and Peru, so from 1540 to approximately 1800, Cuba was a neglected, underpopulated backwater of the Spanish empire. This status changed at the beginning of the nineteenth century with the new importance of tobacco and sugar as crops and with the concurrent importation of African slaves. The number of slaves in Cuba grew enormously, from about 32,000 in 1763 to 286,942 in 1827.

While the rest of Latin America was making moves toward independence during the first two decades of the nineteenth century, there was little such movement in Cuba. One major reason for this seems to have been the large percentage of slaves. It had already been seen in Haiti, a former French colony nearby, that independence had come by way of slave rebellions and eventual expulsion of the whites, a process that Cuban whites did not want repeated on their island. Another major reason was that, with the new importance of sugar, Cuba was simply too valuable a colony for the Spanish to lose it. Further, it was relatively easy to protect because of its insular nature.

As the nineteenth century progressed, there were increasing conflicts between *criollos* (whites of Cuban birth) and *peninsulares* (whites of Spanish, or "peninsular," birth who were sent to administer the colony). Spanish rule became more repressive, and the conflict between the two groups increased.

A series of wars brought Cuban independence. The first, lasting from 1868 to 1878, is commonly referred to as the Ten Years' War. The second unsuccessful attempt for independence was the Little War of 1880. A third attempt began in 1895 and lasted until the United States intervened three years later. Spiritual leader of that movement was José Martí, an intellectual and writer who spent most of the time operating out of the United States. Martí was killed soon after his return to Cuba to fight, but still is regarded as the Father of Cuban Independence. The Spanish reacted savagely, sending in 1896 the notorious General Valeriano Weyler, called "the Butcher" by the Cubans. Weyler put a large number of Cubans into concentration camps and used terrorist tactics against the rebels. Nevertheless, most agree that the rebels were winning when the United States entered the war.

The precipitating factor for United States intervention was the sinking of the battle-ship *Maine* in Havana harbor on February 15, 1898. Although to this day it is not known just who sank the ship, the incident was used as a rationale for United States entry into a war that lasted only four months, but led to United States possession of the Philippines and Puerto Rico and virtual domination of Cuba. After three years of occupation, the United States government forced Cuba to ratify the Platt Amendment and to include it in the country's new constitution before its troops would leave. When Cuban independence came in 1902, it did so with the following stipulations:

(1) Cuba could enter into no treaty with a foreign power that would impair or tend to impair the independence of Cuba or would permit any foreign power to obtain control over any portion of the island;

(2) The Cuban government could incur no foreign debt that ordinary revenues would not cover;

(3) The government consented that the United States could exercise the right to intervene (even militarily) for the preservation of Cuban independence and the maintenance of a government adequate for the protection of life, property, and individual liberty;

(4) For United States defense and protection of the people of Cuba, the government of Cuba would sell or lease to the United States the lands necessary for coaling or naval stations at certain specified points.

Until 1934 at least, when the Platt Amendment was abrogated, Cuban independence was one with strings attached. It was the United States that would decide when the government was not adequate; it was the United States that would decide what amount of debts could be covered by ordinary revenues, unless, of course, they were debts to United States concerns. The naval base that was set up, Guantánamo at the eastern tip of the island, is still a bone of contention between the governments of Cuba and the United States.

United States Interests in the Cuban Economy

The period between independence and the rise of Fidel Castro in Cuba is an example of the complete or nearly complete convergence of interests of United States business and the United States Department of State. Although United States businesses sometimes fought among themselves about policy toward Cuba, the State Department generally favored those groups that wanted to expand trade with Cuba. Cubans were given preferential tariff duties; in exchange, they gave preferential rates to the United States. What developed was an extreme case of the dependency of an underdeveloped country on the United States.

There were clear economic advantages to Cuba from this relationship, at least in the short run. United States private enterprise supplied capital for development of the island that was not available from the Cubans themselves. Much economic infrastructure was introduced by the North American firms, as was technical expertise that was not available in Cuba. In many ways Cuba, with its tropical agricultural products, was a natural trading partner with the industrialized United States. However, both nations did not benefit equally.

One clear example of this unequal power relationship is seen in the establishment of the International Sugar Committee (ISC) in 1917. This committee, made up of five individuals from the United States and Great Britain, limited the Cuban sugar market to those two countries by forcing other nations out of the market. The ISC took on the power to set the price of sugar from the island and to apportion it between the two. Cuba naturally protested this high-handed consumer cartel; however, it accepted the

terms when informed that noncompliance would lead to no more wheat or coal, both of which Cuba imported.

American private companies entered the cultivation of sugar. By 1928, United States groups controlled between 70 and 75 percent of the crop, expanding by buying up the small producers. The high point of their ownership of Cuban sugar came in the years right before the Great Depression.

United States private investment in Cuba was not limited to sugar, as American companies dominated in rubber, chemicals, pharmaceuticals, communications, railroads, and banks. The banks became so important that the Federal Reserve Banks of both Boston and Atlanta opened agencies for United States banks in Cuba. Large loans were granted to the Cuban government, some clearly violating the Platt Amendment. However, the State Department did not interfere with these loans so long as they came from United States banks; furthermore, that government agency used the private banks to bring influence on the Cuban government. Such matters as reduction of the Cuban national budget, tax revision, and even cabinet changes became the preconditions to receiving loans from the American bankers. The Cuban government went farther and farther into debt; by February 1930, it owed $80 million to the Chase Bank of New York alone.

By the 1950s United States capital did not dominate the sugar industry as it had before. Yet, American firms still accounted for 40 percent of the island's sugar production, controlled 40 of the 161 sugar mills, and held 7 of the 10 largest agricultural enterprises. Furthermore, although United States presence in sugar was declining, the opposite was true of influence in the economy as a whole. American companies also controlled 2 of the 3 oil refineries, more than 90 percent of the telephone and electric utilities, 50 percent of the public railroads, much of the mining industry, and much of the tourist industry. Between 1950 and 1958, United States private investments in Cuba rose over 50 percent, from $657 million to $1 billion. The growth areas were petroleum, mining, and service industries. The per capita book value of United States enterprises in Cuba in 1959 was more than three times the value in the rest of Latin America: United States businesses had invested $143 for every Cuban, versus $39 per individual in the Latin American countries.

Political Patterns of the New Nation: 1901–1930

The Constitution of Cuba established a liberal-democratic system, much like that of the United States, with separation of powers and checks and balances. In the early years, leadership in political life and government in Cuba became the province of a relatively small group of individuals who had achieved prominence in the war of independence. Only a small population voted in the elections, which were contested between two parties, the Liberals and the Conservatives.

The Liberals had a more critical attitude toward the United States and called explicitly for the abrogation of the Platt Amendment; they tended to receive more votes from the cities and from the blacks. The Conservatives were more pro-American business and had the support of domestic businesses and rural residents, who were tied in the traditional hacienda, patron-clientele relationships. Nevertheless, at the very foundation of the conflict between the two parties was not ideology, but the struggle to gain and keep the spoils of office.

A constant factor of the period was United States presence. Besides the business interests, there was the constant possibility of intervention under the Platt Amendment. This occurred twice during this period

(1905 and 1917) and indeed was requested by the very first President of the republic, Tomás Estrada Palmas, against his Liberal opponents. People like Estrada, those who used United States intervention and business for their personal fortunes and careers, would pejoratively be called *plattistas* (from the Platt Amendment) or *entreguistas* (ones who "hand over" things to other interests) by later Cubans.

The last President of this period was Gerardo Machado, a Liberal elected in 1924 by promising honesty and a single term of office. However, Machado did not live up to this vow and is remembered today as a heavy-handed, repressive dictator. In 1927 he obtained constitutional amendments that lengthened the term of the President to six years, abolished the vice-presidency, and extended congressional tenures. To silence his opposition he used deportation and assassination. In 1928 he was reelected to a six-year term without opposition.

With the coming of the Great Depression the price of sugar collapsed on the world market. This worsened matters in Cuban domestic politics, and there was much political dissatisfaction, to which Machado replied with repression and terror. All of this resulted in the Revolution of 1933.

The Revolution of 1933 and the Batista Years

The Revolution of 1933 has been called "the lost opportunity" by some students of Cuban politics. Although Machado was deposed by a coup d'état, the events around that fall were much more than a simple changing of people in office. Numerous members of the intelligentsia were rebelling, including professional men, teachers, and students. They called for a new Cuba, without the *entreguismo* ("selling out") of the first thirty years of independence, and they wanted social and economic reform. These intellectuals were organized into various groups, including the Student Directorate, the clandestine organization called only ABC, and the *Auténtico* party. The leader of this latter group was a doctor and professor at the University of Havana, Ramón Grau San Martín.

At the same time, there was a popular uprising in Cuba, centered particularly on the sugar centrales, whose workers had been organized into trade unions by that time. The aims of the workers were revolutionary, calling for a redistribution of income. Indeed, the red flag of communism was seen flying over some centrales.

With the triumph of the revolution, Grau came to the presidency, promising social justice and economic reform. His government, however, was paralyzed by one central factor of Cuban existence: the intervention of the United States Ambassador, Sumner Welles. Welles clearly thought that Grau was not an acceptable ruler, probably because of the radical support that he had. Therefore, the United States government never extended diplomatic recognition to the Grau government, thereby weakening it and being instrumental in its fall in January 1934. Similar intervention by American Ambassadors was common behavior until 1959. A later holder of the post concluded that only the Cuban President had more power on the island than the United States Ambassador.

It has been argued that a revolution in Cuba would have come in peace and without communism if Grau had been supported, or at least not opposed, by the United States government. Hence, the argument continues, the Castro Revolution would never have occurred, since the social and economic reforms would have been carried out some twenty-five years earlier.

Grau's demise came through a military coup, led by Fulgencio Batista, who dominated Cuban politics for the next twenty-

five years. Batista at that time was a sergeant in the military, a man of mixed blood, who had been born in poverty in 1901. He had been instrumental in the original coup that ousted Machado. Although this coup led to the Grau government, by January 1934 the military group was ready to bow to United States pressure. Batista replaced Grau with a colonel, who soon was recognized by the United States, and Batista became the power behind the throne for the next seven years.

From 1934 to 1940, Batista was army chief of staff and really ruled Cuba through puppet Presidents. In 1940, he was elected President for a four-year term. Many people were surprised when he went to Florida in 1944 when his hand-picked candidate lost. In retrospect, Fulgencio Batista was not a repressive ruler during his first ten-year period. Much was done in the area of social reform; a Labor Ministry was established for the first time; social security laws were passed. The Constitution of 1940, generally accepted as very progressive for its time in Latin America, was adopted. Batista at times allied himself with the communist PSP and also made claims to being a nationalist leader, taking credit for the abrogation of the Platt Amendment in 1934.

In 1944, Grau was elected President of Cuba, amid great hopes that the goals of the Revolution of 1933 would be further achieved. Grau and his successor, Carlos Prío Socarrás, were elected by the Party of the Cuban Revolution (generally called the Auténticos, or Authentics), which Grau had founded in 1934. Their platforms were pro-labor and called for extended social security benefits, agrarian reform, increased industrialization, expansion of public health and education, more equitable distribution of income, and nationalism. However, the two Auténtico administrations failed in meeting those goals, although there was slight progress in some of them. Furthermore, the democrats showed that they could be every bit as corrupt as the strong-man governments of Batista and his puppets had been. The result of eight years of democratic government was disillusionment, both because of the corruption and because of the failure to live up to the stated goals of the Auténtico party.

Because of the disillusionment with the Auténticos, the Party of the Cuban People (known generally as *Ortodoxo,* or Orthodox) was founded in 1947 by a young firebrand named Eduardo Chibás. The symbol of the party was a broom, to clean up the government. One means by which Chibás built a popular following was his weekly radio program. At the end of one particularly impassioned speech in 1951, probably disgraced because he had failed to produce promised evidence against a Cabinet Minister, Chibás dramatically shot himself fatally while still on the air. The Ortodoxos had an effect on many young Cubans of the period, including Fidel Castro.

In the presidential election of 1952, there were three major candidates—one Ortodoxo, one Auténtico, and Fulgencio Batista. Apparently, the Ortodoxo candidate would have won, while every indication was that Batista would not. On March 10, 1952, supporters of Batista staged a bloodless military coup, toppling President Prío and returning the former strong-man. Congress was dismissed, and all political parties were dissolved.

Although originally welcomed by some as a way out of corruption and chaos, the second Batista government was an extremely corrupt one. Estimates are that the dictator left Cuba at the beginning of 1959 with upwards of $300 million. Toward the end of the period, Batista was increasingly repressive, and his was a status quo government, neither desiring nor bringing social or economic change. Batista's major organizational strength came from the more con-

servative politicians, the army, and American business. The United States business establishment—and, for that matter, the United States diplomatic representatives—supported Batista nearly to the end of his administration.

By the 1950s, the "generation of 1930" had clearly failed. In the past thirty years, nearly every known mechanism for the transfer of power had been used. *Personalismo* (the personal attraction of a leader) had clearly been more important than organized political groups. The strong leader had emerged, even more than before, as the key to the balance between the army, organized labor, university students, professional associations, major business interests, and, last but not least, the United States diplomatic representatives. The 1933 Revolution had brought to the center stage a dominant group of left-wing nationalists who were concerned with social and economic problems. However, they were never united and accomplished little or nothing due to the intervention of United States Ambassador Sumner Welles, the emergence of Fulgencio Batista as a strong-man, and, equally important, their own inability when they did have power from 1944 to 1952.

Political Dynamics of Cuba Before the Castro Revolution

At this point, it is possible to make some general statements about the political dynamics of Cuba that pertained before the Castro Revolution. Some of these can be traced to the Spanish heritage of the country, while others seem uniquely Cuban.

As in the rest of Latin America, there never was a revolution that established the mobilization of votes as the only legitimate political resource. Therefore, a number of political power resources were equal, or nearly equal, in legitimacy. These resources included this ability to obtain votes (as used by the Auténticos), military power (Batista), and economic power (the United States businesses). The result was a tentative and uneasy situation in which one had to wait to see if so much military power would be more or less effective than so many votes.

Also similar to the rest of Latin America, the political system was built on a philosophical heritage much different than that of the United States. Spanish corporate heritage brought with it a very centralized government, centralized not only in location but also in the hands of one man—the President. The tradition also included patrimonial relationships, which meant, on the individual level, that many members of the lower social classes would be protected by a patrón, as in the case of rural workers on a hacienda. This feature of the patrimonial system was not so prevalent in Cuba as in other Latin American countries, given the different occupational structure. Nevertheless, patrimonialism on a group level meant that people at the top—the elites—would attempt to capture or co-opt emergent groups, such as labor or peasants. Through this patrimonial relationship the new group would receive some of the things that it desired; in return, it would support the people at the top. For example, labor unions have seldom been independent forces in Latin American, or Cuban, politics; they have consistently been tied to political groups or leaders in a co-optative relationship.

While the tradition was similar in Cuba, the groups that were in conflict on the island differed from those in most of Latin America for historical and economic reasons. The group common to them all was the military, gaining prestige from the wars of independence and using force as its power resource.

Along with the military, two other groups that formed the nineteenth-century oligarchy in most of Latin America were the large landowners and the Roman Catholic church. There were large Cuban landowners who were important politically. Nevertheless, the Cuban situation was different because of the large amount of land controlled by foreign interests and because of the market orientation of sugar cultivation. The landed, while powerful, were less influential than in many Latin American countries. Likewise, the church was less powerful. As a rule, the Catholic church in Latin America has been more powerful where it had land and wealth itself and where it had large numbers of obedient followers. Neither occurred in Cuba.

In Cuba, university students and labor unions were important. Students have traditionally played an important part in Latin American politics because they are respected as the new elite; indeed, a very small percentage of college-aged individuals are able to attend the university. Furthermore, they are easily organized, tend to go to universities in the national capitals and other important cities, and generally are reformist, revolutionary, or at least oriented to change in some form. Although the labor unions of Cuba were co-opted, they did have power. Their numbers included not only industrial workers, but also the workers on the sugar centrales. It was much easier to organize workers of the rural proletariat than the atomized members of the peasantry when they lived on squatter farms or in small groups on a patrón-dominated hacienda.

Cuba, also in contrast with much of Latin America, had no powerful group of capitalist entrepreneurs. In much of the area, there are strong upper-class elements that control both agrarian and industrial investment. But in Cuba both the industrial and agrarian enterprises tended to be dominated by United States interests. While a Cuban "sugar bourgeoisie" had emerged (that is,

Cubans with large investments in that economic activity), it did not have the power of similar groups in other Latin American countries.

The groups in Cuba—both Cuban and American—existed in an uneasy equilibrium. It was difficult for any group to do anything that the other groups did not at least acquiesce in.

Two other elements of the Cuban political culture were the traditions of violence and radicalism. A number of civil wars were necessary before independence was obtained. Partly because of this, Cuban politics were more violent than in most other Latin American countries. Students participated in politics, and many times tended to do so violently. The Presidents (especially Machado and Batista) used violence, imprisonment, and execution more than most Latin American presidents.

Another Cuban tradition was that of radicalism. As in most of the rest of Latin America, a communist party had existed since the 1920s, and other radical groups of various philosophies (anarcho-syndicalists, Trotskyites) were also present. The Communist party had lost some of its credibility by cooperating with Batista during his first presidency. It was later outlawed and repressed by him during the post-1952 dictatorship. Nevertheless, the radical tradition had been established.

Life in the Castro Family

Fidel was born into privilege. His father, Angel Castro y Argiz, had amassed a considerable amount of land through hard work, illegal movement of his boundary lines, and persecution of his political opponents. It is estimated that the estate was worth half a million dollars at the time of his death in 1956.

Angel Castro had come from Galicia, Spain, as a conscript in the war of Cuban independence, later deciding to remain on the island. He always blamed the United States for Spain's defeat, and young Fidel first heard anti-American feelings from his father. The elder Castro started out as a manual laborer after the war, probably for the United Fruit Company. His ascent to a man of wealth was extremely unusual in Cuba, for manual laborers were usually preempted from such mobility by the lack of opportunities for education, the social stigma of being a manual worker, and, simply, the lack of any available land. Nevertheless, by the time of the birth of Fidel, Angel Castro had created a large estate and, by selling his sugar cane to the United Fruit Company, had become a wealthy man.

Fidel was the fourth child of the seven born to Angel Castro and his second wife, Lina Ruz González. There had been two children born during Angel Castro's first marriage, and Fidel grew up in a household with a half-brother, a half-sister, four sisters, and two brothers. Fidel, his two older sisters, and his older brother were born out of wedlock, although their parents were later married. It is not clear whether the first wife was still living at the time of Fidel's birth, although it appears so. Hence, the strapping ten-pound baby was born into the household as the fourth child of Angel Castro and his then cook and mistress. Some detractors of Castro today would go so far as to say that his illegitimacy was "the driving force of his personality."

From an early age, Fidel was a very active individual. Even before the age of six, he developed a love for the land, for horses and dogs, and especially for the sea, which was only a few miles north of his home. He liked to go to the nearby port and listen to the fishermen tell their tales of sharks and other adventures.

Family life was filled with tensions and quarrels. The two sets of children did not get along. Castro's father was argumentative, strong-willed, violent, and authoritarian. His mother seems to have been the dominant force in the household, especially in later years as Angel Castro became more infirm and more inclined to drink heavily. There was no family life per se, although the nine children and two parents lived in the same house. The house was dirty and run down, without an inside toilet, despite the fact that the family could certainly have afforded one.

Fidel's relations with his father were always bad. At age six or seven, the boy asked to be sent to school, to which his father replied that it was unnecessary, as he personally had advanced very well in life without any education. The elder Castro gave in when Fidel threatened to burn the house if his request was not granted. At age thirteen Fidel tried to organize the sugar workers on the family estate in a strike against his father, out of a feeling that they were not paid well enough. His father, in turn, tried to have Fidel arrested.

While this childhood must have had some effect on young Fidel, the lack of complete information makes it somewhat hazardous to draw any specific conclusions. Nevertheless, one critic of Castro has concluded that, "by the time Fidel Castro reached young manhood, psychological, and possibly physically traumatic, forces had shaped his character so as to make him receptive to the destructive career he would embark upon." [1]

These family disagreements continued

[1] Nathaniel Weyl, *Red Star Over Cuba* (New York: Devin–Adair, 1962), p. 48.

into later life, even during and after the armed revolution that brought Castro to power. When Fulgencio Batista mistakenly announced the deaths of Fidel Castro and his brother Raúl in late 1956, their mother's first reaction was to go to nearby Santiago, to see about getting the sons' inheritances for herself. Later, during the armed insurrection, Lina Castro worried about her sugar cane fields and feared that the revolutionaries under her son would burn them, a fear that was later justified when the crop went up in smoke. Castro's mother and older brother, Ramón, were incensed when the family farm was nationalized by the land reform enacted by Castro after coming to power, but Ramón had helped during the guerrilla phase by supplying his brother's troops and later worked for his brother's government.

The family member who has been closest to Castro is his brother Raúl, some four years younger. Although they are quite different in appearance, temperament, and perhaps ideology (Raúl reportedly was of leftist persuasion long before Castro), they have worked together since their adolescence. The two brothers were captured together after the Moncada attack in 1953, were in prison at the same time, and fought side by side during the guerrilla struggle. The family member who was never reconciled to the revolution was Castro's youngest sister, Juana ("Juanita"), who apparently could not get over the loss of the family's wealth at her brother's hands. She helped the counterrevolutionaries who were trying unsuccessfully to overthrow her brother in 1962–1963 and finally fled the island in 1964, going to the United States, as one of the many Cuban exiles. Castro helped his sister in her departure, by allowing her to take many of her possessions, while others were permitted to take only the equivalent of five dollars. Juanita later said and wrote many derogatory things about her brother.

Castro's Education

Fidel Castro first entered the local school near the family estate. As was typical of rural Cuban schools at the time, it was inadequate and suitable only for the first several years of grammar school. His later preuniversity education was exclusively in private, religious schools.

The first of these religious schools was the LaSalle School, run by the Marianist brothers in the nearby city of Santiago. He spent several years in LaSalle, but then was moved to the Colegio Dolores, an elementary school run by the Jesuits, in which discipline was required, something that the boy did not appreciate. At one point, he was suspended for leading a strike in a dining hall.

On graduation from the Dolores school at age sixteen, Castro went to another Jesuit institution, the fashionable and expensive Colegio Belén, a preparatory school in Havana. His best subjects there were agriculture, Spanish, and history, all of which were to be of aid to him in his later career. In 1944, he was named the "best high school athletic" in Cuba, participating especially in basketball and baseball. A scouting report of the New York Yankees later stated that Fidel Castro was a good prospect as a major league pitcher.

Yet not all of his activities were in academics and sports. It appears that by this time Castro had developed a feeling for the

Castro playing baseball

(Lee Lockwood/Black Star)

plight of the poor and spent time discussing problems with the manual workers at the Colegio. If the youth could not be found, the teachers first looked in the kitchen to see if he was talking to the cook.

Other activities were disruptive, showing his personality and typical responses even at such an early age. In one case, after an argument with a teacher about a grade, Castro went to get a gun, returning to find that the teacher had wisely fled. Another incident that happened during his years at Belén had to do with a wager that he could ride a bicycle down a hill, at full speed, into a stone wall. This he did, a demonstration of his great courage, to some. Others do not see this as an admirable feat at all, and one report states that young Castro was unconscious for several days and suffered a kind of brain damage called logorrhea, or the tendency to talk incessantly and incoherently. This, the detractors say, accounts for Castro's tendency to give long speeches since coming to power (although few seriously could state that these discourses are incoherent). Yet another incident from this period at Belén has to do with an argument that Castro had with a larger colleague. The story goes that the argument ended in a fight, in which Castro was thoroughly beaten. Yet he recuperated and returned a second and third day, with the same result. This incident supposedly shows his personal courage and unwillingness to accept defeat, with the older and larger boy finally respecting him very much.

In spite of all these conflicts, and those which continued with his father when he returned home, Castro graduated from the Colegio Belén in 1945. The high school yearbook stated,

Fidel distinguished himself always in all the subjects related to letters. His record is one of excellence, he was a true athlete, always defending with bravery and pride the flag of the school. He has known how to win the admiration and the affection of all. He will make law his career and we do not doubt that he will fill with brilliant pages the book of his life. He has good timber and the actor in him will not be lacking.[2]

The University Years

In 1945, at the age of nineteen, Fidel Castro entered the Law School of the University of Havana. As was the custom in Latin American universities, the first-year student entered directly into a semiautonomous *facultad* (school) of a university to begin his professional training immediately. The traditional careers that were favored by university students were law and medicine, both of which led to very respected and well-paid careers. Any student interested in politics would probably go into law, although there are notable cases of medical doctors who entered politics. Indeed, this traditional university system produced more lawyers than there were jobs in private practice. Finding few opportunities in private business or being unwilling or unable to return to agricultural careers, many young lawyers turned to politics and government for social mobility.

Studying law because his mother and others thought that he would be a good lawyer "since he liked to talk so much," Castro entered into student politics immediately. During his first two years he was elected as class delegate in the law school. Not all of his political activity was of an

2 Herbert Matthews, *Fidel Castro* (New York: Simon & Schuster, 1969), p. 22.

378

electoral nature, however. At that time at the University of Havana there existed a number of "action groups," which had originated as leftist groups during the abortive Revolution of 1933. By 1946 they had become little more than opportunist groups that conflicted over campus power, favors with the national government, and lecture notes. They were no longer leftist in any meaningful sense; indeed, the action groups had been responsible for the decline of the power of the Communist party among the students. The groups often fought in the streets, with guns, and Castro himself admits that he carried a gun at times while a university student.

He belonged to one of the two principal action groups, the Revolutionary Insurrectional Union (UIR), although some biographers say that Castro had so much personal power that he was always on the fringes of the group. A "Black Legend" about this period states that he was very much a member; that he took part in the skirmishes; and that he was personally responsible for the death of two or more opponents and was arrested for the deaths, although never indicted or convicted.

It seems clear that young Castro was very active in various rebellious activities. At one point, he went with a group of students to a small town to capture a bell that had been rung to call for the first war of independence in 1868; the students felt that the bell rightfully belonged in Havana. On another occasion, he was in a battle with the police over the issue of university autonomy. At that time, both the police and the military were proscribed from entering universities, even in pursuit of criminals. This rule has led to student-police conflicts all over Latin America for many years, and it is conceivable that Castro would have been involved in such a violent conflict.

Two incidents of Castro's university career are particularly noteworthy. The first was his participation in the planning of an invasion of the Dominican Republic. The second was his activity in Bogotá, Colombia, in April 1948.

In 1947 a group of university students, in particular the UIR, planned to invade the Dominican Republic, on the nearby island of Hispaniola. The President of the Dominican Republic at that time was Rafael Trujillo, a military strong-man who had come to power in 1930 and who had the reputation of being one of the most repressive dictators in Latin America at that time.

The UIR secured arms for the invasion and began to train troops on the small island of Cayo Confites near Cuba; Castro belonged to those troops. For sixty days the young men received military training and learned to use the weapons. They received some aid from the President of Venezuela and were not bothered by the Cuban government, under the democratically elected President, Grau. At the last moment, under pressure from the United States, the government of Cuba stopped the planned invasion by sending navy boats to arrest the rebels.

A number of stories about Castro grew out of this incident. One is that, with the navy boats approaching, he proposed to Juan Bosch, a young Dominican later to be President of his country, that they go to the Dominican Republic and start a guerrilla war against Trujillo. Another story has to do with the way Castro escaped arrest by the forces of the Cuban government. Reportedly, he jumped ship and swam to the shore of the Cuban mainland. This story has been embellished by the additions that the waters were shark-infested and that he swam the distance carrying a submachine gun or a machine gun and wearing an ammunition belt. At any rate, he was not arrested and did make it back to the mainland. The incident does show that at age twenty-one Fidel Castro was enough opposed to dictatorships to train to overthrow the one nearby in the Dominican Republic.

The other dramatic incident was Fidel's presence in Bogotá, Colombia, during the riots in April 1948. He and another Cuban student, Rafael del Pino, were there for a meeting of Latin American students. While there were representatives from several Latin American countries, most of the students were from Cuba and Argentina. Their fares were paid by the dictator of Argentina, Juan Perón, and the meeting was intentionally timed to coincide with the inter-American meeting of foreign ministers of the Pan-American Union, the purpose of which was to reform the structure of that organization. The restructuring done in Bogotá created the Organization of American States, later to be used against Castro in power.

Fidel and del Pino were involved in political activities as soon as they arrived. One incident was the showering of the elite audience of the Teatro Colon with anti-American leaflets on April 3. For this the two Cubans were detained and told that foreigners were not allowed to participate in political activities while in the South American country.

The dramatic event was on April 9. In the early afternoon, while walking in the middle of Bogotá, the populist leader of the Colombian Liberal party, Jorge Eliécer Gaitán, was assassinated by a drifter named Roa Sierra. The city immediately exploded in violence, with looting, burning of shops, and indiscriminate killing. This seems to have been a case of purely anomic, or unplanned, violence, the product of a people who had just had their idol killed.

Fidel Castro and Rafael del Pino were probably involved in the violence, but just how is very much a matter of contention.

Castro later said that he admired Gaitán. He probably had met the Colombian leader a few days before the latter's death, and the two students had a meeting scheduled with Gaitán for later in the day of April 9.

Several people agree that Castro participated in the actual violence, although they disagree in just what way. One report was that he went to the hills and fought for several days; another, that he personally killed several priests. Yet another contention is that Castro was in on the planning of Gaitán's murder; this he did, it is said, because he was a member of the Communist Third International, which was trying to trigger a revolution through killing the idol of the masses.

Several days later, Castro and del Pino were sought for arrest by the Colombian police. They received protection in the Cuban embassy and later flew back to their homeland on a cargo plane. Since this is a period of his life that he prefers not to talk about, the world probably will never know Castro's own version of what happened.

Not all Fidel Castro's political activities during his student years were at the university level; he also became involved in national domestic politics through his allegiance to the Ortodoxo party. Young Castro was strongly influenced by the reformist ideas of Eduardo Chibás, and along with Chibás and a number of other important leaders, he was one of the original founders of the party in 1947. Further, Castro took an active part in the unsuccessful Ortodoxo presidential campaign of 1948, traveling the country in an attempt to arouse the support of the masses for Chibás. Perhaps even at the age of twenty-two, Castro did not believe in the peaceful road to power, for within the Ortodoxo movement he had already created a splinter group, Orthodox Radical Action (ARO), that favored insurrection. Most of the members of that group came to the Ortodoxos with backgrounds in the action groups of the University of Havana. Leaving insurrectional activities to help Chibás in electoral politics was for naught, as he was defeated by the Auténtico Carlos Prío Socarrás.

In spite of all of these political activities during his university years, Castro did have sufficient time to pursue his studies and graduate with a law degree in 1950. His academic record is a matter of controversy. Raúl Castro has shown report cards indicating that his brother was an excellent student. Others say that he was a very mediocre student, probably passed because of his personal power. Even Fidel himself has stated that he was not a conscientious student, rarely studied until right before examinations, and, indeed, chose the wrong university career. Later he was to regret that he had not majored in something that would have been more practical and would have helped him more in facing Cuba's agricultural and economic problems.

Castro's personal relations with other students at the University of Havana are open to argument. Some students nicknamed him *bola de churre* (ball of dirty grease) because of his slovenly personal habits. Apparently he never has been concerned with such matters as personal cleanliness because he is too preoccupied with more important issues. Other biographers say that Fidel was no longer able to use his extraordinary size (he is six feet, one inch) to be an outstanding athlete, as he had been in high school. He participated in debating, although his abilities are disputed. For a time he had a radio program, along with another UIR member, and indeed failed to go for the broadcast one day when another action group attacked and killed his UIR colleague.

One student whom he met was Mirta Díaz Balart, sister of a good friend. They fell in love, and although her family did not approve, they were married on October 12, 1948, in Santiago de Cuba, in a religious ceremony. A son, Fidelito, was born on September 1, 1949. However, the marriage did not last. They were divorced while Fidel was in prison on the Isle of Pines in 1954, as Mirta Castro apparently never approved of her husband's revolutionary activities. She moved to the United States, taking Fidelito with her. The son was educated for a number of years in New York, but had returned to Cuba in time to ride into Havana on a tank with his triumphant father in January 1959. Castro has never remarried, some say because he is too tied up in the revolution to have a normal family life. Detractors state that Fidel has had a number of affairs and children since coming to power although there is no clear evidence of this. He has had a constant companion, Celia Sánchez, since she joined his guerrilla band in the early days of the conflict in 1957. She is his confidant, secretary, and housekeeper—some would add mistress to that list. Fidelito has continued to live in Cuba; during his university career he went under an assumed name, so as to avoid preferential treatment, and later pursued post-graduate studies in the Soviet Union.

A final controversy about Castro's university days has to do with his connection with the Communist party. The maximum leader claimed that he was reading the works of Marx, Engels, and Lenin during his days in law school; that would not have been uncommon at the time and surely is not sufficient to lead to his categorization as a communist. He did have friends who belonged to the Communist party and reportedly admired their discipline and organizational skills. But there is no evidence that Fidel embraced communism at this point.

4

Castro's Middle Years: Moncada and the Guerrilla War

Upon graduation from the university, Fidel Castro entered into private law practice in Havana. From 1950 to 1952 he made little money, since he defended poor clients and an occasional political criminal. Castro himself recalls from this period that he and his young family had a chronic lack of funds, always owing for rent, groceries, and other bills.

Early Political Activities

In spite of his graduation, Castro continued to be active in student politics. In national politics, he continued working with the Ortodoxo party, associating with Eduardo Chibás.

In 1952, Castro was nominated as an Ortodoxo candidate for the lower house of the national legislature. There is serious doubt that he believed things could really

be changed through the democratic route, for in later years he stated that he planned to present a revolutionary program once in Congress. Although he did not expect such a program to be approved, the people could have been mobilized on the basis of it. All of this is speculation: on March 10, 1952, Castro's candidacy, and everyone else's, was terminated by the pro-Batista military coup d'état.

Castro's first reaction to the coup was a legal one, consistent with his university training. On March 24, 1952, he filed a legal brief in the Court of Constitutional Guarantees against the Batista takeover and asked that the usurper be arrested. This young lawyer argued that Batista should be imprisoned for more than one hundred years for treason and sedition, but the court rejected the appeal on the grounds that "the revolution is the fount of law." Perhaps Castro sincerely believed that the legal approach would rid the country of the despot.

More likely, he was simply trying to prove to himself and the other young Ortodoxos that justice through legal channels was futile. Furthermore, it might be contended that the argument of the Court of Constitutional Guarantees, by maintaining that revolution is the fount of law, pushed him in that direction.

The Moncada Attack
Having failed in his attempts to rid the country of Batista through legal means,

Castro turned to tactics more in keeping with what he had learned from the action groups in the university. He began recruiting and training young people who, like himself, abhorred the Batista dictatorship, thought that peaceful means would not be successful in ridding the island of it, and saw a "true revolution" as the means out of the impasse of traditional Cuban politics.

By 1953, Fidel Castro had become convinced that violence had to be used to bring about a basic political, social, and economic

Young Castro addressing a political rally

(Lee Lockwood/Black Star)

383

reordering of the society and not merely to change one political leader for another, as in the traditional coup d'état, nor to reestablish the democratic *status quo ante* of the Auténtico governments. He did not support indiscriminate violence; it had to be directed and purposeful. Further, the decision perhaps was an agonizing one for the young man.

In a military sense the plan that was devised fell into the pattern of the traditional coup d'état, rather than the guerrilla pattern that later proved successful. The armed rebels, about 165 to 170 in number, would stage a surprise attack on the Moncada army barracks in Santiago de Cuba. Moncada was the second largest army barracks in the country, with about one thousand men, while the largest barracks was Camp Columbia, with ten thousand men, near Havana. Moncada was chosen because its size seemed more manageable for a small group of rebels. Furthermore, the people of Oriente Province around Santiago had the reputation of being the most rebellious of the country.

At the same time that the barracks were attacked, there were to be simultaneous strikes at the Bayamo garrison nearby, a hospital, and a radio station. As soon as the latter was seized, a recording of the famous last speech of Chibás was to be broadcast, as well as a call for a popular uprising.

The Moncada plan was Castro's and had no support from the Ortodoxo party. Most of the recruits, poorly armed and hastily trained, were Ortodoxos, but they were bound to him by personal rather than party ties. Thus, Moncada was a personal venture of Fidel Castro, with support from neither the Ortodoxos nor any other party or group.

The attempt was staged at about 5 A.M. on July 26, 1953, now the most famous date on the Cuban calendar. The plan depended very much on the element of surprise. Since July 26 was the second day of Santiago's traditional summer carnival, Castro thought that the soldiers would be either asleep or intoxicated. This element of surprise was lost when a patrol saw the rebels arriving at the barracks. Further, one rebel group got lost and failed to arrive on time. A shot was fired prematurely, and a bloody battle of about two hours ensued. None of the objectives was obtained. About 7 A.M., Fidel ordered a retreat. The human costs of the two hours were immense: the assailants had three killed, sixty-eight summarily executed upon their capture, and forty-six captured and later tried. Only about thirty of the rebels escaped completely, while the army troops suffered the deaths of sixteen enlisted men and three officers. Because Castro had seen little probability of a defeat at Moncada, plans for retreat had been poorly made. The rebels carried no food and did not know the mountains near Santiago well, nor had they made arrangements for a guide. Castro himself escaped to the mountains, only to be captured several days later by government troops. But he had the good fortune of being captured by an army group commanded by a friend and former colleague at the university who saved the future leader from summary execution.

"History Will Absolve Me"
The surviving Moncada attackers were tried in September. Originally Castro was tried along with the others, in open court, with press coverage, and with his acting as the lawyer for all. However, the trial became such a *cause célèbre* that the government claimed that he was ill and proceeded to try the rest of the conspirators.

Castro's trial in October was held in secret in a part of the hospital. He once again defended himself, and the defense has become one of the basic documents of the Cuban Revolution. There is no public record of the trial, nor a transcript, so the leader's defense as the world knows it is that which he reconstructed while in prison. It has been pointed out that if Castro had said all that his reconstructions state he did, it would have been a speech of some six hours. Although no one doubts his capacity to talk that long, there is some serious doubt that the judges listened for such a length of time.

Whether or not all of it was said at the trial, the "History Will Absolve Me" speech is a key to understanding the thought of Fidel Castro at the beginning of the violent stage of the Cuban Revolution. In addition to analyzing the reasons for the attack, the reasons for its failures, and the legal defense of his innocence (rebellion against an illegal government is not a crime), Castro explained in detail what the insurgents would have done, had they been victorious. First of all, the speech called for the restoration of the Cuban Constitution of 1940, a document that was progressive in that it combined liberal democracy with constitutional imperatives for social and economic change. Beyond that, he talked about six areas that required immediate attention, which they would have received upon a victory at Moncada: the landholding system, industrialization, housing, unemployment, education, and health.

There were listed five revolutionary laws, which would have been proclaimed immediately. Besides the reestablishment of the 1940 constitution, they included granting of property to all planters, lessees, sharecroppers, and squatters who worked on small plots; granting workers and employees the right to share 30 percent of the profits of all the large industrial, mercantile, and mining enterprises, including the sugar mills; granting all planters (that is, those working on someone else's land) the right to share 55 percent of the sugar production; and ordering the confiscation of all holdings and ill-gotten gains of those who had committed

frauds during the previous regimes. Nothing was radical about these proposals, which were all within the spirit of the 1940 constitution and, although they demonstrate a large social concern, are not extreme within the Latin American context.

The document was more than a legal defense; it also was to be the basis for the future organization of Fidel Castro's movement. He never gave up, although the court sentenced him to fifteen years in prison. Dramatically, Fidel concluded,

As for me, I know that jail will be as hard as it has ever been for anyone, filled with threats, with vileness, and cowardly brutality; but I do not fear this, as I do not fear the fury of the miserable tyrant who snuffed out the life of seventy brothers of mine. Condemn me, it does not matter. *History will absolve me!* [1]

Imprisonment on the Isle of Pines
Fidel Castro spent the following twenty-two months in prison on the Isle of Pines. His activities there were varied. At one point, he was instrumental in setting up a school for illiterate inmates, teaching basic reading and mathematical skills. The materials used were revolutionary in content, unlike the conventional beginning readers and similar to those used for the entire island of Cuba in 1961. The penal authorities halted the enterprise, but the fact that Castro attempted it while in prison shows something about his character and unwillingness to give up.

Other activities had to do with secret correspondence with his supporters outside of prison. He did not wait until liberty to organize them; rather, he sent instructions on how to do this. In 1954 they started a

[1] Fidel Castro, *Selected Works of Fidel Castro,* ed. Rolando E. Bonachea and Nelson P. Valdes (Cambridge, Mass.: M.I.T. Press, 1972), vol. 1, *Revolutionary Struggle, 1947–1958,* pp. 220–221.

drive to have all political criminals released, which would have included Castro. In the same vein, he wrote his "History Will Absolve Me" speech in publishable form and had it smuggled out to his supporters. Showing a compulsion for detail, which was to continue in his role as maximum leader of Cuba, Castro not only wrote the document, but also told his supporters how many copies to have published, how to distribute it, and even which print to use and how much space to leave between paragraphs.

Another part of the time he was in solitary confinement, a condition that must have been stifling to an individual who had always shown such energy and gregariousness. He passed that time reading such authors as Balzac, Anatole France, José Martí, Carlos Mariátegui (a Peruvian Marxist), and the sociologists Max Weber and Mannheim.

A personal problem during his confinement was the break with his wife. Castro had never provided well for his family, and imprisonment made this even worse. As a result, Mirta Castro had been receiving money from her brother, who was working in the Ministry of the Interior. It turned out that the money was coming illegally from the payroll of the ministry. Whether she knew this or not, Mirta Castro was in effect being paid by Batista during her husband's incarceration. This circumstance added to the personal grief of Fidel at the legal separation.

In 1954, Fulgencio Batista called presidential elections, in which at first he was opposed by the Auténtico Grau. Grau withdrew when he became convinced that a free election was not possible; Batista was "reelected" without opposition. This victory was important for Castro, not only because it showed the continued undemocratic nature of the Batista regime, but also because Batista decided that one way to build his popular standing and legitimacy would be

through a general amnesty for all political prisoners. On May 7, 1955, Batista signed the law granting such an amnesty. Eight days later, Castro and the other twenty-nine survivors of the Moncada attack who were still in prison were released.

Preparation for Guerrilla War

When Fidel Castro was released on May 15, 1955, he embraced the army officer at the door of the prison in order to demonstrate that Moncada had not been an attack against the army, but against Batista. This was the first act of a struggle that was to last a bit more than three and one-half years, was to depose Batista, and was to bring the most sweeping revolution in the history of the American continents.

The First Two Months in Cuba
Castro returned to Havana, to a large, popular welcome, far from a repentant former prisoner. He immediately began to sow dissent with the Batista regime, writing numerous newspaper articles against it. This action left him in bad relations with the dictator, and threats against his life were soon forthcoming. At the same time, he was active in the organization of his movement, which had been begun by fidelistas (a term used because of the personal basis of his movement) during his prison term. The first revolutionary cell was formed.

Not all of his activity was in the organization of the coming violence. At one point, Castro helped write a party manifesto for the Ortodoxo party, criticizing the economic policies of the dictatorship and calling for a return to the Constitution of 1940. This statement got the Ortodoxo party in trouble with Batista, who ordered the closing of their radio and television stations. For such activities, Castro was deprived of the right to make public speeches. But he did not lose the right to write and continued with almost daily columns in the newspapers.

At one point in the two-month period, the Ortodoxo leadership asked Castro to join them as a leader of the party. Stating that he had not done the necessary party work to deserve such a position, he refused. He saw this as an attempt to co-opt him, that is, to make him less radical by giving him a stake in the system, as part of the leadership of the opposition. Castro claimed that he wanted to continue a grassroots level relationship with the people and that the leadership post would restrict his freedom of action to form a revolutionary movement. Clearly, he did not want the restraints that an organized group would place on him.

At this time, much violence was beginning on the island. Various groups were bombing buildings around Havana, seemingly without a master plan, coordination, or a concurrent desire to politicize the masses. Castro disagreed with this strategy. Publicly, he continued to call for a rule of peace and new elections and to state that armed struggle was not necessary, but his real goal was to create an insurrectionary consciousness in the people.

On July 7, 1955, Fidel Castro left Cuba, as a voluntary exile, having concluded that it was impossible to form a revolutionary movement within the country. Government resistance and threats prevented it. He stated that he was off to some place in the Caribbean and that he would return.

Exile in Mexico

For the next year and a half, Castro lived in Mexico and planned his revolution, although his various travels took him to both the United States and Costa Rica. One of his first acts was to establish the 26th of July Movement (M-26-7, for *Movimiento 26 de*

Julio), named for the date of the Moncada uprising. He stated:

The 26th of July Movement is formed without hatred for anyone. It is not a political party but a revolutionary movement. Its ranks are open to all Cubans who sincerely desire to see political democracy reestablished and social justice introduced in Cuba. Its leadership is collective and secret, formed by new men of strong will who are not accomplices of the past.[2]

His other activities were numerous. He kept in contact with fidelistas in Cuba, encouraging the growth of the organization and continuing opposition to accommodation with Batista. The dictator was attempting to get other groups to work with him, toward the possibility of new elections sometime in the future. Castro opposed this vehemently. In August 1955 the national convention of the Ortodoxo party met to consider the possibility of accommodation. A fidelista distributed and read a mimeographed statement from the exiled leader, which was greeted with great enthusiasm by the convention of some five hundred delegates. They voted not to collaborate with Batista. However, the party leadership did not follow that vote, finally leading to the definitive split of Castro from the Ortodoxo leadership in March of the following year.

Meetings with other Cuban revolutionaries also occupied Castro. Among the more important were with Frank País and José Antonio Echevarría, the other two most powerful and charismatic leaders of the resistance and, to a certain extent, his rivals. País was the head of a terrorist group in Oriente, site of Castro's youth and the Moncada uprising. Although reluctant at first, País finally agreed on the part that he

[2] Ibid., p. 68.

would play when Castro and his troops invaded the island.

The meeting with Echevarría was important, not only because of the result, but also because of the conflict of personalities. Echevarría, head of the *Directorio Revolucionario* (DR), a student group, reportedly was just as dynamic and charismatic as Castro. The two had been opponents since university days, when they were affiliated with different action groups. Besides this personal conflict, there was a strategic conflict. Echevarría wanted the revolution to start in urban Havana, through planned assassinations and terrorism; Fidel wanted it in Oriente, with few assassinations, rural guerrilla warfare, and more work with the people. The two leaders finally agreed only in principle—that it was time for a violent revolution—and promised to let each other go ahead in his preferred way.

Another of Castro's activities centered around travel to the United States to build support and to raise money. There were a number of political exiles in that country, plus many Cubans who had left for nonpolitical reasons, looking for better economic opportunities. As a result of his travels, Patriotic Clubs of the 26th of July were set up in a number of large cities. In working with the Cuban community in the United States, he was consciously following the same strategy used by José Martí in the 1890s. Fidel hoped this would raise one or even two dollars a week from each of the two thousand or so members of his patriotic clubs.

At one point, when it was clear that the Cubans were in danger of losing their freedom in Mexico, Castro made an illegal trip to Texas, reportedly swimming across the Rio Grande, to meet with former Auténtico President Prío. Prío gave him between forty and fifty thousand dollars, part of which was used to buy an old, decrepit yacht called the

Granma that eventually was used for the trip back to Cuba.

The most important activity in Mexico was the planning and training for the invasion of the island. Although this was a first priority from Castro's very arrival in Mexico City, its implementation was necessarily delayed until February 1956, when finally there was enough money to begin. The training was done by a Cuban, a veteran of the Spanish Civil War. At first it began in various houses in Mexico City itself, the future guerrilla fighters learning military discipline, the way to make bombs, and the techniques of sabotage. Later the training was moved to a rural area in the mountains near Mexico City. There the troops were taught such things as the art of ambushes, hit-and-run tactics, shooting, mountain climbing, and the manufacture of Molotov cocktails, grenades, and booby traps. As practice for the coming struggle, long marches of ten to fifteen miles a day were undertaken. And there was political training on such matters as the history and sociology of Cuba, including the study of Castro's statements and letters. There is no indication that any Marxist or communist material was important in that training.

Castro himself did not participate in all the military training, such as the long marches. Some of his time was dedicated to organizational work, to contacts with Cubans who came to Mexico to see him, and to the all-important effort of finding recruits for the revolution and raising money. One of the individuals whom he met during these months was Ernesto "Che" Guevara. Although by training a medical doctor and by birth a citizen of Argentina, Che was by desire a soldier of fortune and a revolutionary and by choice a man without nationalistic feelings. He had been a minor functionary of the government in Guatemala during the leftist administration of President Jacobo

Arbenz, who was overthrown in 1954 by troops trained by the Central Intelligence Agency of the United States. Che had then gone to Mexico. He was later to go to Cuba, become an integral member of the guerrilla band, serve in Castro's government for five years, and finally die in the mountains of Bolivia, attempting yet another guerrilla war. Next to Castro himself, Che Guevara was the most important man in the Cuban Revolution.

During this time, Castro and his group had problems with the Mexican authorities. It is clearly against international law for a government to allow its territory to be used by rebels who are planning an attack on another nation, although the law is often ignored. Further, agents of the Cuban government, who knew very well what Castro and his band were up to, urged the Mexican officials to act against the Cuban exiles. At one point, they had to change their camps due to imminent arrest. At another time, all of them were arrested, Castro being released due to pressure from Mexican ex-President Lázaro Cárdenas, while the others remained in jail for some three weeks. There was at least one plot, inspired by Cuban agents, to assassinate Castro, and numerous valuable weapons were seized by the Mexican government. Finally, news came that the Mexican authorities were about to arrest them again; the rebels hurried to the coast and set out for Cuba.

The Guerrilla War

In fear of impending arrest, the Cuban revolutionaries quickly and quietly filed upon *Granma* during the night of November 25, 1956. Eighty-two in all silently sailed from the harbor of Tuxpán, a small port north of Veracruz, stuffed into a yacht designed for only eight to ten people. Fifty other rebels were left behind for want of room. Once on open water, they sang the Cuban national anthem. The insurrection had begun.

The crossing was a difficult one, beginning in freezing rain and with bad visibility. Later the seas were very rough. Few were experienced sailors, and most were seasick. The boat functioned badly, its bilge pumps barely working, if at all, so two buckets were used to bail out the overloaded ship. Even the lifeboats, also designed to accommodate ten people, were unusable.

Castro had publicly announced that he would return to Cuba in 1956. The more specific plans made with Frank País called for a December 1 landing: País would have one hundred armed rebels meet him at Niquero Beach and would at the same time begin an uprising in the city of Santiago. A call for rebellion in Oriente Province would be made.

The *Granma* was delayed by the rough seas and the old motor. When the rebels reached Cuba on December 2, País's rebellion had already failed, and the Cuban navy was expecting a landing. The crossing ended in miscalculation: the designated beach where some fifty rebels were waiting was not reached. The *Granma* ran aground about two hundred yards from the shore and in a most undesirable place. After reaching the shore, the rebels had to wade through a mangrove swamp for several hours before they reached dry land. The grounded *Granma* was sighted by a Cuban patrol vessel, and Batista's troops soon were in pursuit.

Three days later, the rebels stopped to rest in a cane field, feeling somewhat more confident of their safety. They were exhausted, and their feet were blistered. While resting, they were attacked by an army patrol and suffered great losses. They split up into small groups and set out for the prearranged rendezvous point, while Batista loudly proclaimed the annihilation of the rebels and the deaths of Raúl and Fidel Castro. By mid-month, twenty or thirty men had made it to their destination in the Sierra Maestra. (Castro, however, has sometimes referred to the number as twelve, perhaps to achieve biblical imagery.) They had only seven weapons.

Even with thirty men and seven weapons, Fidel Castro was not the kind of person to give up. They rested and on Christmas Day, 1956, climbed Turquino Peak, the highest mountain in Cuba. Besides checking with his altimeter and proving that Cuban geography books were fifty meters off in the true height of the peak, Castro proclaimed, "We have won the war!" While it would take almost two years to perform that feat, this incident portrays accurately the unrelenting confidence of the man.

1957: Discouragement, Conflict, and Hope

The year 1957 started out in discouragement for most of the rebels; indeed, even Castro expressed despair during the year. They were small in number, inadequately supplied, and poorly trained. Their leader was believed to be dead by most of the Cuban people. But three events, one each in the first three months of the year, marked a change in the guerrillas' fortunes.

The basic strategy during this first period of the insurrection was for the rebels to attack isolated army posts and to withdraw immediately, having prepared ambushes for the pursuing army troops. On January 17, twenty-two fidelistas attacked a small, isolated army post. This Battle of La Plata was their first victory. Not only did they obtain material goods, weapons, food, and medicine, but the small battle against outnumbered army troops had other favorable con-

sequences. The morale of the guerrillas was increased, and, equally as important, the people of Cuba learned that a rebel group was operating in the Sierra Maestra.

A month later, on February 17, the Cuban people and the rest of the world found out that Castro was still alive. A reporter for the *New York Times*, Herbert Matthews, traveled to the Sierra Maestra, where he interviewed Castro. With rebel troops marching around the camp continuously (leading Matthews to write that there were about ninety guerrillas, instead of the more accurate thirty) and constant gunfire, Castro told Matthews of his hopes and aspirations. Matthews reported these to the world a few days later. The Cuban people found out that the rebel leader was alive and that the dictator had been wrong in claiming to have killed him.

The third important event of 1957 was the attempt of the Directorio Revolucionario to assassinate Batista on March 13. Apparently they failed only because the dictator had left his office for a few moments. But the significance of the attempt transcended the defeat, for it showed the inefficacy of the urban plan which the DR proposed and about which Echevarría had argued with Castro a few months earlier. In the second place, the attempt was followed by the first of many waves of horror and repression initiated by Batista. These waves, a constant theme of the war, increased the alienation of formerly neutral people. Finally, one of the two strongest rivals for Castro among the revolutionaries—José Antonio Echevarría—was killed right after the attempt. Although Castro was to continue to have difficulties with rivals, an important one had been removed.

In the months that followed, the rebel group in the Sierra Maestra slowly grew and constantly attacked small military outposts. Most of the new supporters came by way of

Santiago, where they were recruited by Frank País. Upon arrival, they were trained in guerrilla tactics, including long marches and strict discipline; they learned how to eat only once a day, how to use the nature of the terrain, and, of some importance in the heights of the mountains, how to sleep without cover.

At the same time, the guerrillas cultivated relationships with the local peasants. Their support was needed for food and supplies, and it was imperative that they not divulge the location of the rebels to the army. But more basically, the problems of the rural poor had to be solved. In the areas controlled by the forces of Castro—small at first, but slowly growing—land reform was initiated in 1958 and legal reforms were made to protect the poor.

On May 28, the first major battle occurred at Uvero, a significant event because it was reported freely by the media to the Cuban people. Furthermore, it led to another repressive reaction by Batista. The best infantry units were sent to the Sierra Maestra and, to eliminate any possible peasant support for the guerrillas, over two thousand families were forcefully evacuated and placed in concentration camps. The infantry units were extremely brutal with noncombatants, and the general result of Batista's move was to alienate even more neutral Cubans.

Yet not all was going well for Castro. In addition to constant pressures from the army, he continued to have difficulties within the rebelling groups themselves. These continued throughout the campaign and after the fall of Batista. One problem for Castro concerned the Cuban exiles who were not part of M-26-7, which included former Ortodoxos and Auténticos, as well as members of the Directorio Revolucionario, who had sought refuge in Florida. They challenged Castro's right to leadership in the anti-Batista campaign.

Yet another group did not challenge his leadership but did question his tactics: members of the Movimiento 26 de Julio who lived in the cities, the *llanos* (plains) members, as opposed to *sierra* (mountain) people. In the first half of 1957, the most outstanding of the llanos leaders was Frank País in Santiago, who argued that the emphasis of the struggle should be on urban terrorism, with the guerrillas in the mountains playing a secondary role. Castro, on the other hand, saw the guerrillas as first in importance, supported by the urban resistance through financing, recruiting, and supplying and also through terrorism, but in a clearly secondary role. País was killed by Batista agents in mid-1957, thus removing Castro's last major challenger to leadership. However, the basic conflict of strategies did not end with his death, as other llanos leaders became even more important, especially in Havana.

1958: Year of Triumph

Through the later months of 1957 and the early part of 1958, the rebel group grew slowly in size. By March there were enough troops to set up a more complex military strategy, and the insurrection entered into its second stage. A guerrilla triangle was established; in addition to the four columns of troops in the Sierra Maestra itself, Raúl Castro was sent north to set up a new front in the Sierra Cristal, while Juan Almeida went to El Cobre, west of Santiago, to set up another.

The progress of the Castro movement in the Sierra Maestra and environs was due not only to their activities, but also to happenings in the outside world. On March 14, the United States government suspended arms shipments to Cuba, as Batista—in conflict with American law—had used the arms for internal security matters rather than the national defense function for which they were intended. One should not underestimate the importance of this act of the United States government, although the fidelistas argued that it was a year or so too late and also too little, since the United States military mission remained. Many Cubans were already withdrawing their support from Batista in reaction to his repressive and brutal measures, and the suspension of U.S. arms (and tacit indication of disapproval of Batista, so important in the Cuban political system) led other groups to withdraw their support from the dictator. In particular, several professional groups stopped support, leaving Batista's power base among only the professional military and the police. Consistent reliance on brute force was seen throughout the rest of the year.

Yet another event that aided the guerrillas indirectly was the failure of the llanos leaders in a general strike, a tactic seen by the latter as an important way of bringing Batista to his knees. The strike called for April 9, 1958, did not succeed. No advance notice was given—presumably in order not to allow Batista to react—and many workers did not get the last-minute message. While the strike was successful in some of the smaller cities, it failed in Havana. This failure discredited the llanos leaders of the M-26-7 and, in turn, helped to consolidate Castro's power in the movement, although he had supported the strike.

In May 1958, Batista ordered an offensive that he felt certain would end the guerrilla movement. Ten thousand troops were sent

Castro during the guerrilla war

(Lee Lockwood/Black Star)

to Oriente to crush the rebels. Most of the troops, along with aerial bombardment, hit the main group under Fidel Castro. One thousand troops were sent to the nearby Sierra Cristal to take care of Raúl Castro and his smaller band. However, the latter managed to negotiate a nonagression pact with the troops and then marched to help his brother.

In spite of this, the bombing was taking its toll on the rebel forces. Castro's response was ingenious and successful. About a dozen private citizens of the United States who were residing in Oriente were kidnapped, and the United States Consul in Santiago was told that they would be released when the bombing stopped. The American government put pressure on Batista to stop the bombing, which he did.

The Batista army had other problems. Their supply lines were extended too far. Fidel began psychological warfare against the troops by lecturing them with a loud-speaker, encouraging them to surrender and help the guerrillas. Many did just that. Finally, on August 7, the army began a disorderly retreat, which the guerrillas used to their advantage and turned into a rout. Ten thousand of the best-armed troops had failed to destroy some eight hundred guerrillas. The army suffered one thousand casualties, while another five hundred soldiers were captured.

The Sierra Maestra rebels immediately began a counteroffensive, and for once there was apparent unity of the various rebel groups around Castro. Fidel now had access to radio broadcasting facilities, which he used daily to talk to the Cuban people. Financial assistance began to appear in great quantities, including money from sugar cane plantation owners, hoping thus to save their fields, and $1 million from the head of the famous Bacardi rum factory.

The counteroffensive was also military, be-

ginning the third stage of the insurrection. By this time probably eight hundred guerrilla troops were in the mountains, divided into four columns. The José Martí column stayed in the Sierra Maestra under Castro's personal direction, while the Frank País column under Raúl Castro remained in the Sierra Cristal. But the third and fourth columns were sent to other parts of the island. One, under Che Guevara, was sent to the Escambray Mountains in Las Villas Province in the central part of the island. Another, under Camilo Cienfuegos, was dispatched to the mountains in Piñar del Río Province, at the western tip of Cuba, although it never arrived. Rather, Cienfuegos's detachment also worked in the Escambray.

For the first time, some of the rebels had moved out of the mountains and crossed the lowlands to reach another mountain range. They did this under the cover of night, at times having to bribe army officials, and other times simply ignored by them. This placed M-26-7 members closer to Havana. It now seemed apparent that Batista could not last much longer. There were other rebel groups in uneasy alliance with M-26-7 and the assumption was that, on the fall of Batista, the first arriving in Havana would have the upper hand in the ensuing struggle for power among themselves. Che was successful in incorporating some of the other rebels into his ranks, therefore lessening the conflict.

By November, the rebels had near complete control of Oriente. Normal transportation was ended, as were all army troop movements. The sugar harvesting nearly had to stop. Army barracks continued to fall to the rebels. On November 17, Castro left the mountains for the first time in the campaign to lead his forces in the plains of Oriente, for the only areas in the province remaining loyal to the Batista dictatorship were a few urban pockets. As the rebels won battle after battle, the army troops fled, leaving more and more weapons for the enemies of the dictatorship. Meanwhile, in Las Villas, Camilo Cienfuegos and Che Guevara were about to cut the island in two. The troops loyal to the government retreated to the capital of the province, Santa Clara, which was besieged by the rebels.

The officers of Batista's army now saw that the dictator had to go. On December 28, General Eulogio Cantillo traveled to see Fidel Castro. The two agreed to a December 31 coup d'état, which Cantillo agreed would open power for the rebels. But the General, really planning to consolidate power himself and to defeat the Castro rebels, returned to Havana and told Batista. His treachery was anticipated by Castro, who refused Cantillo's request that the coup be delayed until January 6.

On December 31, 1958, Santa Clara fell to the troops of Camilo and Guevara. In Oriente, troops commanded personally by Fidel Castro were laying siege to Santiago. The city was encircled and apparently could hold out for only a few days. That night, Fulgencio Batista, dictator for seven years and the most powerful man in Cuba since 1933, fled the island. Incredibly enough, Fidel Castro and his small band had defeated a military dictator with forty thousand troops, well-armed by the United States as part of its Cold War policy.

Why Did Castro Win?

One of the matters relating to the Cuban Revolution that is most surrounded by myth and controversy is why Castro succeeded. Castro and his followers have themselves added to this controversy by reconstructing history. Basically, five reasons for the end

of the Batista regime have been mentioned, all of which are perhaps correct to a certain degree: (1) the military actions per se; (2) the revolutionary potential of the island; (3) the programmatic content of the Castro campaign; (4) the personal attraction of Fidel Castro as an individual; and (5) the lack of support for Batista.

The Military Actions
The military actions, in a conventional sense, were not sufficient in and of themselves for victory. There were no major battles, although the last of the war at Santa Clara came close to being that. The guerrilla strategy (which the Cubans later said that they had used) is to completely control the countryside, leaving the cities isolated and surrounded. While this had happened in Oriente Province, it surely had not happened for the entire island and, especially importantly, it had not occurred around Havana.

Yet another problem in stating that Castro's guerrilla strategy was the reason for his success is the observation that the urban terrorism of his own movement, as well as that of the Directorio Revolucionario, was also very important. Later, Castro gave all credit to the people in the hills, omitting the urban terrorism as being crucial. Other observers of the revolution would state that the opposite was the case. It seems safe to conclude that both parts of the M-26-7 strategy—rural and urban—had their effects in the fall of Batista, although it is difficult, if indeed not impossible, to decide which was the more important of the two.

What the military strategy of Castro did was to prove a nuisance factor to the Batista dictatorship. At least as significant as the tangible results (occupying territory, killing and capturing soldiers, and at the end, interfering with the normal economic activities of Oriente Province) were the consequences that arose from forcing Batista to react. He behaved in an extremely repressive fashion, hence eroding his previous support.

Revolutionary Potential of the Island

Another factor mentioned by several scholars as being the most important was the revolutionary potential of the island. There were many very poor people in Cuba who had very little to lose from a revolution—socially, economically, or politically. While they might have participated in the democracy of the Auténtico years (1944–1952), during the Batista years they had no political rights. Furthermore, many of the rural inhabitants of the island were wage laborers, who tended to be more radical due to the lack of a patrón-clientele relationship such as that existing in Latin American countries with more traditional agricultural patterns. Also, they were more amenable to organization. Since coming to power, the Castro regime has said that its effort was not only a successful guerrilla war, but also a peasant revolution.

It is not even clear that the majority of the individuals who fought in the Sierra Maestra were peasants. Many, if not most, of the rebels were of urban background, recruited by all llanos leaders in the various cities and sent to the hills. Of those who were peasants, it is plausible that most of them were wage laborers, since there was much of the sugar economy in the Oriente area of Cuba. However, in addition to the importance of urban areas to the revolution, there are two other points of caution that should be made before accepting the revolutionary potential of the peasants as the primary cause of Castro's success.

In the first place, the leadership of the Cuban Revolution was not peasant in background. Like Fidel Castro himself, the leaders were middle-income individuals who, for various reasons, did not like the current social, economic, and political systems. However, if a movement must have peasant leadership in order to be "a peasant revolution," then very few, if any, exist in the contemporary world.

Second, and equally significant, the great masses of the Cuban peasants did not actively participate in the Castro Revolution. At its high point toward the end of 1958, there were probably fewer than a thousand troops. The abortive Revolution of 1933, in which great numbers of wage-earning peasants were in revolt, certainly comes nearer to being a peasant revolution (if that phrase means that many or most peasants were in rebellion).

In short, there is no doubt that the economic structure of great inequality and unemployment contributed to the success of the Cuban Revolution. However, this economic structure probably had more direct effect on the route of the Cuban Revolution after the fall of Batista than it did on the success of insurrection.

The Programs of Fidel Castro

Yet another line of argument is that the program presented by Fidel Castro was a major cause of the success of the Cuban Revolution. There are two basic questions that this argument should raise. First, just what was that program? Second, what effect did it have?

During the two years in the Sierra Maestra, the picture of Fidel Castro gained from his private letters and public declarations is one of a man who was deeply attached to the moral doctrine of Eduardo Chibás, but who had an open, rather than a closed, mind. His statements went no farther than his "History Will Absolve Me" speech. Some of his pronouncements were anti–United States. But this was in keeping with general nationalistic feelings in Cuba, and indeed José Martí had said many similar things sixty years before.

Castro's program had a double thrust and hence a double appeal. On one hand, it was libertarian and thus democratic; on the other, it was reformist and tending toward socialism. This program, therefore, was widely appealing to the Cuban people. But it was vague, just as Chibás's had been earlier. The lack of a more detailed program at that point in his career was definitely an advantage for Castro; few people were able to be against something so vague. However, the reason that he was ambiguous is open to dispute. Some admirers state simply that Castro had no greater ideology at the moment and, furthermore, was too involved in the military campaign to think through a program more carefully. Others state that Castro purposefully kept his pronouncements vague in order to hide his membership in the international communist movement.

The effect of this vague program was an asset. Most Cubans could agree with what Fidel Castro was saying. Some few were attracted by his ideas to an active role in the hills, while others agreed sufficiently to participate in urban terrorism. Yet the vast majority of the Cuban people reacted neither favorably nor unfavorably, remaining apathetic. Therefore, it seems justifiable to conclude that the nature of Fidel Castro's program was such that it helped his military victory.

Castro's Personal Attributes

A fourth position is that Fidel Castro personally was the key factor in the success of the Cuban Revolution. Che Guevara said in 1961, "The foremost, most original, and perhaps the most important single factor to render the Cuban Revolution so exceptional was the natural force that goes by the name of Fidel Castro."

There is no doubt that Castro was the unchallenged leader of the movement in the Sierra Maestra. The only executive organ of the 26th of July Movement that functioned perfectly from the beginning to end was Castro himself. The rest of the "collective leadership" in the hills distinguished themselves by generally not meeting and by abstaining from any meaningful political activity. There was no structure of revolutionary education: one might learn politics in the mountains through individual discussions with Fidel Castro, Che Guevara, or Raúl Castro if one happened to be part of their circle. But it was also possible to emerge from the two years in the mountains with no political education, for at no time did the movement run a political training school or organize branches or cells.

The 26th of July Movement was the personal creation of Fidel Castro. It was he who brought together men of differing views to risk their lives; it was he who mediated when there were problems. Wherever he went, he reassured and encouraged people. Quite early in his movement, Castro was criticized by those friends who said that it would have been better if decisions had been made collectively. He promised various times to change his style, but in the end never did.

After coming to power, the leader would be called charismatic, that is, having a personal magnetism that resulted in the people following him. This certainly also applied during his years in the mountains. There was something about the man that led some people to fight in the hills and others to fight in the cities. He promised honest government and one that would change Cuba, albeit in a vague way. Nevertheless, the personal attraction of the leader seems to be more important after his military victory than before.

Batista's Weaknesses

The final argument is that the Castro Revolution succeeded because of the inherent weaknesses of the Batista government. Cuba was not a typical Latin American country in that the traditional power groups of the church and the wealthy landed were not as dominant. Given that situation, the dictatorship depended more on the military, the police, and whatever other groups were willing to support it at any given point in time. These other groups supported him because of his ability to maintain order, but they drifted away from the dictator as he became more brutally repressive in response to the Castro rebellion and clearly no longer could bring order to the society. In the end, Batista had support only from the two armed groups, and they were far from monolithic.

In short, the argument might go that Castro did not win; rather, Batista lost. This of course is an oversimplification. Batista would not have acted the way he did if Castro's rebels had not been in the hills challenging him. Nevertheless, this "Batista weakness" argument is important and later led certain groups, for example the United States Department of State, to withdraw their support from other dictators in Latin America whom they saw as very similar to Batista.

5

Castro at the Top:
The Results of His
Cuban Revolution

The focus of this chapter is on what Fidel Castro's personal revolution has meant to Cuba. It begins with a discussion of the crucial first years of the revolution and the decision to take it to the left; the topics that follow include major policy fields: economic, social, domestic, and international.

As the first section demonstrates, policy makers do not divide the world into neat categories. Any policy will have ramifications in all fields. Throughout this discussion, it can be safely assumed that in any decision of the Cuban Revolution, especially in the 1960s and perhaps to a lesser degree since, Fidel Castro personally has played a major role in the decision-making process, not only in major policies, but also in some very minor ones.

Radicalization
of the Revolution,
1959-1960

When Fidel Castro arrived in Havana in early 1959, hardly anyone expected that the country would change radically in the next two years. But within those years, he transformed the Cuban polity, replacing the old-style Batista dictatorship with a new, revolutionary one. Free elections were initially postponed and then ruled out altogether by 1960. The old anti-Batista political parties were ignored, with the exception of the communist Popular Socialist party (PSP). The judiciary was attacked, ultimately leading to the resignation and self-imposed exile of a number of jurists by the end of 1960. The opposition press was first curtailed and later shut down, while other forms of mass communication were nationalized by 1960. In addition, the labor unions and student movements were purged of dissident elements, ultimately becoming instruments of the regime. Much of the nonagrarian sector of the economy was nationalized by the third quarter of 1960, while agrarian cooperatives and, later, state farms replaced the old *latifundios* as the predominant form of agriculture. The educational system was nationalized in 1961, and the Catholic church was made even less powerful by the expulsion of foreign priests and the closing of private Catholic schools. By 1961 the interest group associations of the prerevolutionary period had been either dissolved or incorporated under state control. The organized associations of big businessmen, landowners, and employers had practically disappeared by mid-1960, while the old professional associations of doctors, lawyers, and architects disappeared as independent entities soon thereafter. At the same time, relations worsened with the United States, leading to a formal diplomatic break in January 1961 and a CIA-sponsored invasion of the island in April of the same year. Meanwhile, relations with the Soviet Union were reestablished, became cordial, and then grew to be very friendly.

The Debate About the Movement to the Left

The Cuban Revolution has been a matter of much debate, both in the United States and in Latin America. No topic has been discussed more heatedly than just why the revolution moved to the left.

One explanation given for why the Cuban Revolution became communist is that Fidel Castro had always planned it that way. He betrayed the revolution because he promised one thing (liberal democracy) and brought another (communist dictatorship). In its simplest form, this reasoning states that Castro had become a member of the "international communist conspiracy" during his university days, had been in Bogotá operating on instructions from that movement, and otherthrew Batista as part of the plan. Yet there is no good evidence that Fidel Castro was a member of either the Cuban PSP or the international communist movement before 1959. Proponents of this explanation state that the failure to find such evidence is simply a matter of Castro's hiding it so well. They point out that it was good strategy for him not to appear to be a communist while

in the hills, as indeed it was. Finally, they remind us that Castro himself stated in December 1961 that "I am a Marxist-Leninist and have always been." Nevertheless, if they would pursue the matter further and read the full speech, they would see that Castro stated that at first even he himself did not realize that he had such a philosophy.

Other explanations of the movement to the left focus on Castro's personality structure, Cuban domestic characteristics, and foreign considerations. One cannot expect a definitive statement about why Fidel Castro took his revolution to the left, particularly in view of the ideological commitments that different scholars have for or against the revolution. The following explanation, however, considers a multiplicity of factors, seems as plausible as any, and is not based on the existence of a clandestine conspiracy.

When Fidel Castro came to power, he had been deeply committed to fundamental social change for a number of years, although he had no firm ideological commitment about how to effect that change. Apparently during his high school days, and surely by the time of his allegiance to the Chibás Ortodoxo party in 1947, Castro saw social and economic inequities in Cuba and wanted to put an end to them. Soon after taking power, he apparently made two decisions. First, these were not reforms that could be attained gradually, but rather they had to be achieved rapidly. This decision was due not only to previous ideological conviction, but also to pressures from the people for change. Second, Castro decided that it was his own personal destiny to bring those changes to Cuba, and indeed the vast majority of Cubans seems to have agreed.

From July through November 1959, there was an increased reliance on members of the PSP, who were entrusted with many responsible posts. In the first year, there is no evidence that the PSP members themselves thought that they were contributing to the birth of a new socialism in Cuba, as they considered the Castro movement to be unfit to lead a socialist revolution. At no time, either before or after Castro's victory, did they attempt to force him into a more radical position. Rather, all their publications show that they tried to do the very opposite —to moderate the reforming zeal of the bearded guerrilla leader lest Cuba come into a direct confrontation with the United States. The statements of the PSP during 1959 were reformist, calling for a return to the Constitution of 1940, for agrarian reform, for the lowering of the voting age, for a return to the system of proportional representation in elections, and for a resumption of diplomatic relations with the communist countries. They clearly did not step into a power vacuum due to the weakness of Castro.

The PSP members were brought into important posts by Castro because they had certain qualities that he could use. Castro could count on the blind allegiance of most of his followers from the guerrilla struggle, but they had few organizational or technical skills. The communists were not a large group, nor were they especially radical or wise in practical politics. But they did have a keen sense of organization and discipline, two qualities that Castro thought essential at the time. Believing in a hierarchical power structure, in which leadership was centralized at the top and socialist ideas and plans were dispensed to the people below, they were accustomed to taking the superiority of their leaders for granted.

In addition to those qualities, the PSP had powerful international allies, most specifically, the Soviet Union. During part of 1959, Castro pursued an independent foreign policy, with aspirations of separation from both superpowers, but it soon became obvious that such a policy would not work. United States business interests were being affected by nationalization of both agrarian and industrial properties. Recalling the long history of American influence in Cuba, Castro and his circle of followers believed that these businesses and the United States government would not stand by and let this happen; they expected a reaction.

The one empirical referent that the Cuban leaders had was the case of Guatemala only five years before. There, the constitutionally elected leftist President, Jacobo Arbenz, had been overthrown by a CIA-sponsored invasion. President Eisenhower later justified this simply by stating that the Guatemalan government was "communist." What had occurred was that members of the local Communist party had reached some posts of importance in the government, which was trying to change the social structure, for example, by nationalizing certain lands of United Fruit Company.

The Cuban leaders (and it should be remembered that Che Guevara had been a minor functionary in the Arbenz government) made two assumptions that entered into their calculations. First, no dramatic social and economic reform could be carried out without adversely affecting United States business interests. Those foreign interests were so important in the economy that changing the economy meant hurting them. Second, if the United States government decided to move against the Cuban Revolution, a strong ally was needed. The only possible one in the basically bipolar world of 1959–1960 was the Soviet Union.

The Deterioration of Relations with the United States
The breakdown of relations between the United States and Cuba was a gradual one over a two-year period. The United States recognized the new government on January 7, 1959, only a week after the flight of Batista. A new Ambassador was named,

Castro and Che Guevara

(Osvaldo Salas/Black Star)

"We must eliminate foreign influences, such as voting by Cubans"

(From *Straight Herblock* [Simon & Schuster, 1964])

Philip Bonsal, who soon came to the island, although he could not see Castro personally until some six months later. As Bonsal recalls it, Castro was immediately "anti-American."

One series of incidents that affected the initial favorable reaction to Castro in the United States had to do with the trials of former supporters of Batista. In the early months of the revolution, they were tried publicly, in a circus-like atmosphere, and then executed by firing squad. The opinion in the United States was that this was a travesty of justice. The Cubans responded that the trials were indeed fair and that many of the judges were of the legal profession and that, at any rate, the *batistianos* were receiving more due process than they had given when they were in power. The second part

of the argument was indeed true, as was seen in the case of the captured survivors of the Moncada attack. Nevertheless, comparing oneself favorably with the Batista regime was faint praise.

Castro made a trip to the United States in April 1959, not as an official visitor, but rather as a speaker before the National Press Club. He did not meet with President Eisenhower, but did have a conversation with Vice President Nixon, after which the latter decided that Castro was a dangerous man and recommended something similar to the eventual Bay of Pigs invasion. One of the controversies about Castro's trip is whether or not he hoped to receive financial aid from the American government. He explicitly instructed his entourage not to talk about such aid, but immediately after his trip to the United States, he went to an inter-American meeting in Uruguay. There he called for a ten-year $30 billion United States aid program to Latin America, leading to the argument that he really did want aid from the superpower, albeit in a multilateral form.

Agrarian reform started in earnest in June 1959. Ambassador Bonsal immediately wanted to talk to Castro about it and did so shortly thereafter. The official position of the United States government was that such reform was acceptable, so long as the Cuban government complied with the international law that aggrieved parties be paid for their lands. Castro later promised to do this, using twenty-year bonds for the amount that the United States businesses had declared their value to be for tax purposes. Needless to say, the property had not been declared at full value, so this solution was not acceptable. Although this loss of property was at first minor, its importance should not be underestimated in the deterioration of relations between the two countries. Some of the individuals and companies affected

402

immediately began to fight the Castro government, by helping Cuban counterrevolutionaries, hence probably accelerating both the nationalization and the deterioration of relations.

Another sore point in the relationship between the two countries was the Cuban-based invasions in mid-1959 of three of its neighbors: Panama, the Dominican Republic, and Haiti. One of the goals of the Cuban leaders was to spread their kind of revolution to other countries in Latin America, a goal that was actively pursued for at least the next half-dozen years. The United States did not favor such aid to revolutionaries.

In October 1959, the Cuban government seized the records of all the companies that had been exploring for oil in Cuba and put restrictions on United States exports to the island. The United States responded by placing an arms embargo on Cuba, attempting to persuade European sellers to do likewise. At the same time, there were a number of flights and movements of men from Florida on anti-Castro missions, which, strictly speaking, were in violation of international law. By November, Castro stated that being anti-communist was a reactionary attitude, and the mass exodus from the island began.

Soviet Vice Premier Anastas Mikoyan visited Cuba in February 1960, making various deals. The Soviet Union agreed to double its sugar purchases in the next five years and offered a low-interest loan of $100 million to buy Soviet goods. But the most dramatic visit of early 1960 was that of the French cargo ship *La Courbe,* laden with arms and munitions for the Cuban government from Czechoslovakia. The ship blew up, causing a serious loss of lives. Castro blamed this on sabotage by the United States, which responded that Cubans had destroyed the ship as an excuse to attack the United States.

A series of events in connection with the American petroleum companies led directly to a definitive break with the United States in June 1960. The Cuban government owed the companies 50 million dollars, which it offered to pay in Soviet crude oil. The companies refused. On June 29 the Cuban government "intervened" in the refineries; that is, it took over their administration without formally nationalizing them. The response of the American government, on July 6, was Eisenhower's announcement of the suspension of the sugar quota for the rest of the year. That meant that Cuban sugar would not be bought by the United States: the Cuban economy thus lost at least $90 million in 1960 alone.

In retrospect, this was the key event in the deterioration of the relationship between the two countries, making the formal breaking of diplomatic relations six months later an anticlimax. The United States government was telling the Cuban leaders that it would paralyze their economy unless they fell into line (presumably by stopping invasion attempts of other countries and moves against American business). The assumption seems to have been that the Cubans had no alternative buyer for the sugar. However, the Soviet Union agreed to buy the sugar and the revolution was "saved." A month later, Castro nationalized the two oil refineries, thirty-six sugar mills, the telephone company, and the electric company. In early January 1961 the United States government broke diplomatic relations with Cuba and in April of the same year sponsored an invasion by Cuban exiles who had been trained by the CIA.

The Dynamics of the Consolidation of the Revolution

The first two years of the Cuban Revolution were ones of consolidating power internally and securing Cuba's position externally. In this consolidation, there were three interrelated questions, which by 1962 had been answered. The first had to do with the nature of the revolution: could fundamental revolutionary changes be carried out through the promised liberal democracy, or would a revolutionary dictatorship be necessary? The latter was chosen. The second involved Castro's allies on the island: could a viable revolutionary regime be formed solely with noncommunist elements from the 26th of July Movement, or was it necessary to have the skills and allies of the PSP? It was decided that, at least for the time being, the PSP was needed. Third, what was to be done about foreign allies? Could the United States be expected to countenance a regime bent on the revolutionary change of Cuba, with its concurrent drawbacks for American business and diplomacy? If not, could Cuba realign itself with the Soviet Union for support? It was decided that the United States would not put up with such a regime; hence the support of the Soviet Union was sought —and received.

All of this happened in a very short time. To explain the rapidity of the changes in Cuba, four factors seem to be especially important.

First, there was the nature of the man. When Fidel Castro came to power he had done the impossible—defeated a military dictatorship with only a few men. He was magnetic and almost superhuman. He had charisma, and large numbers of Cubans were disposed to follow him in whatever direction he took.

Second, there was the economic structure of Cuba. Cuban workers had been organized—not only the urban industrial workers, but also the ones on the sugar centrales. This gave Castro and his government a great advantage over other leaders. The rural proletariat, such as that found in Cuba, is naturally much more radical than are the other kinds of peasants. Further, they are easier to organize from a technical standpoint: it is simpler to work with relatively few large groups (as in a sugar central) than with thousands of small farmers.

Third, Cuba had both radical and nationalist traditions. The radical tradition had included the PSP and had surfaced most dramatically before Castro in the abortive Revolution of 1933. The nationalist tradition was even older and stronger. It had been seen in Martí and later in the entire generation of 1930, which promised to combat the entreguismo of earlier Cuban elites. Although United States business had no doubt performed some valuable functions for the Cuban economy, the Cubans in the 1950s had more than sufficient reason to be nationalistic and anti-American. Castro used that nationalism effectively in building his revolution.

Fourth and finally, Cuban history has been one of generations, of groups of individuals who have banded together during the great struggles of the nation's short existence. The first was the generation of 1868, which made the first attempt for independence. The second was the generation of 1895, brought together in the war that did lead to independence. The third was the generation of 1930, gathered against Machado and in favor of revolution. And when Castro came to power, he came as the representative of the fourth such generation, the generation of 1953. By that time the generation of 1930, with a few outstanding exceptions, had been largely discredited as a political class in the eyes of the young. As a result, there was no reputable political group that could effectively challenge the new, rebel, fidelista generation. Nor were there other institutions (church, landowners, military) that could challenge that new leadership. In short, the new generation had a monopoly of political power very soon after January 1, 1959.

Economic Policies

Fidel Castro's immediate economic program after the revolution combined three goals: income expansion, income redistribution, and structural change. Of these three, income redistribution was the first realized; the earliest policies of the revolutionary government redistributed income from the rich to the poor and, as part of this, from the cities to the countryside.

Agrarian Reform

The First Agrarian Reform was decreed by the Castro government on May 17, 1959. Although it was redistributive in nature, taking land from some and giving it to others, it can be termed a reformist policy since its purpose, above all, was to create and strengthen a small, peasant landholding bourgeoisie. It did not attempt to suppress private property, rather only to change the holdings from large ones to medium-sized ones. State farm enterprises were not created.

The First Agrarian Reform placed a maximum of 402.6 hectares (approximately 1,000 acres) on all holdings. Any above that were redistributed, with the owner allowed to keep the maximum. This redistributed land could not be subdivided either partially or totally (by inheritance, for example). Furthermore, the law established a "vital minimum" of 27 hectares, for the Cuban leaders realized that very small landholdings were an evil as bad as very large ones. Hence, anyone who held less than the vital minimum received enough land to

reach that minimum. Not all the expropriated land was subdivided and redistributed, as some of it was given to cooperative groups as indivisible property. This policy was adopted in order to maintain the economies of scale that exist in some agricultural enterprises, such as livestock raising and, more importantly for Cuba, sugar cane planting. It became significant in later development of agrarian policy, as it made possible state farms (that is, farms run by the government with the workers paid wages, as opposed to cooperatives run by the occupants with the profits shared). The state farm did not appear immediately, however.

The governmental body created to carry out the land reform was the National Institute of Agrarian Reform (INRA). INRA not only saw to the surveying and dividing of lands, but also provided to the new landowners a number of other services, including technical advice, credit, seeds, fertilizers, and rural stores. As other important governmental agencies, INRA was centralized in Havana and directed by key followers of the maximum leader, even by Castro himself at times.

The pace of the reform was slow during the last half of 1959, accelerating rapidly at the beginning of the following year. By June 1961, 3.8 million hectares had been nationalized, affecting 101,000 Cuban peasants who had been resettled and, in many cases, given title. As might be expected, there was opposition to this reform. Both the American owners and the sugar bourgeoisie of Cuba opposed the loss of their property, even though they were told that they would be paid for it at the value declared for tax purposes. These groups moved into open opposition, burning sugar fields and public buildings, mounting assassination attempts, and employing various kinds of sabotage. The reaction of the Castro government was swift and decisive. On

July 6, 1960, the Law of Nationalization of Foreign-owned Enterprises was decreed, allowing the government to seize not only the lands of the foreign businesses, but also their sugar centrales, and providing compensatory payment only when the United States stopped its economic sanctions against the island. In October a similar law enabled the government to seize Cuban sugar mills and their attendant land, about 1 million hectares. The old forces of the status quo had used their most effective weapons against Castro, had lost, and hence were to suffer even more than the original agrarian reform law had called for.

In the next several years, the thinking of the Cuban leaders began to change. By October 1963 they had decided on a more radical agrarian reform. In the first place, the amount of land an individual could keep was decreased to 165 acres. This led to the expropriation of about ten thousand medium-sized farms. In the second place, the new agriculture was to be neither small bourgeoisie nor cooperative. All of the new land went into state ownership, the dominant form of organization becoming the state farm. Setting quotas and production targets, INRA coordinated all these farms, which represented 70 percent of the agricultural land.

Some thirty percent of the land remained in small farms, which were also controlled by the state. They were closely linked to the government by the National Association of Small Farmers (ANAP), which became the sole dispenser of credits, technical assistance, seeds, fertilizer, and other agricultural supplies to its members. Furthermore, INRA itself determined which crops were to be planted by the private farmers; it also set production quotas that the farmer was to meet and to deliver to the purchasing agencies of INRA at prices below the market value.

By late 1963 the agricultural sector—the chief source of economic wealth in pre-Castro Cuba—was completely controlled by the government. Castro and his circle saw this as desirable because it would allow more rational planning of the agricultural sector, as well as removing a possible source of political opposition. Nevertheless, agricultural production has decreased since the agrarian reform, perhaps because of it. Per capita food production and per capita agricultural production declined 28 percent from 1959 to 1969. Several reasons account for these declines. First, certain incentives to work hard were removed by the socialization of the economy. Second, Cuba experienced a very hard run of luck with weather, including the worst drought and the worst hurricane of the century within a few years. Third, the new planners of the economy were inexperienced and perhaps overly ambitious. Under the old capitalist system, most of the people with technical expertise in these matters were either North Americans or Cubans who left the island. The new elite had to learn from scratch. Moreover, they had to develop data collection devices to coordinate an entire agrarian economy, something that had not been done before in Cuba. Finally, the new planners simply made major mistakes.

The result of this decrease in agricultural production, even in foodstuffs, is more complex than it first appears. The decline does not necessarily mean that the great majority of Cubans are eating worse than they were before, although this is certainly true in some cases. Before the revolution, those people with high or middle-range incomes ate especially well, while those of lower income did not. No one starves today in Cuba, but neither are there many cases of obesity. Critics of the regime point out that rationing and long lines to get food have been necessary. What they do not realize is that there was rationing before the revolution, a free enterprise system of rationing in which there were no long lines since so many people did not have the money to buy food or other goods.

The true winner of the Cuban Revolution, because of the agrarian reforms, is the agricultural worker. The island no longer has an unemployment problem; on the contrary, it has a painful labor shortage. There is no unemployment simply because child labor has been abolished, putting the children into schools instead; because eight-hour working days are now constant, even during the sugar harvest; because new labor-intensive crops, such as coffee and citrus fruits, have been introduced; and because many of the former agricultural workers have been drained off to other work, both in industry and in the construction of roads, dams, homes, schools, and hospitals. The dwellers of the Cuban countryside, the agricultural workers, for the first time have both security and increasing real wages.

Industrialization and Diversification

Two other immediate goals of Fidel Castro and his followers were to industrialize the country and to diversify its agricultural component. Both of these goals are common to leaders of countries of monoculture, that is, countries that are largely dependent on one crop or product for their foreign exchange and national wealth.

Cuba had a comparative advantage in the production of sugar; it could grow it better and more efficiently than it could produce other things. However, monoculture makes the entire economy a function of that one crop or product. If the product is agricultural, there are the problems of weather; a drought or a storm can have disastrous effects on the entire country. Whether agri-

cultural or not, the economy becomes subject to the forces of the international market. When there is a scarcity of the product in relation to demand, the prices soar and the economy of the producing country flourishes. When demand goes down (as in war or depression) or when there is a surplus of international production, the price of the commodity goes down, and the entire economy suffers. Such had been the case of Cuba with sugar.

In the first years of the revolution, a twofold solution to this problem was decided upon by the Cuban leaders, and Castro personally: to diversify agricultural production and to industrialize. The first simply meant growing many things, not depending only on sugar. To this end, many producing cane fields were dug up and other crops planted, although some of the diversification took place on lands not previously used. This had a detrimental effect on the Cuban economy in the short run.

The second way was industrialization. Although some manufactures were produced within Cuba before the revolution, most came in finished form from the United States as imports: foodstuffs, clothing, and light and heavy industrial goods. The policy chosen was one of import substitution, that is, constructing factories to produce the goods previously imported in final form. The Cuban leaders started searching for support for this policy, first to construct light industries producing consumer goods and in the long run to initiate heavy industry also. These goals were to be achieved through a centrally directed economy and national planning centered in a Central Planning Committee, which was set up in March 1960. Support for this industrialization came from the communist countries. The Soviet Union lent $100 million for construction of steel factories, electric utilities, an oil refinery, and a geological survey, whereas

China granted $60 million for twenty-four factories. The Czechs supplied an automotive factory, while Rumania furnished capital for fifteen factories; Bulgaria, five; Poland, twelve; and East Germany, ten.

The vision was a Cuba that would be more self-sufficient; however, the policy failed and was abandoned in 1963. The problems with this strategy were many, five of which are most outstanding. First, in the short run, the neglect of sugar meant that the economy produced fewer valuable goods for international trade; less money was coming into the country, and hence there was less money to use to buy needed investment goods. Second, there were critical shortages of skilled technicians, managers, and workers and of needed raw materials. Third, there were planning mistakes. This state planning was a new endeavor, run by individuals with much more revolutionary fervor than practical experience. Fourth, there were breakdowns of plants already in Cuba, those which had been built by the American businesses. Before Castro, when there were breakdowns, the replacement parts came from the United States. An extreme case was one factory in which the first step, when a machine broke down, was to telephone the parent company in Connecticut, explaining what had happened and asking how to fix it. If the instructions given did not work, someone would fly to Cuba from the United States to repair the machinery. This source of parts and technical aid was no longer available in Castro's Cuba. Finally, there was the problem that importing the raw materials and making finished products was, at that stage of Cuba's development, simply more costly than importing the finished product had been.

Sugar Policy

In the long run, especially after 1963, Cuba returned to a dependence on sugar roughly

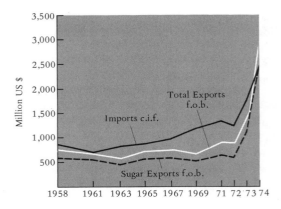

Cuba: Trade trends

(Central Intelligence Agency, *Intelligence Handbook, Cuba: Foreign Trade,* A (ER) 75-69, July: 1975, p. 1)

comparable to that before the revolution. There has been more crop diversification, and there are more factories than previously. Nevertheless, sugar is still king in Cuba.

The major difference was the decision of the Cuban leaders after the revolution to use the profits from the sugar industry in order to reach the goals of industrialization and diversification. Profits from international trade in sugar are not used for consumer goods, nor transferred to foreign owners, who no longer exist, but rather are primarily funneled into capital goods and into the research for and development of other agricultural crops.

For this purpose, sugar production was to be actually increased. This caused the problem of how to cut the cane, as Cuba had never had enough cutters and could no longer bring in seasonal laborers from the Caribbean due to its isolation by the inter-American community. One method that was experimented with was a cane cutting machine supplied by Nikita Khrushchev. Unfortunately, this machine was pretested in the flatter terrain of the Ukraine and did not work on the hillier lands of Cuba. In fact, it was a positive disservice, because cane has to be cut exactly right. Since it is a perennial, the cane stalk must be cut in such a way that the plant sprouts for the next year; the machine did not do that. Hence, it was necessary to use Cuban labor from other occupations during the harvest as well as continuing work on a better machine. The Soviet Union helped in this mechanization and, even more importantly, promised to buy at preferential prices the sugar that Cuba produced. China and some other socialist countries have also bought Cuban sugar, as have some non-communist countries, most notably Japan.

Sugar production continued to lag until the mid-1960s, due to the antisugar policy of the early years of the revolution. Since that time, sugar production has generally trended upward, hitting a high point in 1970. The policy of the leaders during this time was to plant more cane, and in mid-1964, Castro personally, against the advice of some of his counselors, set a goal for a 1970 harvest of 10 million metric tons of sugar. This was not an illogical goal; the purpose of this giant push was to produce enough sugar to give the Cuban government sufficient foreign exchange to increase capital investments dramatically. By 1968, the whole country had come to live with a "sugar obsession." The harvest no longer was limited to one hundred days in the last part of the year, during the coolest temperatures of the Cuban year. Rather, it was extended by several months in 1968, and was up to over a year by 1970. Almost every able-bodied individual was required to cut cane. Government bureaucrats—and the maximum leader himself—took time off to participate. Industrial workers who could be spared were sent to the fields, while those left in the plants were expected to maintain production at previous levels. Teachers and students were expected to cut cane, as were housewives who left their children in day-care centers.

The results of the 1970 harvest were impressive, although the magical 10-million-ton figure was not reached. It was the largest harvest (8.5 million tons) in Cuban history, giving the nation some of the sugar needed to make foreign exchange. The old divisions between country and city and between manual labor and non-manual labor were ameliorated, a social rather than an economic effect, but nonetheless desired by the Cuban leadership. However, the rest of the economy suffered, given the need for both labor and investment in the sugar realm.

Most importantly, Fidel Castro personally failed in the giant harvest. It was an ambitious goal (in the tradition of the Sierra Maestra complex) which he personally had set and on which he placed his personal prestige. He stated, "Ten million less a single pound—we declare it before the world—will be a defeat, not a victory." Cuba then, and Castro himself, suffered a defeat, and he publicly shared part of the guilt. In his analysis, Fidel stated that the defeat came from both objective and subjective factors. The objective ones were the lack of milling capacity, the lack of transportation facilities, and bad planning. But there were also subjective factors—those having to do with the lack of dedication of the people. In this sphere, the harvest failed because not everyone worked as hard as they should have.

The goal of increasing foreign exchange was achieved by the Cuban government during 1973 and 1974, when the world price of sugar soared. While the world price had been around ten cents (United States) per pound in previous years, by 1974 it reached sixty-nine cents. The benefit of this for Cuba is evident, although it was slowed up somewhat when the preferential price being paid by the Soviets suddenly became lower, rather than higher, than the world price. The treaty was renegotiated, although not to the temporarily very high world prices. The Cuban government used this added foreign exchange for capital development. Castro properly predicted in 1974 that the price for sugar could not stay at such inflated levels, and he was proved correct. By early 1976 the world price was back down to nineteen cents per pound.

Cuba today does not set unrealistic goals for sugar harvests, as it did in 1970. Still, the country's economy is centered on sugar production and, to an extent, is a monoculture just as it was before the revolution, at least in terms of foreign trade. However, there have been important changes. The profits from the sugar industry are no longer taken out of the country by private businessmen; they can and are reinvested in Cuba itself, for the benefit of the Cubans. The Cuban economy does not depend as greatly on trade relations with just one country as it did before the revolution. Figures published by the United States CIA, which is unlikely to exaggerate in favor of Fidel Castro's Cuba, indicate that in 1958, 67.1 percent of Cuban exports went to the United States, as compared to the 34.1 percent in 1974 that went to the Soviet Union. On the import side, 67.6 percent of Cuban products came from the United States in 1958, as compared to 50.0 percent from the Soviet Union in 1975. In short, Cuba is dependent on the Soviet Union in economic matters, but not to the extent that it was on the United States before the revolution.

Urban Reform

If the true winners of the Cuban Revolution were the agricultural workers, the ones who lost the most were the urban interests, particularly those centered in the city of Havana. Havana before the revolution was a glittering, dynamic city, the center for many United States businesses and the home for most of the Cuban wealthy. Most production in Cuba was agrarian, but most wealth was urban. The capital city was a center of international tourism, with foreigners coming to the island largely to be able to do things that were not legal in other countries. There were casinos and legalized gambling (some with United States organized crime involved), as well as widespread prostitution.

Castro's revolution has been bad for Havana as it existed before. Most of the wealthy and many of the middle class (who lived in Havana) left the island, in a flood of migration to the United States that included some 700,000 Cubans. United States business interests left, and so did organized crime.

But even more basically, Havana has been the loser of the Cuban Revolution because of the conscious economic decision to use more investment capital in the countryside than in the city. When there is a shortage of building materials, the cities receive them only after all the needs of the countryside have been met—which is to say, seldom. This is a consequence of the Cuban leaders' feeling that the true wealth of the country is agrarian, as well as the guerrilla feeling that virtue is rural, rather than urban. Castro himself has stated that he feels much more at home in the rural areas of the island than in Havana.

The result is a capital city that is not the showcase of the country; instead, visitors to Havana see a "depressed" city, as compared to other Latin American capitals. There definitely has been a redistribution of wealth of the city to the countryside. Nevertheless, there have been positive benefits for the urban dweller. As early as October 1960, stiff rent controls were decreed. Any land-lord was limited to $600 a month in income from his holdings. Later, rents were established at a flat rate of 10 percent of the income of the renter. After ten years an individual stops paying rent and becomes an owner. Furthermore, the resident of Havana also benefited from educational, health, and social programs of the revolution.

One novel policy of the Castro government was the *Cordón de la Habana* (ribbon around Havana), which was dedicated to agricultural work. This presented residents of Havana with the opportunity to raise crops within a short walk of their residences. In part, the policy was motivated by the declining agricultural production in the rest of the country, as well as the preponderant amount of food eaten in the capital. But also, it was another way to break down the old traditional divisions between city and country and between manual and non-manual work. While working on one's crops—vegetables, citrus fruit trees, coffee plants—one could have direct contact with the agrarian world, as well as work with one's hands. Fidel Castro decided that the eight-hour workday is best divided for all between four hours of manual and four hours of non-manual work. There is some indication that the Cordón has not been a great success economically, but no doubt the social dimension is also important.

Yet, none of the above should suggest that Havana is an impoverished city. It is so in relation to other Latin American capitals, which are such centers of wealth, but even today it is still better to live and work in the capital. In 1968, although Havana had only 27 percent of the population, it received 38 percent of the goods and 49 percent of the nation's commercial services. The Havana workers, as a rule, are still better off than their counterparts in other urban centers and than agrarian workers. But the clear thrust of the Castro government has been to narrow that gap—and the government has been successful in doing so.

Socialism in Cuba

Several key features of Castro's economic policy show its socialist nature. The old capitalist class, both foreign and domestic, is now gone. There are a number of collective goods, such as educational and health care, that all share equally, at least in theory. Wage differentials still exist. These are seen as essential in order not to alienate the technicians and managers at the top. However, these higher wages are paid only to those who held those positions before the revolution; new technicians and managers still make more than laborers, but not dramatically more.

As a socialist society, there is a preponderance of ownership by the state itself. Land ownership is about 70 percent in the hands of the government, and evidently Castro is willing to leave that other 30 percent in private hands for some time, at least as long as its owners are responsive to the government through direction by ANAP and INRA. Private nonagricultural business has increasingly been placed in governmental hands. By 1962 all major businesses had been nationalized. In 1968, through the Great Revolutionary Offensive, Cuba became the socialist country with the highest percentage of public ownership in the world. This offensive, launched by Castro personally against the advice of his economic advisers, had as its goal the elimination of the small capitalists who still remained. According to official figures published late in the first month of the offensive, 58,012 stalls, shops, and private service establishments were nationalized, and large stocks of consumer goods were seized.

Likewise, as a socialist society, all economic decisions are made by the central planners. Although beholden to the Soviet Union in many ways, the fidelista regime in the 1960s leaned more toward the antimarket and nonmonetary concepts of nineteenth-century Marxism and early Leninism. The Cubans adopted a highly centralized and radical model for administering the economy and for promoting communist development, which, of course, was under the personal domination of the leader himself. In 1965, Castro settled on a new path for the construction of "genuine communism" in Cuba, which entailed a major reorganization of the economy during the next two years. State enterprises were increasingly regrouped under large industrial and agricultural combines directed by central ministries and state agencies. Organized by industry or commodity, each combine had responsibility for coordinating the entire production, distribution, and marketing activities of its member firms. They did so in accordance with central plans made at the top by what could be called the mathematical approach to socialism. Under this approach, the central planners fix production targets in quantitative terms by setting desired goals and matching those up with projected resources. This is done without regard to profit, or monetary calculations, except for bookkeeping purposes. Each combine is then given its targets, and the perceived necessary resources to reach them.

This system was desired because it gave maximum power to the central elite, unlike "market socialism," as theoretically practiced in the Soviet Union, in which there is room for calculation of profits. It was perceived as a system that would make the radical transformation of Cuba possible most rapidly. Nevertheless, the method is no better than the information received by and the

abilities of the central elite and, in the case of Cuba, of Fidel Castro himself. This is one of the grounds on which the Cuban Revolution was most criticized.

In the 1970s, the direction of the Cuban economy became more like that of the Soviet Union, at least to a certain degree. More stress is placed on price mechanisms, and individual state firms are allowed to make more decisions as to production.

Social Policies

There is no neat separation of economic policies from those which are primarily social. While having all people cut sugar cane was mainly an economic necessity, there also was a beneficial social outcome: the old social distinctions of town and country, of manual worker and non-manual worker, were lessened, as desired by the Cuban leadership. Likewise, it is obvious that policies in education, housing, and health, as well as those relating to women, have economic ramifications even if the primary motivation is social—the desire to change interpersonal relationships.

Education
In late 1960, Fidel Castro announced that 1961 would be "the Year of Education," with the goal of teaching every illiterate to read and write. This skill training was tied together with civic education, thus "instilling in our children and young people an unbounded love of the Fatherland and a feeling of solidarity with the workers and peoples of all lands in their noble struggle for a free and happy life."[1] At the same

[1] Richard Fagen, *The Transformation of Political Culture in Cuba* (Stanford, Calif.: Stanford University Press, 1969), p. 37.

412

time, the literacy workers, or teachers, were to learn the hard realities of underdevelopment. Both the illiterates and the literacy workers were expected to emerge from the experience with a deeper understanding of national problems, a new concept of citizenship, and a new willingness to work for the transformation of Cuba.

Cuba had a relatively easy job in this literacy campaign, simply because the level of illiteracy was low to start with: only about 25 percent in Cuba, compared with much higher figures in most of Latin America. During 1961, some 171,000 literacy workers traveled through the island, teaching the illiterates on a one-to-one basis. There was some danger involved: several were killed in remote areas by the counterrevolutionaries. However, by December, the literacy campaign claimed to have reached 979,000 students, of whom 707,000 were new literates. They learned to read through texts with sentences such as "When the riches of a nation are in the hands of another nation, a revolution is needed to recover those riches. When the humble men and women of a country are without work, without land to cultivate, without education, they must revolt." [2]

The results of this campaign were several. First, a large number of people were involved either as teachers or students, approximately 1.25 million of the 7 million on the island at that time. Second, a number of people, particularly the literacy workers, were mobilized to aid the regime. Third, no doubt the illiterates learned about the revolution and perhaps they acquired some rudimentary literacy skills, although one can seriously question how much these skills

meant in their everyday life and how long they were retained after the campaign. The level of illiteracy was officially lowered to 3 or 4 percent, making Cuba the most literate nation in Latin America.

Since 1961, education has been free, and students have been given all the books and school materials they need, greatly in contrast to the educational system at the time of Fidel Castro's youth. No person is prevented from studying due to the lack of educational resources; indeed, those families who cannot afford another mouth to feed or, for that matter, cannot afford the room and board if the education is away from the home can still send their children to school through scholarships. First begun in 1962, the program provided 277,505 such scholarships by 1970, an incredible number in an island of some 9 million people. The "grand design" of this Cuban educational effort has been fourfold: (1) making education universal from nursery school through the university; (2) developing a Marxist orientation by teaching the children some of the ideology of the regime; (3) combining education with technological principles, productive work, and research; and (4) incorporating the working masses into the educational process.

At higher levels, education has become more diversified. Since 1960 the University of Havana and its two offshoots in Las Villas and Oriente have become vocational training centers. Its former three schools (law, medicine, and letters and arts) have grown to eight (technology, agronomy, medicine, sciences, teaching, economy, humanities, and the workers and peasants faculty— an adult extension division that prepares its four thousand lower-class students to enter one of the other seven faculties). The most important and largest of these is the Faculty of Technology, which at the University of

[2] Ibid., p. 40.

Havana enrolls some fourteen thousand of the fifty-four thousand students, over half of whom are on complete scholarships. This turn toward more pragmatic careers means that technology students are people who can run factories, not do research; doctors can vaccinate, but not transplant organs; economists can become general consultants and planners, with fewer planners in specific fields and no one in training for private business. Professors are promoted by student-faculty committees on the basis of ability to teach and "revolutionary commitment," rather than on research.

Students in higher education are part of the labor force, as some 60 percent of the students are part-time. But even the full-time students spend twenty hours a week in work, quite often related to their studies, as well as twenty hours a week in class and another like period of time in individual study. (This applies all the way down to the level of junior high school.) Further, almost every field of training has a program of preprofessional work that sends professors and students out into the field together, from two weeks to two months a year. Preprofessional work orients the students toward a vocation and gives them a basis for relevance in their academic studies.

Not all students in higher education are in the universities. In the entire country, there are aproximately 40,000 students in schools of agronomy and fishing, which did not even exist before the revolution. Industrial schools have grown from 6,000 to 30,000 students. In all, by the mid-1970s there were some 133,000 students in higher education, of whom 83,000 were in the universities, as compared to 16,000 university students in 1959.

The educational effort has been called the greatest accomplishment of the Cuban Revolution. While this is probably true, some limitations should be mentioned about this effort. First, the quality of education has gone down at the lower school levels, simply because there were not enough teachers at the beginning of the revolution. Second, Cuban education is producing few people with theoretical knowledge and research skills; most are technicians. Third, the autonomy of student groups at the university has been lost; they no longer have the right to be in opposition, to be, indeed, like Fidel Castro was when he was at the university. And fourth, students who are not in favor of the revolution are not allowed in the university, although this seems to be changing recently.

Fidel Castro has replied to those criticisms in the following way. Of course there is a poorer quality of public lower education, but now everyone is receiving some, as opposed to the elite who could afford more than one or two years before the revolution. As far as higher education is concerned, what an underdeveloped country needs in the immediate future is people who have skills useful for the economy—not, for example, a science major who learns to do basic research leading to new knowledge in the field, but rather one who can use the knowledge accumulated by other scientists to get the sugar mills working more efficiently. Therefore, it is appropriate not only that the skills be practical, rather than theoretical, from a general standpoint, but also that those who have the abilities for higher education use them in such a way as to aid the country immediately. As far as student activities are concerned, their time would better be spent in developing a career. And no known antirevolutionaries are admitted (even though those who are neutral might be) simply because there are a limited number of places in the university and technical schools. It does the country no good to train someone who will leave for the United States.

Social Mobilization

The transformation of Cubans into revolutionaries is one of the primary goals of Fidel Castro and the revolutionary leadership. A policy of elite-directed attempts to alter the political culture of the nation is perceived as the means of achieving such individual transformations. The primary mechanism for bringing such changes is through directed participation in revolutionary institutions, that is to say, through social mobilization. The people of Cuba are allowed to participate in the revolution, but only in the ways that Castro and his circle decide are desirable.

A large number of people were mobilized for revolutionary purposes during the literacy campaign of 1961. Both the literacy workers and the illiterates not only learned something useful, but also had the psychological satisfaction of participating in reaching a revolutionary goal. The return of the literacy workers to Havana at the end of the year seemed to many as very similar to the entry of the guerrillas a few years earlier; they had participated in the revolutionary process and had been victors.

While the literacy campaign was a one-year effort, a continuing one has been the Committees for the Defense of the Revolution (CDR). It was launched personally by Castro at the end of 1960 with this statement:

We're going to set up a system of revolutionary collective vigilance. And then we shall see how the lackeys of imperialism manage to operate in our midst. . . . In answer to the imperialist campaign of aggression, we're going to set up a system of revolutionary collective vigilance so that everybody will know everybody else on his block, what they do, what relationship they had with the tyranny, what they believe in, what people they meet, what activities they participate in.[3]

There were five basic functions of the CDRs. First, they were to integrate the people, to bring together all the diverse types of people living and working in Cuba. Second, they were to teach the people the basics of the ideology of the regime. The political education was too short to give its participants any profound knowledge of Marxist-Leninism, but some of the terminology and basic ideas could be introduced. Third, the CDRs were mobilizers, a means of getting the people to participate, enlisting their energies in a number of activities such as cutting cane, collecting scrap metal, or enrolling children in school. Fourth, they functioned as administrators of the programs of the revolution in many fields, including welfare, public health, housing, and education. But most importantly, the CDRs remained a way of collective vigilance.

There is little doubt that this structure did give people a way to participate, within strict limits, in the revolution. Indeed, anyone could join a CDR, and its existence removed any possible excuse for not having an opportunity to demonstrate one's revolutionary fervor. By the mid-1960s, there were 2 million members. Further, the CDR did lead to positive results for the revolution, in all of the five functions mentioned above and particularly in the area of vigilance. Nevertheless, on the negative side it is possible that they led to a loss of legitimacy of the revolution in some cases. The committees were plagued from the beginning by some of their members' using their new power to be arbitrary and, in some cases, self-serving and corrupt. By the late 1960s,

[3] Ibid., p. 69.

the CDRs were deemphasized, vigilance remaining as the primary function.

Another instrument of mass mobilization, for a select group, were the Schools of Revolutionary Instruction (EIR), founded secretly in the latter half of 1960. The single purpose, according to Castro, was the ideological formation of a select group of revolutionaries who then would spread their ideas to the people in general. These schools taught Marxist-Leninism as the leaders of the Cuban Revolution understood it. They were never public or open, and students were chosen to attend.

At its high point in 1962, the EIR consisted of 9 national schools, a consolidated system of 7 provincial schools, more than 200 basic schools, more than 500 instructors, and approximately 10,000 students. However, the schools were discontinued in 1965 for several reasons. Soviet teaching materials were not adequate for the Cuban situation; there was a shortage of qualified teachers. But more basically the Cuban leaders did not believe that revolutionary training could occur in the classroom. Rather, they argued, it is learned from revolutionary activity itself.

The mobilization campaign was successful in getting many people to participate in the revolution. While this was not participation in the sense usually understood in the United States, it should be remembered that Castro personally felt that one of the functions of leadership was to teach people the right kinds of attitudes and behavior. The mobilization was to do that, and it appears to have been particularly successful with the younger generation, in which Castro places his hopes for the future.

Health and Housing
The first objective of the Castro health policy was to nationalize the health care system, making it free to all the citizens of Cuba. In 1959, 83 percent of the medical doctors were in private practice, with only 17 percent working for the state. By 1969, 93 percent of the doctors were working for the state. All health care is free, including office visits, hospitalization, and prescribed drugs.

Nevertheless, this nationalization has not come without difficulties. To meet the ambitious program, the second aim of the health program was to increase the number of doctors. There were some 6,300 in that profession at the time of the revolution; however, between 2,000 and 4,000 of them went into exile. To meet this loss, and the shortage that existed before, there are now three medical schools rather than the previous one, and thirty-two teaching hospitals rather than the four before the rise of Castro. By 1973 there were 8,000 physicians in Cuba.

A related goal was to distribute the medical personnel more evenly. In 1958, 60 percent of the physicians lived and worked in Havana. Thus Havana Province had one doctor for every 420 persons, while Oriente Province had one for every 2,100. The doctors tended to congregate in Havana because of the greater amenities of life there and the possibility of making more money. This maldistribution has been lessened by assigning doctors to the outlying regions and by requiring that all medical students spend two or three years in the countryside.

Another objective has been to increase the hospital and clinic space. The number of public hospitals rose from 54 in 1959 to 180 in 1968, while the number of available hospital beds went from 10,843 to 38,760 during that same period. Forty-eight of the hospitals are rural general hospitals, as compared to only one before Castro. Further, more than 250 clinics have been constructed in both rural and urban areas.

A final objective has been a public health

program, including a vaccination and sanitation program that has eliminated completely the diseases of malaria and polio. Gastroenteritis has been dramatically reduced, and turberculosis and diphtheria have also been almost eradicated.

The results of the health program are impressive. Direct comparisons with the pre-Castro period are hazardous, since statistics were very badly kept. However, it does seem that life expectancy has been increased to about sixty-seven years; infant mortality rates have gone down, from about 52 to 27 per 100,000; maternal mortality has similarly dropped, from approximately 118 to 63 per 100,000.

Yet the Cuban health system at present still has problems. Many of the medical personnel were trained too rapidly, in face of the twin problems of a lack of doctors in 1959 and the subsequent exile of some. One would suspect that if indeed there was insufficient training, it would be cleared up within a matter of a relatively few years, and this seems to have been the case. In the meantime, health care from someone less prepared than desirable is probably better than no health care at all, which was the case for many people in pre-Castro Cuba. Secondly, there has been a chronic lack of drugs, probably having its greatest effect on infant mortality. Before Castro, Cuba received drugs from American business concerns, so the breaking of trade relations with the United States led to a lack of drugs that could not be met by the Eastern European nations and the Soviet Union.

A final reason for the difficulties with the health system is based on economic conditions. During the first decade of the revolution, food production went down. Some indications are that average daily caloric intake has also declined. This is directly translated into health problems, as the great majority of the Cuban people ate too little—and not enough of the right kinds of food—even before the revolution. Any policy that would increase the quality and quantity of food for internal consumption would benefit the health program.

Castro giving a speech

(Lee Lockwood/Black Star)

The housing program has been less of a success. Before the revolution, great numbers of Cubans had inadequate housing, in both the city and the country, especially the latter. Castro has initiated programs that would improve the housing situation, and there has been definite progress. However, much remains to be done. The problem is one common to underdeveloped countries: there simply are not enough construction materials. At the same time, there are many needs for these materials, not only in housing, but also in hospital and school construction. Within that portion of the materials that go for housing, the preference has been given to rural housing, in an attempt to eradicate the thatched huts common in the countryside, but at the detriment of the needs of Havana and the other urban centers.

Racial Minorities and Women

Blacks lived in inferior social and economic positions in pre-Castro Cuba. Although there still are legacies of black cultural deprivations that linger on and although some individual prejudice remains, the most serious manifestations of discrimination—social exclusion and the lack of equal educational and economic opportunities—were terminated by Fidel Castro's revolutionary decrees. Indeed, in the hands of the revolutionaries, the race issue was extremely useful for discrediting the old social order. And, because of what could be called the instant liberation of the black, tens of thousands of disadvantaged Cubans were recruited into the ranks of revolutionary enthusiasts. Castro sincerely felt that racial discrimination was wrong and took actions to end it. Today there is more equality—both legal and real —of the races in Cuba than in any other Latin American country.

Women in Cuba were likewise in a secondary position before the revolution. Several of the policies of the Castro government have changed this situation to a degree. First, prostitution has been ended, in part perhaps because Castro's political ideology is of a "puritanical" nature, but more basically because it represented a form of exploitation not acceptable in the socialist society. At the same time, the revolutionary government has reaffirmed the values of family life—by encouraging civil marriages of those individuals who were living in common-law relationships, for example. Also, the government has encouraged women to enter the militia and to take other jobs in the economy and has established day-care centers to accommodate the children of working mothers.

This policy has been only partially successful. By 1974, women made up only about a quarter of the labor force, compared to about one-fifth before the revolution. One of the reasons for this was seen by the Castro government to be the second-shift phenomenon. Working women soon discovered that they spent eight hours on a job, only to return home to do the cooking, cleaning, and other housework. As a result, the Family Code decreed in 1972 states that when both husband and wife have jobs, they have to share the housework equally. There is no indication whether or not this policy has been successful.

Yet another problem has to do with long-standing attitudes about relations between the sexes, best epitomized by the term *machismo*. From the male perspective, the loss of the dominant role has certain negative results. Since women are now an important part of the labor force, including that of agriculture, they often have to leave offspring in child-care centers, even occasionally for extended periods of time while they are assigned to work in distant places. As a result, the children do not develop feelings of family solidarity. Further, men have more of the child-related responsibilities and are "disemancipated," having less freedom than before. Both of these points are probably true; nevertheless, these changes are seen as desirable by the leader.

The old attitudes of machismo still affect women, too. In the 1974 elections for the Matanzas Assembly of Peoples' Power, only 3 percent of the deputies chosen were women. As Castro pointed out in an interview, this shows that even Cuban women discriminate against themselves; if they accepted themselves as equals, then about half of the deputies would have been women. He concluded, "It is not only necessary to change women's mentality, but also to change men's mentality. This is a struggle the Party must carry on and it is doing just that." [4]

Other Social Policies

The social policies of the Cuban Revolution have not been beneficial for some other minorities. One such group is that which opposes the revolution itself. While apparently a certain amount of verbal disagreement is allowed, no such dissent is allowed at the organizational level. As a result of this policy, about 750,000 Cubans left the island for exile, and another 50,000 to 100,000 are in prisons. Clearly freedom, in the sense that the term is used in the United States, is not allowed in Cuba. But Castro argues,

I believe there are two different conceptions of freedom. You believe that freedom can exist with a class system, and we believe in a system where everyone is equal, where there are no superpowers because there is no pyramid, no millionaires, no multimillionaires, where some

don't even have a job. I wonder if you can compare the freedom of the millionaire with that of the beggar or of the unemployed. However, you believe this is freedom. We believe that is all false, and we believe that without equality there is no freedom because you do have to speak about the freedom of the beggar, the prostitute, the exploited, the discriminated, the illiterate. Freedom to write and speak for a man who cannot write, cannot read? . . . Freedom for an illiterate who does not have any opinion or who cannot even differentiate between good and evil? We believe man can be free only if he is equal. [5]

Although some individuals are in prison because of opposition to the regime, the police under Castro are far less dangerous and repressive than they were during the Batista years. Hence, from their own particular historical perspective, Cubans can deny that they live in a police state.

The other instrument of coercion—the armed forces—has also been changed by the Castro Revolution. One of his first acts after assuming power was to purge the old military of the Batista years. Officers of the rebel army took over many posts. Later in 1959, the regular army was replaced by a militia, which has grown to some 250,000 in number. Today, renamed the Revolutionary Armed Forces and organized after the Soviet military fashion, it is the largest in the Caribbean area, third largest in all of Latin America, and the largest in terms of percentage of population in that geographic area. All young people are required to spend two years in the armed forces, which engages in work related to the economy, such as the sugar harvests, in addition to military tasks. The Castro government realized that there is a potential for an independent polit-

[4] Mankiewicz and Jones, *With Fidel*, pp. 115–116.

[5] Ibid., p. 93.

ical force arising in the military, and a system of indoctrination and controls has been set up to prevent this.

Another group that has been affected negatively by governmental policy is the homosexual community, for Castro believes there is no place for people of such orientation in the new Cuba. They are not allowed to be teachers, and some have been imprisoned.

The Roman Catholic church has also suffered at the hands of Castro's government. Although the church there was never as strong as in most of Latin America, steps were soon taken to weaken its strength. There were several issues at stake. One was the control of education, traditionally in the hands of the religious communities, as seen in Castro's own education. Another was the number of foreign, especially Spanish, priests. These priests were suspected of opposing the revolution, and many were asked to leave the country. Indeed, some priests were discovered participating in the Bay of Pigs invasion.

The low point for the Catholic church was in the mid-1960s when there were only 100 priests in the entire country. However, the churches remained open, and by the end of that decade the number of priests was up to about 230 and two seminaries were operating. A modus vivendi seems to have been reached between Castro and the church: the official policy of the government neither encourages nor discourages church attendance, while the church stays completely out of politics.

Intellectuals, artists, and writers have also been a sore point. At the beginning of the revolution, any intellectual whose works were antirevolutionary had to leave the island. During most of the 1960s the government's attitude toward the artists who remained was a degree of tolerance unsurpassed by other socialist regimes. The various tendencies and schools of arts were allowed to find their own way within the revolution. At the same time, the artists were organized—as was everyone—by the government into the Union of Cuban Writers and Artists (UNEAC), one of whose aims was to "mesh the works of writers and artists with the major tasks of the Cuban Revolution, procuring the latter's reflection and promotion by such works."

One particularly noteworthy incident had to do with the poet, Heberto Padilla. While Padilla had generally been favorable to the revolution in his works, he was arrested in March 1971 for alleged counterrevolutionary activities. More specifically, the charges were that he had talked against the revolution in conversations with a number of European writers who favored the revolution, but questioned some of its means. Padilla was also charged with writing antirevolutionary poetry and with other acts of subversion. Subsequently, in a lengthy confession he admitted the counterrevolutionary activities and was released. The entire incident led to a storm of protest from writers around the world, many of whom had earlier commended the Castro government for its freedoms for the intellectual community.

The other side of intellectual freedom—that having to do with the consumers rather than the producers—shows more positive results. With the higher education of the populace, there is a larger market for all kinds of intellectual pursuits—books, plays, museums, and other entertainments. The Castro government controls closely the contents of these media, including not only the spoken word and books, but also the newspapers. Only official newspapers are allowed to publish, particularly the *Granma,* named for the famous yacht. The books that can be published are controlled, although probably less than in most communist countries. There is a shortage of books for several reasons: there is much demand, many of the books are now free, and, as in many other industries, the Cuban book industry is a relatively new one.

The Accomplishments of Castro's Social Policies

There seems to be little doubt that the chief gains of the Cuban Revolution have been in the realm of social policy, in which the governing elite is less restrained than in economic policy. In general, Cubans are better off in social terms than they were in 1958. This has been because of a conscious decision to use government to bring a different and, in Castro's terms, more just society.

While the leader has admitted that problems exist in the economic realm, some of which he takes responsibility for, he is proud of the accomplishments of the social policies. In his 1970 "Report on the Cuban Economy," he gave the following figures, comparing the late 1960s with the last years of the Batista dictatorship. The outlay for social security services increased from 114.7 million pesos in 1958 to 320.0 million in 1970. In public health, the number of workers went from 8,209 to 87,646, while the budget went from 22.7 million pesos to 236.1 million. In 1958 there were 936,723 people enrolled in schools throughout the nation, as compared to 2,239,464 in 1970. Meanwhile, the budgetary expenditures for education went from 77.0 million pesos to 290.6 million, reflecting an increase in teachers from 23,000 to 127,526 and an increase in the number of scholarship students from 15,698 to 277,505. In the combined fields of social security, public health, and education, the entire budget rose from 213.8 million pesos in 1958 to about 850 million pesos in 1970.

Many people would deny the validity of these figures since they come from Castro and the Cuban government; however, there is no alternative source. Likewise, the figures

as presented do not take into account the growth either of the Cuban population or of the Cuban national budget over the ten-plus year period, nor do they account for inflation and changes in the value of the Cuban currency.

However, there is general agreement that the bright point of the Cuban picture, by 1970, was in the social realm. In the long term, a more successful economic policy would make even more benefits possible in this social sphere. Nevertheless, the Cuban leaders have found these problems to be the most tractable, and it was definitely consistent with ideology to do something about them.

Creation of the New Cuban

One of the policy areas that overlapped the social and economic dimensions had to do with the nature of people in socialist Cuba. Castro and his followers wanted to create a "new Cuban" who would act socially and politically as a member of a society of equals and who would act economically as a diligent worker, hence helping the revolution.

This policy entered into the philosophical realm of how to get people to work if they no longer need to work in order to live. The leaders soon learned that in socialist Cuba people worked less than they had before the revolution. In the earlier period, work was necessary to get money for food, housing, and clothing, among other things. In the new socialist society, many things were collective goods, available to all. Housing was in some cases free, as was public transportation, public entertainment, education, and medical care. One still needed money for food and clothing; however, both of these were scarce and rationed, and one could earn enough money, with guaranteed wages, for what was available from a few hours' work per day. Therefore, people started being absent from work, whether industrial or agricultural.

In the early 1960s the Cuban leadership went through a "great debate" over the incentives that should be used to get people to work harder. One side favored the "material incentives within socialism" position. This argument was that in a socialist society many things would be provided free to all, but there would still be additional pay for those who worked longer and harder. At the time the Soviet Union and a number of Eastern European countries were moving toward such material incentives. The other side, led by Che Guevara, took the "moral incentive" approach. Much like young Marx and Lenin in the early years of the Russian Revolution, this side argued that people fully liberated from the chains of capitalism would continue to work, not because they needed to work to live, but because work is an integral part of everyone's existence. Further, the argument continued, there were certain collective benefits of work, nonmaterial incentives, that would operate. These included patriotism, the long-range good of the country, fear of outside enemies, peer group pressure, and such symbolic things as flags, plaques, photographs, and other gifts from the leaders for good work, and collective rewards for whole production units that met their targets. By 1965 the great debate was over; the advocates of moral incentives had won, at least for the time being.

The way to convert the people into the new Cubans was through social mobilization and the concurrent change of their belief structures. This process was begun in 1961 and continues still today. Yet moral incentives did not motivate the Cubans as expected. From 1965 on—as before—absenteeism, poor discipline, and low productivity became problems in the Cuban economy; nei-

ther appeals of the leadership nor fines solved the problems.

A new model adopted to encourage the people to work was one based on coercion—the military model. By 1968, at the time of the Great Revolutionary Offensive, the Cuban leaders had seen that the productivity levels of the military units cutting sugar cane were much higher than those of the civilian cane cutters. This was credited to the military command structure, which defined the duties and responsibilities of those below, while the agricultural workers did not have a command structure. Moreover, neither did the latter have a system of vigorous discipline, including harsh punishments for disobedience or poor performance, nor did they have well-defined responsibilities. Therefore, the military model was applied to the civilian work force. Although the word *militarization* was never used officially, the whole country was reorganized on that model. Command posts led by the members of the Politburo of the Communist party were set up in every province to coordinate the great agricultural battle of the 1970 sugar harvest. Labor brigades were turned into battalions, each divided into three squads, led by a major and a chief of operations responsible for discipline and work progress.

On August 29, 1969, while Cuba was going through its militarization stage, the regime announced a measure to exert more direct control over all workers. The decree made it mandatory for all workers to have a work-force control card on which their productivity, background, political views, and employment history were recorded. The card was necessary to obtain or change a job and to receive a salary. Moreover, any worker wishing to change jobs needed the permission of a regional officer of the Labor Ministry.

By 1973 the Cuban leadership's policy

moved more toward material incentives for exemplary work. There are no dramatic differences in wages; however, a very good worker might receive certain nonmonetary rewards, such as a week's vacation for his or her family or a preference for new housing or a new refrigerator. The idea of moral incentives has not been discarded, but they are mixed with the material rewards. The long-term hope is placed on the new generation, those who have grown up under socialism. The old generation is still too ingrained with the ideas of capitalism, and increased economic productivity is important enough to warrant a return to modified material incentives.

Foreign Policy

The basic foreign policy of Fidel Castro has called for an end to dependence on the United States and for Cuban independence. In the bipolar world of the early 1960s, this necessarily meant increased reliance on the Soviet Union. Yet another element of Cuban foreign policy has been assistance to other revolutionaries, a position most recently called "proletarian internationalism." This policy has led to conflict with the United States and at times with the rest of Latin America.

The United States and the Inter-American Community

Castro had two clear goals in his early policy toward the United States: to rid his country of North American business interests and to avoid the violent end of the revolution by the United States government. The decision makers in Washington, on their part, had three major objections to the Castro government: seizure of North American businesses

without adequate compensation, sponsorship of invasions of other Latin American countries, and, later, the military presence of the Soviet Union on the island. In all the years of the revolution, Castro's main goal has remained the preservation of the revolution against United States attempts to end it. These attempts took two forms: the use of the Organization of American States (OAS) to impose sanctions and the military or paramilitary removal of Castro or the Revolution.

The United States turned first to the OAS, in 1960, appealing that Cuba was permitting Soviet infiltration of the hemisphere and not fulfilling its responsibilities as a member of the OAS. Both actions were purported to be violations of the inter-American agreements. Subsequently, the foreign ministers of the OAS member-states met in San José, Costa Rica, in August 1960. At that meeting, the United States charged the Soviets with infiltrating the internal affairs of the Americas and thus causing a threat to hemispheric peace and security. Most Latin American governments, however, viewed the Cuban case as merely a dispute between the United States and Cuba, and they did not wish to share responsibility for any action against the Cuban regime. The Declaration of San José, which emerged from the meeting, condemned all types of intervention by extracontinental powers that could endanger American solidarity, but it also declared that no American state can intervene for the purposes of imposing upon another American state "its ideologies or political, economic, or social principles."

Although the declaration did not mention Cuba, its implications were obvious to the Cuban delegation, which walked out of the meeting. In Havana, Castro responded to this OAS action through the Declaration of Havana. In it, he condemned the "open and criminal intervention policy of American imperialism," offered Cuban friendship to the people of the United States, and thanked the Soviet Union for its offers of assistance.

The most dramatic attempt by the United States to end the Cuban Revolution was the Bay of Pigs invasion of April 1961. This was an offensive by Cuban refugees who were living in the United States and were trained by the CIA in Guatemala. Although occurring during the first months of the Kennedy administration, it had been planned at least nine months in advance. The Bay of Pigs invasion was to rid the island of Castro (much like the Guatemalan invasion against Arbenz in 1954) and to replace him with someone who would change the policies of Cuba.

While there were military reasons for the failure of the invasion, the fundamental cause was the CIA's underestimating the degree of domestic support for Castro in early 1961. Most of the anti-Castro Cubans had left the country, and those who remained were closely watched. It was a fact that Castro was a popular man and the leader that the majority of Cubans wanted at that point in time.

The response to the Bay of Pigs invasion was one of Castro's finest military achievements. The victory was overwhelming. About 1,200 rebels were captured, later to be traded back to the United States for bulldozers and other equipment. Castro had anticipated such an eventuality well through his creation of the CDRs and the militia. Both responded immediately. Further, many Cubans who belonged to neither rushed to the area of the invasion to help, as Castro personally commanded the resistance. His regime was even more secure after the defeat of the CIA-trained exiles, and indeed his charismatic authority was increased since he had once again done the impossible. Now he had defeated not only the Batista dictatorship, but also the most powerful nation in the world.

The CIA, both before and after the Bay of Pigs incident, tried to use other violent means against Cuba; its proposed method of ending the revolution was by assassinating Fidel Castro. In 1975, Castro supplied Senator George McGovern with information about twenty-four alleged CIA plots to assassinate him. The same year, the United States Senate Select Committee on Intelligence studied one-third of those attempts, most of which sounded as though they were based on a spy movie. Suggestions for assassination ranged from simple shooting, to more sophisticated methods such as a microscopic hypodermic containing a lethal poison mounted on a fountain pen, a contaminated skin-diving suit, an exploding seashell, and a highly poisonous powder. Yet another plot involved a powder that would cause Castro's beard to fall out, hence detracting from his charismatic image. Whether or not United States Presidents at the time knew about these assassination attempts, as well as those against other leaders, is a question that cannot yet be answered.

After the Bay of Pigs fiasco, the United States government also turned back to a multilateral approach through the Organization of American States to rid the hemisphere of Castro, an approach that not only failed, but in the process discredited the inter-American system. In 1962 at Punta del Este, Uruguay, Dean Rusk urged sanctions against Cuba in the form of a collective break of diplomatic relations and a total trade embargo. However, these sanctions and all others were opposed by the most important Latin American countries on the grounds that they would be meddling in the right of self-determination of the Cuban people. Nevertheless, by a vote of twenty to one the member-states agreed to identify the Castro regime as a communist government allied with the Soviet bloc and declared the adherence of any member of the OAS to the

Marxist-Leninist ideology incompatible with the principles of the inter-American system. Furthermore, by just the two-thirds majority necessary, the foreign ministers voted to suspend Cuba from the OAS as long as it maintained its communist ties. Finally, again by the bare two-thirds majority, the meeting voted to suspend immediately trade with Cuba of arms and war materiel.

Castro's personal reaction to this meeting was the Second Declaration of Havana. In it, he called for violent social revolution throughout Latin America and decried as illusory any hope that the current governments of Latin America would support meaningful social or economic change. Further, in reaction to the United States policy of the Alliance for Progress, started by Kennedy in 1961, Castro stated that the United States government did not seriously want economic or social change, either.

The next use of the OAS by the United States against Cuba was in relation to the Cuban Missile Crisis in October 1962. This crisis centered around the discovery of surface-to-surface nuclear missiles that the Soviet Union was constructing on the island. The United States called immediately for an emergency meeting of the OAS Council, which called for the dismantling and withdrawal of all missiles and other offensive weapons from Cuba and recommended that member-states take all measures necessary to prevent further shipment of war materiel to Cuba. Some Latin American countries immediately contributed units to the United States naval forces engaged in the blockade, some mobilized their armed forces and offered to send troops, and others offered the use of their bases to the United States.

In retrospect, the United States took the least drastic alternative of the three considered. Some members of the White House circle wanted to invade the island, while others wanted "surgical air strikes" against the missiles. The blockade was less dramatic and, as it turned out, effective. Basically the missile crisis was an interaction between the two superpowers, in which Cuba and Fidel Castro were just pawns. Castro tried to play a part, at one point stating that the missiles would not be withdrawn; however, they were when the Soviet Union decided they should be. The Cuban leader's final position, one in which he prevailed, was in preventing the on-site inspections agreed to by the two superpowers. Nevertheless, he was a pawn in this case, a role in which he had had no experience and which he did not relish.

In 1963 the Castro government concentrated its subversive activities in Venezuela, by supplying arms to Venezuelan guerrillas. The discovery of a large amount of Cuban arms for use by these guerrillas prompted the Venezuelan government to request an investigation by the OAS. In July 1964 the foreign ministers of the OAS, meeting in Washington, condemned the Castro regime for its acts of aggression and intervention against Venezuela by a vote of fifteen to four. All member-nations were to break diplomatic and consular relations, and there was to be a complete trade embargo, except for items needed for humanitarian purposes.

Hence, for eleven years, from 1964 to 1975, all nations of this hemisphere were required to break both diplomatic and trade relations with the Castro government. Not all did: Mexico, for example, never broke relations. By 1973 there were moves to end this embargo, and meanwhile more nations reestablished diplomatic and even trade relations with the island. Finally, in July 1975 the OAS, meeting again in San José, Costa Rica, voted to allow each individual nation to decide on its own about relations with Cuba. The multilateral move had failed.

Fidel Castro's reaction to the OAS actions was multifaceted. In the first place, he accepted his suspension from the organization

425

as not very meaningful, because he saw that international organization as merely a tool of United States foreign policy. This view was intensified when, in 1965, the OAS collectively justified the United States military intervention in the Dominican Republic. Second, none of this stopped Castro's intervention in the rest of Latin America. He admittedly helped support guerrilla movements in that area of the world with financial aid and training of the insurgents of those countries in Cuba. The most dramatic assistance to a guerrilla movement was that in Bolivia in 1967. Not only was there financial and propagandistic aid, but a number of Cubans, most notably the honorary Cuban, Che Guevara, secretly went to Bolivia to fight in the guerrilla warfare. This attempt ended in failure and in Guevara's death.

In keeping with the same policy, the Organization of Latin American Solidarity (OLAS) was formed in Havana in 1967, with the attendance of guerrilla and Communist party leaders from all over Latin America; OLAS was to be an alternative to the OAS. At that meeting, Castro ridiculed those Communist leaders of the Latin American continent who believed in the "peaceful road to power." As he told them, quite clearly, "The duty of a revolutionary is to make revolution."

In the end, both sides failed in their efforts. The United States clearly failed to end the revolution by its isolation of Cuba through the OAS and, hence, had given up this route by 1975. On the other hand, Castro clearly failed to make the Andes Mountains of South America into another Sierra Maestra, and OLAS never became an active organization. By the late 1960s and early 1970s, he toned down his support for Latin American guerrilla movements and supported some other governments that did not meet the guerrilla model. One of these was the government of the popularly elected

Chilean socialist, Salvador Allende, a man who had long been Castro's personal friend. The Cuban leader traveled to Chile and spent several weeks visiting and supporting his socialist comrade. The violent overthrow of Allende in September 1973 by the combined forces of the Chilean military, the upper and middle classes, the CIA, and United States business interests seemed to bear out Castro's earlier conclusion that the peaceful road to power would not work.

By mid-1975 it appeared that normal relations between the United States and Cuba were again possible. Castro said that the only precondition for reopening negotiations was the end of the trade embargo, which was possible for all nations of the hemisphere as far as OAS policy was concerned. The United States, however, had broken off trade relations before the OAS called for such a collective act and still had a number of national laws that had to be changed before it could resume trade. Further, there remained the potential issue of the Guantánamo naval base on the eastern tip of the island.

The United States did not seem nearly so ready for a normalization of the relations between the two countries. A few things had been done, most notably an agreement about airplane hijackers. Several United States Senators visited the island, leaving suggestions of a "baseball diplomacy" between the two countries. Nevertheless, a State Department press release stated that there were several conditions for normalization of relations with the Castro government: United States businesses must be paid for their properties that were nationalized at the beginning of the revolution (claims reaching $1.5 billion with interest); Castro must publicly disavow any intentions of spreading his revolution; and the Soviet military presence on the island must be ended. These conditions seemed extreme, probably would have never been acceptable to Castro, and perhaps were just a first bargaining position of the United States government. In spite of official statements, there was slight progress. In August 1975 the State Department allowed subsidiaries of United States businesses in other countries to trade with Cuba, in effect legalizing what had been occurring for several years, as Ford and General Motors plants in Argentina had been selling parts to the Castro government.

Then in late 1975 a new factor entered into the equation: twelve thousand Cuban troops were sent to the African country of Angola in support of one of the three contending groups in the civil war that followed independence from Portugal. The Cuban-backed faction was triumphant in the struggle. At least three factors have been mentioned for the Cuban intervention in Angola: pressure to do so from the Soviet Union, to which Cuba owes much money; a sense of solidarity with black Africa, given the African background of many Cubans; and the feeling of proletarian internationalism, that is, the ideological tenet that one socialist nation should help socialist forces in other countries in their struggles. While all three of these motivating factors might have applied to a certain degree, the key point here is that Cuban activities in Angola eliminated for the time being any possibility of normalization of relations with the United States. In the early months of the Carter administration, contacts between the two countries increased significantly, although short of diplomatic relations.

The Soviet Union and Other Communist Countries

If Cuba was in a dependency relationship with the United States before Castro, it could be argued that it has been in a similar dependency relationship with the Soviet Union since the early 1960s. Most Cuban trade goes to the Soviet Union and other communist countries, as most had gone before to the United States, though to a lesser degree. The Soviets pay the Cubans a price above the current market value for their sugar, as the United States had. Cuba has received large quantities of foreign aid from the Soviets, as it had received small amounts from the United States. This aid has been in the form of loans tied to the purchase of Soviet goods, as early North American loans had been similarly tied. The Cubans have at times been tools of the Soviets in big-power politics, most notably in the missile crisis and perhaps in Angola, as the Latin American countries have been tools of the North Americans. Eventually, Cuba became a big producer of sugar because of the division of labor among the Communist countries of the early 1960s (the same result as had been dictated by the division of world production under the free enterprise system before the revolution).

Nevertheless, there are some notable differences. Cuba now enjoys the protection and assistance of a nation that is six thousand miles away, rather than the mere ninety miles to Florida. This is a positive asset in the sense that small clients of superpowers seem to have more independence if the countries are not nearby, even in this age of jet planes and intercontinental missiles. On the other hand, it is a disadvantage as far as trade relations are concerned. Some would argue that the natural industrial trading partner of Cuba is the much closer United States. Secondly, this new superpower relationship is probably more advantageous for Cuba than was the old one with the United States, simply because the socialist masters do not exploit the island as much as the capitalist ones did.

Yet Cuban relations with the Soviet Union have been less than perfect. One of the basic problems through the years of the Cuban Revolution has been that Fidel Castro has had philosophical differences with Soviet leadership. Castro many times has been more in step with the thought of the Chinese leaders (guerrilla warfare, moral incentives, no peaceful coexistence with the United States), but nevertheless has depended on the Soviet Union economically.

During the first year of the Cuban Revolution, if Khrushchev and the Soviet leadership tried to influence Cuba at all, it was to remain in a position of neutrality in the world, rather than to join the Soviet bloc. In 1959, Soviet relations with the United States were generally good, maintaining a peaceful coexistence called the "Spirit of Camp David." Therefore, the Soviet leaders did not want Cuba to embarrass them by being too anti-American. This soon ended with the U-2 incident of early 1960. Relations between the Soviet Union and the United States deteriorated, and hence the Communist superpower was more willing to aid Cuba in its policies toward the United States.

The period from 1960 to 1962 showed the greatest Soviet-Cuban solidarity. During those years, the Soviets helped by buying the sugar that the United States refused, by lending funds to the abortive industrialization campaign, and finally by convincing the Cubans to rely more on sugar, which they would buy at preferential prices. At the same time, Nikita Khrushchev showed friendship to Castro personally and "rattled his missiles" in support of Castro. However, the missile crisis ended this period of great friendship.

It is still not known exactly why the decision was made to introduce the offensive missiles to this Caribbean island. Reports vary as to Castro's role in this, some saying that he asked for them, others stating that they were forced on him. In either case, the unilateral decision of the Soviet Union to withdraw them, with a guarantee by President Kennedy that the United States would not

"Ve have contingency plans . . ."

(Editorial cartoon by Pat Oliphant. Copyright © 1976, Washington Star. Reprinted with permission, Los Angeles Times Syndicate)

attempt again to end the Cuban Revolution by invasion, was more than Castro could take personally. He had not been consulted. This action, together with the first Escalante affair, completely destroyed the prestige of the Soviet Union in Cuba.

Nevertheless, Cuban-Soviet connections continued with great intensity for the next three years. In an ironic way, the Cuban Missile Crisis made it even more necessary for the Soviet leadership to support the island. Khrushchev needed the help of Castro to convince the former's domestic and foreign critics that the missile venture had been a success in its original aim, that is, the preservation of Cuban independence. Therefore, Castro had more power with the Soviet leader than he had previously enjoyed.

The relations between 1965 and 1968 between the Soviet Union and Cuba were not so cordial. Castro was extremely critical of the Soviet Union's failure to defend North Vietnam, especially after the United States bombing began in 1965. He saw this as a failure to defend the frontiers of the socialist bloc and probably feared that the same would happen to him in similar circumstances. This fear was heightened by the Dominican intervention of the United States in April 1965, when twenty-two thousand United States troops landed on that island so close to Cuba to prevent what President Johnson saw as the possibility of "another Castro." Along with these international relations problems, this was the time of Castro's proclamation of a "Cuban heresy"—that Cuba could go directly to communism, a process that the Soviet line said would take many years of socialism first. Further, in these years he founded the Organization of Latin American Solidarity, in direct contradiction of the Soviet insistence on support for the old-line Communist parties in Latin America and of the peaceful road to socialism. At the same time, the Cuban leadership

became notably friendlier with the Chinese, although this friendship was not translated into significant economic progress for Cuba.

In late 1968, Castro decided to be reconciled with the Soviet Union. This decision, and the honeymoon that resulted between the two countries, came as a complete surprise in Havana. Apparently, by this time Castro had decided that only through close relations with the Soviet Union would economic progress be made on the island.

There was an even greater shock when, on August 23, 1968, Castro gave a speech justifying the Soviet Union's intervention in Czechoslovakia on the previous day. Many were startled, simply because there seemed to be so many parallels between Czechoslovakia in 1968 and Cuba about ten years before. While some would explain Castro's decision in terms of the economic power that the Soviet Union had over him by that time, the Cuban leader justified his support of the invasion on three "pillars": (1) the Communist party must exercise the prerogatives of the dictatorship of the proletariat until socialism and communism are achieved; (2) the socialist community embodies the hopes of all struggling people and of the world revolutionary movement and must be defended at all costs against external and internal enemies; and (3) workers in socialist countries must be willing to make sacrifices to strengthen not only their own countries, but also the socialist community at large.

Since 1968, relations have remained cordial with the Soviet Union. In certain ways Castro has changed his regime so that it is more in keeping with the Soviet model of communism. He has toned down his previous policy of subversion within the Western hemisphere, hence tacitly approving the peaceful road to power in the area. But at the same time, the maximum leader has followed the lead of the Soviet Union in other parts of the world, most notably in Angola.

6

Assessment and Conclusions

In the previous sections, the career of Fidel Castro has been described at some length. The purpose of this final section is to relate that career to currents common within Cuba and, indeed, Latin America. There, both differences and similarities will be seen between the career of the "maximum leader" and those of other leaders.

Background and Training

Fidel Castro's family—regardless of its peculiarities—placed him within the mainstream of Cuban political recruitment. That his father, Angel Castro, had been somewhat active in politics is not very important; rather, the wealth of the father and the benefits it gave the son were extremely important.

During the short independent history before Castro, Cuba had recruited its chief executives in two basic ways. The first, and more common, was through elections between competitive political parties. Generally those individuals who arrived at the highest point of politics in that fashion were university graduates, having the status and connections that came with such a background. University graduates made up a very small percentage of the population, probably less than 2 percent, for in the social class system that existed, university education was the province of the rich. The fact that Castro received such an education had several effects, the most important of which was an opportunity to participate in national electoral politics. Hence, Castro began as an important individual in the Ortodoxo party and at several times had the possibility of pursuing a political career in that way. Furthermore, his study of law at the university put him into the profession that dominated national politics.

The second route to power in Cuban history was through force. The Latin American cultural context is one that allows a variety of power resources to be used. Force had been used in such a way twice before the Castro Revolution: the Revolution of 1933 and the Batista coup d'état of 1952. This route to power was less structured in Cuba and allowed individuals who could not have participated in the electoral method to take part and arrive at the highest posts. Hence, it seems unlikely that Batista would have ever been elected President in 1940 if he had not previously reached the highest levels through force. Nevertheless, this did not mean that armed force could not be used by individuals who fitted into the first pattern. Ramón Grau San Martín had first come to power via the armed route, although he was a university graduate, a doctor, and a professor. In short, Castro was in the group that could choose either of the two basic routes: elections or force. In his career, he attempted both.

While Castro's training was appropriate for his recruitment to politics, there was nothing in it that prepared him either as a guerrilla leader or as the head of socialist Cuba. Indeed, he made two major military mistakes: the storming of the Moncada barracks and the landing of the *Granma*. Likewise, he made a number of mistakes as maximum leader of Cuba—and achieved a number of successes. But in this case, Castro was once again like the other Cubans who reached the pinnacle of power: politics in Cuba, unlike Great Britain or the Soviet Union (albeit in different ways), were never institutionalized to the point that leadership qualities were known before an individual took power.

Unique Characteristics

There are, however, a number of characteristics of Fidel Castro that make him different from other Cuban politicians. These can be divided into two broad categories: political skill and luck.

Before he came to political power, Castro's skill was already evident. He had always the sense that a movement such as his depended just as much, if not more, on the psychological aspects of struggle as on the armed tactics. Violence was never an end in itself; rather, it was to be channeled along with efforts to raise the political consciousness of the people. Hence, he had the "History Will Absolve Me" speech published, lectured opposing army troops with a loudspeaker, and later used a radiobroadcasting setup to let himself be known to the people of Cuba. In essence, this kind of behavior was traditional in Latin America; a *pronunciamiento* is traditionally given along with military actions. However, Castro had the intuition to use this publicity route much more than other political leaders. Likewise, the decision for a guerrilla strategy was a sign of skill. However, it should be remembered that it was, in a sense, the second choice of Fidel, utilized only when Moncada had failed.

Further, the maximum leader seems to have had an incredible string of good luck before coming to power. Two examples are particularly noteworthy. First, it was only by luck that while many of the Moncada attackers were summarily executed upon their capture, Castro was found by a former colleague at the university, who apparently countermanded the orders of a superior in not killing the rebels immediately. Second, luck intervened when Castro's two chief rivals within the insurrection against Batista were killed during the struggle. Thanks to the actions of the Batista forces, Castro did not have to contend with either Frank País or José Antonio Echevarría when he took power. While other examples could be noted, suffice it to say that Fidel Castro (like any other successful leader) did have a certain amount of good fortune in arriving to power.

It is during his government since 1959 that one sees the truly unique characteristics of this man. Two are worthy of mention here. First, he did have that magnetic characteristic of personality called charisma. Many, if not most, of the Cuban people were ready to follow Castro due to the feeling that he was one of history's exceptional individuals who would lead them to the promised land. As one Cuban stated in the early 1960s, "If Fidel is a socialist, so are we." Such charisma is something unique and cannot be manufactured by a leader. It springs from the personality characteristics of the individual and the societal characteristics of the time.

The second truly unique feature is his intelligence. One does not have to agree with the course of the revolution to admit that Castro is a man who is extremely intelligent, who can remember a great number of details and draw logical connections between events, and indeed perhaps can even run an entire country all by himself, with the slight aid of a few friends.

However, since January 1959, Castro has also had his share of luck, both good and bad. Three incidences of good fortune could be mentioned here. First, he was lucky that the Soviet Union was willing to buy Cuban sugar in 1960, hence saving the revolution when the Eisenhower administration tried to paralyze it. One can speculate that things would have been different if a U-2 had not been sent over the Soviet Union by the CIA, if it had not been shot down, and hence if the "Spirit of Camp David" had still prevailed. The Allende administration in Chile (1971–1973) demonstrated that Soviet trade and aid are not guaranteed to any leftist administration that runs into troubles with the United States.

Second, Fidel was lucky that the United States President, along with the CIA, did not decide to send marines to invade Cuba in 1961, rather than several thousand Cuban exiles. Although what would have happened exactly is a matter of conjecture, what is certain is that Castro's government could have been ended militarily in such a fashion.

Finally, Castro was lucky that the CIA (and others) failed in all their attempts to assassinate him. Recent United States history has surely demonstrated that it is relatively easy to assassinate a leader.

Administrative Skills and Failures

In the 1960s, Castro showed the lack of administrative skills in one important sense. Even for someone of his unique intelligence, the first lesson of administration is to delegate responsibilities. This clearly was not done, at least before 1970, and led to some very dramatic failures of the Cuban Revolution.

However, Fidel Castro is in such a position that he does not have to worry about political survival in Cuba and hence to shift responsibility to someone else. The decisions were clearly his; all knew this, and even if they had not, Castro did not have to be concerned that he might lose political power because of his failures. This surely distinguishes him from most other political leaders.

The argument, in brief, is the following: Cuba today is as it is because of the unique characteristics of the island and of its leader. Both sides of the equation are important. One can draw different valid conclusions about whether the Castro Revolution has been good or bad for Cuba, based on different value sets. But there is no doubt that Fidel Castro's unique personal characteristics have dramatically changed the island. Cuba today would be different if someone else had led the revolution or if he had been killed in the process. This is a statement that can be made about very few political leaders.

Selected Bibliography

Two excellent anthologies on the Cuban Revolution are James Nelson Goodsell, ed., *Fidel Castro's Personal Revolution in Cuba: 1959–1973* (New York: Alfred A. Knopf, 1975); and Rolando E. Bonachea and Nelson P. Valdes, eds., *Cuba in Revolution* (Garden City, N.Y.: Doubleday, 1972).

An outstanding discussion of charisma in the Castro case is Edward Gonzalez, *Cuba Under Castro: The Limits of Charisma* (Boston: Houghton Mifflin, 1974).

Two very good book-length interviews with Fidel Castro are Lee Lockwood, *Castro's Cuba, Cuba's Fidel* (New York: Vintage Books, 1969); and Frank Mankiewicz and Kirby Jones, *With Fidel: A Portrait of Castro and Cuba* (Chicago: Playboy Press, 1975).

For a detailed and very readable account of the Cuban Revolution until the late 1960s, see K. S. Karol, *Guerrillas in Power: The Course of the Cuban Revolution* (New York: Hill & Wang, 1970).

To date, the best study of the changes of the 1970s is contained in Carmelo Mesa Lago, *Cuba in the 1970s* (Albuquerque: University of New Mexico Press, 1974).

A recent book, written by the man who brought Fidel Castro to world attention, is Herbert Matthews, *Revolution in Cuba* (New York: Charles Scribner's Sons, 1975).

A very interesting book about the attempt to change the attitudes of Cubans is Richard Fagen, *The Transformation of Political Culture in Cuba* (Stanford, Calif.: Stanford University Press, 1969).

Books critical of the Castro Revolution are numerous. Two very thoughtful and provocative ones were written by Theodore Draper: *Castro's Revolution: Myths and Realities* (New York: Praeger, 1962) and *Castroism: Theory and Practice* (New York: Praeger, 1965).

An extremely anti-Castro tome is Nathaniel Weyl, *Red Star Over Cuba* (New York: Devin-Adair, 1962).

VI

Chou En-lai and Chinese Politics

Lowell Dittmer

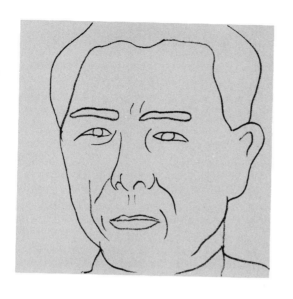

Chou En-lai
Short Biographical Sketch

Chou En-lai was born in 1898 in Huai-an, Kiangsu province, the son of a relatively unsuccessful member of a prominent local mandarin family. He received a modern Western education in Shanghai, Mukden, and Tientsin, then studied abroad in Japan and France, excelling in the humanities and social studies and in extracurricular political activities. He joined the Chinese Communist party in France in 1922. Upon his return to Canton, he married Teng Ying-ch'ao, another middle-class radical whom he had met while both were engaged in the Tientsin student movement. They remained together for the next fifty-one years, during which Teng also pursued a successful political career climaxing in her appointment as Vice Chairman of the Standing Committee of the National People's Congress in November 1976.

Chou En-lai quickly became prominent in both the Communist and the Nationalist parties (which were at that time coaligned), functioning as chief political adviser to the first commander of the military academy at Whampoa. This prepared him to become one of the founders and early leaders of the Red Army when the two parties violently split in 1927.

Chou was named to the Communist party's ruling Politburo in 1927, and he was to remain a member until his death, giving him greater staying power than any other Communist leader, including Mao Tse-tung.

During the first civil war between the Communists and the Nationalists, Chou was occupied primarily with political-military and secret police work. In 1936 he succeeded in convincing the captured Nationalist leader, Chiang Kai-shek, to form a second coalition with the Communists in order to fight the Japanese, and during World War II Chou functioned as the leading Communist representative to the wartime Nationalist capital in Chungking. In 1945 he led the Communist delegation in peace talks with the Nationalists, but the talks broke down in open warfare within a year, resulting in a complete Communist victory on the Chinese mainland in 1949.

After liberation, Chou functioned in a dual capacity: as Premier, he administered the State Council of the Central People's Government; as Foreign Minister, he represented his country on the world stage. Chou died on January 8, 1976, at the age of seventy-eight.

1

Introduction:
China – Land and People

China has the longest continuous history and culture of all the world's great nations. Whereas the United States only recently celebrated its two hundredth anniversary, the Chinese people can trace their history back more than four thousand years. And Chinese culture is as glorious as it is venerable. Though the reckoning is not yet complete, it now appears that the world is indebted to China for the invention of the technology of printing, the merit-based civil service bureaucracy, gunpowder, paper (and paper money), and the compass—not to mention the chain store and pasta! The Chinese people will never forget this great legacy, no matter how they choose to reinterpret it in the light of their more recent experience.

The Chinese have perhaps always been proudest of their political system. Politics has retained such close historical links with morality, education, and philosophy that political mobility was traditionally assumed to be correlated with moral and intellectual

excellence, and conquering armies eventually embraced Chinese political arrangements as a matter of course. From the time of its unification in 221 B.C. to the revolution of 1911, the Chinese political system was a centralized bureaucratic empire ruling over a largely agrarian population. And until the twentieth century, the broad outlines of the political system remained basically stable. Though the system periodically lost its equilibrium, it always seemed to regain it, resulting in a pattern called the dynastic cycle. One dynasty after another would rise to claim the "mandate of heaven" from its discredited predecessor and would bring about a resurgence of economic prosperity and military prowess. After a period of stability varying from only a few to several hundred years, the dynasty would undergo a decline due to internal corruption and barbarian invasion and, finally, would fall. The fall of a dynasty was often marked by civil war, banditry, peasant uprisings, and economic catastrophes; after a short period of such instability, the population was glad to accept anyone strong enough to restore order and unity, and a new dynasty would be established on the foundation of the old one.

With the fall of the Manchu (or Ch'ing) dynasty in the revolution of 1911, however, this cycle was brought to an end, and China made her debut into the modern world of nation-states. Chou En-lai (pronounced *Joe Un-lie*) was born in the waning years of China's final dynasty and lived through the chaos that preceded the establishment of a new political order in China, one based on a Western ideology (Marxism) dedicated to the destruction of the prevailing pattern of Western political-economic organization (capitalism). Chou embraced this ideology as a youth and held fast to it throughout his life, with a steadfastness matched only by his flexibility in interpreting its practical political implications. Although usually overshadowed by the more audacious revolutionary Mao Tse-tung, Chou En-lai was a truer representative of the political genius of the Chinese people and a more accurate prophet of their future than was the brilliant, mercurial Chairman. This remains to be demonstrated in the pages that follow, but first let us take a glance at China's basic geopolitical outlines.

The Land

China's climate and vegetation are similar to those of the United States, for the countries lie largely within the same latitudes (25 degrees north to 45 degrees north). But unlike the United States, China has only one seacoast, giving rise to a historical pattern of development that has begun in the east, in the fertile valleys of the Yellow and Yangtze rivers, and proceeded westward. With an area of nearly 4 million square miles, China is the world's third largest nation, but only about 25 percent of the land is arable. This affords only about half an acre of land to each person in a country where about 80 percent of the population is still engaged in agriculture. Fortunately, the nation seems to be abundantly endowed with natural resources for industrial development,[1] and the economy has made significant gains since the Communists "liberated" the mainland in 1949.[2]

Several features of Chinese ecology have had a direct impact on Chinese political development. The most salient of these are the rural settlement pattern and the parochial tradition of the people. Because most of the population has always eked its livelihood from the soil, the Chinese have traditionally lived in self-contained, cellular communities. This has inhibited the formation of any sense of national consciousness and helps to account for the penchant of Chinese political leaders for centralized, bureaucratic, and despotic measures to achieve a semblance of unity over the country. A scholar named Karl Wittfogel once hypothesized that it was Chinese agriculture's reliance on irrigation that gave rise to a strong centralized state

[1] China has very large reserves in coal and iron ore, produces a great deal of tungsten and some manganese, tin, mercury, molybdenum, and antimony. Oil reserves are also being developed, particularly in Taching in northern Manchuria and at Shengli in the North China Plain. There is also offshore oil in the Pohai Gulf, which China and Japan have agreed to exploit in a joint arrangement whereby Japan will be paid for its investment in petroleum.

[2] China's gross national product has grown from $59 billion in 1952 to $122 billion in 1970, with an average annual growth rate of about 4 percent. Industrial production increased over the same period at an average annual rate of 8 percent. Per capita gross national product rose from $104 in 1952 to $146 in 1970, compared with India's 1970 per capita income of $100 and Japan's of $1,900.

able to supervise and coordinate construction of great waterworks. This theory is belied by the fact that the unification of China took place before an extensive irrigation system was constructed. It seems plausible that once the central government had assumed responsibility for maintenance of the waterworks, the government had an excuse to organize and control the population more extensively, but in fact the waterworks were usually maintained by local government organs. Yet there is still a germ of truth in this theory, for if the waterworks were permitted to fall into disrepair, the result was an increased incidence of floods and droughts, sowing discontent among the peasants, damaging the national economy, and depleting the coffers of the imperial treasury.

A second gross ecological feature that has influenced the historical development of

Administrative divisions of the People's Republic of China

China is the tendency of certain prominent physical features, such as large rivers and high mountains, to divide the country into various physiographic and administrative regions. The dramatic contrast between north and south was partly owing to the differences of climate, vegetation, and terrain between them, but these differences have been sharpened by the presence of the Yangtze and by the absence of natural waterways connecting the two regions. The Yangtze River has thus provided a fairly stable boundary, dividing China into two subcultures in times of national unity and offering a convenient line of demarcation in times of disunity. Of course the importance of physical barriers in dividing the country has been somewhat diminished by the advent of a modern transportation and communications network (particularly the railroads), which has tended to reduce the flow of coastal-inland interactions and to increase the frequency of interactions in a north-south direction.

The People

With an estimated population of over 800 million people, China is the most populous country in the world; [3] and with a population growth rate of about 2 percent per year it will not soon lose this unenviable distinction to second-ranking India. Moreover, despite Communist attempts to disperse the population to the northwest and southwest regions that are more sparsely populated, three-fourths of all Chinese are still concentrated in about 15 percent of the country, mainly in the east and the south.[4] Needless

to say, in this densely settled portion of the country the food-to-population ratio is a serious and constantly growing problem.

More than 90 percent of the population are Han Chinese, the politically and culturally dominant ethnic group throughout most of Chinese history. Although two non-Han nationalities, the Mongols and the Manchus, did succeed in conquering China and establishing barbarian dynasties, they were soon absorbed into the political subculture of the Confucian elite. Most of the 35 to 40 million non-Han minority members are settled in the more arid and mountainous areas in the north and west of China.[5] Neither these minorities nor any of China's historically neighboring peoples have been racially distinct from the Han Chinese, with the happy result that the Chinese sense of superiority (the so-called middle kingdom complex, which assumes that China is the middle of the world) has not been tied to racism. The Chinese have claimed superiority because of their culture, and if barbarians accepted that culture, they found it possible to assimilate without difficulty.

China's three major religious traditions have been Confucianism, Taoism, and Buddhism. Confucian humanism has always been the mainstay of the mandarin elite, while Taoism and Buddhism have found

---

[3] According to Chou En-lai's report to the Fourth National People's Congress in January 1975.

[4] Still, more than 100 million people—only 15 percent of the population, but more than the total populations of many European nations—live in urban areas. The most important cities are

Shanghai, which now claims to be the largest city in the world, with more than 7.5 million people; Peking, the capital throughout most of Chinese history; Tientsin, a great manufacturing center and port; Harbin and Shenyang in northeastern China (formerly Manchuria); Canton on the southern coast; and Nanking, Wuhan, and Chungking on the Yangtze River. Many smaller cities have also grown rapidly since the Chinese Communists launched their industrialization campaign in the 1950s.

[5] In addition to the two mentioned above, the principal ones are the Uigurs, the Chuangs, the Tibetans, the Miao-Yao, and the Yis.

greater support among the masses. But China's peasant masses have not been particularly sectarian about religious dogmas and, in fact, quite freely intermixed the rituals of all three on an eclectic, pragmatic basis. Certain religious tenets became almost universally accepted: filial piety within the family, which entailed respect for the old and care for the young; political relationships based on strict hierarchy, with mutual obligation binding superior and inferior; loyalty among peers; and a situation ethic that prescribed rules of propriety for various different contexts.

2

Chinese Government: An Overview

The fall of the Ch'ing dynasty in 1911 introduced the Chinese people not to the modernizing democratic government that the revolutionaries had promised, but to a half-century of almost unrelieved scission and strife. The disintegration of the republican government within a few years of its establishment led to the fragmentation of power among a number of regionally based warlord governments coalescing and contending with one another; a surviving nationalist revolutionary movement, which soon split into two parties, the Nationalists and the Communists; and the Imperial Japanese Army, eager to take advantage of Chinese disunity to realize Japanese territorial ambitions. The Chinese Communist party (CCP) was born in this turmoil and, by a combination of hard-won political and military skill and sheer luck, was able to survive and prevail over all rivals.

The CCP then proceeded to organize a government based on a combination of Leninist organizational principles and its own revolutionary experiences; the former seemed to have initial priority, but came to be increasingly supplanted by the latter, especially as the Sino-Soviet dispute intensified. It was an authoritarian government, graced, however, with a genuine concern for the poor and the helpless and with a need for enthusiastic mass support. Although the government presented an initial appearance of monolithic unity and single-minded purpose, this appearance was belied by a series of disputes among the leadership, finally resulting in a sharp polarization of society that brought the nation to the verge of civil war in the late 1960s and left enduring cleavages in the polity.

The Historical Legacy

The Chinese imperial system consisted of a centralized monarchy and court, a civil bureaucracy staffed by scholars sifted through a nationwide examination system formally open to all classes, and an agrarian population. The elite was self-enclosed, isolated from the peasantry not by ethnic differentiation (as in a caste or feudal system), but by moral and intellectual self-cultivation and by the masses' desire for local autonomy. The imperial bureaucracy extended its sway only as far down as the county level, allowing local government to be controlled by village and clan leaders. The state ideology was Confucian humanism, which legitimated, but also limited, imperial power. The masses were largely illiterate and normally politically apathetic and could be roused against the central government only by a deep sense of grievance.

Decline and Fall of the Chinese Empire

Memories of the glorious Chinese empire still linger in the minds of its people, and the decline and fall of that empire was a national trauma that established a clear set of priorities for any would-be successor government and still influences Chinese conceptions of its role in international affairs. For although the empire showed signs of decline by the late eighteenth century, its most dramatic failures coincided precisely with the opening of China to the West in the last half of the nineteenth century. China was no stranger to invasions—ranging from the Turks, Tibetans, and Mongols many years before Christ to the Manchus in the seventeenth century—but in the past the Chinese had always been able to assimilate the barbarians into their superior political culture. The Western imperialists, however, successfully resisted assimilation. These were no barbarians moving in from the steppes to occupy the capital and enjoy the spoils of a superior civilization; they remained oriented to their own cultural traditions and political

leadership while systematically pursuing the commercial and religious penetration of what they considered a backward and heathen nation, intervening with military force whenever peaceful intrusion was resisted.

The most famous instance of commercial penetration was the opium trade, undertaken by British merchants in the nineteenth century and resulting in widespread addiction and a negative trade balance. When the Chinese attempted to stanch this pernicious influx, they precipitated a confrontation with Great Britain and were defeated in the Opium War (1839–1842). The punitive terms imposed by the British in the Treaty of Nanking (China forfeited the port of Hong Kong and a large indemnity) set the pattern for a series of unequal treaties: by 1860 the Russians had penetrated into Manchuria, Mongolia, and Chinese Turkestan, laying claim to parts of Chinese territory that are still hotly contested today; France had defeated China to acquire a protectorate over Annam (now Vietnam and Cambodia); Great Britain gained sovereignty over Burma in 1886; and Japan annexed Taiwan after defeating China in 1894–1895. In addition to outright annexations of territory were various leaseholds and spheres of influence established by imperialist powers: Russia established a sphere of influence in Manchuria, Japan in Korea, Germany in Shantung, Great Britain in the Yangtze Valley, and France in southwestern China. Shanghai was divided into several "leased territories" among the United States, France, Japan, and Russia. Only the delicate balance of power among imperialist powers prevented China from being colonized outright; instead, it was carved up like a melon among them.

These defeats and humiliations incited an agonizing reappraisal of China's political system and its ideological underpinnings. Confucianism has always been a highly pragmatic belief system, so as soon as its political efficacy proved inadequate, its ideological legitimacy began to be called into question as well. This reevaluation began in the coastal urban areas among intellectuals most exposed to Western cultural currents and trickled down to the masses. The Western cultural impact was first noticeable in the Taiping Rebellion (1850–1864), led by an unsuccessful candidate for the civil service examinations whose visions of the promised heavenly kingdom bore the unmistakable influence of Christian missionary tracts. The rebellion was suppressed (with great difficulty) and followed by a period of reaction under the tactically skillful, but dogmatically narrow-minded, Empress Dowager. But the government's socioeconomic base was inexorably eroding beneath it: the opium traffic, war indemnities, negative trade balance, and the great costs incurred during the Taiping Rebellion all augured a fiscal crisis. This could not easily be met by raising taxes, partly because the government had lost some of its taxing power to regional authorities and to Western commercial interests, and partly because the taxable economic surplus was slight. The waterworks fell into disrepair, and natural disasters afflicted the land; the government lost its ability to maintain law and order; social insurrections and banditry became pandemic.[1] In order to raise revenue the state began offering official positions for sale after the Taiping Rebellion, thoroughly compromising the examination system, which was abolished in 1905. This left China's traditional education system without any raison d'être, and it

[1] There were revolts in Hunan (1822), Taiwan (1826), Hunan (1833), Shansi (1835), and serious rebellions by the Niens (1853–1868) and by the Moslems in the northwest (1855–1872), southwest (1862–1883), and central Asia (1862–1876 and 1866–1878).

was increasingly displaced by Western education, which brought with it such subversive ideas as democracy, science, and socialism.

The Boxer Rebellion in 1900 was merely the straw that broke the camel's back. The Boxers were superstitious peasants whose initial target was the barbarian Ch'ing dynasty, but the Empress Dowager managed to redirect them against the "foreign devils," particularly the defenseless Christian missionaries and their Chinese converts. After committing various sensational outrages, the Boxers and the regular Chinese troops who had supported them were defeated by a combined force of British, French, Japanese, Russian, and other interested powers, forcing the Empress Dowager to flee Peking in disgrace until a settlement could be reached. The overdue reforms she conceded in the wake of this humiliation could only convince her opponents of the regime's mortal weakness; the dynasty could be shored up another decade only because Western powers saw an interest in preserving a regime committed to repay its indemnities. After her death in 1908, the dynasty began to disintegrate quickly in the absence of any credible succession arrangement. It was toppled with surprising ease by the Revolution of 1911.

Democratic Revolution and National Fragmentation
The fall of the Manchus and the proclamation of a Chinese republic signified a triumph for the radical reformers, who had believed that China must make a sharp break with the past and model herself after the West in order to retain an honorable place among nations. But this brief experiment with democracy turned out to be a disappointment, an embarrassment for proponents of constitutional democracy that has muted its appeal for the rest of the twentieth century. The failure of democracy may be

attributed to three weaknesses: the lack of ideological consensus, the political inexperience and naiveté of the revolutionaries, and structural weaknesses in the constitution.

Overthrowing the Ch'ing was a negative act, signifying only a negative agreement that the Ch'ing must go, without implying any positive consensus on what should replace the old order. Some of those among the revolutionary forces—the usual opportunists and revolutionary hangers-on—were in quest of power or material advantages, while others were engaged by ideological convictions. The latter, however, were not well organized, nor had they worked out their ideology to any practicable level. Their tendency, then, was to compromise too readily with traditional elites, laying themselves open to being used and then dumped. The masses were never appreciably engaged in the revolution. Chinese society thus retained a political stability based on mass indifference, but the revolutionaries were thereby deprived of their natural constituency for democratic reform.

The 1911 revolution was directed in absentia by Sun Yat-sen, a man very much a product of his era. Born near Canton, where Western intrusion was earliest and most marked, Sun was educated first in a British mission school in Hawaii, then trained as a doctor in Hong Kong. He spent much of his life underground or abroad and was perhaps more familiar with the democratic culture of the West than with the realities of power in China. Sun was in Denver, Colorado, when he was suddenly notified that a revolution had succeeded in all provinces south of the Yangtze and was offered the provisional presidency of the Republic of China. Sun accepted, but when Yuan Shih-k'ai, a former military official in the imperial army who was then in command of the strongest military forces in the country,

offered to throw his armies to the support of the revolution in exchange for the presidency, Sun quickly agreed and resigned in his favor. Apparently under the impression that his job was done, Sun magnanimously withdrew from the political arena to devote himself to problems of industrialization, leaving leadership of the Revolutionary party, which he had founded, to his disciples. Yuan was, however, committed neither to the revolution nor to democracy, and he used his power to subvert the fledgling republic.

The constitutional structure of the new government was inherently weak, lending itself to subversion. After a good deal of factional wrangling, a cabinet government was decided upon with a strong Parliament and a weak Prime Minister. This was at odds with the country's authoritarian tradition and set the stage for a power struggle between Prime Minister and Parliament—in retrospect, a presidential system (as in the United States or in Fifth Republic France) might have been preferable. The Revolutionary party held the majority in Parliament while Yuan led his own party in opposition. But neither the Prime Minister nor the Cabinet were given the power to dissolve the legislature when there was irreconcilable conflict, and the legislature could not dissolve the Cabinet by simple majority. Finally Yuan dissolved the legislature by illegally outlawing Sun's party and proclaimed his intention to restore the monarchy, with himself as Emperor.

The republic was ironically spared this step backward by the Japanese, who considered a restoration of the empire to be the only conceivable way China might overcome its vulnerability and resist further Japanese encroachments. In the middle of World War I, Japan presented China with an ultimatum (the Twenty-One Demands), which, if accepted, would have practically placed

China under Japanese protectorate. Yuan temporized, accepting some demands, postponing others, and trying to obtain foreign support to reject the most outrageous. Then in December 1915 a band of Yuan's own generals, financed by the Japanese, rose in revolt and denounced the pretender. In January 1916, Yuan postponed inauguration of his dynasty, and in March he canceled the whole scheme. He died in June, a bitterly frustrated man.

Following Yuan's death, the republic was nominally restored, and for several years after 1916 a succession of weak and ephemeral cabinets occupied the ministries in Peking and endeavored to collect loans from the Western powers, subsisting only as a convenient tool of the surrounding regional military leaders. Sun Yat-sen repudiated the Peking regime and set up what he claimed was the only legitimate government of China in the south, but in fact his republican government was for the time being equally dependent on the grace of local military leaders. In his search for outside assistance Sun turned to Lenin (after meeting rebuff from the United States), accepting the help of Russian advisers in reorganizing his party, now called the Kuomintang (KMT), or Nationalist party, and even allowing members of the infant Chinese Communist party to join on an individual basis. But Sun was never to see his labors bear fruit; this was the heyday of the warlords, when power was grasped by those able to seize it. These men were primarily interested in extracting from their territories the money necessary to keep their armies intact; to do this, they organized the opium trade, sold official posts, overtaxed the peasantry, and made shifting alliances with one another, interacting like sovereign states in a balance-of-power system. China's territorial integrity was even more infringed upon than under the Ch'ing,

as various warlords made concessions to foreign powers to further their short-term interests.

The warlord period lasted from 1916 to 1927, manifesting diverse tendencies. It was an intellectually fertile period that saw the interpenetration of influences from East and West in the coastal cities and, to a lesser degree, in the rural interior. Industrialization began in China's treaty ports, giving rise to a new urban commercial and professional elite. The growth of industry created a demand for cash crops, such as tobacco or cotton, but it also flooded the market with low-priced manufactures and thus drove many of the cottage industries, through which peasants had supplemented their agricultural incomes, out of business. The military competition among warlords increased the tax burden on the countryside, while civil disorder permitted bandits and rent-gouging landlords to prey on the peasantry.

National Liberation and Peasant Revolution

Upon the death of Sun Yat-sen, an ambitious young General named Chiang Kai-shek managed to seize control of the Kuomintang, and he led the KMT-CCP coalition military expedition to the north. This Northern Expedition (1926–1927) was quite successful, enabling Chiang to achieve nominal unity within the country by subduing the warlords and co-opting them into his regime. But Chiang then proceeded to establish ties with China's urban business and rural landlord elites, ties that were incompatible with the Communists' plans for mass mobilization and the redistribution of wealth. The two parties split, and Chiang nearly succeeded in wiping out the smaller party before driving it into the wilderness. For the next twenty years the two parties waged a bitter civil war, interrupted only by an eight-year pause when they formed an uneasy coalition against invading Japanese armies. Civil war resumed shortly after the defeat of Japan in 1945, and although Chiang commanded widespread popularity and seemed to have overwhelming military superiority, he overextended his lines and was outmaneuvered on the battlefield. The defeated Nationalists took refuge in Taiwan, while the triumphant Communists established a revolutionary regime after their own image.

The People's Republic of China

The People's Republic was formally proclaimed by Communist Party Chairman Mao Tse-tung on October 1, 1949, in Peking. The government was based partly on Leninist principles of formal organization and partly on the practical experiences of the CCP during their thirty years as an outlaw group. The former shall be denoted as "formal politics" and the latter as "informal politics."

Formal Politics
Formal politics refers to those principles that have been explicitly formulated in official language and are backed by legal sanction. In the People's Republic, this consists of an official ideology, certain organizational principles, an interlocking set of governmental structures, and a series of constitutional documents in which these are duly codified.

The official ideology of the People's Republic is "Marxism–Leninism–Mao Tse-tung Thought." The fact that the first two terms are *-isms* and the third is *thought* signifies that the former are more basic and central than the latter, which is conceded to be only an adaptation of Marxism–Leninism to the

particular circumstances of China, a "practical" rather than a "pure" ideology.[2] In practice, however, the emphasis is reversed, and the Chinese masses are far better acquainted with the pithy maxims of Mao than with the analyses of Marx, Engels, or Lenin.

Whether Mao has made an altogether original contribution to Marxism is still controversial, but there is no question that his writings have their own distinctive emphases.[3] Most basic is Mao's attempt to base revolution on the peasantry, rather than solely on the industrial proletariat. His faith in the peasant seems at times to approach the mystical, expressing confidence that the peasantry can industrialize and modernize the country without much help from intellectual elites. Second, Mao believes in the efficacy of struggle and contradiction, not only to quell opposition, but also to arouse the enthusiastic support of one's allies. Although struggle is an inevitable part of life, only one side of any contradiction is correct: the revolutionary side. The opposing, reactionary, counterrevolutionary side may be either assimilated or destroyed, but may not retain its independent identity. Who may be accepted into the revolutionary ranks and who may not depends on circumstances, and it is ideologically permissible to enter into alliances of convenience and then to renegotiate or terminate the alliance when expedient.

At the heart of Mao's thought is his military strategy, and it has informed the guerrilla "people's war" that achieved victory on the Chinese mainland as well as influencing Mao's tactic of using antagonistic forces to counterbalance one another in domestic and

[2] Franz Schurmann, *Ideology and Organization in Communist China,* 2d ed. (Berkeley: University of California Press, 1968).
[3] See Benjamin Schwarz, *Chinese Communism and the Rise of Mao* (Cambridge, Mass.: Harvard University Press, 1961).

international politics. But it has also influenced China's distinctive approach to nation building, which departs from the experience of other socialist states in its greater reliance on mass movements than on central planning and strict party organization and is more tolerant toward the peasantry—emphasizing thought reform of conservative elements rather than outright coercion, for example. Whereas the Soviet Union under Stalin gave top priority to heavy industry and bled the peasants white to finance it, China under Mao has geared industrialization to the modernization of agriculture, with greater priority being given to small-scale local industry that uses agricultural products and surplus labor and serves agricultural needs.

Chinese government is based on three organizational principles:

(1) Democratic centralism, meant as a dialectical synthesis of the contradictory needs for democratic consultation and centralized decision, in practice gives greater emphasis to centralism. Democratic centralism entails that everyone within a decision-making unit has the right to discuss various alternatives before a decision is made, but all are bound to absolute obedience after it is made: the individual should obey the organization, the minority should obey the majority, the lower level should obey the higher level, and everyone should obey the Central Committee. These tenets hold for every unit, every member in the CCP.

(2) The mass line governs relationships between the party and the nonparty masses and is meant to involve the masses actively in the implementation of a decision and even to give them some input into its mode of implementation. The mass line is sloganized as "from the masses, to the masses." As Mao explains, "Take the ideas of the masses (scattered and unsystematic ideas) and concentrate them (through study turn them into concentrated and systematic ideas), then go

to the masses and propagate and explain these ideas until the masses embrace them as their own." [4]

(3) Whereas both democratic centralism and the mass line apply to hierarchical relationships among levels, criticism and self-criticism are disciplinary techniques governing relationships among members of the same party committee, government organ, or work unit. In a party that believes in historical determinism, this is a way of coming to grips with misfortune: one member of the group is isolated and criticized for an error, allowing the group to articulate and externalize its sense of grievance; the target of this criticism may then atone for the error by making a sincere self-criticism and may thereby be reintegrated into the group.

The Chinese political system rests on three pillars of power: the Chinese Communist party, the Central People's Government, and the People's Liberation Army. At the highest levels of leadership these three institutions interlock, as their leaders hold positions in all three hierarchies, but at the lower levels there is somewhat more functional differentiation. The function of the party is to make decisions and provide ideological leadership; the function of the government is to implement decisions; and the function of the army is to provide for the national defense and to secure law and order.

Although the CCP is the largest Communist party in the world, with a membership of 35 million by 1977, its size as a percentage of the total population is quite small (less than 3 percent). Although other parties are permitted in China, the CCP is the only one that is free to recruit new members

[4] Mao Tse-tung, *Selected Readings from the Works of Mao Tse-tung* (Peking: Foreign Languages Press, 1971). For an explication of democratic centralism and the mass line, see John W. Lewis, *Leadership in Communist China* (Ithaca, N.Y.: Cornell University Press, 1963).

and has a complete national organization extending to the grassroots level. Three party members at the grassroots can form a party group, five or more can form a branch, fifty or more can elect a committee. The members elect delegates, one level at a time to meetings of peasant brigades, communes, districts, counties, and provinces, right up to the National Party Congress, representing all party members. At each hierarchical level the party congress is entitled to elect a party committee to serve as the executive branch during the periods when the congress is not in session and to report back for endorsement of its activities. The National Party Congress, as the supreme organ of party authority, elects the party Central Committee, which in turn elects a twenty- to thirty-member Politburo with a ten-member Standing Committee to supervise party affairs between plenary sessions of the Central Committee. Actual power in China is concentrated in the Politburo of the Central Committee. National congresses should be held every five years, and in fact ten have been held since the party was founded in 1921. Attached to the party are a number of national auxiliary organizations: the All-China Federation of Women, the Communist Youth League, and the All-China Federation of Trade Unions are the most important of these. These mass organizations were torn asunder during the Cultural Revolution (1966–1968), but were reconstructed with little modification in 1973.

Just as the party leadership is formally accountable to its membership, the Central People's Government is accountable to the Chinese citizenry through the secret ballot: citizens elect delegates to the lowest levels of local government, which in turn elect delegates to the next highest level, the two thousand or so county people's congresses; and they elect delegates to the twenty-nine provincial congresses, and thence to the National People's Congress (NPC), the highest organ of state power. The NPC elects the President of the People's Republic and a Standing Committee to serve between its sessions, which should be held every four years (actually only three NPCs met from 1954 to 1976). The President then appoints a Premier, who is assisted in his work by a State Council. The State Council, which is the locus of real power within the government, has a varying number of ministries according to need, including Foreign Affairs, Planning, Agriculture and Forestry, Industry and Communications, Finance and Trade, Defense, Health, and so forth. A parallel legislative body, the Chinese People's Political Consultative Conference (CPPCC) was set up in 1949 by consultation with other groups and parties who had supported the Communists in their rise to power and was due to be phased out with the establishment of the NPC in 1954. But the CPPCC has continued to persist as a symbol of the united front, containing a thousand or so representatives of various small political parties and functional groups: trade unions, peasant associations, associations of professionals and intellectuals, women, youth, capitalists, and other notables.

The People's Liberation Army (PLA) is of great symbolic importance in China because of the role it played in the Communist victory; high proportions of party leaders were soldiers, and nearly all had some military experience. But the party ideology calls for civilian leadership of the armed forces ("The Party commands the gun," as Mao put it); and until the Cultural Revolution necessitated military intervention into all aspects of civilian life in order to restore order, the civilian leadership was successful in maintaining control. The constitution vests control of the PLA in the Ministry of National Defense within the State Council, but it seems that real direction and policy come from the Military Affairs Committee of the CCP Central Committee. As in the Soviet army, there is a network of political departments and offices within the military structure down to the platoon level, containing political commissars who work alongside the commanding officer of every army headquarters or unit and assume the responsibility for implementing party policies and carrying out educational programs among the troops. Their chain of command ascends not to the military commanders but to the General Political Department (the CCP organ of the PLA's General Headquarters) and the Military Affairs Committee; at the same time, each is responsible to the CCP committee in its own unit. The CCP committee is formally elected by all members within each unit and has the power to supervise all activities and policies within the unit.

As in most governments, the Chinese Communist leadership seeks to legitimate and formalize its political arrangements by codifying them in a constitution. There have been three state constitutions of the People's Republic, including the provisional Common Program, in force from 1949–1954; the first constitution, in effect from 1954–1975; and the most recent constitution, approved by the fourth NPC in 1975. Comparison of these documents reveals certain trends: some of the civil rights that were formally granted the citizenry in 1954 were omitted in 1975, such as freedom of residence and freedom of cultural or research interests; but other, perhaps more meaningful rights were granted, such as the right to criticize the government and to post big-character posters without fear of retaliation. There has been a tendency for the power of the CCP to increase relative to that of the government or the army. And the 1975 constitution concentrates a great deal of power in the office of the Chairman of the CCP, perhaps in order to ensure a smooth succession.

Constitutional revisions do not capture all of the organizational changes that take place in the political system, many of which are precipitated by informal political processes. If the political system consisting of party, government, and army is perceived as a single Gestalt, three distinct patterns of interaction may be distinguished. From the proclamation of the first state constitution in 1954 to the Cultural Revolution in 1966, the CCP maintained command and control over the government and the army, the leadership was functionally differentiated (with some overlap due to multiple-position-holding by leading cadres), and for most of this period there was a three-tiered hierarchical structure consisting of central, regional, and provincial-local levels. During the Cultural Revolution, the party and government organs were in effect abolished at the provincial and regional levels and replaced there by the Revolutionary Committee, which consisted of a triple alliance of soldiers, rehabilitated cadres, and Red Guards. The army constituted the last remaining hierarchical command structure, and soldiers proceeded to move into the leading positions in the civilian political hierarchy at all levels. After 1970, the party was rebuilt, leaving the Revolutionary Committees to function in place of the state administrative organs. PLA personnel have, however, continued to hold leading party and government positions —and without forfeiting their military commissions. After its chief's death in 1971, the power of the PLA was cautiously and gradually reduced, but it remains of key strategic importance.

Informal Politics
The informal aspects of Chinese politics have rarely been set forth in so many words,

Before 1966:

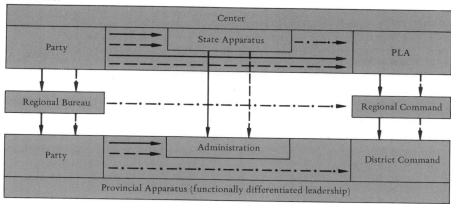

1967-1970:

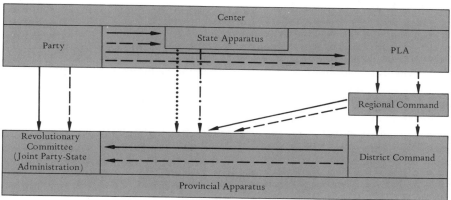

After 1970:

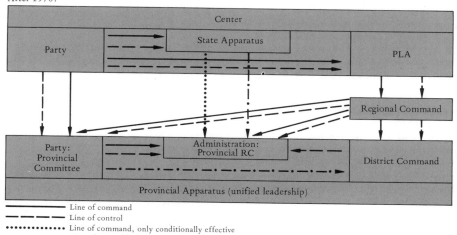

——————— Line of command
— — — — Line of control
•••••••••••••• Line of command, only conditionally effective
—•—•—•— Line of control, only conditionally effective

The changing configuration of Chinese politics

(This figure drawn from "Revolution & Reconstruction in Contemporary Chinese Bureaucracy" by Lowell Dittmer is reprinted from *Journal of Comparative Administration,* Vol. 5, No. 4 (February 1974) by permission of the Publisher, Sage Publications, Inc.)

but have nonetheless occupied a position of increasing importance. The most noteworthy of these seem to be the mass movement, elite factionalism, and two-line struggle.

The mass movement is hardly unique to China—other countries have experienced movements to propagate everything from women's suffrage to prohibition. But no other country's political leadership has so successfully co-opted and guided these mass movements to implement its policies, and no other Communist government has encouraged as much mass activism. The mass movement has been used to implement land reform and marriage reform, to launch a Great Leap Forward in agriculture and industry, to eliminate corruption among officials (known in China as "cadres"), to revolutionize culture, to criticize Confucius, and to do many other things. The mass movement is normally led by party members working in conjunction with a work or school unit; if there are not enough local party cadres available (or if they are not trusted for the task at hand), a party work team is sent from outside. During the Cultural Revolution, the work teams were denounced and withdrawn because of their arrogant attitude toward local units, but they are still employed as a matter of course in any mass movement. The first purpose of any mass movement is publicity—to create public opinion enthusiastically in favor of the policy in question; to this end, various groups are assigned to write and post big-character posters, to march, and to demonstrate. In the later stages of the movement the policy itself is implemented with fanfare.

Factionalism refers to the tendency for members of a leadership group to form informal coalitions and to coordinate planning on an ongoing basis for the sake of some policy or power objectives; it is strictly forbidden, because it disrupts the unity of the leadership. Mao Tse-tung admitted in 1966

that the Communist party has always had factions, but the fact that they are forbidden means that they are concealed. Thus, the only time they are clearly visible is after they have been discovered and announced (that is, during a purge). At this time it is confirmed that they were operative on a clandestine basis long before. On the basis of these periodic announcements and by careful scrutiny of "protocol data" (for example, who stands next to whom in official photographs, who appears when), it is possible to infer that factions indeed exist and that their activities seem to have intensified as a result of the Cultural Revolution.[5] The basis for the formation of these factions may be a common ideology, common origins, a common experience (for example, members of a military faction may have served in the same field army during the civil war),[6] a patron-client tie established on the basis of recruitments and promotions (for example, Chou En-lai's links to those who studied with him in France remained strong, and he consistently promoted and protected them), or any combination of these factors.

The two-line struggle is a dispute over fundamentally differing policy programs and points of view within the party, but it differs from factionalism in that it coincides with cleavages in society (or class struggle). The term thus refers to a coincidence of elite factionalism with a form of mass movement that is mobilized by one faction on its own behalf. Though certain intraparty disputes in the 1930s were considered two-line strug-

[5] One of the best exemplars of protocol data analysis is Roderick MacFarquhar, *The Origins of the Cultural Revolution,* vol. 1, *Contradictions Among the People* (New York: Columbia University Press, 1974).
[6] William W. Whitson, *The Chinese High Command: A History of Communist Military Politics, 1929–1971* (New York: Praeger, 1975), has a good discussion of military factions.

gles, the term was not used again after liberation until 1966, when it was said that the Cultural Revolution involved such a struggle between Mao Tse-tung and his erstwhile heir apparent, Liu Shao-ch'i. At stake in this struggle was the question of which road the Chinese revolution should follow: Mao's "proletarian revolutionary road," which led through self-sacrifice and continued struggle to an objective of complete socialism, or Liu's "counterrevolutionary revisionist road," which led through material incentives, secular expertise, and unprincipled compromise back to capitalism. This great line struggle followed upon Mao's announcement that class struggle and line struggle would never cease, even under socialism, and indeed there has been a recurrence of line struggle in the 1970s, first against Mao's next heir apparent, Lin Piao, and later against the presumptively rehabilitated revisionist, Teng Hsiao-p'ing. Line struggle is quite evidently a method of purge, but it also entails an effort to impress the masses with the meaning of the purge and thus to build popular support for certain policy programs.

455

3

Chou's Early Years: A Revolutionary Comes of Age

Chou En-lai is not the outstanding hero of the Chinese revolution, an honor that must go to Mao Tse-tung. Chou is China's man for all seasons, a complex, charming, and intelligent character who embodies many of the contradictions of an ancient land in rapid transition. An upper-class scion of what he called a "bankrupt mandarin family," Chou has dedicated his life to a party that is dedicated to the destruction of that class and claims to represent the interests of the lower classes. Although Chou has consistently throughout his career deferred to the leadership of others rather than claiming primacy for himself, at the same time he has been a member of the party leadership longer than anyone else in the CCP (including Mao). A Marxist devoted to the eradication of the traditional feudal clan and family system, Chou maintained, according to all reports, a relationship of impeccable filial piety toward his family of origin, and his marriage to Teng Ying-ch'ao was a model of Confucian propriety—he was even hen-pecked!

Although each phase of Chou's career left a visible imprint on his development, the basic outlines of his character and political style emerged clearly in his childhood and youth. This handsome and polished upper-class youth might normally have been drawn into the channels of conventional politics, but like many in his generation he was radicalized by China's political milieu in the early twentieth century, which seemed to call for extreme solutions. Chou's talents made him a gifted agitator and eventually led him to what was then the party of agitators. In school he acquired advanced Western notions of democracy and social justice, and he mastered the written and spoken word. His complex family arrangements imparted a gift for maneuver and subtle intrigue.

Primary Socialization

Chou En-lai was born in 1898 in Huai-an, Kiangsu province, the year of the Hundred Day Reform led by K'ang Yu-wei and two years before the Boxer Rebellion. His family belonged to the landed gentry and was locally prominent, boasting a family compound known as the Hundred-Year Hall because it had once housed five generations under one roof. Chou's father received a classical education and may have passed the imperial examination, but does not seem to have received an official post in a bureaucracy that was by this time already in an advanced state of decay. In marked contrast to Mao Tse-tung's authoritarian but ruthlessly efficient father, who provided a firm target for the young Mao's rebellion, Chou's father seems to have been too passive and ineffectual to invite direct attack, content to fill any minor sinecure that would keep him in wine money. The young Chou shared his father's love for wine and convivial conversation, but apparently harbored a quiet contempt for his weakness. When his penniless and jobless father appealed to his prominent son for support during the war years in Chunking, Chou declined to secure a job for him and gave him only a paltry monthly allowance. Yet when his father died in 1942, Chou observed traditional custom to the hilt, even running obituary notices in the official party news organ that were phrased in exact accordance with old protocol.

This is but the first in a series of instances one could cite of Chou's unusually conspicuous display of filial piety. Filial piety lay at the heart of traditional Confucian political culture, admonishing deference to parents, to older siblings, and by extension to all authorities. As such, it formed a central target of criticism by Communists and indeed by sundry Chinese revolutionaries—and yet

Chou was not above invoking these traditional norms on behalf of Communist political objectives. In a press conference to students and reporters in Chunking following the destruction of the New Fourth Army by Nationalist troops, Chou urged his listeners to forget their fratricidal past and unite against Japan, ending his remarks with an extemporaneous personal aside: "It has been 38 years since I last saw my own home. The poplars in front of my mother's grave must have grown very tall by now." [1] Behind Chou's tears on this occasion, some of his listeners may have conjectured, was a calculating intelligence.

A second example seems to bear out this conjecture. The end of World War II found the KMT and the CCP each occupying different parts of China with their troops, each eyeing the other with acute and well-founded suspicion. Even while Chou negotiated to conciliate the two parties, the Communists launched a land reform campaign in the areas they occupied. When the father of Chou's sister-in-law was jailed as a rich landlord, the sister-in-law (named Ma Shun-yi) sought out Chou to intercede on his behalf. But Chou brushed her off, saying that as far as he knew his half-brother (Chou En-chu, Ma's husband, a lesser CCP official at this time) had something to do with Communist work in that area and that consequently he, Chou, could not believe this was possible. Thus Ma had to sit by helplessly while her father died in prison. When she reported back to Chou's foster mother in Shanghai that her father's dying wish had been that she never again set eyes on another member of the Chou family, the matriarch dragged

[1] Much of the anecdotal material in this chapter is from Kai-yu Hsu's interesting biography, *Chou En-lai: China's Grey Eminence* (Garden City, N.Y.: Doubleday, 1968).

Ma off with her and the two stormed into Chou's office. Chou affected complete surprise, convincing both women that En-chu must have been responsible for this miscarriage. When Ma subsequently fell ill, the matriarch stayed with her at the hospital to care for her; Chou was seen visiting the two quite frequently, while En-chu was never permitted to come. If in these events one can see the artful dodger who survived countless purges to remain a Politburo member continuously since 1927—longer than anyone else in the party (including Mao)—then it must also be conceded that this interpretation did not occur to anyone in Chou's family, all of whom seem to have retained only the highest regard for him.

Yet even the roles one chooses to play on specific occasions probably reflect the personality behind them in some way. Striking in Chou's case is the fact that the parents for whom he exhibited such conspicuous public respect were not even his real parents. His own mother—said to be talented and kind, well-versed in classical Chinese literature—died when Chou was still a child. Young En-lai was then adopted by his second uncle, a prominent citizen in Shanghai who had no son of his own at the time. En-lai's own father meanwhile remarried and had two more sons, perhaps intensifying En-lai's sense of loss or abandonment. His foster father was awesome but distant, fitting the Chinese stereotype of the father, but En-lai's foster mother ran her household with an iron hand, displaying a volcanic temper that no one but En-lai seemed to know how to assuage. She was illiterate, not because she lacked the opportunity to acquire an education, but simply because she refused to study. Yet she also insisted, over the objections of most of her in-laws, on inviting Western missionaries to teach her children the "new knowledge," instead of imparting to them a classical education. When she got angry, she

intimidated everyone but En-lai, who would smile discreetly and, without explicitly taking sides, offer a suggestion to appease her. Though Chou's primary family ties remained with this foster family throughout his life, at the age of ten he was also adopted by his fourth uncle, a police commissioner who took the boy with him to Shenyang in northeastern China (then Mukden, Manchuria). Chou attended elementary school there, relating now to his fourth uncle as his father.

What impact did this complex pattern of family relationships have upon Chou's later political career? Much of Chinese politics at the small-group level requires great tact and finesse at manipulating personal relationships, for which Chou's family experience should have stood him in good stead. The similarity in the relationship between Chou and his authoritarian first foster mother and his later relationships with authoritarian leaders in his career (including Mao Tse-tung most obviously) seems striking. And there is a paradox in the contrast between his punctiliously filial attitude toward his family and his awareness that he was not really a member of that family, that he could not claim true possession of the role he was playing. The volatility of his foster mother's temperament combined with his consciousness of the tenuousness of his own position to engender an overriding need to placate authority.

What Chou may have regarded as his early desertion by his own parents may have led him to suspect the authenticity of authority figures, while also sensitizing him to the plight of those similarly abandoned by legitimate authority figures. It may also have impressed him with the fragility and ephemerality of natural human relationships, an awareness that comes to most of us much later; something so tenuous must be carefully cultivated, he must have concluded. Yet his early insight into the underlying artificiality of the relationships he so assiduously nurtured was to remain with him, giving his ingratiating manners an accompaniment of cool detachment and irony. Whether these relationships between early family experience and later political orientation obtain in the exact manner described must remain conjectural, but these same qualities have been ascribed to Chou throughout his career, both by those who detested him for his mendacity and almost effeminate sensitivity and by those who admired him for his calm savoir-faire and diplomatic agility.

Student Politicization

If Chou's family background gave him what political scientists call his latent political socialization, or set of general dispositions regarding power relationships, then it was during his school days that he acquired his orientation toward the specifically political arena. Chou's years as a student were very important to him: he enjoyed them immensely, excelled as a writer and student leader, and has consistently (if apologetically) identified himself as an "intellectual," with a disposition to take policy positions sympathetic to intellectuals whenever expedient. For example, reminiscing in 1958 about his role in the Shanghai uprising, he said: "I was responsible for leading the armed revolts, but I lacked experience and was weak in understanding political dynamics. I am an intellectual with a feudalistic family background." [2]

As in many developing countries today, a modern education in transitional China tended to foster an "intellectual proletariat," whose members were alienated from their indigenous social milieus but harbored deep resentment toward the imperial power and its pretensions to cultural superiority. They were endowed with an education that raised their consciousness of the meaning of world occurrences and enabled them to discuss abstract questions with other intellectuals in the world, but did not equip them for socially useful employment in their domestic economy. [3] In China, the impact of the West put particular strain on father-son relationships among those sons who embraced Western values because of the wide discrepancy of impact of the West on the two generations. The pattern of avoidance and respect governing traditional father-son relationships facilitated the transferral of traditional attitudes, but led to alienation when youth began to acquire their own vocabulary of reference from Western cultural contacts. Generational rebellion was fostered not only by the widespread attacks on the joint family system, but also by the fathers' attempts to impose traditional ideas on their sons, an action they had been brought to regard as their duty; the sons, in turn, tried to justify their rebellion by identifying themselves with some transcendent social cause. The youth would move to the port city, seek to marry on the basis of free love and sexual equality rather than parental arrangement, and often lead marginal lives of spiritual quest and material poverty. Chou En-lai's unusual family arrangements (that is, the absence of his father, his foster mother's relatively progressive attitudes) enabled him to avoid a sharp break with his family, but in other respects his experiences replicated those of his generation.

[2] *Liu Shao-ch'i, Chou En-lai, Chu Teh t'ung-chih tsai ch'un-chung chung* [Comrades Liu Shao-ch'i, Chou En-lai, Chu Teh among the masses] (Peking, 1958), p. 27.

[3] Cf. Edward Shils, "The Intellectuals in the Political Development of New States," *World Politics*, April 1960.

He attended a missionary-sponsored elementary school in Manchuria, which exposed him to current events and to the most modern political thinking of the day. His teachers introduced him to the essays of contemporary Confucian reformers K'ang Yu-wei and Liang Ch'i-ch'ao. Through Liang's writings, Chou became vaguely aware of the ideas of such Western philosophers as Darwin, Mill, Kant, and Rousseau; from K'ang Yu-wei, he gained his first exposure to utopianism, including K'ang's advanced ideals of common property and the elimination of class, ethnic, national, and sex distinctions.

Upon completing elementary school, Chou took an entrance exam for Tsinghua School (predecessor of the present Tsinghua University), but unfortunately failed the exam. But he passed the exam for the recently founded and somewhat experimental Nank'ai School in Tientsin. Chou enrolled in defiance of the wishes of his uncles, who distrusted the school's openness to Western influences and new ideas, determined to support himself. In contrast to the big, rough country-bumpkin impression left by Mao in school at about the same time, Chou was a rather precocious student of delicate good looks. But like Mao, his talents were in the humanities and social sciences rather than the sciences, and he was a highly talented essayist. "During my last two years at Nank'ai Middle School I received no help from my family," he proudly recounted. "I lived on a scholarship which I won as best student in my class." [4] After a diffident beginning, he displayed a growing leadership ability. He took the lead in organizing a student association called the Ching-yeh lo-ch'un (respect work and enjoy group-life), which also published a journal in which Chou's articles were frequently published. In these early writings, Chou stressed the need for national unification and industrialization, warned of an impending war with Japan, and argued that educated youth should play an important role in the nation's future. When the school presented a play to celebrate its anniversary, no girls were available to play the heroine, a victim of the evils of money. So Chou volunteered for the role, to the consternation of his family.

Chou's years at Nank'ai were exciting and memorable ones. This was the turbulent period of the death of the republic and the short-lived ascendancy of Yuan Shih-k'ai, an excellent time to acquire an education in power politics; in 1913 alone, there were seven major political murders, thirty-two changes in cabinet posts, six large-scale mutinies and riots, and eleven revolts by military leaders who marched their troops on Peking. During his later career, Chou continued to take great pleasure in maintaining the friendships he made at Nank'ai, even while his political orientation diverged more and more from that of most of his classmates. He risked calls on old friends even after the Kuomintang had placed a price on his head, confident that they would not betray him to the Nationalist police. During his wartime sojourn in Chungking, when the Communists and the Kuomintang were cooperatnig against the Japanese, he frequently attended Nank'ai reunions, where he was the life of the party, introducing his wife to all his old classmates. Chou's politically incongruous but apparently sincere delight in his bourgeois contacts continued through the years and may well have influenced his career pattern within the party. As the organizing force behind the People's Political Consultative Conference in 1949, Chou became a symbol of the Communist united front with the bourgeois democratic parties; as Foreign Minister, he served as China's link to the non-Communist world.

[4] Quoted in Edgar Snow, *Red Star Over China* (New York: Grove Press, 1961), pp. 72–73.

460

Upon his graduation from Nank'ai in 1917, at age nineteen, Chou went abroad for further study. At this time many Chinese youth went abroad to study, and the experience often made an indelible imprint on their lives. Those who went to the United States required greater financial support but seemed to enjoy more favorable career prospects upon their return; they typically went into the academic and service professions and became articulate advocates of democratic pragmatism. Those who went to Japan or to Europe (primarily France and the Soviet Union) were more inclined to be radicalized by the experience. Chou went to Japan, relying initially on financial help from four former schoolmates. Though he toyed for a while with the idea of taking the staff entrance exam for a major Japanese university, he never enrolled, instead auditing courses at Waseda University for a year and a half. In 1918 he went to Kyoto, spending his time reading all sorts of political literature on his own and participating in Chinese student activities. He was reportedly influenced at this time by the writings of Kyoto University's socialist scholar, Kawakami Hajime.

For China this was a time of humiliation and turmoil, and Chinese students living in Japan could not escape the repercussions of the difficult situation their country was facing. In 1915 the Yuan Shih-k'ai regime had secretly signed the Sino-Japanese Treaty with its Twenty-One Demands, which agreed to the transfer of German extraterritorial rights in Shantung to Japan, in return for a loan of 20 million yen. These terms did not become known until the World War I peace settlement. China, which had declared war on Germany in August 1917, hoped thereby to attain redress at Versailles, but despite the strong support of President Wilson, the Allies upheld the validity of the Twenty-One Demands and awarded Shantung to the

Japanese. When this news became public in May 1919, it stimulated the mobilization of China's first great mass campaign, the May 4 Movement, which the Chinese Communists regard as the turning point in contemporary Chinese history and the start of a new cultural era. The movement was at first specifically directed against the Chinese politicians who had sold China down the river and against their Japanese patrons. But in its cultural ramifications it included a movement to simplify the written language so that the broad masses could understand it and so to facilitate the spread of the new culture and political ideas, which were then circulating only within the intellectual community, among the public at large. Although the May 4 Movement was essentially a student movement, among its most important consequences was the penetration of the masses by the activist students, which had a mobilizing effect that was to be repeated again and again in the course of China's revolution. Students contacted shopkeepers in order to enforce a boycott on Japanese goods, for example; and they became interested in workers because the latter were employed by numerous Japanese firms, and the students wanted them to go on strike.

Chou learned of the May 4 Movement from Ma Chün, a former Nank'ai classmate who later became one of the earliest members of the Chinese Communist party in Tientsin, meeting his death before a Kuomintang firing squad in the fall of 1927. Chou returned to China immediately, where Ma, as president of the Tientsin Student League, arranged Chou's election as editor-in-chief of the student league newspaper, *Students' United Journal*. He also got a job as part-time secretary to the university president in order to earn his tuition (his relatives—"a spendthrift lot," according to Chou—had ceased to support him) and enrolled at the university, but he devoted most

461

of his time to political activities. He changed the epigraph on the masthead of the *Students' United Journal* to the one he had used on the Nank'ai school paper: "Democracy: of the people, for the people, and by the people." He wrote editorials in the morning in draft form and then discussed the draft at the staff meeting in early afternoon, agreeing to revisions and adjustments where necessary. At the same time as the twenty-one-year-old Chou was writing editorials in Tientsin, Mao Tse-tung, then aged twenty-five, was also editing a student newspaper in Ch'angsha, Hunan. A comparison of the editorial contents is quite illuminating. "What is the greatest question in the world? The question of eating is the greatest," Mao was writing; and, further:

Whose power is greatest? The united power of the people is greatest. What do we not need to fear? Do not fear heaven, do not fear gods, do not fear ghosts, do not fear dead men, do not fear warlords, do not fear capitalists.[5]

Already Mao's writing expressed materialist sentiments and an enthusiasm for struggle between the oppressed and their oppressors. Meanwhile, Chou was advocating that labor and capital should cooperate in the distribution of profits and laying a great deal of stress on education rather than struggle—the workers should improve their livelihoods through education, and China's educated youth offered the best prospect for victory over the warlords and economic modernization. Thus he considered Japan and England as models for China's national development and the educated middle class as models for the Chinese masses.

[5] Quoted in Yen Ching-wen, *Chou En-lai p'ing-chuan* [Critique of Chou En-lai] (Hong Kong: Po-wen shu-tien, 1974), p. 28.

While the May 4 Movement was developing, the Russian Revolution, which was to have an enormous influence on the course of Chinese history, was just beginning to arouse the interest of Chinese student activists. Its first prominent mention in the Chinese press was in a series of three articles on the French and Bolshevik revolutions published in 1918 by Li Ta-chao, one of the future founders of the Chinese Communist party. Li's articles met with no immediate response, but it was not long before the Chinese became aware that a theory of revolutionary socialism existed and that it had been adopted as a system of government by a neighboring country that had many characteristics in common with China, such as large size, backward economy, rural population, feudal social system, and even ethnic diversity. Chou En-lai's initial reaction to news of the revolution was cool, but he was clearly interested. One afternoon in 1919 he took several student delegates with him to Tientsin to call on Sergei A. Polevoy, a Russian teacher at Peking University who served at the same time as a cultural liaison for the Communist International (Comintern), headquartered in Moscow.

In September 1919 Chou was instrumental in establishing the Awakening Society, a political discussion society that began to publish the *Awakening* in January 1920. This society bore a marked resemblance to other organizations formed during the May 4 Movement, including one founded by Mao Tse-tung and others in Ch'angsha. All these organizations later served as nuclei for the CCP, and most of them advocated work-and-study programs to help students study abroad. Meanwhile, Chou's writings were becoming increasingly radical, as the confrontation between the student activists and the local constabulary grew increasingly tense. After Chou presented a petition to the

Governor's office demanding dismissal of the Tientsin Police Chief, he and a number of his fellow activists were thrown in jail. But Chou proved to be a highly resourceful prisoner, organizing his fellow students to hold classes on political and social subjects and leading them in a well-publicized hunger strike. Chou remained in jail for several months, and it was in this unlikely, but perhaps romantic, setting that he met his future wife, Teng Ying-ch'ao.

Teng Ying-ch'ao, later to become one of the leading female officials in the CCP, also hails from China's traditional elite: her father served as a county magistrate before dying at a rather young age. In school she was "active, eloquent, extroverted, and possessed a straight-forward and open character." When Chou went to France, they kept in regular correspondence. "You might almost say we fell in love by post," Teng said later. "He proposed to me in writing only after three years of correspondence." They married upon his return in 1925 (and remained married thereafter, unlike some of their more romantically unsettled comrades); scorning a traditional marriage ceremony, they invited friends to witness their self-marriage. Teng played an active role in party activities throughout their life together, rising to become alternate (1945) and then full (1956) member of the Central Committee, Secretary General of the National Committee of the Federation of Women and a Deputy in the First, Second, and Third National People's Congress. One of the few women to make the Long March, she was incapacitated during most of the trip with an illness later diagnosed as tuberculosis. When the Communists arrived in Yenan, she registered under a fictitious name at a sanitarium in Peking; when the Japanese invaded the city shortly thereafter, she was forced to flee again. The Chous re-

mained childless, reportedly because of permanent injuries suffered during Teng's illness.[6]

In the summer of 1920, Chou arrived in Paris as one of the students in the work-and-study program sponsored by the Awakening Society. "I had little contact with the peasant-worker masses because I had taken no part in the economic process of production," he later recalled. "My revolutionary career started abroad, with very limited knowledge about it obtained from books only." He did no manual labor in France except for a brief period at the Renault plant, devoting himself rather to student political activities. There were more than four thousand Chinese students in France in 1920, most of them from Hunan and Szechuan; this group included a number of Chou's future close associates in the party. As Chou later recalled:

In 1922 I became a member-founder of the Communist Youth League and began to work full time for that organization. Our Communist Youth League had sent delegates to Shanghai in 1922, to request admission to the Party, formed the year before. Our petition being granted, the CYL became formally affiliated with the Party, and thus I became a Communist.[7]

The French section of the CCP grew rapidly, boasting nearly 500 members just before it was driven underground in 1923—more even than the CCP in China at that time. The Party published a number of publications, including the magazine *Red Light*, edited by Teng Hsiao-p'ing, who was known as a "Ph.D. in typography." The list of former members of the French section makes

[6] Li Tien-min, *Chou En-lai* (Taipei: Institute of International Relations, 1970), pp. 27–28.
[7] Snow, *Red Star*, p. 73.

impressive reading.[8] Because Chou was senior among them, a reliable patron-client relationship was established early and persistently nurtured.

As a political movement among Chinese students in a foreign country, the objectives of the French section were limited to the conversion of fellow expatriates, and the movement remained as disembodied from the rest of the populace as was the American student movement of the late 1960s. Within the Chinese student community, there were anarchists, reformers, and international democrats—altogether over forty factions, each with its own organization and program of action. It should be remembered that despite his later renown as a diplomat and administrator, Chou first achieved prominence as a political agitator, and he gave much of his attention through his student years to writing editorials and delivering speeches. In the lively polemics among the various factions, Chou played a conciliatory role, trying to articulate common objectives, such as opposition to the warlords, and to define away basic differences among the CCP, the KMT youth group, and the Third Force group (a predecessor of the bloc of bourgeois democratic parties that was to persistently but futilely seek a middle road between the CCP and the KMT for the next forty years).

Chou also spent about a year organizing in Germany, reportedly supported by a Comintern stipend. In Berlin he organized a socialist youth group and arranged for the admission of another Chinese student to the CCP after the latter's application had been rejected in Shanghai: Chu Teh. A former opium addict and warlord, Chu later became one of the founders of the Red Army (the forerunner of the People's Liberation Army

[PLA]). Chou, the dashing young radical, also reportedly formed a liaison with a German girl, who gave birth to a son. (Though Chou's son died on the Russian front in World War II, his grandson was last reported living in East Germany with his mother.)[9] After three years in France and Germany and even a brief visit to England, Chou decided in 1924 to return and participate in the revolution in China.

The Chinese Communist party was founded while Chou was abroad, holding its first congress in the French Concession of Shanghai in July 1921. Only twelve delegates met, representing a total of fifty-seven members belonging to seven regional groups. The twenty-eight-year-old Mao Tse-tung appeared as a delegate from Hunan, but at least six of the remaining twelve were later to leave the party, including Ch'en Tu-hsiu, who was elected the first Secretary General. The party thus acquired its first leaders and a centralized organization, but the statutes and program drawn up at this time have remained secret. Progress in the mobilization of the masses (particularly the urban proletariat) was to follow shortly. Political progress was slower, not really beginning until 1925.

Conclusion

The period reviewed in this chapter was a disruptive one for China and a formative one for Chou En-lai. The country experienced the success of a national democratic revolution followed by its immediate subversion, leaving a power vacuum to be filled by warlords, foreign imperialists, and other opportunists. This was a period of pluralism

8 Chou En-lai, Ch'en Yi, Li Fu-ch'un, Teng Hsiao-p'ing, and Nieh Jung-chen all eventually became members of the Politburo.

9 *Der Stern* (Frankfurt on the Main), September 1, 1954.

qua power politics, when the issues of China's form of government and future course remained open questions. All in all, it was a good time for political education and a good time for patriotic and idealistic youth to select politics as a vocation, with the realistic hope that their participation might make a difference to the nation's future.

This was the period in which Chou En-lai acquired many of the traits that were to distinguish his later orientation toward political action. From his mother he perhaps acquired his refined tastes; from his father, the convivial aspects of his character and the con-

tempt for weak and corrupt authority. From his cross-adoption into the households of his two uncles he learned to adapt and ingratiate himself in unfamiliar surroundings, to yield to authority in order to prevail ultimately, and to play roles with convincing sincerity. From his whole family background he acquired a respect for scholarship, though his own schooling was short. A descendant of the traditional ruling class, he bore with him the gracious manners and quiet self-assurance characteristic of that class, combined with a sympathy for the underdog that would stand him in good stead in a revolutionary party.

4

Chou's Middle Years:
A Long March

The Chinese revolution is usually classified as a peasant revolution, but it was actually far more complex than that. At different times, it was also an urban insurrection and a national liberation war. In the more than twenty years in which this grand and desperate venture was pursued, there were frequent and radical changes of fortune, and more than once the CCP seemed on the brink of extinction. But through it all, the party survived, or at least a small core of members did, and the experiences they went through together as rebels indelibly stamped the policies they were to pursue in their subsequent careers as elites—but each in his or her own characteristic way.

The story of the Chinese revolution is in part the story of the long and ambivalent relationship of two revolutionary parties: the CCP and the KMT. The two parties came together in alliance twice, and twice split asunder. The first alliance, 1924–1927, was the most intimate one, and the 1927 schism left the most bitter feelings. The first civil war raged from 1927 to 1937, with military clashes taking place in the central, western, and northwestern provinces. The second united front was tenuously maintained from 1937 until the end of the war against Japan in 1945. And the second civil war erupted with the breakdown of talks between the two parties shortly thereafter.

The First United Front

When Chou arrived in Canton from France in 1924, the city was the center of activities for the KMT-CCP alliance; most of the rest of the country was dominated by various warlords, and the revolutionary forces were not unchallenged even in Canton. At this time relations between the KMT and the international Communist leadership in Moscow were quite close, and a group of Soviet advisers came to Canton in October 1923 to carry out a reorganization of the KMT and to facilitate cooperation within the united front. The Communists who entered the KMT on an individual basis participated actively in party work and steadily increased their influence. From January 1924 to May 1926, they occupied about one-fifth of the Central Executive Committee (the KMT equivalent of the CCP Central Committee) and one-third of the Standing Committee seats; in addition, the KMT departments of organization, peasant movements, and propaganda were systematically infiltrated by CCP cadres.

Chou En-lai promptly moved into a line of organizational endeavor for which few of his comrades showed much aptitude, much to the CCP's subsequent regret: the military. He became director of the political department of the Whampoa Military Academy, established by Chiang Kai-shek in 1924 after he studied the organization of the Soviet Red Army in the summer of 1923 in Moscow. Sun Yat-sen attributed the defeat of the 1911 revolution to his lack of armed force, and he set great store in the academy. With the help of Soviet advisers, Chou set up a commissar system at Whampoa and in the KMT's emerging National Army. Under this system every military unit, including those still under training in the academy, had a KMT party representative who was responsible for political control and was required to countersign every order. As head of the political department and chief commissar, Chou gave priority attention to political training and appointed many CCP cadres as party commissars in the army. But Chou and the Communists were unable to penetrate the KMT Military Council or to obtain in the military field the kinds of senior roles they held among KMT political advisers. This was later to prove their Achilles' heel.

Somewhat like the two parties in the

Chou En-lai as a young KMT political commissar at Whampoa Military Academy

(New China News Agency, Peking)

American Congress, the KMT and CCP relationship at this time was a mixed-motive game of cooperation and conflict. In some respects, the two parties complemented one another: the KMT was larger and had more

467

status owing to its leading role in the 1911 revolution, but it badly needed the organizational discipline provided by the CCP and the Comintern advisers, and Soviet aid was of some importance. Collaboration was facilitated by the identical organization of the two parties and by the revolutionary spirit at that time more or less common to both. The Communists, conscious of their weakness (a mere few hundred members as opposed to 200,000 in the KMT) were for the most part cautious and discreet.

But although CCP members were admitted to the KMT individually rather than en bloc, they did in fact maintain their own autonomous organization, or faction, within the KMT, met separately, and were thus able to coordinate strategy and achieve an impact out of all proportion to their small numbers. Chou En-lai, among others, used his power of appointment systematically to infiltrate key organizational units within the KMT, maintaining that the two parties' identity of interests at this stage of the revolution allowed this. There were also certain programmatic conflicts. Both parties conceived of the revolution as a two-stage process: the first stage for national independence against foreign domination, the second for social justice. But the CCP argued that the social revolution was an indispensable part of the national revolution, while the KMT contended that the CCP was giving priority to class struggle over the revolution for national independence and destroying the united front in the process. The CCP would then respond that the KMT wanted only to ride to power on the backs of the people and once in power would do nothing to improve the lot of the people.

Generally speaking, reasonably amicable relations between the two parties lasted through 1924 and 1925 and were not seriously impaired until the Chungshan Incident of 1926. The major factor that intensified

friction was the death of Sun Yat-sen in late 1925 and the succession struggle that ensued, in the course of which all parties sought to maximize power and protect their positions. And when Chiang Kai-shek found his main rival for leadership to his ideological left, he found it in his interest to move to the right.

The Chungshan Incident took its name from a Communist-officered gunboat in the small Nationalist Navy, which Chiang claimed was plotting to kidnap him and deport him to Russia. Whether anything was really behind Chiang's claim is still undetermined. In any case, Chiang suddenly declared martial law, ordered more than fifty CCP members jailed (including his first commissar, Chou En-lai), and directed all Russian advisers and CCP commissars to be dismissed from the army. At this point the CCP leadership was thrown into consternation: some wished to split at once with the KMT, but the party was still militarily weak, and the Russian advisers counseled forbearance. Chiang was placated with the resignation of a few CCP scapegoats from the army, and the alliance was uneasily resumed.

Whether by deliberate design or not, Chiang had used the Chungshan Incident to suppress dissent on his left, and he was now prepared to undertake the long-planned expedition to the north to unify the country. Both parties agreed to cooperate in this venture, the KMT pursuing an orthodox military function and the CCP attempting to weaken the landlords by inciting revolutionary class struggle among their people. Chou En-lai played a key role in this mission at Shanghai, a role later memorialized by André Malraux in his gripping novel, *Man's Fate*. Arriving in the spring of 1927, Chou promptly succeeded in setting up an underground provisional municipal government for Shanghai and a provincial council for the surrounding province. On the eve of March 20, 1927, Chou personally led 300 armed labor-union guards to storm the municipal arsenal and to occupy the police headquarters and the ordinance department; another column seized the railroad station and halted all rail transport. "Within two days," recalled Chou, "we won everything but the foreign concessions." [1] The Communists held the city for three weeks, during which time they installed their citizen's government and implemented a number of reforms.

Meanwhile, Chiang was waiting with his troops outside the city and reconsidering his alliance with the CCP. A month before, KMT forces had broken into the Soviet Embassy compound in Peking, seizing documents that apparently threw some suspicion on CCP loyalties; twenty Communists were executed on the spot, including one of the party founders. There was pressure on Chiang from foreign business interests, who demanded an end to the domestic violence, which had already claimed the lives of six foreign nationals in the Nanking international sector, and reportedly promised Chiang a bank loan of $60 million if he disarmed the Shanghai workers and put them back to work. Chiang resolved to act boldly. On April 11 he gave a secret order to disarm the 2,700 pro-Communist trade union pickets; the disarmament began at 1 A.M. the next morning and was carried out with the help of the secret societies, non-Communist trade union members, and possibly members of the city's underground. The Communist unionists, suddenly under attack from troops they had considered friendly, made easy prey. Official Communist figures for the April 12 Incident stand at 300 dead and 5,000 wounded. From Shanghai, the anti-Communist purge spread to the provinces: in five of the provinces then under Nationalist control, the Communists were either arrested or went underground. Chou En-lai

barely emerged with his life; he was reportedly captured by a KMT general who did not recognize him and escaped with the help of a former student at Whampoa.

Incredible as it may seem, even now the CCP did not withdraw from the KMT, partly because it remained weak, but mainly because the Soviet advisers would not sanction it—Stalin was at this time under attack from Trotsky in Moscow and could not afford to concede error on his China policy. In view of the blood rupture with Chiang, the CCP now sought close cooperation with the left wing of the KMT in Wuhan, hoping to split the left from the right. But although Chou En-lai made initial progress in his negotiations with the KMT left leadership, based on their common opposition to Chiang, an alliance was never brought to fruition.[2] Although the KMT left controlled the central party apparatus, it was as bereft of military power as the CCP; and so when the left dismissed Chiang from all his posts and expelled him from the party, Chiang ignored the order and set up a government of his own in Nanking with the support of the KMT right wing. Moreover, the CCP's continued mobilization of radical peasant associations and labor unions frightened the landlord and urban middle-class constituency of the KMT liberals. Thus when the Comintern delegate in Wuhan showed a somewhat compromising telegram from the Communist party of the Soviet Union to the leader of the KMT left, the latter used this as a pretext to back out of the proposed united front and reconcile with Chiang in Nanking. The first united front was over. On July 20, 1927, the Wuhan government began their purge of all CCP members. Chou fled a few steps ahead of the police.

---

[1] Snow, *Red Star*, p. 75.

[2] Wang Ching-wei, a former protegé of Sun Yat-sen, led the KMT left.

The First Civil War

The military engagements between the Nationalists and the Communists during this period were concentrated in three main theaters: central China (chiefly Kiangsi and Hunan provinces), 1927–1934; the western and northwestern provinces during the Long March (1934–1935); and northern Shensi (Yenan) between 1936 and the conclusion of the second united front a year later. With regard to military strategy, the party line changed from an early period of direct assaults on large cities (the Nanch'ang Uprising, the Autumn Harvest Uprising, the Canton Commune, and the attacks on Ch'angsha and Hankow) to a relatively conventional defensive strategy designed to protect the rural bases in central China. When the party departed Kiangsi, it also abandoned its conventional military strategy in favor of the guerrilla warfare tactics of Chu Teh and Mao Tse-tung. With regard to political policy, the party abandoned its attempts to mobilize an urban proletarian constituency except on a clandestine level and began to promote land reform and to organize a peasant army.

The Urban Uprisings

On August 1, 1927, the Communists attempted a military putsch at Nanch'ang, the economic and political center of Kiangsi province, marking the beginning of the military phase in the party's history, which was to last for over 20 years and to have a far-reaching impact on both its spirit and its structure. As director of the Military Department of the party's Central Committee, Chou En-lai led in planning the uprising from the beginning. He intended the uprising to recruit its own army, pointing out that a number of CCP officers were then functioning in KMT units stationed in the

area and that if a pretext were provided, these men might leave the KMT for the CCP and bring their troops with them—otherwise, they would eventually be purged. The uprising might then be joined by worker and peasant masses in the surrounding countryside. Because Nanch'ang was vulnerable to attack from four sides that could not easily be defended, Chou recommended that after its departure the army should move to the East River region of Kwangtung to form a base there with Swatow as the provisional capital (Swatow was the seaport from which Chou hoped to make contact with the Soviet Union).[3]

Chou arrived in Nanch'ang in July 1927 and set up his headquarters in a downtown hotel, where he was joined by a number of very able colleagues.[4] According to a leading participant, Chou proved a cool but decisive leader:

He dealt very calmly with complex affairs, both day and night. He took on both work and blame, disregarding criticism. . . . This period also marked the beginning of his being treated with respect by comrades in general and the growth in importance of his status.[5]

Chou set zero hour at 4 P.M. on August 1, 1927. Despite an intelligence leak to the

[3] Jacques Guillermaz, "The Nanchang Uprising," *China Quarterly,* no. 11 (July–September 1962), pp. 161–168.
[4] These included Chu Teh, now a senior KMT officer; Ch'en Yi, Li Li-san, Hsü T'e-li, and Nieh Jung-chen, all comrades from French student days; and two KMT generals who were also clandestine CCP members, Ho Lung and Yeh T'ing.
[5] Chang Kuo-t'ao, *The Rise of the Chinese Communist Party, 1921–1927,* 2 vols. (Lawrence: University Press of Kansas, 1971), vol. 1, passim.

local authorities, the rising seemed to achieve complete surprise. After five hours of fighting, the city was seized: most of the non-Communist troops were disarmed, while others were driven back to the northern suburbs. No looting or disorder took place; in fact, the population understood little of what was going on and took scarcely any notice. Chou announced the formation of a new regime the following day, called the Central Revolutionary Committee, to which he appointed several left-wing KMT leaders, such as Madame Sun Yat-sen. This was essentially a symbolic gesture representing continued CCP desire to appeal to the left KMT—those KMT leaders who had won appointments had not even been consulted, all decision-making positions went to the Communists, and the Front Committee continued to operate behind the scene. The Central Revolutionary Committee issued a proclamation and covered the town with slogans, but the hoped-for mass uprising did not materialize. The party could only attract a few hundred new recruits. At this point the local KMT commander marched on the town. The Communists began to retreat on August 3, and by August 5 they had evacuated the town without a blow being struck, taking with them $100,000 (Chinese) in booty and confiscated supplies.

The rebel forces were split into three groups, all of which ran into KMT armies and fought pitched battles along the escape routes. The Red Army lost a third of its strength in the first few days, completing the march with only about two thousand soldiers. Chu Teh led his troops eastward into Fukien, eventually joining Mao Tse-tung for their famous rendezvous in Chingkangshan (in Kiangsi province), where together they founded the Kiangsi soviet. With the rest of the troops and the Central Revolutionary Committee, Chou En-lai marched toward

Swatow, where they were met by a sustained KMT attack. Though ill with a fever of 104 degrees, Chou went on the front line to direct the troops under fire: "My illness is no problem; I think I can hold on," he said. Red soldiers held this great seaport from September 23 to September 30 before falling back to Hailufeng. Chou was so ill with malaria during the retreat that he barely made it, having been deserted several times by his stretcher-bearers. He managed to make his way to Hong Kong via sampan, where he received medical attention.

The immediate verdict of the party leadership was that "the Nanch'ang Uprising turned out to be an unsuccessful experience in military opportunities by the Front Committee, which had been affected by the baneful influence of the previous opportunists." But like other heroic losses, Nanch'ang later acquired a mystical dimension. The political resolution accepted at the Sixth Party Congress in 1928 interpreted the Nanch'ang Uprising as a correct military action, and in 1934, August 1 was officially proclaimed the anniversary of the founding of the Red Army. After all, the uprising achieved its purpose of drawing a number of able and later famous military officers and men from their positions in the Nationalist Army into the core of what became the Red Army, saving them from likely execution at the hands of the KMT.

The Nanch'ang Uprising was the first blow in what became known collectively as the Autumn Harvest Uprising, a group of rebellions based on the populist assumption that the peasants were oppressed and rife for spontaneous revolt. Mao Tse-tung led the Hunan contingent of the uprising, and Chou En-lai tried to instigate an uprising in Hangchow. The uprising encountered the same difficulties everywhere—general peasant apathy, a shortage of cadres, lack of arms, bad coordination, and an effective counter-attack by Nationalist armies—and failed utterly. Canton was captured for a few hours in December 1927, allowing time for proclamation of a Canton Commune, with sweeping confiscations, nationalizations, redistribution of wealth, and cancellation of debts. But the Nationalist forces counterattacked the same day, and the townspeople remained impassive while the Communists were crushed. During the fall of 1927 there were small uprisings in Kwangtung, Hunan, Hupei, and Hopei; in 1928 there were uprisings in Chekiang, Kiangsu, Kiangsi, Hopei, Honan, and Shensi. All failed and were crushed. The toll taken by these struggles was heavy; by the end of 1927 the party was reduced to less than a fifth of the almost fifty-eight thousand members claimed in April, and only 34 of April's 121 top Communist leaders were still active. The one factor of great significance that did emerge from the experience was the formation of a Communist-led peasant army. Although the top leadership of the party remained predominantly intellectuals, the enrollment of peasant soldiers into the party reduced the proportion of workers from more than half in early 1927 to no more than 8 percent in 1930.

The party dealt with the failure of these uprisings, as it has customarily dealt with misfortune, by changing its leadership. Although he was a leading advocate of the erroneous policy (Soviet leader Bukharin chided Chou specifically for leading "blind actions of armed revolt"), Chou survived the transition (as he always has), partly because he was not the supreme leader, partly because he was adroit in switching sides and making self-criticisms. But although the director was changed, the tune remained the same, and the reason was that Moscow, not the CCP leadership, was calling the tune. In the summer of 1930, Red Army forces at-

tacked the three largest cities in the region: Ch'angsha, Wuhan, and Nanch'ang. A temporary success was won in Ch'angsha, but all of the attacks were eventually repulsed with heavy losses. The sole lasting result was that the party's secret organizations in the cities were flushed out and destroyed.

This debacle precipitated another change of leadership, as the so-called returned students (returned from study in Moscow, also called the 28½ Bolsheviks) came to power, but this time there was a slight change of tactics. In concession to those who advocated a shift from the cities to the countryside, the leadership authorized Mao Tse-tung and certain others to establish rural base area governments, or soviets. In the cities, the party abandoned its putschist policies and went on the defensive, attempting to shield the remnants of its underground organization from increasingly effective KMT secret police work. More than 24,000 CCP cadres and agents were arrested from 1928 to 1931, including more than 40 officials at the central level, 829 cadres at the province and city levels, and 8,199 at the local levels.[6] Chou En-lai was placed in charge of CCP counterintelligence work in 1930–1931, and, according to one informant, the work done under Chou's direction in Shanghai was one of the factors that saved the party from complete extinction. As copies of Chou's photograph (taken when Chou was Chiang's chief commissar in 1925) began to appear in railroad stations with an $80,000 price on his head, Chou began to cultivate a thick black beard and masquerade as a priest.

This first phase in the history of the CCP had begun auspiciously, but ended in a series of crushing setbacks—the counterrevolutionary coup in Shanghai, the ouster from the KMT, and the failure of the urban uprisings. From 1919 to 1931, activities had been cen-

[6] Yen Ching-wen, *Chou En-lai,* p. 106.

tered in the cities, where the party had achieved impressive gains in mobilizing students, intellectuals, and workers. Party membership grew from 57 in 1921 to 57,967 in 1927; in addition, Chinese trade unions by 1927 included 2.8 million members, and Communist influence in the trade union movement was second to none. Yet in one fell swoop, Chiang had almost succeeded in annihilating the party. In 1927 alone, CCP membership fell from nearly fifty-eight thousand to about ten thousand—and perhaps less than half of these survivors remained active. And the party's attempt to recapture the cities encountered one defeat after another.

Why did the first phase of Communist mobilization come to so grievous an end? Partly because there are intrinsic limits to an urban-based revolution. Many aspects of the city make it ideal as a revolutionary center; the congregation of intellectuals at the various schools there, the ready accessibility to new ideas from abroad, the ease and rapidity of communication all made possible the organization and rapid growth of a new party. With the process of industrialization came also a burgeoning urban proletariat and assorted other displaced and disprivileged people, many of them available for mobilization in a movement promising to improve their social conditions. And yet the same factors that made the urban setting so accessible to revolutionary activities also made it vulnerable to police control by the KMT. The interdependence of sectors and the high degree of organizational integration made it impossible for the CCP to achieve partial liberation of a city, and they had to fight all-or-nothing positional warfare against more numerous and better equipped opponents. Once the KMT had consolidated its hold on the government, it could use its superior control of modern weapons and communications to crush the Communists in pitched battle

and to make it very difficult for their organizations to survive in urban centers.[7] For these many reasons, the party was soon to withdraw from the cities and retreat to the vast rural countryside.

The Kiangsi Period
The remainder of the Central Committee abandoned Shanghai in 1931, moved to the Kiangsi soviet, and soon became involved in a dispute over military strategy with the local soviet chairman and political commissar, Mao Tse-tung. Chiang Kai-shek had not abandoned his relentless pursuit of Communists and now took the offensive in a series of encirclement campaigns designed to annihilate the "Communist bandits." The Red armies of Chu Teh and Mao Tse-tung had successfully repulsed the first three encirclement campaigns in 1930 and 1931, capturing many men and rifles. As Chiang prepared to launch his fourth encirclement, the CCP held an important meeting to discuss military strategy.[8] Mao argued in favor of mobile guerrilla warfare, luring the enemy deep into soviet territory, cutting their supply lines, and attacking at two weak points. Chou En-lai disparaged this guerrilla approach; he was willing to use the lure tactic behind enemy lines, but to defend the base areas he advocated a swift frontal counterattack outside the soviet area, meeting the KMT army unit by unit with a highly centralized Red Army before the enemy had a chance to deploy its troops. Whereas Mao's "scorched earth" tactics risked alienating the native peasantry (whose crops would be destroyed), Chou's policy would engage the

[7] Ying-mao Kau, "Urban and Rural Strategies in the Chinese Communist Revolution," in *Peasant Rebellion and Communist Revolution in Asia,* John W. Lewis, ed. (Stanford, Calif.: Stanford University Press, 1974), pp. 253–270.
[8] Held in August 1932 in Ningpo, Kiangsi.

enemy outside the soviet area. Mao acknowledged this, but argued that exposing the people to KMT depradations would test their will and determination, cementing their loyalty through personal sacrifice. Chou's position was accepted at the meeting, and Chou replaced Mao on the Military Committee of the party's Central Bureau for Soviet Areas and a few months later succeeded him as political commissar of the consolidated Red Army as well. This was perhaps the nadir of Mao's fortunes, and he fell ill for the next four months, absenting himself from all central meetings.

In the fourth encirclement campaign, Chou's military strategy appeared to be successful, confirming the view of many CCP leaders that Mao's guerrilla tactics were obsolete. But the outcome was somewhat inconclusive, for Chiang was diverted by Japanese incursions into northern Hopei. Chiang launched his fifth encirclement in October 1933, mobilizing an estimated 500,000 men against the Communists. This year-long offensive was no longer limited to military operations, but included elaborate political and economic activities as well. On the recommendation of German military advisers, Chiang abandoned his attempt to launch frontal offensives—a policy that had shown itself futile—and tried to strangle the Communists in their own territory. To this end he virtually barricaded the Kiangsi periphery with barbed wire fences and blockhouses bristling with machine guns and light cannons. The Red soldiers could neither fight their usual guerrilla war of attrition nor could they assault frontally because of their inferior numbers and equipment.

In the winter, spring, and summer of 1934, Chou worked feverishly to strengthen the Red Army as the encirclement tightened. The spring of 1934 saw the Kiangsi base in serious difficulty: food and clothing were scarce, and salt was an increasing rarity.

Chou wrote exhortations in various party and Red Army journals, gave speeches, and toured the front lines to mobilize every available resource in defense of the base. In April 1934 the Communists lost a decisive battle in the Fukien-Kiangsi border area, leaving four thousand dead on the battlefield and taking twenty thousand wounded away with them. Chou remained on the line under fire until forced back to the second line of resistance. On August 30, the second line also collapsed, exposing other defensive positions, which fell like dominoes.

In a small village within earshot of the battle, the party leadership went into emergency session and agreed to try to break out from the encirclement. Chiang's fifth encirclement had cost the Communists sixty thousand men already, but a quick count showed there were still some eighty thousand men under arms, ready to leave. On October 16, 1934, they broke out, moving southwest toward the line held by the politically less reliable Kwangtung provincial troops, leaving only a few thousand Red regulars and partisans to fight rearguard actions.[9] At the time of the break-out, Mao and Chou were both weak with illness. The Reds did not break through KMT fortifications until November 29 and suffered fearful losses: one-third of their forces had been destroyed, and tons of equipment had to be abandoned or hidden in caches. There does not seem to have been any clear idea as to the CCP's ultimate destination. Subsequent party historians pictured the battle-weary heroes marching forth to fight the Japanese, but an eyewitness recalls, "Isolated as we were, we were rather vague about 'resistance to Japan.'"[10]

[9] Chiang and the military leaders of the officially pro-KMT provincial forces of Kwangtung and Kwangsi were not on good terms, and these formed the weak side of his trap.
[10] Chang Kuo-t'ao, The Rise, 2: 384.

The Long March

The six-thousand-mile Long March was an unmitigated military disaster, but a spiritual triumph, leading the party ever after to take an ambivalent view of apparent disasters and to harbor suspicions about prosperity. The Communists had no transportation other than their feet and a few horses and pack mules. The KMT bombed and strafed the fleeing troops from the air and mounted obstacle after obstacle in their path. Thousands of KMT troops pursued them; other thousands were sent to precede them on the Yangtze River, where Chiang was certain to crush them completely. The crossing points of the Yangtze were reinforced with men and weapons; boats and ferries were brought to the southern bank of the river; and at all strategic points, blockades were raised.

After about three months on the march, the Reds entered Kweichow province and took Tsunyi, a central market town and transportation hub. They occupied the town for eleven days, their longest rest during the trip. They confiscated money from the banks and supplies from the warehouses, distributing what their own troops did not use to the city poor. They also captured the Governor's headquarters and residence, where they held an enlarged Politburo conference in January 1935. The flight from Kiangsi had been a misfortune for which the incumbent leadership could be blamed, and Mao intended to replace them at the helm.

Mao relied on his supporters among Red Army generals to champion his guerrilla tactics and to condemn the positional warfare that Mao claimed was responsible for the Communist defeats. While some of the incumbents attempted to defend their positions, Chou En-lai made a clean breast of the strategic errors of the Politburo and himself, moving that Mao be given the leadership of the Red Army and voluntarily retiring from the Military Committee. This left the others

Chou En-lai on the Long March

(New China News Agency, Peking)

in the leadership little choice but to concede their errors as well, greatly facilitating Mao's victory. So when Mao was elected chairman of the Military Committee and reorganized the committee, he retained Chou as his vice chairman. Chou could be quite useful to him, and he was too powerful and well-connected to risk offending. Mao reportedly had no particular aptitude for directing military action in the field—his genius lay in deciding upon general strategic principles and military policies—so he continued to rely on Chou. Until Tsunyi, Chou had been the highest military figure in the party, present at the Red Army's creation and closely identified with it ever since, receiving a great deal of support among leading cadres in all nineteen of the armies present at Kiangsi (only one of which was Mao's Chingkangshan unit). At the time of Mao's challenge he was, of course, full member of the Politburo, and Mao was a mere CC member. But he must have recognized that the party had reached a watershed in its development and that the rise of Mao represented the upsurge of a leadership faction with strong indigenous roots after fourteen years of foreign direction. Henceforth the party could operate with much more autonomy from Moscow, taking advantage of those aspects of the Chinese situation the Soviets had been unable to see—the salience of the peasant problem and the intense feelings of nationalism to be tapped.

In the course of the Long March, this small and desperate band of survivors endured awesome hardships. Partly because he was wracked with disease during much of the trip, partly because he had to stay up every night to chart the next day's escape route, attend late-night Politburo conferences, or evaluate intelligence reports (which usually arrived at night), Chou often spent the day taking cat naps while being carried on a stretcher. The marchers lived off the land, foraging provisions where they could find them. They crossed burning deserts and treacherous swamplands and snow-capped mountains, still fighting a rearguard action against pursuing KMT troops. In late 1935, more than a year after they had fled Kiangsi, the exhausted survivors arrived in Yenan, having lost 80–90 percent of the individuals they had started with.[11]

[11] The best account of this period is Dick Wilson, *The Long March* (New York: Viking Press, 1971).

The War of National Resistance

Once the party had settled in Yenan, the logic of a second united front with the KMT soon presented itself: they were now much weaker militarily than they had been in Kiangsi and badly needed respite to recover; moreover, the Japanese were making incursions not far from their new base area, and there was already a sizable popular constituency in support of a united front for national resistance. Chou En-lai first approached KMT officials in Shanghai in the summer or autumn of 1935 to discuss prospects of a united front, but the CCP proposals fell on deaf ears. Chiang was still determined to place domestic pacification before repulsion of foreign threats.

But thanks to Chou's expert preliminary diplomacy, an incident now occurred that succeeded in changing Chiang's mind. Chiang's local commander in northeastern China was "Young Marshal" Chang Hsueh-liang, the son of a former Manchurian warlord. Chang cherished a deep animus against the Japanese, who had driven him from his stalking grounds in Manchuria in the early 1930s (and killed his father) without encountering any resistance from Generalissimo Chiang. After extended negotiations, Chou convinced Chang that the Chinese Communists were also anti-Japanese Chinese patriots who sincerely wished to subordinate their forces to the Generalissimo's command and to cooperate against the invaders. The Young Marshal finally consented to a secret local truce with the CCP, pending an attempt to persuade Chiang Kai-shek to adopt the same policy at a national level. This local truce paralyzed Chiang's attempt to mobilize northeastern troops in his offensive against the Red Army and cleared the way for expanded CCP activities in the area.

Meanwhile in Nanking, Chiang Kai-shek, growing increasingly impatient with Chang Hsueh-liang's failure to join in the offensive against the CCP, flew to Sian in December 1936. In a meeting there, Chiang declined the Young Marshal's entreaties for a more aggressive anti-Japanese campaign and announced plans for a new anti-Communist offensive to begin December 13. He also signaled his intention to replace Chang as commander of the "bandit suppression headquarters" in the northeast. Before dawn on December 12, the Young Marshal's outraged supporters reacted, arresting the Chief of State.

This unexpected turn of events caused alarm and confusion in all quarters. According to available eyewitness reports, most Communist leaders, including Mao Tse-tung and Chu Teh, initially rejoiced at their windfall good fortune and planned a public trial to be climaxed by Chiang's execution. His death would disorganize the Nationalists, possibly even split them, and give the Communists a new lease on life and an opportunity to gain control over the disorganized anti-Japanese resistance movement. However, the Comintern's advice to the CCP leaders was more cautious. Moscow considered Chiang to be the only figure of sufficient prominence to rally the nation against the Japanese; the kidnapping was a gross mistake brought about by Japanese intrigues to block the unification of China, and Chiang should be released, preferably after extracting commitments from him to cooperate with the CCP. The Comintern telegram to this effect provoked intense debate within the CCP Politburo. "We didn't sleep for a week, trying to decide," Chou later recalled. "It was the most difficult decision of our whole lives." But after a good deal of debate, the Comintern's viewpoint prevailed.

Chang Hsueh-liang, finding himself astride a tiger he could not easily dismount, turned to Chou En-lai for advice. Chou came to Sian and entered into direct, but confidential, negotiations with Chiang Kai-shek, his former commander-in-chief. He maintained an air of respect and submission toward Chiang throughout, without any sign of coercion, so that no trace of unpleasantness would mar the chance for future interviews. The CCP by no means entertained ideas unfavorable to the interests of the Nanking regime, Chou assured him. The CCP would rather support Chiang as a national leader in resisting Japan, but it was necessary to remove old prejudices and forge unity to resist foreign aggression. At one point Chou relieved the tense atmosphere by engaging in small talk with Chiang about his family, reassuring him on the basis of his own contacts that his son, Chiang Ching-kuo (present-day KMT Chairman in Taiwan) was enjoying good treatment in the Soviet Union, where he had been studying for several years.[12]

Chou remained in close touch with Mao in the CCP headquarters in Paoan throughout the negotiations. Chiang, while indicating that the CCP's conditions were not entirely unacceptable, refused to bargain under duress or to sign any written agreement. This greatly disquieted Mao Tse-tung, who suspected another betrayal, but Chou sent him a reassuring telegraph: "Chiang, with the vainglory of a self-appointed hero, would probably not go back on his word." Seized by a sudden patriotic impulse, the Young Marshal suddenly released his exalted captive, even accompanying him in his flight

[12] During the period of the first united front, when cordial relations existed between the KMT and the Soviet Union, the Soviets established a university for Chinese revolutionaries of both parties. Young Chiang Ching-kuo went there to study and remained for twelve years, marrying a Soviet woman. Yueh Sheng, *Sun Yat-sen University in Moscow and the Chinese Revolution* (New York: Paragon Book Gallery, 1971).

back to Nanking (where Chiang promptly had him placed under arrest). With the situation now out of their hands, the Communists watched nervously to see whether Chou had indeed won the Generalissimo's confidence.

Upon his return, Chiang asserted publicly that nothing had changed, but he quietly called off the projected offense against the CCP and reassigned the forces assembled for that purpose elsewhere. Whether he could no longer mobilize support to wipe out the Communists while the Japanese were attacking, or whether he was displaying the "vainglory of a self-appointed hero," Chiang remained true to his word. Gradually, the blockade was loosened, and visits were exchanged. Chou En-lai himself made several trips into the government zone, visiting Nanking, and even Kuling, the Generalissimo's summer residence. The Marco Polo Bridge Incident of July 7, which initiated the Sino-Japanese War, did much to allay lingering mistrust on both sides and to speed acceptance of a formal agreement to cease civil war in September 1937. The CCP was not permitted to enter the KMT either as a "bloc within" (individual members) or a "bloc without" (formal alliance between the two parties); this was a much looser arrangement, based not on formal agreements, but on "consultation in settling whatever problems occur." [13] The CCP remained illegal in KMT areas, but it became possible for the party to extend its influence and widen its organization. On the Communist side, concessions included abandoning the more radical aspects of their land reform program (for example, confiscation of landlords' land), cessation of anti-KMT propaganda,

and a guarantee of equal legal and political rights to all citizens regardless of class origin.

In 1937 the CCP held an intraparty discussion of the implementation of united front policy. Mao proposed that the Communist forces pay little attention to KMT directives, avoiding confrontation with the Japanese army and harboring strength for the eventual renewal of civil war with the KMT. Although CCP troops would nominally be incorporated into the Nationalist armed forces, they should keep the original organization of the Red Army intact and maintain absolute independence from the KMT. The returned student faction, with Comintern backing, bitterly attacked Mao's self-serving proposal, pointing out that open defiance might tempt Chiang to dissolve the united front and form an anti-Communist alliance with Japan. Tactfully, Chou joined in criticism of Mao's proposal, seeking, however, to formulate an acceptable compromise position. Emphasizing the importance of public opinion, he noted,

There were many ways to practice independence. We could tell Nanking frankly that the battle tasks assigned to the 8th Route Army should be those that give full play to its guerrilla expertise. It was possible to carry out the orders of the government nominally but preserve our own spirit in fact. If the 8th Route Army fought only guerrilla battles and avoided the enemy's real strength, people might think we were not doing our utmost for the War of Resistance. Under favorable conditions, the 8th Route Army should engage in mobile warfare against the Japanese on a large scale.[14]

Sensing the majority against him on this matter, Mao accepted Chou's compromise,

[13] James P. Harrison, *The Long March to Power: A History of the Chinese Communist Party, 1921–1972* (New York: Praeger, 1972), p. 288.

[14] Chang Kuo-t'ao, *The Rise,* 2: 537.

and the CCP henceforth implemented a policy combining unity and struggle.

Chou and Teng Ying-ch'ao spent most of the war years in Chungking as Communist officials within the United Front National Government. Chou's work with the Nationalists and independents in Chungking was in some ways as important to CCP victory as Mao's leadership in building the base areas or Liu Shao-ch'i's in establishing the underground organizations in the White (or enemy-occupied) areas. Overt Communist activities were confined to Chungking after the first years of the united front, though there was considerable work among students in several wartime university centers. In August 1937 the KMT invited Chou and Chu Teh to sit in on meetings of the Supreme National Defense Council; Chou was also invited to attend the National Executive Congress, as in the old days at Canton, and even appointed Deputy Minister of Political Training in the army. His wife was one of seven Communists invited to participate on the party's Political Council established in 1938. Though these positions were all essentially honorific, they gave the Communists a high-level forum from which they could present their views and demands to representatives of the smaller parties and independent groups and beyond them to the people.

The party also gained access to mass communications media in the Nationalist zone. The *New China Daily,* with a circulation of about twenty-five thousand in 1940, was the main source of Communist news and propaganda; it operated under Chou's jurisdiction. The New China News Agency established offices in Chengtu and several other cities, where they supported numerous leftist bookstores. The CCP press in the government zone was directed by talented journalists, many of whom had sound foreign training.

The Communists had not only permanent representatives in Chungking, but liaison offices in several other large cities, where they organized the migration of volunteers to Yenan. During this period the CCP was supporting democracy (and protesting KMT suppression of it) in order to enhance its appeal to the middle-class liberal groups—and with considerable success. The creation of the China Democratic League was generally conceded to have been a notable testimony to Chou's ability to mobilize anti-KMT sentiment among these groups.

During the War of National Resistance, Chou engaged in three rounds of negotiations with the KMT leadership altogether, and with each successive round the positions of the two parties grew wider apart. Chou was unquestionably the best negotiator on the CCP side, having a good grasp of international affairs, a command of French and English, and good contacts with both CCP and KMT officials. The issues involved in these negotiations need not be discussed here, especially since they invariably wound up in deadlock. Between the first and second round of negotiations, Chou returned to Yenan to participate in the party's rectification movement (1942–1944), in which the last vestiges of Mao's intraparty opposition was publicly discredited. In the final round of negotiations in May 1945, the salient issue at stake was control of China in the imminent postwar period. The KMT insisted here on national unification under Chiang Kai-shek before everything else, while the CCP refused to surrender its army and territory without guarantees. Both parties soon set about trying to build a national front regime including third parties but excluding and isolating each other. After leaving Chungking at the end of the third round of negotiations in 1945, Chou flew back to Yenan to prepare for a coalition government excluding the KMT, while the KMT prepared to convene a national assembly excluding the CCP.

Behind the emergence of the CCP as a credible challenger to the KMT's hegemony in China lies a remarkable success story. This success did not rest on the CCP's victories against the Japanese, but on the CCP's consistent adherence to a policy formulated near the outset of the war by Mao Tse-tung. Instead of taking up a position on the front alongside the government units, the Eighth Route Army remained largely behind Japanese lines. The KMT forces had largely evacuated these occupied areas, and lack of adequate troops forced the Japanese to restrict their occupation to the chief towns and lines of communication. In this partial power vacuum, the Red Army began the political, administrative, and military organization of the population, while at the same time gathering together isolated or abandoned elements that belonged to the former national and provincial armies and willing elements that belonged to the former administrative structure. The three Communist divisions gradually spread beyond Shansi, using Mao's guerrilla tactics to avoid encounters with the enemy except at times of decisive superiority. As time went on, about fifteen different bases with shifting boundaries grew up and were subsumed under three regions: northern China, central China, and a small southern China region. It was in these base areas that most of the party's wartime expansion took place. By the end of 1944, according to Chou En-lai, the Communists controlled 12 regional administrative structures and 591 districts. CCP membership rose from 40,000 in 1936 to 1 million in four years and more than 2 million by the end of the war.

There has been some controversy among theorists purporting to explain the success of the Chinese Communist revolution. Some

have emphasized its nationalist aspects, whereas others point to its social revolutionary appeal. The former, led by Chalmers Johnson, have contended that the CCP was unsuccessful prior to the War of National Resistance and that only the Japanese invasion created circumstances permitting them to succeed. The Japanese army contributed to this paradoxical outcome by holding the Nationalist forces at bay—which allowed the CCP to assemble a constituency behind Japanese lines—and by unwittingly mobilizing the Chinese peasantry against them through their excessively harsh occupation regime and indiscriminate counterinsurgency tactics.[15] The critics of this argument emphasize the continued CCP tactics of pointing to unequal wealth and power to mobilize the have-nots against the haves, particularly in Yenan.[16]

Actually, both theories are to some degree correct. It is true that the Japanese invasion diverted the KMT from their relentless offensives against the CCP and provided the latter with a sheltered opportunity to expand; and it is also true that Communist propaganda abandoned its more radical policy of land reform in favor of more inclusive nationalist themes, leading some Western observers to conclude that the CCP was not really Communist at all. But at the same time, while the KMT grew increasingly conservative during the war years, under the pretext that it could not lead a revolution and fight a war at the same time, the CCP continued to offer a far more radical platform for social and political change throughout this period, successfully combining war

[15] Chalmers Johnson, *Peasant Nationalism and Communist Power: The Emergence of Revolutionary China, 1937–1945* (Stanford, Calif.: Stanford University Press, 1962).
[16] Mark Selden, *The Yenan Way in Revolutionary China* (Cambridge, Mass.: Harvard University Press, 1971).

with revolution. It was the party's progressive platform that was responsible for its success in recruiting growing numbers of the nation's idealistic student youth, while the KMT leadership became an increasingly aged and corrupt collection of competing elite cliques. Nationalism was a more effective slogan in the more populous areas behind Japanese lines, which furnished the bulk of the new recruits, but recruits in the original Red base areas and the top party organs continued to be primarily committed to the social revolution.

The Second Civil War

The period from the capitulation of Japan in August 1945 to the accession of the People's Republic of China in October 1949 can be divided into two main phases. The first was dominated by negotiations and continued until the Chinese Communist delegation left Nanking on March 5, 1947. During this period Chou En-lai played a prominent role as leader of the CCP negotiating team. From mid-1946 to mid-1947, the Nationalists were on the offensive and were usually victorious—but the CCP avoided battle and allowed the KMT to overextend its lines. The second phase, lasting from the spring of 1947 until the end of 1949, was one of uninterrupted military operations on a larger scale than ever before, spreading to all theaters of the war. Beginning in mid-1947, the CCP stabilized its lines and went over to the offensive, and by mid-1948 the KMT began to collapse. Yet contact was secretly maintained and official negotiations took place even at the beginning of 1949.

Although victory against Japan made the conflict of interest between the KMT and CCP more explicit, in the general state of euphoria and popular relief at the end of the war, it was hard for either side to refuse negotiation and thus to shoulder the onus for renewed civil war immediately after the war of resistance. Mao, Chou En-lai, and a number of other Red leaders flew to Chungking in August 1945 for direct talks with Chiang Kai-shek, escorted by the American Ambassador to China, Patrick J. Hurley. Mao's meeting with Chiang was brief and ceremonial. Substantive talks were conducted subsequently between Chou and the KMT's Chang Ch'un. Negotiations were conducted for forty-one days, and a joint communiqué was released on National Day (October 10, 1945). Both parties agreed to accept three general principles: democratization and constitutional government were to be heralded by the calling of a political consultative conference that would be followed by a national assembly; administrative autonomy was to be encouraged (though the government still refused to recognize the administrative structures of the liberated areas); and the CCP agreed in principle to the nationalization of their armed forces. The agreement was written with a frustrating lack of precision, however, withholding all details as to how the principles agreed upon were to be put into effect. The principal achievement of the talks concerned the delimitation of the territory under each party's control. The area south of the Yangtze, it was agreed, would be Nationalist territory, while the Shen-Kan-Ning border region would be Communist. Other areas were to be contested.

This vague, fragile agreement was rendered invalid less than two weeks later, as military clashes broke out between the two parties now intent upon laying claim to disputed territories. Hurley resigned in November 1945 after the October agreement had broken down. Upon his return to the United States, he claimed that his efforts had been sabotaged by a section of the United States State Department that aided the CCP

481

—a charge that reechoed in Joseph McCarthy's Communist witch hunts in the early 1950s. To replace him, President Truman now sent his personal representative, General George C. Marshall, to China to mediate the dispute. In the ensuing discussions with Marshall, Chou served as the principal Chinese Communist negotiator. Although Marshall bore secret instructions from Truman to support the Nationalists regardless of whether they cooperated with American mediation attempts, Marshall's appointment was welcomed by all sides: Nationalist, Chinese Communist, and Russian.

In 1946 a committee of three, consisting of Marshall, Chou En-lai, and Chang Ch'un, was established to implement a preliminary cease-fire agreement negotiated under Marshall's direction on January 10. On the same day that this was signed, the Political Consultative Conference, for which the Communists had so long been agitating, opened in Chungking. Both Chou En-lai and Teng Ying-ch'ao sat on this body, together with thirty-eight other delegates from the CCP, the KMT, and the minor political parties and independent groups. At its first session, a truce agreement was signed by Chou En-lai and Chang Ch'un. The moment the Political Consultative Conference adjourned, Chou flew back to Yenan to go into night session with the CCP Central Committee; two days later he returned to Chungking with the announcement that Yenan was deeply gratified with the improvement in the situation.

But an achievement of even greater potential significance was the agreement by the committee of three on the reorganization and new deployment of armies, signed on February 25, 1946. This stipulated the zones where each party was to station its troops and set forth a schedule for the mutual demobilization of troops; had it been implemented, it would have enabled a coalition government to be constituted and forestalled the

outbreak of civil war. Three days after its signing, the committee of three set out from Chungking to inspect military lines in northern China. During his inspection of Yenan, Marshall met Mao Tse-tung, who drank a toast to him and agreed to return to Nanking "whenever Chairman Chiang wants me to go."

But the cease-fire order, issued by Chiang and Mao on January 10 to take effect on midnight three days later, did not take effect. The Communist high command warned its field commanders to expect surprise attacks shortly after the cease-fire was to take effect and instructed them to launch immediate counterattacks. Whoever srtuck first is unclear, but there were clashes all along the front lines. The CCP took advantage of this breach in the truce to move their troops northward into highly industrialized Manchuria, which the KMT was scheduled to occupy according to the cease-fire agreement. At the same time, the KMT advanced its divisions along the main channels of communication. The two came into violent conflict in May 1946.

The breakdown of the truce took a bitter personal note for Chou when a group of Chinese Communist officials, including some of Chou's close associates, were killed while flying from Chungking to Shensi; Chou suspected that the plane had been sabotaged. Still Chou persisted in his efforts to convince General Marshall of the validity of the CCP position, rather than breaking off negotiations altogether. At the same time, he continued to devote regular attention to press relations, meeting both Chinese and Western correspondents in Nanking with unfailing tact and eloquence. Even after full-scale civil war broke out in the summer of 1946, spreading from Manchuria southward, Chou remained at the seat of the national government in Nanking to preserve a channel of communication. American attempts at mediation continued through the summer and fall of 1946. But as the Nationalist military position was initially favorable, they refused to comply with the truce proposals; later, when the tide turned, the Communists would refuse to comply. Chou En-lai finally left for Yenan on November 19, 1946 (when the Nationalists were winning), stating that he saw no possibility of early resumption of talks and that he did not know whether he would return to Nanking even if such talks were to be resumed. However, the CCP did not completely close the door to renewed negotiations, leaving a small liaison mission headed by one of Chou's deputies through the winter of 1946. On February 1, 1947, the CCP released their pamphlet *Greet the New High Tide of Revolution,* which amounted to a tacit declaration of war; on July 4, 1947, Chiang Kai-shek responded by ordering "Mobilization for the suppression of rebellion." General Marshall acknowledged the hopelessness of the situation with his withdrawal in August 1947.

Chou spent the critical months of the Chinese civil war in the countryside of northern China with Mao Tse-tung and the top political leadership of the CCP. In the spring and summer of 1947 the Nationalist troops launched a general offensive and gained the upper hand virtually everywhere. In March of that year a Nationalist drive even forced the Communists to evacuate Yenan. At this juncture, the Central Committee split up to ensure continuity of leadership in case one headquarters should be captured or destroyed; Chou, Mao and Jen Pi-shih fled to a village near the Great Wall, while Liu Shao-ch'i, Chu Teh, and an alternate working committee moved into the Shansi-Chahar-Hopei base area. But between the summer of 1947 and the summer of 1948 the tide gradually turned, as the Communists won a foothold in central China and managed to break the chief Nationalist communication links in northern China and Manchuria, isolating their adversary in several large cities and the surrounding areas.

In the winter of 1947–1948 the Nationalist government, disheartened by the unfortunate turn the war had taken, approached the Communists in view of reopening negotiations. But the intransigence of the Communists and the obstinacy of the Generalissimo himself condemned these efforts to failure. The final phase of the war began with a general offensive by the Communists that shattered all Nationalist positions. In the spring of 1949 the Communists crossed the Yangtze, the historic boundary between northern and southern China. By the fall of 1949, Communist armies had reached Canton and Szechuan, and by the end of the year the entire continent had fallen except for Yunnan, Sinkiang, and Tibet. The surviving Nationalist forces retreated to Taiwan, where they prepared to make a last-ditch stand against the expected Communist invasion. For reasons having to do with the rapidly polarizing international context (especially the invasion of South Korea, which contributed to the rise of Republican anti-Communism in the United States), the anticipated invasion never ensued, though the Communists did invade and seize Hainan Island to the south of Taiwan. Since 1949, the two governments have hence competed on the international stage, both claiming to be the sole legitimate government of China.

The speed of the Nationalist collapse exceeded the hopes of the CCP leadership, which found itself suddenly faced with all the problems of establishing control over a nation of more than 500 million people that was afflicted by rampant inflation and economic chaos. In the international arena, the Chinese soon found themselves embroiled in a struggle with the most powerful nation on earth, the United States—first in Korea, then over the Taiwan Strait question, as the

Americans sent their Seventh Fleet to the strait to insulate Taiwan from the mainland. Yet the new regime embarked upon its imposing new responsibilities with the self-assurance engendered by their remarkable success over seemingly insuperable odds, an experience that reinforced their Marxist belief that the laws of history could be understood and mastered.

Conclusion

In twenty-eight years, the vagaries of history and will had borne this forlorn band of rebels through one crisis after another to the pinnacle of the Chinese power structure. And near the top of the greasy pole throughout this period was Chou En-lai, now an international figure of some renown. The same qualities that had made him an assiduous and clever, though quite conventional, military leader would now make him a capable administrator and a brilliant diplomat. He combined a charismatic public presence with an acute attention to detail, and the charm and social grace he displayed as a descendent of China's traditional ruling class made him acceptable company for the diplomatic elite of other countries, who usually stemmed from similar class backgrounds. His cosmopolitan experiences and interests enabled him to translate Chinese slogans and policies into language his foreign interlocutors could understand, dispelling images of the doctrinaire Communist and giving an impression of being more flexible than he actually was.

The rise of Chou En-lai and the CCP unfortunately coincided with a period of great distress for the Chinese people. To be sure, industrial development began to gather momentum during these years: industrial production in China (including Manchuria)

grew at an annual rate of 9.3 percent in 1931–1936, reaching its peak in 1936, just before the Sino-Japanese War. Stimulated by a wartime economy, production reached a peak for the pre-Communist period in 1942 and thereafter declined, disrupted by the ravages of war. But politically the picture was one of a nation demoralized by internal corruption and torn asunder by civil war and foreign invasion.

The national democratic revolution led by the KMT ultimately foundered, while the socialist revolution led by the CCP went on to triumph. The CCP proved more capable not only of addressing the social question of distributive justice that the KMT ignored, but also of outbidding the KMT in capturing the spirit of Chinese nationalism that the KMT claimed to represent. The onset of industrialization and the commercialization of agriculture had unleashed social dislocations in both city and countryside that the Communists were prepared to exploit, first to organize the urban workers and intellectuals, later to build peasant armies in the countryside beyond the reach of Chiang's military and police apparatus. The withdrawal of the major democratic powers (particularly the United States) from active world involvement and the consequent failure of the League of Nations to enforce the international status quo, created a situation in which militaristic Japan felt at liberty to annex by force those portions of China that it had long coveted. The Sino-Japanese War permitted the CCP to revive from its near annihilation during the Long March and to expand behind Japanese lines. The Japanese invasion also drove the KMT from its urban base and precipitated its economic and political downfall.

Why did the KMT fail—while the Meiji Restoration in neighboring Japan, based on similar ideological principles, succeeded? For one thing, imperial China had been much more thoroughly penetrated by foreign powers than had Tokugawa Japan. Also the KMT attempt at nation building occurred several decades later, after the Bolshevik Revolution had already provided a precedent and an international headquarters for domestic insurgency. But perhaps the most important single factor responsible for the KMT's failure was its inability to appreciate the importance of public opinion and mass participation in politics, the recognition of which has transformed modern politics more than any other development. During the War of National Resistance, the KMT was unable to shift the resistance to a national scale and to give it authentic popular expression. This failure might be ascribed to several possible factors—the influence of a Western military strategy that tended to ignore the political aspect, loyalty to a traditional elitist political culture that left the people to shift for themselves, and the fear that the creation of semi-independent theaters of operation would destroy national unity. The Chinese Communist party, on the other hand, with democratic centralism as a principle of organization, was able to found and direct isolated bases behind Japanese lines without the slightest risk that they would rebel or shift their loyalties, combining great tactical flexibility with overall strategic control. Ideologically, the KMT proved vulnerable, by attempting to revive a neo-Confucian ethos while operating on the basis of Machiavellian power politics and by propagating Sun Yat-sen's Three Principles of the People while losing its revolutionary commitment. By drawing public attention to these blatant inconsistencies while skillfully masking its own, the CCP was able to attract widespread support to its revolutionary ideology.[17]

[17] Jacques Guillermaz, *A History of the Chinese Communist Party, 1921–1949* (New York: Random House, 1972).

485

5

Chou at the Top:
A Man for All Seasons

When the Communists seized power in 1949, their priorities were suddenly reversed: their major task at hand was no longer destruction of the established order, but reconstruction of a new one. Yet the organization's mobilizational techniques that had been developed during its thirty years of life beyond the law were all revolutionary ones designed for the destruction of established power. These techniques functioned to arouse the people with a sense of indignation about their condition and an optimistic idealism about the improvements their own active participation in politics might bring about. The political implications of institutionalization in some respects ran counter to the effects of mobilization: institutionalization resulted in the devolution of power to those trained in certain specialized fields, which entailed a progressive disenfranchisement of the masses, who lacked such training. The result was that the construction of socialism in postrevolutionary China was characterized by ambivalence: some revolutionaries adapted quickly and effortlessly to the tasks of institutionalization and rapid economic growth, while others felt that the revolution had not been pushed far enough and were primarily concerned with its continuation.

Chou En-lai accommodated himself gracefully to both mobilization and institutionalization, though his heart seemed to be in the latter. His activities during the postliberation era may conveniently be divided into three categories: those having to do with the consolidation and administration of a modern state, those concerned with the attempt to continue and expand the revolution, and those concerned with Chinese foreign policy.

State Building

On May 1, 1949, the Central Committee announced its plan to call a new Chinese

People's Political Consultative Conference (CPPCC), bringing together the leaders of all parties and groups (including even the left-wing rump of the KMT) to form a People's Republic of China. At this time Chou En-lai, as the Chinese Communist leader with closest connections with the smaller parties and independent political groups, began to talk with their leaders in China and Hong Kong. Six months after the party occupied Peking, Chou En-lai met with a committee of 23 delegates from various groups in order to draft a Common Program outlining the structure and main policies of the new regime. On September 1, 1949, Chou convoked 683 delegates to the first session of the CPPCC to approve this document. The Common Program and the other fundamental laws adopted by the CPPCC were to constitute a provisional constitution for the state during the transitional period of 1949 to 1954, when a formal constitution was adopted. The National Committee, elected by the CPPCC to exercise its functions during its recess, was to serve as a provisional National People's Congress during the same period. When the First National People's Congress was convened in September 1954, the status of the CPPCC was changed from that of an organ of state power to a consultative body; but because the CPPCC symbolized the "democratic united front of the entire Chinese People," representing "all democratic classes and all nationalities throughout China," it was not dissolved as originally planned, but has continued to serve as a liaison office of the various bourgeois democratic parties.[1] As a public tribute to Chou's contribution to the

[1] The size of the CPPCC has undergone an unbroken accretion, its National Committee alone growing from 180 delegates to 550 in December 1954 to 1,200 in 1964. Cf. William L. Tung, *The Political Institutions of Modern China* (The Hague: Martinus Nijhoff, 1964).

united front with these non-Communist parties, he was elected Vice Chairman of the growing but increasingly powerless body from 1949–1954, and in 1954 he succeeded Mao Tse-tung as Chairman of the conference; he was reelected to this post in the Third and Fourth CPPCCs in 1959 and 1965. In addition he was elected Chairman of the State Council and Minister of Foreign Affairs. Thus since 1950, Chou has simultaneously served as chief administrator of the large government bureaucracy created by the party to carry out their domestic program, the first foreign minister of the Central People's Government, and the principal spokesman of the government on the accomplishments, shortcomings, and programs of the regime.

In the early days of the People's Republic, Chou established himself as the ubiquitous political figure, engaging in a remarkable range of political activities. As Donald Klein has pointed out, he attended the majority of the 34 meetings of the Central People's Government Council and the 224 meetings of the Government Administration Council (the cabinet) held between 1949 and 1954. His reports before these two bodies alone would fill many volumes, and many more would be required to include still other addresses before the CPPCC National Committee, various mass and professional organizations, and national conferences of progressive workers and peasants. Many of these reports were technical in nature and of only passing interest, but others represented the official Chinese position on key domestic and foreign issues. Although Chou's lengthy reports did not attempt to interpret Marxist theory or to declare any important new policies, his collected speeches and reports provide one of the richest sources of basic data about China, especially during the first ten years of the People's Republic.

In 1949, China had only twelve thousand miles of railways and forty-eight thousand miles of usable roads, all in chaotic condition and in need of major construction. Industrial production had declined by 56 percent and agricultural output by 25–30 percent, as compared to the previous peacetime peak year of 1936. Population had also increased significantly, to a total of about 550 million, and continued to expand at an annual rate of about 2 percent. Because only part of the vast countryside is arable, and because decades of civil war had left the water conservancy and flood control works damaged or neglected, this increase in the population was critical. Not enough food could be grown to feed the population. And the Great Powers, led by the United States, were trying to strangle the new regime with a trade embargo.

In view of these outstanding problems, the policy of the leadership in 1949 was to give first priority to restoring industrial and agricultural production to their prewar levels, to bring about a measure of financial stability by curbing inflation, and to rebuild the transportation network. Thereafter, the broad outline of economic development would follow that of the Soviet Union: agricultural collectivization, industrialization, and abolition of private enterprise. In contrast to the Soviet Union, however, China proceeded in implementing this program at a moderate pace with minimal use of violence, making provision wherever possible to co-opt rather than destroy the members of the former ruling classes who opposed them. Thus, overall economic production rose throughout the 1949–1952 period, so by 1952 it was back to prewar levels. In addition, inflation was curtailed, the rail network was largely restored, and new construction was started.

The first step in the collectivization of agriculture was land reform, promulgated in the Agrarian Reform Law of June 1950. In the process of implementing land reform, the local party leadership divided China's vast peasant population into five classes: landlords, who owned land, but did not work it; rich peasants, who owned land and employed labor, but also worked the land; middle peasants, who may have owned land, but depended mainly on their own labor to make a living; poor peasants, who usually rented land or worked part-time for others; and farm laborers, who depended entirely on sale of their labor for a livelihood. Although only farm laborers are technically analogous to the urban proletariat, the Communists tried to isolate the landlords by uniting all the other classes against them. Cadres did not implement land reform simply through bureaucratic channels, as KMT cadres had been accustomed to do, but mobilized the peasants to participate in enforcing the law. They did this not only by pointing to the inequitable distribution of property but also by accusing the landlords of cruelty and by encouraging the peasants to do likewise in mass trials and "speak bitterness" meetings, thereby overcoming traditional deferential attitudes toward authority. By appealing to the interests of the peasants while at the same time allowing them to unleash repressed hostilities against their former oppressors, the Communists secured the voluntary cooperation of the majority of the peasants with the land reform policy and their enthusiastic support of the new regime.

Following land reform, there was reportedly some controversy within the leadership over whether to press on with great speed toward the socialization of agriculture or to pause at this stage and concentrate more attention on urban industrialization. All revolutionary developing regimes are apt to face a dilemma of this sort, necessitating a choice between developmental and redistributive policies: the mass constituency is apt

Chou En-lai among the masses
(New China News Agency, Peking)

to lay claim to the spoils of victory, but future development calls for its reinvestment. Land reform in China resulted in the fragmentation of landholdings into small private plots, which satisfied the peasants and increased production, but reinforced their passive attitudes about their newly acquired property, thus threatening to impede collectivization. It is conceivable that Chou En-lai, Liu Shao-ch'i, and other moderates in the regime favored a longer pause before moving ahead with collectivization, in order first to develop the agricultural machinery that would make collectivization profitable. Mao stressed striking while the iron was hot and pressing to the next phase of the revolution. A compromise seems to have been reached to resume the collectivization of agriculture, but to do so at a measured pace while simultaneously proceeding with socialization of the means of industrial production.

The first step on the road to agricultural collectivization was the formation of voluntary mutual-aid teams, comprising from three to five households each and operating only during the busy seasons. Gradually these were converted into permanent mutual-aid teams of six to ten households, in which communal use was made of still privately owned tools and resources. Income was based on the amount of land and resources invested into the common fund and the amount of work done. The second step in the process was the formation of agricultural producers' cooperatives, or APCs, comprising about forty households. Again, the peasants retained nominal ownership of their property and could in theory opt out of the cooperative at will; income was distributed on roughly the same basis as in the mutual-aid teams. The APCs were introduced in some areas as early as 1952, but were not widely promoted or accepted until 1953–1955. By mid-1956, more than 90 percent of all peasant households had joined the

APCs, most of them of the advanced type. The main difference between elementary and advanced APCs was that in the former, the peasant owned the land; in the latter, the APC did. By mid-1957, more than 96 percent of all peasant households were in advanced APCs.

This sudden acceleration in the pace of collectivization in 1956 was stimulated by Mao Tse-tung, a consistent proponent of a faster pace. Now impatient with what he regarded as his colleagues' undue timidity, he scornfully denounced the dissolution of 200,000 immature APCs by Teng Tzu-hui, Chou's deputy for agricultural affairs, and circumvented established procedure to call for a national upsurge. Mao's intervention was highly successful in accelerating the pace of collectivization, giving him greater confidence in his ability to intervene arbitrarily in mass movements based on his own intuition of the masses' interests. But Chou En-lai, along with the rest of Mao's staff, opposed Mao's speed-up, as Chou admitted a decade later: "I bore the responsibility for the opposition to adventurism in 1956 [and] I made a [self-critical] examination." [2]

In the cities, the leadership adopted a policy to use, restrict, and transform the capitalist industrial and commercial sector from 1949 to 1957, initially allowing private industry to play a dominant role in the interest of a speedy economic recovery. In 1952–1953, the government began to restrict private enterprise with respect to sales, profits, and production, also launching a "five-anti" campaign in early 1952 to purge antagonistic members of the urban bourgeoisie on charges of bribery, theft of state secrets, and so on. The transformation of

2 Donald W. Klein and Anne B. Clark, eds., "Chou En-lai," in *Biographic Dictionary of Chinese Communism, 1921–1965* (Cambridge, Mass.: Harvard University Press, 1971), 1: 210–219.

private industry proceeded in 1954–1957 in two stages. In the first, private enterprises were transformed into state-private enterprises, with the operations of the plant being directed by the state in accord with the national plan while ownership was retained by the original investors. The second stage, joining operation by whole trades, was launched in late 1955, bringing virtually all of private industry under state control by the end of 1956.

The first Five-Year Plan was introduced in 1953, though it was not publicly announced until mid-1955. In it, the Chinese indicated their determination to follow the Soviet model of economic development, concentrating resources on the construction of a heavy industrial base while neglecting light industry and agriculture.[3] According to the best estimates by both Communist and Western economists, this allocation of resources resulted in impressive industrial development during the first plan, with an average annual growth rate of industrial production of no less than 19 percent. However, the neglect of light industry and agriculture resulted in a somewhat unbalanced development: agricultural production in-

creased by an annual average of only 4.5 percent during the same period. On the whole, however, the first Five-Year Plan was a success, resulting in an increase in gross national product of 6–10 percent per annum during the entire period. This was achieved primarily on the basis of internal investment, although the Soviet Union did supply some valuable technical assistance.

Meanwhile, the institutionalization of the governmental structure was proceeding in good order. In January 1953 it had been announced that the National People's Congress would be convened at an early, but unspecified date to approve the first constitution of the People's Republic. The congress actually convened over a year and a half later (September 1954) and adopted the constitution that has defined the structure of the People's Government from that time to the present. The delay, however, suggested disagreements among the top leaders over the form of the proposed organization of the state structure. This suggestion of intraparty dissension was confirmed with the purge of Kao Kang and Jao Shu-shih. Publicly announced in 1955, the purge may have actually taken place as early as January 1954, the date of the last official mention of Kao Kang in the press.

Kao and Jao, who had been leaders in the industrialized Manchurian and eastern China regions, apparently called for the replacement of several top leaders, including Chou En-lai and Liu Shao-ch'i. Kao Kang supported this demand with a theory of two parties, one the party of the revolutionary bases and the army (the Red areas) and the other the party of the White areas controlled by the Nationalists during the war. Kao argued that the party was the creation of the army and that those who stemmed from the Red areas should therefore have preferential consideration. This interpretation of party history was of questionable accuracy (Kao's

---

[3] At the beginning of 1956, the Central Committee promulgated the draft regulations concerning Mao's program of agricultural development, which became part of the general upsurge of economic activities that the regime consistently pressed during the early part of the year. But in the course of the year, Chou and his deputies on the State Council frequently warned against the danger of adventurism, placing themselves in implicit opposition to Mao's initiative. For example, the 1956 session of the NPC was highlighted by Chou's report on the work of the government; in this report he defended reasonable income differentials and denied the need for radical change. As a result of the opposition to adventurism put up by Chou and his cabinet in the summer of 1956, the Leap Forward approach to development was firmly rejected at the Eighth Congress in September 1956.

foremost associate was Jao Shu-shih, a prominent member of the party underground during the war), but its implications struck directly at Chou En-lai and Liu Shao-ch'i, who had spent much of the war years in the White areas (Chou in Chungking, Liu in the Japanese-occupied areas) and who held the very posts to which Kao aspired. Kao and Jao also allegedly advocated preferential investment in China's old industrialized areas in the east and northeast rather than a diversification of industry to the interior, arguing on the basis of the relative advantage of investing on an established industrial base. This first serious threat from within to the unity of the leadership was quietly checked. The State Planning Committee, which had been chaired by Kao Kang, was dissolved and reorganized as the State Planning Commission under the cabinet. Neither Kao nor Jao were heard from again.

Politics and the Intellectuals

In the latter part of 1955, the CCP apparently decided to heighten participation of the non-Communist intellectuals in public affairs. Because the party's long banishment to the wilderness had deprived it of the opportunity to train its own experts, a not inconsiderable portion of these were still nonparty members. Modernization requires the contribution of intellectuals no less than the mobilization of the masses, the leadership decided, and it began to try to mobilize their support. To inspire these intellectuals with patriotic and hopefully pro-Communist enthusiasm and to attract other intellectuals to the Communist cause, it was considered necessary to liberalize the party's administration of the intellectual world. During December 1955 the non-Communist parties held meetings and passed resolutions, the

main thrust of which was that the upsurge of socialism had brought about a new situation in which the intellectuals would be called upon to make greater contributions to socialist construction than ever before.[4]

All of this was part of the public preparation for a large conference convoked by the Central Committee on January 14–20, 1956, and attended by 1,279 party officials to discuss the problems of the intellectuals. Chou En-lai delivered the main speech, emphasizing the shortage of educated manpower available for the national economic effort and outlining the measures the party was prepared to take to make the best use of existing talent. "The fundamental question concerning the intellectuals now is that the forces of our intelligentsia are insufficient in number, professional skills and political consciousness to meet the requirements of our rapid socialist construction," he announced. Chou estimated the total number of intellectuals in China at 3,840,000 in all fields, of which 100,000 were higher intellectuals (that is, college graduates). But he claimed only some 40 percent of this total as active supporters of the CCP. The remainder, he said, should be reeducated by the party, but "it is impossible to settle the problem crudely. There are people who persist in their wrong thinking. If they do not turn against the people in speech and action, and, even more, if they are prepared to devote their knowledge and energies to serving the people, we must be able to await the gradual awakening of their consciousness and help them patiently while at the same time criticizing their wrong ideology." The party's three tasks in mobilizing intellectuals

[4] Thus, during the period of the first Five-Year Plan, 56 percent of total state investment was allotted to industry (87 percent of which went to heavy industry), 18.7 percent into transport and communications, and only 8.2 percent for agriculture, forestry, and water conservation.

were to employ them in more appropriate positions, to give them confidence in "extended academic discussions of socialist construction," and to ensure better working conditions and appropriate treatment.

Chou En-lai was probably the most suitable man to say these things. More familiar than any of the other four members of the Politburo's inner circle with the non-Communist intellectuals and their attitudes, he consistently acted as the party's spokesman to the intellectuals. During the War of National Resistance, as noted earlier, he spent much of his time in Chungking eliciting support for the Communist cause from non-Communist intellectuals. In 1950, Chou initiated thought reform of the intellectuals with his lecture, "Reforming the Intellectuals," which also bespoke his desire to co-opt this elite group into the Communist apparatus.

What Chou En-lai had initiated in his speech was eventually to become famous as the Hundred Flowers Movement. But the policy implications of this movement were to change considerably from the time of its inception to its eventual culmination more than a year later. The divergence between Chou's original purpose in initiating this mild liberalization and its ultimate upshot has to do with an apparent difference between Chou's and Mao Tse-tung's purposes. Chou apparently wished for nothing more than to awaken and to employ the talents of the intellectuals, many of which lay untapped. In this he succeeded: his speech was followed immediately by practical measures alleviating the plight of the intellectuals. Their living conditions were improved; salaries were increased; political, social, and administrative duties were reduced; working conditions were improved. Some unemployed intellectuals were now employed, and intellectuals were encouraged to apply for membership in the CCP. A planning com-

mittee for scientific development was set up later in the year to formulate a twelve-year plan for the natural and social sciences.

Mao, however, seemed to see in this liberalization an opportunity to mobilize intellectuals outside the party to criticize various people inside the party whom he blamed for bureaucratism. Thus in a speech on May 2, 1956, Mao called to "Let a hundred flowers blossom, let a hundred schools of thought contend," advocating freedom of criticism. Inasmuch as the suspicious intellectuals still hesitated to reply, Mao delivered another address on February 27, 1957, his most ambitious theoretical essay since liberation, "On the Correct Handling of Contradictions Among the People," in which he encouraged people to "dare to criticize and dare to debate." Again in a speech to the party's National Conference on Propaganda Work the following month, Mao repeated his invitation. Finally, in May the dam burst, and the criticisms that appeared were sharper than Mao had anticipated, including among their targets the dictatorship of the proletariat, Mao's own leadership, and other fundamentals of the Communist regime. On June 8 the regime suddenly retaliated, stanching the outpour of criticism and initiating a purge of rightists who had taken advantage of the relaxation to manifest their opposition. Altogether it is estimated that 300,000–400,000 rightists were seized in 1957. At this point Mao claimed that the purpose of the campaign had been to trap the rightists into incriminating themselves all along, although it seems more likely that Mao erred on the side of optimism in his original assessment of the intellectuals' political loyalty.

The failure of the Great Leap Forward and the withdrawal of Soviet technicians in the summer of 1960 impelled the party once more to embark on a policy of attempting to win the cooperation of the intellectuals through a policy of liberalization in order to rehabilitate the economy from the "three bitter years" of 1959–1961. This led to a partial revival of the Hundred Flowers in 1961–1962, the "small blooming" campaign (*hsiao ming fang*). This time, although a strict framework was laid down to separate academic from political expression, the intellectuals used their academic freedom in some cases to launch, by historical analogy, subtle criticisms of the Maoist policies they considered responsible for the economic depression. There is little question that Chou supported these liberalization policies, as did many of his more outspoken lieutenants on the State Council, such as Ch'en I. But when Mao abruptly terminated the policy in the summer of 1962 because of the opposition it had permitted, he immediately and unquestioningly acquiesced, as did most of the other leaders involved in that policy. Only P'eng Chen, Politburo member and Mayor of Peking, manifested reluctance over the campaign launched in the mid 1960s to purge the ranks of the intellectuals of political dissidents. His resistance was the immediate precipitant of the Great Proletarian Cultural Revolution.

The Great Leap Forward

Who was responsible for the Great Leap Forward, what was its purpose, and why did it fail? To answer the first question, it seems clear that the main moving force behind the Leap was the Chairman, who was probably the primary source of innovation in Chinese politics since the CCP's rise to national power in 1949. Chou En-lai retreated into the background, maintaining a guarded neutrality that would allow him to shift with the currents as events unfolded. Neither his

report nor that of his deputy (Ch'en Yun) to the Third Plenum of the Eighth Central Committee was published, and in April 1959 in his speech to a National People's Congress session he emphasized the need for centralized leadership over local industry and a pressing need to consolidate the People's Communes. Mao's principal supporters seem to have been Liu Shao-ch'i and the party bureaucracy. It is plausible that Mao's retirement from his position as chief of state on Liu's behalf in December 1958 was Mao's way of purchasing Liu's support for the Great Leap in the face of general reluctance to venture so bold a program. And as a reward, the Communist party was allowed to intervene in the implementation of many policies that had previously been undertaken by the state apparatus. Chou En-lai had opposed Mao's attempt to leap forward for the second time in a row, and it is perhaps no coincidence that he was replaced as Foreign Minister in February 1958. If so, however, he gave no hint of disappointment nor even diminished his activities in the foreign policy field.

If Mao's role as prime mover in the Leap cannot be denied, it is also important to recognize that his purposes were more than a product of subjective megalomania, an interpretation that has subsequently gained favor in the light of the Leap's obvious failure. As noted, although industry, particularly heavy industry, had expanded rapidly during the first Five-Year Plan, agriculture had not responded nearly so well, and it was becoming clear in the latter stages of the plan that there was a bottleneck in the agricultural sector, which supplied most of the raw materials for light industry and the exports needed to pay for industrial imports and for new capital investment. Thus the leadership was torn between its desire to continue its successful industrialization program and its awareness that industrialization could not proceed indefinitely without diverting more resources to the agricultural sector. Mao's Great Leap was in effect an attempt to do both things at once: industrialization would continue, but new investment would take place in the rural countryside, and it would rely chiefly on labor rather than on capital investment, utilizing the underemployed pool of rural farm labor.

Vast water conservation and irrigation projects were organized in the winter of 1957–1958, mobilizing 100 million people on an unprecedented scale. These projects quickly soaked up the surplus labor and even created a shortage, which was exacerbated by the campaign to build small-scale native industries (such as back-yard steel refineries) in the rural areas in the spring of 1958. Clearly the collectives were too small a unit of organization to administer these vast numbers, and moreover, the shortage of labor required a change in rural organization to permit women to work in the fields while their husbands were engaged in the construction and operation of small factories. It was on this basis that the People's Communes were launched. The first commune was reportedly initiated voluntarily on an experimental basis in Honan in April 1958, and after Mao remarked to a reporter, "The People's Commune is good!" during a tour of the province, the nationwide movement to establish communes spread with lightning speed. By September of the same year, more than 90 percent of all peasant households in China belonged to communes. The smallest commune embraced about ten times the land and population as contained in an advanced APC, and all property was communally owned. The commune offered the putative advantage of combining industry and agriculture as well as education and military affairs, obtaining greater output by improved rural organization, greater economies of scale, and increased investment funds.

The Great Leap collapsed as a result of a coincidence of natural disasters, to which the leadership gave most of the blame, and organizational mismanagement, to which the peasantry and Western economists gave most of the blame. The dissolution of private plots and the communist wind of egalitarianism that swept away material incentives in favor of barracks communism reduced the incentives of middle peasants to produce, and productivity fell. The faith in mass voluntarism and the denigration of expertise resulted in the construction of water conservation and irrigation projects without prior geological exploration, converting millions of acres into alkaline land. The statistical system collapsed under the pressure to report more optimistic results to the leadership, making planning impossible. Many of the products of the new factories were of inferior quality, while machinery in the established enterprises was overtaxed and often ruined by the high quotas.

The Communist leadership began its retreat from the Leap as early as December 1958, but this retreat was then briefly reversed by a manifestation of high-level opposition to Mao. On July 14, 1959, P'eng Teh-huai wrote a long memorandum tactfully, but devastatingly, outlining his criticisms of Mao's leadership. Throughout the month of July there was heated discussion as the lines were drawn between the P'eng and Mao contingents. Mao grudgingly accepted partial blame, but considered P'eng's criticisms illegitimate because P'eng had voiced no objections when the programs in question had been approved, waiting until they had failed before objecting. Mao also alleged that P'eng had engaged in conspiratorial faction building and had sought support in the Soviet Union for his position.

These considerations were sufficient to secure P'eng's dismissal as Defense Minister, but not wholly persuasive. Chou En-lai, Liu Shao-ch'i, and the rest of the leadership rallied to Mao's support in the dismissal of P'eng, but then endorsed a series of revisions to Great Leap programs that tacitly suggested the validity of many of P'eng's criticisms and led to a revival of controversy over the general question of "revisionism" in the 1960s.

The Specter of Revisionism

The Great Leap Forward and concurrent poor weather precipitated the most serious economic depression to hit China since 1929. At the low point of 1960–1962, gross national output dropped by 20–30 percent from the high point reached during the Leap, per capita income by roughly 32 percent, and industrial production by 40–45 percent. Although the Great Leap Forward was at no time publicly repudiated, the next three years witnessed a gradual, but comprehensive, rollback of its programs. In November 1960 the party dispatched a secret directive restricting the power of the commune and making the smaller brigade the operational unit of planning, production, and accounting; two years later, the production team became the basic accounting unit. In effect, this signified a retreat to the level of collective organization under the lower-level agricultural producers' cooperatives, since both units had about 20 households. Under the pressure of a large budgetary deficit, the many small educational institutions that had been set up in the communes and factories in order to expand educational opportunity were abandoned, leaving only the quality schools in operation and eliminating

the prospect of education for those unable to pass the entrance exams to these elite institutions. The small private plots were restored, and a rural free market, in which their produce could be exchanged, was allowed to develop. Because of the pervasive disillusionment that made idealistic incentives implausible, material incentives were introduced to both industrial and agricultural workers, making it possible for those who worked hardest or had better resource endowments to acquire incomes substantially higher than those who did not.

All of these measures were concessions to China's depression and budgetary deficit that would probably not have been tolerated under normal circumstances, because they diverged from Communist ideological objectives. Or at least this was the view of the Maoists. But the Maoists also sensed that a powerful contingent of the leadership had become so committed to this recovery program that they were unwilling to lead the nation onward along the road to communism even after the economy showed signs of reviving. Given the vastness and complexity of the bureaucratic hierarchy, they did not seem to be clear about who belonged to this contingent, so they reviled them in the abstract as revisionists or "Party persons in authority taking the capitalist road." Mao himself retired from active participation in managing the economy during this period, while he and his most intimate advisers occupied themselves with theoretical concerns. Thus they felt they could absolve themselves from the politics they condemned.

Chou En-lai's role in this implicit contradiction between the forces of institutionalization and of revolution was characteristically one of a balancer. While remaining an active participant in the formation and implementation of policy during this ideologically tainted period, he at the same time joined spiritedly in the rhetorical repudiation of revisionism, thus taking care to define himself outside this abstraction, whose substantive content had not yet been defined. For example, two enlarged party and Central Committee work conferences (attended by no less than seven thousand party officials) were held in January–February 1962. At both conferences, Chou En-lai and Lin Piao apparently backed Mao's program and called for the more intensive study of Mao's thought to solve various problems. Liu Shao-ch'i, however, contrasted the "very favorable . . . political situation" described by Mao in his address with what he termed a "very unfavorable" economic situation. He also called for greater democracy within the party and the right to dissent in intraparty discussions, which could be construed as an attempt to reverse the verdict on P'eng Teh-huai. And again in his report to the Third National People's Congress held in Peking from December 21, 1964, to January 4, 1965, Chou En-lai bitterly denounced those in rural areas who had taken advantage of "temporary difficulties" in the past to expand the area of private enterprise at the expense of the collective economy. He added that it was "imperative to revolutionize the leading Party and government organs at all levels and likewise our cadres at all levels," a statement hinting in advance of Chou's sympathy for Mao's revolutionary aspirations.

It seems to have been the unsuccessful Socialist Education Movement, more than anything else, that brought class struggle to an acute stage and revealed the location of the party persons in authority taking the capitalist road to be within the top ranks of the leadership. Though the movement was launched with the dissemination of Mao's "First Ten Points" in May 1963, it never really gathered momentum because of con-

troversies among the leadership as to its method of implementation. Mao Tse-tung favored the broad mobilization of the poor and lower-middle peasants through peasant associations, whereas Liu Shao-ch'i, Teng Hsiao-p'ing, and the second line of the leadership (in charge of practical implementation of Mao's policies) tried to circumvent this policy because it threatened to alienate the productive middle peasants and to split the party apparatus. Instead, they proposed the extensive use of party work teams sent down from the higher levels to aid in the reorganization of local party committees. Chou En-lai prudently evaded the entire controversy, except to issue a general repudiation of capitalist tendencies in the countryside. By January 1965 the conflict between Mao Tse-tung and Liu Shao-ch'i seemed to have reached an acute stage, leading Mao to issue this warning:

The key point of this movement is to rectify those people in positions of authority within the Party who take the capitalist road, and progressively to consolidate the socialist battlefront in the urban and rural areas. Of those Party persons in authority taking the capitalist road, some are in the open and some are at the higher levels. . . . Among those at higher levels, there are some people in the commune districts, hsien, special districts, and even in the provincial and Central Committee departments, who oppose socialism.[5]

[5] On January 12, People's Daily, the official party newspaper, started running a series of articles by intellectuals developing two main themes. First, while the CCP policy toward intellectuals was generally sound, many cadres did not attempt to help the intellectuals with their political problems, did not associate with them, did not trust them, and even looked down on them. Second, many improvements were needed in the intellectuals' living and working conditions.

The Great Proletarian
Cultural Revolution

Roots of the Cultural Revolution
Much of Western sociology places institutionalization at one end of a polar continuum at the opposite side of which is anomie, or anarchy. For example, Huntington defines institutionalization as "the process by which organizations and procedures acquire value and stability," contrasting it with "a Hobbesian world of unrelenting competition among social forces." [6] But within the Marxist sociological tradition, institutionalization is viewed with ambivalence. It tends to be contrasted with revolution and equated with a trade-union mentality and false consciousness, a way of deluding people about their true interests so that they accept the status quo. Well imbued with the suspicions implicit in such a perspective, Mao and his colleagues have retained a good deal of ambivalence about the institutionalization of their revolution. On the one hand, they wish to establish the revolution securely against the constantly impending threat that it will somehow be reversed or devalued, as they feel that the Yugoslav and Soviet revolutions have been. On the other, they suspect that in thus establishing the revolution, they are inadvertently creating an Establishment: a vast, Kafkaesque bureaucracy without a human face.

Because of their fundamental ambivalence about institutionalization, the Communist leadership is apt to view systemic crises quite differently than they are viewed in the West. Whereas Western pluralist democracies typically view crises as disequilibrating interruptions in the process of orderly growth—per-

haps an inevitable consequence of the tendency to suppress problems on behalf of stability, but dangerous all the same—many in the Communist leadership seem to view crises as political situations in which the masses can be led to accept radical reforms that they would not accept under more normal circumstances. Hence the more radical Chinese Communist leaders try not to suppress or even merely to manage crises, but to exploit or even precipitate them, in order to effect fundamental changes. In the ensuing atmosphere of general alarm, the masses can be persuaded to accept sacrifices and to contribute goods or labor they would not ordinarily consider necessary. Thus the campaign against alleged American germ warfare during the Korean War was used to justify launching an annual Patriotic Health Drive. Thus were crises induced throughout the 1950s at regular intervals in order to create mass movements whose objectives were to educate the participants and to implement reforms outside the formal bureaucracy. Chou En-lai is not by nature the type of leader deliberately to precipitate a crisis, but he has proved indispensable in steering the movement toward its objectives in the midst of crises while preventing the situation from getting out of hand.

The Great Leap Forward convinced Mao that further progress toward socialism could not be achieved until the people's thinking was changed; he took an increasingly idealistic perspective on the course of human history and called for a cultural revolution to chart the course for further changes in the material infrastructure. But a majority of the leadership gave culture much lower priority in the scheme of things. These men seem to have concluded that the nation could not afford artificially induced crises for the time being, and they thus quietly frustrated Mao's attempt to precipitate another. When

[6] Samuel P. Huntington, *Political Order in Changing Societies* (New Haven, Conn.: Yale University Press, 1968), chap. 1.

Mao unilaterally triggered the Cultural Revolution, the subsequent mass movement thus coincided with an unresolved cleavage among the leadership. Because of their failure to cooperate with the movement, Mao turned the masses against them and finally purged them. But Mao's purpose was not merely to eliminate rival leaders, a goal that could have been achieved more simply and quickly some other way, but to encourage the masses to criticize the line attributed to those to be purged, thereby reflexively committing the people to the realization of a contrary, "revolutionary" line.

The Cultural Revolution provides an excellent opportunity to observe Chou En-lai as a crisis manager in action. As one of the largest and most ambitious mass campaigns to date, which in its course opened to question some of the basic premises on which the Chinese Communist regime was founded, the Great Proletarian Cultural Revolution constitutes a watershed in Chinese politics.

Sparks of Revolutionary Uprising
The Cultural Revolution was launched conventionally enough through bureaucratic channels in September 1965 and took on its radically iconoclastic character only later, as Mao grew impatient with the officials he had chosen to launch it. The man Mao selected to launch the movement was P'eng Chen, who had distinguished himself in denouncing Soviet revisionism and rectifying Peking Opera. P'eng Chen was also Mayor of Peking, however, with a long liberal record toward the intellectuals. And one of the men Mao specifically mentioned as a prospective target in the campaign was Wu Han, P'eng Chen's Vice Mayor and a former intellectual satirist of Mao Tse-tung. If P'eng Chen displayed considerably less enthusiasm in criticizing this revisionist on his own municipal party committee (and he did), this was be-

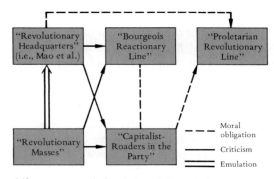

The purpose of the Cultural Revolution

cause Wu Han's purge would tend to cast a pall on P'eng's own position as Wu Han's patron. So when a young polemicist wrote an article attacking Wu Han, P'eng Chen refused to publish it. Even after P'eng learned that Mao himself was behind the critique, he refused to publish—a measure of the erosion of Mao's authority. Only after Mao had the article published in the Shanghai paper, *Liberation Army Daily,* did Peking publish it, even then attempting editorially to minimize its impact.

For the next few months P'eng Chen continued to pursue a Janus-faced policy of criticizing Wu Han enough to placate Mao, but not enough to necessitate Wu's purge or any other changes in his organization. Mao continued to increase the pressure on P'eng Chen, with a mounting sense of frustration. In February 1966, P'eng sought to bring the criticism movement to a close by drafting an "Outline Report on the Current Academic Situation," which limited debate to the academic community and sought to avoid a political conclusion. Throughout the entire winter of 1965–1966, Chou En-lai was conspicuously absent from the scene.

Then, in the spring of 1966, the movement finally began to gain momentum, as university and high school students began participating in mass demonstrations against Wu Han and other dissident intellectuals.

At a meeting of the Central Committee Secretariat held April 9–12, Chou En-lai joined other members of the leadership in criticizing P'eng Chen for grave errors, including opposition to the Chairman. "Concerning P'eng Chen," Chou En-lai recalled in a later speech, "the Party Central carried out debates for as long as twelve days in continuation, and upon P'eng Chen's personally recognizing his crimes, the Central decided, for the first time, that he is an anti-Party element."

P'eng Chen disappeared from the public eye at the end of March. On April 30, Chou lauded Mao's thought no less than eleven times in a speech to a visiting Albanian delegation and warmly praised the Cultural Revolution, publicly signaling his support for the forthcoming campaign. P'eng's purge—and the attendant reorganization of the Peking municipal committee and the Propaganda Department of the Central Committee—was announced without further explication to a stunned nation on June 1. This precipitated the mobilization of students on the campuses, first occurring in Peking and the large cities, then radiating from the urban centers throughout the country.

Chou En-lai participated only briefly in the Cultural Revolution in June–July 1966, when Liu Shao-ch'i and Teng Hsiao-p'ing, as acting leaders of the Central Committee during Mao's absence from Peking, sent work teams down to the schools and local government units to supervise the movement. But during his brief participation he saw enough to sense that the movement was not being implemented as Mao intended. He joined a party task force on May 26 to assess the situation on the Peking University campus after the first big-character poster had been posted there and undertook other inspection trips in early June. "The Chairman has not been in Peking in several weeks and is thus not responsible for the comrades who badly interpret his instructions, and in particular he does not know about the work teams sent to the universities and municipal governments," he said, drawing a clear line between the Chairman and the acting Liu-Teng leadership. He then departed on a convenient diplomatic trip to Eastern Europe.

By early August, when Chou returned to Peking to attend the Eleventh Plenum of the Eighth Central Committee, the whole character of the Cultural Revolution had changed dramatically. Mao Tse-tung had returned to Peking in late July and, after a brief inspection tour, had roundly denounced Liu's and Teng's handling of the situation on the campuses, calling for an immediate withdrawal of work teams. In the course of the plenary session, the rank order of the Politburo was changed, demoting Liu Shao-ch'i from second to eighth place in the listings. In the sixteen points issued on August 8 as an agenda for the forthcoming campaign, there were indications that Chou En-lai's influence had been heeded in its drafting: points two, three, and five promised that the public criticism would be directed against the party (not the government). In points twelve and fourteen, certain occupational groups, scientists and technicians, were specifically exempted from participation in the Cultural Revolution. And an explicit connection was made between the movement and the need to stimulate production, a theme Chou was to reemphasize repeatedly in the coming months.

The Spreading Prairie Fire
As the news spread across the country that Chairman Mao himself had donned one of the armbands of the young Red Guards, thus giving public sanction to their attacks on constituted authority, young people in different parts of the country all thronged to form Red Guard units of their own and to join the revolution. The transportation system was

soon glutted with young rebels who were traveling across the country to make liaisons with other groups or to tour various revolutionary sites. The revolutionary activities of the young rebels initially consisted of the desecration of symbols of traditional authority (such as religious shrines or the homes of China's residual bourgeoisie), but their movement underwent a radicalizing trend that soon brought them into conflict with the moderates in the Communist party. Chou's basically pragmatic outlook and his paramount interest in preserving the continuity of essential government functions during this period made him a natural ally of the revisionists who came under attack. If this is true, why did Chou neither prevail in subduing the young rebels nor fall victim to their criticisms?

The answer is that while Chou may have been in Liu Shao-ch'i's corner concerning general policy line and political style, he differed with Liu in his approach to the question of law and order, adopting a much more flexible strategy of response. Whereas Liu seemed willing to stand or fall with the Leninist party system, Chou made survival his *sine qua non*, abandoning one policy position after another as soon as it looked untenable. Thus he avoided involvement in the sort of polarizing conflict spiral that destroyed Liu. Chou En-lai explained his strategy of survival during the Cultural Revolution with unusual candor: one's "personal opinions," he said, should "advance or beat a retreat" according to the decision of the majority. In other words, one should "shift with the wind." "The one danger is a tendency to turn conservative." Chou had already exhibited his characteristically supple way of dealing with such difficulties as early as 1945. When he was in Chungking, a mob of students demonstrating against the Russians for plundering Manchuria after the Japanese surrender turned their rage upon

the local Communist mission, and Chou's office was besieged. "We must be patient," he warned his staff coolly;

We must be ready to give in to them, and we must at all costs avoid bloodshed. Otherwise we shall be falling into the trap of the enemy. If they break in, we retreat. If they enter the front gate, we withdraw to the hall. If they come into the hall, we go upstairs.[7]

A quantitative analysis of Chou's public appearance during the first year of the Cultural Revolution suggests that he functioned as a fireman, appearing most frequently during revolutionary high tides, to cajole, reprimand, pacify, or compromise with the radicals and retiring from public view during periods of conservative retrenchment. He adopted a diplomatic forensic style in his many speeches to the Red Guards, initially agreeing wholeheartedly with what his audience was doing and then going on to suggest that they do something else, often the opposite of what they were in fact doing. He continually endeavored to draw subtle distinctions that would break down the simplistic black-white, all-or-nothing categories of the polemics—for example, subdividing the "capitalist-roaders" into those who had merely "made mistakes" and those who were "counter-revolutionary," with the obvious purpose of saving the former. And he made use of his access to the Chairman (he was the only moderate leader to retain such access) to report and thereby subtly reinterpret Mao's "latest instructions." Though Mao was the leader of the Cultural Revolution, he himself did not appear before the revolutionary masses again after his ceremonial appearances to Red Guard rallies in the fall of 1966, nor did he make a speech of more

[7] Lung Fei-fu, *Eleven Years with Vice-Chairman Chou* (Peking: Foreign Languages Press, 1955).

than a few sentences, and this permitted the thought of Mao Tse-tung to emerge primarily through the mouths of those close to him. Mao himself retired to his official residence near Peking and even complained that the Red Guards made too much racket criticizing his neighbor, Liu Shao-ch'i.

An examination of Chou's speeches in the fall of 1966 illustrates how he used the resources at his command to calm the rising torrent. As the Red Guards began to sally forth to the streets in mass demonstrations, traveling to all parts of the country to spread the flames of revolution, Chou admonished them to remain in their own cities, work units, and schools. He added that they should not try to invade the factories or government offices to incite revolution there, should not use newspapers or radio stations or propaganda organs, and should not take it upon themselves to purge officials. In contrast to Lin Piao and to the radical members of the Cultural Revolution Group (CRG), Chou tended to play down the struggle-between-two-lines theme and initially his impulse was even to defend Liu Shao-ch'i and Teng Hsiao-p'ing. Most of the State Council directives issued in the course of the Cultural Revolution were also meant to restrict the scope of mass mobilization and to protect central leaders from attack. Because the enforcement machinery of the government broke down under the onslaught, most of these directives were quite ineffectual, however, and the success of Chou's resistance came to depend more on his personal political skills than on his institutional power base.

Movement to Seize Power
The power seizure movement climaxed the Red Guard invasion of the factories and mines that took place at the end of December 1966 for the purposes of spreading the revolution to the workers. It was soon found that isolated enterprises could not be seized

without seizing those who controlled them, and the Red Guards began seizing municipal governments and finally provincial governments and central government ministries; virtually every political organization in China became liable to a power seizure.

The power seizure movement seems to have started at the factory level as a way of satisfying radical demands while putting the factories back into operation. Workers had taken advantage of the general breakdown in authority to extort higher wages from their frightened management, who was happy to raise wages if it would waylay further criticism, writing off the expense to radical disruption. Chou called this tendency to succumb to workers' demands "economism" and encouraged the workers to seize power in the factories in order to end it. Economism had to be arrested because it was bad for production, and the purpose of the Cultural Revolution, according to Chou, was to increase production. But only certain groups would be permitted to seize power, namely, those who qualified to run the factory after they had seized it. Chou recommended first of all that the rebels organize in advance according to profession or industry, depending on the local situation; only after there was unity and proper organization could a power seizure take place. Second, power seizures had to be carried out by members of the unit in question, and outside agitators were thus precluded. Preferably the power seizure should take place before the rebels had the chance to link up with a national organization, which would place the rebel group under cross-pressures once they had seized power. Finally, the rebels should bear in mind that the purpose of the power seizure was to restore production in the unit in question and not to simply use that unit as a steppingstone to a more general power seizure, which was certainly not necessary seventeen years after the

Chou En-lai addresses the Red Guards

(New China News Agency, Peking)

Communists had seized national power.

Whereas the radicals viewed the Cultural Revolution as a revolutionary struggle aimed at power seizure at the highest levels from the very beginning, Chou viewed it as a "chain reaction" that was exploited by radicals who "wanted to bombard the powerholders whether or not they were powerholders taking the capitalist road." He construed the proper function of the Cultural Revolution not as a real revolution by the proletariat against the bourgeoisie, but rather as a dress rehearsal for a future occasion when political power might fall into the hands of the revisionists. He did this by exploiting the logical inconsistency of the radical position, in insisting at once that revisionists had usurped command while simultaneously recognizing that Chairman Mao had been in command uninterruptedly for the last thirty years.

There was a natural tendency for the Red Guards to wish to proceed from word to deed, from the criticism of the capitalist-roaders to their humiliation and purge. Chou sought to forestall this process by drawing a distinction between the error committed by the official in question, which could become the symbol of mass controversy, and the official in person, who could remain on the job while his error was fully aired in public. Thus on January 8, Chou En-lai turned his back on a rebel audience when there were shouts of "Down with Liu Shao-ch'i and Teng Hsiao-p'ing" and only turned around again when there was a call to overthrow the reactionary line of Liu and Teng. "There is some difference in the slogans that you shouted just now," he explained.

We should thoroughly criticize the bourgeois reactionary line represented by Liu and Teng, and we should smash it. However, the other slogan is open to question. Under the decision made by the 11th Plenum of the Central Committee, these two men are still Party Central Committee Standing Committee members. I am speaking to you, representing the Party. Your shouting that slogan in my face places me in a difficult position.[8]

In the same speech, Chou tried to protect five of his Vice Premiers on the State Council who had come under criticism, and throughout the Cultural Revolution he continued vigorously to defend those Vice Premiers, Ministers, Vice Ministers, state committee chairmen, and their deputies who were most important to the successful operation of the State Council, even when they had been associated with revisionist policies. Though he allowed Ch'en I (who openly defended Liu Shao-ch'i before the Red Guards) to be publicly criticized, he kept him on the job under the pretext that he could not be purged without the approval of the Central Committee. Eventually he was to lose T'an Chen-lin and Po I-po to the rebels, but only after a defense in depth.

Not only were the highly visible central leaders attacked—and the local and provincial committees, which were equally visible to their own local constituencies—but there were also power seizures within Chou's own government ministries, which threatened his own immediate power base in exactly the same way that the attack on Wu Han threatened P'eng Chen. And Chou's response was really not essentially different from P'eng Chen's: he resisted. But he resisted more skillfully, more subtly, and more sucessfully. Unlike P'eng Chen or Liu Shao-ch'i, he engaged in direct negotiations with the elite patrons of the radicals, the Cultural Revolution Group, and the leaders of the People's Liberation Army, ingratiating himself with them by becoming an adviser to the CRG

[8] *Mainichi* (Tokyo), January 11, 1967.

and attending the expanded conferences of the Military Affairs Committee.

Having appeased the elite leaders of the rebel groups, Chou was prepared to deal forcibly with the rebels. He formed a number of supervisory committees, staffed by a mixture of radicals and State Council personnel, to preside over the various functional systems under the central bureaus; and any power seizures at the central level that did not meet with the approval of the appropriate committee were suppressed. He tried to prohibit the participation of outsiders in bureau power seizures, except as observers. Certain bureaus that he deemed critical to

national security he placed off limits altogether: the Ministry of Public Security, the Ministry of Finance, the Science and Technology Commission, all central news media, and all banks—but by the same token he advocated a thorough power seizure in those organizations that had no functional work, such as the Communist Youth League or the Federation of Women.

The first condition for determining whether power should be seized in a particular unit was thus that it should not disrupt vital services. The second criterion had to do with whether the masses had been thoroughly mobilized in advance. It will be

Organization of the government of the People's Republic of China

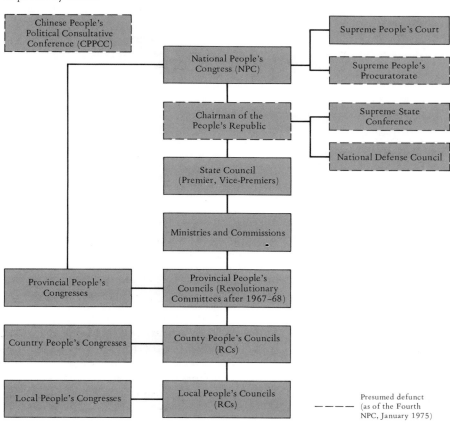

Presumed defunct
– – – – (as of the Fourth
NPC, January 1975)

noticed that neither criterion had anything to do with the ideological question of whether a unit was in fact led by capitalist-roaders, which was the essential issue for the radicals, who would not hesitate to seize power again if they felt that those who had first seized it were not true leftists. When the radicals complained about the sham power seizures made by the moderate mass organizations, Chou replied: "One should not talk in absolute terms, this one is false and that one is true. Often the appearance of matters is not clear. . . . The problem of whether [power seizure] is real or false should be solved through compromise." The Agricultural Ministry, for example, underwent what the radicals regarded as the "model of a sham power seizure," but Chou supported the rightist Red Guards who had come to power. In a confidential interview, Chou warned them that "still there will be a struggle for counter-power seizure. You must firmly fight that battle." He showed undisguised disgust with radicals who expelled party members from the party although they themselves were not even party members.

At present [students] of schools do not pay any attention to study, and just like to go out and put up big-character posters, sometimes opening a big rally of several ten-thousand people without much preparation. . . . The big-character poster becomes a simplistic slogan: the movement has been promoted for half a year but it cannot drift in such a way any more.[9]

[9] *Hung-se chan-pao* [Red Battle News], February 17, 1967; cited in Hong Yung Lee, "The Political Mobilization of the Red Guards and Revolutionary Rebels in the Cultural Revolution," Ph.D. diss. (University of Chicago, 1973). I owe much of my information on Red Guard activities to Lee.

The February Adverse Current

By the end of January, the Red Guards and Revolutionary Rebels had succeeded in seizing power in about half of China's provinces, and yet several factors made the consolidation of power far more difficult. Because the radical criteria for power seizure were ideological—concerning which there was a consensus on general principles but not at all on specifics—once power had been seized, another rebel faction would often call it sham and attempt to seize it again. Moreover, the young rebels had no experience in running the organizations they had seized, as Chou pointed out. To the radicals who seized the power of the Ministry of Railways he said tauntingly: "You cannot relinquish power. You can neither assign it to the lower level nor submit it to me. I won't accept it even if you give it to me. You must stand on your own feet." Thus it quickly became obvious that the failure of the rebels to formulate radical organizational alternatives to the existing set of arrangements was a salient weakness in their program. The "Paris Commune" they tried to set up according to the notions of CRG Chairman Ch'en Po-ta proved impracticable because it renounced any reliance on experienced cadres and was unable to deal with the problem of factionalism. Chou En-lai took advantage of this Achilles' heel in the rebel program to articulate his own alternative organizational structure: the Revolutionary Committee. Comprising a combination of rebel faction representatives, PLA men, and liberated civilian cadres (that is, those who had repented), this form of organization made certain concessions to the rebels, while adult officials were in most cases able to maintain majority control.

In the adverse current that followed the decision to make the Revolutionary Committee the organizational objective of the

Cultural Revolution, conservative cadres launched a strong counterattack on the young rebels. In a series of meetings of the party center held at Huaijent'ang around the middle of February 1967, these cadres gave vociferous expression of their grievances to the Chairman, evoking bonds of loyalty based on shared experiences dating from the Long March to protest the public humiliation of veteran cadres. Mao responded with a number of concessions: the polemics should be more genteel and well reasoned, targets should henceforth be limited to "dead tigers," raids on government files (to collect incriminating "black materials") were prohibited, and Red Guards were ordered to return to their homes to make revolution while increasing production.

But in putting these policies into effect, conservative cadres either misjudged Mao's intentions or overstepped the bounds of his tolerance, taking advantage of their temporary upper hand to suppress and punish the young rebels and to launch a sweeping reversal of verdicts to rehabilitate purged officials. For example, though the Revolutionary Committee was Chou's own idea, he succeeded in preventing any from being set up in any State Council organ with the exception of the State Committee on Science and Technology, and he also excluded the army from participating in State Council affairs. Although nearly every ministry or committee experienced a power seizure, they did so only with Chou's explicit authorization, and the postrevolutionary organization was based on a restoration of the Party Committee. When a young Vice Minister led a power seizure in the Ministry of Finance without Chou's permission, Chou had him arrested.

The Wuhan Incident

In response to rising rebel protests against conservative retrenchment policies in Feb-

ruary and in "Black March," a series of meetings was held in the Politburo and Military Affairs Committee in the last two weeks of March. There it was decided that the rebels should be permitted to launch another general offensive. This time, however, the mass media were intended to function as a Pied Piper for rebel criticisms, leading them in a coordinated attack on the bourgeois reactionary line of Liu and Teng and thereby distracting them from factional fights or attacks on the army or additional cadres. The central propaganda apparatus, by then in the hands of the CRG, set up a writing group consisting of thirty polemical journalists to publish keynote articles on various topics that would be reproduced in magazines and newspapers throughout the country.

This attempt to contain and continue the revolution was unsuccessful, because the center was unable completely to control the publicity apparatus, let alone the myriad rebel organizations. From its beginning in June 1966 with the writings of big-character posters, a nationwide Red Guard press had developed (in some ways similar to the American underground press), publishing several hundred tabloid titles and countless pamphlets, all devoted almost entirely to polemics. These publications would appropriate the symbols disseminated by the central media for their own factional purposes, calling their opponents representatives of the line being denounced. When Mao announced that the Cultural Revolution was a continuation of the struggle between the CCP and the KMT, for example, each faction denounced the other as today's KMT; when the center called upon the Red Guards to practice more self-criticism, each faction would denounce the other for failing to practice self-criticism.

Thus factional warfare intensified continuously through the spring and summer of

1967, in many areas involving a coalition of moderate groups and the local PLA headquarters against a radical faction backed by the Cultural Revolution Group. This conflict reached a culmination in armed warfare in July and August, as the radical forces began raiding army headquarters or ammunition trains bound for Vietnam to seize weapons, having been encouraged by Chiang Ch'ing's slogan, "Attack non-violently, defend with force!" The Wuhan incident revealed graphically how close the nation was to civil war and resulted in a pause in the Cultural Revolution.

Two delegates from the center arrived in Wuhan on July 14, 1967, continuing an investigation mission that had already taken them to Chengtu, Chungking, and Honan provinces. In their function as arbiters, the two indicated that their sympathies lay with the radical minority. Thus they attempted to reverse verdicts in a locally famous case of a rebel headquarters that had been disbanded by the local PLA commander. This verdict was patently unacceptable to the local troop commanders, who at this point laid siege to the building and took the two representatives of the center into custody. Although this action was taken at the time to be tantamount to open insurrection against the center, the local military commanders may have been banking on support for their *fait accompli* from the central PLA leadership in Peking. In any case, Chou En-lai flew at once to Wuhan, deciding at the last moment to land at another airport south of the city because of rumors that the main airport had been blockaded by the One Million Heroes (a radical faction). In settling the incident, Chou flew to Wuhan altogether four times to negotiate. Finally he attained the release of the two captives, who returned to Peking for a hero's welcome.

When news of this incident spread, it in-cited widespread indignation focused on the PLA, and the various radical organizations took advantage of this to launch attacks on the army and other pillars of established authority. The upsurge of radicalism in Peking paralyzed the government ministries. Most seriously disrupted was the Ministry of Foreign Affairs under Ch'en I, who was unable to defend it because he personally was deluged by criticism. Ch'en had reasserted himself during the February Adverse Current by retracting his self-criticism under the pretext that it was given under duress and then by removing the radicals from his ministry. But in August the ministry was surrounded and blockaded by radicals who finally stormed the building and took over the ministry for five days (according to some reports, fifteen days). During this time, they "dispatched telegrams to foreign countries, sent notes to the country of XX, appointed diplomats to foreign countries, searched out and closed the Party Committee of the Foreign Ministry, and detained the vice-foreign ministers." Chou En-lai himself was trapped in his office in the Great Hall of the People for two days and nights by 500,000 leftist Red Guards who apparently wanted to lead a public struggle rally against him for his role in obstructing the purge of other rightist officials, and he was able to dissuade them only after negotiating incessantly with them, one delegation after another. Such a large movement could not have occurred in the heart of Peking without the knowledge of the CRG, the public security bureau, and the PLA, and yet the Maoist leadership made no effort to interfere until Chou had already persuaded his antagonists to disperse. The leftists posted big-character posters claiming that Mao considered Chou a former supporter of the International Faction and a dubious ally. But Mao (who had left the capital during this episode) wrote a letter in support of Chou, in which he revealed his ambivalence:

Several members of the CRG are very angry with Chou En-lai. It is mostly his habit of always combining and compromising that infuriates them. Recently, Red Guards began to criticize him in their big-character posters. Of course, no one would ever pretend that honesty is En-lai's main quality, but on the other hand he has proved to be extraordinarily useful. His talents make him practically irreplaceable in our Party . . . we should thus endeavor to keep him. Provided that he clearly dissociates himself from Liu Shao-ch'i and Teng Hsiao-p'ing we should, I think, associate him with our proletarian headquarters, and leave him a certain freedom of initiative. As to whether in the future we shall always be able to rely on his loyalty, this is a question to which only he can provide the answer.[10]

It was at about this time that the rightists reacted vigorously to the leftist tide that the Wuhan Incident had precipitated, and the balance of forces swung in Chou's favor once again. The CRG radicals who had called for a campaign to cleanse the ranks of the PLA of capitalist-roaders were removed from their mouthpiece, the party journal *Red Flag,* and purged. Although Chou now attacked the leftists openly, he also defended Chiang Ch'ing from the rightists, who wanted to take advantage of the situation to eliminate her, seeking to reconcile the PLA and the CRG. The CRG returned the favor by restraining the Peking radicals who had been attacking Chou. He also persuaded Mao to tour the provinces and to observe the chaotic conditions firsthand, as a result of

[10] Quoted in Simon Leys, "The Grand Master's Checkmate," *Far Eastern Economic Review* 87, no. 3 (January 17, 1975): 30–33.

which the Chairman also gave support to a moderation of the movement.

Thus, at the beginning of October, a campaign was launched against "anarchism, small-group mentality, sectarianism, individualism, and pragmatism in our ranks," a list of slogans that signified the leadership's desire to turn the spearhead of criticism away from the revisionist leaders and point it at the revolutionary masses. Throughout the fall and winter of 1967–1968, the consolidation continued. Fourteen provincial Revolutionary Committees were established between November 1967 and April 1968, and these bodies contained a lower proportion of mass representatives than did the six Revolutionary Committees that had been established during the revolutionary high tide from January to March 1967. In January 1968 the emphasis shifted from the Revolutionary Committee to party rectification, in manifest preparation for a reconstruction of the purge-weakened CCP. Chou En-lai announced on January 17 that "the working class is now to take the lead in revolution, just as the intellectuals and students did at an earlier stage," with the evident intention of demobilizing the most radical elements of the Red Guard movement. This coincided with a campaign against petty bourgeois factionalism, which the PLA used to justify suppressing the radicals, defining any group not represented in the Revolutionary Committees as a faction.

The Paradoxical Triumph of the Cultural Revolution

At the end of March 1968 a purge of the PLA leadership occurred, which was generally interpreted by the left to signify a vindication of their own position and a repudiation of the army's consolidation policies. On this cue, the ultraleftist groups that had been barred from participation on the Revolutionary Committees rose once again. The big-character posters and polemical tabloids, forbidden during the winter, reappeared, and mass rallies were held. But attempts by the CRG to lead the criticism movement in a nonviolent direction were even less successful than they had been the previous summer. The CRG again attempted to invoke Liu Shao-ch'i as a symbol for all grievances, but the Red Guard press made almost no mention at all of Liu Shao-ch'i in their increasingly vehement denunciations of their local opponents. The claim was generally made that the main contradiction was now between the Revolutionary Committees and the revolutionary masses, and that the former represented the new bourgeois authority that suppressed the latter. Serious struggle by force between opposing rebel groups or with the PLA was reported in many provinces in the summer of 1968, both sides using modern weapons.

By August, Mao Tse-tung had lost all patience with the young revolutionaries, and he decided to announce the victorious conclusion of the movement. To the radicals, this triumph was not without its ironies. To restore order to the movement, Mao called forth a vehicle similar to the one he had repudiated at its outset: the work team, now referred to as the worker-peasant propaganda team, was sent to each Red Guard and Revolutionary Rebel unit to hold "Mao Tse-tung Thought study classes," where the errors of that unit would be pointed out according to the team's interpretation of Mao's thought. Rather than being welcomed to the revolutionary leadership, radical organizations underwent voluntary disbandments, and their members were sent down to the countryside to do manual labor. At the Twelfth Plenum of the Central Committee in October 1968,

Liu Shao-ch'i was denounced for an unlikely series of villainies (which did not, however, include reference to anything that occurred after 1949, signifying the leadership's reluctance to tamper with the basic postliberation political structure) and thrown on the trash heap of history.

After the Revolution

What, finally, had the Cultural Revolution achieved? The Cultural Revolution was unique in that it was invoked from above, indeed by the leader of the government that became its principal target, but in many other respects its consequences were similar to those of other revolutions. Although the Red Guards themselves probably suffered the most grievous casualties, the political leadership was badly decimated: about two-thirds of the officials of the central bureaucracy were purged, including 68.5 percent of the 169 members of the Eighth Central Committee, 78.8 percent of the Politburo members, and 86.2 percent of the provincial first party secretaries. Chou En-lai's State Council survived with fewer losses than the party, but even so, nearly half the ministries were left without a politically active minister in command. The fallen officials were not killed or imprisoned, as they were during Stalin's great purge of the 1930s, but instead were sent to May 7 Cadre Schools, where they could reform through labor.

In addition to personal changes, there was considerable alteration of China's political and cultural institutions, though the economic system remained basically unchanged. The most important political change was the introduction of the Revolutionary Committee in place of the old governmental organizations, for the first time providing an authorized role for nonparty mass representatives in running the government. Nonparty members were also invited to participate in the "open-door rectification" sessions that accompanied the reconstruction of the party in 1971. The emphasis on greater mass participation (plus the decimation of the central bureaucracy) led to the devolution of certain major fields of responsibility—education and medicine in particular—to lower levels and the introduction of new procedures to keep the level of routine decision making at as low a level as possible. A campaign was launched in 1968 for better troops and simpler administration, resulting in the wholesale dismissal of secretarial and staff personnel and the simplification of China's immense bureaucracy. Chou En-lai boasted in 1970 that organs of the State Council had been reduced from ninety to twenty-six, with a corresponding cut in staff from sixty thousand to ten thousand—a reduction of more than 80 percent. (Actually, Chou seems to have exaggerated somewhat: of the fifty ministries known to have existed before 1966, twenty-one are known and seven presumed to have survived).[11]

In the cultural superstructure, even sanitized plays and novels featuring prerevolutionary heroes and villains were abolished and ten revolutionary model plays, revised by the masses under the supervision of Chiang Ch'ing, became the national standard for emulation. In the school system, primary and middle schools remained closed until 1969 and colleges until 1971–1972, while a major overhaul of admissions criteria and curriculum took place. Entrance examinations were abolished and replaced by ideological and class criteria for admission, including a minimum of two year's manual labor at a commune or factory. The curric-

ulum was revised to stress immediately practical subjects and to abbreviate course requirements. The politically suspect teaching staff was placed under surveillance by worker-peasant-soldier teams. Workers and peasants themselves taught some classes on practical subjects, while teachers participated part-time in manual labor, in order to abolish the distinction between mental and manual labor.

But the Cultural Revolution was unique not simply because it was invoked from above, but also because it was arbitrarily terminated from above. And it was terminated not because the revolutionary objectives had been fully achieved, but because the strife had become intolerably disruptive to the economic system on which the population relied for its subsistence. The revolution was thus left half-finished: the revolutionaries did not win power in the new administration, but were sent out to the communes to work, often for the rest of their lives. The main beneficiaries of the revolution were the last mainstays of discipline, the soldiers. As the demobilization of the radicals removed this countervailing force, and as Lin Piao was anointed as Mao's sole Vice Chairman and heir-apparent, China began to take on the aspect of a military dictatorship—still very dedicated to certain revolutionary goals, but only within the bounds of law and order.

The Quest for Postrevolutionary Equilibrium

In the eight years following the Cultural Revolution, Chinese politics has been dominated by two basic issues: how to reestablish a new equilibrium without reversing the changes that had been introduced by the

[11] Cf. Harry Harding, "The Organizational Issue in Chinese Politics, 1959–1972," Ph.D. diss. (Stanford University, 1973).

Cultural Revolution and how to provide for the succession to the declining first generation of revolutionary leadership in China.[12]

The first issue was created by the various trends that the Cultural Revolution had set in motion: rising expectations for greater economic rewards and political participation among formerly disprivileged groups, feelings of alienation and sometimes vengefulness among humiliated elites, insecurity and a felt need to push the revolution to its conclusion among those radicals who had attained tenuous positions within the leadership. Public conflict had been legitimated as a means of making policy decisions, but the upshot was an uncontrollable factionalism that was clearly incompatible with political stability and economic growth. Yet as soon as the Red Guards were demobilized, the radicals in the leadership found themselves isolated and left without a popular base. And the PLA members who supplanted civilian cadres in the regime proceeded to impose a military rule on the country that was much more strictly regimented than the civilian populace had been accustomed to. This period of austerity under Lin Piao's military stewardship lasted from 1968 to 1970–1971, and it was a period in which Chou remained on the sidelines.

But Lin Piao was one of those radicals who had risen to power through the Cultural Revolution and had felt his power ebb away with the demobilization of the mass movement, placing him in an uncomfortable position of total dependence on Mao Tse-tung. Rather than broadening his base of support by forming coalitions with other leaders or

factions, he alienated them by insisting on a punitive policy toward purged civilian cadres and by seeking to appoint PLA men to all vacant positions. Even the PLA was not entirely under his control, however; Mao began to challenge his command of the PLA, and indications began to appear that the eleven regional commands in China displayed considerable autonomy and could by no means be assumed to belong to Lin's loyalty group. Thus, although Lin had been named as Mao's heir-apparent in the Constitution drafted by the Ninth Party Congress in 1969, his continued sense of insecurity led him to try to consolidate his position. But Mao began to construe Lin's search for security as a threat to his own position and quickly took steps to render Lin impotent. Following the Second Plenum of the Ninth Central Committee in September 1970, where Lin first aroused Mao's suspicions by betraying an ambition to become Chief of State (a position that had remained vacant since the purge of Liu Shao-ch'i in 1968), the Chairman proceeded to purge some of Lin's supporters and to transfer others, leaving Lin in a severely weakened position.

At this point Lin Piao, aware that he had lost the Chairman's favor and probably faced public humiliation and purge, decided to resort to a desperate strategem. With the assistance of his son, his wife, and a few trusted military advisers, he began to plot a coup d'état to assassinate the Chairman and to seize power before his own fate was sealed. But the plot misfired, reportedly because Lin's own daughter informed Chou En-lai in time for the latter to take action, and Lin Piao and his co-conspirators, aware that they were in grave danger, hastily boarded a small jet and set off for the Soviet Union. On the night of September 12–13, 1971, their plane crashed in Outer Mon-

[12] The information in this section is collected from *The New York Times, Far Eastern Economic Review* (Hong Kong), and other current news media.

golia near the Soviet border; all passengers were killed.

In the criticism campaign that followed Lin's death it was alleged that Lin's betrayal and attempted coup were a continuation of the struggle between two lines; and, according to various commentators, a number of policies may have been in dispute between the two men: Lin may have opposed the *démarche* to the United States, advocated a more radical agricultural program, favored greater investment in heavy industry (particularly the military-industrial sector), and so forth. But to all appearances policy differences were less important than personal mistrust and a subsequent power struggle. Certainly this struggle had important policy implications, however. The most important of these was that the most powerful radical obstacle to the restoration of the status quo had been removed, and reconstruction of the CCP proceeded apace. By August 1971, within a year from Lin's fall from favor, party committees had been reestablished in all twenty-nine provinces. Just as the Ninth Party Congress in 1969 had symbolized the rise of Lin Piao and the PLA, the Tenth Party Congress in August 1973 marked the rise of Chou En-lai and the reassertion of civilian control: the proportion of Central Committee seats held by the military declined from 45 percent to 32 percent, and the number of military officers in the Politburo fell from ten to four. There was a sweeping rehabilitation of cadres who had been purged during the Cultural Revolution, and more rehabilitated cadres turned up in Chou's State Council than anywhere else, including no less than ten Ministers and fifty Vice Ministers. Undoubtedly the most startling of these rehabilitations was the reappearance of Liu Shao-ch'i's old crony Teng Hsiao-p'ing.

From 1971 to 1973, the bureaucratic right

thus co-opted the criticism themes against Lin Piao to launch a strong attack on the left, with the result that many of the programs introduced during the Cultural Revolution were partially rescinded. In agriculture, the radicals had paid no attention to concrete historical conditions, but sent orders down from above without regard for the desires of the masses. In industry, the "politics in command" slogan was misused and necessary rules and discipline were disregarded, the result of which was that production was impaired. In culture, production of new art was inhibited by sharp criticism of everything that was not perfect from the beginning, and artists did not dare to experiment. In education, the emphasis on practice resulted in a neglect of theoretical knowledge, and the quality of texts suffered from too frequent quotations of the thoughts of Mao, making them appear ludicrous.

But the radicals still had powerful resources at their command: from the cultural and propaganda ministries in Peking they controlled a major sector of the nation's propaganda apparatus, four of the radical leaders held positions in the party Politburo, and they could still count on the support of the Chairman. They launched their counterattack early in 1973, beginning by redefining Lin Piao's crimes as ultrarightism rather than ultraleftism so that the criticism of Lin could now be turned against the right. A campaign to criticize Confucius was launched, and the crimes of Confucius sounded suspiciously like the policies of Chou En-lai. Confucius sought to "restore old families" who had been deposed from the aristocracy and to "call back to office those who had retired into obscurity." The ancient sage was denounced as a "suave liar . . . skilful at compromising . . . crafty double-dealer . . . cultivating aristocratic tastes . . . always advocating moderation . . . always impeccably dressed." Though he was never named in these oblique attacks, Chou was clearly intended. The criticism gathered sudden momentum just before the convention of the Tenth Party Congress in 1973, deploring the evisceration of radical educational reforms and the other "new-born things" introduced by the Cultural Revolution and rousing the revolutionary masses to "go against the tide." This slogan, allegedly coined for the occasion by the Chairman himself, implied that the main current of the time was an erroneous one, and that blame could be attributed to "the fact that some bourgeois elements, careerists and conspirators have got a certain hold inside the Party."

Had Chou En-lai reacted to this affray by stiffening his position, as Liu Shao-ch'i did, he would probably have confirmed the suspicions of his accusers and have fallen. However, he adopted a far more subtle strategy containing elements of retreat (to placate the Chairman) and indirect counterattack (to keep the younger leftists at bay). Retreat was evident in his speech to the Tenth Party Congress, in which he defended and praised the "new-born things" of the Cultural Revolution and implied he would not permit further attempts to abridge them. He counterattacked by using his influence over the Peking media to co-opt, reinterpret, and finally emasculate the radical criticism themes. One could rebel, agreed the *Red Flag,* but this should always be done within the framework of party discipline:

To go against the tide and to observe Party discipline are two attitudes in complete harmony, for both of them have one common purpose: upholding the correct Party line. Our great leader Chairman Mao always dared to go against the tide; yet at the same time he was always maintaining resolutely the principle of centralized Party organization and respect for Party discipline. However, some chieftains of the opportunist line, in order to promote revisionism, constantly endeavor to sabotage these principles of Party organization and oppose Party discipline.[13]

This emphasis on discipline in the Peking press (which, of course, thwarted radical attempts to mobilize the masses outside party channels) was enthusiastically taken up by most provincial propaganda organs. To defuse the allegorical attack on Confucius, Chou linked this criticism to the ongoing campaign against Lin Piao, who was suddenly discovered to have been a covert worshipper of Confucius. The fact that the anti-Confucius movement was successively designated by three different names (first "denunciation of Confucius," then "denunciation of Confucius and Lin Piao," and finally "denunciation of Lin Piao and Confucius") reflects Chou's victorious progression in diverting, controlling, distorting, and neutralizing the movement. By February 1974 it had been conclusively established that "the denunciation of Confucius is nothing but a means to denounce Lin Piao." Although the radicals tried to revive the criticism movement in the spring and summer of 1974, the provincial authorities refused to follow them, and a wave of strikes by radical workers in a number of mines, factories, and railroads throughout the country served only to discredit the movement.

Chou En-lai on the World Stage

The Institutional Infrastructure
To begin at the top, there have been only two regular Foreign Ministers in the regime's

[13] *Red Flag* (Peking), no. 12 (December 1973).

514

history, Chou En-lai and Ch'en I, and Chou has maintained a guiding influence over foreign policy throughout, despite his replacement as Foreign Minister in 1958. In 1949 the Foreign Ministry was put together from the small circle of negotiators and propagandists who worked in four diplomatic operations prior to liberation. First and foremost was a liaison group headed by Chou En-lai in Chungking; second was a branch of the same group at Kweilin, which ran a news service. A third group worked out of Hong Kong, and a fourth was represented on the truce teams that the Marshall mission operated in northern China and Manchuria at the end of the war.

The Ministry of Foreign Affairs was formed in 1949 as one ministry under Chou's State Council, led by a Foreign Minister (Chou) and a variable number of Vice Ministers. Although the nature of the foreign policy-making process has of course been kept confidential, it is thought that decisive initiatives were (and are) made in the Politburo and that the Foreign Ministry is in charge of implementing these decisions. But the locus of routine foreign policy formation was (and remains) in the State Council. The larger Central Committee plenums seldom deal with foreign policy issues (except in the broadest sense), whereas the State Council frequently hears reports on foreign affairs. Over the years, Chou En-lai's voice was heard in direct pro-

Chou En-lai reports to the National People's Congress on Chinese foreign policy

(New China News Agency, Peking)

portion to the intensity of the crises that have arisen. Even after his resignation as Foreign Minister in 1958, he made major pronouncements during the Lebanese crisis of 1958, the Quemoy embroilment of the same year, and the Tibetan affair of 1959. Chou doubled as the Chinese equivalent of an American press secretary.

By the time the Foreign Ministry was a year old, the professional diplomats (including Ministers and department heads as well as personnel staffing the missions abroad) probably numbered no more than 150, plus another 100 technical personnel—interpreters, researchers, and so forth. By the mid-1960s, these figures had grown tenfold, perhaps twentyfold if the numerous people's organizations engaged in international relations are included. Yet there has been remarkable continuity at the top levels— only three purges have affected the Foreign Ministry since 1949, each involving relatively minor figures. During the Cultural Revolution purges, Foreign Ministry personnel dropped to a low point of one thousand, but by late 1972 the number had grown back to two thousand and was still expanding.

During the early years of the Cold War, geographic specialization within the ministry was simple, as was China's foreign policy: the world divided into socialist countries and "the rest," each under one Vice Minister. Later there was a division and subdivision of the world into more specialized departments. During and after the Cultural Revolution there was some simplification of this division of labor, but today there are four geographic departments (Asia, Eastern Europe, western Asia and Africa, and the West), plus several functional departments concerned with information, protocol, and so forth. The Foreign Ministry has developed good research facilities and an efficient security apparatus. There are a number of people's organizations operating in tandem

with the Foreign Ministry, such as the People's Institute for Foreign Affairs or the Association for Friendship with Foreign Countries. These associations serve a number of functions, for example, receiving certain guests on an unofficial basis and gathering information.

The first diplomats to be sent abroad were mainly ex-generals with little diplomatic experience, while those with greatest diplomatic talent remained at home in the ministry. To rectify the shortage of diplomatic personnel, immediate steps were taken in 1949. The Peking Foreign Languages College, the Russian Language School, the Institute of Diplomacy, and the Institute of International Relations of the Academy of Sciences (suspended since the Cultural Revolution) were all established to help train diplomatic cadres. By the early 1960s the Foreign Ministry had eliminated most of the ex-military men who had served in the early 1950s, and Chinese diplomats of the younger generation scored high in terms of language proficiency, knowledge of subject matter, negotiating ability and general personal affability; the Foreign Ministry was able to operate at a relatively high level of efficiency. The Communist bloc nations began in the 1960s to be used as a testing ground in the training of officials, while the better educated and more experienced people were placed in the non-Communist world.

In mid-December 1949, Mao went to Moscow for talks with Stalin, taking with him only a small group. On January 20, 1950, Chou arrived with a larger delegation, composed largely of officials from the economic organizations of the government. And at the Kremlin on February 14, 1950, Chou signed the thirty-year Sino-Soviet Treaty of Friendship, Alliance and Mutual Assistance, which formed the cornerstone of Chinese foreign relations during much of the next decade. The treaty provided for

Russian economic, technical, and military assistance to China amounting to $300 million (but not as much as the Chinese leaders wanted), affirmed the independent status of Outer Mongolia, and provided for the joint administration and ultimate transfer to China of the ports of Port Arthur and Dairen.

When the party first assumed power in 1949, they seemed to have ambivalent attitudes toward the establishment of diplomatic relations with non-Communist nations. Initially, most contacts concerning establishment of diplomatic relations were exchanged with Communist nations; those exchanged with non-Communist countries were worded to stress that "new China" was the complete master of its own house and would tolerate nothing less than absolute equality in its foreign relations. Chou also attempted to undercut the international standing of the Nationalist government in Taiwan, stipulating nonrecognition of the Nationalist regime as a precondition for establishing relations. Despite such preconditions, within the six months ending April 13, 1950, Chou had succeeded in establishing diplomatic relations with twenty-six nations, including eight Asian countries. China's initiatives on the diplomatic front might have attained further successes but for the outbreak of the Korean War in June 1950.

Chou is credited with intense but futile efforts to avert a direct Sino-American confrontation in Korea. Chinese intervention was probably motivated by defensive considerations. Encroachments on China's sovereignty by Western powers and by Japan had in the past begun with the annexation of outlying areas such as Indochina or Korea, and the Chinese apparently feared that American involvement in the Korean conflict might presage a foray into Manchuria. The United States for its part saw itself as acting to prevent yet another step in a coordinated international Communist plot to conquer the world. Despite President Truman's assurance that the United States had no intention to use its armed forces to intervene in China proper, when General MacArthur's forces reached the thirty-eighth parallel (then the dividing line between North and South Korea) and prepared to cross it, the Chinese threatened to intervene. On August 20, Chou cabled a warning to the United Nations: "Korea is China's neighbor. The Chinese people cannot but be concerned about the solution to the Korean question." On September 30, Chou issued a warning to Truman through the Indian Ambassador in Peking that China would send troops to North Korea's aid if the Americans crossed the thirty-eighth parallel. Convinced that the Chinese were bluffing, MacArthur launched his brilliant Inchon landing and drove north toward the Yalu River, which separated Korea from Manchuria. By mid-October, Chinese People's Volunteers were crossing the Yalu and taking up position on North Korean territory. A Communist counteroffensive forced MacArthur to retreat to the southern tip of Korea, but failed to defeat United Nations forces, and the Korean War soon developed into a seesawing, long-drawn-out, essentially stalemated struggle in which neither side seemed able to effect a victory. After two major, but unsuccessful, Chinese offensives in April–May 1951, truce talks began at Soviet initiative. The talks were to prove long, vituperous, and inconclusive; not until June 1953, after newly elected President Eisenhower threatened to use the atomic bomb, was a Korean armistice signed.

The Korean War was to consolidate the Sino-Soviet alliance and to freeze Sino-American relations for many years, contributing to the formation of a tight bipolar international system. The attack on South Korea led President Truman to interpose the

American Seventh Fleet between Taiwan and the mainland on grounds that a Communist occupation of Taiwan would threaten United States forces in the Pacific.

American negotiations with Japan, which had become an essential base and rear support area for United Nations forces in Korea, began immediately, leading to a peace treaty in 1951 and then to a Japanese-American mutual-defense treaty. Massive Soviet aid to both North Korea and China during the Korean War likewise brought about a close liaison between Moscow and Peking.

In March 1953, Chou went to Moscow for Stalin's funeral as head of the Communist delegation. At the funeral ceremony, he was permitted to walk abreast of the senior Soviet leaders just behind Stalin's bier, an honor that gave him precedence over all non-Soviet Communist leaders at the funeral ceremony. Stalin's death opened the way for the conclusion of the Korean War. Upon his return to Peking, Chou set forth new proposals on March 30, 1953, providing the basis for an agreement on the exchange of prisoners of war, signed on June 8, and for the armistice agreement, signed on July 27. The Chinese Communists had not won a clear-cut victory in Korea, but they had achieved their objective of preventing imperialist encroachment on their border in a contest with the world's mightiest industrial power, and Chou was to derive maximum political advantage from this situation in the international arena.

The Spirit of Bandung

In April 1954, when a conference of nine powers convened in Geneva to work out a settlement of the Indochinese conflict following the crushing French defeat at Dienbienphu, Chou attended his first meeting of world statesmen, in his first (and last) visit to an industrialized democracy since his student days in Japan and Western Europe.

He made a generally favorable impression by his calm, dignified manner, but when he offered his hand to the anti-Communist John Foster Dulles, the latter folded his arms stiffly behind his back and shook his head. Hoping to thwart Dulles' efforts to encircle and contain China with a ring of bases and alliances, Chou proposed an international guarantee of the neutrality of Southeast Asia. Dulles, however, insisted that Western troops were necessary in Indochina to deter Chinese aggression, pointing to the Chinese invasion of Korea in justification. Chou responded that Chinese intervention there had prevented the United States from "playing the old game of the Japanese militarists of invading Korea to establish a base for invasion of the mainland of China."

When no progress was made in the discussions over Korea, this phase of the conference was terminated on the initiative of the United States, and the nations with a direct interest in the Indochina conflict turned to this problem. June 23, 1954, French Premier Pierre Mendès-France and Chou En-lai drew up the framework of the basic agreement to be signed by representatives of France and the Viet Minh.

Chou En-lai's performance at Geneva won praise not only from the French, who welcomed his assistance in extricating themselves from a politically embarrassing situation, but also from more detached observers. The agreement also helped to buttress Chou's contention that the settlement of Asian political problems necessarily involved direct negotiations with the People's Republic of China. But the elections promised in the accords were never held, reportedly because President Eisenhower had been informed that Ho Chi Minh would win them. This led Chou En-lai to remark bitterly in 1971, "We were badly taken in during the first Geneva conference."

During the temporary adjournment of the

Geneva Conference in June–July 1954, Chou returned to Asia to hold talks with the Prime Ministers of India and Burma, two countries that had expressed interest in freeing themselves from tight bloc alignments and taking a more neutral position in world affairs. On June 28, Chou joined with Prime Minister Nehru of India in issuing the *Panch Shila* (five principles) that should guide relations between the two states: (1) mutual respect for each other's territorial integrity and sovereignty; (2) nonaggression; (3) noninterference in each other's internal affairs; (4) equality and mutual benefit; and (5) peaceful coexistence. It was agreed during Chou's visits to New Delhi and Rangoon and by the reciprocal visits of Nehru and U Nu to Peking that India and Burma would maintain strict neutrality in the Cold War and friendly relations with China, while the Chinese in turn agreed to refrain from aggression or the export of revolution along Indian and Burmese frontiers.

Chou's meetings with Nehru and U Nu and other such discussions paved the way for Chinese participation in an Afro-Asian Conference held at Bandung, Indonesia in April 1955. During the Bandung meetings, Chou added further elements to the Panch Shila affirmations: recognition of racial equality and respect for the rights of the people of all nations to choose their own way of life and their own political and economic systems. Chou scored a personal triumph at the conference, exceeding even his impressive performance at Geneva and identifying China with the anti-imperialist, antimilitarist attitudes of the emerging Third World.

Chou En-lai's appearance at Geneva and at Bandung had done much to allay the impression of China as a bellicose nation, a view that had been prevalent in much of the world's non-Communist press since the Korean War, and thereby to hamper American attempts to build an anti-Communist

alliance system around China's periphery. There were, to be sure, some logical inconsistencies in China's new soft line. First, China sought to pose as leader of a nonaligned bloc at the same time that it maintained a close affiliation with one of the bloc leaders in the world bipolar system, the Soviet Union. This was to prove particularly embarrassing during Soviet suppression of a similar drift toward looser bipolarity in Eastern Europe. Second, it remained ideologically committed to promote revolution against the very governments it sought now to befriend. For both reasons, the soft line could easily be construed in hostile eyes as a mere tactical shift, a change in window dressing.

An unexpected result of the Afro-Asian Conference of April 1955 was the initiation of an extended diplomatic encounter between China and the United States. At Bandung, Chou made a public offer to enter into negotiations with the United States to discuss "the question of relaxing tensions in the Far East and especially the question of relaxing tension in the Taiwan area." Hopes for fruitful talks with the United States were heightened on May 13 when Chou for the first time expressed his willingness to "strive for the liberation of Taiwan by peaceful means so far as it is possible." Chou's offer was accepted, and on August 1, 1955, the Sino-American ambassadorial-level talks began in Geneva, later shifting to Warsaw. The talks began auspiciously, leading to agreement in their first year on the repatriation of Americans and Chinese from the two countries concerned, but then became stalemated over the Taiwan issue.

Meanwhile, Chou En-lai's performance at Bandung was bearing fruit in the form of extensive interaction between China and the Third World. The increasing contacts set the stage for Chou's extended good-will tour of southern and southeastern Asia in 1956, visiting North Vietnam, Cambodia, India, Burma, and Pakistan and resulting in agreements with Indonesia and Burma.

Chou En-lai's tour was interrupted by the tumultuous events of 1956 within the Communist bloc. Khrushchev's famous "secret speech," which featured a sweeping repudiation of Stalinism, triggered an uprising in Poland and a more serious revolt in Hungary, both of which were suppressed with the aid of Soviet troops. This naturally flew in the face of the assumption upon which Chou had built his bridge to the Third World, namely that "Western colonialism and Western military pacts were the only real dangers threatening the independence of the new nations of Asia and Africa." Chou returned to Peking from India, spent several days in consultation, then flew to Moscow to seek the reestablishment of bloc solidarity. After three days of conferences with Soviet leaders, he flew on to Warsaw and Budapest, where he issued a joint communique with Kadar and Gomulka; he then returned to Moscow and offered to mediate between the Soviet Union and Poland and Hungary. Beginning in 1957, Chou and his associates in the Foreign Affairs Ministry maintained the somewhat contradictory positions that unity and solidarity were necessary in the socialist camp and that various paths to socialism were unavoidable.

Beginning in 1958, a radical line tended to hold sway in Chinese foreign policy. The impact of this line was to lay greater emphasis on encouraging revolutionary groups in other countries, a policy that embarrassed attempts to establish friendly contacts with the governments of those countries. This more radical policy was accompanied not only by a more militant stance against the United States, but also by the deterioration of relations with India, the Soviet Union, and much of the Third World, which in-

creasingly sought a policy of detente with Washington.

By 1965, China's militant foreign policies of the past few years appeared to have run bankrupt. Dahomey and the Central African Republic broke diplomatic relations with Peking, and Nkrumah was overthrown by a coup in Ghana while he was visiting Peking. Chou had been shut out of black Africa, either outbid by the superpowers or dismissed for revolutionary double-dealing. The largest Communist party in the non-Communist world, the Indonesian PKI, which had been closely aligned with Peking, attempted a coup without adequate military backing and was wiped out with the loss of more than 200,000 lives. The escalation of guerrilla warfare in Vietnam had so far resulted only in an escalation of American military support to South Vietnam, including the introduction of American combat troops and the bombing of the north. Pakistan's 1965 attempt, with Peking's support, to decide the Kashmir question in its favor by force of arms had been repulsed, and the status quo ante was negotiated by Moscow, greatly enhancing Soviet prestige as a peacemaker in the region and emphasizing the widening rift between the Soviet Union and China.

The Sino-Soviet Dispute
The Sino-Soviet dispute is the story of the disintegration of international communism, which had once seemed so monolithic that all revolutionary movements in the world seemed to be directed from a single nerve center in the Kremlin. Chou had been prominent during both China's alliance with the Soviets and during their schism, but seems in balance to have been among those Chinese leaders who first advocated the latter course.

Chou made eight trips to Moscow altogether, and almost all the important treaties between the two Communist regimes were negotiated and signed by Chou. From the first three of these—in January 1950, August 1952, and March 1953—he brought back treaties and alliances greatly benefiting China. The Soviet Union relinquished some of its historical interests in China, advanced substantial loans to Peking, and sent technicians to help build dams, steel plants, and railroads. Between his fourth trip in April 1954, which mainly concerned the Vietnamese war then under negotiation in Geneva, and his fifth in January 1957, the relationship began to show signs of strain.

Perhaps the basic difference predisposing the two nations to part company was one of development: the Soviet Union had grown to full economic maturity and, while its ideology did not permit her to admit it, was basically satisfied with its status in the world and unwilling to risk it; China was still a developing, revolutionary power dissatisfied with its progress at home or its position in the world arena and willing to take more risks to rectify its disadvantage than the Soviets were willing to vouchsafe. The Soviets had tacitly supported India in the 1958 border crisis and allowed themselves to be bluffed by the United States in the Taiwan Strait crisis during the same year, unwilling to risk nuclear war for a few offshore islands. The evident Chinese willingness to run such a risk may have figured in the Soviet decision in 1959 to abrogate an earlier promise to supply China with nuclear weaponry.

With the Great Leap Forward and the People's Commune, China made a dramatic departure from the Soviet pattern of development that seemed dangerously adventurist. Claiming that Chinese overestimation of the native abilities of the unlettered masses had resulted in scrapping Soviet plans and ignoring or even harassing Soviet experts, Khru-

shchev unilaterally withdrew 1,300-odd Soviet advisers from China in the summer of 1960, abandoning 154 key development projects.

Through the early 1960s a bitter and increasingly explicit controversy raged in the leading newspapers and journals of both nations, as the Chinese accused the Soviets of bourgeois revisionism at home and social imperialism abroad. Eventually the dispute was even extended to Communist parties throughout the world, resulting in a factionalism of many of them into pro-Soviet and pro-Chinese wings.

In March 1963 the Chinese, angered by Khrushchev's taunting reference to colonial vestiges at Hong Kong and Macao, raised the issue of the Sino-Soviet boundaries, referring specifically to the unequal treaties imposed on China by the tsarist government at the end of the nineteenth century. These issues were extremely vexing to the Soviet Union, which also had latent boundary conflicts with Japan and with its Eastern European satellites, and raised the fear that an overpopulated China might aspire to expand into Siberia. Relations between the two countries reached a new low during the Cultural Revolution, manifested in quick Chinese denunciation of the Soviet invasion of Czechoslovakia in August 1968 and culminating in an armed clash between Soviet and Chinese forces over the disputed Ussuri River in the spring of 1969. Boundary negotiations were resumed shortly thereafter, but they went nowhere.

As Chinese nuclear capacity grew steadily through the 1960s, the Chinese became apprehensive about the possibility that the Soviet Union would launch a preventive attack to destroy their nuclear capability, particularly after the 1968 invasion of Czechoslovakia and the border clashes the next year. This apprehension over Soviet intentions is widely believed to have contributed to the Chinese opening to the United States.

China Enters the World Community

Having suffered from the self-inflicted wounds of internal convulsion and diplomatic isolation during the Cultural Revolution, China turned to a new, vigorous, and imaginative foreign policy in the early 1970s, through which it was to achieve its most dramatic successes in the world since the mid-1950s. One aspect of the new foreign policy was almost certainly aimed at winning admission to the United Nations.

In order to ingratiate himself with the Third World nations who had come to dominate voting in the General Assembly, Chou revived the practice of people-to-people and banquet diplomacy with great élan. Prominent Third World statesmen were invited to China, where they were wined and dined with fanfare. In 1971 alone, some 290 delegations from eighty nations were invited to China, while the People's Republic in turn sent some 70 delegations to forty nations. The Chinese also launched a major drive to expand the scope of state-to-state relations. Between October 1970 and 1971, the People's Republic established diplomatic relations with fourteen nations, resumed relations with Burundi and Tunisia, and elevated diplomatic relations with Britain and Holland to the ambassadorial level. Finally, the People's Republic also increased its aid to underdeveloped nations at an unprecedented rate.

During the twenty-sixth session of the United Nations, the admission issue was once again brought to a vote. The General Assembly on October 25, 1971, voted overwhelmingly to admit the People's Republic and to expel the Republic of China. On November 1, 1971, the red flag with five gold stars of the People's Republic of China took its place in front of the United Nations in New York along with the flags of 130 other members.

Since China's admission to the United Nations, Peking has taken up the anticolonial, antiracist, nationalist, and anti-imperialist issues of putative concern to the Third World, frequently attacking superpower hegemony. Yet it has played this radical role in this world forum with considerable decorum and diplomatic adroitness, using the veto very sparingly (unlike the Soviet Union, which in the early years resorted incessantly to the veto to paralyze the Security Council), not exploiting the General Assembly as a propaganda forum against the United States, and pursuing the usual logrolling tactics with considerable finesse. In fairness, however, it should be noted that the majority within the United Nations has shifted substantially toward an anti-American, Third World consensus, making Chinese vetoes less necessary.

Sino-American Rapprochement

Probes for a Sino-American detente had been initiated by the Nixon administration soon after the President's election as part of his plan to settle the Vietnamese conflict by negotiating the withdrawal of external support to North Vietnam. In his third month of office, Nixon informed DeGaulle that he was withdrawing from Vietnam and was desirous of a normalization of relations with China, a message that was conveyed to Peking by the French Ambassador. The Chinese responded favorably. In 1969 and 1970, the United States manifested its interest in a settlement by relaxing trade and travel restrictions and by beginning the withdrawal of American troops from Vietnam.

As Chou later recounted the gradual process leading to a rapprochement between the two old antagonists, Mao Tse-tung himself took the initiative at several crucial points. When Edgar Snow visited Mao on December 18, 1970, the latter quite unexpectedly suggested to Snow that Nixon could come to Peking. In April 1971 an American table-tennis team visited the People's Republic: a mere variant of people-to-people diplomacy. But within three months these contacts were elevated to a state-to-state level. In a dramatic television broadcast on July 15, Nixon revealed that Henry Kissinger had just returned from secret negotiations in Peking and that he himself had accepted an invitation to visit the People's Republic.

From the Chinese point of view, the primary purpose of the visit was unquestionably to resolve the Taiwan issue before that issue had become utterly intractable owing to the growth of Japanese economic interests there. Its secondary purpose was to acquire a counterweight to growing Soviet power on China's northern border. The primary American objective was to promote peace negotiations in Indochina by persuading the Chinese to stop supporting hawkish policies in Hanoi, under the assumption that, despite the disintegration of the Communist bloc, Hanoi would still heed Peking's injunctions because of her dependence on outside aid. The secondary purposes were to facilitate detente with the Soviet Union by creating a competitive relationship between Peking and Moscow and to promote Nixon's reelection chances in the 1972 elections by making his visit a media spectacular. The Chinese gave only partial satisfaction to the primary American objective, partly because a too blatant sellout of North Vietnam would have discredited its revolutionary credentials, partly because Peking's ability to influence Hanoi was much more limited than Washington had thought. But detente with China undoubtedly facilitated detente with the Soviet Union, and the Chinese were only

too happy to grant full publicity to the Nixon trip in order to build up public expectations for substantive agreements between the two powers.

From February 21 to February 28, 1972, in what he called "a week that changed the world," the President of the United States visited the People's Republic of China at the invitation of Premier Chou En-lai. During his trip, Nixon held "extensive, earnest, and frank discussions" with Chou En-lai and "a serious and frank exchange of views on Sino-US relations and world affairs" during a brief interview with Chairman Mao. In the Nixon-Chou communiqué issued at the end of the visit, the United States acknowledged that "all Chinese on either side of the Taiwan Strait" maintained that "there is but one China and Taiwan is a part of China," thus for the first time agreeing tacitly with the Chinese position that the liberation of Taiwan was China's internal affair in which no other country had the right to interfere. The United States, however, reaffirmed "its interest in a peaceful settlement of the Taiwan question by the Chinese themselves." With this prospect in mind, the United States affirmed "the ultimate objective of the withdrawal of all US forces and military installations in Taiwan," promising meanwhile progressively to reduce such forces as tension in the area decreased. Regarding the Indochina war, the United States stressed the principle of self-determination in South Vietnam, the desirability of a negotiated solution, and the significance of the withdrawal of American troops. China, on the other hand, expressed its firm commitment to the Indochinese peoples for attainment of their goals.

The Sino-American detente had accomplished many of the immediate purposes of both parties, as well as opening a new vista in Sino-American relations that the two countries were left free to pursue as it suited their interests. Nixon gained additional time for settlement of the Indochina war by relieving him of domestic pressure on the war issue; he also gained credit for initiative and flexibility in foreign policy, as well as a public relations coup through the media exposure he received during his visit. This publicity placed the prestige of both nations behind the visit, raising popular expectations on both sides for increased cultural contacts. Since the visit, American groups ranging from the Philadelphia Symphony Orchestra to scientists and radicals have visited China, whereas Chinese acrobats, doctors, and scientists have toured the United States; about ten thousand Americans and several hundred Chinese have been involved. China gained a stronger bargaining position for its confrontation with the Soviet Union, a pledge from the United States for eventual settlement in Vietnam, and, most importantly, American acknowledgement that Taiwan was a part of China. As an indirect but immediate consequence of detente, the way had been cleared for China's admission to the United Nations, and Japan felt at liberty to initiate formal relations with the People's Republic.

Death and Succession

Succession is important and problematic in all Communist regimes—important because power is concentrated at the top and politics is highly variable, problematic because no reliable means for the transfer of power has yet been devised in any Communist system. "Pre-mortem" succession offers the best way of reducing uncertainty, for it allows successors to consolidate their power with the help of retiring chiefs; the problem is that the latter may harbor unresolved ambivalence about their succession, fearing that

Chou En-lai and Japanese Prime Minister Tanaka Kakuei, September 1972

(United Press International)

their chosen successors may precipitate their premature retirement or repudiate their policies once they are out of the way.[14] This was the case with Mao Tse-tung's attempts to arrange his own pre-mortem succession by Liu Shao-ch'i and then by Lin Piao. Thus most Communist leaders leave an ambiguous situation upon their demise, and it usually takes some time for a dominant leader to emerge from the struggle among various contenders for power. This period of ambiguity is a critical one for the system, when the leadership finds itself torn between fear of renewed tyranny and a need for leadership; for the time being no significant decisions can be made, for each such decision raises the prior question of who is to resolve it. Because this question cannot be decided until the succession crisis itself is resolved, significant decisions tend to be deferred or compromised.

14 Cf. Myron Rush, *How Communist States Change Their Rulers* (Ithaca, N.Y.: Cornell University Press, 1975).

524

Chou En-lai reportedly knew that he was dying of cancer as early as 1973 and that he had but a short time to live, and so he set about trying to arrange his own pre-mortem succession with great deliberation. In 1973 he reappointed his old Paris classmate Teng Hsiao-p'ing as Vice Premier, and Teng began to assume Chou's functions during Chou's increasingly frequent absences. At the Tenth Party Congress in 1973 Teng became a member of the Central Committee, and by January 1974 he had been identified as a member of the Politburo. In June 1974, Chou retired to the hospital, explaining that "I am not very well because I am old," and Teng now appeared frequently in his place. Beginning in September 1974, Teng began to appear at the audiences Mao Tse-tung granted foreign visitors, appearing with him no less than ten times in 1975; this seemed to signify that Teng had ingratiated himself with the Chairman. At the Fourth National People's Congress in January 1975,

Teng was elected a Vice Chairman of the Central Committee and a member of the Standing Committee of the Politburo and was also listed as first-ranking Vice Premier in Chou's State Council. Chou had thus clearly signaled his choice of heir apparent, and Teng seemed to have widespread support within ruling circles—he was even assumed to be next in line to succeed the aging Chairman.

Chou wished not only to designate his successor, however, but to leave clear policy guidelines intact for the next generation of political leaders. He unveiled his plans for the future in his report to the Fourth NPC, which he delivered in person in one of his last public appearances. Praising Chiang Ch'ing and reciting no fewer than seventeen of Mao's sayings as a talisman against radical criticism (the Chairman himself had conspicuously absented himself from the congress), Chou outlined an ambitious long-term plan for economic development: by the

Chou En-lai plans his succession, August 1975

(New China News Agency, Peking)

end of the fifth Five-Year Plan in 1980, China will have built "an independent and relatively comprehensive industrial and economic system," and "by the end of the century there will be a comprehensive modernization of agriculture, industry, national defense, science and technology." He assigned the State Council under Teng Hsiao-p'ing's acting leadership to draw up "a long-range and a ten-year plan, five-year plans, and annual plans," with plans to be worked out on all levels down to the industrial and mining enterprises and the rural production teams. Teng Hsiao-p'ing and the State Council promptly set to work, and by September 15 they were prepared to convene a month-long National Study Tachai Conference in the county containing the Tachai Brigade (a famous radical agricultural model in China). An ambitious agrarian program for the coming fifth Five-Year Plan was presented to the 3,700 cadres in attendance.

Chou's attempt to chart political developments for the twenty-five years after his death excited the apprehensions of the radicals that these plans foresaw rapid, but unprincipled, development and gave relatively low priority to continued progress toward socialism. Thus in the summer of 1975 the radicals, with Mao Tse-tung's support, launched yet another campaign, this time to defend the dictatorship of the proletariat from those capitulationists (as exemplified by the hero of the popular novel, *Water Margins*) who wish to give way to "bourgeois right." However, response to this criticism in the provinces seemed sluggish and sporadic, while the provincial media treated the Tachai conference as a major milestone in the history of the People's Republic.

Chou En-lai died on January 8, 1976, at the age of seventy-eight. Teng Hsiao-p'ing delivered a eulogy at the memorial service on January 15 on behalf of the Central Com-

mittee, the State Council, and the PLA, praising his "immortal contribution" to the Chinese revolution and mourning his death as a "gigantic loss." Mao Tse-tung did not attend the memorial service, but the eulogy was published in all papers and read on the radio.

Henceforward, Chou En-lai's well-laid plans for his own succession went quickly awry. On February 8, 1976, a former Minister of Public Security named Hua Kuo-feng was named Acting Premier, vaulting over five more senior Deputy Premiers, most conspicuously Teng Hsiao-p'ing. Only four days later, a poster campaign was launched against Teng in several cities, preempting plans by Teng and others to launch a Learn from Chou En-lai campaign. These criticisms continued through February and March, and Teng Hsiao-p'ing did not reappear in public again after giving his funeral eulogy. But the popular response to the campaign was hardly wholehearted: the PLA did not respond, and only about half of China's twenty-nine provincial administrations took a position on the campaign; for the most part debate was confined to a few institutions of higher learning in Peking and Shanghai.

In early April 1976 the campaign was brought to a climax that brought posthumous vindication to Chou En-lai. In preparation for the Chinese Ching Ming festival for remembrance of the dead, floral wreaths were placed on Chou's grave. But two days later these wreaths had been quietly removed, and rumor had it that Chiang Ch'ing and the radicals were responsible. A crowd of thirty thousand people gathered, apparently spontaneously, and sought to present a petition to the Great Hall of the People; when they were prevented, a riot ensued. Demonstrations spread to over half a dozen other major Chinese cities, including Nanking and even Shanghai. The response of the leadership to this completely unexpected show of support for a figure whose relationship to Mao had always been somewhat ambiguous was to blame the demonstrations on Teng Hsiao-p'ing: Teng was now officially removed from all his posts and Hua Kuo-feng formally appointed Premier and first Deputy Chairman of the CCP. But the radical faction of the leadership did not appear again for several days, and the campaign to criticize Teng was now led by the provincial party secretaries and other establishment figures, who had presumably been assured that public criticism would be limited to this single target.

The reason Chou had failed to prevail in choosing his own successor was partly that Teng's more brusque and uncompromising manner made him personally unacceptable to the leading radicals and partly that his record in the Cultural Revolution was more vulnerable; but the chief reason seemed to be simply that Chou died before Mao did, and the radicals saw their opportunity and seized it. But although Chou was unable to handpick his successor, he had managed to institutionalize the development policies that he wished to see continued after his death, inspiring elites to pursue them in a well-planned series of meetings and winning mass enthusiasm through a publicity campaign. And although Teng himself was ousted, the pool of acceptable candidates on

the State Council from whence his replacement had to be picked were all Chou appointees who had worked closely with Chou and shared his goals. Although Hua Kuo-feng had a reputation as a Mao protégé on the basis of his work in Hunan, he had worked closely with Chou in Peking since 1971 as Director of the General Office of the State Council.

Mao Tse-tung, on the other hand, with his well-known animus against institutionalization, had not only failed to institutionalize the revolutionary policies he stood for (admittedly a contradiction in terms), but omitted, after two previous embarrassing misjudgments, to pick a successor. Thus within a month after the Chairman's death on September 9, 1976, all four of the leading radicals were suddenly arrested and accused of plotting a coup. Hua Kuo-feng seized the chairmanship of the party with the support of the established military and political figures and proceeded to consolidate his position. The policies he intended to pursue sounded very similar to the long-term developmental plan first presented by Chou in December 1975. And the image he presented to the Chinese people was one of a man who is "loyal, selfless, open and straightforward, modest and prudent"—a description taken almost word for word from Teng Hsiao-p'ing's funeral eulogy to Chou En-lai.

6

Assessment
and Conclusions

At this point it is appropriate to ask, why did Chou En-lai succeed in the vortex of Chinese politics while so many around him failed? When a person decides to adopt a political career, he or she brings to this vocation various personal resources that can then be adapted with more or less flexibility to the situation at hand. Thus any politician's success may be seen as a product of personal character and its congruence with the repertoire of situations encountered.

Some politicians ride to prominence on a particularly burning issue, such as William Jennings Bryan in his campaign against the gold standard or Eugene McCarthy in his antiwar candidacy. Mao Tse-tung may be said to have been this type of politician, and the central issue he came to stand for in Chinese politics was revolution. This has been an issue of such resonance in modern China that it assured him of a permanent popular following. But if Mao was first in

the hearts of his countrymen, he was not always first in the hearts of his colleagues. His close identification with this issue made it difficult for him to adapt to a situation of peaceful growth, with the result that he either became irrelevant or found some way of stimulating artificial revolutions.

Chou En-lai, on the other hand, always avoided becoming identified with any particular policy, remaining quite content to mouth whatever policy seemed appropriate to the particular situation. Even the recent, historic opening to the West was attributed by Chou to Mao's personal initiative. It is true that there are more restrictions on the attribution of credit in Chinese politics than in, say, the United States—most of it goes either to the supreme leader or to the faceless masses. But Chou's lack of identification with any particular policy was on the one hand a source of his political resiliency in a party prone to purge those identified with

528

particular policies when those policies are abandoned, and perhaps a token of his personal modesty as well. But on the other hand it may explain why he hovered near the top ranks of leadership for so long without ever having risen to a position of supremacy, for as supreme leader he would have had to decide upon and symbolize a specific set of policies, not merely to implement them.

Another resource available to the politician in China no less than in the United States is identification with a particular constituency, or reference group. Just as George Wallace and Nelson Rockefeller have different and clearly defined constituencies in American politics, which are reflected in the policies preferred by these politicians and even in their syntax and political styles, so Mao Tse-tung, Lin Piao, Liu Shao-ch'i, and Chou En-lai had different constituencies in Chinese politics. Mao was clearly identified with the peasants, and he exhibited this identification in his homespun public manner and in his policies; Liu Shao-ch'i, the "iron Bolshevik," was identified with the Leninist party apparatus; and Lin Piao was clearly identified with the PLA.

The ability of politicians to achieve identification with any particular reference group is limited by their ascriptive characteristics, which define their styles: it would be very difficult for Rockefeller to achieve identification with lower-middle-class southern whites, for example, or for Wallace to achieve identification with the electorate of east-side Manhattan. Unlike Mao or Liu or many other members of the leadership who hail from marginal elites (the rich peasantry, for example) or from downwardly mobile or déclassé families, Chou had a pedigree from China's traditional ruling class. A scion of the landed scholar-gentry by birth, he received a progressive and cosmopolitan education, making him perhaps the party's

closest facsimile to an intellectual. He never bothered to deny his nonproletarian class background, sometimes seeming almost to flaunt it—albeit jokingly. Chou En-lai's natural political constituency was China's intellectual and professional middle class, and throughout his career he functioned as the party's bridge to this important group. He displayed many of the qualities this group admires in a politician: charm, tact, duplicity, caution, quick intelligence, an ever-present concern for appearances. During the war years in Chungking, he assiduously courted the small parties and independent groups making up the Third Force in Chinese politics, leading many of them into a united front with the CCP that was later incorporated into the structure of the regime. The government bureaucracy he administered since liberation employed more nonparty intellectuals than any other elite institution. The only significant policy initiatives contained in the innumerable reports he delivered were calculated to facilitate closer cooperation between the regime and the intellectual community: the report on problems of reforming intellectuals issued just before the 1950 thought reform campaign and his report on the intellectuals in January 1956, which initiated the Hundred Flowers Movement. But the commitment of the intellectual community to an intellectual liberalism contained within it the seeds of political opposition that led them into repeated confrontations with a new regime still sensitive to criticism. At each confrontation, Chou abandoned his wayward clientele with characteristic dispatch while sanctions were imposed, only to restore some of them to favor afterward.

Lacking any identification with a specific set of substantive policies and identified with an ideologically disreputable constituency, Chou En-lai may be said to have owed much of his success to his political style. In an attempt to analyze more clearly this elusive but important political resource, one political scientist has defined style as the way leaders address the responsibilities of their job. And most political jobs consist of three major responsibilities: rhetoric, personal relations, and homework.[1] Although Chou's greatest talent seemed to lie in personal relations, he was also an outstanding rhetorician and an assiduous believer in homework.

As a rhetorician, Chou was skilled, fluent, and highly persuasive. He began his career as a full-time rhetorician: as a student editor, orator, and overall agitator, he was at the time very talented at mobilizing the masses with his words. And throughout his career his rhetoric retained its sharp edge. For example, when asked in 1965 whether the Americans in Vietnam were stepping up the fighting in order to save face by gaining a strong bargaining position before beginning negotiations, he answered with a vivid turn of phrase: "Saving face? A brigand who has committed an armed robbery—can he save face by committing a second or third? How many crimes are required before America's face is, as you put it, saved? In my view, the best way this bandit can save his face is by giving back the property he has stolen."[2] But during his later career, as Chou became increasingly involved in administrative and diplomatic activities, the function of his rhetoric tended to shift from the mobilizational to the devotional. An example is this excerpt from a 1964 interview:

Now that the economic situation in China has changed for the better, some people are saying that everything is wonderful. They always fail to form a correct picture of China. As far as we are concerned, we have found the right road. And while marching along this road, difficulties and shortcomings will continue to crop up, and we have to work continuously in order to overcome them as we go forward, and we also have to sum up the experience continuously so as to find better methods for advancing our cause. The same is true of both revolutionary struggles and of production and construction. . . . Man constantly sums up experience from practice, continues to make discoveries and inventions, and keeps on creating and advancing.[3]

A host of distinguished visitors to China have testified to Chou En-lai's extraordinary charm in personal relations, including Lord Bernard Montgomery and former United Nations Secretary General Dag Hammarskjöld. He left Edgar Snow with "the impression of a cool, logical and empirical mind."[4] "He is a very different person from Mao," Montgomery reflected in a 1960 interview. "He is intellectual and very clever . . . a quick and clear thinker, very lucid in his speech, with a most pleasing personality and a nice sense of humor." James Reston of *The New York Times* remarked that "he has the coolest eye and most penetrating way of looking at you of any man I think I've ever seen." Kissinger is said to have spent twenty of his forty-nine hours in Peking talking to Chou, for whom he had the highest praise.[5]

Although surprisingly little systematic study has been applied to so crucial a political resource as charm, a few of its more obvious components stand out in Chou's case. Chou was always a strikingly handsome man, slim, impeccably dressed, with jet black

[1] James D. Barber, *The Presidential Character: Predicting Performance in the White House* (Englewood Cliffs, N.J.: Prentice-Hall, 1972).
[2] K. S. Karol, *China: The Other Communism* (New York: Hill and Wang, 1967), appendix.

[3] Quoted in Edgar Snow, *The Long Revolution* (New York: Random House, 1971), p. 187.
[4] Snow, *Red Star,* p. 76.
[5] Snow, *The Long Revolution,* p. 187.

hair and thick eyebrows pointing straight
back to his temples. He enjoyed talking to
people and did so for hours on end, bom-
barding guests with questions about every
aspect of life in their countries. He typically
approached his interlocutor from a disarm-
ingly self-effacing position, which was often
flattering. When visiting some college students assigned to manual labor on a Sinkiang
commune in 1965, he began: "Once I was
far more politically unversed than you girls.
In my younger days I had a pigtail on my
head, which was so full of the old, old stuff
that there was not room for even capitalism
—which got in there later. And it was a
long time before I found Marxism-Leninism." [6] Finally, Chou simply always took
great pains to cultivate people. For example,
he would personally attend to all the details
of the dozens of delegations who toured
China to ensure that everything left a pleasant impression on the visitors, whenever possible memorizing the delegates' names to
address them personally, speaking a few
words in their language, and so on. Until he
was hospitalized for cancer, he greeted every
state visitor at the airport, made personal appearances at state banquets, and saw every
state visitor off at the airport. He was prin-
cipally responsible for all negotiations with
important state guests and attended all Mao's
receptions for visitors.

Another important aspect of personal relations is a politician's interactions with his
colleagues, who are less interested in his charisma than in his collegiality on a long-term
basis. This is particularly important in Chinese politics, where the elite is small, extremely close, and highly sensitive. How
Chou's early family relationships equipped
him magnificently for this delicate task was

shown earlier. Though his ceremonial rhetoric was egalitarian, in practice he always
took careful note of his interlocutor's status
and deferred to it. He seemed particularly
proficient at subordinating himself to and
ingratiating himself with powerful authority
figures, beginning with his foster mother
and continuing through Li Li-san, the CCP's
fiery leader of the later 1920s, and Mao Tse-
tung. He cooperated with Mao for more
than thirty-seven years without ever seeming
particularly close to him personally. Their
relationship seemed mutually complementary, however: Chou welcomed the detailed
execution of a plan, and the more complex
a problem, the better; he was likely to compli-
cate the problem while solving it. Whereas
Mao tended to discuss matters in abstract,
simple terms suggesting his breadth of vision
and impatience with detail, Chou spoke in
practical, operational terms. Edgar Snow,
who knew both men, describes their relationship well: "In talks I have had with China's
two great men it usually is Chou who meticulously answers the main questions and Mao
who listens, adds a few words of caution or
elucidation, and enlarges the broad and dialectical view." [7] But equally important,
Chou showed great delicacy concerning his
Politburo colleagues less senior to him, such
as Chiang Ch'ing or Yao Wen-yuan, who
rose suddenly on the basis of the Cultural
Revolution and were quite sensitive about
their status. Whereas his would-be successor, Teng Hsiao-p'ing, could not contain his
ire about these "helicopters," Chou actually
pushed the youthful Wang Hung-wen as a
possible candidate for the succession.

It is hard to see where the ubiquitous
Chou still found time for homework, but the
fact that he ran China's vast government apparatus since liberation indicates that he was
a capable administrator. A man of indefati-

[6] Committee for Concerned Asian Scholars, *China:
Inside the People's Republic* (New York: Bantam Books, 1972), p. 335.

[7] Snow, *The Long Revolution,* p. 187.

gable energy, he once said he had taken a single week-long vacation in ten years—and this because he was ill. He attended countless official banquets, gave innumerable ceremonial addresses, apparently with relish, and sometimes regaled his guests with conversation deep into the night. He was often so well informed about the situation in other countries that he surprised his visitors. For example, in the course of a July 1971 interview with members of an American delegation to the People's Republic, Chou informed his visitors of four detailed facts. First, according to American estimates, within the past 10 years the United States had spent $120 billion on the Indochinese war. Second, the output of steel in Japan in 1970 approached 100 million tons. Third, in the fourth Japanese defense plan, from 1972 to 1976, that nation planned to spend more than $16 billion. The total amount spent on military expenditures since World War II (up to 1971), in the first three defense plans, was only a bit more than $10 billion. And finally, the internal debt of the United States was approaching $400 million, so the annual interest paid on the debt ($19 billion) nearly equaled the total amount of the largest budget prior to World War II ($20 billion in 1940–1941).[8]

Chou En-lai in truth may be said to have been China's man for all seasons. If Mao Tse-tung was the country's great symbol of revolution, master of the art of the impossible, Chou En-lai was master of the art of the possible, China's compleat politician. It is hazardous to forecast in this ever-surprising country, but as of now it seems that the road to China's future is not that of Liu Shao-ch'i or even that of Mao Tse-tung, but that of Chou En-lai.

---

[8] Committee for Concerned Asian Scholars, *China: Inside the People's Republic* (New York: Bantam Books, 1972), pp. 331–371.

Selected Bibliography

The best (albeit dated) book-length biography of Chou En-lai remains Kai-yu Hsu's *Chou En-lai: China's Grey Eminence* (Garden City, N.Y.: Doubleday, 1968). Excellent capsule biographies are contained in Howard L. Boorman and Richard C. Howard, eds., *Biographical Dictionary of Republican China* (New York: Columbia University Press, 1967); and Donald W. Klein and Anne B. Clark, eds., *Biographic Dictionary of Chinese Communism, 1921–1965* (Cambridge, Mass.: Harvard University Press, 1971). See also Thomas W. Robinson's perceptive article, "Chou En-lai's Role in China's Cultural Revolution," in *The Cultural Revolution in China,* Thomas Robinson, ed. (Berkeley: University of California Press, 1971).

Among many fruitful attempts to apply social science theory to the Chinese political system, a few of the more noteworthy are Chalmers Johnson, *Peasant Nationalism and Communist Power: The Emergence of a Revolutionary, 1937–1945* (Stanford, Calif.: Stanford University Press, 1962); Franz Schurmann, *Ideology and Organization in Communist China,* 2d ed. (Berkeley: University of California Press, 1968); Richard Solomon, *Mao's Revolution and the Chinese Political Culture* (Berkeley: University of California Press, 1971); and Lowell Dittmer, *Liu Shao-ch'i and the Chinese Cultural Revolution* (Berkeley: University of California Press, 1974).

Excellent historical overviews of the Communist rise to power are provided in James P. Harrison, *The Long March to Power: A History of the Chinese Communist Party, 1921–1972* (New York: Praeger, 1972); and in Jacques Guillermaz's two volumes, *A History of the Chinese Communist Party, 1921–1949* (New York: Random House, 1972), and *The Chinese Communist Party in Power, 1949–1976* (Boulder, Colo.: Westview Press, 1976).

Edgar Snow's vivid story of the Chinese revolution, based on close personal acquaintance with many of its leaders (including Mao Tse-tung and Chou En-lai), is recounted in *Red Star Over China* (New York: Grove Press,

1961), *The Other Side of the River* (London: Victor Gollancz, 1963), and *The Long Revolution* (New York: Random House, 1971). William Hinton's books, which include *Fanshen* (New York: Monthly Review, 1967) and *Hundred Day War* (New York: Monthly Review, 1972), are based on extended sojourns in China. Among the most informative of the recent spate of travelers' accounts are Ross Terrill, *800,000,000: The Real China* (New York: Dell, 1971); and Committee of Concerned Asian Scholars, *China: Inside the People's Re-*

public (New York: Bantam Books, 1972).

For reasonably comprehensive overviews of Chinese foreign policy see Harold Hinton, *Communist China in World Politics* (London: Macmillan, 1966); Ishwer Ojha, *Chinese Foreign Policy in an Age of Transition* (Boston: Beacon Press, 1969); J. D. Simmonds, *China's World: The Foreign Policy of a Developing State* (New York: Columbia University Press, 1970); and Peter Van Ness, *Revolution and Chinese Foreign Policy* (Berkeley: University of California Press, 1970).

Index